C0-DKN-515

ISBN: 9781313725705

Published by:
HardPress Publishing
8345 NW 66TH ST #2561
MIAMI FL 33166-2626

Email: info@hardpress.net
Web: http://www.hardpress.net

HISTORICAL COMMENTARIES

ON THE

STATE OF CHRISTIANITY

DURING THE FIRST THREE HUNDRED AND TWENTY-FIVE YEARS

FROM

THE CHRISTIAN ERA:

BEING

A TRANSLATION OF

"THE COMMENTARIES ON THE AFFAIRS OF THE CHRISTIANS BEFORE THE TIME OF CONSTANTINE THE GREAT,"

BY JOHN LAURENCE VON MOSHEIM, D.D.

LATE CHANCELLOR OF THE UNIVERSITY OF GOTTENGEN.

In two Volumes.

VOL. II.

VOLUME I. TRANSLATED FROM THE ORIGINAL LATIN,

BY

ROBERT STUDLEY VIDAL, Esq. F. S. A.

VOLUME II. TRANSLATED, AND BOTH VOLUMES EDITED,

BY

JAMES MURDOCK, D. D.

NEW-YORK:

PUBLISHED BY S. CONVERSE.

1853.

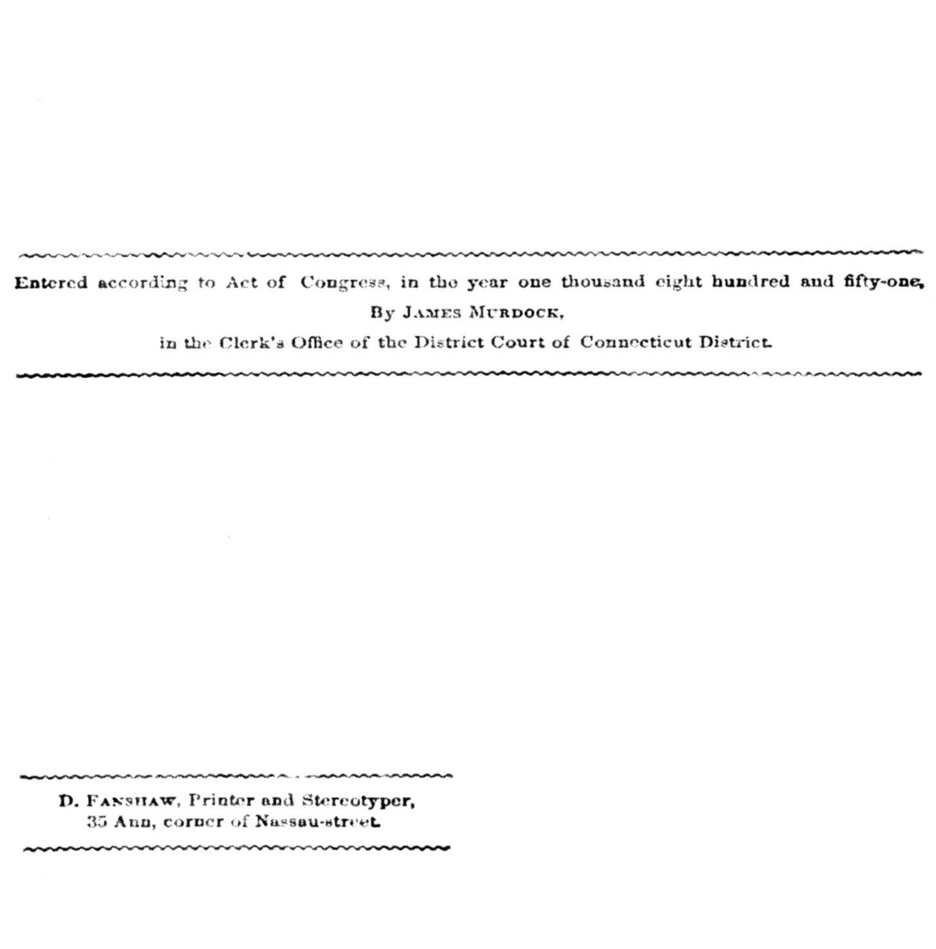

D. Fanshaw, Printer and Stereotyper,
35 Ann, corner of Nassau-street.

CONTENTS OF VOL. II.

THE
ECCLESIASTICAL HISTORY
OF THE
THIRD CENTURY.

---

§ I. **Propagation of Christianity in Arabia.** That the [p. 448.] limits of the Christian commonwealth were much extended during this century, no one hesitates to admit; but, in what manner, by whose instrumentality, and in what parts of the world, is not equally manifest, the ancient memorials having perished. While Demetrius ruled the Alexandrian church, over which he is said to have presided until the year 230, a certain Arabian chieftain, (that is, as I suppose, the head and leader of a tribe of those Arabs who live in tents, and have no fixed and permanent residence,) sent letters to this prelate, and to the prefect of Egypt, requesting that the celebrated *Origen* might be sent to him, to impart to him and his people a knowledge of Christianity. Origen, therefore, went among these Arabs; and, having soon dispatched the business of his mission, he returned to Alexandria.(1) He undoubtedly took with him from Alexandria several Christian disciples and teachers, whom he left with that people, as he himself could not be long absent from Alexandria.

(1) We have a brief narrative of these events in *Eusebius*, Hist. Eccles. lib. vi. c. xix: p. 221.

§ II. **Propagation of Christianity among the Goths.** To the Goths, a most warlike and ferocious people, dwelling in Moesia and Thrace, the wars they waged with various success against the Romans, during almost the whole of this century, produced this advantage, that they became friendly to Christian truth. For, in their incursions into Asia they captured and carried away several Christian priests, the sanctity of whose lives and manners, together with their miracles and prodigies, so affected the minds of the barbarians, that they avowed a willingness to [p. 449.] follow Christ, and called in additional teachers to instruct them.(1) There is, indeed, much evidence that what is here stated, must be understood only of a part of this race, and that no small portion of them remained for a long time afterwards addicted to the superstitions of their ancestors; yet, as in the next century *Theophilus*, a bishop of the Goths, was a subscriber to the decrees of the Nicene council.(2) there can be little doubt that quite a large church was gathered among this people in a short space of time.

(1) *Sozomen*, Hist. Eccles. l. ii. c. 6. *Paulus Diaconus*, Hist. Miscellan. l. x. c. 14. *Philostorgius*, Hist. Eccles. l. ii. c. v. p. 470. Philostorgius states, that the celebrated *Ulphilas*, who in the next century translated the Christian Scriptures into the language of the Goths, was descended from those captives that were carried away by the Goths from Cappadocia and Thrace, in the reign of Gallienus. This is not improbable; and yet there are some other things in the narrative of Philostorgius, which perhaps are false.

(2) *Socrates*, Hist. Eccles. l. ii. c. 41.

§ III. **Christianity in Gaul, Germany, and Scotland.** In Gaul a few small congregations of Christians were established by Asiatic teachers, in the preceding century. But in this century, during the reign of Decius, seven holy men, namely, *Dionysius*, *Gatianus*, *Trophimus*, *Paulus*, *Saturninus*, *Martialis*, and *Stremonius*, emigrated to this province, and, amidst various perils and hardships, established new churches at Paris, Tours, Arles, Narbonne, Toulouse, Limoges, and in Auvergne;(1) and their disciples, afterwards, gradually spread the knowledge of Divine truth over the whole of Gaul. With these seven men, some have associated others, but it is on authorities obscure and not to be relied on.(2) To the same age is now ascribed, by men of erudition, who are more eager for truth than for vain glory, the origin of the churches of Cologne, Treves, Metz, and other places in Germany; although the old tradition is, that the founders of these churches, Eucharius, Valerius, Maternus, Clemens, and others, were sent forth by the apostles themselves, in the first century; and there still are some who fondly adhere to these fables of their ancestors.(3) And, it must be confessed, that those have the best of the argument, who thus correct the old opinion respecting the origin of the German churches. The Scots, also, say that their country was enlightened with Christianity in this cen- [p. 450.] tury; which, although probable enough in itself considered, rests on proofs and arguments of no great force.

(1) This we learn, in part, from the Acta Martyrii Saturnini, in the Acta Martyrum Sincera of *Ruinart*, pa. 109; and, in part, from *Gregory* of Tours, Historia Francor. l. i. c. xxviii. p. 23, ed. Ruinart. The French anciently referred these seven persons, and the origin of the churches they founded, to the first century. In particular, *Dionysius*, who was the chief man of the seven, and the founder of the church at Paris, and its first bishop, was for many ages believed to be *Dionysius* the Areopagite, mentioned in the 17th chapter of the Acts of the Apostles. But in the last century, men of the greatest erudition among the French did not hesitate to correct this error of their predecessors, and to assign Dionysius and his associates to the third century and to the times of Decius. The tracts and discussions on this subject by Launoi, Sirmond, Petavius, Puteanus, Nic. Faber, and others, are well known. The ancient opinion, however, still remains so fixed in the minds of not a few, and especially among the monks of St. Denys, that it cannot be eradicated; which is not at all surprising, since great numbers make the glory of their church to depend very much on its antiquity. But the arrival of these seven men in Gaul, is involved in much obscurity. For it does not sufficiently appear, whence they came, nor by whom they were sent. *Gregory of Tours*, Historia Francor. l. x. c. xxxi. p, 527, says: Gatianum a Romanæ sedis Papa transmissum esse: from which it is inferred, that the other six also came from Rome. The fact may be so, and it may be otherwise. It is equally uncertain whether they emigrated to Gaul together, and all at one time, or whether they went at different times separately. And other points are involved in the like obscurity. I indeed suspect, that these devout and holy men, during the Decian persecution in Italy, and especially at Rome, voluntarily, and for the preservation of their lives, rather than by the direction and authority of the Romish bishop, removed to Gaul, where they could enjoy greater safety than at Rome and in Italy.

(2) The people of Auxerre, for instance, commemorate one *Peregrinus*, who, as they think, came likewise from Rome in this century, and laid the foundation of their church. See *Le Beuf*, Memoires pour l'Histoire d'Auxerre, tom. i. p. 1–12. There is also mention of one *Genulphus*, as an apostle of the Gauls, in this century. See the Acta Sanctor. mensis Januar. tom. ii. p. 92. &c. And others are also mentioned by some writers.

(3) What the French believed respecting those seven men, with none to gainsay them, the Germans also believed of *Eucharius*, *Maternus*, *Clemens*, and others; namely, that they were disciples of the apostles, and that in the [p. 451.] first century they established Christian churches in Germany, on this side the Rhine and in Lorraine, at Cologne, Treves, Metz, and in other cities, and governed the Churches they gathered, as their bishops. This opinion became suspicious to some learned men in the last century; and in the present century, it has been boldly assailed by *Augustine Calmet*, in a dissertation prefixed to his History of Lorraine, written in French, tom. i. in which he contends

(p. vii.) that Eucharius and Maternus founded the Churches of Cologne and Treves, in the third century, and (p. xvii. xx.) that Clemens did not found the church at Metz prior to that time. To this learned man stands opposed the commentator on the Acta S. Auctoris, in the Acta Sanctor. Antwerp. tom. iv mensis Augusti, p. 38. who not unlearnedly labors to sustain the ancient opinion. But the recent writer of the Historia Trevirensis Diplomatica, John Nic. *ab Hontheim*, a man of vast learning, after considering the whole subject with great care, and weighing accurately the testimony, in a Dissertation de Æra Fundati Episcopatus Trevirensis, prefixed to the first volume of his history, has fully shown, that more credit is due to Calmet than to his opponent. For, having maintained at great length, that those rely on witnesses not to be credited who carry back the founding of the church at Treves, and the other German churches, to the apostolic age, and make the holy men above mentioned to have taught in the first century, he demonstrates (section vi. p. xxxii. &c.) by arguments the strongest possible in such a case, that *Maternus* in particular, did not live in the first century, nor in the second, but near the end of the third: and as to the church of Cologne, that it is referable to the beginning of the fourth century.

(4) The Scotch historians tell us, that their king, *Donald I.* embraced Christianity, while Victor presided over the Romish church. See Sir Geo. *MacKenzie's* Defence of the Royal Line of Scotland, ch. viii. p. 219. But, as the strongest proof of their position is derived from coins of this Donald, never inspected by any one, there can be no doubt as to the credit they deserve. And yet it appears, for other reasons, adduced by *Usher* and *Stillingfleet* in their Antiquitates et Origines Ecclesiæ Britannicæ, that the Scotch church is not of later date than the third century.

§ IV. **Causes of the progress of Christianity.** We give credence to the many and grave testimonies of the writers of those times, who cannot be suspected of either fraud or levity, that the successful progress of Christianity in this century was, in a great measure, attributable to divine interpositions, by various kinds of miracles, exciting the minds of the people, and moving them to abandon superstition.(1) Neither can we easily either reject altogether, or [p. 452.] seriously question what we find testified by the best men of the times, that God did, by dreams and visions, excite not a few among the thoughtless and the enemies of Christianity, so that they at once, and without solicitation, came forward and made a public profession of the Christian faith:(2) and their examples, without doubt, served to overcome the timidity, or the hesitation, or the indecision of many. And yet, I suppose, it will be no error to maintain, that causes merely human and ordinary, so operated on the minds of many as to lead them to embrace Christianity. For the earnest zeal of the Christians, to merit the good will of all men, even of their enemies; the unparalleled kindness to the poor, the afflicted, the indigent, to prisoners, and to the sick, which was peculiar to the church; the remarkable fortitude, gravity, and uprightness, which characterized their teachers; their unwearied assiduity in translating the Sacred Books into various languages, and publishing copies of them; their amazing indifference to all human things, to evils and sufferings, and even to death itself;—all these, and other equally distinguishing traits of character, may, very justly, have induced many to admire and to embrace the religion of Christians, which produced and sustained so great virtues. And if, as I would by no means deny, pious frauds found a place among the causes of the propagation of Christianity in this century, yet, they unquestionably held a very inferior position, and were employed by only a few, and with very little, if any success.

(1) Numerous testimonies of the ancients, respecting the miracles of this century, might easily be collected. See *Origen*, contra Celsum, l. i. p. 5–7, and in various other places; *Cyprian*, Epist. ad Donatum, i. p. 3, on which passage *Steph. Baluze* has collected many testimonies of like import, in his Notes there; *Eusebius*, Hist. Eccles. l. vi. c. v. p. 208, &c. The reported miracles of *Gregory* of New Cesaria are well known; and yet there are some among them which may be justly called in question. See *Ant.* van *Dale's* Preface to his work de Oraculis, p. 6.

(2) The ancients record many instances of this kind. See *Origen*, contra Celsum, l. i. p. 35; and Homil. in Lucae, vii. Opp. tom. ii. p. 216. *Tertullian*, de Anima, c. xiv. p. 348. *Eusebius*, Hist. Eccles. l. vi. c. v. p. 208, &c. &c. Among these examples, there are some which may, I am aware, be explained by referring them to natural causes; but there are others which demand a higher cause.

§ V. **Persecution under Severus.** This zeal of Christians [p. 453.] for extending and enlarging the church, was often much favored by the circumstances of the times. For, although they never enjoyed perfect security, the laws against them being not repealed, and the people frequently demanding their condemnation, yet, under some of the Roman emperors of this century, their enemies, in most of the provinces, seemed to be quiet, and to dread the perils to which a legal prosecution exposed them. Still, seasons of the severest trial frequently occurred, and emperors, governors, and the people, disregarding the ancient edicts, came down as furiously upon the Christians as they would upon robbers: and these storms greatly impeded the work of extirpating the old superstitions. The commencement of this century was painfully adverse to the Christian cause. For, although Severus, the Roman emperor, was not personally hostile to Christians, yet, from the records of that age, still extant, it appears that, in nearly all the provinces, many Christians, either from the clamorous demands of the superstitious multitude, whom the priests excited, or by the authority of magistrates, who made the law of Trajan a cloak for their barbarity and injustice, were put to death in various forms of execution. To these evils, originating from various causes, the Christians themselves undoubtedly gave some impetus, by a practice which had for some time prevailed among them, with the approbation of the bishops, that of purchasing life and safety by paying money to the magistrates.(1) For the avaricious governors and magistrates would often assail the Christians, and direct some of the poorer ones to be put to death, in order to extort money from the more wealthy, and to enrich themselves with the treasures of the churches.

(1) I cannot regard this practice as one of the least of the causes of the frequent wars of the magistrates and men in power against Christians, contrary to the laws and the pleasure of the emperors. For what will not avarice venture to do? The Montanists strongly condemned this practice; and hence *Tertullian* is vehement and copious in reprobating it; and, in his book de Fuga in Persecutionibus, c. xii. p. 696, he says: Sicut fuga redemptio gratuita est; ita redemptio nummaria fuga est. - - - - Pedibus statisti, curristi nummis. And then, after some bitter but unsound remarks, he proceeds: Tu pro Christiano pacis- [p. 454.] ceris cum delatore, vel milite, vel furunculo aliquo præside, sub tunica et sinu, ut furtivo, quem coram toto mundo Christus emit, immo et manumisit. Who can wonder, that informers and accusers were never wanting, so long as the Christians, (as appears from this passage,) would pacify informers with money? Felices itaque pauperes (for these, being without money, were obliged to suffer,) quia illorum est regnum cœlorum, qui animam solam in confiscato habent . . . Apostoli persecutionibus agitati, quando se pecunia tractantes liberaverunt? quae illis utique non deerat ex praediorum pretiis ad pedes eorum depositis. But not only individual Christians consulted their safety in this way, but whole churches also compounded with the governors for peace, by pecuniary contributions, and paid a sort of annual tribute, not unlike that assessed on bawds and panders and other vile characters. It is not amiss, to transcribe here the indignant language of *Tertullian*, c. xiii. p. 700.: Parum denique est, si unus aut alius ita eruitur. Massaliter totae ecclesiæ tributum sibi irrogaverunt. Nescio dolendum, an erubescendum sit, cum in matricibus Beneficiariorum et Curiosorum, inter tabernarios et lanios, et fures balnearum, et aleones et lenones, Christiani quoque vectigales continentur. Moreover, as

appears from Tertullian, the Christians sometimes bargained with those, who threatened to turn accusers if money was not given them, at other times with the governors themselves, and sometimes with the soldiers; which last deserves particular notice, because we learn from it, that the magistrates directed the soldiers to watch for, and break up, the assemblies of Christians: and therefore, these were to be pacified with money, in order that Christians might safely meet together for the worship of God. Says Tertullian: Sed quomodo colligemus, inquis, quomodo Dominica solemnia celebrabimus? Utique, quomodo et Apostoli, fide, non *pecunia* tuti: quae fides si montem transferre potest, multo magis *militem*. Esto sapientia, non praemio cautus. Neque enim statim, (mark the expression,) *et a populo eris tutus, si* officia militaria redemeris. What the bishops thought of this practice, is abundantly shown by *Peter* of Alexandria, who was a martyr of this century. In his canons, extracted from his Discourse dePoenitentia, Canon xii. (in *Wm. Beverege's* Pandectae canonum et concilior. Tom. ii. 20.) he not only decides, that those are not to be censured who purchase safety with money, but are to be commended; and he encounters Tertullian with his own arguments. I will quote only the Latin, omitting the Greek: Iis, qui pecuniam dederunt, ut omni ex parte ab omni malitia imperturbati essent, crimen intendi non potest. Damnum enim et jacturam pecuniarum sustinuerunt, ne ipsi animae detrimento afficerentur, vel ipsam etiam proderent, quod alii propter turpe lucrum non fecerunt, &c.

§ VI. **The Edict of Severus against conversions to Christianity.** [p. 455.] These evils were greatly augmented, when the emperor, in the year 203, for some cause not known, became somewhat differently disposed towards the Christians, and issued an edict, forbidding Roman citizens, under a severe penalty, from abandoning the religion of their fathers, and embracing Christianity. This law, although it opposed only the increase of the church, and affected only those recently converted, and those who wished to join the Christians after the publication of the law, yet afforded occasion for the adversaries of Christians to persecute and harass them at their pleasure; and especially because the ancient laws, and particularly that most vexatious one of Trajan,—that persons accused, and refusing to confess, might be put to death,—remained unrepealed, and in full force.(¹) Hence, so great was the slaughter among Christians, especially of such as could not, or, from conscientious motives, would not redeem their lives with money, that some of their teachers supposed the coming of Antichrist to draw near. Among others, many of the Alexandrian Christians lost their lives for Christ, of whom was *Leonidas*, the father of Origen; and in Africa, the celebrated Christian females, *Perpetua* and *Felicitas*, whose *Acta*, illustrious monuments of antiquity, have been often published; and *Potamiena*, a virgin of Alexandria, and her mother, *Marcella*, with various others. Respecting the termination of this persecution, the ancient writers are silent; but, as it appears from reliable authorities, and especially from Tertullian, that the Christians were also persecuted in some places under *Caracalla*, the son of *Severus*, it seems to be judging correctly to suppose that the persecution did not cease till after the death of *Severus*.

(1) On the persecution of the Christians under Severus, *Eusebius* treats, Hist. Eccles. L. vi. cap. 1. &c.; but only in a general way: for he neither reports the law, nor the time and cause of its enactment. Other Christian writers incidentally mention the severity of the persecution, the cruelty of the judges, and the constancy of certain Christians; yet they say very little of the mode and the grounds of the persecution. *Spartian*, however, the writer of the Life of Severus, has told us the year, and stated the reason, of the persecution: Vita Severi. c. 16, 17. in the Scriptores Histor. Augustae, p. 617, 618. For he says, that the emperor, in the year that he invested his son Antoninus with the Toga [p. 456.] virilis, and designated him consul with himself, which was the tenth year of his reign, as he was passing through Palestine into Egypt, enacted a law equally severe against the Jews and the Christians: Palaestinis jura plurima fundavit: Judaeos fieri sub gravi poena vetuit: Idem etiam de Christianis sanxit. This language shows, that Severus did not enact *new* laws against the Christians, nor command the extirpation of the professors of christianity, but only resolved to prevent the increase of the church, and commanded those to be punished, who should forsake the religion of their fathers and embrace that of the Christians. Persons, therefore, who were born Christians, or had become Christians before this law was enacted, might indeed be exposed to some trouble and danger from the old laws, and especially from the noted rescript of Trajan, which subsequent enactments had not abrogated; but from this new law of Severus they had nothing to fear. But some learned men are not ready to believe this. For, perceiving what a multitude of Christians suffered death, under Severus, they say, the fact is not to be accounted for, if Severus wished evil to none but the deserters of their former religion. They therefore conjecture, either that Spartian has mutilated the law of Severus, and omitted a large part of it, or that the emperor issued other and severer laws against the Christians, which have not reached our times. But I can easily overthrow both these conjectures. That Spartian did not mutilate the law of Severus, his own words show. For he compares the edict against the Jews, with that against the Christians, and says that the latter was of the same tenor with the former. But Severus neither interdicted the Jewish religion, nor compelled those born of Jewish parents to embrace the religion of the Romans; but merely forbid accessions to the Jewish community from people of other nations. And therefore he was no *more* severe against the Christians, seeing his decree against them was precisely the same as against the Jews. That Severus enacted other laws against the

Christians, than the one mentioned by Spartian, is contrary to all probability. For, not to mention the silence of the ancient writers, it appears from explicit passages in Tertullian, that the emperor did not repeal those ancient laws which favored Christians; which he undoubtedly would have done, if he intended they should be treated more severely than in former times. In his book, *ad Scapulam*, which was written after the death of Severus, in the reign of Antoninus Caracalla, *Tertullian* thus addresses that governor, (c. 4, p. 87.): Quid enim amplius tibi mandatur, quam nocentes confessos damnare, negantes autem ad tormenta revocare? Videtis ergo quomodo ipsi vos contra mandata faciatis, ut confessos negare cogatis. This passage shows, most beautifully and admirably, how the emperors, and among them the recently deceased Severus, would have the judges deal with Christians. In the first place, sentence of death was to be passed *in nocentes confessos*. The *nocentes* here, are those "accused and convicted in a regular course of law." This is put beyond controversy [p. 457.] by various passages in Tertullian, and also in this very passage, in which the *nocentes negantes* follow the *nocentes confessos*. Who could be a *nocens negans*, except the man who was accused of some crime or fault, and convicted by his accuser, and yet denied that he was guilty? We will, however, let Tertullian himself teach us, how to understand the expression. Among the examples which he shortly after adduces, of governors that favored the Christians, he extols one Pudens, in the following terms: Pudens etiam missum ad se Christianum, in elogio, concussione ejus intellecta, dimisit, scisso eodem elogio, *sine Accusatore negans se auditurum hominem, secundum Mandatum* (ss. *Imperatoris.*) Under Severus, therefore, as is most manifest from these words, the law of Trajan remained in full force; and it enjoined, that no Christian should be condemned, unless he was legitimately accused and convicted. And, moreover, those accused and convicted, but who yet denied themselves to be Christians,—the *nocentes negantes*, might be put to the rack, and be compelled by torture to confess guilt. This was not expressly enjoined by Trajan, but it was in accordance with Roman law. But, thirdly, the laws did not permit the magistrates, to urge confessing persons to a denial or a rejection of christianity, by means of tortures. This was a liberty which the governors assumed contrary to the laws, as I suppose, and from motives of avarice. For when the confessors declared that they would not redeem life by paying money, the governors hoped, that if put to torture, they would change their determination. That the laws of Hadrian and Antoninus Pius, ordering that Christians should not be put to death unless convicted of some violation of the Roman laws, were in like manner not repealed by Severus, appears from another example of the governor Circius Severus, mentioned by the same Tertullian; Circius Severus Thysdri ipse dedit remedium, quomodo responderent Christiani ut dimitti possent. By cautious and circumspect answers to the judges, therefore, Christians could elude the malice of their accusers: and in what manner, it is easy to conjecture: viz. they confessed that they followed a different religion from the Roman, namely the Christian; but that the emperors forbid a Christian to be punished, unless he was convicted of some crime, and *they* had never been guilty of any crime. With an upright judge, this plea was sufficient. And it is not only certain, that

Severus did not abrogate the imperial edicts favorable to the Christians, but it also appears from Tertullian, that he constantly and to the end of his life retained his former kind feelings towards them. For Tertullian says of him, after his death: Sed et clarissimas feminas et clarissimos viros Severus sciens ejus sectae esse, non modo non laesit, verum et testimonio exornavit, et populo furenti in eos palam restitit. How could Severus have been a protector of Christians against popular rage, and also their eulogist, if he had enacted se- [p. 458.] verer laws against them, than the preceding emperors? It must therefore be certain, as Spartian has stated, that he ordered the punishment, not of all Christians universally, but only of such as became Christians after the enactment of the law.

But how was it, you may ask, that so great calamities fell on the Christians, in his reign, if Severus directed only the new converts to be punished? An answer is easily given. In the *first* place, let it be remembered, that the Christians had been miserably persecuted in most of the Roman provinces, before the law of Severus existed. This we have shown in the history of the second century, from the Apologeticum of Tertullian; and the fact cannot be denied. The avaricious governors finding the Christians willing to redeem their lives with money, suborned accusers, and inflamed the people, in order to extort money; and they actually put some confessors to death, to strike terror into the more wealthy, and make them willing to compound for their lives. In the *next* place, it is to be supposed, that Severus gave power to the governors to investigate the case of such as forsook the Romish religion and embraced Christianity; and, in these investigations, the magistrates and their minions, as is very common, did many things not warranted by the law. *Thirdly*, as the persons who forsook the religion of their fathers were to be punished, undoubtedly the same penalties, or perhaps greater, awaited those who caused their apostacy. For he who instigates another to commit a crime, is more culpable than the transgressor. It was therefore a necessary consequence, that many of the Christian teachers were condemned. *Lastly*, those conversant in human affairs well know, that when new laws are enacted on any subject, the old laws relating to it acquire new life. It would therefore not be strange, if on Severus' prohibiting conversions to Christianity, the number of accusers should be suddenly increased. I say nothing of the probability, that the more unfriendly governors extended the prohibitions of the law, and summoned to their bar persons who became Christians before the law was enacted.

What some of the learned maintain, respecting the cause of this edict, has little or no weight. The most probable conjecture is that of *Henry Dodwell*, in his Dissert. Cyprian. Diss. xi. § 42. p. 269.; namely, that the emperor's victory over the Jews, who had disturbed the public tranquillity by a recent insurrection, gave rise to this edict. That this Jewish insurrection induced Severus to prohibit Romans from becoming Jews, lest the augmentation of the resources of that people should prove injurious to the commonwealth, is beyond all controversy. But Spartian couples the law against the Christians with that against the Jews, and tells us, that both were enacted at the same time: and we may reasonably suppose, therefore, that some ill-disposed persons suggested to the emperor, that there was equal danger from the Christians, and that if their numbers and strength should become augmented, they might make war upon the Romans who worshipped the gods. This argument had great effect upon the superstitious emperor. And there is little force in [p. 459.] what is opposed to this supposition, by certain learned men, who, following *Tillemont* (Memoires pour l'Histoire de l'Eglise, tom. iii. P. I. p. 487.) say, it appears from Jerome's Chronicon, that the war against the Jews occurred in the *fifth* year of Severus, but that the law was not enacted till his *tenth* year. For there might be various reasons for several years to intervene between the war and the promulgation of the law. *Dodwell*, however, and those who follow him, have erred in supposing that Severus did not distinguish between the Jews and the Christians, but confounded them together. For, not to mention, that Spartian's language is opposed to this idea, he distinctly stating that there were *two* laws, one against the Jews and the other against the Christians; Severus could not be so ignorant of the affairs of his own times, as to confound the Christians with the Jews. There were Christians in his own family; and with some of them he lived in intimacy.

§ VII. **The state of Christians under Caracalla and Heliogabalus.** Severus, having died at York, in Britain, in the year 211, was succeeded by his son, *Antoninus*, surnamed *Caracalla*, who better deserved the title of tyrant than that of emperor. Yet, under him, the persecution which his father had excited against the Christians, gradually subsided :(1) and, during the six years of his reign, we do not learn that they endured any very great grievances. Whether this is ascribable to his good will towards Christians, or to other causes, does not sufficiently appear.(2) He being slain, after the short reign of *Macrinus*, who instigated the murder, the government of the Roman empire was assumed by *Antoninus Elagabalus*, a prince of the most abandoned character, and a monster of a man. Yet, he also, did nothing against the Christians.(3) After a reign of three years and nine months, he was slain, with his mother, Julia, in a military tumult at Rome; and *Alexander Severus*, the son of Mammaea, whom Elagabalus had adopted, and had constituted Cæsar, was hailed emperor in the year 222, and proved to be a very mild and excellent prince.

(1) We have a work of Tertullian addressed to *Scapula*, a most bitter enemy of the Christians, and written after the death of Severus, from which it appears that the commencement of Caracalla's reign was sullied by the execution of many Christians in Africa.

(2) Some learned men think, Caracalla had kind feelings towards Christians; and in favor of this opinion they cite the authority of Tertullian and [p. 460.]

Spartian. The former, in his work *ad Scapulam*, c. 4. p. 87, records, that Antoninus Caracalla *lacte Christiano educatum fuisse*, which, undoubtedly means, that he was nursed by a Christian mother. The latter, in his life of Caracalla, (in the Scriptores Hist. Augustae, tom. i. p. 707,) relates of him, that when seven years old, Quum collusorem suum puerum ob Judaicam religionem gravius verberatum audivisset, neque patrem suum, neque patrem pueri, vel auctores verberum diu respexisse: that is, he was exceedingly offended at the injury done to his companion. From these two testimonies, learned men have supposed, that it may be inferred, the Christian mother of Caracalla instilled into him a love of her religion, along with her milk; and that this led him to so great indignation towards the persons who had punished his companion on account of his religion. They, moreover, do not hesitate to say, that by *Judaica Religio* in the passage from Spartian, should be understood the *Christian religion;* because it is certain, that Christians were frequently confounded with Jews by the Romans of those times. But to me, all this appears very uncertain. To begin with the last assumption, I cannot easily persuade myself, that Spartian meant Christianity when he wrote Jewish religion; for it appears from other passages in his book, that he was not ignorant of the wide difference between the Jews and the Christians. And again, it was not a love of the religion, which his companion professed, but attachment to the person of his friend and play-fellow, that made him angry with those who punished him. Lastly, it is not easy to conceive, how a sucking child could be imbued by his mother with the love of *any* religion. The ancient Christians do not mention Caracalla among their patrons; and the tranquillity they enjoyed under him, was due perhaps to their money, which they would spend freely in times of trouble, more than to the friendship of this very cruel emperor.

(3) There is a passage in the life of Heliogabalus by *Lampridius*, (c. 3. p. 796.) which seems to indicate, that this emperor, though one of the worst of men, was destitute of hatred to the Christians. It is this: Dicebat praeterea (Imperator) Judaeorum et Samaritanorum religiones et Christianam devotionem illuc (viz. *Rome*, where he would have no other god to be worshipped, besides Heliogabalus, or the sun, of which he was himself priest,) transferendam, ut omnium culturarum (i. e. all forms of divine worship,) secretum Heliogabali sacerdotium teneret. Although this passage is more obscure than I could wish, yet the following things can, I think, be learned from it. I. That Heliogabalus wished to abolish all the deities worshipped by the Romans, and to substitute in their place one deity, the sun, of which he himself was priest. Nor was this very strange; for among both the Greeks and the Romans, there were persons who supposed that all the Gods represented only the sun. II. That, on this taking place, he wished to have the Jewish, Christian, and Samaritan religions transferred also to Rome. And III. That his aim was, that the *sacerdotium*, that is, the priests of Heliogabalus or the sun, might learn the [p. 461.] secret ceremonies, of all religions, and be able, perhaps, from these ceremonies to improve and embellish the worship paid to the sun. Heliogabalus, therefore, did not wish to extirpate the Christian religion, but he would have Christians live at their ease in Rome itself, and worship God in their own

way, so that the priests of the sun, by intercourse with them, might learn their most secret discipline. Such an emperor could have no thoughts of persecuting the Christians.

§ VIII. **State of Christians under Alexander Severus.** Under Alexander Severus, the Christians saw better times, than under any of the preceding emperors. The principal cause of their peace and tranquillity, was *Julia Mammæa*, the emperor's mother, who influenced and guided her son; and, having the greatest respect for Christianity, once invited Origen, the celebrated Christian doctor, to visit the court, that she might profit by his instructions and conversation.(1) Yielding himself, therefore, wholly to the judgment and pleasure of his mother, Alexander not only adopted no measures adverse to the Christians, but he did not hesitate to show, by various tokens, his kind feelings towards them. And yet, if we examine carefully all the evidences of these his kind feelings, which history records, they do not appear sufficient to prove, that he regarded Christianity as more true or more excellent than other religions. If I can rightly judge, Alexander was one of those who supposed, that but one God was worshipped by all the nations, under different names, in differing modes and forms, and with diversity of rites. This opinion, it is well known, was held by many of the philosophers of that age, and particularly by the Platonists. And, if so, he would think, that the Christian mode of worshipping God might be tolerated as well as the others; and perhaps, also, he deemed it in some respects more consentaneous to reason than some of the others.(2) Yet his estimate of Christianity was not sufficient to lead him to abrogate the old laws against Christians, if it was true, as it seems to be, that in his reign, Ulpian collected all the laws enacted against the Christians, so that the Roman judges might understand how they were to proceed against them. And hence, perhaps, we must not regard as fictitious, all the examples of martyrdom endured by Christians under him, in one place and another, of which we find mention.

(1) All the modern Christian historians represent *Julia Mammaea*, the mother of Alexander, as a convert to Christianity. See Joh. Rud. [p. 462.] *Wetstein:* Præfatio ad Origenis Dialogum contra Marcionitas; who thinks, with others of great authority and learning, that credit must be given to so numerous testimonies. But the older historians, *Eusebius* (Hist. Eccles. L. vi. c. 21.

p. 223.) and *Jerome*, (Catal. Scriptor. Eccles. c. 54.) speak dubiously. The former characterises Julia as θεοσεβεστάτη, and the latter styles her *religiosa.* And both tell us, that Origen was invited by her to the court, which was then at Antioch, and that she heard him discourse on religion. But neither states, that she yielded to Origen's views, or that, abandoning superstition, she became a professed Christian. Neither are the two words, by which Eusebius and Jerome express her piety, of such import as clearly to imply her conversion; for they are applied by the ancients, in general, to all persons, Christians or not Christians, who were solicitous for salvation, and reverenced a supreme Being. On the other hand, we find manifest indications, in the life of Julia, of real superstition, and of the worship of the false Roman gods. These and other considerations induce several excellent men to believe, that she continued an adherent to the religion of her ancestors. A fuller discussion of this subject may be found in Fred. *Spanheim's* Diss. de Lucii Britonum Regis, Juliæ Mammaeæ et Philiporum Conversionibus, c. 2. Opp. tom. ii. p. 400. I will add a few things, corroborative, as I think, of this opinion. And first, *Lampridius,* in his life of Severus, c. 14. (Scriptores Hist. August. tom. i. p. 901,) styles her *Sancta Mulier*, an expression corresponding with the epithets used by Jerome and Eusebius; yet no one supposes that *Lampridius* intended, by this language, to indicate that she embraced Christianity. Again, I deem it worthy of remark, that Eusebius states in the passage specified, that Origen did not remain long at Antioch with the empress, but (ἔσπευδε) *quickly returned* home. If I am not deceived, this is evidence, that the avaricious Julia, who was very greedy of wealth, found no great satisfaction in the discourses of Origen, who was a despiser of wealth, and contented with poverty; and therefore, she soon sent back the austere teacher to Alexandria. There can be no doubt, however, that Julia was well disposed towards the Christians and their religion; and, though her manners differed widely from theirs, yet she felt respect for the Christian discipline, and for those who practised it. And hence it is not strange, that her son also, Alexander, should be very well disposed towards Christians. For both in his childhood and his manhood, as historians inform us, he was governed solely by her authority, and always considered her decisions perfectly right. Says *Lampridius*, (in Vita Severi, c. 14. p. 901.): Quum puer ad imperium pervenisset, fecit cuncta cum *matre*, ut et illa videretur pariter [p. 463.] imperare, mulier sancta, sed avara et auri atque argenti cupida. And a little after, (c. 26. p. 924.) he says: In matrem Mammæam unice pius fuit. The distinguishing kindness, therefore, of the emperor towards Christians, would seem to be attributable, not so much to his judgment and wisdom, as to his deference to his mother.

(2) There are some who rank *Alexander Severus* himself among the Christians. And though this opinion stands opposed by numerous proofs of the depraved superstition by which his life was deformed, yet a man of great learning and worth, Paul Ernest *Jablonski*, not long since, found a way to solve the difficulty. In an ingenious dissertation, de Alexandro Severo Christianorum sacris per Gnosticos initiato, he endeavors to render it probable, that Alexander listened to some Gnostic teacher, and embraced that form of Christianity which

the Gnostics professed: but that he dissembled his real opinions before the people, which was a thing allowable among Gnostics, and publicly worshipped the Roman Gods, but privately worshipped Christ. This dissertation of the learned Jablonski, is found in the *Miscellaneis Lipsiensibus novis*, of the excellent Fred. Otto *Mencken*,(tom. iv. P. i. p. 56–94.) The sole foundation of this opinion, (for all that is brought from Lampridius and others in support of it, falls to the ground without it,) is an ancient gem, published by James de Wildé, on which appears the well known Monogramm of Christ, together with this inscription: *Sal. Don. Alex. Fil. Ma. Luce.* These notes he would have us read and interpret thus: *Salus Donata Alexandro Filio Mammæae Luce* (ss. Christi, this name being expressed by the Monogramm.) Charles du Fresne had previously referred this gem to Alexander Severus, in his Diss. de Inferioris ævi Numismat. § 24. contrary to the views of Gisbert *Cuper*, who (in his notes on Lactantius de Mortibus Persequutor. p. 239.) would refer it to some emperor's son of the name *Alexius.* Tobias *Eckhard* also, (in his Testimonia non Christianor. de Christo, p. 157.) professed to regard this gem as no contemptible proof, that Alexander and his mother privately embraced Christianity. But it was the celebrated *Jablonski* who undertook formally to state and defend this opinion: and he finds (§ II. p. 71.) in this gem, not a probable argument, (as *Eckhard* deemed it to be,) but certain and unanswerable proof, that Alexander was privately initiated a Christian. But this his certain and strongest possible proof, rests solely on the two letters *Ma.* which are subjoined to *Alex. Fil.* in the gem; and which he thinks cannot possibly denote any other person than *Mammæa.* He says, (§ II. p. 70.): Sunt autem illæ Litteræ indicio certissimo, nullis machinis elidendo, Gemmam hanc sculptam esse in honorem et memoriam Alexandri Filii Mammæae. But, to tell the truth, I must [p. 464.] confess that I do not see what there is, that compels us to understand by these letters no person but *Mammæa.* There were many names, as every one knows, both of males and females, which began with the two letters *Ma.* And if any person should insert one of these instead of *Mammæa*, I see not how he can be forced to give up his conjecture. If the word *Imperator*, or the abbreviation *Imp.* had been prefixed to the name *Alex.* the person might feel some embarrassment. But in the gem, as the learned author admits, there is nothing that indicates imperatorial rank.

Leaving the more full dijudication of this point to others, I will bring forward all the testimonies of the ancients concerning Alexander's friendship for the Christians, and will show that nothing more can be inferred from them, than that he deemed Christianity worthy of toleration, and its religious worship neither absurd nor injurious to the commonwealth; but that he by no means preferred Christianity to all other religious, or regarded it as more holy, more true, or more excellent. In the first place *Lampridius*, in his Life of the Emperor, (c. 22. p. 914.) says: Judaeis privilegia reservavit. Christianos esse passus est. From this, only a moderate degree of benevolence can be proved. The emperor favored the Jews, more than he did the Christians. For he restored to the former, the privileges of which they had been divested by preceding emperors; while to the latter he granted no rights, but merely suspended

the operation of the ancient laws against them; in other words, he made no enactments against them. Yet he did not abrogate the old, unjust, and vexatious laws, as we shall presently see; so that the favor which he conferred on the Christians, though real, was yet but moderate. It is meritorious to suspend the operation of iniquitous laws; but far more so, to rescind and abolish them; and most of all, to guaranty rights infringed upon by the former laws. But to proceed: this same *Lampridius*, (c. 29. p. 930.) tells us, that the emperor had an image of our Saviour, together with the likenesses of certain great men, placed in his chamber for private worship, for he says: Matutinis horis in Larario suo. (in quo et divos et principes, sed optime electos et animas sanctiores, in queis et *Apollonium*, et quantum scriptor suorrum temporum dicit, *Christum*, *Abraham* et *Orpheum*, et hujuscemodi *Deos* habebat et *majorum effigies*.) rem divinam faciebat. A very learned dissertation was written, a few years ago, by the distinguished Charles Henry *Zibich*, and which the celebrated *Mencken* deservedly placed in the Nova Miscellanea Lipsiens. (tom. iii. p. 42.) This learned man aims to prove, and, in my opinion, does successfully prove, that it cannot be inferred from this passage, that Alexander paid divine honors to our Saviour. All that appears from it, is, that Christ had a place assigned him by the emperor, among the *animæ sanctiores*, i. e. the men distinguished for sanctity, piety, and wisdom; and that he was accounted not inferior to Apollo-
[p. 465.] nius, Abraham and Orpheus. But, not to be too strenuous, we will grant, that a degree of probability is attached to the opinion, that *Lampridius* intended to signify that a sort of worship was paid by the emperor to Jesus Christ: we will admit also the truth of the facts stated, although a strenuous disputant might call them in question, since Lampridius mentions only a single witness for them; and lastly, we will admit, that the historian here gives to Christ the title of *Deus*, or "God;" and that the words: *Et hujuscemodi Deos habebat*, are the correct and true reading, although many think they are not. Yet, after all these admissions, it will not be proved, that Alexander considered the Christian religion as better and more holy than the other religions. On the contrary, the language clearly shows, that the emperor placed Christianity among the plausible and allowable forms of religion, and that he coincided in opinion with those men of his age, who considered all religions as equal, differing only in rites, regulations, and modes of worship. For he coupled together the three chief personages of the three most distinguished religions of his times, the Gentile, the Christian, and the Jewish; namely, *Orpheus*, (that great master of the mysteries and theology, and the eulogist of the gods,) and *Abraham* and *Christ:* and this shows, that he attributed the same dignity to each of those religions. Moreover, all those whom Alexander honored with a place in his principal *Lararium*, and esteemed as *Divi*, were not in his opinion holy persons, and patterns of virtue and wisdom. For, as *Lampridius* tells us, (c. 32. p. 936.) Consecraverat in Lario majore inter divos et optimos (etiam) Alexandrum Magnum. And yet he was far from denying, that in *him* were enormous vices, as well as virtues. Our author says (c. 30. p. 932.): Condemnabat in Alexandro ebrietatem et crudelitatem in amicos. Of no more weight is the third thing, relative to Alexander's reverence for Christ, recorded by *Lampridius*, (c. 43.

p. 993.) namely: Christo templum facere voluit, eumque inter divos recipere. He would, therefore, only assign Christianity a place among the other religions, and not recommend it to his people as the only religion that was true and worthy of God. This will appear more clearly from the grounds of his giving up the design: Sed prohibitus est ab iis, qui consulentes sacra, repererant, omnes Christianos futuros, si id optato evenisset, et templa reliqua deserenda. For this passsage does not refer (as many have supposed) to the emperor *Hadrian*, who formed the same project, but to our *Alexander*. He was therefore, not unwilling to have divine honors paid to Christ; but he would have it so done, that the Roman gods should not be neglected. And when he learned, that these gods would be despised, if *Christ* should be enrolled among them, he would rather have divine honors withheld from Christ, though worthy to receive them, than see the gods neglected and despised. I can conceive how the emperor may have been led to think of enrolling Christ among the [p. 466.] gods of the Romans. The old imperial laws against the Christians were an obstacle to his placing them beyond all danger of punishment or injury, which his mother ardently desired; and yet he was afraid to annul these laws precipitately, lest he should irritate the people and the priests. And therefore, to accomplish what he and his mother had at heart, he tried to get Christ admitted among the gods of the republic; because, if this were done, those old edicts against the Christians would of course fall to the ground, and yet would not be subverted by him, but by the Senate who sanctioned Christ's apotheosis.

As for what Lampridius tells us (§ 45. p. 997.) of his copying the Christians' method of appointing public functionaries, though it was in some measure paying honor to the Christians, yet in a less degree than learned men suppose. The statement is: Ubi aliquos voluisset vel rectores provinciis dare, vel præpositos facere, vel procuratores, nomina eorum proponebat - - - dicebatque grave esse, quum id Christiani et Judæi facerent in prædicandis sacerdotibus, qui ordinandi sunt, non fieri in provinciarum rectoribus, quibus et fortunæ hominum committerentur et capita. Not to notice that the Christians are here associated with the Jews, the comparison which the emperor makes between Christian priests and the Roman governors of provinces, shows that, in his view, the functions of a Christian priest were less important and salutary, than the functions of magistrates. For, in the language of the schools, he reasoned from the less to the greater. If such caution is exercised in the election of Christian priests, what caution should be exercised in appointing magistrates, to whom are entrusted the lives and fortunes of the citizens? No man could talk thus, if he believed that the Christian priests showed men the way to salvation, and taught them the true method of obtaining peace with God. Such a man could not esteem the temporal life and prosperity of the citizens, as more important than the salvation of their souls, for which the Christian priests labored.

Similar remarks are applicable to the judgment which Alexander is said to have passed, in a litigated case between some Christians and the hucksters; in *Lampridius*, c. 49. p. 1003: Quum Christiani quemdam locum, qui fuerat publicus, occupassent, contra propinarii dicerent, sibi eum deberi; rescripsit, melius esse, ut quomodocunque illic Deus colatur, quam propinariis dedatur. These words show a religious mind, and are somewhat commendatory of the Christian religion; for the emperor admitted that the Christians worshipped God; and, on that account, the state could tolerate them. And yet he indicates, that the Roman mode of worshipping God was preferable to the Christian; or, at least, the word *Quomodocunque* leaves it doubtful, whether the Christian mode of serving God was to be approved or was faulty. Such language does not indicate a man who viewed Jesus Christ as the Son of God, and the only (I will not say *Saviour*, but) *Instructor* of the human race, and whose doctrines and precepts [p. 467.] were more just and holy than any others. What the same *Lampridius* tells us, (c. 51. p. 1007.) that Alexander was so much pleased with this precept, (which he had learned either from Jews or from Christians) *Quod tibi fieri non vis, alteri ne feceris*, that he ordered it to be inscribed on the palace and on the public works, has plainly no decisive force in the question before us. For the most virulent enemies of the Christians did not deny, that Christianity contained many beautiful and incomparable moral precepts. Nor does the statement of *Eusebius*, (Hist. Eccles. l. vi. c. 28. p. 228.) that *the family of Alexander was full of Christians*, much assist those who maintain, that he regarded Christianity as the best and holiest of all religions, notwithstanding he declined a public profession of it. For what wonder is it, if an emperor, obsequious in everything to a mother who loved the Christians, suffered her to take Christians into her family? One who placed all religions upon a level, and considered them as differing only as to forms or modes of worshipping the Deity, might consistently admit men of all religions to become his servants.

(3) *Lactantius* says (Divinar. Instit. l. v. c. 11. p. 627. ed Bünem.): Nam et constitutiones sacrilegæ et disputationes jurisperitorum (in Christianos) leguntur injustæ. *Domitius* de officio proconsulis rescripta principum nefaria collegit, ut doceret, quibus pœnis adfici oporteret eos, qui se cultores Dei confiterentur. The most learned men have no hesitation in saying, that this *Domitius*, an enemy of Christians, was *Domitius Ulpianus*, whom Alexander entrusted with the chief administration of the state. See Francis *Baldwin's* Comm. ad. edicta Principum Roman. de Christianis, p. 101. &c. ed. Gundling. This man, therefore, by collecting together the imperatorial laws against the Christians, may have aimed to moderate the benevolence of his master towards Christians, and to intercept in a measure the effects of his clemency. And of course, it is not beyond credibility, that under this mildest and best of emperors, the judges in several places governed their conduct towards Christians, by the laws which *Ulpian* thus spread before them in a collated form, rather than by the wishes of an emperor who had not courage to repeal those laws. Certain it is, that in the Martyrologies and other books, we meet with not a few examples of Christians put to death under Alexander. See the Martyrologium Romanum, diem 11mam Octob. et diem 22dam Novemb. Yet Theodore *Ruinart*, (Præf. ad Acta Martyr. sincera et Selecta, § 47. 48.) does not conceal the facts, that he regarded most of them as dubious.

§ IX. **The Persecution under Maximin.** This tranquility of the Christians was disturbed by *Maximin the Thracian*, whom the soldiers created emperor, when Alexander Severus was slain, in the year 235. Maximin was actuated, not so much by [p. 468.] hatred of Christianity, as by *fear*, lest the Christians should seek to avenge the slaughter of their beloved Alexander; and he therefore did not order all Christians promiscuously to be executed, but only the bishops and doctors; hoping that when these were removed, the Christians, being deprived of their leaders and guides, would remain quiet and attempt nothing to his injury.(1) Perhaps also, the tyrant did not purpose the death of *all* Christian bishops, but only of those whom he had known to be the friends and intimates of Alexander. It is certain, that very few cases are recorded of bishops or doctors, who honored Christ by martyrdom, or by any severe sufferings, under this emperor.(2) We know, indeed, that in some of the provinces, during this reign, the sufferings and calamities of the Christians were more extensive, and reached all classes; but these extensive calamities are not to be traced to the emperor's edict, but either to insurrections of the populace, who regarded Christianity as the cause of their misfortunes, or to the injustice and cruelty of the governors. And hence, we readily agree with those who maintain, that the Christians were harrassed, in various places, during the whole three years reign of *Maximin.*(3)

(1) *Eusebius* states, (Hist. Eccles. L. vi. c. 28. p. 225.) that Maximin, burning with hatred to the family of Alexander Severus, which was filled with Christians, commenced a persecution against the Christians. But he adds, that the emperor ordered only the *bishops* (ἀρχοντας τῶν ἐκκλησίων,) to be slain, as being the *authors of evangelical instruction* (αἰτίους τῆς κατὰ Ε'υαγγέλιον διδασκαλίας). These statements are in conflict; if I am not greatly mistaken. If his hatred to the *family* of Alexander, had been the cause of this persecution, he would not have poured his wrath upon the *bishops*, who, none of them, belonged to the family of Alexander, but must have attacked and slain the family of Alexander itself. This course would have gratified his passion; but the punishing of the bishops, brought no evil or detriment to the surviving ministers and servants of Alexander's household. This difficulty will be removed, if we understand the (κάτος) *anger* or *hatred*, in Eusebius, to denote *fear combined with hatred:* for those whom we dread or *fear*, we naturally *hate.* The tyrant was afraid, lest the family of the murdered emperor should conspire against him, and strive to avenge the death of their excellent lord; and therefore, he pursued them with violent hatred. To free himself from this *fear*, he resolved on the slaughter of the Christian bishops, hoping that when they were put out of the way, the adherents and servants of Alexander, being deprived of [p. 469.]

their advisers and guides, would attempt nothing very formidable against him. Undoubtedly, some one who professed to be acquainted with Christian affairs had suggested to the emperor, that the Christians followed implicitly the guidance and will of their bishops; and therefore, that he would have nothing to fear, if these bishops were out of the way. Unless this explanation be admitted, I see not how the slaughter of the Christian bishops could originate from hatred to the family of Alexander.

(2) Although *Eusebius* says, that Maximin commanded all the Christian bishops and teachers to be put to death, I yet very much doubt, whether the tyrant's edict was so dreadfully cruel. I suspect, rather, that the emperor's enmity extended only to those Christian teachers, who had been intimate with Alexander and his mother, and whom the former knowingly permitted to instil the Christian faith into a large part of his family. The chief of these was *Origen*, who was well known to have been invited to the court, not long before: and therefore him especially, the tyrant wished to have arrested and put to death. This we learn from *Orosius*, who says, (Histor. L. vii. c. 19. p. 509. ed. Havercamp.): Qui maxime propter christianam Alexandri et matris ejus Mammaeae familiam, persequutionem in sacerdotes et clericos, id est, doctores, *vel praecipue propter Origenem* presbyterum miserat. And it is well known, that in order to avoid the emperor's fury, Origen kept himself concealed at Caesarea for two years. Being unable to find him, the tyrant vented his indignation upon his two most intimate friends, *Ambrose*, a man of great distinction, and *Protoctetus* a presbyter; who were first treated with great indignity and abuse, and then banished to Germany by order of the emperor. See *Eusebius*, Hist. Eccles. L. vi. c. 29. p. 229. Besides these, very few only, here and there one, of the Christian priests and bishops, suffered greatly under Maximin. Says *Sulpitius Severus*, (Hist. Sacra, L. ii. c. 32. p. 247.): Maximinus *nonnullarum* ecclesiarum Clericos vexavit. Now, whence this paucity of martyrs and confessors among the bishops and teachers, if the edict of Maximin commanded *all* Christian bishops every where, to be seized and put to death? Numerous examples of martyred clergymen under this very cruel emperor, would have come down to us, if the edict had ordered the bishops and teachers to be indiscriminately put to death. But all that is obscure in this matter, becomes clear and obvious, if we suppose that hatred or fear of the *family of Alexander* was, as ancient writers expressly state, the cause of this persecution of the Christian teachers; and this alone may lead us to conclude, that the emperor's rage was only against those priests, who had been intimate with Alexander and his family.

[p. 470] (3) Those who treat of the persecution under Maximin, trace all the evils of the church during his reign, to this edict of the emperor. But in this they certainly err. The emperor only wished to get rid of some of the bishops and teachers. And therefore, the proceedings against all classes of Christians, in one place and another, must be ascribed to other causes. And of this fact, those early writers who treat of these general persecutions, have not left us in ignorance. *Origen* tells us, (tom. xxviii. in Matth. in his Opp. tom. i. p. 137, ed. Lat.) that earthquakes occurred in some places, and that the people, as usual, attributed the calamity to the Christians, and therefore inflicted great evils upon them. See also his *Exhortatio ad Martyres*, which he wrote in the reign of Maximin. The same cause, and not the cruelty of Maximin, produced the sufferings of the Christians in Cappadocia and in the adjacent regions; which, however, were augmented by the injustice of Serenianus the governor. Thus *Firmillian* testifies, (in his Epistle to Cyprian, among the Epistlolae Cyprianicæ, No. lxxv. p. 146, ed Baluz.): Ante viginta et duos fere annos, temporibus post Alexandrum Imperatorem, multae, istic conflictationes et pressurae acciderunt, vel in commune omnibus hominibus, vel privatim Christianis; terrae etiam motus plurimi et frequenter extiterunt, ut et per Cappadociam et per Pontum multa subruerent, quaedam etiam civitates in profundum receptae dirupti soli hiatu devorarentur, ut *ex hoc* (not in consequence of the imperial edict,) persecutio quoque gravis adversum nos Christiani nominis fieret, quae post longam retro aetatis pacem repente oborta de inopinato et insueto malo ad turbandum populum nostrum terribilior effecta est. Serenianus tunc fuit in nostra provincia praeses, acerbus et dirus persecutor. Hence, the Christians were not persecuted in *all* the Roman provinces, but only in those which had previously suffered greatly from these natural calamities. For thus Firmillian proceeds: In hac autem perturbatione constitutis fidelibus, et huc atque illuc persecutionis metu fugientibus, et partrias suas relinquentibus, atque in alias partes regionum transeunti bus, (erat enim transeundi facultas, eo quod *persecutio illa non per totum mundum, sed localis fuisset,*) emersit, &c. But, certainly, the persecution would have pervaded every part of the Roman world, if it had been commanded by an imperatorial edict. To express frankly my own views, I can hardly persuade myself that Maximin issued any decree against the Christian priests and bishops; but I suppose that, after the death of Alexander, he merely ordered the arrest of *Origen* and a few others, whom he knew to have been intimate with the murdered emperor and his mother; and that, after a short time, other objects occupying his mind, and the state of things being changed, this sudden burst of passion subsided.

§ X. **The tranquillity under Gordian and Philip.** *Maximin* being slain, by the African legions, in the year 238, *Gordian*, a mere boy, was created emperor; and, by means of his father-in-law, *Misitheus*, a man of great energy, he so conducted the government for six years, as to place the Christians in perfect safety. But, being unable to prevent the murder of Misitheus by *Philip* the Arabian, he was, the next year, himself slain by the same man, who had usurped the office of Prætorian Præfect. From the year 244 this *M. Julius Philip*, with his son of the same name, as the Cæsar, governed the Roman empire for almost five years, and showed himself exceedingly friendly to the Christians. From this fact arose the report, which was propagated in the subsequent ages with great unanimity among the writers, that both these *Philips* privately renounced the superstition of the futile gods, [p. 471.]

and embraced Christianity. But whether this report states a fact, or only a vulgar fable, originating from the kindness of the emperors towards Christians, has been disputed with great earnestness by the learned. Whoever will candidly and impartially weigh the arguments on both sides of the question, will see, that arguments are adduced by both parties, which, on examination, appear weak and powerless; and that there is nothing to fully settle the point, and compel us to accede to either party in the dispute.(1)

(1) There are extant many very grave and learned discussions respecting the renunciation of the old superstitions and reception of Christianity by the two *Philips;* some exclusively devoted to the subject, and others treating of it incidentally and cursorily. The most important of them are enumerated by Jo. Alb. *Fabricius*, (Lux salutaris Evangelii toti orbi exoriens, p. 235) But to his list, if it were necessary, large additions might easily be made of persons of high reputation, among both the ancients and the moderns. Omitting a work of so little importance, we will recount the principal arguments on both sides, so that those desirous to understand the controversy, may obtain their object with but little labor. In the first place, the reader should be apprised, that arguments are adduced on both sides, which scarcely deserve to rank among slender conjectures. Such, for example, are those from certain coins,—from Origen's journey to Arabia,—from the austerity of the younger Philip,—from certain just and equitable laws of the elder Philip, and from other topics adduced in proof of the sincere regard of the Philips for Christ, but which are of no weight, and vanish when touched. Nor are those more solid which are de- [p. 472.] rived from the celebration of the secular games by Philip,—from the superstitious marks on coins bearing his likeness,—from the apotheosis of Philip,—and from some other topics, in proof that the emperors were averse from Christianity. We propose to bring forward only those arguments which seem worthy of some regard, and may have influence on sober minds.

Among the arguments of those who wish to prove Philip a Christian, the first place is due to the testimony of *Eusebius*, (Hist. Eccles. l. vi. c. 34. p. 232,) who reports from tradition: "That on the vigils of Easter, the emperor wished to be a participator with the rest of the people in the prayers of the church, but that the bishop would not permit him to be present, until he had made confession of the enormous sins he had committed, and had taken his stand among the penitents: and that the emperor was not displeased, but conformed to the bishop's wishes." *Eusebius* mentions neither the place where this occurred, nor the name of the bishop who ventured to exclude the emperor from the church. But from the narrative of *Leontius*, bishop of Antioch, (an ancient writer who lived in the time of Constantius,) preserved in the *Chronicon Paschale*, edited among the Byzantine Historians, by *Carol.* du *Fresne*, it appears, that it was *Babylas*, bishop of Antioch, and afterwards a martyr under Decius, who assumed so much authority over the emperor. See the *Chronicon Paschale*, thes. x. et xiii. ad ann. 253. p. 270. *Chrysostom* also, in his Oration in honor of St. Babylas, (opp. tom. i. p. 658, 659, ed. German.) mentions this heroic act of the bishop, but without giving the name of the emperor. To this testimony of *Eusebius*, learned men add his declaration in his *Chronicon*, ad ann. 246. in the translation of Jerome: *Philippus primus omnium ex Romanis Imperatoribus Christianus fuit:* with which *Jerome* himself agrees, in his *Catalog. Scriptor. Eccles.* cap. *de Origene.*—To break down this chief bulwark of those who place Philip among the Christians, those of the contrary opinion exert themselves greatly: and Fred *Spanheim*, (in his Dis. de Christianismo Philippi Arabis, § 11 &c. Opp. tom. ii. p. 418.) has carefully collected all the arguments, which can be thought of. Yet they all resolve themselves into a few, if we carefully examine the prolix discussions of these great men. The amount is, that *Eusebius* does not cite any specific and suitable testimony, in support of his narrative; but says himself, that he learned what he states from common fame: his words are, Κατέχει λόγος, *fame has it:*—that *Leontius* also drew his account merely from public rumor, handed down by tradition, κατὰ διδαχὴν, *per traditionem:*—that *Chrysostom*, in his statement, committed more than one error, and moreover, does not give the name of the emperor. But all these objections will not be sufficient proof, to discerning minds, that the conversion of Philip to christianity *must* have been a fable. For who would deem it conclusive reasoning, to say: This or that is reported only by fame, and not in any book or author; and therefore it is not true? We know innumerable things, which [p. 473.] have come to us only through the medium of fame or continuous tradition, without being written down by the contemporary writers: and yet they *may* be perfectly true. And on the other hand, many things are false, for which the testimony of many ancient writers may be adduced. Fame is a reporter both of truth and falsehood. It is, therefore, not sufficient proof of the falsehood of a story, to show that the historians base it only on fame: Investigation is to be made, whether reliance should, or should not, be placed on this fame. Now the testimonies adduced, put it beyond controversy, that in the fourth and fifth centuries, over a great part of the Christian world, fame declared Philip to have been a convert to christianity. In the thing itself, there is nothing absurd, or incredible. On the contrary, there are some things to support it: among which, and not the least, is this: that what, in his History *Eusebius* states as derived from *fame*, in his Chronicon he states as being *certain:* and in this he is followed by *Jerome*, as already shown. Consequently, unless the truth of this *fame* can be overthrown by other and more potent arguments, there must be reason for doubting at least, whether this fame is to be credited or disbelieved.

Another argument adduced by those who contend for Philip's conversion to Christianity, is drawn from the Epistles written by *Origen* to this emperor and to his consort Severa, mentioned by *Eusebius*, (Hist. Eccles. l. vi. c. 36. p. 233.) To elude the force of this argument, the learned men who exclude Philip from the class of Christians, advance many things, which truly had better have been omitted. They, for example, question the genuineness of these epistles; they doubt whether Eusebius ever saw them, &c. They remark, that *Eusebius* and

Jerome, who both speak of these epistles, do not in all respects agree; for *Eusebius* says, Origen wrote to the emperor's spouse, and *Jerome*, that he wrote to the emperor's mother. But these are trivial objections, and easily answered by the opposite party. The case did not require so elaborate a discussion; for there is nothing in these epistles merely, which can materially aid the advocates of Philip's Christianity, because neither Eusebius nor Jerome tells what was in them. No wise and careful man will ever reason thus: A certain Christain teacher wrote a letter to this or that man, therefore the person written to was a Christian. For why may not a Christain write to one who is not a Christian? A Christian may, by letter, exhort a person alienated from Christianity, to become a Christian. Or he may intreat him to be kind and indulgent to Christians; or may address letters to him on other subjects. And, assuredly, if Eusebius had found in these epistles any clear proofs of the conversion of Philip and his mother to Christianity, he would not have omitted the notice of [p. 474.] so important a fact; neither would he, when just before treating of Philip's exclusion from the Christian worship by a bishop, have appealed solely to the authority of tradition. He would, doubtless, have said: "I have seen the epistles of *Origen* to *Philip*, from which I know with certainty, that he adhered to the Christian religion."

Of no more weight is the *third* argument of those who make Philip a Christian, derived from the *Acta S. Pontii;* (edited, with improvements, by Steph. *Baluze*, Miscellaneor. tom. ii. p. 493.) For, the advocates of the Romish church themselves dare not deny, that these *Acta* are of no authority, or at most, of very little; and that they state many things, respecting *Pontius*, the reputed instrument of Philip's conversion, and respecting Philip himself, which no sober, intelligent man, acquainted with antiquity, will ever admit to be true. It is probable that this whole fable was invented by some person who wished to add strength and authority to the old story of Philip's being a Christian. *Lastly*, those who place Philip among Christians, adduce a host of witnesses from the *sixth* century downwards. For all the Greek and Latin historians, since that century, and among the Arabians, *Eutychius* (in Annal. Eccles. Alexandr.) and *Abulpharaius* (in Historia Dynastiarum.) with united voice, declare that *Philip* was a Christian. But those who deny that Philip was a Christian, treat this great army with contempt, and pronounce them unworthy of regard: because they all borrowed from the narrative of *Eusebius*, so that the whole story falls back upon him. And learned men say this, with some appearance of truth. For many of these witnesses use the very words of Eusebius in his *Chronicon*, and others depart very little from them. Yet it must be confessed, that some of them express themselves as if they had other authorities for their statement, besides Eusebius.—As to the various other arguments in favor of Philip's Christianity, derived from some of his coins,—from certain of his enactments,—and from the regard for Christ, exhibited by his wife *Severa;* though deemed very weighty by some great men, they are too far-fetched to be arguments of any real force. We will therefore pass over to the other side, and examine the arguments of those who maintain that Philip was not a Christian. These also adduce many arguments, which may be easily confuted. We will only notice those arguments, in which there appears a degree of weight not to be contemned.

In the *first* place, they remind us of the fact, that all the writers of imperatorial history are wholly silent, as to any conversion of Philip to the Christian faith. And they add, that many of the Christian writers, and *Eusebius* at the head of them, (in Vita Constantini Mag.) distinctly state, that *Constantine* the Great, was the first of all the emperors that embraced Christianity. But the dissidents are far from quailing before this argument. They say, that Philip did not profess Christianity, openly and publicly, but only in private [p. 475.] and secretly; so that he publicly worshipped the gods, and dissembled his change of faith, while in private he attended the Christian worship. And hence the writers of Roman history, and also *Julian*, and some others, were ignorant of his renunciation of the old religions. And they say, that the Christian authors, who declare *Constantine* to be the first Christian emperor, are not to be understood as speaking absolutely, but only as representing *Constantine* to be the first of all to profess Christ, openly, fully, and without disguise; and, on that account, he was properly and deservedly called the *first Christian emperor.* This reply, it is difficult to divest entirely of all force; although it is not free from exceptions. It appears to me, that *Eusebius* himself affords it some support, in his Life of Constantine, (L. IV. c. 74. p. 563.) where he speaks of Constantine as being the first of all the emperors up to that time, who *openly* professed himself a Christian. Ἐπὶ μόνῳ τῶν πώποτε χριστιανῶν διαφανῶς ἀποδειχθέντι Κωνσταντίνῳ. When he says that Constantine was the first who *openly* (διαφανῶς) worshipped Christ, he seems to intimate, that there were others before him, who (ἀδιαφανῶς) *secretly* and *covertly* professed Christ; and thus he apparently explains the meaning of all those, who, with himself, had placed Constantine first among the Christian emperors.

Secondly, the very flagitious life which Philip led, both before and after his access to his imperatorial power, is urged by learned men, in opposition to such as would account him a Christian. Although many go too far in explaining and amplifying this argument, and set down some things as flagitious, which deserve a milder and softer name; yet it is beyond controversy, that very deep stains are found upon the life and conduct of this emperor. But I think, those change the question, who would infer, from the vices and crimes of Philip, that he disbelieved the Christian religion. The question is not, whether Philip was worthy of the name of Christian, and lived a life conformable to the precepts of Christianity. If such were the question, the argument from his flagitious life, would be wholly unexceptionable. But the question is, whether he regarded the Christian religion as more excellent and true than the Roman, or, in other words, as divine. This he might do, and still lead a very wicked life. If all those are to be stricken from the list of Christians, whose morals and actions violate the precepts of Christianity, Constantine himself, can hardly, if at all, maintain his place among Christian emperors.

Thirdly, learned men say, the secular games, celebrated by Philip with great pomp, in the thousandth year of the city, are opposed to the supposition that he had embraced Christianity. For these games originated in the superstition of the old Romans, were sacred to the gods, and embraced rites that were [p. 476.] absurd and wholly incongruous with Christianity; and yet Philip omitted none of these sacrilegious ceremonies, he immolated victims to the gods, and exhibited the customary spectacles in the Campus Martius, in the circus. and in the theatre; and of course, he sedulously performed all those acts, which it would be an abomination for a Christian to perform. I will not deny, that here is the strongest evidence that Philip was not such a Christian as he ought to have been, if indeed he was a Christian, at the time when he celebrated these games, of which there is doubt and uncertainty. Yet all these unbecoming acts might be done by a prince, who fully believed the truth of the Christian religion, but was eager to give stability to his government, solicitous to please the Roman people, studious to conceal his real opinions respecting religion, and willing to give the name of prudence to this impious dissimulation. Men of such a character think many things to be allowable, which others, very justly, regard as criminal. And who does not know, that the Christian emperor *Honorius*, permitted the secular games to be celebrated at Rome, in the fourth century, with the omission of some of the most impious of the ceremonies?

The *fourth* argument adduced by the learned, to disprove the Christianity of Philip, is derived from his *coins*, on which are found images of the gods, and other indications of the grossest superstition. This argument has already been impugned, by the remarks before made. And, not to repeat what has long since been urged by others, that we find not a few marks of the ancient superstition on coins of the acknowledged Christian emperors; who can think it strange, that an emperor, solicitous to keep the people ignorant of his secret conversion to Christianity, should have suffered his coins to be struck in the ancient form of the state? Even if Philip had been truly pious, there would have been a very plausible excuse for his conduct; and the more so, in proportion to the certainty that conclusive evidence of a prince's religious creed, cannot always be deduced from his coins. It is also to be remembered, that many of these coins were not struck by his order, but by the colonies and free towns, in honor to him.

Upon a deliberate and candid comparison of the arguments on both sides of the question, the religion of *Philip* appears to me to be one of those subjects, on which a controversy may be so maintained, that the victory shall ever remain dubious. All parties, however, must acknowledge the fact, that under him. the Christians enjoyed peace and prosperity, and that he gave many proofs of his marked kindness to them. And yet, just before his death, (as we learn from *Eusebius*, or rather, from *Dionysius* of Alexandria, as quoted by *Eusebius*, Hist. Eccles. L. vi. c. 41. et L. vii. c. 22.) there was a serious insurrection of the infuriated populace of Alexandria against the Christians. Such assaults were experienced under the mildest and best emperors.

[p. 477.] § XI. **The Persecution under Decius.** Philip, after reigning five years, was slain in the year 249, and was succeeded by *Decius Trajanus*, a prince, in many respects commendable, but superstitious, and immoderately attached to the old Romish religion. He, in the very beginning of his reign, either from fear of the Christians, whom he knew to cherish the memory of Philip, or from the promptings of superstition,(1) issued terrible edicts against the Christians, commanding the governors and magistrates, on pain of incurring themselves the severest animadversions, to either wholly exterminate the Christians, or recover them to the service of the gods by tortures and the rack. From what is handed down to us respecting this persecution, it appears that it was conducted differently by those intrusted with its execution; some proceeding more violently, and some more gently; and this seems to prove, that the emperor, only in general, ordered the Christian worship to be suppressed, and the Christians forced to return to idolatry; but left the mode of proceeding, and the kinds and degree of punishment, to the discretion of the governors.(2) Very many lost their lives during this persecution, in all parts of the Roman empire, and among them the distinguished bishops of the larger cities, as *Fabian* of Rome, *Babylas* of Antioch, *Alexander* of Jerusalem, and many others. But, to the extreme grief of their pastors, vast numbers of Christians, preferring the enjoyments of this life more than religion, procured for themselves safety, by sacrifices or incense presented to idol gods, or by the purchase of certificates that they were idolaters. And hence arose the reproachful titles of *Sacrificati*, *Thurificati*, and *Libellatici*, denoting those guilty of these several forms of perfidy towards Christ.(3)

(1) *Eusebius* (Hist. Eccles. L. vi. c. 39. p. 234.) says, that Decius assailed the Christians, (πρὸς Φίλιππον ἔχθους ἕνεκα,) *from hatred to Philip:* but *Gregory of Nyssa*, (in Vita Greg. Thaumaturgi, Opp. tom. iii. p. 567. 568.) says, that his attachment to the religion of his country, which was everywhere shorn of its dignity and respectability by Christianity, and the vast numbers adhering to it, alone induced this emperor to enter on a persecution of the Christians. These motives are not so incongruous, but that they might both coexist. Perhaps, however, it will not be rash to suppose, that the same motive influenced *Decius* as had before influenced *Maximin;* namely, a fear lest the Christians [p. 478.] should seek to avenge the death of Philip, who had greatly patronised them, and by raising insurrections, endanger the new administration. I am the more inclined to favor this conjecture, because the violence of this persecution very quickly abated. For we learn from *Cyprian*, (Epist. 36. 37. 40.) that scarcely a year elapsed, before tranquillity was, in a great measure, again restored to the church. The emperor finding his power well established, and perceiving that the Christians made no disloyal attempts against him, silently abrogated the

edict, which his fears had dictated. His impassioned cruelty would have been more permanent and abiding, if it had originated from his superstition.

(2) The tenor of Decius' edicts against the Christians, can be learned only from some passages in the early writers who advert to them, and from the proceeding of the masgistrates who executed them; for the edicts themselves are lost. Bern. *Medonius*, indeed, published at Toulouse in 1664, 4to. what he termed, *Decii Augusti Edictum contra Christianos*, taken professedly from an ancient manuscript book. But *Tillemont* has shown, (Memoires pour servir a l'Hist. de l'Eglise, tom. iii. P. ii. p. 400.) that the document contains many things, which make its genuineness doubtful, although it contains much that agrees very well with the statements of the ancient writers. If I can judge, this edict was copied from the *Acta* of some *Saint*, and enlarged in some respects, and corrected in others, by the publisher, to make it agree better with the statements of the ancients. And, undoubtedly, *Medonius* would have told us, to what book he was indebted for so great a treasure, if he himself had ventured to rely on its authority.—It is beyond all dispute, that this edict of Decius was more cruel and unjust than all that preceded it, and particularly, than the rescript of *Trajan*. *Dionysius* of Alexandria, (apud *Euseb.* Hist. Eccles. L. vi. c. 41. p. 238.) pronounces it (φοβερώτατον) *horrible* or *terrible*: and he says, it was such, *ut ipsi etiam electi, si fieri posset, scandalum paterentur*; and he adds, that *all Christians*, on hearing of it, were *exceedingly terrified.* It must, therefore, have threatened evils before unheard of, and have prescribed a new method of assault on Christians, more formidable than any preceding it. *Gregory* of Nyssa, (in Vita Gregorii Thaumat. Opp. tom. iii. p. 568.) states—1. "That the emperor in his edict, commanded the governors and magistrates to bring back the Christians to the worship of the gods, by every species of punishment and terror."—2. That he threatened the governors and magistrates with severe and signal penalties, if they were remiss and negligent in the execution of this his mandate.—3. Hence, all the governors, in obedience to the mandate, neglecting all other business, immediately commenced torturing the Christians; and expounding to them the edict, they signified to them, that such of them as refused to renounce Christianity, would be subjected to every species of punishment, and even to death, [p. 479.] for such refusal.—4. That various kinds of torture, before unheard of, were invented; and the terrible instruments for lacerating and torturing their bodies, were exposed in public for all to behold.—5. That all this produced amazing terror, and universal commotion.—What we learn from other writers, Origen for instance, respecting the tenor and import of this horrid law, only confirm these statements in general, without adding any further light concerning them. Undoubtedly, the edict embraced all sorts of Christians, or those of every order, age, and sex: for this appears from the examples of those who suffered at Alexandria, as narrated by *Dionysius* of Alexandria, (apud Euseb. Hist. Eccles. L. vi. c. 41. &c.) There is, however, a noticeable passage in *Cyprian*, (Ep. 52. ad Antonianum, p. 69. ed. Baluz.) from which we learn, that *Decius*, (as *Maximin* before him had done,) wished to have the Christian priests and bishops made the principal subjects of the persecution; and therefore, when *Fabian*, the Romish bishop, had been slain, he prevented

the election of another bishop to fill his place. *Cyprian* says of Cornelius, the successor of Fabian: Sedit intrepidus Romæ in sacerdotali cathedra eo tempore, cum tyrannus *infestus sacerdotibus Dei* fanda atque infanda comminaretur, cum multo patientius et tolerabilius audiret levari adversus se æmulum principem, quam constitui Romæ Dei sacerdotem. If we consider the statements of *Dionysius*, (in the above-named passage of *Eusebius*,) those of *Cyprian*, (in his tract *de Lapsis*, and in various of his *Epistles*.) and those of some others, respecting the zeal of the governors and magistrates in executing the emperor's edict, there will appear a great diversity in the modes of proceeding and punishing. As *Cyprian* expressly states, (Epist. 7. 8. 15. 26. 37. 53.) Some cast the Christians who boldly confessed Christ, into prison: and, after some delay, such as utterly refused to submit, they sent into exile. Others subjected the Christians who confessed, to exquisite tortures, variously modified and protracted for many days, and then remanded them almost lifeless to the jails, where they left them to languish out life. And hence at the death of Decius, many Christians were found lying in the prisons, and were set at liberty: of which number the celebrated *Origen* was the most distinguished, he having suffered exceedingly under Decius; but he was restored to his liberty after the slaughter of Decius. See *Eusebius*, (Hist. Eccles. L. vi. c. 39.) Others, first tried the effects of imprisonment in overcoming the resolution of Christians; and then tried the efficacy of tortures; and, these proving insufficient, they sentenced them to a capital punishment; but not all in the same form. The more cruel doomed them to the flames, the more lenient ordered them to be decapitated; and thus, some in one way, and others in another, they inflicted death on those they accounted pernicious and guilty citizens. Yet amid this variety in the mode of proceeding, there was still one constant aim. For we see, that they all tried, in various ways, to induce the Christians to renounce the profession of Christianity; they all proceeded tardily and reluc- [p. 480.] tantly to the punishing with death; and, lastly, they all pursued a more severe and rigorous course with the ministers, and especially with the bishops, than with others, and put them to death with less delay. What the mode of proceeding was in Africa, may be learned, in some measure, from the tract of *Cyprian de Lapsis*, (in his opp. p. 182.) In the first place, the accused or suspected were allowed by the judge a certain number of days, during which they might consider and make up their minds, whether to profess Christ, or to deny him. *Explorandæ fidei præfiniebantur dies.* During this period they remained at home and free; and, as appears in the sequel, no one opposed their seeking safety by absconding. This was sufficiently humane. In Egypt, as we learn from an epistle of *Dionysius*, (apud Euseb. ubi sup.) immediately after accusation, confession was extorted; confession was followed by imprisonment, imprisonment by torture, and torture by capital punishment; and very often all these followed in rapid succession. Many of the Christians did not hesitate to avail themselves of the liberty granted them by the indulgence of the governors, to take time for deliberation. But *Cyprian* was displeased with it, and enjoined upon his flock to decline the favor: Sed qui sæculo renuntiasse meminit, nullum sæculi diem novit; nec tempora terrena jam computat, qui æternitatem de Deo sperat. Nemo, fratres dilectissimi, nemo hanc gloriam mutilet, nemo incorruptam stantium firmitatem maligna obtrectatione debilitet. From the concluding words of this exhortation, it would appear, that the more courageous among the African Christians would not avail themselves of the privilege offered by the governors, and were blamed for it by some, who, undoubtedly, accused them of imprudence. After the time for deliberation had elapsed, those who remained silent, and would neither profess Christ nor deny him, were held by the judge to be confessed Christians: Cum dies negantibus præstitutus excessit, quisquis professus intra diem non est, Christianum se esse confessus est. Therefore, such of them as had not fled away, and could be found, were apprehended and thrown into prison. But many fled, before the time expired; and these were publicly proscribed, and their goods confiscated. Says *Cyprian:* Primus victoriæ titulus, gentilium manibus apprehensum Dominum confiteri. Secundus ad gloriam gradus est, cauta secessione subtractum Domino reservari. Illa publica, hæc privata confessio est.—Hic fortasse dilatus est, qui *patrimonio derelicto,* idcirco secessit, quia non erat negaturus. *Cyprian* himself fled, and suffered the penalty of flight, the loss of his property. Those whose constancy could not be overcome by imprisonment, were sometimes banished, with no additional punishment; sometimes they were put to the rack; and frequently, when nothing would induce them to renounce Christ, they were subjected to capital punishment.

To one who attentively considers what has now been stated, it will be evident, that the persecution of the Christians by the mandate of *Decius* differed [p. 481.] from all the former persecutions; and that the mode of proceeding in it, was not according to the first rescript of *Trajan,* nor according to the edicts of the succeeding emperors. The governors now possessed the amplest powers for inquisition, whereas before they had to wait for an accuser to appear; any one so disposed might act the accuser, without regard to legal forms; nor was there any danger attending accusations: public accusations of the people, which the former imperatorial laws forbid, were now admitted; as appears from the example of Cyprian; those who professed adherence to Christ, and refused to renounce their faith, were not ordered at once to execution, as the law of *Trajan* directed, but were exposed to severe tortures; neither were all who withstood the force of torture, put to death; but many were either kept in perpetual imprisonment, or were sent into exile. It is easy, therefore, to conjecture what the edict of *Decius,* of the atrocity and cruelty of which the Christians so much complained, prescribed. The emperor did not order the Christians to be slaughtered: he did not absolutely command, that even those who could not be subdued by sufferings and torture, should be put to death: for, if he had commanded the capital punishment of all, whom torture and the rack could not bring to renounce Christ, the governors would not have dared to discharge many from the prisons alive; and to shut up others who had been tortured, in places of confinement; and to grant to others a season for consideration, after they had with great constancy professed themselves Christians; as was sometimes done in Egypt, according to *Dionysius* as quoted by Eusebius. The emperor, therefore, must have charged the magistrates only, in general, to destroy the Christian religion; to carefully search out all the professors of it, and to punish those who refused to worship the gods with all sorts of torture and sufferings, until they would return to the religion of their fathers. Perhaps, however, he commanded that bishops and priests, on refusing compliance, should be at once put to death in order to strike terror into others. He did not prescribe the mode of proceeding against those who, on being admonished, refused to renounce Christ, but left it to the judgment and discretion of the governors: and hence that diversity in the proceedings of the magistrates with Christians, some proceeding more mildly, and others more harshly. That many of the governors consigned to the sword or the flames, a large part of those whom the rack and the prison could not subdue, can by no means prove, that *Decius* commanded the execution of all the persevering. For the governors had power, without any mandate from the emperor, to put those to death, whom neither force nor fear, neither arguments nor persuasives, could induce to worship the gods; by virtue, not only of the law of *Trajan*, which threatened death to such as would not forsake Christ, but also by the common law of the empire, which declared all who should not obey the imperatorial edicts unworthy to live.—As to the rewards and honors which, I find some moderns say, were proffered to those who would apostatise from Christ, I do not discover a notice of them in any ancient writer. Perhaps some of the governors attempted to entice here and there an individual, [p. 482.] to whom they were favorably inclined, by this allurement; but that any emperor should have sought to secure the obedience of his subjects, by promises, persons of any acquaintance with Roman affairs will not easily believe.

(3) All the persecutions sustained by the Christians in preceding times, had not produced so many deserters and apostates from divine truth, as this single short one under *Decius*. Persons of all ranks, and, what is especially remarkable, even bishops and priests, scarcely waited to be informed of the tyrant's threats, before they hastened to the tribunals of the governors and magistrates, and professed themselves ready to worship the gods and to disclaim Christ. This defection or fall of so many Christians, was deeply deplored by *Cyprian*, among others, in his eloquent treatise *de Lapsis*. This distinguished writer attributes the evil to the indulgent, luxurious, and degenerate course of life produced in Christians by the long continued peace, particularly under Alexander Severus and the two Philips; for only a very few, in certain provinces, experienced the hostility of Maximin. Freed from solicitude and caution, the Christians had relaxed much of their contempt of this life and its concerns, and had in many places contracted vicious habits. This must be believed, on the authority of a man perfectly acquainted with the state of Christians in his own times. And yet, I apprehend, there will be no mistake in assigning an additional cause, and supposing that the peculiar nature and form of the persecution instituted by Decius, induced more persons to violate their plighted faith to Christ, than ever before. *Trajan* decreed death to every avowed Christian who refused to forsake Christ, making no mention of tortures and racks: and much the same were the edicts of the other persecutors of the Christians: but *Decius* threatened,—not a capital punishment, but long and painful sufferings, to the despisers of the gods; and a lingering, protracted death, amid varied

successive tortures, to the more resolute professors of christianity. And his governors executed his threats with great exactitude: they ordered no one to be put to death, unless he was first subjected to numerous tortures, and exhausted and almost dead in consequence of his pains and horrid sufferings; and many also were tortured, until they actually expired. Some of the governors, in order to strike greater terror into Christians, ingeniously contrived new modes of torture, and exposed the instruments of the executioners, publicly, before the eyes of all. This was a far more efficient way to destroy courage, and inspire dismay, than the punishments of the preceding times. Men who are not afraid to die, will look with horror on long continued writhing pains, and lacerations of the body; and this horror will be increased by seeing many examples of such extreme cruelty and inhumanity.

Among the lapsed during this bloody persecution, in addition to the *Thurificati* and *Sarificati*, that is, those who had presented incense before the images of the gods, or placed victims and sacrifices on their altars, we find notice of a new class of which there is no mention before this period, namely, the *Libellatici*. Who these were, the learned are not agreed. In regard to this question, [p. 483.] the following particulars are true beyond all doubt:—*First*, that the term *Libellaticus* was derived from (*libellus*) the *written paper*, which those called *Libellatici* either presented to the judge, or received from him:—*Secondly*, that these persons had redeemed their lives, and procured safety from the emperor's edict, by means of money. And this, as we have before seen, was neither a new thing, nor regarded as base and improper. By the disciples of *Montanus*, indeed, it was considered as impious to purchase life and safety with money; but the rest of the Christians condemned this Montanist opinion:—and *thirdly*, this is certain, that the *Libellatici* did not renounce Christ, either in words or deeds; that is, they neither payed worship and honor to the gods, nor concealed or dissembled their own religion. And yet they committed an act bearing some affinity with this crime, and one which, when carefully considered, might seem to be a tacit proof of a denial of Christ.—*Lastly*, that the *Libellatici* were the least criminal, or if you please, the best among the lapsed, and, with little trouble, obtained reconciliation with the church. The two following questions, however, have been especially debated: Whether the *Libellatici* were so denominated, from the (*libelli*) *papers* they *gave* in, or from such as they *received*? and, What was the *tenor or contents* of these *libelli*, from which they derived their name? This discussion is founded wholly on the interpretation of some rather obscure passages in *Cyprian*: for *he* only makes distinct mention of the Libellatici; notwithstanding there is good evidence, that such persons were found in other countries than Africa; for avarice reigns every where, and life is every where more valued than money. To recite the various opinions and conjectures of the learned, is not in accordance with my plans, nor would it be of much use. It will be more pleasant, and more profitable, to cite the passages of Cyprian, and give their true interpretation. In the first place, it is clear that those learned men have not duly considered the subject, who suppose the *Libellatici* were thus named on account of their (*libelli*) *petitions* presented to the governor or magistrate, requesting the judge, on the payment of a certain sum of money, to spare the petitioner, and not demand of him a public renunciation of his religion. For, not to mention that it cannot be shown that such petitions to judges were allowed of, and that on the contrary, it appears from Cyprian, (as we shall soon see,) that the *Libellatici* appeared personally, or by their agents, before the judge, and implored his clemency, not in writing, but by oral statements only;—I say, not to insist on this, although it is of great weight in this controversy,—the Christians, by presenting such petitions, would have been guilty of no offence. For, as already shown, the laws of the church allowed Christians to petition the judge, either orally, or in writing, to spare them, and to offer him money as an inducement. A *Libellaticus*, therefore, was a Christian who obtained from the magistrate, by some pecuniary consideration, a (*libellus securitatis*) *certificate of security*, in which it was stated, that he had complied with the emperor's edict, that is, had sacrificed to the gods, although in fact he had done no such thing, and had told the judge that his religion utterly forbid his doing it. On account of this certificate, which the Christian produced if occasion required it, he was publicly by the citizens regarded as a deserter from his religion, while in reality he [p. 484.] was no deserter of it. The judge practised deception, by giving the certificate; and the Christian practised deception by it, and suffered himself to be mistaken for an apostate. And herein properly consisted the offence of the *Libellatici;* for this tacit profession of perfidy, although it was mere simulation, seemed to differ but little from a real and open profession of it. This view of the subject is, for the most part, admitted by *Prudentius Maran*, in his life of Cyprian, (§ vi. p. liv. &c.) prefixed to the Baluzian edition of Cyprian's Works. Yet he rejects it in part; for he denies, that these certificates declared the holders of them to have complied with the emperor's edict: this, he thinks, would have been too gross a falsehood. He therefore supposes, that the judges entered upon the public *records*, that the persons holding certificates had sacrificed and renounced Christ, but they omitted this in the certificates. This worthy monk was not destitute of erudition, but he had little acquaintance with human affairs; and aiming to bring forth something new, he brought it forth; but under unfavorable auspices. Good sense forsook him. As to the (*Acta*) *public records*, in which he thinks it was written, that the holders of certificates or the *Libellatici*, had offered sacrifices, I shall say nothing. He took this from a passage in Cyprian, misunderstood; so that the fact of such a record, is not proved; although it is not contrary to all probability. But when he maintains, that what was written in the book of Records, was not inserted in the certificates of safety, he forgets the demands of Decius' edict, which required the governors to extirpate the Christian religion, and to compel all Christians to offer sacrifices and worship the gods. The governors, therefore, could not, unless they were willing to incur the penalties, with which, as before shown, the emperor's edict threatened them, grant safety, and certificates thereof, to any others besides those who had complied with the emperor's edict. And therefore, beyond controversy, it must have been stated in the certificate, that the holder of it had done what the emperor required. Such a public testimonial was supposed to be written in good faith, although written in bad or deceptive faith; and therefore it exempted those who produced it, from all fear and danger. It may be added, moreover, that *Cyprian*, (as we shall presently see,) calls those certificates, not only *impious*, but also *certificates of idolatry*. (Epist. 68. p. 119.): Basilides et Martialis *nefando idololatriae libello* contaminati sunt. These certificates could not have merited such epithets, if they had simply assured certain Christians of their safety, making no mention of their having paid honour to the gods. What, I would ask, is *a certificate of idolatry*, (*libellus idololatriae*,) but a certificate declaring the person an *idolater*, or asserting that he has worshipped the gods?—*Lastly:* if the fictitious crime of the Christian *Libellatici* had been entered on the records of the court, but not mentioned in the certificates, the holders of the certificates could not have made that use of them, which they especially desired to do, before other judges; because these judges might demand of them, to commit in their presence the act, of which there was no mention made in the certificate.

Let us now turn to the principal passages in *Cyprian*, relative to the *Libel-* [p. 185.] *latici*, and see whether they accord with what has been stated. The most noted of all the passages is in his Epistle to Antonianus (Epist. 52. p. 70.) : Cum ergo inter ipsos, qui sacrificaverunt, multa sit diversitas, quæ inclementia est et quam acerba duritia, *Libellaticos* cum iis, qui sacrificaverunt, jungere, quando is, *cui libellus acceptus est, dicat:* Ego prius legeram et episcopo tractante cognoveram non sacrificandum idolis, nec simulacra servum Dei adorare debere, et ideirco ne hoc facerem, quod non licebat, *cum occasio libelli fuisset oblata*, quem nec ipsum *acciperem*, *nisi ostensa fuisset occasio*, ad magistratum vel veni, vel alio eunte mandavi, Christianum me esse, sacrificare mihi non licere, ad aras diaboli me venire non posse, dare me ob hoc præmium, ne quod non licet faciam. Nunc tamen etiam iste, qui libello maculatus est, posteaquam, nobis admonentibus, didicit, nec hoc se facere debuisse, etsi manus pura sit, et os ejus feralis cibi nulla contagia polluerint, conscientiam tamen ejus esse pollutam flet, auditis nobis, et lamentatur. From this extract the following things are manifest:—1. The *Libellatici* had paid no worship to the gods, they had not even touched meats offered to the gods, and consequently they were far more innocent than the *Sacrificati*.—2. They procured certificates, lest possibly, if arraigned before the tribunals, they might commit these crimes through dread of torture.—3. Not at their own solicitation, but at the suggestion of others, the judges asked them to order certificates to be written for them ; or, as *Cyprian* expresses it, while they were not contemplating such a thing, an *occasion was offered* them for petitioning for a certificate. That is, the avaricious magistrates perceiving a prosperous, wealthy person among the Christians, signified to him, privately, through their satellites or friends, that his safety might be secured, and exemption from suffering purchased, with a moderate sum of money; thus proffering him the clemency of the judges.—4. The *Libellatici* did not present *written* petitions to the magistrate, but went to the judge, either personally or by some friend, and orally made known their wishes, presenting, at the same time, the price of the favor asked for. *Cyprian* reports the language they used. This method of proceeding was necessary to the magistrate's safety. If they had allowed written petitions to be presented by those who wished to obtain certificates of safety without sacrificing, the very petitions might lead to the easy detection of the fraud. Those conversant with the proceedings of men, well know that such transactions being derogatory to the law, and counteracting the designs of the sovereign power, are never done in writing, but always orally. This leads me to wonder the more at those who conceive, that the *Libellatici* were so called from the (*libelli*) *written petitions* which *they* presented.—5. Some of these *Libellatici* applied personally to the judges, while others signified their wishes through the medium of friends. For some supposed they would be less criminal, if they did not themselves attempt to bribe the judge, but employed others to do it. Some, again, I suspect, were afraid to appear personally, lest the judges, on their professing themselves Christians, should at once seize them, and cast them into prison; and, therefore, they employed some worshipper of idols, who had nothing to fear, to present [p. 486.] the request, pay the money, and receive the certificate in their name.—6. It is manifest that the *Libellatici received* a writing from the judge whom they had bribed; for *Cyprian* twice mentions the (*libellus acceptus*) *writing* or certificate *received.* And this writing or certificate protected them against all prosecutions, or attempts to compel them to worship the gods.

Another passage, in an Epistle of the Roman Clergy to Cyprian, (inter *Cypriani* Epistolas, Ep. 31. Opp. p. 42.) is not quite so lucid, and yet sufficiently so to confirm the preceding statements: Superioribus litteris nostris (a letter not now extant,) vobis sententiam nostram dilucida expositione protulimus, et adversus eos, qui seipsos infideles illicita nefariorum libellorum professione prodiderant, quasi evasuri irretientes illos diaboli laqueos viderentur, quo non minus quam si ad nefarias aras accessissent, hoc ipso quod ipsum contestati fuerant, tenerentur, sed etiam adversus illos, qui acta fecissent, licet præsentes quum fierent, non affuissent, quum præsentiam suam utique ut sic scriberentur mandando fecissent. Non est enim immunis a scelere qui ut fieret imperavit: nec est alienus a crimine, cujus consensu, licet non a se admissum crimen, tamen publice legitur, et cum totum fidei sacramentum in confessione Christi nominis intelligatur esse digestum, qui fallaces in excusatione præstigias quærit, negavit, et qui vult videri propositis adversus Evangelium vel edictis vel legibus satisfecisse, hoc ipso jam paruit quod videri se paruisse voluit.—From these words of the Roman clergy we may learn:—1. That the *Libellatici* were accustomed *libellos nefarios profiteri*, in presence of the judge; and by such *professione se ipsos infideles prodere.* What is here meant by *libellum profiteri,* the writers of the Epistle presently show; it is, *to direct* or require that something *be written*, or that a *libellus* be drawn up. This will be perfectly manifest, to one comparing the expression with what follows it. Those therefore greatly err, who make *profiteri libellum* here to be equivalent to *offerre judici libellum.* It is rather, to profess to the judge, that they stand ready to receive a *libellum* at a certain price, or to request one from the judge, tendering him money 2. What was written in the certificate thus asked for, is clearly indicated in the following words: *cujus Consensu, licet non a se admissum crimen, publice legitur.* The person then who solicited a certificate, *consented, that a crime, which he had never committed, should be publicly imputed to him.* The crime referred to, was, undoubtedly, that of *sacrificing.* It is therefore certain, that the certificates stated that such and such persons had sacrificed to the gods. And this, moreover, is confirmed by the following words: *Videri vult propositis adversus Evangelium vel edictis vel legibus satisfecisse; paruit, quia paruisse videri voluit.* Consequently, the governor testified in his certificate that Caius or Seius had complied with and satisfied the emperor's edict; and he who (*profitebatur*) declared his willingness to receive the certificate, consented that the judge should so state concerning him, although the statement was false. The [p. 487.] words *publice legitur* may lead some to conjecture, that the certificates thus granted were posted up publicly in the Praetorium, so that all might read them. And perhaps they were so; but it is not necessary to put this construction on the words. For any thing may be said (*publice legi*) *to be publicly read*, which is frequently read in public, which is shown and must be shown, to all who ask to see it; and therefore is liable to be read by every one. *Maran*, who thought it evident from this expression, that the fictitious criminal act was not stated in the certificate, but only recorded on the court records, did not recollect, that these *court records* were not read publicly, nor could all have access to read them. Moreover, the language here used shows most conclusively, that it must be understood of written papers *received* from the judge, and not of papers *presented* to him. For how could a *Libellaticus*, in a paper of his own, confess a crime which he had not committed? How could he affirm that he had complied with the emperor's edict?—3. Hence it is clear what the Roman priests mean, when they say that the exhibitors of these certificates *proclaimed themselves unbelievers.* For when a man professes before a judge, that he is willing to have a crime publicly attributed to him, which, however, he would shudder to commit, he *betrays his infidelity;* that is, he makes it known, that he will not publicly profess Christ, and that he is unconcerned, if the public should regard him as an apostate.—4. These things being kept in sight, it will not be difficult to apprehend the meaning of the Roman Clergy, when they say: *Libellaticos irretientes diaboli laqueos evadere velle, at non minus teneri, quam si ad nefarias aras accessissent, quod hoc ipsum contestati fuerant.* The *Laquei Diaboli*, which might *irretire*, or lead men to forsake Christ, were imprisonment, the rack, and the tortures wherewith the governors, by command of Decius, sought to bring Christians to a renunciation of Christ. And the *Libellatici*, although they had not gone to the forbidden altars, nor offered sacrifice to the gods, yet were equally guilty, in the view of the Roman priests, because they had attested to (*hoc ipsum*) this *very thing*, namely, their going to the altars and offering sacrifice. They had not indeed themselves attested to this; but, with their consent, the judge had attested it; and he who approves the act of another, by consenting to it, is justly considered as a cause and author of it; and one who authorises another to charge him publicly with a crime, in a sense charges it upon himself.—5. What we learned from the former passage, is also manifest from this, namely, that the *Libellatici* did not present (*libellos*) *written requests* to the judge, but either went to him themselves, or sent their authorised agents to solicit from him a (*libellus*) *written certificate.* Prudentius Maran fancies that the words *Acta fecissent*, here indicate the (*Acta Judicii*) *Records of the Court;*

a most unhappy conceit: as if truly, entries on the court records might be made by the petitioners to the court; that was the business of the public notaries. In this place, *Acta facere* is the same with *libellum profiteri:* for the Roman clergy are here speaking of those (*Acta*) *acts*, which were unavoidable, by such Christians as would secure their safety by means of a (*libellus*) certificate.

We subjoin a third passage from the tract of *Cyprian* (*de Lapsis*, [p. 488.] c. 27. p. 190.): Nec sibi quo minus agant poenitentiam blandiantur, qui etsi nefandis sacrificiis manus non contaminaverunt, *libellis* tamen conscientiam polluerunt. Et illa professio denegantis contestatio est Christiani quod fuerat abnuentis. The learned hesitate in regard to the meaning of this passage; because it is concise and rather obscure; and yet, by proper attention, we may easily discover its import. The *Professio denegantis* is, the *Professio libelli* of a Christian, who denies before the judge, that he can or will offer sacrifice. This will appear, if we compare the first passage above cited with the one before us. This *Professio libelli* is the *Contestatio* or testimony of a Christian, *abnuentis id, quod fuerat*, i. e. denying that he is any longer a Christian, which he before was. For, he who permits it to be stated, (in libello) in the certificate, that he has offered sacrifice, virtually denies that he is a Christian, by allowing the title and glory of a Christian to be taken from him. Fecisse se dixit (namely, by the judge, who wrote as he desired,) quicquid alius *faciendo* commisit. Cumque scriptum sit; non potestis duobus Dominis servire, servivit saeculari Domino qui obtemperavit ejus edicto (i. e. the person who consented to have it written, that he had obeyed the Decian edict,) magis obaudivit humano imperio, quam Deo. Viderit an minore vel dedecore vel crimine apud homines publicaverit, quod admisit. Deum tamen Judicem fugere et vitare non poterit. To avoid prolixity, I will not continue the explication of this passage, notwithstanding it is ill understood by many; for it contributes but little to elucidate the subject under consideration.—Among the other passages in *Cyprian* relative to the *Libellatici* and their certificates, there are none which throw additional light on the subject, or add weight to the arguments already adduced, except a passage in his Epistle to Fortunatus, (de Exhortatione Martyrii, c. 11. p. 271.) where he cites the example of Eleazur, in 2 Maccab. 6. to rebuke the crime of the *Libellatici*. He says: Ac nequis vel libelli vel alicujus rei oblata sibi occasione qua fallat amplectatur decipientium malum munus, nec Eleazarus tacendus est, qui cum sibi a ministris regis offerretur facultas, ut accepta carne qua liceret sibi vesci ad circumveniendum Regem simularet se illa edere, quæ de sacrificiis ingerebantur, consentire ad hanc fallaciam noluit, dicens, nec ætati suæ, nec nobilitati convenire, id fingere, quo ceteri scandalizerentur et in errorem inducerentur, existimantes Eleazarum ad alienigenarum morem transiisse. A cursory reading of this passage will show, that the *Libellatici* practised an imposition upon the emperor, and feigned obedience to him; and also, that they were invited to do this by others; for *Cyprian* says, they embraced the opportunity *proffered* to *them*. It is likewise evident that they did not present the (*libellum*) *written paper* to the judge, but received it from him; for *Cyprian* calls these (*libellos*) written papers *malum munus;* which single expression is nearly a sufficient confutation of the false opinions and conjectures of many. For a [p. 489.] *munus* is something received; and a *malum munus* is, undoubtedly, a gift that is injurious to the receiver. There must, therefore, have been something written in the (*libellus*) certificate, which might bring reproach and criminality on the *Libellaticus*.

This whole subject might have been more clear and easy to be understood, if the edict of *Decius* had come down to us. For, as there is no mention whatever of such (*libelli*) certificates, by any writer who lived anterior to the times of this edict, although we know that, before that period, Christians purchased to themselves safety by money and presents, it seems that this whole matter originated from the severe law of this emperor. He, if I am not mistaken, not only required all the Christians that could be found, to be seized, and by tortures compelled to pay homage to the gods; but also, lest some might evade the law, and falsely pretend to have sacrificed, he ordered the judges to give a *libellum*, or public testimonial, that the thing had been actually done, according to the emperor's requisition. A man, therefore, destitute of a *libellus*, or testimonial from the judge, was liable to be accused of disobeying the law and being a rebel: but the man who could produce his *libellus*, was free from all danger. This idea, in my opinion, throws much light on the hitherto incomprehensible cause for these *libelli*. To all Christians who would be safe from molestation, the *libellus* or testimonial of the judge, that he had sacrificed, was indispensable. Vast numbers procured a *libellus* by actually doing what the emperor required: others, too conscientious to follow their example, and not knowing what to do, remained trembling at their homes. And to these timid and hesitating persons the money-loving judges caused it to be secretly intimated by their retainers, that there was a way to obtain a *libellus*, without sacrificing; that the judges would give the testimonies required by the imperitorial edict, to persons who would not sacrifice, provided they would show due gratitude to their benefactors.

§ XII. **Contests respecting the Lapsed.** This great multitude of apostates caused a large portion of the Christian community to be thrown into commotion; and here and there it produced inveterate contests. For while those persons wished to be reinstated in the church, without undergoing the long penances prescribed by the ecclesiastical laws: and some of the doctors, from a propensity towards lenity, favored that course; and others of a sterner mould, and more rigidly adhering to the ancient discipline, resisted it: parties very naturally arose among the Christians. Very many of the lapsed, especially in Egypt and Africa,(¹) in order to obtain more readily a reconciliation with their bishops and churches, employed the *martyrs* to intercede for them. For, as the reputation and influence of martyrs and confessors among the early Christians were amazingly great, and their decisions were regarded as almost divine, it had become the custom, [p. 490.] even in the preceding century,(2) to admit to the communion those among the lapsed who could procure a testimonial of fraternal love from a martyr, on their exhibiting to him a few signs of contrition. Such testimonies from a martyr, signifying that he could forgive and hold fellowship with certain persons, were usually called *Libelli Pacis*. During this Decian persecution, some martyrs in Africa abused this prerogative immoderately; and some of the bishops and presbyters, either from fear or veneration of the martyrs, or from ignorance of ecclesiastical law, were too ready to receive the offenders who were provided with these certificates.(3) To the evils which were to be apprehended from this inprudence and ready acquiescence, *Cyprian*, the bishop of Carthage, placed himself in strong opposition. Being then absent from his church, he wrote Epistles, recommending that this lenity should be tempered with due severity, and that proper limits be set to the rule respecting the certificates of peace. And hence he became involved in a troublesome controversy with the martyrs, the confessors, the presbyters, the lapsed, and the people; but from it he came forth victorious.(4)

(1) Respecting Egypt, see *Dionysius* Alexandrinus, (apud *Euseb.* Hist. Eccles. L. vi. c. 44.)—As to Africa, *Cyprian's* Epistles are full on the subject.

(2) The learned have long remarked, that *Tertullian* is the earliest writer who mentions this custom; towards the close of his book, *de Pudicitia*, (c. 22.) and in his book, *ad Martyres*, (c. 1.) See Gabr. *Albaspinaeus*, (Observ. Eccles. L. i. Observ. 20. p. 94.)—Hence it is concluded, that this custom was not older than the middle of the second century.

(3) Under the title of *Martyrs* were included, those on whom a sentence of death had already been passed, and also those who had sustained very grievous sufferings for Christ's sake, and were still detained in prison, uncertain what was to befall them. As to the right of these martyrs to give certificates of peace when so requested, there was no dispute. Neither did any one deny, or pretend to deny, that a shorter and lighter penance was to be imposed on the persons presenting such certificates to the bishop. Whoever should have controverted either of these points, would have been accused of violating the sanctity and dignity of the martyrs; nay, of high treason against the majesty of God, who, as many supposed, spoke and gave his decisions through the martyrs. The only controversy was, respecting the manner in which this right was to be used, and the extent of the influence to be allowed to these certificates. These *Libelli Pacis* were not introduced by any law or canon, but only by custom; and therefore, it was uncertain how far this right extended. And this uncertainty occasioned many things to be done by the martyrs, during the

Decian persecution, whch were highly detrimental to the welfare of the church, [p. 491.] and which, therefore, *Cyprian* and other bishops felt bound to censure.—In the first place, whereas certificates had formerly been given by the martyrs to only a few individuals, and this after a careful examination of each case; in the present persecution, they were distributed among all, without discrimination or distinction: and the bishops were of course overwhelmed with a multitude of these certificates of peace. Says *Cyprian* (Epistola xiv. p. 24.): Cum comperissem, lapsos exambire ad martyres passim, confessores quoque, importuna et gratiosa deprecatione corrumpere, ut *sine ullo discrimine atque examine* singulorum, darentur *quotidie libellorum millia* (a definite number is here rhetorically used for one indefinite,) contra Evangelii legem, litteras feci, quibus martyres et confessores, consilio meo quantum possem ad dominica præcepta revocarem. There are several other passages in *Cyprian*, which speak of the immense number of the certificates given by the martyrs. On the evils resulting from them, there is no need to expatiate. With the full expectation of obtaining such certificates, everybody hurried away to the judicial tribunals, and publicly renouncing Christ, offered sacrifice to the gods; and then, as if they had done right, they proceeded to the prisons, where the more resolute Christians were detained awaiting their final sentence, and requested certificates of peace; and, having readily obtained them, they repaired to the bishops, and asked to be restored to fellowship in the church, on the ground that the martyrs recognised them in their certificates as brethren. In the persecutions of former times, the prudence of the bishops had laid checks upon this evil, arising from the indiscretion of ignorant and illiterate martyrs. For they sent discreet and well informed deacons to the prisons, to advise the martyrs, and prevent their giving certificates indiscriminately, or to any but persons worthy of their kind offices. But under Decius, this wise course was neglected; and hence arose the sad confusion, and the unmeasured liberality of the martyrs. Let us hear *Cyprian* on the subject (Epistola x. p. 20.): In præteritum semper sub antecessoribus nostris factum est, ut diaconi ad carcerem commeantes martyrum desideria consiliis suis et scripturarum præceptis gubernarent. Sed nunc cum maximo animi dolore cognosco, non tantum illic vobis non suggeri divina præcepta, sed adhuc potius impediri. Most earnestly, therefore, the holy man conjures the martyrs to follow the example of their predecessors, and not to give their opinion in any case, without close inspection and examination. Quoniam audio, fortissimi et carrissimi fratres, impudentia vos quorundam premi - - oro vos quibus possum precibus, aut Evangelii memores et considerantes quæ et qualia in præteritum antecessores vestri martyres concesserint, quam solliciti in omnibus fuerint, vos quoque sollicite et caute petentium desideria ponderetis, utpote amici [p. 492.] Domini, et inspiciatis et actum et opera et merita singulorum, ipsorum quoque delictorum genera et qualitales cogitetis, ne si quid abrupte et indigne vel a vobis promissum, vel a nobis factum fuerit, apud gentiles quoque ipsos ecclesia nostra erubescere incipiat. From this language it is very manifest that it was not the *right* of the martyrs to give certificates of peace to the lapsed, recommending them to the churches, but only the *use of this right*, which was the subject of controversy.

This error was accompanied by another of no less magnitude. The martyrs, in this *Decian* persecution, did not always insert the names of the persons to whom they wished the church to be reconciled, but naming an individual, they connected with him a company who were not named; that is, they recommended to the communion of the church, all those whom the bearer of the certificate might bring forward as his friends and associates. Whoever, therefore, had obtained such a vague and indeterminate certificate, might, at his discretion, make all he pleased partakers with him in the benefit conferred. And some, if I am not deceived, so abused this pernicious power, as actually to sell the privilege of sharing in the certificate. This, I think, I can discover in the somewhat obscure language of *Cyprian* (Epist. x. p. 20.): *Intelligentes et comprimentes eos,* (he is addressing martyrs,) *qui personas accipientes in beneficiis vestris,* (i. e. who extend your favors, not to those worthy of them, but to those they choose, however unworthy,) *aut gratificantur,* (i. e. either give them away,) *aut illicitæ negotiationis nundinas aucupantur,* (i. e. or search for buyers of the priviliges contained in the certificate, thus making merchandise of the privileges they had obtained.) On discovering Christians of such corrupted morals and perverse minds, in this early age of the church, we need not greatly wonder at the temerity and licentiousness of the subsequent ages, in making everything sacred venal, and converting the sins of men into a source of gain. But this was then a new crime; for the martyrs of earlier times did not give such certificates. At this period, doubtless, there were evil-minded and cunning men, who did not stop with renouncing Christ, but were willing to add sin to sin, and therefore blandly persuaded the honest but uneducated martyrs, who had none to direct and guide them, to issue such certificates. Of this wrong conduct, *Cyprian* himself complains, (Epist. x. pp. 20. 21.): Sed et illud ad diligentiam vestram redigere et emendare debetis, ut nominatim designetis eos, quibus pacem dari desideratis. Audio enim quibusdam sic libellos fieri, ut dicatur: "Communicet ille cum suis:" quod *nunquam* omnino a martyribus factum est, ut incerta et cœca petitio invidiam nobis postmodum cumulet. Late enim patet, quando dicitur: "Ille cum suis;" et possunt nobis viceni et triceni et amplius offerri, qui propinqui et affines et liberti ac domestici esse asseverentur ejus, qui accepit libellum. Et ideo peto, ut eos, quos ipsi videtes, quos nostis, [p. 493.] quorum pœnitentiam satisfactioni proximam conspicitis, designetis nominatim libello, et sic ad nos fidei ac disciplinæ congruentes litteras dirigatis.

Some of the martyrs, before dying for Christ, gave direction to certain of their friends to issue certificates in their names, when dead, indiscriminately, to all who should ask for them. An example of this we have in the Epistle of *Lucian*, a Confessor, to *Celerinus*, (among the Epistles of *Cyprian*, Epist. xxi. p. 30.): Cum benedictus martyr Paulus, adhuc in corpore esset, vocavit me et dixit mihi: Luciane, coram Christo dico tibi, ut si quis post arcessitionem meam, (i. e. after I am put to death,) abs te pacem petierit, da in nomine meo. And *Cyprian* informs us, (Epist. xxii. p. 31.) that this *Lucian*, whom he pronounces a man of piety, but not well informed on religious subjects: Libellos manu sua scriptos gregatim nomine Pauli dabat. Cyprian adds: Lucianus, non tantum Paulo adhuc in carcere posito, nomine illius libellos manu sua scriptos passim dedit, sed et post ejus excessum eadem facere sub ejus nomine perseveravit, dicens hoc sibi ab illo mandatum. And this same *Lucius* gave certificates in the name of another martyr, *Aurelius*, who was unable to write: Aurelii quoque adolescentis tormenta perpessi nomine, libelli multi dati sunt ejusdem Luciani manu scripti, quod litteras ille non nosset. The martyrs who were so liberal as to order certificates to be given to all applicants, when they were dead, appear to have cherished a great error by believing, that so great was the efficacy of the death they were about to suffer, that it could expiate the sins of other persons; and that the injunctions of a deceased and triumphant martyr were perfectly satisfactory both to God and to men. Thus much is certain, and is manifest from *Cyprian's* Epistles, and from his book *de Lapsis*, that most of the martyrs were ignorant of the true grounds of these certificates of peace; and they imagined grounds for them quite inconsistent with the Christian religion. This *Cyprian* in some measure perceived, as appears, among other things, from his reprehension of *Lucian's* proceedings, (Epist. xxi. p. 32.): Cum Dominus dixerit, in nomine Patris et Filii et Spiritus Sancti gentes tingi, et in baptismo præterita peccata dimitti, hic præcepti et legis ignarus mandat pacem dari et peccata dimitti in Pauli nomine, et hoc sibi dicit ab illo esse mandatum. This is a frigid and futile argument; as also are, it must be confessed, many others occuring in the writings of *Cyprian*. This excellent man is not entirely self-consistent, on this whole subject; and he especially vacillates in regard to the force and the ground of these certificates; yet he partially apprehended the subject. Those who gave the certificates, whether from their ignorance, or from rash and hasty judgments, really believed that martyrs received power from God to forgive sins, and remit the penalties incurred by transgressors. And *Cyprian* effected nothing, either by the preceding argument, or by any others. For this [p. 491.] *Lucian*, whom he endeavored to set right, being provoked and irritated by Cyprian's letters, burst every bond of modesty, and, getting others of the confessors to join him, issued, in his own name, and in that of all the confessors, a general certificate of peace, requiring that all the lapsed, without exception, should be restored to the church. Says *Cyprian* (Epist. xxii. p. 31.): Postquam ad Confessores litteras misi, ut quasi moderatius aliquid et temperantius fieret, universorum Confessorum nomine idem *Lucianus* epistolam scripsit, qua pæne omne vinculum fidei et timor Dei et mandatum Domini et Evangelii sanctitas et firmitas solveretur. Scripsit enim omnium nomine *universis* (lapsis) eos pacem dedisse, et hanc formam per me aliis episcopis innotescere velle: cujus epistolæ exemplum ad vos transmisi.

This improper conduct of the martyrs, who were generally illiterate and unacquainted with the Christian discipline, might perhaps have been easily checked and corrected, if the presbyters and bishops had done their duty. But they, actuated by hatred of Cyprian and by other motives, shamefully increased the evil, and wished more to be conceded than the martyrs asked for. It was not the aim of the martyrs to subvert all order and to prostrate the authority of the bishops by means of their certificates, nor to exempt those whom they undertook to patronise entirely from ecclesiastical penalties. This is clear, from the language of *Lucian* himself, the most audacious and indiscreet of them all:

(*Cyprian*, Epist. xxi. p. 30.): Et ideo, Frater, peto, ut, sicut hic, cum Dominus coeperit ipsi ecclesiae pacem dare, secundum praeceptum Pauli (not Paul the apostle, but Paul the martyr, in whose name Lucian issued the certificates,) et nostrum tractatum, exposita caussa apud episcopum, et facta exomologesi, habeant pacem non tantum hae, sed et quas scis ad animum nostrum pertinere. It appears therefore,—1. That he did not wish the lapsed to be immediately restored to the church, from which they had excluded themselves by sinning; but he would have the matter postponed, till the return of more tranquil times.—2. That he did not ask to have the lapsed restored to communion, without the cognisance and assent of the bishop.—3. That he would have the lapsed publicly confess their fault, and humbly ask the forgiveness of the church: *Exomologesin facere.* He by no means wished all the lapsed, who held certificates, to be received without any punishment, but only those who, after their fall, lead a manifestly pious and holy life. This condition Lucian expressly added, in that general certificate, which was so particularly offensive to Cyprian. Says Cyprian, (Epist. xxii. p. 31.): Additum est plane, de quibus ratio constiterit, quid post commissum egerint. *Lucian* therefore allowed enquiry into the conduct of those presenting certificates, and would deprive of the benefits of their certicates those guilty of new transgressions. Similar prudence and moderation were observed by other martyrs in giving certificates of peace; as *Cyprian* has recorded in repeated instances. Thus, (Epist. ix. p. 19.): Martyres memores loci nostri ad me litteras direxerunt, et petierunt tunc desideria sua [p. 495.] examinari et pacem dari, quando ipsa antea mater nostra ecclesia pacem de misericordia Domini prior sumpserit et nos divina protectio reduces ad ecclesiam suam fecerit. And (Epist. x. p. 20.) addressing the martyrs, he says: Litteras ad me direxistis, quibus examinari disideria vestra et quibusdam lapsis pacem dari postulastis, cum persecutione finita convenire in unum cum clero et recolligi coeperimus. See also Epist. xi. p. 21. Many also of the lapsed, though possessed of certificates, wished nothing to be done preposterously, but very modestly submitted their case to the judgment of the bishop. Says *Cyprian*, (Epist. xxviii. p. 38.): Scripserunt mihi nuper quidam de lapsis humiles et mites et trementes et metuentes Deum, et qui in ecclesia semper gloriosè et granditer operati sunt. - - - Et quamvis libello a martyribus accepto, ut tamen a Domino satisfactio sua admitti possit, orantes scripserunt mihi, se delictum suum cognoscere et poenitentiam veram agere, nec ad pacem temere aut importune properare, sed expectare praesentiam nostram, dicentes pacem quosque ipsam, si eam nobis praesentibus acceperint, dulciorem sibi futuram. Certain of the presbyters, however, at the mere sight of these certificates, in utter disregard of the respect due to the bishop, and contrary to all order, not even requiring any public confession of their faults, admitted all sorts of lapsed persons, at once, not only to the assemblies of the church, but even to the Lord's supper;—than which, nothing in that age could be more indiscreet, or more injurious to the church. Says *Cyprian*, (Epist. x. p. 20.): Presbyteri quidam nec timorem Dei, nec episcopi honorem cogitantes—contra Evangelii legem, contra vestram quoque (he is addressing the martyrs,) honorificam petitionem. (mark the circumspection he uses,) ante actam poenitentiam, ante exomologesin gravissimi atque extremi delicti factam, ante manum ab episcopo et clero in poenitentiam impositam, offerre pro illis et eucharistiam dare, id est, sanctum Domini. corpus prophanare audent. With grief he repeats the same in the following Letter, (Epist. xi. p. 21.) These presbyters, envying Cyprian the honors paid him, stirred up the martyrs and confessors to demand that more respect should be given to their certificates than heretofore, and that disregarding the authority of the bishops, the lapsed should be restored, with no delay whatever. Says *Cyprian*, (Epist. xl. p. 52.): Hi fomenta olim quibusdam Confessoribus et hortamenta tribuebant, ne concordarent cum episcopo suo, ne ecclesiasticam disciplinam cum fide et quiete juxta præcepta dominica continerent, ne confessionis suæ gloriam incorrupta et immaculata conversatione servarent. Hence those great and turbulent movements, both of the confessors and the lapsed; the former demanding that their certificates should have the effect of laws and mandates, and the latter, that instant admittance should be allowed them to all the sacred rites, on the ground of their certificates. In our province, says *Cyprian*, (Epist. xxii. pp. 31, 32.): Per aliquot civitates in præpositos (the bishops,) impetus per multitudinem factus est, et pacem, quam semel cuncti a martyribus et confessoribus datam clamitabant, confestim sibi repræsentari coëgerunt, territis et subactis præpositis suis, qui ad resistendum minus virtute animi et robore fidei prævalebant. Apud nos etiam quidam turbulenti, qui vix a nobis in præteritum regebantur, et in nostram præsentiam differebantur – – velut quibusdam facibus accensi plus exardescere et pacem sibi datam extorquere cœperunt. Some of the lapsed had the audacity to send insulting letters to Cyprian, in which they did not ask for reconciliation, but claimed that they had already obtained it. (Epist. xxix. p. 39, 40.): Quorumdam lapsorum conspirata temeritas, qui pœnitentiam agere et Deo satisfacere detrectant, litteras ad me fecerunt, pacem non dandam sibi postulantes, sed quasi jam datam sibi vindicantes, quod dicant Paulum omnibus pacem dedisse.

[p. 496.]

(4) *Cyprian* endeavored to repress the disturbances produced by the certificates of peace, in their commencement, by three grave and explicit Epistles, addressed, respectively, to the Confessors, the priests, and the people. In these Epistles he urged to have the subject postponed until he should return to his see; and the Confessors he exhorted to use prudence and moderation, and the people to wait quietly till the persecution should terminate. But, for various reasons, these Epistles only created still greater disturbances, as we have already intimated. The confessors and martyrs, especially, urged their rights with earnestness; and open opposition to them would have been hazardous. The *Lucian* before mentioned, in that general certificate of peace which he wrote in the name of all the confessors, threatened Cyprian pretty distinctly, that if he persevered in resisting the wishes and demands of the martyrs, the result would be, that himself and other martyrs would exclude Cyprian from their communion. This short, but threatening and arrogant Epistle of *Lucian*, is worth inserting here, from *Cyprian*, (Epist. xvi. p. 26.): Universi Confessores Cypriano Papæ salutem! Scias, nos universis, de quibus apud te ratio constiterit, quid post commissum egerint, dedisse pacem. Et hanc formam per te et aliis episcopis innotescere volumus. *Optamus te cum sanctis martyribus pacem habere.*

Præsente de clero et exorcista et lectore. What Lucian here says of his wishing Cyprian *pacem habere cum martyribus*, amounts undoubtedly to this: *We will deprive you of our peace, unless you confirm the peace given by us*; notwithstanding all the efforts of *Stephen Baluz*, (in his notes on the passage,) to extenuate the folly of this language. Had they carried these threats into execution, they would doubtless have brought the good man into great trouble. He was therefore obliged to yield a little, and to treat this dangerous subject cautiously and prudently. While he was laboring and trembiing, the Roman priests and confessors afforded him aid, by their epistle addressed to the priests and the people of Carthage, in which they approved and lauded the course he had pursued. They also wrote to *Cyprian* himself, who had by his letters endeavored to bring them to espouse his cause. These epistles from Rome seem to have set this controversy nearly at rest; for we meet with few or [p. 497.] no traces of it afterwards.—When Cyprian returned to his church on the termination of the Decian persecution, he called a council at Carthage, the Acts and Canons of which are mentioned by him in several of his Epistles, (See Epistt. lii. liii. lv. lvi. lxviii.) A principal subject of discussion in the council, was the case of the lapsed, and the penance they should perform. But it does not appear, that the influence which certificates of peace given by martyrs ought to have, was discussed and settled. This subject seems to have been designedly passed over, and consigned to oblivion. For it was full of danger and difficulty; because, while consulting the interests of the church, the honors and authority of the martyrs and confessors, whom the people venerated excessively, could not be safely underrated. *Cyprian* in all his Epistles upon this subject, proceeds as if treading on the treacherous embers of a sleeping volcano, and is exceedingly careful not to appear to depreciate the honors and the dignity of the martyrs. Yet with all his prudence he could not escape entirely the indignation of the martyrs and the complaints of the people. What then would have occurred, if he had ventured, in the council, in the presence of so many living confessors, idolized by the people, to call their prerogatives in question, and to set definite limits to the effects of their certificates of peace? What contention, what clamors, what disputes would have arisen? After this contest, I find no further mention of certificates of peace, in any ancient history of the Christians. I therefore suspect that the bishops, becoming more cautious and prudent, in view of this troublesome case, whenever a persecution broke out, pursued the old custom, and sent presbyters and deacons to the prisons, to instruct and guide the martyrs, and prevent their being too liberal and indiscreet in the issue of such certificates.

§ XIII. **Contest between Cyprian and Novatus.** The controversy just described, was accompanied by another more trivial and limited in its nature, but, on account of its source and origin, greater and more formidable; for it arose from hatred and the indulgence of unrestrained passion; and it was protracted, and was conducted with an animosity, perhaps, greater than the case demanded, till it ended in a deplorable schism.(¹) *Novatus*, a presbyter of Carthage, even prior to the persecution under Decius, had had disagreement with *Cyprian*, his bishop, for some cause not now known, and had drawn off some of the brethren from him; that is, he had persuaded them not to follow the demands of the bishop in everything.(²) If we give credit to his adversary's statements, *Novatus* was not only factious, vain, and rash, but also guilty of many offences and crimes. *Cyprian*, therefore, purposed to call him to a judicial trial, and to exclude [p. 498.] him from the communion of the church. And the day for his trial had been appointed, when, suddenly, the publication of the emperor's edict intervened; and, as it obliged *Cyprian* to betake himself to flight, *Novatus* remained safe in his former position.(³) This was the first act in this protracted drama.

(1) The history of the two-fold schism, produced by *Novatus* and *Novatian* at Rome, and by *Felicissimus* at Carthage, in the midst of the Decian persecution, must be gathered from the Epistles of *Cyprian*, from *Eusebius*, from the Fabulæ Hæreticorum of *Theodoret*, and from detached passages of other ancient writers. Yet the few documents we have relative to this protracted contest, are insufficient to give us a full and perfect knowledge of it. The primary and, so to speak, interior causes of this conflict, are, in great measure, undiscoverable; nor will equity or reason permit us to believe everything true, which is told us by *Cyprian* and the other bitter enemies of *Novatus* and his friends. If I am not greatly deceived, there were faults on both sides; but which was most blameable, the scantiness of the records that have reached us, make it very difficult to decide. The short statement of this controversy given above, differs in some respects, from that heretofore given by the learned. Yet I have stated nothing without good reason; nor can the order and connexion of the events be apprehended differently. The affairs of *Novatus*, of *Felicissimus*, and of *Novatian* were certainly connected; and yet, in some sense, they were disconnected. This connexion in some respects and disconnexion in others, have not been carefully discriminated, by most of those who have written on the subject; and often they so mix up things, that their readers are left in great perplexity and uncertainty. I make no exceptions among even the most distinguished expounders of the affairs of Christians.

(2) *Novatus*, with whom this whole controversy originated, was undoubtedly a Carthagenian presbyter. For no one who reads the Epistles of *Cyprian* censuring him, will give credit to *Baronius*, who would make him a bishop. And yet, if I can judge, he was not one of the presbyters who served the principal church and were always near the bishop, but he presided over a separate congregation distinct from the principal church. I think this may be inferred from the fact, that he created *Felicissimus* a deacon; of which *Cyprian* so bitterly complains, (Epist. xlix. p. 63.): Ipse (Novatus) est, qui Felicissimum

satellitem suum diaconum, nec permittente me, nec sciente, sua factione et ambitione constituit. Whether this occurred while Cyprian was at Carthage, or in his absence during the persecution, I think we must come to the conclusion stated. If *Novatus* ventured to do this, before the persecution, and while Cyprian was in Carthage, (which is quite supposeble,) it must be [p. 499.] manifest, that *Novatus* had charge of a separate congregation distinct from that of *Cyprian.* For how could an individual presbyter create a deacon in the bishop's own church, and the bishop be present, and not know of it? How could he have so obtruded this deacon upon the bishop? If this occurred during the absence of Cyprian, we must come to the same conclusion. For although some of the presbyters and a portion of the people were not very partial to Cyprian, yet the greater part of the church had the highest respect and reverence for him; and therefore, no presbyter could so manage as to cause a deacon to be appointed without the bishop's knowledge and contrary to his pleasure. The whole, or at least the greater part of the church would have resisted it, and have cried out that the head of the church must be consulted and have a voice in the matter. But the congregations that were separate from the mother church and the bishop, and had their own appropriate presbyters, had likewise their own deacons; and if *Novatus* had charge of such a church, he might have created Felicissimus a deacon in *his* church, without the knowledge or consent of the bishop. And this supposition is confirmed by the language used by *Cyprian.* For it appears, that *Novatus* did not create a deacon by his own sole authority and choice, but, as *Cyprian's* language shows, (*sua factione et ambitione,*) in his factious ambitious spirit, by flattery and intrigue, he persuaded the church under him to elect Felicissimus deacon. Had *Novatus* simply assumed, contrary to ecclesiastical law, the power of constituting a deacon in his own church, there would not be ground for charging him with either faction or ambition. Besides, Cyprian does not blame him for recommending to his church the election of Felicissimus to the office of deacon, which it was lawful and right for him to do; but he complained, that *Novatus* undertook and carried through the whole business, without consulting him, or letting him know anything of it. *Novatus*, doubtless, believed that such a congregation, distinct from the mother church, had the right and the power of electing their own servants, with consent of the presbyter who had charge of them. But *Cyprian*, who was a most strenuous defender of episcopal rights and authority, contended that nothing whatever, even in those minor Christian assemblies, ought to be undertaken or transacted without the approbation and consent of the bishop; and he therefore considered *Novatus* as censurable for recommending to his church the choice of Felicissimus for deacon, before he had been approved of and judged worthy of a deaconship by the bishop. Perhaps *Novatus* intentionally neglected to consult the bishop, because he knew that *Cyprian* had a dislike to the man. The church over which *Novatus* presided, worshipped on a certain hill in Carthage. This, I think, *Cyprian* intimates, (Epist. xxxviii. p. 51.) where he says of *Felicissimus:* Comminatus est fratribus nostris - - - potentatu improbo et terrore violento, quod secum *in monte* non communicarent, qui nobis obtemperare voluissent. Many copies, both [p. 500.] manuscript and printed, here read, *in morte.* But this reading is destitute of meaning; and Felicissimus would have been a fool to have threatened such a thing to his adversaries, when it would have frightened nobody. The learned have therefore long considered the true reading to be, *in monte.* And this reading is much confirmed by the appellation of (*Montenses*) *the Hill People*, given to the Novatians at Rome, according to *Epiphanius*, (in Ancorato, c. 13. Opp. tom. ii. p. 18.) They were probably so called, because they considered that portion of the Carthagenian church, which worshipped on some hill or mountain of the city, to be the only true church of Carthage. Hence *Felicissimus* threatened the friends of *Cyprian* with exclusion from communion in the *Hill Church:* which was unquestionably the church in which Felicissimus officiated as deacon, and, of course, had some authority; and, as this was the church over which *Novatus* presided, it must be clear, that I am correct in stating, that *Novatus* had charge of a small congregation, distinct from the mother church, which assembled on some hill in Carthage.

If we may give credit to *Cyprian* and his adherents, there were few worse men among the Christians of that age than *Novatus.* Cyprian says of him, (Epist. xlix. p. 63.): Rerum semper cupidus, avaritiæ inexplebilis, rapacitate furibundus, arrogantia et stupore superbi tumoris inflatus, semper istic episcopis male cognitus, quasi hæreticus semper et perfidus omnium sacerdotum voce damnatus, curiosus semper ut prodat, ad hoc adulatur ut fallat, nunquam fidelis ut diligat, fax et ignis ad conflanda seditionis incendia, turbo et tempestas ad fidei facienda naufragia, hostis quietis, tranquillitatis adversarius, pacis inimicus. So many and so great diseases of the mind, he had manifested by his great enormities and crimes. For, not to mention his seditious conduct towards his bishop, he was a thief, a robber, a parricide, and a perpetrator of sacrilege. Spoliati ab illo pupilli, fraudatæ viduæ, pecuniæ ecclesiæ denegatæ has de illo exigunt pœnas. - - - Pater etiam ejus in vico fame mortuus, et ab eo in morte postmodum nec sepultus. Uterus uxoris calce percussus, et abortione properante in parricidium partus expressus. What can be more base and detestable than such a man? The best informed ecclesiastical historians have no hesitation as to the entire truth of these statements, because they come from a very holy martyr, in whose affirmation implicit confidence must be placed. And far be it from me, to accuse the holy man of falsehood or intentional misrepresentation. But I suppose, candid and well-informed men will readily concede, that a martyr *might* commit mistakes and errors; that under the influence of strong passions and an excited imagination he might exaggerate in some things, and extenuate in others. And therefore, if we suppose something of this nature, in the present case, occurred in regard to the otherwise excellent *Cyprian*, we shall do no injury to his reputation. In recounting the vices of *Novatus* he is manifestly declamatory, and plays the orator; and those who understand human nature, know that we are never more liable to err, than in describing the character of other men, and especially of our enemies. That *Novatus* was [p. 501.] contentious, prone to innovation, and also factious, I can readily admit; but the good *Cyprian* could sometimes discover faults where there were none, and was too virulent against those whom he regarded as hostile to his reputation and dignity. To express my own opinion, I cannot look upon *Novatus* as so black a character as *Cyprian* represents him; because he neither sought nor obtained for himself any great advantages, throughout this long and vehement contest. He allowed others to be created bishops, and enjoy the fruits and rewards of the dissension; but for himself, he was contented with his situation and the rank of a presbyter, and chose rather to minister than to bear rule. This indicates his moderation. The crimes, with which Cyprian charges him, were doubtless the subject of common talk, and were, therefore, collected from common fame; but it is observable, that *Novatus* was never convicted of them. He could not, indeed, after he left Africa, be summoned to a trial; but Cyprian might have substantiated the crimes of the absent man by examining the witnesses, and have legitimately passed sentence on him if found to be guilty. But it is manifest, that he did neither; nor does he let fall a single word, even in the passages where he shows the most anger, from which it can be inferred, that Novatus was *proved* guilty of the crimes which common fame charged upon him, and that on such ground he had been deposed from office and ejected from the church. It is therefore no rash conjecture, to suppose that the truth of these enormous imputations could not be substantiated. *Felicissimus* the friend of Novatus, *Cyprian* condemned and excommunicated: and why should he spare *Novatus*, if he knew him to be guilty of such enormities?

But let us pass over these points, which it is absolutely impossible at this day to clear up, because no writings of *Novatus* have reached us; and let us look into the controversy, of which *Novatus* was the prime cause and author. The learned are agreed, that *Novatus* was the original cause of the African disturbances. And this is explicitly stated by *Cyprian*, (Epist. xlix. p. 63.): Idem est Novatus, qui apud nos primum discordiæ et schismatis incendium seminavit.—But I cannot agree with those who think, that these contests and disturbances commenced in the absence of *Cyprian*, and in the midst of the persecution, and that, before the Decian persecution, *Novatus* had never plotted against his bishop. We have testimony to the contrary, in the epistle already cited, and proof that before *Cyprian's* retirement, *Novatus* was hostile to him. *Cyprian* clearly discriminates between the offences of *Novatus* before the persecution, and those during the persecution; and he says, that *Novatus*, before the persecution, had alienated brethren from the bishop: Qui quosdam istic ex fratribus ab episcopo segregavit, (this he did before the persecution began; next follows his criminal conduct during the persecution;) qui in ipsa persecutione ad evertendas fratrum mentes alia quædam persequutio nostris fuit. And who, let me ask, can doubt, that a controversy had arisen between *Cyprian* and *Novatus*, before the Decian persecution, when he hears *Cyprian* [p. 502.] himself declaring, that he should have arraigned Novatus before the tribunal of bishops. and have cast him out of the church, if he had not been prevented by the emperor's edict? He says, indeed, that the crimes of *Novatus*, and not any *private* or personal offence, had caused him to form that purpose. But of the crimes of *Novatus*, we have already given our views; they were not so clear and manifest as to demand public animadversion. Neither does *Cyprian*, as we have already seen, disguise the fact, that the enormity of his evil deeds was augmented by some offence against the honor and right of his bishop. What it was that set the presbyter and the bishop at variance, does not fully appear. But I strongly incline to believe, that *Novatus*' conferring the office of deacon on Felicissimus, without the consent and approbation of *Cyprian*, irritated the feelings of the bishop, who held his episcopal dignity in the highest estimation; and that here commenced the whole sad conflict. I am aware, that some learned men suppose that *Felicissimus* was constituted deacon while *Cyprian* was absent, and they censure John *Pearson*, who maintains, (Annal. Cyprian, § 20. 22. p. 25.) that he had been put into that office, before the quarrel began. But they can allege nothing in support of their opinion, except the question, "Who consecrated or ordained *Felicissimus?*" What bishop would have presumed to do it, if *Cyprian* had been at home! See *Tillemont*, (Memoires pour servir á l'Histoire de l'Eglise, tom. iv. P. I. p. 393.) To this question, I answer: *Novatus, himself*, consecrated his deacon; and he thought this to be lawful. Those Presbyters who, like *Novatus*, had charge of separate churches, enjoyed many prerogatives, which did uot belong to the other presbyters who were connected with the bishop. But *Cyprian* deemed this to be unlawful. And so he intimates, I apprehend, when he says, that (*ambitione Novati*) through the *ambition* of Novatus, the man (*constitutum fuisse*) was *constituted* deacon, (*se non permittente*) without his permission. According to *Cyprian's* views, *Novatus* should have asked leave of his bishop to initiate his deacon; but, being inflated by *ambition*, and presiding over a church situated perhaps in the suburbs, or on some neighboring hill, he supposed the permission of the bishop not necessary to the transaction. And here lay his chief fault.

(3) See *Cyprian*, (Epist. xlix. p. 64.): Hanc conscientiam criminum (Novatus) jam pridem timebat. Propter hoc se non de presbyterio excitari tantum (be excluded from the class of presbyters,) sed et communicatione prohiberi pro certo tenebat. (But how could the worthy *Cyprian* know this, and here assume power to judge of the thoughts of another?) Et urgentibus fratribus imminebat cognitionis dies, quo apud nos caussa ejus ageretur, nisi persecutio ante venisset, quam iste voto quodam evadendæ et lucrandæ damnationis excipiens, (i. e. he rejoiced in this occurrence. But who had told Cyprian that fact?) hæc omnia commissit et miscuit; ut qui ejici de ecclesia et excludi habe- [p. 503.] bat, judicium sacerdotum voluntaria discessione præcederat: quasi evasisse sit pœnam, prævenisse sententiam.—Many, both ancients and moderns, have understood the last part in this quotation, as referring to the journey of *Novatus* to Rome; and they suppose *Cyprian* intended to say, that *Novatus* escaped the sentence impending over him, by his flight. But in this they are clearly mistaken. The (voluntaria discessio) *voluntary departure*, of which *Cyprian* speaks, was a withdrawal from the church, as is manifest from what precedes. *Novatus* withdrew himself from the bishop and the church, to prevent being excluded by the priests.

§ XIV. **The Schism of Felicissimus at Carthage.** After the departure of *Cyprian*, and so long as the African magistrates kept up a vigorous persecution of the Christians, these movements were dormant. But when the fury of the persecution gradually subsided, and *Cyprian* began to prepare for returning to his church, now fast recovering its former tranquillity, *Novatus*, doubtless, fearing that the returning bishop would revive the prosecution which he had commenced before his flight, deemed it necessary to organize a party which should obstruct the return of his adversary to his church, and thus to deprive him of the means of annoyance to himself.(1) And, therefore, by means of *Felicissimus*, the deacon whom he had ordained against the pleasure of the bishop, he drew off a portion of the church from *Cyprian;* and, particularly, with the aid of one *Augendus*, he resisted the regulations which *Cyprian* had sanctioned, in reference to the poor. To his party belonged, not only many of the people, but especially five presbyters, who had long indulged animosity towards *Cyprian*.(2) This turbulent faction were able to retard somewhat the return of *Cyprian*, but they could not frustrate it. Therefore, after a short delay, which prudence suggested, the bishop returned to Carthage, and assembling a council, principally on account of the lapsed, he began to repress the rashness of his adversaries; and he expelled *Felicissimus*, the author of the sedition, and the five presbyters, his associates, from the church. The ejected persons, unawed by this punishment, set up a new church at Carthage, in opposition to *Cyprian's* congregation, and placed over it, as bishop, *Fortunatus*, one of the five presbyters, whom *Cyprian* had excommunicated.(3) But this company had more courage than efficiency, and sinking into discord, seems, not long after, to have become extinct, for none of the ancients make mention of its progress.

(1) *Cyprian* does not expressly say that *Novatus* induced *Felicissimus* to organize this opposition to him; but this is inferred, from the fact, that he throws on *Novatus* all the blame of the divisions and discords in the church. He says, (Epist. xlix. p. 64.): Circa cæteros autem fratres elaboramus, quos ab eo (Novato) circumventos dolemus, ut veteratoris perniciosum latus fugiant, ut lethales laqueos sollicitantis evadant, ut de qua pelli ille divinitus meruit ecclesiam repetant: quos quidem, Domino adjuvante, per ejus misericordiam regredi posse confidimus. In the same Epistle, he calls *Felicissimus* (*satellitem Novati*) a satellite of Novatus; which pretty distinctly implies that *Novatus* used *Felicissimus* as his agent or instrument for disturbing the peace of the Church, and setting it at variance with its bishop. But, as I observed at the first, many [p. 504.]

things relating to this contest are unknown to us; and *Cyprian* himself sometimes speaks, as if *Felicissimus* did not act from the instigation of another, but from the impulse of his own mind. In his 38th Epistle, (p. 51.) in which he descants warmly on the criminality of *Felicissimus*, he makes no mention whatever of *Novatus*, but represents *Felicissimus* as the cause of all the evil. He says: Nec loci mei honore motus, nec vestra auctoritate et præsentia fractus, *instinctu suo* quietem fratrum turbans proripuit se cum plurimis, *Ducem se factionis* et *seditionis principem* temerario furore contestans. The affairs of *Novatus* and *Felicissimus* were undoubtedly connected; and that each of them aided the other, is beyond controversy: yet the two movements seem to have stood disconnected, in some respect, which we are unable even to conjecture. In the progress of the controversy, this disconnexion becomes manifest. For *Novatus* joined the followers of *Novatian*, from whom *Felicissimus* kept aloof. *Novatus* set up one *Maximus* as a bishop at Carthage, and *Felicissimus* set up another, in the person of *Fortunatus*. This shows, that the two sects had nothing in common at that time, except their hatred of *Cyprian*. In the commencement of the controversy, however, their connexion seems to have been more intimate.

(2) *Felicissimus*, as a man, was not much better than his presbyter *Novatus*. For *Cyprian* charges him not only with *fraud* and *rapine*, but also with *adultery:* Ad fraudes ejus et rapinas, quas dilucida veritate cognovimus, adulterium etiam crimen accedit, quod fratres nostri graves viri deprehendisse se nunciaverunt et probaturos se asseverarunt. This occurs in Epistle 38. (p. 51.): and in another Epistle, (55. p. 79.) he is branded with marks of still greater infamy; for he is pronounced, Pecuniae commissae sibi fraudator, stuprator virginum, matrimoniorum multorum depopulator atque corruptor. It was not therefore *one* act of adultery, but *many*, that he committed; and not satisfied with that form or wickedness, he violated the chastity of many virgins. I confess, I must here [p. 505.] doubt a little, and must suspect that *Cyprian*, in the ardor of his indignation, expressed more than he intended. But let us dismiss our suspicions, and listen to the martyr. This debauchee, then, who was unworthy of the name of a man, stirred up the sad conflict, while *Cyprian* was absent. *Cyprian* in his exile had sent four deputies to Carthage, the two bishops *Caldonius* and *Herculanus*, and two very distinguished confessors, the priests *Rogatianus* and *Numidicus*, who, in the bishop's name and stead, should distribute among the poor the moneys due to them, and carefully examine the lives and the condition of those who were living on the bounties of the church, in order to advance the most worthy of them to sacred functions. I will give the substance of this commission in the holy man's own words; (Epist. xxxviii. p. 51. ed *Baluz.* which is the edition I always quote;) addressing the deputies, he says: Cumque ego vos pro me vicarios miserim, ut expungeretis necessitates fratrum nostrorum sumptibus (i. e. with the money collected by the church for the poor,) si qui etiam vellent suas artes exercere, additamento, quantum satis esset, desideria eorum juvaretis: simul etiam et aetates eorum et conditiones et merita discerneretis, ut jam nunc ego, cui cura incumbit, omnes optime nossem et dignos quoque et humiles et mites ad ecclesiasticae administrationis officia pro-

moverem. It appears then—First: That *Cyprian* intended, by these deputies, *necessitates expungi fratrum sumptibus;* i. e. to relieve the wants of the brethren from the funds of the church. For *expungere necessitates*, is simply to satisfy and remove the wants of the poor.—Secondly: That he wished those among the poor, who were disposed to labor at their trades, to be supplied with money from the church treasury sufficient for purchasing the necessary tools and means for business.—Thirdly: That he wished those among the poor, who were fit for deacons and other sacred functions, to be removed from the class of the poor who were supported by the church, in order to their admission to the class of officers of the church; in short, he wished the fund for the poor to be relieved of a part of its burden. All these measures were honorable, pious, and useful. But *Felicissimus* resisted them. He would not have (*necessitates expungi*,) the wants of the brethren relieved, nor have such an examination of the indigent as the bishop directed. Says *Cyprian:* Intercessit, ne quis posset expungi, (being a deacon, he held the church funds, and therefore was able to prevent the giving of relief to the embarrassed; he refused to pay over to the bishop's deputies the moneys in his hands:) neve ea, quae desideraveram, possent diligenti examinatione discerni. The necessities of many were indeed relieved; that is, as *Cyprian* soon after states, through the hands of the deputies, (stipendia episcopo dispensante percipiebant,) they received the stipends which the bishop dispensed. For *Felicissimus* had not the whole treasury in his hands, but only that of the Hill Church, of which he was deacon. But as he held out severe threats against those who did not reject the relief [p. 506.] profferred by *Cyprian's* deputies, many abstained from it, and would not avail themselves of the kind offers of the deputies. And these, undoubtedly, *Felicissimus* relieved from the funds in his hands. Comminatus est fratribus nostris, qui primi expungi accesserant potentatu improbo et terrore violento, quod secum in monte non communicarent, qui nobis obtemperare noluissent; i. e. he threatened, that he and the Hill Church, of which he was deacon, would not hold those as brethren, who, being in want, should make application to the bishop's deputies.—Here we have the crime of *Felicissimus.* But the cause or pretext for the criminal act, *Cyprian* does not mention; nor has any one, so far as I know, attempted its investigation. This, therefore, is a problem for us to solve: and it is not so abstruce, as to require great ingenuity for its solution. *Felicissimus*, as we have seen, was a deacon; and therefore to him belonged the care of the poor, and the administration of the treasury of the church. Now the authority and dignity of deacons, were far greater in the African church than in the other churches, as might be shown from various testimonies. They, equally with the presbyters, had a seat in the councils, as appears from *Cyprian's* 55th Epistle, and other places. They were dispatched to the prisons, to look after the martyrs and confessors, and be their counsellors, as before shown. In the absence of the presbyters, they could receive the confessions of offenders, and absolve the penitent. This *Cyprian* admits, in his 13th Epistle, where he allows the lapsed to make their confession to the deacons. They also had some share in the government of the church. Therefore *Felicissimus*, inflated with the pride of office, maintained, that the distribution of money to the poor and other matters, should have been assigned by the bishop to himself and the other deacons, and not to deputies commissioned by him; and he complained, that by his commission, *Cyprian* trespassed on the rights of the order of deacons. This solution will at once suggest itself to a person familiar with Christian antiquities, and duly considering the case. But, perhaps, this daring man meditated something still more criminal. He contended, perhaps, that by forsaking his church in the time of persecution, and seeking his own safety by flight, *Cyprian* forfeited his dignity, and deprived himself of the honors and the rights pertaining to a bishop: and therefore, that his orders, communicated through his deputies, were to be disregarded, as being those of a man no longer possessing authority; and that another head must be placed over the church. And it is well known, that others, likewise, called in question the prudence of *Cyprian*, in withdrawing from his church when conflicting with its enemies.

Cyprian, on being informed of the criminal conduct of *Felicissimus*, immediately addressed to his legates a letter which has come down to us, ordering the man to be ejected from the church. The legates obeyed their instructions, without delay, and declared unworthy of communion in the sacred rites, not only *Felicissimus*, the author of the disturbance, but also one *Augendus*, his associate, concerning whom we have no knowledge, and some others of both sexes. This appears from a letter of the legates, among the Epistles of [p. 507.] *Cyprian*, No. xxxix. This act certainly betokens a man of a vehement and hasty temper, rather than of a discreet and prudent mind; and it is one of the things which, in my judgment, show that *Cyprian* was more studious of his own honor, than of the public good. In the first place, he assumed the office of a judge, in his own cause, contrary to the rules of justice; for the contest was respecting the extent of the bishop's rights, and those of the order of deacons. And that *Felicissimus* was not destitute of arguments, by which to defend his conduct, is sufficiently manifest from the fact, that *Cyprian* most carefully conceals from us the cause which produced the controversy. For if the cause alleged by his adversary for his bold resistance to the bishop, had been manifestly unjust, or destitute of all plausibility, *Cyprian* certainly would not have passed silently over it, but would have assailed it in his usually eloquent and severe manner.—In the next place, *Cyprian*, by his deputies, expelled from the church one of its ministers or deacons, unheard and unconvicted of crime, by his sole authority, and without consulting the people; which a bishop had by no means a right to do. He therefore went far beyond the limits of his power. He mentions, indeed, (in the Epistle before cited,) *three* grounds for his sentence: the threats of *Felicissimus*, his frauds and rapines, and his adultery. But, as *Cyprian* himself tacitly admits, *Felicissimus* had never carried his threats into execution; the frauds and rapines of which the bishop says he had the most certain knowledge (*se dilucida veritate cognovisse*,) had not been brought forward and spread out before the people; and as to the adultery, as he again admits, it had never been substantiated by proof. It was therefore unavoidable, that this rash decision should produce still greater dissensions. Among the Carthagenian presbyters, there were *five*, who had dissented and opposed the elevation of *Cyprian* to the episcopate.

These had previously manifested, by various signs, an aversion to him; and now they openly forsook him, and went with the party of *Felicissimus;* and undoubtedly, for the purpose of obtaining the appointment of another bishop in his place. Some learned men think *Novatus* was one of the *five;* to which opinion we shall soon give attention. These presbyters, in order to accomplish their object more readily, promised to the lapsed, towards whom *Cyprian* had been somewhat severe, that if they would separate themselves from the bishop, they should be restored to the fellowship of the church without any penance whatever. Says *Cyprian*, (Epist. xl. p. 52.): Conjurationis suæ memores, et antiqua illa contra episcopatum meum - - - venena retinentes, instaurant veterem contra nos impugnationem suam. - - - Nunc se ad lapsorum perniciem venenata sua deceptione verterunt, ut ægros et saucios, et ad capienda fortiora consilia per calamitatem ruinæ suæ minus idoneos, et minus solidos, a medela vulneris sui avocent, et intermissis precibus et orationibus, quibus Dominus longa et continua satisfactione placandus est, ad exitiosam temeritatem mendacio captiosæ pacis invitent. Most bitterly does this holy man complain of the rashness of the five presbyters, in this Epistle addressed to the Christian people. But among his complaints and accusations, there are some which are extravagant, and would better become an orator laboring to excite odium against [p. 508.] a criminal, than a Christian bishop. One thing of this character, as it strikes me, is his comparing the five presbyters to the five *principal men of Carthage*, who were joined with the magistrates for suppressing and exterminating the Christians. Quinque isti presbyteri nihil aliud sunt, quam quinque primores illi, qui edicto nuper magistratibus fuerunt copulati, ut fidem nostram subruerent, ut gracilia fratrum corda ad lethales laqueos prævaricatione veritatis averterent. In searching for the import of this passage, learned men have labored wonderfully. But it manifestly refers to the five principal citizens, whom *Decius*, in his edict, had coupled with the magistrates, for the more sure accomplishment of his purpose of exterminating Christianity. By this formidable schism, the return of *Cyprian* to his diocese was, for a time, retarded; yet, very soon, casting away all fear, he returned, and by his presence put an end to the strife.

It now remains for us to inquire, whether the famous *Novatus*, whom *Cyprian* terms the standard-bearer of all the Carthagenian tumults, was one of those five presbyters who joined the party of *Felicissimus?* The learned, with great unanimity, affirm it: one only, so far as I know, denies it; namely, John *Pearson*, in his Annales Cyprianeæ; and he offers no proof of his opinion. It *Novatus* were one of these presbyters, the cause of his hatred, and of the sedition against *Cyprian*, would be manifest. But, all things considered, I apprehend *Pearson* was right, and that *Novatus* is not to be numbered among those adversaries of *Cyprian*. In the first place, it has been already shown, clearly, that *Novatus* was at enmity with *Cyprian* some time before *Felicissimus* attempted to make disturbances in the church at Carthage; and that *Cyprian* was prevented from bringing him to trial, and ejecting him from the church, solely by the sudden outbreak of the Decian persecution, which obliged *Cyprian* to go into retirement. But those five presbyters did not withdraw themselves from *Cyprian*, until after the sedition excited by *Felicissimus*. Before that time, they had dissembled their alienation, and the bishop had no controversy with them. In the next place, it appears, from the 49th Epistle of *Cyprian*, (p. 64.) that sentence was never pronounced by the council of Carthage against *Novatus*, but that he prevented the sentence by his flight. Says the bishop: Ejici de ecclesia et excludi habebat. - - Quasi evasisse sit pœnam, prævenisse sententiam. And he afterwards says: He *merited* expulsion from the church, (cum *meruisse* de ecclesia pelli.) and not that he *was expelled.* In fact, *Novatus*, to prevent being condemned, withdrew himself from the church of Carthage, and from Cyprian's jurisdiction. But those five presbyters, as we shall presently see, appeared before the council of bishops which Cyprian assembled after his return, made their defence, and, by a decree of the council, were excluded from the communion of [p. 509.] the church. I am aware that Cyprian says, (Epist. xlix. p. 63.) that *Novatus* was condemned by the voice of all the priests, (*perfidus omnium Sacerdotum voce damnatus.*) And hence the learned have inferred, that he was condemned in the council, in conjunction with the other presbyters, the enemies of Cyprian. But the words may very properly be understood of the private condemnation of individuals; and they undoubtedly prove, that all the teachers of the church disapproved of his temerity and improbity. Besides, unless I am wholly deceived, *Novatus* had already reached Rome, and joined the partizans of *Novatian*, when Cyprian, after his return, instituted a process against the faction of *Felicissimus* and the five presbyters. The whole history will become disjointed, and be very difficult to arrange, unless we take this to be certain. And when Cyprian says, explicitly, that *Novatus* (*sententiam prævenisse*) prevented sentence being passed by retiring; he clearly intimates that *Novatus* had gone away, and was residing at Rome, before *Cyprian* returned to his church.—Lastly, omitting other things for the sake of brevity, it is certain, that although *Novatus* aided *Felicissimus*, and was favorable to his cause while in Africa, yet, he did not adhere to his party at Rome, but joined a very different one, namely, that of *Novatian*. Neither did he recognize the bishop, *Fortunatus*, whom the faction of *Felicissimus* had set up in opposition to *Cyprian*; but he established another bishop at Carthage, namely, *Maximus*, one of the Novatian party.

(3) On the subsidence of the Decian persecution, *Cyprian* returned to Carthage, and immediately summoned a council of bishops, to settle the controversy respecting the lapsed, and to try the cause of *Felicissimus* and the presbyters associated with him. It were much to be wished that the Acts of this council, or at least, the epistle of Cyprian and the African bishops concerning it, of which Cyprian makes mention, (Epist. xlii. p. 57.) had come down to us. But they are all lost, and we have to form our judgment of the whole affair, from a few words of *Cyprian*. From these it appears, *first*, that *Felicissimus* and the five presbyters were present and had a hearing before the council. *Cyprian*, writing to Cornelius, bishop of Rome, says, (Epist. xlii. p. 57.): Quantum vero hic ad presbyterorum quorundam et Felicissimi caussam pertinet, quid hic actum sit, ut scire posses, litteras ad te collegae nostri (the assembled bishops) manu sua subscriptas miserunt, qui, *auditis eis*, quid senserint et quid pronunciaverint, ex eorum litteris disces. *Secondly*, from another of his Epistles to the same Cornelius, (Epist. lv. p. 87, &c.) it appears, that not only the bishops

of the African province, but also the presbyters and deacons, and not in a small but in a large number, were present in the convention. Si eorum, qui de illis priore anno judicaverunt, numerus cum presbyteris et diaconis computetur, plures tunc affuerunt judicio et cognitioni, quam sunt iidem isti, qui cum Fortunato (the bishop set up by the factious in opposition to *Cyprian*,) nunc videntur esse conjuncti. From the same Epistle, it appears that all of them were ejected from the church by the united suffrage of the bishops; yet not [p. 510.] without the prospect of a pardon of their offences, provided they would reform. Says *Cyprian*, (p. 88.): Nec ecclesia istic cuiquam clauditur, nec episcopus alicui denegatur. Patientia et facilitas et humanitas nostra venientibus praesto est. Opto omnes in ecclesiam regredi. Neither does Cyprian omit to mention the offences, which called forth this sentence; but, to my astonishment, he gives most prominence to that one, which is the most excusable, and was never numbered among the capital crimes which exclude a man from the church; namely, compassion for the lapsed, and defence of the Certificates of Peace heretofore mentioned. Let us hear the eloquent man's own words: Taceo itaque de fraudibus ecclesiae factis, (i. e. the interception and misapplication of the money of the church,) Conjurationes et adulteria et varia delictorum genera praetereo. (These the good man considers as minor offences, and as not so much against God, as against men and the bishop. But now comes the huge crime against God himself, and for which alone they were deemed worthy of punishment.) Unum illud, in quo non mea, nec hominum, sed Dei caussa est, de eorum facinore non puto esse reticendum, quod a primo statim persecutionis die - - *communicare cum lapsis, et poenitentiae agendae intercedere* non destiterunt: i. e. they wished those, who brought Certificates of Peace from martyrs, to be received again by the church. In magnifying this crime, he pours forth all his eloquence, and consumes a large part of his Epistle, as if nothing could be more atrocious and offensive to God. Now I suppose, that an adulterer, a sacrilegious man, an enemy of the public peace, a plunderer of the funds devoted to the poor, is a far greater sinner, than the man who, being of a mild temperament and aware of human frailty, shows himself kind and lenient towards those, who apostatised from Christ through fear of death, and themselves abhorred the crime. But to tell the truth, it was neither this fault, nor the bulk of the others, which cast *Felicissimus* and his associates out of the church; but (as the whole Epistle shows,) it was this single one, that *Felicissimus* dared to oppose the mandates of the bishop, and to raise up a party against him. And that excessive lenity towards the lapsed, was so great and heinous a crime, in the view of *Cyprian*, because it was not only contrary to his judgment in the matter, but also weakened his authority. We shall see, in another place, with what zeal this holy man labored to defend and exalt the episcopal dignity, at the expense of the people's rights.—In what way the accused conducted their defence, or with what arguments they justified their conduct, *Cyprian* has no where informed us. We should have been able to judge much better of the merits of this controversy, if some of those arguments had reached us. I am very confident that they accused *Cyprian* of thirsting for power and lordship; and that they urged the rights of the presbyters, the deacons, and the people. *Felicissimus* and the presbyters, when condemned by the council, were not disheartened by the [p. 511.] contumely, but sought to establish a new congregation at Carthage, separated from *Cyprian's* church. And over their flock, they made one *Fortunatus* bishop, obtaining consecration for him from five bishops who are named and severely castigated by *Cyprian*, (Epist. lv. p. 82.) And thus there were three bishops at Carthage, at one and the same time; namely, *Cyprian*, whom the greater part of the people followed, *Maximus*, set up by the legates of Novatian from Rome, and *Fortunatus*, whom the faction of *Felicissimus* had created. This last party, in order to strengthen their new church, sent *Felicissimus* with quite a number of delegates to Rome, to endeavor to bring the Romish bishop *Cornelius* to espouse their cause, and renounce the support of *Cyprian*. *Cornelius* was a little perplexed, being terrified by the threats of the legates, and stumbled by their false statements. For they threatened to expose (*turpia multa ac probrosa*) many base and reproachful things, if he refused to receive the letter they had brought for him, (*Cyprian*, Epist. lv. p. 80.); and they asserted, that *twenty-five* African bishops attended the consecration of *Fortunatus*. *Cyprian* contends, that this was a gross falsehood; and I believe, he was correct. And yet he seems to admit, that there were more than *five* bishops present on that occasion; bad ones, however, either lapsed, or heretical. Si nomina (of the five-and-twenty bishops) ab eis quaereres, non haberent vel quos falso nominarent. Tanta apud eos etiam malorum (*episcoporum*, undoubtedly; for he is speaking of bishops,) penuria est, ut ad illos nec de sacrificatis, nec de haereticis viginti quinque (episcopi) colligi possint. In the assembly, therefore, besides the *five* who consecrated *Felicissimus*, there were several other bishops, but they were either *sacrificers* who, of course, must have been deposed, or they were, in Cyprian's estimation, heretics. *Cornelius* assumed courage, his first fears subsiding, and rejecting the overtures of *Felicissimus*, he remained friendly to *Cyprian*. And this was necessary, for his own sake; for he was hard pressed by the faction of *Novatian*, which also assailed *Cyprian*, and inclined towards the party of *Felicissimus*. What *Cornelius* would have done, had he been free and not in need of *Cyprian's* friendship, is another question, and we offer no conjectures about it. What occured after this,—whether *Fortunatus* had any successor, or whether those who separated from Cyprian, returned again to the church,—no ancient writer has informed us. Perhaps, this whole faction became amalgamated with the Novatians.

He who shall impartially examine this controversy, will perhaps admit, that it may be pronounced the last struggle of expiring liberty, in the African church, against episcopal domination. *Cyprian*, although he frequently speaks modestly enough of himself, and respectfully enough of the martyrs and confessors, the rights of the presbyters and deacons, and the authority of the people, yet wished to concentrate all power in his own hands, and, subverting the ancient form of government, to subject the whole church to the absolute au- [p. 512.] thority and good pleasure of the bishop. This was the source of all these conflicts. The confessors, the presbyters, the deacons, and the people, made a partial resistance; but the fortitude and perseverance of *Cyprian* finally triumphed. No one will approve of every thing done by his antagonists; yet that

they contended for the rights of the clergy and people, in opposition to a bishop affecting to have absolute dominion over them, is placed beyond all controversy by the scanty and obscure documents which have come down to us.

§ XV. **The Schism of Novatian at Rome.** Before the return of *Cyprian* from exile, *Novatus,* dreading the severity of the bishop, had retired to Rome; where discord and strife were no less prevalent than at Carthage. *Novatian*, one of the Roman presbyters, a learned, eloquent, and grave man, but rigid and austere, denied that any persons falling into the grosser sins, and especially the persons who had forsaken Christ in the Decian persecution, were to be received again to the church; and, perceiving that *Cornelius*, a man held in the highest estimation among the Romish presbyters, and also some others, differed from him on this subject, he made the most strenuous opposition to the election of *Cornelius* to succeed *Fabian*, as bishop of Rome.(1) From hatred, perhaps, of *Cyprian*, who was much attached to Cornelius, *Novatus* became an associate and co-adjutor of *Novatian.* Nevertheless, *Cornelius* was elected bishop, and *Novatian* withdrew from communion with him, and was followed, at the instigation of his friend, *Novatus*, by five presbyters, several of the confessors, and a portion of the people.(2) Both parties, by their letters, appealed to *Cyprian;* and he, after dispatching legates to Rome, and carefully examining the case, gave his decision in favor of *Cornelius.* And, on the other hand, *Cornelius* followed the example of *Cyprian's* fortitude; and, in a numerous council, which he assembled at Rome, in the year 251, procured the ejectment of *Novatian* and his adherents from the church, since nothing would persuade them to entertain milder sentiments in regard to the lapsed.(3) The issue of this affair was as unhappy as that of the African contest; and it was the more lamentable, on account of the long continuance of the evil, whereas the African schism was comparatively of short duration. Those whom *Cornelius* had excluded from the Romish church formed themselves into an associated body, over which they placed, as bishop, *Novatian*, the parent of the association. This new company of Christians, although detested by most of the bishops, who approved the decrees [p. 513.] of the Roman council, respecting the lapsed, enjoyed, nevertheless, staunch patrons, and was at once diffused through many parts of Christendom, and could not be suppressed before the *fifth* century. For this, its good fortune, it was indebted to the gravity and probity of the teachers who presided over it, and to the severity of its discipline, which tolerated no base characters, none guilty of the grosser sins.([4])

(1) The authors of most of the schisms among Christians, have been charged, justly or unjustly, with many crimes and faults; but this *Novatian* was not only accused of no criminal act, but was commended, even by those who viewed him as warring against the interests of the church, by *Cyprian*, *Jerome* and others, on account of his eloquence, his learning, and his philosophy. See *Cyprian*, Epist. lii. and lvii. His adversary *Cornelius*, indeed inveighs against him with much bitterness, in an Epistle to *Fabius*, bishop of Antioch, (preserved in part by *Eusebius*, Hist. Eccles. L. vi. c. 43. p. 244. &c.); but still he does not impeach his life or moral conduct. And nearly all the charges he brings against him, great as they may seem to be, relate to the intentions of the mind, which are known only to God: and some of the charges reflect more disgrace on *Cornelius* himself than *Novatian*. But he has been taxed with ambition; for it is said that he stirred up this great controversy, merely because *Cornelius* received most votes for the vacant bishopric, which he himself coveted. This is an old charge; and it has acquired so much strength and authority by age that all the moderns repeat it with entire confidence; and they tell us, that *Cornelius* and *Novatian* were competitors for the episcopate, and that the latter failing of an election, disturbed the church, in his lust for office. But I have no hesitation to pronounce this a false accusation; and I think there is no good proof that *Novatian* acted in bad faith, or that he made religion a cloak for his desire of distinction. His enemy, *Cornelius*, does indeed say this, (in his Epist. apud *Euseb.* Hist. Eccles. L. vi. c. 43. p. 244.): Προπάλαι ὀρεγόμενος τῆς Ἐπισκοπῆς ὁ θαυμάσιος οὗτος, καὶ κρύπτων ἐν ἑαυτῷ τὴν προπετῆ ταύτην αὐτοῦ ἐπιθυμίαν. Admirandus ille vir episcopalis loci cupiditate jampridem accensus, et præcipitem illam ambitionem suam tegens, diu omnes latuit. But the very words in which he is here accused, carry with them his acquittal. For *Cornelius* clearly shows, that he *concealed* his ambition, which long remained *unknown*. Now, if this was true, *Novatian* certainly did nothing from which his desire of the episcopate could be inferred, nor could he have labored to secure votes or have attempted to corrupt the electors and draw them into his party. For the man who so conceals his ambition, that everybody believes him to seek no self-aggrandisement, cannot surely be a competitor with another man for the [p. 514.] episcopal office. But Cornelius supplies us with still stronger testimony to the innocence of his adversary. For he acknowledges, that when they were deliberating at Rome respecting the choice of a bishop, and Novatian declared that he wished some other person than *Cornelius* might be chosen, he affirmed, with a tremendous oath, that he *himself* did not wish for the office: Ὁ γὰρ τοι λαμπρότατος καὶ δι' ὅρκων φοβερῶν τινῶν πιστούμενος τὸ μὴ δὲ ὅλως Ἐπισκοπῆς ὀρέγεσθαι. *Egregius ille vir tremendis quibusdam sacramentis*

affirmaverat, se Episcopatum non concupiscere.—Now, whoever neither does nor attempts anything that could awaken a suspicion of his being ambitious, and morever declares, on oath, that he has no desire of the episcopate, can not possibly be a competitor for the episcopal office. But, some may say: The villain perjured himself; and although he made a great show of modesty, yet he opposed the election of Cornelius, in order to secure the appointment to himself. To this many things might be said in reply; I will mention only one. *Novatian* was not a man to whom a suspicion of perjury can be attached; he was a man, whom his very enemies pronounced upright, inflexible and rigorous, and whom no one ever charged with impiety towards God, or with being of a perverse and irreligious disposition. What then could *Cornelius* have designed by writing to Fabian, and probably to others, that *Novatian* had long secretly burned with desire for the episcopal office? I answer: to confirm a conjecture, and that a very dubious and intangible one. He reasoned in this manner: *Novatian*, on being expelled from the church, allowed himself to be created bishop by his adherents; therefore, he had long coveted the office of a bishop, although he pretended to the contrary. How fallacious and unworthy of a bishop such reasoning is, I need not here show. There would indeed be a little plausibility in it, though very slight, if *Novatian*, immediately after the election of Cornelius, had wished his friends to create *him* also a bishop; a thing entirely within his power to effect. But he postponed all movements for erecting a new church, and patiently awaited the decision of the approaching council. And after he had been condemned and excluded from the church, together with his adherents, he thought there could be no sin in his taking the oversight of his own company. The invidious representations of this affair by *Cornelius*, can not at this day be refuted, owing to the want of documents; yet, as they come from an enemy, they are not to be received implicitly by those who would judge equitably.

Novatian, before he became a Christian, was a philosopher, and most probably a Stoic. From the account *Cornelius* gives of him, he appears to have been of a melancholy temperament, and consequently, gloomy, austere, and fond of retirement. Those who forsook him and came back to the Romish church, said they found in the man, what *Cornelius* calls (apud *Eusebium*, p. 242.): τὴν ἀκοινωνησίαν καὶ λυκοφιλίαν, which *Valerius* translates *abhorrentem ab omni societate feritatem, et lupinam quamdam amicitiam.* He therefore shunned society, and was wolfish towards even his friends; i. e. he was harsh, [p. 515.] austere, and ungracious in his intercourse. That these things were objected to him with truth, I have no doubt; for manners like these are entirely accordant with his principles. He was led to embrace Christianity by a deep melancholy, into which he had fallen, and from which he hoped to be recovered by the Christians. At least, so we must understand. in my judgment, what *Cornelius* has stated, (nor will any who are familiar with the opinions and phraseology of the ancient Christians, understand *Cornelius* differently,): Ἀφορμὴ τοῦ πιστεῦσαι γέγονεν ὁ Σατανᾶς, φοιτήσας εἰς αὐτὸν καὶ οἰκήσας ἐν αὐτῷ χρόνον ἱκανόν. *Caussam atque initium credendi ipsi Satanas in ipsum ingressus atque in ipso aliquamdiu commoratus.* This in our style and mode of speaking, would be: *A deep and settled melancholy had fastened on his mind: and the Christians who knew him said, that an evil spirit had got possession of him, and that if he would profess Christ, the evil spirit would go out of him; so, from a hope of recovering his health, he professed Christianity.* Perhaps his melancholy was attended by convulsions. I have not here put a hasty and unwarrantable construction on the statement; for it is not credible that *Novatian* himself, being a Stoic philosopher, would refer his malady to an evil spirit. This notion was instilled into him by the Christians; who, undoubtedly, were desirous to bring a man of such correct morals to become a Christian; and they gradually made him a convert to their faith. Impatient of his malady, *Novatian* yielded to their exhortations. But by the regulations of the ancient church, he could not be baptized so long as he appeared to be under the power of an evil spirit. Exorcists were therefore sent to him, to expel the foul demon by their prayers. But they failed of success; and *Novatian* at length being seized with a threatening disease, while under their operations, was baptized in his bed, when apparently about to die. On recovering from the sickness, he seems to have hesitated whether he should in health confirm what he had done in his sickness, and thus persevere in the Christian religion. For, as Cornelius invidiously says of him, he could not be persuaded to submit to the other rites prescribed by the church, and be confirmed by the bishop, or be *signed*, as the term used expresses it. For this pertinacity, and disregard of the Christian regulations, unquestionably the only assignable cause must have been, that his mind was fluctuating between the philosophy he had before followed, and the Christian religion which he had embraced from a hope of recovering his health. Nor can I much wonder at this dubitation: for the Christians had assured him of the restoration of his health by the exorcists, who had failed in the undertaking. Nevertheless, the bishop, *Fabian* perhaps, a while after, made him a presbyter in his church, contrary to the wishes of the whole body of priests, and of a large part of the church. (See *Cornelius*, apud *Euseb.* l. c. p. 245.) It was altogether irregular and contrary to ecclesiastical rules, to admit a man to the priestly office, who had been baptized in bed; that is, who had been merely sprinkled, and had not [p. 516.] been wholly immersed in water in the ancient method. For by many, and especially by the Roman Christians, the baptism of *Clinicks*, (so they called those, who, lest they should die out of the church, were baptized on a sick bed,) was accounted less perfect, and indeed less valid, and not sufficient for the attainment of salvation. This also was even more strange and unheard of, that a man should be admitted among the teachers and leaders of the Christian people, who disregarded the laws of the church, and pertinaciously rejected the authority and confirmation of the bishop. The belief of this age was, that the Holy Spirit was imparted by the confirmation or *signing* of the bishop; so that all those lacked the Holy Spirit, whose baptism had not been approved and ratified by the bishop, by prayers, imposition of hands, and other rites. Ample proof of this is given by *Cornelius*, who expressly states, that *Novatian* was destitute of the Holy Spirit because he neglected the *signing* of the bishop. Τούτου δὲ μὴ τυχὼν, πῶς ἂν τοῦ ἁγίου πνεύματος ἔτυχε; *Hoc autem* (the *signing* of the bishop,) *minime percepto, quo tandem modo Spiritum sanc-*

tum potuit accipere? The Roman bishop, therefore, committed a great fault, by conferring the honored office of a presbyter on a man, who resisted the laws of the church, and whom he knew to be destitute of the Holy Spirit. And not only the body of presbyters, but also the people, perceived the magnitude of this fault; and both entreated the bishop not to confer that honor upon *Novatian*. But I can easily see, what may have induced the prelate to violate the laws of the church in regard to this man. He feared lest the man should forsake the Christian religion and revert to his former errors, of which disposition he had perhaps given some proofs. And therefore, to bind him to the church, and prevent his apostatizing, he conferred this honor upon him. In this opinion I am much confirmed by what is stated by *Cornelius*, (apud *Euseb.* p. 245.) that *Novatian* was raised to the rank of a presbyter, immediately after receiving baptism: Πιστεύσας κατηξιώθη τοῦ πρεσβυτερίου κατὰ χάριν τοῦ ἐπισκόπου, (which is not badly translated by *Valesius*): *Post susceptum baptismun* (properly, *as soon as he had believed*) *Presbyteri gradum fuerat consecutus, idque per gratiam episcopi.* Very justly said to be *by the favor of the bishop:* for it was contrary to the laws and customs of the church, to admit a man to the office of presbyter almost as soon as he was baptized, and before he had filled the office of deacon. This very honorary and unusual benevolence of the bishop, retained *Novatian* in the church, but it did not so heal and confirm his diseased mind, as wholly to extinguish all propensity to leave the church. For, on the rise of the Decian persecution, when the deacons called on him to quit his chamber, where he kept shut up, and perform the functions of a presbyter among his toiling and oppressed brethren, he refused to do it; nay, openly declared, that the office of presbyter was irksome to him, and that he had thoughts of returning again to his philosophy: Μὴ γὰρ ἔτι βούλεσθαι πρεσβύτερος εἶναι ἔφη, ἑτέρας γὰρ εἶναι φιλοσοφίας ἐραστής. *Respondit, non amplius se velle* [p. 517.] *presbyterum esse, sed alterius philosophiæ amore teneri.*—I have introduced these remarks on the life of Novatian, because they show that he was far from being an evil-minded man, though he was of a melancholy and singular character; and they explain the cause of that schism which originated from him. *Novatian* wrote much, but nothing that has reached us, except a tract *de Trinitate;* which is commonly printed with the works of *Tertullian*, and, a few years since, was published separately, with Notes and Observations by *Jackson*, in London. But some learned men contend, and not without apparent reason, that it is uncertain whether *Novatian* was the author of this tract.

(2) That the African presbyter *Novatus*, who fled from Carthage to Rome to avoid the sentence of *Cyprian*, became an associate and a coadjutor of *Novatian*, procured him many friends, and with vast zeal and effort cherished and promoted his cause, is abundantly proved by the Epistles of *Cyprian*, by *Jerome*, by *Pacian*, and many others. *Novatian*, a man gloomy and retiring, would have given way to admonition, or would have been easily overcome, had not his irresolute mind been excited and fortified by the various appliances of that factious, active, eloquent man, an adept at kindling the passions, who was influenced, undoubtedly, by his hatred of *Cyprian*, the partizan of *Cornelius*. And necessity also urged *Novatus* to embrace and defend the party of *Novatian*, with

all his might, and even to the establishing of a new church at Rome. He had repaired to Rome as to a haven of security, in order to be safe from the shafts of *Cyprian* and the Africans. But if *Cornelius*, the intimate of his adversary, should continue at the head of the Romish church, he himself would most assuredly be rejected and expelled from it. It was therefore necessary for him either to seek another asylum, or to cause *Cornelius* to be deposed from the bishopric, or lastly, to establish a new church in which he would find shelter. He therefore, more for his own safety, than for the honor of *Novatian*, prevailed by his eloquence on the Roman *confessors*, i. e. on that portion of the church which possessed the greatest influence and efficiency, to place themselves in opposition to *Cornelius;* a thing, which *Novatian* either could not, or would not attempt. Says *Cyprian* (Epist. xlix. p. 65.): Novato illinc a vobis recedente, id est, procella et turbine recedente, ex parte illic quies facta est, et gloriosi ac boni confessores, *qui de ecclesia illo incitante discesserant*, posteaquam ille ab urbe discessit, ad ecclesiam reverterunt. The same man, and not *Novatian*, who was a quiet man, though austere and rigid, induced a portion of the people at Rome to abandon *Cornelius*. Says *Cyprian:* similia et paria Romae molitus est, quae Carthagine, a clero portionem plebis avellens, fraternitatis bene sibi cohaerentis et se invicem diligentis concordiam scindens. He also [p. 518.] persuaded *Novatian*, a timid man, and perhaps reluctating, to allow himself to be created bishop: Qui istic (at Carthage,) adversus ecclesiam diaconum fecerat, illic (at Rome,) episcopum fecit; i. e. he ceased not to urge *Novatian* and his friends, until he prevailed with the latter to elect a bishop, and with the former to take upon him that office. He likewise consented to be despatched to Africa, with others, by the new bishop; and thus empowered, he established, at Carthage and other places, bishops adhearing to the Novatian party. Every thing was planned and executed by the active *Novatus*, and nothing or but little by *Novatian*. These acts were criminal, and they indicate a turbulent spirit, thirsting for revenge, and more solicitous for victory and self-advancement than for either truth or tranquility. Neither would I become the patron of the man: and yet there is one thing, in which he appears to me less culpable than is commonly thought. All the ecclesiastical historians, whom I have read, add this to his other crimes, that at Rome he approved opinions directly opposite to those which he maintained in Africa: whence they conclude, that he showed his malignity, by this whiffling and inconsistent course: At Carthage, say they, he was mild and lenient to the lapsed, and thought they ought, especially such of them as presented Certificates of Peace, to be kindly received, and be admitted to the church and to the Lord's supper, without undergoing penance; and this was intended to vex Cyprian. But at Rome, with *Novatian*, he excluded the lapsed forever from the church; and was so austere and uncompassionate, in order to overthrow *Cornelius*. Now whether the learned have judged correctly in this matter, I very much doubt. *Cyprian*, the most bitter of *Novatus*' enemies, enumerates all his faults, real or fictitious, in a long catalogue; but he does not mention this. Such silence in his enemy, is alone sufficient, in my view, to clear his memory from this charge. *Cyprian* likewise touches on the opinion, which, after the example of *Novatian*, he maintained at Rome: but he does not add, that while in Africa he held a different and opposite opinion: which he would doubtless have not omitted, if *Novatus* could be justly charged with the inconsistency. With an affectation of wit, *Cyprian* says: Damnare nunc audet sacrificantium manus, (i. e. he denies that persons who have sacrificed with their hands, should be received again into the church,) cum sit ipse nocentior pedibus, (i. e. when he had himself been more guilty with his feet: very bad taste!) quibus filius qui nascebatur occisus est. *Novatus* was reported to have kicked his pregnant wife in her abdomen. *Cyprian* would have used other language, if *Novatus* had been chargeable with changing his opinions respecting the lapsed. He would have said: *Damnare nunc audet sacrificantium manus, quum pedes eorum antea osculatus sit,* (he now dares condemn the hands of sacrificers, whereas before he kissed their feet.) This comparison would have more force and more truth. The learned have no other reason for believing that *Novatus* at Rome condemned the lapsed, whom in Africa he patronized, except their persuasion, that he was one of the five presbyters, who deserted *Cyprian* at Carthage; for *Cyprian* complains of them, that they were too indulgent towards the lapsed. But we have before shown that *Novatus* was not one of them; for it is evident that he had his [p. 519.] contest with *Cyprian,* long before the five presbyters had theirs.

(3) Of the Roman council, in which *Novatian* was condemned and ejected from the church, an account is given by *Cyprian,* (Epist. lii.) by *Eusebius,* and by others of the ancients. *Novatian* was present; but he could not be brought to agree with the bishops, that pardon should be granted to the Christians who lapsed in the time of persecution. He had not always held the same opinion; for before his contest with *Cornelius,* he had decided that pardon should be extended to all the lapsed, who relented, confessed, and submitted to the ecclesiastical penalties. This we learn, not only from *Cyprian,* (Epist. lii.) but also from others. But, in the heat of contention, as often happens, he insensibly became more strenuous than he was before. We are informed, not only by *Cyprian,* but also by *Socrates,* (Hist. Eccles. L. iv. c. 28. p. 245.) that *Novatian's* reason for opposing the advancement of Cornelius to the See of Rome, was, that he held friendly intercourse with the lapsed, before they had made satisfaction to the church. Nor does *Cyprian* venture to deny that fact, but only to apologise for it. He says, (Epist. lii. p. 69) : Sed et quod passim (here *passim* is equivalent to *promiscue*) communicare sacrificatis Cornelius tibi nunciatus, hoc etiam de apostatarum fictis rumoribus nascitur. He here seems to deny the fact; but a little afterwards, he admits pretty plainly, that *Cornelius* had given reconciliation to the lapsed in case of sickness, and had not required of them to do penance when restored to health. Si qui infirmitatibus occupantur, illis, sicut placuit, in periculo subvenitur. And that he treated the *Libellatici* with still greater lenity, is also not dissembled. It was not, therefore, a sheer fiction, that *Novatian* charged upon *Cornelius.* Perhaps some, at Rome, were less cautious than *Cyprian* in their defence of *Cornelius,* and while they admitted the charge to its full extent, contended that it was a trivial fault, and not derogatory to the character of a bishop. By the reasoning of these men, the bilious and morose *Novatian* was so irritated, that he affirmed,

at last, that the lapsed ought to be forever excluded from communion with the bishop and the church; and in this way he aimed to strip the bishop's advocates of all arguments in his favor. And having assumed this ground in the heat of controversy, he afterwards would not abandon it, lest he should appear vacillating and unstable in his opinions. And undoubtedly, *Novatus* urged him not to yield to any admonitions.

(4) I will not enumerate the patrons and favorers of *Novatian*, some of whom were men of high character, nor trace the progress of the sect. It appears from *Socrates*, (Hist. Eccles. L. iv. c. 28. p. 245.) that the Epistles, which *Novatian* sent throughout the Christian world, had great effect on the minds of many, and drew them over to his party. From *Eusebius*, (Hist. Eccles. L. vi. c. 44. p. 246. et c. 46. p. 248.) it appears, that *Fabius*, the bishop of Antioch, and many others, leaned towards his opinions, from fear lest too great indul-[p. 520.] gence to the lapsed should produce peril and damage to the church. It also appears, that the Novatians collected congregations of considerable magnitude, first in Africa, and then in various parts of Europe, Asia, and Africa, at Rome, Constantinople, in Spain, in Gaul, and in Phrygia. And the causes of this success are noticed by the ancients. In the first place, as *Socrates* remarks in the passage before cited, the severity of the sect towards those who stained their characters by sin, procured for it a high estimation among those very studious of piety. And then, the gravity, and the purity of morals, which most of their teachers exhibited, could not fail to procure for them respect from the people. And hence, *Constantine* the Great exempted them from the liabilities of the other heretics; and, by a law enacted A. D. 326. (inserted in the Codex Theodos. tom. vi. p. 124.) he allowed them to enjoy the temples and property they had legitimately acquired. But the subsequent emperors were not equally indulgent to them; and a law of the younger *Theodosius*, A. D. 423, (found also in the Codex Theodos. tom. vi. p. 202.) decreed the same penalties against them, as against the other sects. He had previously, in the year 413, enacted a severe law against a branch of the Novatian sect, who bore the name of *Sabbatians* or *Protopaschites*. The name was taken from one *Sabbatius*, who, near the beginning of the fifth century, separated from the other Novatians, because he thought the feast of Easter should be celebrated at the same time with the Jewish Passover. See Ja. *Gothofred* on the Codex Theodos. (tom. vi. p. 222.) From the fifth century, it appears, the sect gradully died away; and yet some slight relics of it were apparent in the sixth century.

§ XVI. **The Novatian Doctrines.** As to the Christian religion, generally, there was no disagreement between the Novatians and other Christians. But that which especially distinguished them from the great body of Christians was, that they denied a re-admission into the church, to all who fell into the greater sins after baptism, and especially to those who, under the pressure of persecution, revolted from Christ and sacrificed to the gods: and yet they did not exclude these persons from all hope of eternal salvation.(1) In close connection with this doctrine was another, that they could not look upon a church as anything short of an assembly of unoffending persons; persons who, since they first entered the church, had not defiled themselves with any sin which could expose them to eternal death. And this error obliged them to regard all associations of Christians, that allowed great offenders to return to their communion, (that is, the greatest part of the Christian commonwealth,) as unworthy of the name of true churches, and destitute of the Holy Spirit; thus [p. 521.] arrogating to themselves alone, the appellation of a genuine and pure church. And this they ventured publicly to proclaim. For they assumed to themselves the name of *Cathari* (*the Pure*), thereby obviously stigmatizing all other Christians as impure and defiled; and they re-baptized the Christians who came over to them, thereby signifying that the baptisms of the churches from which they dissented were a vain and empty ceremony.(2) The other things reported concerning the faith of this sect, are either uncertain, or altogether incredible.

(1) Of the ancient writers who mention and condemn the principal error of *Novatian*, respecting the perpetual exclusion of lapsed Christians from the church, some express themselves obscurely and ambiguously, and others seem to disagree with each other. It is therefore not strange that the moderns, also, in treating of the Novatians, should vary in their statements, and advance diverse opinions. This, in general, is undoubtedly true, that *Novatian* and his adherents excluded for ever from the church, those who fell into sins after baptism. But there are two things which admit of dispute: *First*, who were meant by the *Lapsed?—Secondly*, whether he excluded the lapsed from the church only, or also from heaven and eternal salvation? As to the first point, it is certain that the contest between *Cornelius* and *Novatian*, in its origin, related solely to those who had fallen away in the Decian persecution. And yet it is no less certain, that *Novatian*, as Cyprian gravely charges upon him, (Epist. lii. p. 74.) placed all persons whatever, whose conduct showed a deficiency of Christian firmness, in one and the same predicament; and he inflicted the same penalties on the *Libellatici* as on the *Sacrificati* and the *Thurificati*. And as the laws of the ancient church considered certain other transgressors, especially adulterers and murderers, as equally guilty with the apostates, *Novatian*, also, seems to have comprehended them all in one sentence, and to have ordered the church doors to be for ever closed against others, as well as against apostates. And those writers of the fourth and fifth centuries, who mention this Novatian doctrine, whether they refute it, or only explain it,

all so understood it, telling us that *Novatian* prohibited all persons, guilty of any great fault, from re-admission to the church. And this rule certainly was practised by the Novatian churches in those centuries. This is most explicitly affirmed by *Asclepiades*, the Novatian bishop of Nice, in the fourth century (apud *Socratem*, Hist. Eccles. L. vii. c. 25; p. 367.): Ἐκτὸς τοῦ ἐπιθῦσαι καὶ ἄλλαι πολλαὶ κατὰ τὰς γραφάς εἰσιν ἁμαρτίαι πρὸς θάνατον, δι' ἃς ὑμεῖς μὲν πρὸς τοὺς κληρικοὺς, ἡμεῖς δὲ καὶ τοὺς λαϊκοὺς ἀποκλείομεν. Præter sacrificium idolo-[p. 522.] rum sunt et alia multa peccata ad mortem, ut loquuntur scripturæ, propter quæ vos quidem clericos, nos vero etiam laicos a communione removemus. In nearly the same manner, *Acesius*, another Novatian bishop, explains the views of his sect, (apud *Socrat.* Hist. Eccles. L. i. c. 10; p. 38). He says, that from the times of Decius, there prevailed among his people this *austeram legem* (αὐστηροῦ κάνονος): Neminem, qui post baptismum ejusmodi crimen admiserit, quod peccatum ad mortem divinæ scripturæ pronuntiant, ad divinorum mysteriorum communionem admitti oportere. None of the ancients, so far as I know, has left us a catalogue of the sins which the Novatians accounted mortal; and, of course, it is not fully known how far their discipline reached, though all pronounce it very rigid. *Gregory Nazianzen*, (Orat. xxxix. Opp. tom. ii. p. 636.) is dissatisfied, because they did not include *avarice* among the mortal sins, since the Scriptures pronounce this sin as great as that of Pagan worship, and declare it to be a *species of idolatry*. But the good man is mistaken. The Novatians did not punish vicious mental habits, such as avarice and the like, but acts contravening any of the greater commands of God, or what are called *crimes*. *Gregory*, also, in the same Oration, states that the Novatians reckoned second marriages among mortal sins; which is attested by *Epiphanius*, *Augustine*, *Theodoret*, and many others. Neither is this utterly false; for *Socrates*, who was well versed in Novatian affairs, informs us, (Hist. Eccles. L. v. c. 22; p. 288.) that not all the Novatians, but only those of Phrygia, excommunicated the persons who contracted second marriages. This fact suggests to us the origin and source of this custom. There were followers of *Montanus* still residing in Phrygia, in the fourth century, and they condemned second marriages. These mixed with the Novatians, whom they admired for their severe discipline, so congenial to their own practice, and undoubtedly persuaded them to adopt this part of the Montanist discipline.—It is therefore beyond a question, that the Novatian church, in its maturity, refused to commune, not only with apostatizing Christians, but also with all persons guilty of the grosser sins. But the inquiry still remains, whether the church, at its commencement, and also the founder of it, held the same opinion. That there is ground for doubt on the subject, appears from the 52d Epistle of Cyprian, who sometimes speaks as if Novatian allowed a place in his church to adulterers, and to other equally great sinners, and excluded only deserters of Christianity, or apostates. He says, (p. 74.) · Aut si se cordis et renis scrutatorem constituit et judicem (Novatianus), per omnia æqualiter judicet - - et fraudatores et mœchos a latere atque a comitatu suo separet, quando multo et gravior et pejor sit mœchi, quam libellatici caussa, cum hic necessitate, ille voluntate peccaverit. A little after he adds: Nec sibi in hoc novi hæretici blandiantur, quod se dicant idololatris non communicare, quando sint apud illos adulteri et fraudatores, qui teneantur idololatriæ [p. 523.] crimine, secundum Apostolum. And a little after: Ita fit, ut si peccato alterius inquinari alterum dicunt, et idololatriam delinquentis ad non delinquentem transire sua asseveratione contendunt, excusari secundum suam vocem non possint ab idololatriæ crimine, cum constet de Apostolica probatione mœchos et fraudatores, quibus illi communicant, idololatras esse. One cursorily reading these passages, might easily fall into the belief that Novatian tolerated *adulterers* and *defrauders* in his congregation, or did not forbid this class of offenders, after undergoing the penances prescribed by the church, to be again received among the brethren; and, therefore, that he closed the doors of the church only against falsifiers of their faith. But, if I do not greatly mistake, one who shall attentively and sagaciously examine all that Cyprian says on the subject, will come to a different conclusion. He is not treating of manifest *adulterers* and *defrauders*, but only of clandestine and concealed ones; and his mode of reasoning is this: It may be that there are dishonest men among the followers of Novatian, who, while they profess chastity and uprightness, secretly defile themselves with adultery and fraudulent dealing: and it is most probable, that there are such degenerate Christians contaminating all societies of Christians, and, of course, also the Novatians. If, then, it be true, as the Novatians maintain, that a man becomes a sinner himself, by associating fraternally with a sinner, the Novatians must be in perpetual peril, and may not escape the stains and spots of sin, whatever pains they may take. That such is the import of Cyprian's reasoning, is, I think, manifest from the first part of it: Si se cordis et renis scrutatorem dicit et constituit Novatianus, fraudatores et mœchos a latere suo separet. Had he been speaking of persons, whose adulteries and crimes were publicly known, there would have been no need of searching the heart and the reins, in order to discriminate the evil doers from the other Christians. But for detecting and discriminating secret adulterers and defrauders, a sagacity more than human, an exploration of the hearts of men was requisite. To show how difficult it is to remove all sinners from the congregation of the just, Cyprian selected two out of many crimes, adultery and fraud, which are commonly committed with so much secrecy and caution, as to escape public notice. There are, indeed, in this same Epistle of Cyprian, the following words, relative to adulterers: Quibus tamen et ipsis pœnitentia conceditur et lamentandi ac satisfaciendi spes relinquitur secundum ipsum Apostolum, 2 Cor. xii. Some learned men think that these words warrant the belief, that *Novatian* allowed adulterers to expect a re-admission to the church. But, in my opinion, they are most certainly mistaken. For, so far is this passage from showing that *Novatian* allowed a reconciliation to adulterers, that it does not show that all other Christians, except Novatians, would receive them. *Cyprian* says no more than this, that *St. Paul* left to adulterers a hope of penitence and satisfaction. And, [p. 524.] therefore, although the controversy commenced with those unfaithful Christians, who apostatized in the Decian persecution, yet, it is most probable, that the Novatian church, from its origin, decided that all persons violating the principal laws of God, after baptism, ought for ever to be excluded from the assembly of the brethren.

I come now to the other point, on which I stated there was room for some doubt. A great number of modern writers tell us, that *Novatian* cut off all those who fell into the greater sins after baptism, not only from the hope of re-admission to the church, but likewise from the hope of eternal salvation. And they have respectable authorities for their assertion, in writers of the fourth and fifth centuries, namely, *Eusebius*, (Hist. Eccles. L. vi. c. 43. p. 241.) *Jerome*, (in Iovinianum, c. 2.) and all those who affirm (and there are many that do so,) that *Novatian* discarded and abolished all penances. But the more carefully I examine the best and most reliable documents of this controversy, the more certain do I feel, that *Novatian* was not so destitute of clemency, and that those who so represent him, attribute to him a consequence, which *they* deduce from his principles, but which *he* did not allow. Very many in that age believed, that the road to heaven was open only to members of the church, and that those who were without the church must die with no hope of eternal salvation: and therefore they baptised Catechumens, if dangerously sick, before the regularly appointed time; and they restored to the church the unfaithful or the lapsed Christians, when alarmingly sick, without any penances or satisfaction, lest they should perish for ever. Our *Cyprian* decides, (Epist. lii. p. 71.) thus; *Extra ecclesiam constitutus, et ab unitate atque caritate divisus, coronari in morte non poterit.* As there were many holding this doctrine, they must have reasoned thus: *Novatian* would leave the lapsed to die excluded from the church: but there is no hope of salvation to those out of the church. Therefore he excluded the lapsed, not only from the church but also from heaven. *Novatian*, however, rejected this conclusion, and did not wholly take from the lapsed all hope of making their peace with God. For this assertion, our first great authority is *Cyprian*, who otherwise exaggerates the Novatian error quite too much. He says, (Epist. lii. p. 75.): O haereticae institutionis inefficax et vana traditio! hortari ad satisfactionis poenitentiam et subtrahere de satisfactione medicinam, dicere fratribus nostris, plange et lacrymas funde, et diebus ac noctibus ingemisce, et pro abluendo et purgando delicto tuo largiter et frequenter operare, sed extra ecclesiam post omnia ista morieris; quaecunque ad pacem pertinent facies, sed nullam pacem quam quaeris accipies. Quis non statim pereat, quis non ipsa desperatione deficiat, quis non animum suum a proposito lamentationis avertat? And after illustrating these thoughts with his usual eloquence, he concludes thus: [p. 525.] Quod si invenimus (in the scriptures,) a poenitentia agenda neminem debere prohiberi - - admittendus est plangentium gemitus et poenitentiae fructus dolentibus non negandus. So then *Novatian* exhorted sinners ejected from the church to weep, to pray, to grieve over their sins, in short to exercise penitence. But why did he so, if he believed there was no hope of salvation for the lapsed? Undoubtedly, he urged sinners to tears and penitence, that they might move God to have compassion on them, or, as Cyprian expresses it, (*ut delictum abluerent et purgarent,*) to *wash and purge away their sin.* Therefore, he did not close up heaven against them, but only the doors of the church; and he believed, that God had reserved to himself the power of pardoning the greater sins committed after baptism. And this opinion of their master, his disciples continued to retain. The Novatian bishop *Acesius*, at the council of Nice, in the presence of Constantine the Great, according to the testimony of *Socrates*, (Hist. Eccles. L. i. c. 10. p. 39.) thus stated the doctrine of his sect: Ἐπὶ μετανοίαν μὲν ἡμαρτικότας προτρέπειν, ἐλπίδα δὲ τῆς ἀφέσεως μὴ παρὰ τῶν ἱερέων, ἀλλὰ παρὰ τοῦ Θεοῦ ἐκδέχεσθαι, τοῦ δυναμένου καὶ ἐξουσίαν ἔχοντος συγχωρεῖν ἁμαρτήματα. Ad poenitentiam quidem invitandos esse peccatores, remissionis vero spem non a sacerdotibus expectare debere, verum a Deo, qui solus jus potestatemque habet dimittendi peccata. A similar statement by *Asclepiades*, another Novatian bishop, is found in *Socrates*, (Hist. Eccles. L. vii. c. 25. p. 367.): Θεῷ μόνῳ τὴν συγχώρησιν ἁμαρτιῶν ἐπιτρέποντες. Soli Deo potestatem condonandi relinquimus. And *Socrates* himself, (L. iv. c. 28. p. 245.) obviously explains the doctrine of Novatian in the same manner. Let us now rest upon these lucid and strong testimonies, and not vainly strive to enervate them, as some learned men do, by other far inferior and less explicit testimonies. This, however, I must not disguise, that from the very testimonies which in some measure vindicate the Novatian sect, it appears, that this species of Christians did not hold out to sinners a sure and undoubting hope of salvation. They would not indeed, have the persons whom the church excluded, sink into utter despair; but, while committing their case to God alone, and urging them to persevere in their penitence through life, they declared that the lapsed might *hope*, but must not feel assured, or that they were unable to promise any thing certain in regard to the judgment of God. This surely was sufficiently hard and discouraging. One utterly uncertain of his salvation, is not much happier, than one who is in despair; for he must pass his life in continual fear.—In what condition those of the lapsed were placed, whom the Novatians admitted to penitence, is manifest; they remained through life in the class of penitents. They could therefore be present at the public discourses to the people, for this was allowed to penitents; and in a particular place, distinct from that of the faithful, they could manifest the sorrows of their heart, in the sight of the brethren; and they could live and converse with their kindred and relatives: but from the common prayers, and from the sacred supper, they remained excluded.

(2) The error of the Novatians, in itself, appears to be of no great moment, as it pertained merely to the external discipline of the church; but in [p. 526.] its consequences, it was of the greatest importance, as being in the highest degree adapted to rend the church, and to corrupt religion itself. The Novatians did not dissemble, and conceal these consequences, as other sects did, nor did they deny, but avowed them openly. In the first place, as they admitted no one to their communion who had been guilty of any great sin after baptism, they must have held, that the visible church of Christ is a congregation of holy and innocent persons. And this principle might have been borne with, somehow, provided they had allowed, that salvation was also attainable in the other churches, which permitted sinners to become reconciled by penitence; although they might hold its attainment to be more difficult than in the churches denying restoration to the lapsed. But this they utterly denied, or at least, represented it as extremely dubious and uncertain. And by assuming to themselves the arrogant title of *Cathari*, or the "Pure," they charged all the churches that received back transgressors, with defilement, or impurity and, as we have just

heard from *Cyprian*, this impurity, they said, arose from their intercourse with sinners. How they explained this doctrine, is not stated by any ancient writer, nor need we here attempt its investigation. Whether they supposed the vitiosity of the guilty, like a contagious disease, communicated itself to the innocent, or whether they believed this guilt and pollution to arise from the sin of too great lenity towards sinners; it is certain, they regarded it as of no small moment, and indeed so great, that it could deprive men of those divine aids which are necessary for the attainment of salvation. That such were their sentiments, no one can doubt, if he considers, that they regarded the baptisms of all the churches that re-admitted transgressors, as being invalid, and that they rebaptised the members of other churches that came over to them. See *Cyprian*, (Epist. lxxiii. p. 129.) It was the almost universal opinion of that age, that it is by baptism men obtain forgiveness of sin, on account of their faith and their profession of it: but that the gifts of the Holy Spirit are conferred, by what they denominated *consignation*, or the Confirmation of the bishop. So taught *Dionysius* Alexandrinus in Egypt, as appears from his Epistle, (apud *Euseb.* Hist. Eccles. L. vii. c. 8. p. 254.); so also *Cornelius*, at Rome; and so likewise *Cyprian* in Africa, who uses this doctrine particularly, in the controversy respecting the rebaptizing of heretics, of which we shall soon have occasion to speak. He says, (Epist. lxxiii. p. 131.); Manifestum est autem, ubi et per quos *remissa peccatorum* dari possit, quae *in baptismo* scilicet *datur*. And soon after, he thus describes the effects of *Confirmation:* Qui in ecclesia baptizantur (and consequently have already obtained remission of their sins,) praepositis ecclesiae offeruntur, et per nostram orationem et manus impositionem *Spiritum Sanctum* [p. 527.] consequuntur et Signaculo Dominico consummantur. More, to the same purpose, may be found in this Epistle. I acknowledge it to be uncertain, whether *Novatian* attributed the same efficacy to episcopal Confirmation, as other Christians did. Novatian himself, as we have seen objected to him by Cornelius, had no reverence for episcopal Confirmation; and satisfied himself with baptism only: and *Theodoret* tells us, (Haeret. Fabul. L. iii. c. 5. Opp. tom. iv. p. 229, 230.) that his followers made no account of unction or Confirmation, and of course, other rites accompanying unction. Nor was it, in my judgment, a bad conjecture of Jo. *Morin*, (Comm. de sacris Ordinationibus, tom. iii. p. 127.) that the Novatians, in this matter, followed the example of their master, who had contemned the so called seal of the bishop. But concerning *baptism*, and its effects, it clearly appears from *Cyprian*, (Epist. lxxvi. p. 154.) that the opinion of Novatian was the same, as that of his adversaries: indeed he must have attributed greater efficacy to baptism than they did; and must have supposed that the Holy Spirit was imparted by it, if he ascribed no virtue to confirmation. And therefore, as *Novatian* denied all efficacy to the baptisms of the Christians who received the lapsed to communion, he denied that any of those dissenting from him had obtained from God the pardon of their sins, or had received the gifts of the Holy Spirit purchased by the blood of Christ. But what hope of salvation can be left, to men laboring under the burden of their sins, and destitute of the aids of the Holy Spirit? And here I would have particularly noticed, that the lapsed, or those excluded from the church for their offences, were in a better condition, according to *Novatian's* doctrine, than those Christians who admitted the lapsed into their assemblies. For he taught the lapsed to hope they might succeed in appeasing God, by persevering in their prayers and tears, and other acts of penitence: but those Christians who disagreed with Novatian neglected this, the only ground of safety to them, because they did not suppose that they had fallen from a state of grace; and, therefore, they had nothing at all in which they could trust. How inhumane and dangerous such doctrines were, and whither they tended, I need not explain more fully. Neither is it necessary here to admonish those who may read the ancient writers, respecting *Novatus* and *Novatian*, to beware of falling into their errors; for they often confound the two very different, but associated men, being deceived by the affinity of the names, *Novatus* and *Novatian*. But learned men have long since given warning on this point.

§ XVII. **The Persecution under Gallus.** While these controversies among Christians were rife, in the year 251, *Decius* was slain, with his sons; and *Gallus* succeeded him in the government, with his son, *Volusian*. The year following, the persecution against the Christians, which had been less vigorously prosecuted during the last years of *Decius*, was renewed, either by [p. 528.] the publication of new edicts, or by the revival of the old ones; and again the Christians had to undergo many evils, in various provinces of the Roman empire, which, however, they seem to have endured with more fortitude than under *Decius*.(1) The fury of the people was augmented by the calamities with which the Roman empire was at the time much afflicted, and in particular by a pestilential disease, which carried off an immense number of persons in various parts of the country. For it was supposed that the gods inflicted these penalties on the nations on account of the Christians. This opinion occasioned *Cyprian* to write his tract, *ad Demetrianum*, in which he attempts to confute it.(2) This persecution ceased in the year 254, when *Gallus* and his son being slain at Interamnia, *Valerian*, and his son *Gallienus*, were placed at the head of the Roman empire; for *Valerian* immediately restored peace to the Christian world.

(1) That *Gallus* again attacked the Christians, and renewed the persecution commenced by Decius, admits of no controversy. *Dionysius* of Alexandria, (apud *Euseb.* Hist. Eccles. L. vii. c. i. p. 250.) expressly says, that when Gallus saw things moving on according to his wishes, he trod in the steps of Decius, and persecuted (τοὺς ἱεροὺς ἄνδρας) the holy men. That his Christian subjects in Italy, and especially at Rome, were persecuted, is demonstrable from the 57th and 58th Epistles of Cyprian. And that the Christians of Africa were exposed

to numerous perils, is manifest from *Cyprian's* Tract, *ad Demetrianum*, and from other testimonies. But it is not equally apparent, by what law or rule he would have proceedings against them regulated; whether he imitated the cruelty of *Decius*, or directed to some other mode of proceeding. *Cyprian* mentions (Epist. lv. p. 82.) an edict published at Carthage, respecting sacrifices; and he says, that it occasioned the people to demand him to be cast to the lions: His ipsis diebus, has quibus ad te litteras feci, ob sacrificia quæ edicto proposito celebrare populus jubebatur, clamore popularium ad leonem denuo postulatus in circo fui. But as Cyprian, in this Epistle, makes no mention of evils and perils arising from this edict to the Christians, and writes as if all was then quiet, I can readily accord with the learned in supposing that this edict merely admonished the people to placate the gods by sacrifices, in order to avert the pestilence and other calamities; and that it did not order a persecution of the Christians. In this opinion I am confirmed by the fact, that Cyprian does not complain of any actual sufferings, but only of the threats of the Gentiles: Et Gentiles et Judæi *minantur* et hæretici. All things considered, I am induced to [p. 529.] believe that *Gallus* was not so cruel and unjust to the Christians, as is commonly supposed; that he did not, like Decius, come down with fury upon them, but only terrified the people who believed in Christ, and ordered their principal bishops into exile. And I am led to this belief, *first*, by the language used by *Dionysius* of Alexandria, (apud *Euseb.* Hist. Eccles. L. vii. c. 1.), who says that the (ἱεροὺς ἄνδρας) *venerable or holy men* were assailed by him. This language, if I am not much deceived, denotes, not the common people, but the bishops and priests. And, as to the evils which these venerable men suffered, he uses a mild term, which seems to exclude capital punishment, viz.: Ἤλασεν, insectatus est, *he chased away*. As to any martyrs, neither he nor others say one word. And then the occurrences at Rome, in this persecution, as they are fully stated by *Cyprian* in his Epistle to *Cornelius* (Epist. lvii. p. 94, &c.), strongly confirm this opinion. *Cornelius*, the bishop, was there apprehended, and required to defend his cause before the prætor; and as soon as the people heard of it, the greatest part of them hastened spontaneously to the judge, and not only professed Christ fearlessly, but declared themselves ready to lay down their lives with their bishop. Prosilierat adversarius terrore violento Christi castra turbare. Sed quo impetu venerat, eodem impetu pulsus et victus est. - - *Unum* (the bishop) primo aggressus, ut lupus avem secernere a grege, ut accipiter columbam ab agmine volantium separare tentaverat. - - Sed retusus adunati exercitus fide pariter et vigore, intellexit milites Christi vigilare - - vinci non posse, mori posse, et hoc ipso invictos esse, quia mori non timent. - - - Quale illud fuit sub oculis Dei spectaculum gloriosum, quale in conspectu Christi ecclesiæ suæ gaudium, ad pugnam, quam tentaverat hostis, inferre non singulos milites, sed tota simul castra prodiisse! Omnes enim constat venturos fuisse, si audire potuissent, *quando accurrerit properanter et venerit quisquis audivit.* And yet not one of this multitude was either sent to prison, or subjected to torture, or put to death. The bishop only, *Cornelius*, was sent into exile. And no greater punishment was inflicted on *Lucius*, his successor; and, such was the clemency of the times, that he was soon recalled from the exile into which he was sent. On this his recall, (which was procured, I suspect, by the money of Christians), *Cyprian* congratulates him in his 58th Epistle (p. 96). There is, indeed, an old tradition, supported by authorities of some respectability, that both *Cornelius* and *Lucius* were afterwards put to death. This tradition I could resist, if I were so disposed. This is certain, that Cyprian's calling each of them, (*beatum martyrem*) *a blessed martyr* (Epist. lxvii. p. 117), is no solid proof of this tradition; for it appears, that Cyprian used the word *martyr* in a broader sense, applying this honorable title to the *Confessors* also. But, suppose there was no doubt of the violent death of Cornelius and Lucius, these two examples of the execution of bishops, would rather [p. 530.] demonstrate the moderation than the cruelty of Gallus; since it is manifest, from the Epistles of Cyprian to each of them, that no one, besides them, suffered death at Rome. In Africa, Cyprian lived at Carthage without fear, during this persecution; although, shortly before, he had been demanded by the furious populace to be thrown to the lions. Neither was his presence in the city unknown by the magistrates; for *Demetrianus*, that violent enemy of the Christians, to whom Cyprian wrote a Tract, a man, doubtless, of no little authority, and, perhaps, one of the inferior judges, often called on Cyprian, and disputed with him about religion; as Cyprian himself states, in the exordium of his Tract. Neither is there anything in his Epistles, from which it can be inferred, that any Christian in Africa suffered death under *Gallus*. It would seem, therefore, that only exile and the milder punishments were inflicted on certain individuals. I acknowledge that the learned men, who think Gallus was no milder than Decius, have some show of arguments for their opinion. *First*, they observe that *Cyprian*, by divine inspiration, predicted, before the persecution of Gallus commenced, that there would be one of great magnitude and turbulence. See his 54th Epistle, (ad Cornel. p. 79.): Spiritu Sancto suggerente, et Domino per visiones multas et manifestas admonente, hostis imminere prænuntiatur et ostenditur. . . Protulimus, diem certaminis appropinquasse, hostem violentum cito contra nos exsurgere, pugnam, non talem qualis fuit (i. e. under *Decius*) sed *graviorem* multo et *acriorem* venire. And he writes the same thing in his 56th Epistle, (ad Thibaritanos, p. 90.): Nam cum Domini instruentis dignatione instigemur sæpius et admone amur. - - Scire debetis ac pro certo credere ac tenere, pressuræ diem super caput esse cœpisse, et occasum sæculi atque Antichristi tempus appropinquasse. . . Gravior nunc et ferocior pugna imminet. But, to confess the truth, the prophecies and visions which Cyprian often announces, are fallacious and of dubious credibility. He was certainly a pious and good man, but of a fervid temperament, and not sufficiently governed by reason; and he often rashly supposed the suggestions of his excited imagination to be dictated to him by the Holy Spirit. To demonstrate this by examples from his life and Epistles, cannot be necessary, since this very prophecy of an impending, direful persecution, manifests its human origin and its falsity. He predicts, not only greater evils than under *Decius*, but likewise (*occasum sæculi et Antichristi tempus*) *the coming of Antichrist and the end of the world:* and even those who may account him the greatest of prophets in other things, must admit, that he was here egregiously mistaken. And when a part of the prediction has been confuted by the event, it cannot be doubtful how the whole of it is to be regarded. Moreover, Cyprian himself frankly owns, that his predictions and visions were ridiculed by many, (Epist. lxix. p. 124.): Qamquam sciam somnia ridicula et vaticinationes ineptas quibusdam videri, sed utique illis, qui malunt contra sacerdotes credere, quam sacerdoti. With these people he is very angry, but I consider them not so wild in [p. 531.] their opinions as he judged them to be. But a stronger support to those who think *Gallus* was as cruel to the Christians as *Decius*, is derived from Cyprian's Tract, *ad Dematrianum.* That this tract was written in the reign of *Gallus*, can be shown by many unexceptionable proofs; and in it the writer bitterly complains of the very great wrongs suffered by the Christians. He says, (c. xii. p. 220.): Innoxios, justos, Deo caros domo privas, patrimonio spolias, *catenis premis, carcere includis, gladio, bestiis, ignibus* punis. Nec saltem contentus es dolorum nostrorum compendio et simplici ac veloci brevitate pœnarum. Admoves laniandis corporibus longa tormenta, multiplicas laceran-dis visceribus numerosa supplicia, nec feritas atque immanitas tua usitatis potest contenta esse tormentis; excogitat novas pœnas ingeniosa crudelitas. Now, if all these things occurred at the time Cyprian was writing that Tract, it must be acknowledged, that the times of *Gallus* were not more happy than those of *Decius.* But it must be remembered, that Cyprian plays the orator in this book, and rather declames than teaches or discusses. And hence we are not obliged to consider all that he states respecting the sufferings of Christians, as then taking place before him, or as occurring at the very time he wrote. He is speaking, generally, of the injustice and cruelty of the Roman governors and magistrates; and, therefore, the things he states may fairly be referred to the previous times of *Decius.* Orators are wont to speak of things of recent oc-currence, and things always to be feared, as if they saw them. And that this is no groundless conjecture, but a correct interpretation of the passage, appears from the fact, that in his Epistles, written about the same time, Cyprian makes no mention at all of the sufferings of his people. Besides, the undisturbed quiet which he himself enjoyed, while writing that Tract, is evidence that the Christians were not then struggling under any great evils.

(2) At that time a very destructive and inveterate pestilence afflicted a large part of the Roman empire; and it was accompanied by other great calamities. Therefore, as was usual for the idolaters, many persons in Africa declared the Christians to be the cause of these great calamities. Among them there was, in particular, one *Demetrianus.* And, as he often called on *Cyprian* to dispute with him, and continued to repeat this accusation, *Cyprian* undertook to refute it in an appropriate Tract. Near the beginning of this Tract, (ad Demetrianum, c. 2.), he says: Cum dicas plurimos conqueri, quod bella crebrius surgant, quod lues, quod fames sæviant, quodque imbres et pluvias serena longa suspendant, nobis imputari, tacere ultra non oportet, ne - - dum criminationes falsas con-temnimus refutare, videamur crimen agnoscere. - - Dixisti per nos fieri et quod nobis debeant imputari omnia ista, quibus nunc mundus quatitur et urgetur, quod Dii vestri a nobis non colantur. Hence, as before stated, when the people of Carthage were admonished by the edict of the proconsul to appease the

anger of the gods with sacrifices, they immediately demanded that Cyprian, the Christian bishop, should be cast to the lions; because they believed [p. 532.] that this man, and the community of Christians over which he presided, were the causes of their calamities, and that sacrifices and supplications would be fruitless, unless these enemies of the gods were put out of the way.—In this discussion, Cyprian is often eloquent and ingenious, but he is not always solid. With regard to this *Demetrian*, who so foolishly assailed the Christians, learned men suppose him to have been a man of very high rank, perhaps the proconsul of Africa; and they infer this from Cyprian's accusing him of inflicting many wrongs on the Christians, and manifesting great cruelty. We have already, in the preceding note, exhibited a part of this accusation. But, as before stated, Cyprian, throughout this Tract, discourses in the style of an orator; and, therefore, what he seems to charge upon Demetrian, personally, may fairly be referred to the Roman judges and magistrates generally. When I read over the exordium of the Tract, he does not appear to me so great a man as he does to these learned gentlemen. Cyprian does not address him in a modest and respectful manner, such as all persons should employ, in their intercourse with men of very high rank, and especially with the vicegerents of the supreme ruler; but he bursts forth in a strain of unbridled reproach and contumely: Oblatrantem te et adversus Deum ore sacrilego et verbis impiis obstrepentem frequenter, Demetriane, contemseram, verecundius ac melius existimans errantis imperitiam silentio spernere, quam loquendo dementis insaniam provocare. What an accumulation of reproachful terms are in these few words? Who can think that Cyprian would be so delirious as to compare a proconsul, or governor, a representative of the emperor, a man who held the power of life and death, with a *barking cur*, and to call him *sacriligious*, *impious*, *ignorant*, *stupid*, *insane?* Cyprian, although he was of a vehement temperament, could admirably curb his impetuosity, and restrain his passions, when occasion required or danger threatened; as appears from his Epistles. And who does not know that the ancient Christians, after the example of Christ and the Apostles, approached magistrates of all ranks with great caution and respect? Neither let any one imagine that these expressions may have escaped from Cyprian through inadvertence, and that in the progress of the discussion, their harshness is corrected by milder and more gentle language. He proceeds with the same virulence with which he commenced, and heaps on his adversary all the reproaches which an exasperated mind is prone to dictate. Scarcely had he uttered what was just cited, when he adds, that Demetrian was one of the *dogs* and *swine* to which Christ had forbidden the casting of what is holy. A little farther on, he terms him *rabid, blind, deaf, brutish;* Labor irritus, offerre lucem *cæco*, sermonem *surdo*, sapientiam *bruto*. Nor do these suffice: Demetrian is still further complimented with the terms, *raging* and *impious.* He says: Conticui, cum nec docere *indocilem* possem, nec *impium* religione comprimere, nec *furentem* lenitate cohibere. And many more such flowers of rhetoric might be gathered from this Tract. Undoubtedly, those eminent men, *Baronius*, *Pearson*, *Tillemont*, and others, must have read these passages; yet, it is strange that [p. 533.] they could have read them, and yet believe *Demetrian* to have been the governor or proconsul of Africa; or, at least, a magistrate of very high rank. Either Demetrian could not have been a man of such high rank, or Cyprian, in assailing him as a man of no character or worth, lacked common sense, and had not the full use of his reason. But these worthy men supposed, they were obliged to consider Demetrian so honorable a man, because they believed that those great sufferings of the Christians which Cyprian deplores, all proceeded from *Demetrian:* and if this had been the fact, then, doubtless, he must have been the supreme judge and proconsul. We have above cited the leading accusations of Cyprian, at the same time observing, that it is not necessary to refer them to Demetrian, personally, because the language of rhetoricians will admit of a laxer interpretation. As to my own views, I suspect that this adversary of Cyprian, was a man of the same occupation and rank with Cyprian, before his conversion, that is, a Rhetorician or Teacher of Eloquence at Carthage. A Philosopher I would not venture to call him, because he supposed the gods had afflicted the human race with pestilence, war, and famine, on account of the Christians; an opinion incongruous with the views of a philosopher. He lived in intimacy with Cyprian, visiting him quite frequently, and discussing religious subjects with him. But it is not to be supposed, that this intimacy commenced after Cyprian abandoned superstition and became a Christian. I therefore suppose they became intimate at the time when Cyprian taught eloquence at Carthage. The similarity of their pursuits, perhaps, brought them to associate together, and the bond which united them could not be entirely severed by the change of religion in Cyprian. This fact, moreover, of the intimacy existing between these two men, appears to me to afford a strong argument against the opinion, that Demetrian governed Africa as the proconsul. For who that is well acquainted with Roman and Christian affairs, will believe, that a proconsul, the governor of a province, who was bound by the emperor's mandate to persecute the Christians, would pay frequent friendly visits to a Christian bishop, and converse and dispute with him familiarly on religious subjects? Between Christians, and especially between Christian bishops and persons of such an exalted station, there must have been as great discord as, to use the words of *Horace,* (*lupis et agnis quanta sortito contigit,*) "naturally exists between wolves and lambs."

§ XVIII. **Disputes respecting the Baptisms of Heretics.** This external tranquillity gave rise to internal conflicts among Christians. How persons should be treated who left heretical congregations, and came over to the Catholics, had never been determined by any general rules. Hence some, both in the East, and in Africa, and elsewhere, placed reclaimed heretics in the class of Catechumens; and, though already baptized, received [p. 534.] them into the church by a second baptism. But the greater part of the Europeans considered the baptisms of erroneous churches as conveying forgiveness of sins for Christ's sake, and therefore they received the heretics who came over to them, solely by the imposition of hands and prayers.(1) This difference of practice, however, had not hitherto prevented their having fraternal intercourse. The Asiatic Christians, in councils held at times not ascertained, in Iconium, Synnada, and other places, changed their former usage into an established law, by enacting, that all heretics coming over to the true church, should be purified by a second baptism. On learning this, *Stephen*, bishop of Rome, esteeming the other custom more sacred, and as being derived from the Apostles, excluded those oriental Christians from the communion of the Romish church, but not from the church universal. Nevertheless, *Cyprian*, after consultation with certain African bishops, in a council held at Carthage, assentea to the oriental doctrine, to which many of the Africans had long been adherents; and this he signified, though modestly, to *Stephen*. But so offended was Stephen, that he not only gave Cyprian a severe reprimand, but when Cyprian replied with firmness, and by a unanimous vote in a second council at Carthage, pronounced the baptisms of all heretics destitute of any efficacy, *Stephen* declared him and the African bishops unworthy of the name of Brethren, and loaded them with severe reproaches. An end was put to this contest, partly by the prudence of the Africans, who were unwilling to render evil for evil, and partly by the death of Stephen, and the occurrence of a new persecution under Valerian; each party persevering in its opinions.(2)

(1) These facts we learn from several sources, but the most clearly from *Eusebius*, (Hist. Eccles. L. vii. c. 2. p. 251. and c. 7. p. 253, 254). Those who disagreed on this subject, all admitted that persons received the pardon of the sins of their past lives by baptism, on account of that faith in Christ Jesus which the candidates for baptism professed; but that the Holy Spirit is conferred by the bishop's imposition of hands and prayers. As I have already stated, such was the common opinion of that age. Those, therefore, who received heretics without re-baptizing them, believed that the persons baptized among heretics, had received remission of their sins, because they had professed Christ, and had been baptized in his words or in his name; but they denied that such persons were endowed with the Holy Spirit, because the heretical leaders and bishops [p. 535.] were destitute of the Holy Spirit, and therefore could not communicate the gifts of the Spirit to others. And, of course, they delivered over such persons to the bishops to be confirmed or sealed. But those who rejected the baptisms of heretics, and re-baptized the persons baptized among them, maintained, that

none but a pure and true faith was by God deemed a proper ground for the remission of sins; and, as the heretics taught their people to profess a corrupt and false faith at baptism, no remission of sins could be expected from such baptism. This argument is pursued at great length by *Cyprian*, (Epist. lxxiii. *ad Jubaianum*, p. 130). I will quote a few sentences to illustrate and confirm what I have said. The reasoning of those disagreeing with him, he thus states, (c. 4.): Quærendum non est quis baptizaverit, quando is, qui baptizatus est, accipere remissam peccatorum potuit secundum quod credidit: i. e. It is not necessary to enquire who administered the baptism, seeing the person received remission of his sins, on the ground of the faith in Christ which he professed. He then replies to this reasoning at considerable length; and, among other things, he says, (c. 5.): Quomodo potest videri, qui apud illos baptizatur, consecutus esse peccatorum remissam et divinæ indulgentiæ gratiam per suam fidem, qui ipsius fidei non habuerit veritatem? Si enim, sicut quibusdam videtur, secundum fidem suam quis accipere aliquid foris extra ecclesiam potuit, utique id accepit, quod credidit. Falsum autem credens verum accipere non potuit, sed potius adultera et profana, secundum quod credebat, accepit. - - (c. 6.): Quod si secundum pravam fidem baptizari aliquis foris et remissam peccatorum consequi potuit, secundum eandem fidem consequi et Spiritum sanctum potuit, et non est necesse, ei venienti manum imponi, ut Spiritum sanctum consequatur et signetur. Aut utrumque enim fide sua foris consequi potuit, aut neutrum eorum, qui foris fuerat, accepit. The theology of the early divines, who lived before the times of Constantine, if viewed generally, did not differ from ours; but viewed particularly, and with impartiality, it differed wonderfully. Nor will this appear strange to a person acquainted with antiquity. For the few doctrines which make up the sum of the Christian religion, had not then been inculcated, so to speak, after being subjected to a manipulation, and legitimately defined and inclosed in determinate formulas of language; and, therefore, the individual doctors explained them as they judged proper. And the explanation which commended itself to a man of some influence and ingenuity, was approved by many others who were less learned, just as at the present day; and so it passed for the common doctrine of the whole church.

(2) The history of the controversy between the Roman bishop, *Stephen*, and certain African and Asiatic bishops, respecting the efficacy of the baptisms of heretics, the writers belonging to the Romish church labor with all their might to pervert and involve in obscurity. For since it affords the most lucid documents, from which it can be proved that the power of the Romish bishop, although he held a very conspicuous rank among the Christian prelates, was yet [p. 536.] very small in that age, and that his decisions were disregarded and repudiated with the utmost freedom; these writers jumble up and confuse every thing, partly by idle conjecture, and partly by violently wresting the meaning of the ancients, lest, as is abundantly manifest, the truth should too clearly shine out and arrest attention. One of them, perceiving clearly that by such artifices the truth might be disguised, but could not be extinguished, concluded to cut the inexplicable knot, like Alexander, which the patrons of the Roman

Pontiff could not untie; or, to apply the sponge, as Augustus to his Ajax, to all the most important documents of this contest that have reached us. I refer to *Raymundus Missorius*, a Franciscan friar, who, in a book appropriately on the subject, (printed at Venice, 1733, 4to.) attempted to prove that the Epistles of *Firmilian* and *Cyprian*, in which they censure the decision of Stephen, and some other works, were forgeries got up by the African Donatists. But this astonishing temerity has been met and rebuked as it deserved, by our Jo. Geo. *Walch*, in a Dissert. printed at Jena, in 1738, and by Jo. Henry *Sbaralea*, an adherent to the Roman Pontiff, in a very learned work printed at Bologna, 1741, 4to. With the single exception of Jo. *Launoi*, who boldly lays open this contest, although more spiritedly in some respects than was necessary, (in his 15th Epistle, addressed to Ja. Boileau;) the Romish writers, who otherwise hold moderate opinions of the dignity and authority of the Roman Pontiff, yet study to give some coloring to this history, and to extenuate the vehemence of the disputants, especially of Stephen, lest they should appear to judge the bishop of the first see in Christendom with too much harshness. Those who are separated from the Romish church, exhibit greater fidelity in their treatment of this controversy. And yet I would not deny, that they sometimes go too far, and are especially faulty in this, that they make *Cyprian* to have been the author of the contest. Into this opinion they were led by *Eusebius*, who tells us, (Hist. Eccles. L. vii. c. 3; p. 251.) that *Cyprian* first condemned the baptisms of heretics; and yet, he himself subsequently refutes that assertion. It is most fully attested, in my view, that the Asiatic bishops gave occasion for this contest by their decrees, and that *Stephen* was in conflict with them before *Cyprian* took up the subject.

So long as the Apostles of Jesus Christ lived, there were either no sects of heretics, or only such as were very small and obscure. Hence they established no rules respecting the effects of baptism by heretics, nor did they determine in what manner churches should receive those who came over to them from the heretics. But in the second century, when by degrees various sects of corrupters of the ancient religion arose, and often individuals abandoned them and came over to the orthodox, the question naturally arose, whether these individuals were to be considered as already members of the church, or as aliens? Whether they were to be initiated by baptism, or were to be considered as already initiated? And that there was no uniformity of sentiment on [p. 537.] this subject, might easily be shown, if it were necessary. Nor could there be uniformity in that age, when no one arrogated to himself the office of judge and legislator among Christians, and when assemblies of the whole church could not be convened, and the heretical sects were of different characters, some better, and some worse. The Romans, whom the other Europeans followed, seem to have always held, that reclaimed heretics, who had been already baptized in the name of Jesus Christ, did not need a second baptism. In Asia and Africa, some received heretics without baptizing them, while others held that they must be baptized; and each bishop followed his own judgment. In the third century, the heretical churches being greatly multiplied and amplified, this question was perpetually coming up, and calling forth deliberation and discussion. For the custom of holding councils having first originated in Greece, as has been already shown, and quickly extending itself over the Christian commonwealth, those things which had before been left to the discretion of individual bishops, were brought under public discussion, and were determined by the suffrages of the bishops. Some dissension on this subject having arisen in Africa, at the commencement of this century, *Agrippinus*, the bishop of Carthage, called a *council*, in which it was decided, as Cyprian informs us, (Epist. lxxi. p. 127, and Epist. lxxiii. p. 130.): *Baptizandos esse, qui ab hæreticis ad ecclesiam veniunt*: Persons coming over to the church from the heretics, are to be baptized. Many of the African bishops followed this decision, but not all, as appears from these Epistles of Cyprian, and as will be manifest from what will soon be stated. Besides, what need was there of new councils and deliberations, if all the bishops of Africa had been obedient to the decision of Agrippinus? With the modesty which characterized the early bishops, Agrippinus and his associates had uttered their *opinion*, but not enacted a *law*. And the African church, as will soon be shown, had always regarded this as an open question, concerning which either side might be advocated, without danger to religion or to fraternal harmony. But, in process of time, when the minds of the Asiatic bishops became divided on this subject, and especially when dubitation arose about the baptisms of the Montanists, many of them assembled at Iconium and Sennada, cities of Phrygia, and in other places, and after mature deliberation, unanimously decided, that heretics coming over to the church ought to be again baptized. The fullest witness to this fact is *Dionysius* of Alexandria, (apud *Eusebium*, Hist. Eccles. L. vii. c. 7; p. 254). Concerning the council at *Iconium*, in particular, *Firmilian*, the bishop of Cæsarea, in Cappadocia, gives testimony in his Epistle, printed with those of Cyprian, (Epist. lxxv. p. 145). All these proceedings either remained unknown at Rome, or, which is more probable, were considered of so little importance, as to be overlooked. But after many years, when *Stephen* was at the head of the Romish church, the scene changed, and what had been regarded as free and harmless at Rome, assumed the nature of a crime. What occasioned this change, none of the ancients [p. 538.] has informed us. But it is most probable, that in the time of Stephen, a contest respecting the baptisms of heretics arose at Rome also; and that there were some there who maintained, that heretics ought not to be received without a new baptism, as was the custom of the church of Rome. Perhaps these persons had come from the East, and contended that the rule in their country was preferable to that followed at Rome. But *Stephen*, believing the Romish custom to be derived from the apostles, not only decided that it should be retained, but also that the Asiatic churches, by following a different rule, were cherishing a great error. To reclaim his eastern brethren from this error, he wrote them a letter: and, as they would not obey him, but defended their own opinions, he excluded them from his communion, and from the brotherhood of the Romish church. Those are mistaken, who suppose that these Asiatic Christians, and subsequently the African, were by Stephen *excommunicated* from the church. In that age the Romish bishop did not claim to have so much power, as to think he could eject others from communion in the universal church; nor did any one hold the opinion, that the persons whom the Romish bishop excluded from the communion of *his* church, forfeited their privileges throughout the Christian world. These opinions first originated long afterwards. But at that period, each individual bishop could exclude from his communion, or pronounce unworthy of the privileges of fraternal embrace, all those whom he, either justly or erroneously, judged to be contaminated with gross sins, or guilty of any conduct inconsistent with the obligations of a Christian teacher. But his judgment, every one was at liberty to follow or to reject, as he saw fit. By this rule *Cyprian* acted; by this *Victor* of Rome; by this *Stephen;* and by this many others in that age. Moreover, it is very incorrect to call these private decisions *excommunications;* and to say, e. g. that Stephen *excommunicated* Cyprian: for the two expressions, to *excommunicate,* and to *deprive one* of *our communion*, are of very different import.—But to return to Stephen: Respecting his unkind conduct towards the Asiatics, these few things only are preserved in the Epistle of *Dionysius* Alexandrinus, by *Eusebius*, (Hist. Eccles. L. vii. c. 5; p. 252.): Ἐπεστάλκει μὲν οὖν πρότερον καὶ περὶ Ἑλένου καὶ περὶ Φιρμιλιανοῦ καὶ πάντων τῶν τε ἀπὸ τῆς κιλικίας καὶ καππαδοκίας καὶ γαλατίας καὶ πάντων τῶν ἑξῆς ὁμορούντων ἐθνῶν, ὡς οὐδὲ ἐκείνοις κοινωνήσων διὰ τὴν αὐτὴν ταύτην αἰτίαν, ἐπειδὴ τοὺς αἱρετικοὺς (φησιν) ἀναβαπτίζουσι. Antea quidem (Stephanus) litteras scripserat de Heleno et de Firmiliano, de omnibus denique episcopis per Ciliciam, Cappadociam, cunctasque finitimas provincias constitutis, sese ob eam caussam ab illorum communione discessum, quod hæreticos rebaptisarent. On this passage, *Valesius* (Adnot. ad Euseb. p. 141.) puts a milder construction, by supposing that Stephen did not actually break off communion with the Orientals, but only threatened to do it, and never carried his threats into execution; and this opinion is embraced by several learned writers among the Romanists, who would, as far as possible, excuse the outrageous conduct of Stephen. But, without insisting that the language of the passage will not admit so mild an interpretation, there is now extant a testimony above all exception, that Stephen actually [p. 539.] did break communion, not only with the Africans, but also previously with the Orientals and others. I refer to the Epistle respecting this controversy, written by *Firmilian* (one of those bishops whom Stephen condemned,) to Cyprian, and published among *Cyprian's* Epistles, (Epist. lxxv.). In the first place, this whole epistle is hostile in its tone, and shows, that at the time it was written, harmony between *Stephen* and *Firmilian*, and his associates, was wrent and dissipated; for Firmilian does not condescend to give Stephen the ordinary title of brother, but assails him as an enemy and an adversary, with contumelious language. Had Stephen merely *threatened* to break friendship with him, Firmilian should, and would have used very different language respecting him. *Secondly*, not far from the end of the Epistle, (c. 24.) Firmilian most manifestly represents, that Stephen had declared war, not only against the African churches, but also against many others, and among them against the Oriental; for he thus addresses him: Lites et dissensiones quantas parasti per *ecclesias totius mundi?* Peccatum vero quam magnum tibi exaggerasti, quando *te a tot gregibus scidisti? Excidisti* enim *te ipsum.* Noli te fallere. Siquidem ille est vere schismaticus, qui *se a communione ecclesiasticæ unitatis apostatam* fecerit.

Dum enim putas omnes a te abstineri posse, solum te ab omnibus abstinuisti. - - (c. 25) Quid enim humilius aut lenius, quam *cum tot episcopis per totum mundum* dissensisse? *Pacem* cum singulis vario discordiæ genere *rumpentem*, *modo cum Orientalibus*, (so then fraternal intercourse with the Orientals was actually suspended, and not merely threatened,) quod nec vos latere confidimus, modo *vobiscum*, qui in meridie estis.—Whether the Asiatics retaliated the injury they had received from Stephen, and in like manner excluded him from *their* fraternal love, is found nowhere stated. But this Epistle of Firmilian, so full of gall and excessive bitterness, renders it most probable they did so. For if the Asiatics had remained friendly and patient under the outpoured indignation of Stephen, this very influential and dignified man would have expressed his views and feelings in milder language.

As already stated, nearly all the learned, relying on the expressions of *Eusebius*, place the controversy with the Asiatics *after* the African controversy with Cyprian, and suppose that the Asiatics only became implicated in the African disputes. It is, therefore, necessary for me to show, that in this they err, and that the controversy commenced in Asia, and thence was carried into Africa. My *first* argument is derived from the Epistle of the celebrated Firmilian *to* Cyprian, which has been already cited. We have seen, that when Firmilian wrote that Epistle, friendly intercourse with the Orientals had already been interrupted by Stephen. Now, *Firmilian* there replies to an Epistle addressed to [p. 540.] him by *Cyprian*, immediately after Stephen had commenced his controversy with Cyprian. And therefore Stephen had *suspended intercourse*, (*abstinuerat*)—to use an ecclesiastical term—with the Asiatics and with Fermilian, *before* he assailed Cyprian. *Secondly.* When Firmilian writes, that he conceives Cyprian cannot be ignorant of the hostile conduct of Stephen towards the Orientals, *Pacem cum singulis rumpentem, modo cum Orientalibus, quod nec vos latere confidimus;* when he writes thus, I say, he manifestly indicates that Stephen's Asiatic contest preceded his African contest with Cyprian. *Lastly*, *Dionysius* Alexandrinus, (apud *Euseb.* Hist. Eccles. L. vii. c. 5, p. 252,)—than whom a better and more reliable authority cannot be given, most clearly states that *before* (*πρότερον*, *prius*,) Stephen commenced his attack on *Cyprian* and the Africans, he had pronounced *Firmilian* and the Asiatic bishops unworthy of his communion. The passage has been already cited.

Cyprian involuntarily became implicated in this controversy with the Asiatics. Having assembled a council at Carthage, in the year 256, the question was proposed by the bishops of Numidia, *Whether those apparently baptised among heretics and schismatics, ought, on coming over to the catholic church, to be baptized?* Cyprian and the thirty-two bishops present in council, replied, *That no one could be baptized outside of the church, because there is but one baptism instituted in the holy church:* and they added, *that they did not bring forward a new opinion, but one established long ago by their predecessors.* See the Epistle among those of Cyprian, (Epist. lxx. p. 124.) But, as the number of bishops in this council was not great, Cyprian called another shortly after, in which were seventy-one bishops, and submitted this and other questions to a second discussion; and all the bishops, as Cyprian informs us, (Epist. lxxiii. p. 129.) decided:

Unum baptisma esse, quod sit in ecclesia catholica constitutum, ac per hoc non rebaptizari, sed baptizrari, quicunque ab adultera et prophana aqua veniunt abluendi et sanctificandi salutaris aquæ veritate. This decision of the second council was defended by Cyprian, in his long Epistle to Jubaianus, (Epist. lxxiii. p. 129,) just as he had before vindicated the decision of the former council, in his Epistle to Quintus, bishop of Mauritania, (Epist. lxxi. p. 126.) But as he was aware that a different custom prevailed at Rome, and perhaps had heard something about the rupture between Stephen, the Roman bishop, and the bishops of Asia on this subject, both he and the council thought it advisable to communicate this decision of the council to *Stephen*, and to take measures to prevent his getting into a passion and breaking off communion with them. The Epistle addressed to Stephen, in the name of the council, is still extant among the Epistles of Cyprian, (Epist. lxxii. p. 129.) Every person reading the Epistle will at once see that it was not written for the purpose of acquainting the Romish bishop with the doings of the council, but solely to forestall his anger and indignation. For they pass silently over nearly all the many important decisions of the council, and mention only two of them, the one concerning the baptisms of heretics, and the other concerning priests and deacons coming over [p. 541.] to the church from the heretics. Yet, despairing of Stephen's approving their sentiments, they wisely intimate, at the end of the Epistle, that they have no wish to enter into controversy with any one differing from them in opinion. They say, (c. 4,) Cæterum, scimus quosdam quod semel imbiberint nolle deponere, nec propositum suum facile mutare, sed salvo inter collegas pacis et concordiæ vinculo quædam propria quæ apud se semel sint usurpata retinere. Qua in re nec nos vim cuiquam facimus aut legem damus, *quando habeat in ecclesiæ administratione voluntatis suæ arbitrium liberum unusquisque præpositus rationem actus sui Domino redditurus.* Now, he who sees the Africans writing in this manner to the Roman bishop, and still contends that the Roman bishops in that age had any power or jurisdiction whatever over the other bishops, surely must be beyond measure obstinate and perverse, or he must be excessively blinded by his early received opinions. If it was true in the *third* century, as the African council assert, *that every individual bishop had free arbitriment in the administration of the affairs of his church, and would have to give account of his conduct to the Lord only*, then, beyond all question, that which many at this day account true, was at that time absolutely false: namely, that God had subjected all the bishops to a certain one of them, and that a certain one was to enact laws in Christ's name for the church, and that every thing in the church must be conducted and administered according to *his* pleasure.—But to proceed, it is clear then, that the African church, although it decided that heretics must be again baptized on entering the purer church, yet did not regard the contrary opinion as tearing up the foundations of religion. On the excited mind of *Stephen*, however, this moderation of sentiment proved rather irritating than sedative; because, doubtless, it provoked him to see the Africans take ground with those whom he had pronounced enemies of his church. He therefore, in the name of the Roman church, wrote to *Cyprian*, or rather to the African church, in whose name Cyprian had addressed him, no less imperiously than bitterly and revilingly, and doubtless in the same strain as previously to the Asiatic bishops, declaring that he would have no communion with persons who said the baptism of heretics ought to be repeated. The Epistle is lost through the fault, if I do not misjudge, of those in former times, who thought it beneficial to the church to cover up the faults and errors of the Roman Pontiffs. But the tenor of it may still be known, partly from the Epistle of *Cyprian*, to Pompeius, (Epist. lxxiv.) and partly from the Letter of *Firmilian*, bishop of Cæsaræa, to Cyprian, which is the next in order among the Epistles of Cyprian, (Ep. lxxv.) According to *Cyprian's* account of it, it contained *many arrogant things, irrevelant to the subject, and adverse to his own cause, unadvisedly and unskilfully written:* and that this representation is not entirely false, an impartial person can without difficulty believe; and yet, to be perfectly frank, the same might, to some extent, be said of *Cyprian's* own Epistle, for it employs vain and futile arguments, and abounds much in sarcasms. But there is this commendable in [p. 542.] Cyprian, that he does not retaliate upon Stephen, by excluding him from fellowship, but calls him *Our Brother*, which title is a manifest indication of a disposition for peace and a dread of discord. Learned men have greatly lauded this temperate conduct of Cyprian; and not wholly without reason. But, in my judgment, it will detract somewhat from this commendation to reflect that Cyprian *could not* deny to Stephen the privileges of a brother, without contradicting his own principles. Stephen might consistently do so, because he regarded the opinion of the Africans as militating with true religion; but Cyprian and the Africans could not do it, because they judged the opinion of Stephen to be one of the minor errors which were to be tolerated. The man must doubtless be heartless, and destitute of all kind feelings, who can deprive another of the rights of a brother, while he acknowledges him to have erred but slightly, and to have not wounded the vitals of religion.—But we will proceed. It appears from the Epistle of *Firmilian*, already mentioned, that *Stephen*, in his Epistle to the Asiatics, derived the custom which prevailed in the Roman church from Peter and Paul, the founders of that church, and appealed to continuous *tradition*. He says, (c. 6. p. 144.) Adhuc etiam infamans Petrum et Paulum beatos Apostolos, quasi hoc ipsi tradiderint. But the Asiatics defended their opinion in the same way; indeed they carried their pretensions still higher, and declared Christ himself to be the author of *their* tradition. Says *Firmilian*, (p. 149.) Nos veritati et consuetudinem jungimus, et consuetudini Romanorum consuetudinem, sed veritatis, opponimus, ab initio hoc tenentes, quod a *Christo et ab Apostolis* traditum est. In this controversy, therefore, *tradition* was opposed to *tradition*, the Asiatic tradition from Christ and the Apostles to the Roman tradition from Peter and Paul. But it should be remembered, that even in that early age, the institutions, which no one was able to trace to their origin, were called the *traditions of Christ and the Apostles*. And Firmilian himself attests, that the Asiatics accounted their custom an Apostolical one, solely because they were ignorant of the time of its introduction. He says: Nec meminimus hoc apud nos aliqando cœpisse, cum semper istic observatum sit, ut non nisi unam Dei ecclesiam nossemus, et sanctum baptisma non nisi sanctæ ecclesiæ computaremus. From this Epistle of Firmilian it appears, moreover, that *Stephen* had greatly lauded the dignity of his church, and its eminence among the churches. Atque ego in hac parte juste indignor ad hanc tam apertam et manifestam Stephani stultitiam, quod qui sic de episcopatus sui loco gloriatur et se successorem Petri tenere contendit, super quem fundamenta ecclesiæ collocata sunt, multas alias petras inducat, et ecclesiarum multarum alia ædificia constituat, dum esse illic baptisma sua auctoritate defendit. This, doubtless, was the part of Stephen's letter, for which Cyprian branded him with the epithet *proud.* I wish we had the reply of the Africans to this [p. 513.] panegyric on the chair of Peter. But it has been lost, undoubtedly, because it was not honorary to the Romish church; as we may easily infer from the other Epistles of Cyprian, in which he expresses his opinion of the rights of the bishops. The other topics in this Epistle of *Stephen*, or rather, of the Romish church, I omit, as they throw no light upon history. On receiving this Epistle the African bishops did not abandon their cause, but, in another Epistle addressed to the Romish church or to Stephen, refuted all his arguments for the efficacy of baptisms by heretics. The learned men who have investigated this history of this controversy, take no notice of this second Epistle of the Africans. But no one who attentively reads the Epistle of Firmilian to Cyprian, can doubt that it was actually written. He says, (c. 4, p. 143.) Nos vero quæ a vobis scripta sunt quasi nostra propria suscepimus, nec in transcursu legimus, sed sæpe repetita memoriæ mandavimus. Neque obest utilitati salutari aut eadem retexere ad confirmandam veritatem aut et quædam addere ad cumulandam probationem. After a few remarks, he proceeds, (c. 7): Sed et ad illam partem bene a vobis responsum est, ubi Stephanus in epistola sua dixit hæreticos in baptismo convenire. And a little after: Quo in loco etsi vos jam probastis, satis ridiculum esse, ut quis sequatur errantes, illud tamen ex abundanti addimus. The Africans, therefore, had replied to Stephen, and *Firmilian* had the reply in his hands: and in his own Epistle he, in part, (*retexebat*,) *reconstructed*, as he expresses it, and in part confirmed the reasoning of it, by new arguments. Perhaps some may conjecture, that the Epistle which Firmilian had before him was that of Cyprian to Pompeius, or his 74th Epistle, in which he confutes the Epistle of Stephen. But this conjecture must be abandoned, if we consider that Firmilian cites from the Epistle which he mentions and examines, several things which do not occur in the Epistle to Pompeius. Besides, it is manifest from the words of Firmilian above quoted, that he is not speaking of a private Epistle of one individual to another, but of a common Epistle of the assembled African bishops. He says: Quæ a *vobis* scripta sunt, legi. *Vos* jam probastis: *Vos* respondistis. *Stephen* was so irritated by this Epistle, that he not only replied more harshly and angrily than before, but he assailed *Cyprian*, whom he regarded as the author of the African contumacy, with direct maledictions, and excluded the Africans from his communion. This also may appear perhaps to be news, because we do not find it any where expressly stated. But here, again, the Epistle of Firmilian will show that this is no vain or rash conjecture. At the time Firmilian wrote, all communion between the Africans and the Romans had certainly been suspended by Stephen. For Firmilian says: (c. 6, p. 144): Quod nunc Stephanus ausus est facere, *rumpens adversus vos pacem*, quam semper antecessores ejus vobiscum amore et honore mutuo custodierunt. And towards the end: (c. 24, p. 150): Peccatum vero quam magnum tibi exaggerasti, quando te a tot gregibus scidisti! I omit more passages of the same [p. 544.] tenor. But in the first Epistle of Stephen, which Cyprian refutes in his Epistle to Pompeius, Stephen had not proceeded beyond threats; notwithstanding *Augustine* has stated, (de Baptismo contra Donatistas, L. V. c. 25, Opp. tom. ix. p. 106,) that Stephen, abstinendos generatim putaverat, qui de suscipiendis hæreticis priscam consuetudinem convellere conarentur. There must, therefore, have followed a *second* Epistle, in which he carried out the determination he had formed, and declared non communion with the Africans. Moreover, Firmilian testifies, (c. 26,) that in his last Epistle Stephen assailed Cyprian with invectives: Et tamen non pudet Stephanum, talibus (hæreticis) adversus ecclesiam patrocinium præstare, et propter hæreticos asserendos *fraternitatem scindere*, insuper et *Cyprianum pseudochristum et pseudoapostolum et dolosum operarium dicere*. Firmilian would, doubtless, never have said this, had not Stephen written it. But, in his first Epistle, he had not yet uttered these reproaches, for Cyprian would not have passed them in silence in his Epistle to Pompeius, if they had then been uttered. It was, therefore, in another Epistle, written after the first, that he inveighed so reproachfully against Cyprian. The wiser Africans thought they ought to spare no pains to allay this storm, and therefore sent a legation to Rome, to restore peace if possible. But Stephen forbid the Roman Christians to receive into their houses the bishops of the legation, whom he had deprived of his communion, and would not admit them even to a conference. Says Firmilian, (c. 25, p. 150,) A vobis, qui in meridie estis, legatos episcopos patienter satis et leniter suscepit, ut eos nec ad sermonem saltem colloquii communis admitteret, adhuc insuper dilectionis et caritatis memor præciperet fraternitati universæ, ne quis eos in domum suam reciperet, ut venientibus nor solum pax et communio, sed et tectum et hospitium negaretur! So the legation returned home, leaving the business where it was. I see not what could demonstrate more clearly than this fact does, that Stephen excluded from the communion of the Roman church not only Cyprian, but the whole African church, of which these bishops were the legates.—After this many things were, doubtless, said and done, of which no record has reached us. Stephen, we may believe without testimony, being a man of weak mind, endeavored to excite the christian world against the Africans; and many councils were held on the subject here and there, as I recollect Augustine some where intimates. And therefore Cyprian, that he and his Africans might not stand alone, thought proper to look about him for friends. And, knowing that the Asiatics had been attacked in the same manner, he dispatched Rogatian, his deacon, with a letter to the oft-mentioned *Firmilian* a man of very great influence, and sent him documents which would acquaint him with the whole case. Firmilian responded according to his wishes; and, as his Epistle (among those of *Cyprian*, Ep. lxxv.) [p. 545.] shows, approved of all that had been done and written by the Africans; and, in the severest terms and even with contumely, censured *Stephen*, who had treated the Asiatics with the same abuse as the Africans. At the same time *Cyprian*, to prevent any of the African bishops from taking sides with

Stephen, convoked a council in the month of September, A.D. 256, from the three provinces of Africa, Numidia, and Mauritania. The Acts of this council have been transmitted to us by *Augustine*, (de Baptismo contra Donatistas, L. vi. and vii. Opp. tom. ix.) They are extant also among the works of Cyprian, p. 329. There were present 87 bishops, and not only presbyters and deacons, but also (*plebis maxima pars*) a large portion of the people. In his address to the attending bishops, Cyprian reiterated what he had before repeatedly declared, that the question to be discussed was one of those on which men might differ in opinion, without a violation of fraternal harmony; and he chastised the arrogance of Stephen, but without naming him. His words are worthy to be here repeated, as they express the sentiments of that age in regard to the independence of bishops, and render perfectly certain that no one in that age, not even Stephen himself, had ever dreamed of any judge and legislator for the universal church. That Stephen himself had not thought of any such judge I confidently assert; for, certainly, if he had supposed such high dignity to be conferred on himself by Christ, he would have pursued a very different course than he did with the Africans. Said Cyprian: Superest, ut de hac ipsa re singuli quid sentiamus, proferamus, *neminem judicantes*, aut a jure communicationis aliquem, si diversum senserit, amoventes. Neque enim quisquam nostrum episcopum se esse episcoporum constituit, aut tyrannico terrore ad obsequendi necessitatem collegas suos adigit, quando habeat omnis episcopus pro licentia libertatis et potestatis suæ arbitrium proprium, tamque judicari ab alio non possit, quam nec ipse potest alterum judicare. Sed expectemus universi judicium Domini nostri Jesu Christi, qui *unus et solus* habet potestatem et præponendi nos in ecclesiæ suæ gubernatione, et de actu nostro judicandi. At that time, therefore, Christ had no vicar here on earth, but was himself (*solus et unus*) the sole and only judge of his church. All the bishops concurred in the opinion of Cyprian, and decided that heretics should be re-baptized. The unanimity and modesty of this great council, and the friendship between the Asiatics and the Africans, I suppose, repressed the violence of Stephen and other bishops; for we do not learn that this contest continued afterwards. *Dionysius* Alexandrinus also, as we learn from *Eusebius* (Hist. Eccles. L. vii. c. 2, &c.) endeavored by his letters to bring the mind of Stephen to acquiescence and peace; and perhaps others, who foresaw danger from a continuance of the contest, followed his example. For some time, therefore, the Africans adhered to their opinion, the other christians not taking offence at their constancy; but gradually they went over to the opposite opinion, and finally, in a council which *Augustine* styles *plenarium* (de Baptismo, L. I. c. 7,) held at Nice or Arles, (for [p. 546.] the learned are not agreed as to this council,) they universally embraced the Romish custom.

It remains for us to ascertain the precise sentiments of the two parties. *Cyprian* and *Firmilian* state with sufficient perspicuity, what they and their brethren maintained. Says Cyprian, (Epist. lxxiv. ad Pompeium, c. 12, p. 142): Omnes, qui ex quacunque hæresi ad ecclesiam convertuntur, ecclesiæ unico et legitimo baptismo baptizantur, exceptis his, qui baptizati in ecclesia prius fuerant, et sic ad hæreticos transierant. Illos enim oportet, cum redeunt, acta pœnitentia per manus impositionem solam recipi. By heretics, Cyprian under stood, not merely corrupters of the true religion, but likewise all who withdrew themselves from the principal church, and formed separate congregations. And hence, he required the *Novatians* to be re-baptized on their coming over to the church, (as we learn from his 76th Epist. ad Magnum, p. 151, &c.); and yet he acknowledged that the Novatians were free from all gross errors. This pious and good man, but too zealous about his official dignity and office, viewed all who were separated from the bishop as also separated from Christ, and his benefits, and believed that salvation was attainable no where but in the visible church under the bishops of the Apostolic succession: and this obliged him to decide, that there could be no saving baptism except it was administered by such bishops, or by their direction and authority. He would surely have entertained different ideas about the effects of baptism, if he had not been strangely captivated with a love of the dogma of the unity of the visible church, and had not exalted extravagantly the rights and authority of bishops. The opinions of his adversary *Stephen*, are not equally manifest. Those solicitous for the reputation of Stephen, and such, with few exceptions, are nearly all the adherents to the Romish church, to whom it appears hard and difficult to believe that any of the ancient Pontiffs differed from the modern, or that the church, in the third century, was divided between two errors—those in favor of *Stephen*, I say, tells us that he taught just as the Romish church does at the present day, not that the baptisms of *all* heretics, but only of those who in baptizing invoked the names of the Father, Son, and Holy Spirit, were valid baptisms. See *Tillemont*, (Memoires pour servir a l'Hist. de l'Eglise, tom. iv. P. I. p. 419, &c.) and *Natalis Alexander*, (Selecta Hist. Eccles. Capita. tom. iii. p. 691, &c.) who treats this subject in his usual scholastic rather than historical manner. But others for the most part, to whom the reputation of the ancient Roman Pontiffs does not appear of very great importance, think that Stephen believed all persons baptized in the name of Christ, might be received into the fellowship of the better church, without another baptism. Respecting these, see in particular Peter *Allix*, (Diss. de vita et scriptis Tertulliani, c. 4, p. 30, &c.) not to mention *Blondell*, *Launoi*, and others. The former party defend their position by the authority especi- [p. 547.] ally of *Eusebius*, *Augustine*, *Vincent* of Lirins, and *Facundus*: who say that Stephen accounted no baptism valid, unless it was administered in the words prescribed by Christ. But to these comparatively recent authorities the latter party oppose other more ancient and higher authorities; and first *Stephen* himself, whose words, in his Epistle to the Africans, preserved by *Cyprian*, (Epist. lxxiv. c. 1, p. 138.) are these: "Si quis ergo *a quacunque hæresi* venerit ad vos, nihil innovetur nisi quod traditum est, ut manus illi imponatur in pœnitentiam, cum ipsi hæretici proprie alterutrum ad se venientes non baptizent, sed communicent tantum." Moreover, *Cyprian*, who, almost invariably, represents Stephen as holding *all* baptisms administered in the name of Christ to be legitimate, says, (Epist. lxxiv. c. 5, p. 139.) Si effectum baptismi *majestati nominis* tribuunt, ut *qui in nomine Jesu Christi* ubicunque et *quomodocunque* baptizentur, innovati et sanctificati judicentur; cur non, &c. And farther, the ancient, but unknown author of the *Liber de Rebaptismate*, who takes sides with Stephen, and whose book is commonly printed with the *Opera Cypriani*, (p. 353.) with the following title prefixed: Non debere denuo baptizari qui semel in nomine Domini nostri Jesu Christi sunt tincti; seems to decide the question respecting Stephen's views. I omit other testimonies of less importance. These testimonies, I confess, seem to have great weight; yet I have some hesitation to admit their conclusiveness, because *Firmilian*, an opposer of *Stephen*, in his Epistle to Cyprian, (c. 9, p. 145.) states Stephen's opinion thus: Illud quoque absurdum, quod non putant quærendum esse quis sit ille qui baptizaverit, eo quod qui baptizatus sit, gratiam consequi potuerit *invocata trinitate nominum Patris et Filii et Spiritus Sancti*. Firmilian writes what he had found stated in the Epistle of Cyprian, or of the Africans to Stephen, and he also himself was well acquainted with the opinions of Stephen; and, therefore, his testimony is worthy of consideration. Yet, perhaps, he aimed only to explain the point, and attributed to Stephen the conceptions of his own mind. To confess the truth, I can believe that Stephen expressed his views only in general terms, and did not accurately define them; and, therefore, they were explained differently. Men very frequently, at the present day, in theological controversies, affirm and deny, attack and defend, only in a general way, and without defining the conflicting opinions. And why may we not suppose this to have occurred in the present controversy.

§ XIX. **The Persecution under Valerian.** After showing himself kind and indulgent towards the Christians until the fifth year of his reign, suddenly, by the persuasion of Macrianus, his bosom companion, a man of very high rank and reputation, but exceedingly superstitious, *Valerian*, in the year 257, changed his policy towards them, and ordered the governors of pro- [p. 548.] vinces to inhibit the meetings of Christians, and to send their bishops and teachers into exile.(1) But these milder mandates rather animated than disheartened the Christians, who had been accustomed previously to greater evils. Therefore, in the following year he issued a much severer edict, in the execution of which the magistrates put to death no small number of Christians throughout the provinces of the Roman empire, and frequently inflicted on them punishments worse than death.(2) Eminent among those that fell in this persecution were *Cyprian*, the celebrated bishop of Carthage, who was beheaded; and *Sixtus*, the Romish prelate, who is said to have been crucified; and *Laurence*, the Roman deacon, famous among the martyrs, who is said to have been roasted to death on a slow fire: some, however, refer this last martyrdom to the Decian period. But *Valerian* being taken captive in a war with *Sapor*, king of Persia, his son *Gallienus*, by a rescript addressed to the provincial governors in the year 260, restored full peace to the Christians, after four years of suffering.([3]) Yet they were not placed in entire security; for the ancient laws of the Emperors against them were not abrogated, and, therefore, such of the governors as were so disposed, could put those Christians to death who were regularly accused and acknowledged their faith, if they refused to sacrifice to the gods.([4])

(1) Respecting the clemency of *Valerian* to the Christians in the first years of his reign, and the author of the subsequent change in his feelings towards them, the most important witness we have is *Dionysius* Alexandrinus, in his Epistle to Hermammon, the latter part of which is preserved by *Eusebius*, (Hist. Eccles. L. vii. c. 10. p. 255.) But as *Eusebius* cites two passages from this Epistle, in one of which *Dionysius* does not mention the name of the person who induced Valerian to persecute the Christians, and in the other tells us that *Macrianus* advised the Emperor to this course, a dispute has arisen among the learned, whether this persecution is to be traced to one man as its author, or to two. In the first passage *Dyonisius* says: Ἀποσκευάσασθαι δὲ παρέπεισεν αὐτὸν ὁ διδάσκαλος καὶ τῶν ἀπ' Αἰγύπτου μάγων ἀρχισυνάγωγος, τοὺς μὲν καθάρους καὶ ὁσίους ἄνδρας κτιννύσθαι καὶ διώκεσθαι κελεύων. Verum magister et Archisynagogus magorum Aegypti ei (Valeraino) tandem persuasit, ut ab hoc instituto desciseeret, jubens, ut castos quidem et sanctos viros persequeretur atque occideret. But a little after he says: Ὁ μὲν γαρ Οὐαλεριανὸς εἰς ταῦτα ὑπὸ τούτου (Μακριάνου) προαχθεὶς εἰς ὕβρεις καὶ ὀνειδισμοὺς ἐκδοθεὶς. Nam Vale-
[p. 549.] rianus quidem, qui ad hujusmodi facinora a Macriano (for he is the person spoken of,) impulsus fuerat, contumeliis et opprobriis fuit expositus et deditus. It is, therefore, made a question, whether this *Macrianus* is the same person who was before called Chief of the Synagogue of the Egyptian Magicians, or a different person. Not a few, deeming it scarcely credible, that so distinguished a man as *Macrianus* was, an intimate with the emperor, and holding the highest position, "than whom," (as *Tremellius Pollio* says in his Gallienus, Scriptor. Hist. August. tom. ii. 189.) "none of the generals were deemed more wise, none more competent for business, none more opulent," should be prefect of the Egyptian Magicians,—have supposed this Magician of Dionysius to be a different person from Macrianus; and, of course, that there were two persons who prompted *Valerian* to show cruelty to the Christians. Among these authors, Gisbert *Cuper*, (in his Notes on *Lactantius* de mortibus persequutorum, p. 152.) goes so far as to suppose this Magician was a *Jew*, infering it from the Jewish words διδάσκαλος and Ἀρχισυνάγωγος applied to him; and Ja. *Basnage* in vain attempted to confute that idea, while he himself did not believe *Macrianus* and the Magician to be the same person. (see Letters de Critique, Histoire, Litterature par M. Cuper, p. 386, 390, Amst. 1742, 4to.) But, as Dionysius most explicitly states, that *Macrianus* recommended the persecution to the emperor, and that *Valerian* received the sad reward of his docility, while he adds nothing which can lead to the supposition that *Macrianus* had an associate in the transaction, the supposition has

not the least probability; on the contrary, we must believe that Dionysius designated one and the same person in this two-fold manner. Nor will this interpretation be weakened by the two epithets above mentioned. The first of them, διδάσκαλος, *magister*, should not be referred to the Magicians, as is manifest from the Greek. *Valesius* has not expressed properly the meaning of Dionysius; and this has occasioned some, who did not inspect the Greek, to fall into a mistake. He should have rendered it (*Magister ejus*) *his* (*Valerian's*) *master*, and *chief of the synagogue, &c.* For this word undoubtedly has reference to *Valerian*, who yielded to the opinions of *Macrianus* in every thing, and always defered to him as to a master. *Valerian* himself, in a speech to the senate, said: Ego bellum Persicum gerens, *Macriano totam rempublicam tradidi.* See *Trebellius Pollio's* 30 Tyrants, (in the Scriptor. Historiæ Augustæ, tom. ii. p. 288.) And as to the title *Chief of the Synagogue of the Egyptian Magicians*, it is a sneer of Dionysius at Macrianus, and not the title of his office or position in society. As Macrianus was exceedingly devoted to magic, and delighted greatly in magical sacrifices, according to Dionysius, he represents him as qualified, by his skill in the art, to fill the office of Chief or President of the Egyptian Magicians. As to the motive which led Macrianus to inflame the Emperor's mind against the Christians, Dionysius states it to have been this, that he knew there were persons among them who could frustrate the ma- [p. 550.] gical rites, and destroy their effects by a word or a nod. Being himself greatly devoted to magic, he "prompted the emperor to celebrate impure rites of initiation, abominable incantations, and execrable sacrifices;" for example, "to immolate infants, and explore the entrails of new-born children." See *Dionysius*, as quoted by *Eusebius*, (L. vii, c. 10.) But he well knew, not only that the Christians universally held these nefarious mysteries in abhorrence, but also that some of them possessed the power of disconcerting and controlling demons, so that they could not manifest their presence by oracular responses and the other signs. Says Dionysius: Καὶ γὰρ εἰσὶν καὶ ἦσαν ἱκανοὶ παρόντες καὶ ὁρώμενοι, καὶ μόνον ἐμπνέοντες καὶ φθεγγόμενοι, διασκεδάσαι τὰς τῶν ἀλιτηρίων δαιμόνων ἐπιβουλάς. Erant enim et sunt etiamnum (inter nos) ejusmodi, qui vel præsentia et aspectu suo, et insufflantes duntaxat ac vocem edentes, dæmonum præstigias disturbare possunt. And, therefore, he prevailed on the emperor to endeavor to extirpate a sort of men injurious and terrible to the art he loved and to the demons he consulted. But, we may suppose, the good man here gives us his conjectures rather than what he knew to be facts. Respecting the power of the ancient Christians to confound and put to silence demons and their servants and idols, of which many others also speak, I shall not go into any discussion: but this is easily perceived, we ought not to look there for the cause of Macrianus' hostility to the Christians. If he had believed that Christians possessed such power, that they could control the demons he loved and worshipped, I think he would not have dared to assail them, but would rather have feared and stood in awe of them. For, why cannot they who have the demons under their power, and who control them at their pleasure, also bring, if they choose, various evils upon the worshippers of demons! And who but a madman, destitute of reason, would voluntarily and eagerly worship beings whom he knew to be paralyzed and stript of all power by others more powerful! Whoever seeks for himself a lord, will, if he be in his senses, prefer the more powerful to one of less power. But suppose Macrianus was so insane as to think the demons and their worship frustrated by the Christians, he might have forestalled the evil much more easily than by a resort to edicts, and laws and punishments: for, by a little vigilance he could have excluded all Christians from being present at his infernal rites and mysteries. Let us concede, what is not to be denied, that the ancient Christians often supposed their enemies to reason just as they themselves would, and so attributed to them designs very foreign from their real ones. I think his superstition alone was sufficient to prompt Macrianus to inflame the emperor against the Christians. And I am the more inclined to think so, because I learn from *Trebellius Pollio*, (Thirty Tyrants, c. 14, in the Histor. Augustæ, tom. ii. p. 297.) that this was a hereditary disease in the family of the Macriani. For all the males and females of this family wore an image of Alexander the Great on their rings, [p. 551.] their garments, and their ornaments, influenced by a peurile conceit of the vulgar, (*juvari in omni actu suo, qui Alexandrum expressum in auro gestitarent vel argento,*) that whoever carried a likeness of Alexander impressed on gold or silver, would be aided in all their acts. Who can wonder that a man who could promise himself success from a likeness of Alexander the Macedonian, should have been extravagantly attached to the Roman Gods and their worship, and have wished evil to the enemies of his country's religion?

The first assault of Valerian upon the Christians was such as could be endured; as appears from the *Acts* of *Cyprian*, and of *Dionysius Alexandrinus*, (apud *Euseb.* Hist. Eccles. L. vii. c. 11). For he merely decreed the banishment of all bishops and presbyters who would not worship the Roman gods, and prohibited the religious assemblies of Christians. *Cyprian* was exiled to Carubia, by the proconsul Paternus, after refusing to sacrifice to the gods; and *Dionysius* was sent by the præfect Aemilius to a place called Cephro, in the parts of Libya. But let the proconsul Paternus state to us the pleasure and the mandate of the emperor, according to the *Acta Cypriani*, (in Theod. *Ruinart*, Acta Martyr. sincera et selecta, p. 216). When *Cyprian* was arraigned before him, Paternus thus addressed him: Sacratissimi Imperatores Valerianus et Gallienus litteras ad me dare dignati sunt, quibus præceperunt eos, qui Romanam religionem non colunt, debere Romanas cæremonias recognoscere. *Cyprian* had no sooner declared that he could not obey this mandate, than the proconsul pronounced sentence of banishment upon him, and then proceeded: Non solum de episcopis, verum etiam de presbyteris mihi scribere dignati sunt. From this it is very manifest that the emperor's mandate extended only to the bishops and presbyters; against the deacons and the people nothing was decreed. Neither was capital punishment ordered for bishops and presbyters, but merely exile. Lastly, the proconsul added: Præceperunt etiam, ne in aliquibus locis conciliabula fiant, nec cœmeteria ingrediantur. Si quis itaque hoc tam salubre præceptum non observaverit, capite plectetur. Capital punishment, then, was enacted against those who persisted either in holding religious assemblies, or in attending them. The emperors prohibited first in general, all religious assemblies, which they designate as *Conciliabula;* and then, in particular, the conventions which were held in *Cemeteries.* By this term, it is well known, the places were designated in which the Christians interred their dead; and as there were frequently martyrs and confessors among their dead, they assembled at these Cemeteries on certain days for religious worship, and to commemorate those holy men. Perhaps, also, at other times the Christians might assemble in their Cemeteries to offer prayers at the sepulchres of the saints and martyrs. And as they commonly came away more resolute and more determined to endure every evil for Christ's sake, it is not strange that such as wished the extinction of the Christians should oppose their resorting to these places. Here, then, we have the whole contents of the first edict of Valerian against the Christians: [p. 552.] and with this account fully accords all that Dionysius states, (apud *Euseb.* L. vii. c. 11.) respecting his own sufferings and those of his colleagues. Aemilian, the prefect of Egypt, said to them: Mittemini in partes Libyæ ad locum Cephro. Hunc enim locum *jussu Augustorum nostrorum elegi.* Nullatenus autem licebit vobis conventus agere, aut ea quæ vocantur cœmeteria adire. Here, however, learned men oppose to us not a few examples of persons, who, in this first persecution of Valerian, were either put to death, or thrown into prisons, or bastinadoed, or condemned to the mines. Among other proofs adduced is the 77th Epistle of *Cyprian,* addressed *ad martyres in metallis constitutos,* in which he represents (p. 158.) a part of the people of his charge, as having already gone forth to receive from the Lord the crown of their merits, by the consummation of their martyrdom, and a part as remaining still within the bars of their prisons, or at the mines in chains: and he then states, that not only bishops and presbyters, but also many of the people, and among them virgins and boys, were bastinadoed, fettered, and thrust into the mines: Denique exemplum vestrum secuta multiplex plebis portio confessa est vobiscum pariter et pariter coronata est, connexa vobis vinculo fortissimæ caritatis, et a præpositis suis nec carcere, nec metallis separata. Cujus numero nec virgines desunt. - - In pueris quoque virtus major aetate annos suos confessionis laude transcendit, ut martyrii vestri beatum gregem et sexus et ætas omnis ornaret. These examples, I say, learned men have cited, to show that the first rescripts of Valerian and his son were more cruel than we have represented, and that not only bishops and presbyters, but Christians of every order and sex were subjected to heavy penalties. But whence this severity on many, notwithstanding the law was not very rigorous, may be learned from the latter part of the imperatorial mandate. For this ordained capital punishment against all who either held assemblies or entered the cemeteries. All, therefore, bishops and others, who suffered death, bastinadoing, imprisonment, or other punishments worse than exile, undoubtedly incurred these penalties because they *would* hold meetings contrary to the will of the emperor, and were caught in the cemeteries. For, as we shall soon see, the major part of the Christians were bold in violating the imperatorial mandates. This is fully confirmed by the 82d Epistle of *Cyprian,* ad Successum, (p. 165.) where he writes: Xystum autem *in cimiterio* animadversum sciatis octavo Iduum Augustarum die, et cum eo Diaconos quatuor. Sed et huic persecutioni quotidie insistunt præfecti in urbe, ut si qui sibi oblati fuerint (in the cemeteries, undoubtedly,) animadvertantur et bona eorum fisco vindicentur. The proconsul of Africa, doubtless, had apprehended a great multitude of Christians of both sexes and of all classes, who were assembled for the purpose of religious worship; as may be inferred from the mention of [p. 553.] boys and virgins. To condemn such a mass of persons to death, as the Letter of the emperor required to be done, appeared to the proconsul too hard and cruel; and, therefore, he ordered only a few to be executed to terrify the rest, and the others he ordered to be bastinadoed, and to be sent in chains to the mines.

This persecution by Valerian had so much in it new and diverse from the former persecutions, that I cannot but wonder at some learned men, who tell us that Valerian proceeded against the Christians according to the laws of the earlier emperors. *First*, the ancient laws required that there should be an accuser, but now no accuser was needed, for the governors themselves had inquisitorial powers. The proconsul Paternus required Cyprian to declare who were his presbyters; and when he refused to do it, the proconsul said: Ego hodie in hoc loco *exquiro:* A me invenientur. See the Acta Cypriani in *Ruinart's* Acta martyr. p. 216.—*Secondly*, the emperor's law ordered the punishment, not of all professed Christians, but only of the bishops and presbyters. No one compelled the *people* to change their religion and worship the gods: only the pastors of the flocks were required to adore and pay homage to the gods. When Dionysius replied to the prefect Aemilius, who urged him to the worship of the gods, that he worshipped the one God, the Creator of all things, the prefect said: The emperors allow you to do so, provided you also worship the gods: Quis vero vos prohibet, quo minus et hunc, si quidem Deus est, cum iis, qui natura Dii sunt, adoretis. This we have from Dionysius himself, (apud *Euseb.* Hist. Eccles. L. vii, c. 11; p. 258).—*Lastly*, those who declared that they would not worship the gods, were not put to death, but were only torn from their flocks, and sent into exile. The people, thus bereaved of their guides and teachers, were forbidden by the emperor to assemble and hold meetings; and, as I think, for this among other reasons, that they might not choose new teachers and bishops in the place of those exiled; for the Romans knew that such functionaries could not be created except by election in a popular assembly. And the emperor hoped, if their conventions were abolished and their teachers removed, their religion itself would gradually become extinct among the common people, and the ancient superstition would occupy its place.

(2) In the second year of this persecution, *Valerian* issued another and much severer edict, which, through nearly all the provinces of the Roman empire, caused the death of numerous Christians, and particularly of bishops and presbyters, and exposed others to severe punishments of every sort. When vague and uncertain rumors of this new imperial law reached Africa, *Cyprian* sent messengers to Rome to learn the truth respecting it; and from their report he gives the following summary view of the new edict, (Epist. lxxxii. p. 165.): Quæ autem sunt in vero ita se habent: Rescripsisse Valerianum ad Senatum, (I) ut episcopi et presbyteri et diaconi incontinenti animadvertantur. The dea- [p. 554.] cons had before been exempted, but now they are added to the bishops

and presbyters; undoubtedly, because the enemies of the Christians had learned that they supplied the place of the bishops and presbyters, and carried relief to those in captivity. By this law, therefore, all the men of the holy order, if they refused to pay honor and worship to the gods, were to be immediately put to death; that is, they were to be led from the tribunal to the place of execution, without being for a time kept in prison. This is strikingly illustrated in the death of Cyprian himself, as described in his *Acta*, (apud *Ruinartum*, et alios). When brought before the proconsul, he was first asked whether he was a *papa* or bishop of Christians; and he confessed that he was. He was then commanded *cæremoniari*, that is, to worship the gods in the Roman manner; which he persisted in refusing to do. Then sentence of death was passed upon him; and, after sentence, he was conducted from the prætorium to the place of execution, and there beheaded. This was the uniform mode of proceeding against men in holy orders, during the Valerian persecution. The policy of the law I can easily see. It was scarcely possible to prevent the people from flocking to their teachers lodged in prison; and their last words and exhortations had a wonderful effect upon the minds of the people, animating them, and preparing them to meet death voluntarily and cheerfully for Christ's sake; of this there are extant many examples. The kind of capital punishment to be inflicted, was not prescribed by the law, but was left to the discretion of the magistrate. Hence, we perceive that the officers of Christian churches were put to death in this persecution in a diversity of modes.—(II.) Senatores vero et egregii viri et equites Romani, dignitate amissa, etiam bonis spolientur, et si ademptis facultatibus Christiani esse perseveraverint, capite quoque multentur, matronæ vero ademptis bonis in excilium relegentur. There were, then, among the Christians of that age, persons of both sexes, who were of the first rank and the highest respectability; for, otherwise, this part of the law would have been superfluous. What the emperor decreed respecting matrons, must, doubtless, be construed in the same manner as the decree respecting senators and knights: viz. that they should first be stripped of their property, and then, if they continued to be Christians when their goods were confiscated, they were to be sent into exile. It is most probable that both, after the first part of the sentence, were sent to prison, and time allowed them to deliberate, whether they would return to idolatry or persevere in the Christian religion.—(III.) Cæsariani autem quicunque vel prius confessi fuerant, vel nunc confessi fuerint confiscentur et vincti in Cæsarianas possessiones descripti mittentur. Subjecit etiam Valerianus Imperator orationi suæ exemplum litterarum, quas ad præsides provinciarum de nobis fecit: quas litteras quotidie speramus venire. The *Cæsariani* were, undoubtedly, the persons whom St. Paul (Philip. iv. 22.) calls: τοὺς ἐκ τῆς καίσαρος οἰκίας, the domestics, the servants, the freedmen, belonging to the emperor's household, and residing in his palace. Why the emperor particularized them, we may learn from *Dionysius*, (apud *Euseb.* L. vii. c. 10; p. 256.) who tells us that Valerian's house or family, at the commencement of his reign, was com- [p. 555.] posed, in great part, of Christians: πᾶς ὁ οἶκος αὐτοῦ θεοσεβῶν πεπλήρωτο, καὶ ἦν ἐκκλησία Θεοῦ. Tota ejus familia piis hominibus abundabat, ac Dei ecclesia esse videbatur. Some of these servants of Cæsar, therefore, had already, in the beginning of the persecution, frankly acknowledged that they were Christians, and refused to apostatize from Christ: nor had this proved injurious to them, because the first mandates of the emperor reached only the bishops and presbyters among the Christians. But now, both those who had before confessed, and those who should hereafter confess, were condemned by one and the same law. Provided they still refused to renounce the Christian worship, the emperor commanded them to *be confiscated;* that is, not only their estates and property, but also their *persons* were to be transferred to the public treasury, and they were to be distributed in bonds over the domains, or the estates and farms of the emperor, to perform servile labor there. Respecting the people, or the Christians of the middle and lower ranks, the emperor decreed nothing. These, therefore, were out of danger, and could, without hazard, attend the execution of those put to death under this law. The *Acts* of Cyprian (ed. *Ruinart*, § 5. p. 218.) tell us, that when the proconsul pronounced sentence of death on Cyprian, (*turba fratrum*) a throng of the brethren were present; and, after the sentence was pronounced, this throng cried out: Et nos cum ipso decolemur. Propter hoc tumultus fratrum exortus est, et multa turba eum prosecuta est. In this throng also there was a presbyter and several deacons, and one sub-deacon, who ministered to the dying man. Yet, neither on these, nor on the Christian people that fearlessly accompanied their bishop to execution, did any one lay a hand, or offer them any violence. More examples are not needed. We know, indeed, from Dionysius, (apud *Euseb.*) and from other sources, that a considerable number of the common people either lost their lives or were severely punished in this persecution; but as the emperor had decreed no punishment against that class of persons, it must be considered as certain, that these persons had been found, either in assemblies or in the cemeteries, and were punished for the violation of the imperitorial law on that subject. For no one can doubt, although Cyprian omits the mention of it, that the former edict against holding assemblies and going to the cemeteries was repeated in the new edict. Indeed, we know from two rescripts of *Gallienus*, (cited by *Eusebius*, Hist. Eccles. L. vii. c. 13; p. 267.) that Valerian provided, as far as he could, that the Christians should find it difficult to disregard that law. For, in the first rescript, *Gallienus* having stopped the persecution of Christians, says to certain bishops, that he had given orders, ὅπως ἀπὸ τόπων τῶν θρησκευσίμων ἀποχωρήσωσι: ut cuncti (*milites*, as I suppose,) a religiosis locis abscedant. Therefore *Valerian* had ordered the soldiers to keep guard about the sacred places of the Christians, or the places where they assembled to worship God. In the second rescript he permits the bishops, τὰ τῶν καλουμένων κοιμητηρίων ἀπολαμβάνειν χωρία: ut cœmeteriorum suorum loca recuperarent. The cemeteries, therefore, had been taken from the Christians by order of the emperor, and undoubtedly confis- [p. 556.] cated. Whether both rescripts refer to the same subject, or whether the "religious places" of the former are different from the "cemeteries" of the latter, is not clear, and I will not therefore decide. Yet, the former appears to me the more extensive, and to remove soldiers from *all* the sacred places, because the recovery of the cemeteries is made the subject of a special grant.

The cause of the change of the first and milder edict into this far severer and more cruel one, though not expressly stated by any ancient writer, may still be easily inferred from the transactions of those times. Neither the bishops and presbyters, nor the christian people, obeyed the emperor's law respecting assemblies and the cemeteries. The people resorted, in great numbers, to the places where the bishops lived in exile; and the bishops, regardless of the imperitorial mandate, not only held assemblies in those places, but also did what might seem to be of a more treasonable character, namely, they labored to convert the pagans to Christianity, and to enlarge the boundaries of the church. We ought to praise these holy men for their magnanimity: but it may be questioned whether it would not have been better to temper that magnanimity with prudence, and give way to the iniquity of the times, for the sake of avoiding a greater evil. The emperor and the governors, in these circumstances, supposing themselves to be contemned by the Christians, especially by the bishops, determined to coerce them by sterner laws. That this is no fiction appears from the history of *Dionysius* Alexandrinus and *Cyprian.* We learn from *Eusebius*, (Hist. Eccles. L. vii. c. 11, p. 258.) that when Dionysius was sent into exile, the præfect said to him: Nullatenus autem licebit vobis (you and the presbyters) conventus agere. Quod si quis in conventu aliquo fuerit inventus, is sibi ipse periculum arcesset. How he obeyed this interdict of the emperors he tells us directly after. *First,* though absent, he took care that the Christians remaining at Alexandria should meet together frequently, contrary to the law: Eos, qui in urbe erant, perinde ac si adessem, majore studio congregavi in ecclesiam, absens quidem corpore. This he was able to accomplish by means of the four presbyters whom he had left at Alexandria, together with several deacons, as he afterwards states. *Secondly,* in the place of his exile he held assemblies of the Christians who followed him from the city, and others who resorted to him from every quarter: Apud Cephro vero nobiscum magna fidelium adfuit multitudo, partim eorum, qui ab urbe nos sequuti fuerant, partim aliorum, qui ex reliqua Egypto confluebant. *Lastly,* he labored to bring new converts into the church: Ibi quoque januam nobis patefecit Deus ad prædicationem verbi sui. - - Non pauci ex gentilibus, relictis simulacris, ad Deum conversi sunt. All these things were excellent in themselves, and worthy of so great a bishop: but they implied contempt for the emperor's mandates. It is, therefore, not strange that soon after the prefect, who had knowledge of all this, removed Dionysius to more distant and inhospitable regions; and the indignation against the Christians increased daily. In very nearly the same manner *Cyprian* conducted, in his exile at Curubis, as appears evident from his life, written [p. 557.] by his deacon *Pontius.* For he went thither, attended by many persons, and a number of the brethren there visited him. (See § 12.) Neither were these only the poor aud humble, but likewise the most noble and distinguished. Says *Pontius* (§ 14.): Conveniebant plures egregii et clarissimi ordinis et sanguinis, sed et sæculi nobilitate generosi. And these congregated together, he instructed very frequently with his discourses and exhortations: Ille servos Dei exhortationibus dominicis instruebat, et ad calcandas passiones hujus temporis contemplatione superventuræ claritatis animabat. Thus the Christian bishops and presbyters themselves, because they would prosecute their work of advancing the Christian cause, rather than obey the emporor's will, provoked the tyrant to enact severer laws against them.

(3) Dionysius of Alexandria, (apud *Euseb.* Hist. Eccles. L. vii. c. 10, p. 255.) thought the words of St. John, in the Apocalypse, (ch. 13 : 5.) were fulfilled in *Valerian* : whether he was correct or not does not effect the present argument: Et datum est illi os loquens magna et impia: Et data est illi potestas et menses quadraginta duo. Hence learned men have rightly inferred that the Valerian persecution continued into the *fourth* year. And that after Valerian was captured by the Persians, his son Gallienus sent rescripts throughout the Roman world, staying the persecution, and giving Christians liberty freely to profess their religion, is fully attested by *Eusebius*, (Hist Eccles. L. vii. c. 13, p. 262.) where he confirms his statement, by quoting the very words of the rescripts. *Gallienus* seems to have regarded the sad fate of his father as a punishment inflicted on him by the Christian's God, for the persecution of his servants.

(4) A memorable example of this kind is stated by *Eusebius*, (Hist. Eccles. L. vii. c. 15, p. 263.) *Marinus* was put to death at Cæsarea, after the restoration of peace to the Christian community by Gallienus. He was wealthy, prosperous, and of a good family, and he aspired to the honor of a centurionship among the Romans. But when near the attainment of his object he was accused of being a Christian, before Achæus the judge, by some one who was his rival candidate for the office. Marinus confessed the charge. The judge gave him three hours to consider whether he would sacrifice to the gods or persevere in the Christian faith. When the time had elapsed, Marinus professed Christ with greater promptitude than before, and cheerfully submitted to capital punishment. The proceeding with this man, most evidently, was not according to the edict of *Valerian*, which had already been abrogated by *Gallienus*, but according to the ancient law of *Trajan*. For an accuser appeared : The criminal, on confession, was required to renounce Christ, and, as he would not do it, he was forthwith led to execution. From this example, therefore, it appears that the ancient laws of the emperors against Christians retained all their force, even when milder ones had been enacted; and, therefore, under the milder emperors, [p. 558.] and in times of tranquillity, the governors could pass sentence upon the Christians who were formally accused and confessed the charge. The corps of *Marinus*, one Asturius, a Roman senator, and a man of the highest respectability, bore away on his own shoulders, and committed to burial ; as we learn from the same *Eusebius*, (Hist. Eccles. L. vii. c. 16, p. 264.) And this he could do with impunity and perfect safety : and the reason is obvious. According to to *Trajan's* law, the judge could not punish without an accuser, and a man of such high reputation and distinction, and the personal friend of the emperors, no one either dared or wished to accuse before the court.

§ XX. **Persecution under Aurelian.** If, therefore, a few examples be excepted, of Christians put to death by governors who abused their power, the Christians enjoyed a good degree of tranquillity under *Gallienus*, who reigned eight years with his brother

Valerian, and also under his successor *Claudius,* who reigned two years.(1) *Aurelian,* who succeeded Claudius in the year 270, although immoderately given to idolatry, and possessing a strong aversion to the Christians, yet devised no measures for their injury during four years.(2) But in the fifth year of his reign, either from his own superstition, or prompted by the superstition of others, he prepared to persecute them:(3) and, had he lived, so cruel and ferocious was his disposition, and so much was he influenced by the priests and the admirers of the gods, that this persecution would have been more cruel than any of the preceding. But before his new edicts had reached all the provinces, and when he was in Thrace, in the year 275, he was assassinated by the instigation of Mnestheus, whom he had threatened to punish. And, therefore, only a few Christians suffered for their piety under him.(4)

(1) That in the reign of *Claudius,* a few Christians here and there were put to death by the governors, undoubtedly under cover of the ancient laws, is evident from the instances adduced by *Lupius,* in his Notes on the *Epitaph of Severa,* (§ ii. p. 6, &c.) Among these examples is that of *Severa* herself, whose particular Epitaph was dug up in the *Via Salaria,* A. D. 1730, and has been elucidated by a long and erudite commentary.

(2) With great unanimity, the modern writers have stated, that *Aurelian* in the first years of his reign was kind and friendly to the Christians, but on what grounds or authority I know not. For I no where find any testimony that he had this goodwill, nor do I meet with any specimen of it. I know that *Eusebius* tells us, (Hist. Eccles. L. vii. c. 30. p. 282.) that when the Christians appealed to this emperor against Paul of Samosata, who refused to quit the house of the church, after he was condemned in a council for corrupt sentiments concerning Christ, the emperor ordered him to be put out by force; and this decision against Paul *Eusebius* seems to regard as evidence of his friendly regards for the [p. 559.] Christians. But, if I am not greatly deceived, the followers of Eusebius infer from this act of Aurelian, more than is found in it. We will grant that, at that time, Aurelian had not indulged feelings of hostility to the Christians, nor determined on their extirpation. But how he could have entertained kind and friendly feelings towards them, I cannot understand, while he was burning with zeal for the worship of those gods which the Christians execrated, and, moreover, spoke contemptuously of the sacred rites of the Christians. For thus he wrote in an Epistle to the Senate, (preserved by *Vopiscus* in his *Aurelius,* c. 20. Histor. Augustæ, tom. ii. p. 463.): Miror vos, patres sancti, tamdiu de aperiendis Sybillinis dubitasse libris, *perinde quasi in Christianorum ecclesia,* non in templo Deorum omnium, tractaretis. In this language there is a very invidious comparison between the Christian religion and the worship and sacred rites of the gods;

and it indicates a mind wholly averse from the Christians, and paying all reverence to the gods. He seems to suppose that a certain divine and celestial influence prevailed in a temple of the gods, which illuminates the minds of those who deliberate there, and shows them what to do; but that the churches of Christians lack this influence, and, therefore, everything proceeds tardily and heavily in their councils. But this very representation is honorary to the Christian assemblies of that age: for it shows that nothing was done in them in a headlong and tumultuous manner, but everything was maturely considered and carefully weighed, so that the consultations continued often for a long time Moreover, when we come to treat of Paul of Samosata, we will show that *Aurelian's* decision against him is no evidence of any love for Christians, but of his hatred to Zenobia, a queen of the east.

(3) Eusebius tells us (Hist. Eccles. L. vii. c. 30; p. 283.) that Aurelian was prompted to persecute the Christians (τισὶ βουλαῖς,) *by certain counsellors*. Perhaps this was true. It might be that either the Platonic philosophers, who possessed great influence in those times, or the heathen priests, who had many friends at court, and especially among the ladies of rank, represented to the emperor that the destruction of the Christians would prove useful to the empire. But whoever will survey the life of Aurelian, will perceive that he needed no external influences to bring him to assail the Christians, for his innate cruelty and superstition were sufficient of themselves to prompt him to such a nefarious resolution. Scarcely any one among the emperors, before Constantine the Great, was more superstitious, or more devoted to the imaginary deities. His mother was a priestess of the sun: (see *Vopiscus* in his Aurelian, c. iv. p. 420). And her son, in consequence, all his life reverenced the sun as the supreme deity. He closes an oration, in which he thanks Valerian for the honors he had received from him, in these words: Dii faciant et *Deus certus Sol*, (so then he placed more confidence in the sun than in all the other gods,) ut et senatus de me sic sentiat. (Ibid. c. xiv. p. 451). When the forces of Zenobia had [p. 560.] been vanquished at Emessa, he supposed that he was indebted for the victory to the good providence of the sun; and, therefore, "immediately after the battle, he repaired to the temple of Heliogabalus, as if to pay his vows for the public favor." (Ibid. c. xxv. pp. 478, 479). And "the garments enriched with jewels," which had been stripped from the vanquished Persians, Armenians, and other enemies, he consectrated in the temple of the sun. (Ibid. c. xxviii. p. 483). When Palmyra was captured, and the infuriate soldiers had plundered the temple of the sun, he was more solicitous for nothing than to have that sacred edifice magnificently repaired and dedicated anew. To Ceionius Bassus, whom he had intrusted with this business, he wrote: Habes trecentas auri libras e Zenobiæ capsulis: habes argenti mille octingenta pondo. De Palmyrenorum bonis habes gemmas regias. Ex his omnibus fac cohonestari templum: mihi et Diis immortalibus gratissimum feceris. Ego ad senatum siribam, petens, ut mittat Pontificem, qui dedicet templum. (Ibid. c. xxxi. p. 491). Afterwards he erected a very magnificent temple of the sun at Rome, (Ibid. c. xxxix. p. 522,) and placed in it much gold and jewelry. (Ibid. p. 523). And hence, after his death, Aurelianus Tacitus said, in his oration before the senate: Quindecim millia

librarum auri ex ejus liberalitate unum tenet templum (solis): omnia in urbe fana ejus micant donis (Ibid. c. xli. p. 527). On one of his coins, mentioned by Ezechiel *Spanheim*, (de usu et præstantia numismat. vol. ii. p. 485.) is this legend: *Sol Dominus imperii Romani.*—Now, who can wonder that a prince inflamed with such insane zeal for the worship of the sun, should have determined to assail with the sword, and to persecute with edicts, those Christians who deemed the sun unworthy of divine honors?

(4) Eusebius states (Hist. Eccles. L. vii. c. 30; p. 285, &c.) that *Aurelian* fell by parricidal hands, while preparing for his intended assault upon the Christians, and, as it were, *in the very act of subscribing the edicts against them.* This obscure statement is explained by *Lactantius*, (de mortibus persecutorum, c. 6.) who informs us that his edicts had reached only to the provinces bordering on Thrace, and says: Protinus inter initia sui furoris extinctus est. Nondum ad provincias ulteriores *cruenta ejus edicta* pervenerant, et jam Cænofrurio, qui locus est Thraciæ, cruentus humi jacebat.

§ XXI. **Efforts of the Philosophers against the Christians.** While the emperors and magistrates were striving to subvert the Christian commonwealth by means of laws and punishments, it was assailed with craft and subtly, during this whole century, by the philosophers of the Ammonian school; who assumed the name of Platonists, extended their discipline over nearly all the Roman empire, and gradually obscured the glory of all the other sects. For, as most of the people who cultivated piety and virtue, [p. 561.] more readily repaired to the Christians than to the schools of the Philosophers, and many went also from the schools of the Platonists themselves,(1) they were induced to resist to the utmost a sect which threatened ruin to their prosperity and fame. Hence *Porphyry*, a Syrian or Tyrian, the coryphæus of the Platonist sect in this century, (according to *Plotinus*,) a man distinguished for his subtlety and acuteness, composed a long treatise against the Christians; which, it is to be regretted, the laws of the Christian emperors have caused to disappear: for the few fragments of it still remaining, show that *Porphyry* was no very formidable adversary.(2) Others of this sect adopted into their creed the best and most sublime precepts of Christianity, and especially those relating to piety and morality, so that they might appear to teach religion and virtue with as much purity and sanctity as the Christians. Others, again, in order to weaken the Christians' argument from the life and miracles of the Saviour, labored to show, that among the more devout worshippers of the gods, there had been men not inferior, and perhaps actually superior, to *Jesus Christ*, both in their origin and virtue, and in the number and magnitude of their miracles; and for this purpose they drew up the lives of *Archytas* of Tarentum, *Pythagoras*, *Apollonius* Tyanæus, and other men of great fame; and, stuffing these biographies with silly fables, they put them into the hands of the common people.(3) The men of this class did not revile Jesus Christ, nor deny that the precepts which the Christians taught as coming from him, were, for the most part, excellent and commendable, but they devised a sort of harmony of all religions, or a universal religion, which might embrace the Christian among the rest. This plan, which was contrived by *Ammonius*, the founder of the sect, required the admission of only so much of the Christian system as was not utterly repugnant to idolatry, or to the ancient popular religions.

(1) Respecting the conversion to Christianity of many Platonists, and especially of the disciples of *Plotinus*, the head man of the Platonist school in this century, we have the following very lucid passage in the writings of *Augustine*, (Epist. lxviii. ad Dioscorum, cap. v. § 33. Opp. tom. ii. p. 260.): Tunc Plotini schola Romæ floruit, habuitque condiscipulos multos, acutissimos viros. Sed aliqui eorum magicarum artium curiositate depravati sunt, aliqui Dominum [p. 562.] Jesum Christum ipsius veritatis atque sapientiæ incommutabilis, quam conabantur attingere, cognoscentes gestare personam, *in ejus militiam transierunt.*

(2) On the work of *Porphyry* against the Christians, may be consulted Lucas *Holstenius*, (de Vita Porphyrii, c. xi.) Jo. Fran. *Buddeus*, (Isagoge in Theologiam, tom. ii. p. 1009, &c.) and Jo. Alb. *Fabricius*, (Lux Evangelii toti orbi exoriens, p. 154). To the observations made by these authors I have nothing to add.

(3) The Life of *Pythagoras* was written in this century by *Porphyry*, and in the next by *Jamblichus*, and both, unquestionably, in order to make that philosopher appear in all respects the equal of *Jesus Christ*, but especially so in his miracles and in the wisdom of his precepts. This is demonstrated by Ludolph *Küster*, in the notes to his edition of the Life of Jamblichus; and any one will readily see it, if he will compare either of these biographies with the history of our Saviour: (See *Küsteri* Adnot. ad Jamblichi, cap. ii. p. 7. et cap. xix. p. 78). No two lambs could be more alike than Christ and Pythagoras, if all were true which those two biographers have stated. The fable of *Apollonius* Tyanæus, which *Philostratus* composed in this century, by command of *Julia*, the empress, wife to the emperor Severus, is abundantly known; and none among the learned need to be informed that *Hierocles*, a Platonic philosopher of the fourth century, contrasted Pythagoras with Jesus Christ, and that *Eusebius* of Cæsarea

wrote a special treatise against the book. That *Philostratus* aimed, in his very splendid, and yet most stupidly mendacious book, to suggest such a comparison between Christ and Apollonius, has long been shown by the learned men who are cited and approved by Godfrey *Olearius*, the editor of Philostratus; (Præfat. p. xxxix). Moreover, as Christ imparted to his friends and legates the power of working miracles; so also, to make the resemblance perfect, these Platonists represent *Pythagoras* as imparting the same power to several of his followers, to Empedocles, Epimenides, Abaris, and others. See *Jamblichus*, (Vita Pythagoræ, c. 28. p. 114). To exhibit the designs and the impudence of this sect, I will cite a Latin translation of the words of Jamblichus in the above cited place. Having spoken of some miracles of Pythagoras, he adds: Millia alia, hisque diviniora, magisque miranda, quæ de viro traduntur. - - Quorum compotes etiam facti Empedocles Agrigentinus, Epimenides Cretensis et Abaris Hyperboreus, multis in locis talia facinora designarunt. Satis autem nota sunt ipsorum opera.

Moreover, these comparisons were made, not so much to disparage Christ, as to injure Christianity. For those who compared Christ with Pythgoras, with Apollonius Tyanæus, with Empedocles, with Archytas, &c. tacitly admitted that Christ was a divine person, far superior to the common order of men, [p. 563.] the Lord of demons, the controler of nature, and a great benefactor to the human race: but they affirmed that the Christians misunderstood and perverted the opinions of their master and guide. As they wished to reduce all modes of philosophising, whether Grecian or barbarian, to the one mode of the *Platonists*, and explained this mode according to the Egyptian notions of God and nature; and, moreover, labored to bring all the religions of the world into harmony with this Platonico-Ægyptian system, and as they did not deny that Christ taught a religion which was good and useful, it became necessary that they should maintain, that what the Christians inculcated was, in great measure, diverse from the opinions of [Christ] their master. They, therefore, wished to accomplish *two* objects by the above-mentioned comparisons:—*First*, to prevent any credit being given to the assertion of the Christians, that Christ was *God*, or the *Son of God*. For if there were to be found among men, individuals possessing the same power of changing and controling the laws of nature, as had been possessed by Christ, then the Christians' argument for Christ's divinity, derived from his miracles, would fall to the ground. Their *second* object was, to bring men to believe that Christ had no design to subvert the ancient pagan religions, but merely to purify and reform them. Now, if among the most devout of the pagan worshippers, there were found persons the equals, and perhaps the superiors of Christ in great achievements, then it would necessarily follow, that those are mistaken who suppose Christ wished to abolish the temples and the ceremonies of the pagan worship.

To the list of Platonists who labored to subvert the Christian religion by cunning devices, *Apuleius* was, not long since, added by the very learned and ingenious William *Warburton*, in his English work, *The Divine Legation of Moses Demonstrated* (vol. ii. p. 117). For he thinks that *Apuleius*, a man excessively superstitious and hostile to the Christians, both personally and from zeal to his sect, wrote his well-known *Metamorphosis*, or fable of the Golden Ass, for the purpose of making it appear that the mysteries of the gods possessed the highest efficacy for purifying and healing the minds of men, and were therefore greatly to be preferred to the Christian sacred rites. With his accustomed penetration and skill in matters of antiquity, this distinguished man has discovered in Apuleius some things never before observed by any one. Among these, the most noticeable is, that he thinks it may be inferred with much probability from the *Defence* of Apuleius now extant, that the *Licinius Aemilianus*, who accused *Apuleius* of magic before the proconsul of Africa, was a Christian. But as to the object of the fable of the Ass, which this very learned man supposes to have been to exalt the pagan mysteries, and throw contempt on Christianity, I have my doubts; because I see nothing adduced from that fable, which it would be difficult to explain in a different manner.

§ XXII. **The First Movements of Diocletian.** *Diocletian* was advanced to the government of the empire A. D. 284; and being by [p. 564.] nature more inclined to clemency than to cruelty, he suffered the Christians to live in tranquillity, and to propagate their religion without restraint. But in the subsequent year, 285, he took for his colleague in the government *Maximian Herculius*, a man who is represented as most inveterately hostile to the Christians, and as having punished many of them, both in Gaul and at Rome, with extreme rigor; nay, as having put to death the whole Thebæan legion, composed of Christians, because they refused to sacrifice to the gods at the Leman lake. I say, he is so *represented;* for the alleged examples and proofs of such atrocity are not of so high authority that they cannot be called in question and invalidated.(1) It is more certain that, near the end of the century, *Maximian Galerius,* (whom the two emperors had created a Cæsar, together with *Constantius Chlorus*, in the year 292,) persecuted both the ministers of his palace and the soldiers, who professed Christianity, removing some of them from office, harassing others with reproaches and insults, and even causing some to be put to death.(2) But this hatred of *Galerius*, because it did not reach very far, and seemed to be tolerated rather than approved by the two emperors, did not prevent the daily advance of the Christian cause; and the Christians, rendered secure by long-continued peace, deviated sadly from the primitive sanctity and piety.(3)

(1) Roman Catholic writers mention numerous martyrs, put to death during the first years of *Diocletian's* reign, in Gaul, at Rome, and elsewhere; but as the early writers say nothing of them, and especially *Eusebius*, who tells us

that the condition of the Christians during the eighteen first years of *Diocletian* was very quiet, and almost wholly free from perils; (see his Hist. Eccles. L. viii. c. 1, p. 291.) these writers either contend that Eusebius was better acquainted with the Eastern church than the Western, or they tell us, that these martyrs were overlooked by the ancients, because they were put to death not by a public mandate of the emperor *Diocletian*, but only by the private orders of *Maximian Herculius*. Such as choose may rest satisfied with this explanation; but I must confess, there is no rashness in doubting the reality of all these martyrdoms. The whole history of them is based on the credibility of certain Acts and martyrologies, to which no one will commit himself, if he judges that confidence is to be placed in none but certain and approved authorities. No one can be ignorant, that the catalogues of martyrs in use in some churches, are of a most uncertain character, and are collected for the most part from dubious ancient and obscure reports; nor are the narratives, [p. 565.] which have in various places been current for several centuries, entitled to any greater respect. How few are the undisputed *Acts* of the saints and martyrs in the three first centuries, may be learned from Theodore *Ruinart*, who attempted to collect them all, and did make a collection. This learned man published a moderate sized volume; and he would have made out a very little one, if he had determined to admit nothing but what is above all suspicion.

Of all the martyrs whom *Maximian Herculius* is said to have sacrified to his gods, there are none more celebrated and noble than those that composed the *Thebæan legion*, who, from the place where they were slain, were called the *Agaunian Martyrs*. Their relics are spread almost all over the Romish church, and are held in special reverence in France, Switzerland, and Italy. Nor is this reverence of recent date, originating in those centuries in which all Europe was involved in ignorance; when superstition every year created new martyrs. For it appears from the works of *Avitus*, of Vienne, (published by Ja. *Sirmond*,) who flourished near the beginning of the sixth century, that at that time there was at Agaunum, a church dedicated to these martyrs, and that in it a festal day was observed in memory of them. (See Ja. *Sirmond*, Opp. tom. ii. p. 93–97.) This I mention, because I perceive that some learned men, who are opposed to these martyrs, maintain that the knowledge of them was first brought to light in the middle of the sixth century, nay, in the *seventh* century. As *Maximian Herculius* was marching an army into Gaul to quell some commotions there, having passed the Alps, he arrived at the parts of Valais on the Leman lake; and to prepare his troops for contending under better auspices, he ordered a general lustration, and that the troops should swear fealty on the altars of the gods. This mandate of the general was resisted by the Thebæan legion, which had *Mauritius* for its commander, had just come from the East, and was wholly composed of Christians. *Maximian* therefore twice decimated it, that is, caused every tenth man to be put to death; and as this rigor was wholly insufficient to overcome its constancy, he ordered his army to fall upon it and slay the entire legion. This is the substance of that *Passio Sanctorum Mauritii ac sociorum ejus*, which is said to have been composed by *Eucherius*, bishop of Lyons, in the sixth century, and which, after others,

Theod. *Ruinart* published, with learned notes, in his *Acta* Martyrum sincera et selecta, p. 271, &c. The adversaries of the Romish church, who have controverted so many of the other alleged martyrdoms, all left the "*Happy Legion*," as this legion was called, untouched down to the eighteenth century, except by here and there an individual. Nor was this strange, because there is scarcely any other narrative of martyrdom that is confirmed by so many very ancient documents and testimonies as this is. Perhaps, also, many feared they should de-
[p. 566.] tract from the honor of Christianity if they brought under discussion this so illustrious and extraordinary example of early Christian fortitude and constancy. Others may have been so charmed with the story of the *Thundering Legion*, of which we have before spoken, under *Marcus Antoninus*, that they could see nothing improbable in this Christian *Thebæan Legion* serving under *Maximian Herculius*. For if a whole legion of Christians was admitted into the Roman army under Marcus, much more might such a legion be countenanced under *Maximian*, when the Christian cause had been more widely extended and better established. But in this eighteenth century, John *Dubordieu*, a very learned man, who had seen the supposed bones of Mauritius and some of his fellow-soldiers honored with great superstition at Turin, made a formal attack upon the Thebæan legion, and was the first to class it among the fables of former ages, in a book published at Amsterdam, in 1705, 8vo., under the title: "Dissertation critique sur le Martyre de la Legion Thebeenne." Three years after, Ja. *Hottinger*, in his Ecclesiastical History of Switzerland, (tom. i. L. ii. § 23, &c.) followed the example of Dubordieu, and confirmed his positions with new arguments of no inconsiderable weight. Both reasoned ingeniously and learnedly. But the dissertation of the latter, as it constituted a small part of a large volume, and was written in the German language, did less harm to the Thebæan legion than the treatise of the former; which, being written in an elegant style, was soon circulated over a large part of Europe, and forcibly urged those of moderate learning, as well as the more learned, to place the *Happy Legion* among the *pious fictions* of former ages. A defence of the Happy Legion was at once contemplated by *Claret*, the Abbot of St. Maurice, in the Valais, to whom, more than to any other, the task appeared to belong; but being burdened with too much business, he devolved the task upon his friend *Joseph de l'Isle*, Abbot of St. Leopold, at Nancy; and he, after a long interval of thirty-five years, came out against the opposers of the holy soldiers, in a French work, printed at Nancy in 1741, 12mo. entitled, "Defense de la verité de la Legion Thebeenne pour repondre a la Dissertation du Ministre du Bordieu." This writer, deficient neither in learning nor ingenuity, pours upon his antagonist a great abundance of testimonies and documents, among which are some of sufficiently high antiquity, and now first adduced by him; but in replying to the arguments of his opponent, and particularly to those brought against the *Acta Sti Mauritii*, attributed to *Eucherius*, his strength fails him, and he hardly maintains his ground: neither does he meet the whole controversy, for he was ignorant of the arguments which *Hottinger* had added to those of the first assailant. Yet the erudite man fully satisfied his own church, and especially those members of it who live sumptuously and merrily at the ex-

pense of St. Maurice and his companions, that is, on the resources of the Happy Legion, contributed and consecrated by well-meaning people; but the minds of those whom *Dubordieu* and *Hottinger* led astray, he could not convince and reclaim. After some years, *Dubordieu* being dead, the attack was renewed by one of the prefects of the Genevan library, *Boulaire*, [p. 567.] if I remember correctly, a man of uncommon sagacity and industry; nay, he fortified the attack by new arguments, in a French Epistle, which is inserted in the *Bibliotheque Raisonnée*, (tom. xxxvi. p. 427, &c.) This learned man deserves special praise, not only for ingenuously admitting that *Dubordieu*, whom he patronizes, had committed some mistakes, but also for laboring to ascertain the origin of the fable, and to show that it was brought from the East into Rhetia. A little afterwards, a rather brief, but ingenious and well-digested opinion on the subject, was given by the very respectable Loysius *Bochat*, in his Memoires Critiques sur l'Histoire ancienne de la Suisse, (vol. i. p. 557, &c., edit. of 1747.) He had no doubt that every intelligent person who shall feel himself at liberty to express his real sentiments, after examining the whole subject, will place the history we are considering among the pious frauds.

Whoever compares with a calm and unbiassed mind the arguments on both sides, will readily adopt the opinion, that this controversy is not yet decided; the learned men already mentioned have indeed rendered the story of the Thebæan Legion dubious, and some parts of it they have divested of all probability, but they have not overthrown the whole story. For, as already observed, the advocates of the Blessed Legion bring forward a mass of testimonies, some of which have great antiquity; and although the other party oppose to these testimonies the silence of the cotemporary writers, and those of the age next after the legion, and also arguments derived from the nature of the case, yet all this proof seems insufficient to wholly overthrow the evidence of so many proofs from both facts and testimony. Whoever shall carefully and accurately weigh all the arguments, however, will, I think, conclude, that the side of the opposers has the advantage over that of the defendants. The most ancient witness for the legion lived in the *fifth* century, and wrote the Life of Romanus, Abbot of Mount Jura, in Burgundia, who died after the middle of the fifth century. This Life is in the *Acta Sanctor. Antwerp.* (tom. iii. Februar. ad diem 28, p. 740,) and was undoubtedly composed soon after the death of Romanus by one of his associates. From this author we learn, that in the time of Romanus, and consequently about the middle of the *fifth* century, there was at Agaunum a church dedicated to Maurice, the commander of the legion; and that his whole history was then inserted in the *Acta*, and was considered altogether true. For thus he writes (c. iv. § 15, p. 744): Basilicam Sanctorum, immo, ut ita dixerim, castra Martyrum in Agaunensium locum, sicut passionis ipsorum relatio digesta testatur, quæ sex millia sexcentos viros, non dicam ambire corpore in fabricis, sed nec ipso (ut reor) campo illic potuit conspire, fidei ardore deliberavit (Romanus) expetere. And in his preface (p. 741,) he explicitly mentions Maurice, the commander of the legion, and not obscurely tells us, that his *urn*, i. e., his sepulchre, was to be seen in the church of Agaunum: Prior (Romanus) priscum secutus Johannem supra *urnam S. Mauritii*, id est [p. 568.] Legionis Thebaeorum martyrum caput, velut ille eximius Apostolus supra salutiferi pectus recumbit auctoris. This church, having fallen by its age or otherwise, near the close of the century, needed to be rebuilt. Accordingly, it was rebuilt, and *Alcimus Avitus*, archbishop of Vienne, preached a sermon in the new built church near the commencement of the *sixth* century. The sermon is lost, or at least has not been discovered; but *Sirmond* found the beginning of it in an ancient manuscript, with the following inscription: Dicta in Basilica sanctorum Agaunensium, in innovatione monasterii ipsius vel passione martyrum. Although the exordium thus recovered is short, yet it places beyond dispute, that some *Acta Legionis Thebaeæ* then existed, that they agreed with those we now have, and were publicly read in the presence of the assembly immediately before this discourse. The *Acta* now extant are attributed to *Eucherius*, bishop of Lyons, in the sixth century, a man of respectability on many accounts; and therefore they hold the third place in the list of documents on which rests the credibility of this story. The documents of the sixth and following centuries, being much inferior to those of the first class above mentioned, I pass them without notice.—It is therefore clear, unless I wholly misjudge, that as early as the beginning of the *fifth* century, and perhaps also in the fourth, the inhabitants of Rhætia and the Valais, firmly believed what is at this day stated respecting the Thebæan Legion; they possessed and read the *Acta* of this legion; dedicated a church to it, and in that church annually celebrated the memory of those illustrious soldiers; they preserved the bones of Maurice, the commander of the legion; and they pointed out the plain where the slaughter of it took place by command of *Maximian Herculius*. It remains then to be inquired, whether these arguments are sufficient to place the truth of the story beyond all controversy. This the very learned opposers deny; and on what grounds I will now shew, with the same impartiality with which I have stated the arguments in favor of the story.

First. Many, and especially *Dubordieu*, in opposing the *Acta felicis Legionis* which have come down to us, deny that these *Acta* were written by *Eucherius;* they contend that they contain various errors; and they would attribute the compilation of them to some ignorant monk of the *seventh* century. But if we admit that these objections are urged with as much truth as erudition and ingenuity, yet, unless I greatly mistake, they avail nothing against the truth of our historical facts. For these facts do not rest solely on the authority of those *Acta*, but, as we have shown, upon stronger and more ancient testimonies, which cannot in any way be confuted. Let us suppose that these *Acta* were compiled in the *seventh* century, or even in the eighth or ninth, and by some ignorant and fraudulent person; it would still be certain, that as early as the *fifth* century there were other *Acta* in the hands of the Rhætians, which, in regard to the main facts, agreed with these.

Secondly. Much stronger is the argument derived from the silence of the writers, who lived at and near the time when the legion is said to have been butchered. *Eusebius*, the father of ecclesiastical history, and otherwise a careful recorder of the sufferings of the martyrs, knew nothing respecting this [p. 569.] legion. *Sulpicius Severus*, of the *fifth* century, who lived in Gaul, and wrote a (*Historia Sacra,*) History of Religion, knew nothing of this legion; Paul *Orosius*, who commented on the expedition of Maximian into Gaul, knew nothing of it; *Lactantius*, who, in his book De Mortibus Persequutorum, describes the cruelty and the tragical death of Maximian, knew nothing of it; *Prudentius*, a distinguished Christian poet, who sung the praises of the known martyrs of his times, knew nothing of it. In short, all the writers of the *fourth* century whose works have come down to us, knew nothing respecting this legion. The weight of this negative argument, which surely is great, was felt by Joseph de l'Isle; who, of course, does all he can to evade it. But fairness requires us freely to admit, that, while it is impossible wholly to destroy it, it may be in a measure weakened. In the first place, the advocates for the legion say, it is not strange that an occurrence in Europe, and in the valleys of the Alps, should have been unknown to *Eusebius*, and to all the Asiatic and African writers; nor can it be denied, that *Eusebius* is silent as to many occurrences in the West, and that his history, for the most part, treats of the affairs of the East. With regard to *Sulpitius Severus*, there is greater difficulty; because he lived in Gaul, where this legion is reported to have been butchered; and, as he was of a light and credulous disposition, he would undoubtedly have mentioned it in his history, if there had been a popular rumor spreading throughout Gaul, in his age, of the glorious death of so many soldiers. But I am suspicious, that Sulpitius himself affords a plausible answer. After briefly but nervously speaking of the grievousness and severity of the Diocletian persecution, in the following terms: Hac tempestate omnis fere sacro martyrum cruore orbis infectus est. - - Nullis umquam magis bellis mundus exhaustus est; he proceeds to say explicitly, that for the sake of brevity, he should not particularly mention any of the martyrs, although their *Acta* were extant: Extant etiam mandatæ litteris præclaræ ejus temporis martyrum passiones: quas connectendas non putavi, ne modum operis excederem. (See his Historia Sacra, L. ii. c. 32, p. 248.) Here, it appears to me, he clearly explains the reason of his silence. Paul *Orosius* and *Prudentius* lived in Spain; and therefore it might be that they were ignorant of an occurrence on the borders of Italy. *Orosius*, moreover, (Hist. L. vii. c. 25,) treats very summarily of the affairs of Diocletian and Maximian, and of the persecution of Christians by them; so that he could not well repeat so long a story as that of the Thebæan Legion; and, like *Sulpitius*, he mentions no particular martyr. But in regard to *Lactantius*, whom I asssume to be the author of the celebrated treatise *de Mortibus Persequutorum*, the most ingenious apologist will find himself staggered. For he might well know the story, since his book shows, that he was not only familiar with all the occurrences in the empire and the imperial court in those times, but also with the vices and crimes and flagitious deeds of *Maximian;* nor can any reason whatever be assigned, why he should omit an occurrence so intimately connected with the subject of which he was [p. 570.] treating, and yet describe very copiously the hostility of *Maximian* towards the Christians, and the many sufferings they endured at his hands.

Thirdly. Another argument against the legion is drawn by learned men from the story itself, which, they say, contains many things utterly incredible.

They contend, first, that it is incredible there should be in the Roman army, at that time, a whole legion made up of Christians; and it is still more incredible that *Maximian*, when marching against enemies, and just ready to meet them, should slaughter so great a portion of his army, recently summoned from the East to ensure his success, and should thus willingly weaken his forces, and deprive himself of the means necessary to a victory; for, however savage his disposition, he was most skilful in military affairs, and a consummate general. Again, they contend, that it seems by no means probable, that among so many soldiers, not one was disposed to consult his safety, either by dissimulation or by flight. And, finally, they say it was strange, and a thing unheard of, for so great a body of armed men patiently to resign themselves up to their executioners, and make no effort to defend their lives with their arms. All these considerations are urged with much ingenuity and address by very learned men; and yet it must be admitted, that if the story of the Thebæan Legion can be proved by irresistible testimony, then it has nothing to fear from these arguments; for none of them are so strong as to be wholly unanswerable.

For myself, next to the silence of *Lactantius*, I regard as the strongest of all arguments against the story of this legion, what the above-mentioned prefect of the Genevan library states to us, from Cæsar Barronius, (Adnot. ad diem 22, Septembr. Martyrologii Romani, p. 375,) respecting a *Maurice* among the Greeks, very similar to the Gallic commander of the Thebæan Legion. For the Greeks very devoutly observe the twenty-first day of February, in memory of a certain *Maurice*, a military tribune, whom the emperor Maximian commanded to be put to death on account of his Christian faith, at Apamea, in Syria, and with him seventy Christian soldiers. The *Acta* of this Maurice are given by the Jesuits of Antwerp, (Acta Sanctor. tom. iii. Februarii, p. 237,) and are undoubtedly of modern date, and of no historical value. Yet this *Maurice* was held by the Greeks of the *fifth* century to be a martyr of the highest order; as is attested by *Theodoret*, (Græcar. Affectionum L. viii. p. 607.) Now, it is contrary to all probability that there were two *Maurices*, both tribunes, and both put to death by the same emperor; the one in Syria and the other in Gaul, and at about the same time, and each with the soldiers under him. And therefore, it would seem that the story of Maurice and his companions must have been borrowed, either by the Latins from the Greeks, or by the Greeks from the Latins. But *Theodoret*, above cited, affords objections to our supposing the Greeks received the story from the Latins; and therefore it is most probable that the Latins transferred the Maurice of the Greeks from Syria to Gaul, and augmented and embellished his history with many fables, invented doubtless for the sake of gain. Yet I will not strongly object if some should conjecture, perhaps, that something actually occurred [p. 571.] in the Valais, or near the Leman Lake, which afforded occasion for the perpetration of this fraud, by some priest desirous to procure sustenance and wealth from the credulity of the people. Perhaps Maximian, while marching his army into Gaul, actually ordered a few of his soldiers, who refused to sacrifice to the gods for the success of the war, to suffer the penalty of their constancy. Perhaps, soon afterwards, a little chapel was erected in memory of those holy soldiers, on the spot where they were slain; for such was the custom of that age. But as that little chapel had not sufficient fame and celebrity to render it very lucrative to its guardians, they, in order to allure people thither, and thus enrich their domicile, expanded the brief history of its humble origin, and summoning to their aid the *Maurice* of the Greeks and his military companions, they represented *Maximian* as slaughtering a whole legion in the Valais. And the multitude of human bones in those parts afforded support to the fable. For, those familiar with ancient history know, that great battles were formerly fought in that part of Gaul, and many thousand persons slain; so that the ground, where now is seen the splendid and prosperous monastery of St. *Maurice*, was formerly rich in dead corpses.

(2) This is attested by *Eusebius*, (Hist. Eccles. L. viii. c. 1, p. 292, c. 4, p. 295; and in the end of the book, p. 317.) So learned men long since observed; nor can there be any doubt of it. But as to the author of this first persecution of the soldiers and officials of the palace, some doubts have arisen in my mind, while comparing *Eusebius* with *Lactantius;* which, I am surprised, have not occurred to the learned. *Eusebius* clearly represents, that before Diocletian had made any decrees against the Christians, *Maximian Galerius* persecuted the soldiers and servants of the palace. But Lactantius, (de Mortibus persequutor. c. 10, p. 85, &c.) although he inveighs vehemently against the cruelty of Maximian in other instances, and charges him with extraordinary zeal for exterminating the Christians, yet is entirely silent as to this crime of Maximian; and he tells us, on the contrary, that *Diocletian* first assailed the soldiers and officials of the palace, but without shedding blood. He represents *Diocletian* as being then in the East, and as searching in the livers of beasts which he had slain, to obtain auguries of future events. But some of his ministers who were standing by, being Christians, made the sign of the cross on their foreheads: *quo facto, fugatis dæmonibus, sacra turbata sunt.* The soothsayers repeated their sacrifices several times, but in vain; they could not discover the customary appearances on the entrails of the victims. At length the chief soothsayer declared, *non respondere sacra, quod rebus divinis profani homines* (namely, Christians) *interessent.* Then Diocletian, in a rage, ordered all the persons in the palace to offer sacrifices, and such as refused were to be scourged. And by letters addressed to their commanders, *milites ad nefanda sacrificia cogi præcepit, ut qui non paruissent, militia solverentur.* He adds: *Hactenus furor ejus et ira processit, nec amplius quidquam contra legem* [p. 572.] *aut religionem Dei fecit.* Neither was he afterwards disposed to go farther. For when, after some years, *Maximian* wished to have public edicts of a bloody character enacted against the Christians, he refused, and said: *Satis esse, si palatinos tantum et milites ab ea religione prohiberet.* (c. 11, p. 99, ed. Bauldrian.) Whether, therefore, this first light and moderate persecution of soldiers and officials, which preceded the great Diocletian persecution that commenced in the third year of the following century, is to be attributed to *Diocletian* or *Maximian*, appears to be uncertain, because of the disagreement of the principal authorities on the subject. Those who would reconcile these disagreeing statements, may say that both emperors committed the same fault, and assailed

their soldiers and palace servants at the same time; *Diocletian* in the East, and *Maximian* in Illyricum, which was the province under *his* jurisdiction. And there is, I confess, a shade of difference between the military persecution described by *Eusebius*, and that which is mentioned by *Lactantius*, which might seem to make them distinct from each other. *Lactantius* says, that *Diocletian* punished no one capitally; but *Eusebius* represents some as being put to death by *Maximian*. In fact, I do not look upon this conjecture with contempt. Yet, not to dwell on the improbability that the two emperors, when far separated from each other, should, at the same time, commit the same outrage; what could have induced *Lactantius* to state the crime of *Diocletian*, and to omit the similar crime of *Maximian*, on whom he at other times charges all the evils brought by Diocletian on the Christians? If you say he was ignorant of the fact; I answer, *first*, this is altogether incredible: and, *secondly*, I ask, how could *Eusebius*, a man not less well informed respecting the events of those times, than was the author of the treatise *de Mortibus Persequutorum*, and who represents the first outrage as that of *Maximian*,—how could he be ignorant that *Diocletian* committed the same outrage?—Another method of removing the difficulty seems to be intimated by *Lactantius* himself, in his *Institutiones Divinæ*, (L. iv. c. 27, p. 546, ed. Bünemann.) In treating of the interruption of the sacred rites of the haruspices by the Christians crossing their foreheads, he speaks as if not *Diocletian* solely, but also *Maximian*, were offering those sacrifices; for he speaks of (*Domini*) *lords*, in the plural, as being present: Quum enim quidam ministrorum e cultoribus Dei sacrificantibus *Dominis* assisterent, imposito frontibus signo, deos *illorum* fugaverunt. And, a little after: Aruspices adegerunt *Principes* suos in furorem, ut expugnarent Dei templum. Now if, as these words seem to imply, *Diocletian* and *Maximian* were together, and both united in the sacrifices, then neither *Lactantius* nor *Eusebius* is wholly wrong; but each has erred, by attributing an act of the two emperors to only one or the other of them. But from adopting this opinion, we are withheld by *Lactantius* himself, (de Mortibus Persequutor. c. 10, near the end,) where [p. 573.] he not obscurely shows, that the emperors were in different places at the time when Diocletian was enraged at the Christians for interrupting his religious rites. And why, I ask, if Maximian was then with Diocletian, does he not mention his name, since he wished to make his villanies as notorious as possible? Besides, every body knows, the plural number is often used instead of the singular, especially by those who, like Lactantius, speak or write in a rhetorical manner. In short, that the great persecution which the Christians suffered under Diocletian in the subsequent century, commenced with this slight preclude at the close of this century, and was hurtful only to the soldiers and the residents in the palace, can admit of no question; but against the supposition of a twofold prelude, the one in the East and the other in the West, both *Eusebius* and *Lactantius* stand equally opposed, for each of them mentions but one; and, whether *Diocletian* or *Maximian* commenced the tragedy, remains in uncertainty.—I will subjoin a few remarks on the motive which, according to Lactantius, induced Diocletian to maltreat the Christian soldiers and officials of the palace. I cannot doubt that something of the kind narrated did occur; but that the Christians, by crossing their foreheads, put demons to flight, and disturbed the emperor's divination, I cannot easily believe. The soothsaying art, we know, was a deception, invented to impose on the common people; and this was well understood by the wiser among the Romans, as appears from *Cicero's* second Book *de Divinatione.* We therefore suppose that the crafty soothsayers, who were watching for an opportunity to bring down great evil upon the Christians, pretended that they could not sacrifice successfully, on account of the presence of Christians, aiming to exasperate the feelings of the superstitious emperor; and the design succeeded. But the Christians, who supposed that the evil spirit enacted all the frauds of the priests, had a belief in divination; which, however, they could not have had, if they had consulted their reason.

(3) Respecting the prosperous state of the Christians, before the commencement of the Diocletian persecution in the year 303, *Eusebius* treats at some length, (Hist. Eccles. L. viii. p. 291.) He says, the emperors showed great kindness to the Christians; committed the government of provinces to some of them; allowed their domestics, with their children and servants, full liberty to profess the Christian religion; and even seemed to have peculiar affection for their Christian attendants and servants. The governors of provinces also, and the magistrates, paid great respect to the bishops. And hence, the Christian community daily received much enlargement, and churches were built in the several cities: neither could the calumnies and artifices of the ill-disposed disturb their tranquillity. But at the same time Eusebius freely acknowledges, with grief, that the Christians in the enjoyment of liberty fell into licentiousness and great vices; they had internal broils and contests, congregation with congregation, and prelates with prelates; frauds and dissimulation also, reached a very high pitch; neither did that moderate chastisement [p. 574.] of the soldiers correct these vices; but rather the Christians waxed worse and worse: the pastors disregarded the rules of religion in their mutual contests, affected the despotism of princes, and did various things unbecoming their character. These facts should be borne in mind, if we would justly appreciate the causes of the violent persecution soon after, under Diocletian. For the Christians, by their imprudent conduct, put weapons into the hands of their adversaries. For who can doubt, that the friends of the gods took occasion, from the vices and the broils of the Christians, to instil into the emperors, that the interests of the republic required the utter extirpation of so turbulent a sect; a sect that would not be quiet, but, abusing its prosperity, produced so great commotions in the state?

§ XXIII. **Constitution and Government of the Church.** The form or Constitution of the Christian church, which had been introduced in the preceding century, not only continued, for the most part, to exist in this century, but became confirmed and strengthened. Over the individual congregations of the larger cities, one person presided, with dignity and authority, entitled the *Bishop;* but he was allowed to decide nothing in private matters, without taking counsel with the *Presbyters;* and nothing in public matters pertaining to the whole church, without assembling and consulting the people.(1) All *Bishops,* as well as all *Presbyters,* were perfectly equal in rank and authority; yet, for keeping up the consociation of the churches, the Bishop who governed the congregation in the principal city of a province, was entitled to some precedence and honór above the others. And the necessity for this regulation became greater, as councils were more frequently called together throughout the Christian commonwealth, in which the representatives of the churches deliberated and established rules for the common welfare of the whole province, or of several provinces. The cause which led one Bishop in a province to have a sort of preëminence over the rest, also procured a primacy and some authority for the Bishops of the primary cities in Asia, Africa, and Europe; among whom, unquestionably, the first place was assigned to the Bishop of the city of Rome. But as for any common judge of the whole church, or a Bishop of Bishops, performing the functions of a vicegerent of Christ, those times knew nothing of it.(2) To the *Deacons,* in the larger and more opulent churches, there were [p. 575.] added functionaries of lower rank, *Subdeacons, Acolythists, Janitors, Lectors,* and *Exorcists;* in consequence, as I apprehend, of the fastidiousness and pride of the *Deacons,* who, finding themselves in greater affluence, were unwilling to discharge the humble offices which they had previously never declined.(3)

(1) Respecting the authority and rights of *presbyters* in this century, declarations of the ancients have been collected in abundance, by David *Blondell,* in his *Apologia pro sententia Hieronymi de episcopis et presbyteris,* (p. 136, &c.) and many more, by Claud. *Fonteius,* (the assumed name of a celebrated theologian of the Parisian school, James *Boileau,*) in his treatise, *de antiquo jure presbyterorum in regimine ecclesiastico,* (Taurini, 1676, 12mo.) But there is one witness who may be a substitute for all, namely *Cyprian,* one of the most strenuous vindicators of the high rank and authority of bishops. Although he lays claim to the highest distinction and prerogative, especially when heated by conflict with those who resist his pleasure, yet he freely acknowledges in many passages of his Epistles, that he could decide no great question without consulting the clergy and presbyters. And although he sometimes acts inconsistently with his principles, and disregards the rights and prerogatives of the people, yet when properly master of himself, and more obedient to the law of

right than to self-will, he does not fail to show, that, in the government of the church, and in ecclesiastical jurisdiction, by no means the least part belongs to the common people. To save the reader from the trouble of searching them out, I will cite some passages to this purpose, so that my assertions may not appear unsupported. To his presbyters and Deacons he thus writes, (Ep. v. p. 11; al. Ep. xiv. c. 4): Ad id vero, quod scripserunt mihi compresbyteri nostri Donatus et Fortunatus, Novatus et Gordius, *solus rescribere nihil potui, quando a primordio episcopatus mei statuerim nihil sine consilio vestro,* (i. e., of the presbyters and deacons,) *et sine consensu plebis mea privatim sententia gerere.* Sed cum ad vos per Dei gratiam venero, tunc de iis, quæ vel gesta sunt vel gerenda, *sicut honor mutuus poscit, in commune tractabimus.* Here Cyprian expresses himself with precision; for he says he *ought*, in the more important cases, to ask the (*consilium*) *advice* of the presbyters and deacons; but that only the (*consensus*) *consent* of the people was requisite. The bishop, therefore, deliberated on business matters with the presbyters, and not with the people; and the course which he and the clergy deemed suitable, was proposed to the people assembled for the purpose, and they either approved or rejected it. For the common people could either sanction or annul; they were not obliged to ratify, whatever the bishop and his counsellors had decided upon. A similar passage occurs in Epistle xiii. (p. 23, al. Ep. xix. ad Presbyteros et Diaconos, c. 2.) Hoc et verecundiæ *et disciplinæ* et vitæ ipsi omnium nostrum *convenit, ut Præpositi cum clero convenientes, præsente etiam stantium plebe, quibus et ipsis pro fide et timore suo honor habendus est, disponere omnia consilii communis religione possimus.* Being requested by the presbyters and [p. 576.] deacons to decide the case of two deacons and an acolythist, who, having lapsed, again returned to the church, he replies most explicitly, (Ep. xxviii. p. 39; al. Ep. xxxiv. ad presbyt. et Diaconos, c. 4): Desiderastis quoque, ut de Philumeno et Fortunato hypodiaconis et Favorino Acolytho, qui medio tempore recesserunt, et nunc venerunt, quid mihi videatur, rescribam. *Cui rei non potui me solum judicem dare, cum multi adhuc de clero absentes sint,* nec locum suum vel sero repetendum putaverunt, *et hæc singulorum tractanda sit et limanda plenius ratio, non tantum cum collegis meis, sed et cum plebe ipsa universa.* When he had created a lector and a subdeacon, without consulting the presbyters, he excuses the deed to his clergy on the ground of necessity, (Ep. xxiv. p. 33; al Ep. xxix. ad Presbyt. et Diacon.): Fecisse me autem sciatis lectorem Saturum et hypodiaconum Optatum confessorem, *quos jam pridem communi consilio clero proximos feceramus.* - - Nihil ergo a me absentibus vobis *novum* factum est: sed *quod jam pridem communi consilio omnium nostrum cœperat, necessitate urgente, promotum est.* Cyprian then, by his own confession, would have done something (*novum*) *new*, and contrary to former usage, if he had constituted even the lowest officials of the church, lectors and subdeacons, without consulting the presbyters. There are examples, I am aware, of Cyprian's creating presbyters and lectors, without the consent of the clergy and people; e. g. *Numidicus*, whom he created a presbyter, (Ep. xxxv. p. 48; al. Ep. xl.) and *Celerinus* and *Aurelius*, and perhaps others, whom he made lectors with the concurrence of only a few of the clergy, (Ep. xxxiii. et xxxiv.

p. 46, &c.; al. Ep. xxxviii. et xxxix.) But all these were *Confessors*, and had given proofs of their constancy and fortitude. And *Confessors* enjoyed this prerogative in the ancient church, that they seemed to be elected and designated for the sacred office, as it were, by God himself; and therefore they might be received into the sacred order, by the bishop alone, without the suffrages of the clergy and the people. And so, in this act, the ancient usages were not violated, but rather followed out. The correctness of these statements will be seen by such as read those Epistles of Cyprian to his presbyters and people, in which he relates the admission of these men to offices, or, in the phraseology of *Tertullian*, their (*Collectio in Clerum*) enrollment among the clergy. The Epistle which relates to Aurelius, (Epist. xxxiii. al. xxxviii. ad clerum et ad plebem,) commences thus: Cyprianus presbyteris et diaconis et plebi universæ salutem! In ordinationibus clericorum, fratres carissimi, solemus vos ante consulere et mores et merita singulorum communi consilio ponderare. (Here we have the common and ordinary usage; the extraordinary usage, or the prerogative, so to speak, of Confessors, next follows.) *Sed expectanda non sunt testimonia humana, cum præcedunt divina suffragia;* that is, the suffrages of the clergy and people are not necessary in the case of *Confessors*, whom God has declared worthy of the sacred office, by the grace [p. 577.] which he has given them. And yet Cyprian had not acted alone in this case, but in conjunction with some presbyters; for he adds, (ibid, c. 2): Hunc igitur, fratres dilectissimi, *a me et a collegis, qui præsentes aderant*, ordinatum sciatis. In like manner he speaks of *Celerinus* the lector, (Epist. xxxiv. p. 47; al. Ep. xxxix. c. 1): *Ego et collegæ mei, qui præsentes aderant*, referrimus ad vos, Celerinum fratrem nostrum virtutibus, pariter et moribus gloriosum clero nostro, *non humana suffragatione*, (i. e. not by the suffrages of the clergy and people,) *sed divina dignatione* (which God manifested, by giving him fortitude under tortures,) *conjunctum*. After a sentence or two, Cyprian adds: *Nec fas fuerat, nec decebat sine honore ecclesiastico esse, quem sic Dominus honoravit cœlestis gloriæ dignitate.* Those unacquainted with ancient customs and opinions, may not know the meaning of this last citation; and the annotators on Cyprian pass it over, as they do many things which need to be explained by reference to ancient usages. I will therefore explain how God *cœlestis gloriae dignitate honoraverit Celerinum*, an illustrious Confessor, who for nineteen days had been under torture, and bore in his body many scars of his wounds. The souls of Martyrs and Confessors, on leaving the body, were supposed to ascend immediately to glory, but not so the souls of other Christians, which had to await the final advent of the Judge, in a certain intermediate state. See, among others, Tertullian, (de Anima, c. 55, p. 353, &c.) where he says: Nullis romphæa paradisi janatrix cedit, nisi qui in Christo decesserit (the Martyrs,) non in Adam? Nova mors pro Deo, *et extraordinaria pro Christo*, alio et privato excipitur hospitio. Habes etiam de paradiso a nobis libellum, quo constituimus, *omnem animam* (leaving the body by a natural death,) *apud inferos* (in an intermediate place,) *sequestrari in diem Domini.* He therefore who, by God's assistance, had been superior to tortures, obtained a title to celestial glory, and he was by God publicly *honored with that distinction.* Cyprian then means to say: That to the man whom God has declared an heir of celestial glory, and to whom he has assigned a place among the glorified souls immediately after death, ought to be assigned a place among the leaders and ministers of the church militant.—The same account is given by *Cyprian*, in the case of Numidicus, a distinguished Confessor, whom he had received among the presbyters, without the consent of the clergy and people, (Ep. xxxv. p. 49; al. Ep. xl.): Nam admonitos nos et instructos sciatis, *dignatione divina*, (this is explained above,) ut Numidicus presbyter adscribatur presbyterorum Carthaginensium numero et nobiscum sedeat in clero, luce clarissima confessionis illustris. We here learn the ground of the custom, in the ancient church, of receiving into the sacred order *Confessors*, though unlearned and not duly qualified. They reasoned thus: Confessors, by the resolution and firmness of their minds in confronting tortures and death, have obtained through grace a title to celestial felicity, which [p. 578.] other Christians have not; it is therefore right and proper, that those to whom God has vouchsafed so great honor, should also be honored by the church, and be elevated above other Christians. Neither is it necessary that the clergy and people should, as in other cases, approve of their admission to the rank of fathers of the church. The divine suffrage is sufficient; and the bishop, on ascertaining that fact, may proceed, without a consultation with the clergy and people, to admit them to the sacred order.

But we return from a digression. There is no passage in *Cyprian* which more clearly demonstrates, that the clergy and the people shared with the bishop the power of governing the church, than one in his 27th Epistle, (p. 37, 38; al. Epist. xxxiii. c. 1.); and I wonder that it should escape the attention of the learned, who have treated of this subject. The Epistle commences thus: Dominus noster, cujus præcepta et monita observare debemus, episcopi honorem et ecclesiæ suæ rationem disponens in evangelio loquitur et dicit Petro: Ego tibi dico, quia tu es Petrus, et super istam petram aedificabo ecclesiam meam, et portæ inferorum non vincent eam, &c. - - - Inde per temporum et successionum vices episcoporum ordinatio et ecclesiæ ratio decurrit, ut *ecclesia super episcopos constituatur, et omnis actus ecclesiæ per eosdem præpositos gubernetur.* Cum hoc itaque *divina lege fundatum sit*, miror, quosdam audaci temeritate sic mihi scribere voluisse, ut ecclesiæ nomine litteras facerent, *quando ecclesia in episcopo et clero et in omnibus stantibus sit constituta.* The reasoning of *Cyprian* in this passage deserves contempt; for no one can suppose, with him, that the words of Christ to Peter here cited, define the rights of the church and of the bishops. The doctrines, however, which he professes, deserve regard; for, *First*, he most explicitly declares the church to be *super episcopos constitutam*, or, to be superior to the bishops; from which it follows, that supreme power in ecclesiastical affairs is vested in the church; and that the bishop, without the church, can decide and determine nothing. *Secondly*, he tells us what he would have us understand by the word *church*: and affirms that to the church belong, not merely the clergy, but also *omnes stantes*, that is, the whole multitude of persons who have not, by any of the greater sins, nor by defection from Christianity, merited exclusion from the number of the brethren, and therefore continue stedfast in the faith. *Thirdly*, he teaches that *actum omnem ecclesiæ gubernari ab episcopo*, or that the biohop presides in the meetings of the church, states the subjects to be discussed, and collects the suffrages or opinions given. More than this cannot be here intended by the word *gubernari*, because he had declared the church to be the greater and superior to the bishop. For the church would be the lesser and inferior to the bishop, if *gubernare* here meant to prescribe the decisions and demand an approbation of the bishop's own personal judgment. The church must necessarily be free to [p. 579.] act its own pleasure, if it be true, that it has more power and authority than the bishop. *Lastly*, he decides that all these are the precepts of Christ, or *divina lege fundata:* with what truth he could so affirm need not be inquired; it is sufficient that he thought it to be so. From this language therefore the learned men may correct their views, who attempt to persuade us that Cyprian, whenever he calls the clergy and people to his aid, and associates himself with them, does so, not in obedience to law and right, but only from modesty and a regard for prudence. He himself denies the truth of this opinion, and bids us believe, that the bishop who shall decide any matter of much importance without consulting the clergy and people, will violate a mandate and law of our Savior.

(2) So numerous and strong are the testimonies to the liberty and equality of the Christian churches in this century, adduced long since by learned men, in the great controversy respecting the primacy of the Roman bishop, that it would seem the persons who maintain that one church had power and a sort of jurisdiction over the rest, must be chargeable with a greater devotion to their sect and to their early imbibed opinions, than to the truth. Those who contend that in this century, as well as in subsequent times, all the European churches were subject to the bishop of Rome, think they find great support for their opinion in the writings of *Cyprian;* which may seem very strange to the impartial judges of the subject, who know, that from this same writer the defenders of the opposite opinion derive their principal arguments in support of the opinion that the church, in this century, recognized no visible head or supreme bishop. One of two things must be true; either one or the other of the contending parties must have misinterpreted Cyprian, or Cyprian is not consistent with himself, and had very obscure and indeterminate ideas respecting the nature of the church. I will exhibit the arguments on both sides, and then give my own judgment in the matter. *First:* The still extant Epistles of *Cyprian* to Cornelius, Lucius, and Stephen, bishops of Rome, and also some Epistles of Cornelius to Cyprian, are written in a manner that makes it evident that no one of them even thought of any difference as to jurisdiction, rank, and station among them. In that age, as well as in this, when inferiors wrote to their superiors, or superiors to their inferiors, they distinguished themselves from the persons they addressed, by certain titles and modes of expression; although the propensity for adulation and for arrogance had not then reached the height to which it subsequently arose. But nothing of this kind can you discover in the Epistles I have mentioned. *Cyprian* addresses the Romish bishops in the same style as he addresses other bishops, and calls them simply (*fratres et collegas*) *Brothers* and *Colleagues;* and *Cornelius* addresses Cyprian

in the same style, and drops not a syllable which can be considered as indicative of any jurisdiction or authority. Indeed, *Cyprian* is himself the most assuming, and not only reproves Stephen severely for claiming some dignity and power, but also most freely censures Cornelius, when he thought him in error, and recalls him to his duty. I well recollect, that *Peter* de *Marca*, (de concordia sacerdotii et imperii, L. vii. c. 1, p. 988,) as well as many [p. 580.] others, attempts to prove from Cyprian's Epistle to Stephen, concerning Marcian, bishop of Arles, (Epist. lxvii. p. 115; al. Ep. lxviii. c. 2,) that Cyprian acknowledged the primacy of Stephen in the church; for, in this Epistle, Cyprian exhorts Stephen "*to write in the fullest manner to the bishops of both Gauls, that they should no longer suffer Marcian, the friend of Novatian, to insult the college of bishops:*" from which the great *de Marca* infers, that Stephen had some jurisdiction over the bishops in Gaul. But Stephen *Baluze*, (in his notes on the passage, p. 488,) is more cautious, and concludes that *Cyprian* well knew "*that the defence of the canons was committed to the bishop of Rome;*" that is, this learned man interprets the passage according to the views of the Gallican church. But I will leave it to all impartial persons to judge whether there is any force in such reasoning as this: Cyprian admonishes Stephen to write to the bishops of Gaul about excluding Marcian; therefore Cyprian believed that Stephen had some jurisdiction over the Gallic bishops. Who does not know, that even we ourselves are accustomed every day to exhort those over whom we have no kind of authority or power?

Secondly: Cyprian's contest with the Roman bishop Stephen, respecting the baptisms of heretics, which we have stated above, has vast weight, in proof that nobody, in that age, ascribed to the Romish prelate the honor of being supreme judge in all religious controversies. Indeed, those on the opposite side cannot deny this; and therefore they resort to every expedient to cast this great contest into the shade. *Cyprian*, having assembled several bishops, decided with them, that all heretics coming over to the church, ought to be again baptized; and this decision of his council he transcribed and sent to the Roman Stephen, not on account of any official relation to him, or any law requiring it, but solely as a matter of courtesy. He says (Epist. lxxii. p. 129, c. 4,): Haec ad conscientiam tuam, frater carissime, et pro honore communi et pro simplici dilectione pertulimus. *Stephen* disapproved this decision, and answered Cyprian haughtily: the latter, despising his menaces, held firmly to the decision, and, assembling a still larger council, fortified it with new and stronger supports. Stephen, thus situated, did not, as is commonly stated, cast *Cyprian* out of the church, but only declared him unworthy of *his* communion. *Cyprian* contemned this ebullition of wrath; and the other bishops felt very indignant at it. These were most certainly the facts; and who that reads or hears them, can bring himself to believe that the Roman pontiff or bishop then possessed any supreme power or sovereignty? Some perhaps will say, that Cyprian did wrong, and being heated by passion, overstepped the boundaries of respect due to the Roman bishop. But this is a hasty and futile objection. For if Cyprian had done any thing inconsistent with his duty, he would have been reproved and deserted by the other bishops. They, however, did not think that Cyprian had done wrong, but that *Stephen* was in fault. And this seems to put it beyond [p. 581.] all controversy, that if perhaps, some priority in honer, yet none in power or jurisdiction was then conceded to the Romish prelate.

Thirdly: The writings and acts of *Cyprian* while this contest was going on, afford also very clear testimony on this subject. In his 71st Epistle, (ad Quintum, p. 127, c. 3,) he denies that *Peter* had any primacy of authority: Nam nec *Petrus*, quem primum Dominus elegit, et super quem aédificavit ecclesiam suam, - - - vindicavit sibi aliquid insolenter aut arroganter assumsit, ut diceret, *se primatum tenere*, et obtemperari a novellis et posteris sibi oportere. If then, according to Cyprian, *Peter* himself held no primacy, and neither could enact any inviolable laws, nor wished to do it, how could he ascribe any primacy to Peter's successor, so much his inferior? In his 73d Epistle, (p. 137, c. 26, and elsewhere,) he teaches, that *all bishops* are independent, and subject to the power of no one: *Unusquisque episcoporum, quod putat, faciat, habens arbitrii sui liberam potestatem.* How very different is this declaration from the opinion of those who say, all bishops ought to be in subjection to the bishop of Rome? Still more clearly and fully does he express himself in his Address at the opening of the Concilium Cathaginense de hæreticis baptizandis, (p. 329): Neque enim quisquam nostrum episcopum se esse episcoporum constituit, aut tyrannico terrore ad obsequendi necessitatem collegas suos adigit, *quando habeat omnis episcopus pro licentia libertatis et potestatis suæ arbitrium proprium, tamque judicari ab alio non possit, quam nec ipse potest alterum judicare. Sed expectemus universi judicium Domini nostri Jesu Christi, qui unus et solus habet potestatem et præponendi nos in ecclesiæ suæ qubernatione et de actu nostri judicandi.* This language needs no interpreter.

I pass over other passages of similar import, and will add only one more, which is the more pertinent and forcible, because it occurs in an Epistle to the Roman bishop himself, Cornelius, (Epist. lv. p. 86; al. Ep. lix. c. 20): Nam cum statutum sit ab omnibus nobis, et æquum sit pariter ac justum, *ut uniuscujusque caussa illic audiatur, ubi est crimen admissum, et singulis pastoribus portio gregis sit adscripta, quam regat unusquisque et gubernat, rationem sui actus Domino redditurus*, oportet utique eos, quibus præsumus, non circumcursare, nec *episcoporum concordiam cohærentem - - collidere, sed agere illic caussam suam, ubi et accusatores habere et testes sui criminis possint;* nisi si paucis desperatis et perditis minor videtur esse auctoritas episcoporum in Africa constitutorum, qui jam de illis judicaverunt. Felicissimus and Fortunatus, two enemies of Cyprian, had gone to Rome, and implored the aid of Cornelius. *Cyprian* felt greatly troubled at this. He first wrote to Cornelius, reminding him that it had been established by the common consent of all the bishops, that every criminal should be tried where the crime had been committed. Now, from this it clearly appears, that all Christian bishops were on a level with each other, or [p. 582.] were equals as to power; and that no individual among them held the office of supreme judge. What follows will make this still more evident. For he says: (ii.) That to the bishops severally, portions of the flock of Christ were committed, to be governed by each bishop according to his own discretion and judgment only. (iii.) That no bishop had any judge, lord, or master, who could call him to account for his acts, except *Jesus Christ.* Therefore, (iv.) that a sentence passed by one bishop, cannot in any way be corrected or changed by the others. And he adds (v.) lastly, that the authority of the African bishops was not inferior to that of the Roman prelate; and that those who would account them inferior to him (*homines esse desperatos et perditos*) were men of a desperate and abandoned character.

But to these testimonies, so clear and unequivocal, the friends of the Roman pontiff oppose others, in which *Cyprian* himself seems to enervate what he had so often said respecting the equality of all bishops, and to attribute to the Romish prelate a sort of sovereignty and superior authority. For they observe, that in many passages Cyprian affirms: *Jesum Christum ecclesiam suam super Petrum originem unitatis et rationis fundasse.* I will cite only one passage of this kind, which occurs in Epistle lxxiii. (p. 131, c. 7): Nam *Petre* primum Dominus, super quem aedificavit ecclesiam, et unde unitatis originem instituit et ostendit, potestatem istam dedit, ut id solveretur in cœlis, quod ille solvisset in terris. Et post resurrectionem quoque ad Apostolos loquitur, &c. —Again, they urge, that on account of this dignity conferred on *Peter* by Christ, *Cyprian* (Epist. lv. p. 86; al. Ep. lix. c. 19,) calls the Romish church: *Petri cathedram atque ecclesiam principalem, unde unitas sacerdotalis orta est.*—But they especially urge a passage from his treatise *de Unitate Ecclesiæ*, (p. 195, &c., c. 4.) I will cite the passage as it stands in the edition of *Baluze;* but it is well known that the ancient copies disagree, and it is justly suspected, or rather proved, that zeal for the honor of the Romish church has induced some learned men in time past to corrupt and enlarge the passage to suit their own views and desires. Loquitur Dominus ad Petrum: Ego tibi dico, inquit, quia tu es Petrus, et super hanc petram aedificabo ecclesiam meam. - - Et iterum eidem post resurrectionem suam dicit: Pasce oves meas. Super illum unum aedificat ecclesiam suam, et illi pascendas mandat oves suas. Et quamvis Apostolis omnibus post resurrectionem suam *parem* potestatem tribuat, et dicat: Sicut misit me Pater, et ego mitto vos, accipite Spiritum sanctum - - tamen ut unitatem manifestaret, unitatis ejusdem originem ab uno incipientem sua auctoritate disposuit. *Hoc erant utique et ceteri Apostoli, quod fuit Petrus, pari consortio præditi et honoris et potestatis,* sed *exordium* ex unitate proficiscitur, et primatus Petro datur, ut una Christi ecclesia et cathedra una monstretur. - - Hanc ecclesiæ unitatem qui non tenet, tenere se fidem credit? Qui ecclesiæ renititur et resistit, qui cathedram Petri, super quem fundata [p. 583.] est ecclesia, deserit, in ecclesia se esse confidit? From these extracts, distinguished men think it can be proved, that *Cyprian* regarded the Roman bishop as presiding over the whole church, and represented him to be its common judge and legislator; and that this opinion was not held by *Cyprian* alone, but by that age, and by the whole church. Those who, in reply, would cut the matter short, may say: *First,* that *Cyprian* here states his own private opinion; but that there is no evidence to show, that the whole church thought as he did. Others indeed, in times subsequent to Cyprian, said nearly the same things; but they copied from him. For the influence of this bishop and martyr among Christians was immense, and his opinions were regarded by many as divine oracles. Yet *Cyprian*, as will not be denied, even by those who consider him a very great and holy man, had imbibed many futile, vain and superstitious notions, and also cherished some remarkable errors; and hence we ought to enquire, whether his opinion accords with the truth, or whether it should be placed among the errors which he indulged. If this dogma of his is to be estimated by the arguments and proofs which he adduces to support it, I fear it cannot be ranked with those which no man of sound mind can reject.—*Secondly:* Let it be considered, that Cyprian nowhere ascribes that *primacy* of which he speaks, to the Romish *bishop*, but to the Romish *church*. But the (*ecclesia*) *church*, as we have before shown, in *Cyprian's* estimation, was above or superior to the bishop, and consisted of the bishop and the clergy, and the whole multitude of the (*stantium*) the faithful, united. If then it were perfectly certain, as some learned men think it is, that Cyprian attributed to the Romish *church* a primacy over all churches, his opinion cannot by any means be transferred to the Romish *bishop* or pontiff; for his opinion will be precisely this: The entire Christian population of Rome, together with their clergy and bishop, have power over the universal church. But how wide is this from the opinion of those who think the Romish prelate sustains the office of Christ's vicegerent!

But, laying aside these answers, although they are not to be despised, let us come to close combat. The passages from *Cyprian*, cited on the side opposed to the Pontifical claims, beyond all controversy, contain these principles: All the bishops in the Christian church, have equal powers and prerogatives; none of them is under any other lord or judge, than Jesus Christ. And, the African bishops are in no respect inferior to the bishop of Rome. But the passages cited on the side of the defenders of the Pontiff, contain, according to their interpretation, the following doctrine: There is one bishop in the church, who rules over all the rest, namely, the bishop of Rome; and, therefore, the African bishops are inferior to the bishop of Rome, and ought to yield obedience to his commands and decrees. These two opinions, as is manifest, contradict each other. And, therefore, one of two things must be true; either Cyprian contra-
[p. 584.] dicts himself, and brings forward directly opposite opinions on different occasions; or the passages on one of the sides must be so explained and understood, as not to conflict, but to harmonize, with those on the other. Now let the learned men, who are so solicitous about the dignity of the Romish church and the supreme Pontiff, choose which side they please of this alternative. If they choose the first, and admit that *Cyprian* has advanced contradictory opinions, his authority is gone, and nothing can be proved or inferred from his declarations. For what credit or authority is due to the man, who talks absurdly and advocates opinions contradictory to each other? The latter part of the alternative therefore must be tried, and the passages of one sort must be so explained that they will accord or harmonise with the others. Now, by universal consent, it is an established rule, that light controls and illumines darkness; that is, the obscure and ambiguous passages of a book, are to be elucidated and explained by the passages which are clear and perspicuous: for it would be preposterous to guage and measure the import of passages in which there was

no obscurity or ambiguity, by other passages which are enigmatical and admit of many explanations. Now if this rule is to be applied in the present case, as undoubtedly it should be, I think all will agree, that the passages of Cyprian which speak of the unity of the church, its being founded on Peter, and the primacy of the Romish see, must be understood and explained in such a way as not to conflict with the passages which affirm the parity and independence of all bishops: for the latter passages are clear and perspicuous, and will not admit of various interpretations; but the former, relative to the unity, &c. though of frequent occurrence, are not perspicuous, and will admit of diverse explanations. According to the rules of correct reasoning, then, we cannot suppose that Cyprian ascribed to the Romish church a sort of primacy of power, and a sort of *civil unity* of the universal church, a unity as to authority and control, like that in states or republics, which are governed by the will of one man. For such a primacy and such a *unity* would subvert and destroy that independence and equality of all the bishops, which he most strenuously maintains. On the contrary, in our judgment, it must have been, that the holy man revolved in his mind such a *unity* of the church, as would accord with his belief of the equal rights of all bishops; and such a *primacy* of the Romish church, as would comport with his decision, *That the African bishops are not inferior to the bishops of Rome, and that what they decree, cannot be reversed or altered, either by the Roman bishop, or by all the other bishops ;* which decision Cyprian states in almost these very terms.

If any one should here ask for a correct explanation of this *primacy* and this *unity* as maintained by Cyprian, I will readily answer, respecting the *primacy.* Among all the Christian churches, Cyprian assigned the *first place* to the Romish church; for reasons, indeed, that are very weak and futile, yet such as satisfied *him.* Whether this was his private opinion, or whether he expresses the general views of the church, is another question, which I shall leave untouched. And yet I will not deny, that from the time the Christians embraced the idea that the Christian church had in some sort the form of a body politic, the commencement or origin of the combination was always traced to the [p. 585.] Romish church. But, as to the *unity* which Cyprian attributed to the church, and which he says originated from the Romish church, it is not so easy to answer. And I suspect, that Cyprian himself would have felt himself embarrassed, if he had been called upon to explain the nature of this unity in clear and definite terms. For, on this subject, which he represents as being of very great importance, he yet speaks so vaguely and with so little uniformity, that we can readily perceive, he had no very distinct conception of it in his own mind. Those are exceedingly mistaken, who suppose that Cyprian, Tertullian, and the other Christian writers of that age, clearly understood whatever they taught and inculcated with great earnestness: so far from it, they annex different ideas to the same terms, as the subject and convenience seem to call for them; which is evidence, that their minds needed light, and that they entertained vague and indeterminate notions. And yet this *unity* of the church, which Cyprian so highly extols, and the commencement of which he places in the Romish church, *may* be elucidated, in some sort, provided we may, from a part of the

unity, judge of the whole. That unity, which ought to prevail in the universal church, actually existed, and ought to exist, in the African church, over which Cyprian presided; as he tells us repeatedly, and it cannot be questioned. Therefore, from the *unity* in the African church, we may learn what kind of unity Cyprian supposed to exist in the universal church. Now the African bishops were upon a footing of perfect equality, as to power and jurisdiction: each could sanction and establish what he deemed salutary and proper in his own church, without being accountable for his acts to any one save Jesus Christ. This we learn from the lips of *Cyprian* himself. And yet there was a *primacy* in this same church, composed as it was of members all equal; and that primacy was in the church of Carthage. Moreover this *primacy* was necessary, because *unity* was necessary in the African church. As, therefore, the *sacerdotal unity* in the universal church, emanated from the church of Rome, so in the African, it originated from the church of Carthage. That *unity*, with the *primacy* on which it was based, was no obstacle to the parity, and equality in powers, of the bishops; and, on the other hand, the equality of the bishops was no obstruction to the *primacy* and the *unity*. All that this *unity* required, was, that all the bishops in the province of Africa, should concede the first place in point of rank, to the bishop of Carthage: that on subjects of graver moment, they should communicate with him, and ask his opinion; but that they should follow that opinion was not necessary; that they should go to the conventions or councils held on great questions, at the summons of the primate; and, lastly, that they should observe and follow out what was decided upon by common consent in those councils. The manner of proceeding in these councils, we learn distinctly from the *Acta magni Concilii Carthaginensis de baptizandis haereticis*, in the Works of *Cyprian*, p. 329. The primate, or head of the *unity*, stated the business for which they were assembled, and gave his colleagues the fullest liberty to express their opinions. His own opinion was given last of all. If they disagreed, and the subject did not pertain to an essential point of reli-
[p. 586.] gion, each bishop was at liberty to follow his own judgment; as the oration of *Cyprian*, at the opening of that council, puts beyond all controversy. Such a *unity*, and such a *primacy* in the universal church, *Cyprian* conceived of: nor could he have conceived of any other, unless we would make the holy man to be totally ignorant of his own sentiments and meaning. That is, he conceived that all bishops ought to be so connected with the Romish church, as to concede to it the same rank which *Peter* had among the Apostles, namely, the first rank; and so as to recur to it in doubtful cases of great moment, reserving to themselves, however, the right of dissenting from its judgment, but still remaining in its communion if practicable. If he had any thing more than this in his mind, and I will not affirm positively that he had not, yet this, at least, is evident, beyond all question, that he contemplated nothing of such a nature as would invest the Romish prelate with any sovereignty or power over the whole church.

Into this my opinion, I am confident all those will come, who shall attentively consider what Cyprian has said respecting the *unity* of the church, and the consequent *primacy* of the Romish church. The whole subject may be comprehended in the following propositions: the truth or falsehood of which I leave out of consideration. (I) Jesus Christ founded his church on Peter. Yet (II) He did not give to Peter any power over the other Apostles, or any sovereignty and primacy of jurisdiction over them. But (III) after His resurrection, he conferred the same power on all the Apostles. (IV.) On Peter, however, he conferred this power first, and afterwards on the Apostles; in order to indicate that, *unitatis originem ab uno incipere debere.* I choose to use *Cyprian's* words rather than my own: for I must confess, I am unable to comprehend perfectly the force of his reasoning, or the meaning of his language. (V.) *Omnes igitur Apostoli,* says Cyprian himself, *id erant, quod Petrus fuit, pari consortio præditi et honoris et potestatis.* We may here observe, that Cyprian does not leave to Peter even a primacy of *honor* or rank. (VI) *At quoniam exordium ab unitate proficiscitur, ideo primatus* (but of what sort? Having very clearly divested Peter of any *primacy of power or honor,* what primacy could he leave to him? If a man is not superior to others either in *honor* or in *power,* in what respects can he be superior to them?) *Petro datus est, ut una Christi ecclesia et cathedra una monstretur.* Let others explain this: I will not attempt it. (VII) The Romish bishop represents Peter; the other bishops represent the Apostles. (VIII) The respect, therefore, which the other Apostles paid to Peter, must the bishops show to the Romish prelate. (IX) But Peter was not superior to the other Apostles, either in power or in honor: therefore, also, all the bishops, the successors of the apostles, are not inferior to Peter's successor, neither in power nor in honor. (X) Yet as Christ made Peter the beginning and source of the church's unity, therefore the other apostles, although perfectly his equals, owed him some honor as being the source of the church's unity. And of course, the same thing is [p. 587.] incumbent on the bishops, towards the successor of Peter. (XI) Consequently, the Romish church is the principal church, and from it flowed the *sacerdotal unity,* namely, through Peter. (XII) Therefore whoever separates himself from the chair of Peter, tears himself from *the church,* which is *one,* and has the source of its unity in the church of Rome. Yet, according to Cyprian's views, those do not forsake the chair of Peter, who reject the decisions and decrees of the Romish bishop, and think differently from him in religious matters. For he himself had rejected the decision of Stephen respecting the baptisms of heretics; and had rebuked, not only Stephen, but also Cornelius; and yet he had not forsaken the chair of Peter, but remained still in the church's unity.—Those who are able, may digest and comprehend all this: it is sufficient for my purpose, that *Cyprian* has so stated, and nearly the whole in the very words now given. And how greatly these propositions differ from the opinion of those writers, who would make the Roman bishop the *judge* and *legislator* of the universal church, must be obvious to every one.

(3) Yet I will not contend, if any persons are disposed to offer a more honorable reason for the creation of those minor officers, and should say, perhaps, that they were devised, in order that the candidates for holy orders might go through a sort of preparation and trial of their fitness for the office of deacons. To the office of a deacon, and especially in the African church, much

dignity and honor were attached in this century. It might therefore be thought hazardous, to receive aspirants to this office, without some previous trial of their fitness.

§ XXIV. **The Prerogatives and Powers of the Bishops much enlarged.** Although the ancient and venerable form of church government which was sanctioned by the Apostles, might seem in general to remain undisturbed, yet it was gradually deflected more and more from the ancient model, and, in the larger congregations especially, assumed the nature of a monarchical government. For, as is common in human affairs, the bishops, who presided over the congregations, arrogated to themselves much more dignity and authority than they had before possessed, and the ancient rights, not only of the people but also of the presbyters, they first abridged, and then wholly subverted, directing all the affairs of their communities according to their own pleasure. And, lest this should appear to be done rashly and wrongfully, they devised and set forth new doctrines respecting the church and the office and authority of bishops, which they seem not to have fully understood themselves. In this business, *Cyprian* was an example to his brethren in this century; for, being himself a bishop, and, as cannot be denied, of an aspiring and ambitious disposition, he contended most strenuously for the [p. 588.] honor and the power of bishops, and, lest those prerogatives, which he thought belonged to them, should in any measure be wrested from them, he labored to establish them on stable and immoveable foundations. And, as the influence of this man, both while he lived and after his decease, was very remarkable, and such that he might almost be called the common master and guide, his inventions for establishing the dignity and power of bishops, without any difficulty, spread through the church universal, and were received with implicit faith.(1)

(1) Having some knowledge of the course of human affairs, I am neither greatly surprised, nor indignant, when I see the progress of episcopal power and dignity in the ancient church, and contemplate the rights of the people first, and then those of the presbyters, gradually extinguished. This might very easily occur: indeed, would almost necessarily occur. As men are naturally fond of ruling, it is usual for those of elevated positions in society to endeavor to enlarge the boundaries of their authority and power; and commonly their efforts are successful, and are aided by their colleagues or by combinations. For where

power or authority is equally distributed among many, disagreements and trying contests often arise, which it is hardly possible to repress, without increasing the authority and prerogative of the head man of the company. To this cause many others may be added; such as zeal for certain objects, ambition, poverty, the desire of wealth, &c., which stimulate the governors of the society, even though naturally sluggish, slow in movement, and unaspiring, and thus elevate them and place them on a higher level. And those who, in these ways, whether by accident, or by their own efforts, or by the folly of others, obtain elevation, are very apt to claim the standing they hold as justly due to them; and to search for reasons and arguments to prove, that the authority they possess did not come to them fortuitously but in a legitimate manner. And hence arise frequently obscure, futile, perplexing discussions, which yet are necessary for those that would defend what they have obtained. To apply these remarks to Christian affairs and the gradually increasing power of the bishops, is not necessary; the wise will readily see, that the same thing occurred among Christians, which is common in all human affairs; and that the primitive equality of all, and the joint administration of sacred things, gradually disappeared, and the rank of those entrusted with the chief management of the church's affairs, was of course amplified. Councils having been every where introduced in the preceding century, and a consociation of the churches in each province being established, it was a natural consequence, that the bishops, who alone deliberated in these councils on all great questions, and framed their canons, should appear more exalted characters than formerly, and that the prerogatives, not only of the people, but also of the clergy, should suffer diminution. Yet a semblance, and, indeed, not merely a semblance, but a real part of the ancient liberty, and of the common participation in the government, remained: [p. 589.] nor was any of the bishops of this century so bereft of modesty, as to dare maintain, that he had a right to transact any great business, without consulting the clergy and the people. Strong testimonies to this point, have already been adduced from Cyprian. But this same Cyprian, who, when he has selfpossession and is apprehensive of some danger, acknowledges the church to be superior to the bishop, and attributes much importance to the clergy and the people, at other times so exalts the authority and dignity of bishops, as to subvert and destroy all the prerogatives of the people and presbyters, and strenuously maintain that the whole government of the church belongs to the bishop alone. That is, this man of unquestionable excellence and worth, but too fond of power, follows prudence and yields to circumstances, when he admits associates in the government of the church, but speaks out the sentiments of his heart when he extols bishops and makes them sovereigns of their churches. And in this direction he is so indulgent to his natural propensity, that no one before him, not even *Ignatius*, the great patron of episcopal dignity, has, in my opinion, spoken more magnificently of the sovereign power and authority of bishops, no one has exalted their authority more highly.

In the *first* place, whenever occasion offers, he very carefully inculcates, that the bishops do not obtain their office by the suffrages of the clergy and people, but from the judgment, testimony and good pleasure of God himself. He says, (Epist. lii. p. 68, al. Ep. lv. c. 7.): *Factus est autem Cornelius episcopus de Dei et Christi ejus judicio.* This he repeats in numerous passages; and it is customary language with him: *Deus sacerdotes suos facit.* (See Epist. xlv. p. 59., lii. p. 68, 69., lv. p. 82., lxv. p. 113., lxix. p. 121.) I will cite but one notable passage, which may stand for them all. It is in his 69th epistle, p. 121. al. Ep. lxvi. c. 1., where he says to Florentius, one of his adversaries: Animadverto, te *post Deum judicem, qui sacerdotes facit* velle, non dicam de me (quantus enim ego sum?) sed *de Dei et Christi judicio,* (which he received, according to *Cyprian's* views, when he was constituted a bishop,) *judicare.* The man whom he here reproves, had doubted whether Cyprian was the true and legitimate bishop of Carthage. Cyprian replies, that this is sacrilege, and an attack upon God himself and his Son: for men do not make bishops, but God. He goes on to say: Hoc est in Deum non credere. hoc est rebellem adversus Christum et adversus evangelium ejus existere, ut tu existimes, sacerdotes Dei sine conscientia ejus in ecclesia ordinari. How explicit! how positive! Now in this declaration, which is always on his lips, *Deus sacerdotes suos facit,* by the words *sacerdotes,* he means the *bishops.* There are indeed some passages of his writings, in which he honors *presbyters* with the appellation, sacerdotes; and hence some learned men, *Blondell, Salmasius,* and others, have hastily concluded that Cyprian regarded presbyters, as equal in official power and authority with bishops. But whenever he asserts that God creates the priests, [p. 590.] he, beyond all controversy, uniformly means the bishops; and sometimes he employs the very word *episcopus* instead of *sacerdos.* Neither did this holy man suppose, that *presbyters* are made and created by God: this glory he ascribed only to the bishops.—How Cyprian understood this assertion, of which he is so fond, I do not know exactly: for he never explains it, and always uses that vague method of stating and defending his opinions, to which he had been accustomed among the rhetoricians when he was himself a rhetorician, before he became a Christian; and, therefore, he defines nothing. But I suppose him to mean, that whenever an assembly was collected to choose a new bishop, God so illuminated and influenced those who had the right of voting, that they could not create or nominate any other than the person to whom he had decreed the office. If this was not his meaning, I know not what was. That he could not intend that common and ordinary law of divine Providence, which wisely controls all human affairs, is most certain, and will soon be shown. But his opinion, as thus explained, is attended by many difficulties. For men were often created bishops, who were wholly unworthy and unfit for the office; and a wise man can never think that these persons were elected by an extraordinary divine impulse or influence. Moreover, as is well known, the votes of the electors were often divided, so that they could not agree upon any one man. But these difficulties the good Cyprian neither perceived nor heeded. Yet there is one thing he must undoubtedly have believed, that to constitute a *divine decision* in the election of a bishop, the harmonious or unanimous consent of the whole church was not necessary, but only the suffrages of the major part of it. For he himself was not elected by the voice of the whole Carthagenian church; five of the presbyters, and doubtless, a portion of the people, went with them, wished another man to be made bishop. His opinion, therefore, doubtless, was, that whenever the major part of a church pronounced a man worthy of the episcopal office, God is to be supposed to have spoken by the church, and to have made him *his priest.* Of the arguments on which he rests this opinion, I will mention only the one on which he places most reliance; and the force of the others, which he himself deems less conclusive, may be estimated from this. He assumes, that bishops are the successors of the apostles. Epistle xlii. (p. 57. al. Ep. xlv. c. 4.): Laborare debemus, ut unitatem a Domino et *per Apostolos nobis successeribus* traditam obtinere curemus. This was the common opinion of that age. On this assumption, he thus reasons: But the Apostles were created and constituted by Christ himself; therefore also, the successors of the Apostles, the bishops, are created by God himself and by Christ. I shall presently cite a fine passage relative to deacons, in which this argument is most distinctly exhibited. But in this connexion, higher claims are raised by that argument, which he bases on the authority of Jesus Christ. For Cyprian solemnly affirms, that by divine revelation, and [p. 591.] from the mouth of Christ himself, he received the declaration *Deus sacerdotes suos facit.* Thus he writes, (Epist. lxix. p. 122. al. Ep. lxvi. c. 10.): *Memini enim, quid jam mihi sit ostensum, immo quid sit* servo obsequenti et timenti *de dominica et divina auctoritate præceptum :* qui inter caetera quæ ostendere et revelare dignatus est, et hoc addidit: Itaque, *qui Christo non credit sacerdotem facienti,* et postea credere incipiet sacerdotem vindicanti. Now, if what Cyprian would have us regard as true, were true, namely, that Christ himself had dictated to him these denunciations against those who will not believe (*Christum sacerdotes facere*) *that bishops are appointed by Christ ;* then it would be impious, to doubt the validity of this principle!

I will now subjoin the opinions of Cyprian respecting the origin of the functions of *presbyters* and *deacons*, as this will more fully and perfectly disclose to us his entire doctrine respecting the office and prerogatives of bishops. It is a pleasure to know the opinions of an age supposed to be distinguished above others for sanctity and the cultivation of true religion, and to see from what beginnings those dogmas originated, which are still held to be divine by many, and are brought forward to interrupt the peace of the Christian commonwealth. Neither is this merely pleasant, but it is especially useful and necessary, since learned men of all parties have begun strangely to pervert and involve in obscurity the opinions of the early ages. To whom the *presbyters* owe their office and rank, how extensive their power, and how far they are inferior to bishops, Cyprian nowhere clearly states. And those who shall carefully peruse his writings that have reached us, will perceive that, when treating of *presbyters*, he is very cautious not to offend persons of that order, which included quite a number who were unfriendly to him. Yet this may be inferred, from what he has said here and there in his cautious manner, that he placed presbyters far below the bishops, and would not have applied to them his favorite maxim or declaration, that *God makes the priests.* That is, he supposed that *the church*, and not God, created presbyters. He has not, I admit, said this in so many words in any of his writings; but it is a necessary consequence from what he says respecting the judge to whom presbyters are accountable. A *bishop* has no human judge, and is accountable to God only; because it is God that makes the bishops; but the *church*, collectively, not merely the bishop, is the judge of *presbyters*,—and, doubtless, because the presbyters receive their office from the church. But let us hear him, (Epist. xi. p. 19; al. Ep. xvi. c. 4): Interim temerarii inter vos (he is addressing his *presbyters*,) Deum timeant, scientes, quoniam si ultra in iisdem perseveraverint, utar ea admonitione, qua me uti Dominus jubet, ut interim prohibeantur offerre, acturi et apud nos et apud confessores ipsos et apud *plebem universam* caussam suam cum, Domino permittente, in sinum matris ecclesiæ recolligi cœperimus. Cyprian here claims for himself some power over the offending presbyters; for he threatens them, if they continue to offend, that he will *prohibere offerre*; that [p. 592.] is, prohibit them from administering the Lord's supper. But he very cautiously adds, that he assumes this authority by a divine command: *qua me uti Dominus jubet*; thereby acknowledging, that ordinarily a bishop could not restrain a presbyter from performing his functions; but he signifies, that this power was given to him by God in a *vision*, such as he declares and affirms had been often made to him, as his writings show. But from the trial of their offence and their judicial sentence, he wholly separates himself; and decides, that the matter must go before an assembly of the whole church. Because, it would seem, that to the church which made them presbyters, it belonged to judge of the magnitude of their offence. Neither had God, although declaring many things and committing many things to him in visions, or believed to do so, signified his pleasure to have this prerogative of the church abolished.—Concerning *Deacons*, he speaks more distinctly. For he very clearly states, that they are constituted neither by God nor by the church, but by the bishop. And he thence infers, that if they violate their duty, the bishop alone can punish them, without consulting the church. One Rogatianus, a bishop, had been very ill treated by his deacon; but remembering the ancient prerogatives of the church, he would not himself avenge the injury he had received, but stated his grievance to Cyprian and to the church of Carthage, undoubtedly asking their counsel. Cyprian replied, (Epist. lxv. p. 114; al. Ep. iii. c. 1): Tu quidem honorifice fecisti, ut malles de eo nobis conqueri, *cum pro episcopatus vigore et cathedrae auctoritate haberes potestatem, qua posses de illo statim vindicari*, certus quod collegæ tui omnes gratum haberemus quodcunque circa diaconum tuum contumeliosum sacerdotali potestate fecisses. This decision is followed by a long and most invidious descant on the reverence and honor due to bishops, and the punishments which those merit who treat bishops with indignity; which, I could wish, had been written by some other person than *Cyprian* the martyr; for, in truth, it is quite futile, and unworthy of so great a man. He first shows, from the law of Moses, (Deut. xvii. 12, 13,) that God decreed capital punishment against the despisers of the Jewish priests, who, he thinks, did not differ from the Christian priests; and then he mentions Corah, Dathan, and Abiram, with their friends and associates, who suffered terrible punishment at the hands of divine justice for their impiety. His own words are: *Ut probaretur, sacerdotes Dei ab eo, qui sacerdotes facit* (in speaking of bishops he could not omit his favorite maxim: *Deus sacerdotes facit.*) *vindicari.* Other arguments of similar strength then follow, from the Old Testament. Lastly, he gravely asserts, that Jesus Christ himself has taught us, by his example, that bishops are to be treated with the highest respect; for Christ said to the leper (Matth. viii. 4,) "*Go and show thyself to the priest;*" and when, at his trial, he was smitten on the cheek, (John, xviii. 22, 23,) he uttered nothing reproachful against the Jewish high priest, (ibid. c. 2): Quæ omnia ab eo ideo facta sunt humiliter atque patienter, ut nos humilitatis ac patientiæ haberemus [p. 593.] exemplum. *Docuit enim sacerdotes veros legitime et plene honorari, dum circa falsos sacerdotes ipse talis exstitit.* But all these arguments, if indeed they prove anything, only prove that great respect is due to bishops, and that those who despise or revile them should be punished very severely; and not that a bishop is the proper judge of the deacons, and may punish them if they resist him. And therefore he now proceeds to establish this prerogative as belonging to bishops. His reasoning is this, (ibid. c. 3.) Because *the bishop makes a deacon,* he says: Meminisse autem Diaconi debent, quoniam Apostolos, id est, episcopos et prapositos *Dominus* elegit diaconos autem post ascensum Domini in, cœlos *Apostoli sibi constituerunt* episcopatus sui et ecclesiæ ministros. Quod si nos aliquid audere contra Deum possumus, *qui episcopos facit,* possunt et contra nos audere diaconi, *a quibus fiunt.* Much is wrapt up in these few words: For, *first,* he shows why we must believe his darling principle, that God makes the bishops. Christ made the Apostles; but the bishops have succeeded to the place of the Apostles; therefore, not men, but God and Christ make the bishops. *Secondly,* he shows that to bishops belongs the power of making deacons, by this argument: The Apostles appointed the first deacons; but the bishops have the same prerogatives as the Apostles, for they are their successors; therefore deacons derive their office from the bishops, or, the bishops make the deacons. This reasoning may surprise those who recollect that according to the Acts of the Apostles, it was the *church,* or people, acting according to a suggestion of the Apostles, and not the Apostles themselves, that first of all constituted deacons. But either this fact did not occur to Cyprian while writing with excited feelings, or he deemed it expedient not to notice it. According to Cyprian, then, inasmuch as the bishops make deacons, it must be clear also, that they have the right to coerce and punish offending deacons; as he attempted to show to his fellow bishop Rogatianus. *Lastly,* arguing still from his assumptions, which he takes for facts, he shows that deacons must never oppose a bishop. For, bishops must never oppose God, by whom *they* were constituted; and therefore deacons must never oppose the bishops, by whom *they* were constituted. Admirable reasoning, truly! But we should recollect that Cyprian was a rhetorician.—Having settled all these points, as he supposed, by sound reasoning, undoubtedly, (for I am unwilling to believe that he acted in sincerity,) he gives the following as his deliberate opinion, (ibid. c. 3): Ideo oportet diaconum præposito suo plena humilitate satisfacere. - - Quod si ultra te provocaverit, fungeris circa eum potestate honoris tui, ut eum vel deponas vel abstineas. And still more liberal, he assigns to Rogatianus authority also over the associates and friends of the deacon: Et quoniam

scripsisti, quendam cum eodem diacono tuo se miscuisse et superbiæ ejus atque audaciæ participem esse, hunc quoque et si qui alii tales extiterint et contra sa- [p. 594.] cerdotem Dei (so he commonly designates a bishop,) fecerint, vel coërcere potes vel abstinere. But, may the *manes* of St. Cyprian forgive me! In this, as in other things, he abandoned and changed the ancient law of the church, through his excessive anxiety to extend the prerogatives of bishops. By the ancient law, the bishop could neither make deacons nor deprive them of their office, at his pleasure; but to the whole multitude, or the church, pertained both. And this, strange to tell, he himself confesses and maintains on another occasion and in another place. For, being of a fervid temperament, he at times forgets in the ardor of debate, what he had elsewhere inculcated. In his 68th Epistle, (p. 118; al. Ep. lxvii. c. 4,) after maintaining the rights of the people in the creation of bishops, and asserting that *the ordination of a bishop is legitimate and right only, quæ omnium suffragio et judicio fuerit examinata,* he immediately adds, that he would have the same rule applied to deacons; and he denies that the Apostles alone constituted the deacons: Nec hoc in episcoporum tantum et sacerdotum, *sed et in diaconorum ordinationibus* observasse Apostolos animadvertimus, de quo et ipso in Actis eorum scriptum est: Et convocarunt, inquit, illi duodecim totam plebem discipulorum.—Quod utique idcirco tam diligenter et caute convocata plebe tota gerebatur, ne quis ad altaris ministerium vel ad sacerdotalem locum indignus obreperet. Now, therefore, it will be manifest, how *Cyprian* makes bishops, presbyters, and deacons to differ from each other. God makes the priests or bishops; the church makes the presbyters; and the bishop makes the deacons. And therefore, God only is the judge of the bishops; the church the judge of presbyters; and the bishop the judge of deacons.

On this, his darling maxim, that *God makes the priests or bishops,* which he deduces from the parity of bishops with the Apostles, Cyprian erects a large superstructure of prerogatives and honors, which, in his judgment, bishops ought to enjoy. For his *first* inference from it is, that all the prerogatives which belonged to the Apostles whom Christ himself created, belong also to the bishops their successors. *Secondly,* he infers from it, that no one should judge of the actions of bishops but God only, by whom they were made. And hence he is often very angry with those who call in question the things done by bishops. He writes to Florentius, (Epist. lxix. p. 121; al. Ep. lxvi. c. 1): Animadverto te - - in mores nostros diligenter inquirere, et post Deum judicem, qui sacerdotes facit, te velle - - de Dei et Christi judicio judicare. Hoc est in Deum non credere. - - Nam credere quod indigni sint qui ordinantur, quid aliud est, quam credere, quod non a Deo nec per Deum sacerdotes ejus in ecclesia constituantur? And, after much of the same import, he adds, (c. 4, 5): Dolens hæc profero, cum te judicem Dei constituas et Christi, qui dicit ad Apostolos ac per hoc ad omnes præpositos, qui Apostolis vicaria ordinatione succedunt; qui audit vos, me audit: et qui me audit, eum audit, qui me misit. Inde enim [p. 595.] schismata et hæreses obortæ sunt et oriuntur, dum episcopus, qui unus est et ecclesiæ præest, superba quorundam præsumtione contemnitur, et *homo dignatione Dei honoratus* indignus hominibus judicatur. Quis enim

hic est superbiæ tumor, quæ arrogantia animi, quæ mentis inflatio, ad cognitionem suam præpositos et sacerdotes vocare! What force there is in all this, and whither it tends, is sufficiently manifest! But he goes even farther than this, and maintains, that the whole church is comprised in the bishop: whence it follows, that no person is a member of the church unless he is obedient to the bishop, or in subjection to him. But the church is a *unity;* and in the establishment of this doctrine Cyprian spent much labor and pains; and his treatise *de unitate ecclesiæ* is still extant. Of course all bishops also, as they properly constitute the church, must form a unity of some sort, and be held together by an indissoluble bond. And if this be so, then we must believe, that a person who separates himself from one bishop, separates himself from all, and at the same time from the whole church; and he excludes himself from heaven, as well as from the church. This Cyprian maintains in his 69th Epistle, (p. 123; al. Ep. lxvi. c. 8.) He first gives his definition of the church: *Ecclesia est plebs sacerdoti adunata et pastori suo grex adhærens.* Assuming this, his *first* inference is: *Unde scire debes episcopum in ecclesia esse, et ecclesiam in episcopo, et si quis cum episcopo non sit, in ecclesia non esse.* Very true, provided the definition is faultless! And there are other instances, from which we may learn that Cyprian well understood the great power there is in definitions, and that any thing may be proved, if a neat and suitable definition can be devised. But he supposes some one may come forward with this objection: I dissent indeed from you, and from some other bishops; but I fully accord with another, or several other bishops: if then the man is in the church who *adheres to his own bishop,* I am in the church, for I adhere to the pastor whom I have chosen. By no means, says Cyprian: Whoever dissents from *me*, dissents from *all:* he who forsakes the bishop under whom he lives, forsakes them all, (Ibid. c. 8): *Et frustra sibi blandiri eos, qui pacem cum sacerdotibus Dei* (that is, with the bishops in whose congregations they live,) *non habentes, obrepunt, et latenter apud quosdam* (other bishops,) *communicare se credunt, quando ecclesia, quæ catholica et una est* (add: *et in episcopis posita,*) *scissa non sit neque divisa, sed sit utique connexa et cohærentium sibi invicem sacerdotum glutino copulata.* Subservient to the support and confirmation of this doctrine, is that whole topic, so often and so carefully discussed by Cyprian, respecting the *unity of the church;* a topic broached by others long before him, and in Africa, by Tertullian in particular, but never investigated, elucidated, and made as intelligible as its importance required. In explaining and illustrating this topic, the holy man is so little consistent with himself, so unsettled and indeterminate in his views, that we readily perceive he indistinctly grasped his subject, and his greatest [p. 596.] admirers will not deny that he made some mistakes.—But magnificent as these views were, and extravagantly as they honored episcopacy, yet they did not satisfy Cyprian: to make the dignity of Bishops completely inviolable, he deemed it nessessary to add, that they represent Christ himself, and that they not only guide and rule us as his vicegerents, but also sit in judgment upon us. And this, he thinks, is easily inferred from the divine origin of bishops. Now if the bishops represent the person of Christ among men, if they act and decide in his stead, then it is manifest, that to resist and oppose them, or to refuse to obey

their mandates, would be to offend the divine majesty and despise Christ himself. And the excellent Cyprian would have us believe it is really so. This sentiment he nowhere maintains with more vehemence and eloquence than in his 55th Epistle, *ad Cornelium*, (p. 81, 82, &c. al. Ep. lix. c. 2. 7;) an Epistle, which, I confess, I never read without some pleasure and admiration. The Carthagenian bishop writes to the bishop of Rome, who ought to know, the best of all men, what were the powers and what the prerogatives and honors belonging to Christian bishops, he being himself, as Cyprian admitted, the *(princeps) chief* of all the bishops. And yet the Carthagenian prelate instructs the Roman, just as a master would one of his least pupils, very minutely, respecting the powers and the dignity of bishops; and, pretty clearly taxes him with ignorance on this most important subject. For *Cornelius*, the good bishop of Rome, was more modest than Cyprian wished him to be, and seemed not fully to understand the immense amplitude and elevation of his prelacy: he conceded much to his clergy: and much to the people: and moreover suffered himself to be terrified by the threats of Cyprian's adversaries who had gone to Rome. And therefore Cyprian thus addresses him, near the commencement of the Epistle, (c. 2.): Quod si ita res est, frater carissime, ut nequissimorum timeatur audacia, - - actum est de episcopatus vigore, et de ecclesiæ gubernandæ *sublimi ac divina potestate*, nec Christiani ultra aut durare, aut esse jam possumus. This rebuke he protracts to a considerable length, and then adds a long oration, in which he informs *Cornelius*, by citing many passages of holy Scripture, (which no competent judge will deem to be in point,) that a bishop is a great man, and has no superior among mortals, except Jesus Christ. This instruction took effect on *Cornelius*, and on all his successors; among whom it is well known, not one has been so ignorant of his own authority and importance as to need so stern a monitor and instructor. Let us see how Cyprian closes that oration, (Ibid. c. 7.): cum haec tanta et talia et multa alia exempla præcedant, quibus sacerdotalis auctoritas et potestas de divina dignatione firmatur, quales putas eos, qui sacerdotum hostes, et contra ecclesiam catholicam rebelles nec præmo-
[p. 597.] nentis Domini communicatione, nec futuri judicii ultione terrentur? Neque enim aliunde hæreses abortæ sunt, aut nata sunt schismata, quam inde, quod sacerdoti Dei non obtemperatur, nec *unus in ecclesia ad tempus sacerdos, et ad tempus judex vice Christi cogitatur; cui si secundum magisteria divina obtemperaret fraternitas universa, nemo adversum sacerdotum collegium moveret.* The rest I omit. Here then we have the author of that proud title, *Vicar of Jesus Christ*, which the Roman Pontiffs at this day claim as exclusively theirs. The author of it was not born at Rome: but an African bishop first taught the Roman prelate, that all bishops ought to assume it. And it was commonly adopted, from this time onward, by all bishops; as has been proved by Joseph *Bingham* in his *Origines Ecclesiasticæ*, (vol. i. p. 81, 82. Lib. ii. c. ii. § 10.) I will add, that down to the *ninth* century, it was customary to speak of all bishops as the *Vicars of Christ:* for *Servatus Lupus*, a writer of that century, (or rather, all the bishops in the part of Gaul denominated *Senonia*, in whose name *Servatus* wrote,) honored Aeneas, the bishop of Paris, with this title. (Epist. xcix. p. 149. ed. *Baluze.*) *:* Consolationem recipimus, dum vos sub pastore bono (Christo)

agentes, qui summe bonus est. *vicarium ejus* (boni pastoris) scilicet *visibilem*. ministeriique nostri consortem, absque dilatione expetere - - cognovimus. But after this period, the Roman Pontiffs were accustomed to appropriate this, as well as the other honorary titles of the ancient bishops, exclusively to themselves. In short, whatever prerogatives the greatest of the Roman Pontifs at this day arrogate to themselves, with perhaps the single exception of infallibility, were all ascribed by *Cyprian* to the bishops universally; which fact shows, how greatly his views differed from the modern, respecting the nature and government of the church. And as he thought, so he acted. For whoever candidly surveys and considers those contests which distracted his life, will perceive, that most of them originated from his zeal for innovations on the ancient rights of the Carthagenian church, and amplifying the powers and the dignity of the bishop. Most of the business he managed according to his own pleasure and volition, regardless of the consent or opinions of either presbyters, or deacons, or the people. And hence frequently the presbyters, the deacons, or a portion of the people, resisted his wishes, and complained that they were injured. But he rose above them all, being a vigorous and fearless man; and his doctrines respecting the unity of the church and the authority of bishops, were propagated by means of his Epistles, over the whole church. It is amazing to see, what influence he acquired throughout the Christian world, after his magnanimous martyrdom for Christ, so that he was accounted almost the common teacher and oracle of all. Those who would look into this subject, may read the 18th Oration of *Gregory* Nazianzen, in commemoration of him. [p. 598.]

§ XXV. **The Morals of the Clergy.** Many complaints occur here and there in the writers of this century, of the corrupt morals of the clergy; and these complaints cannot be supposed to be vain and groundless: and yet splendid examples of primitive integrity and sanctity are frequently to be seen, both among the bishops and among the presbyters and deacons; examples well adapted to impress the human mind, and to exhibit the power of religion. Bad men were therefore commingled with the good; and those deserve not our confidence, who, as many in fact do, would measure the happiness of this age by the examples of either of these descriptions.(¹) I will therefore only observe, that the growing errors among Christians, respecting the nature of true piety, had such influence on not a few of the ministers of religion, that by striving to obtain a reputation for sanctity, they brought upon themselves disgrace and a suspicion of criminal conduct. A striking example of this is afforded by those in Africa, and perhaps also in other provinces of the East, who received into their houses females who had vowed perpetual chastity, and even made them partakers of their bed, at the same time most solemnly protesting that nothing occurred incompatible with modesty. For, extravagant ideas of the sanctity of celibacy having grown up, and consequently those among the priests being regarded as most venerable, and the most acceptable before God, who had no wives, many wished so to consult their reputation, as still to retain a measure of social comforts and enjoyments. The bishops, by their exhortations and precepts, resisted this custom, which was very offensive to the people: but, so very powerful is every thing which favors our natural instincts, that this practice could not be wholly exterminated, either in this century or the next.(2)

(1) Complaints respecting the vices of the clergy in this century, are made by nearly all the Greek and Latin fathers, who attempt to assign the causes of the calamities, with which the Christians of this century often had to conflict. See *Origen's* Commentatory on Matthew, (P. I. Opp. edit. Huet. p. 420, 441, 442.) *Cyprian*, in many of his Epistles, *Eusebius*, (Hist. Eccles. L. viii. c. 1.) and others. Those of the present day, who read these complaints, which often resemble the declamations of rhetoricians, are apt to conclude that almost nothing of the primitive piety of the church remained in this age. But it is not difficult to collect from the same writers, many testimonies to the innocence and the pure morals of the pastors and ministers of the churches: and therefore others are induced by these high commendations, to assert, that, with perhaps a few [p. 599.] exceptions, all the clergy were free from every vice. And from such wide sweeping general commendations, and accusations, dictated for the most part, and colored by impassioned feelings, in my opinion, little or nothing can be inferred with certainty. And the judgment which *Origen* passed, appears to me more probable: (Contra Celsum, L. iii. p. 129, ed. Spencer.) He admits that there were some among the Christian bishops and teachers, who did not do their duty as they ought; but, he adds, it is nevertheless certain that if the Christian prefects and senators are compared with the pagan senators, magistrates and judges, the latter will fall far behind the former, in probity, virtue, and integrity. Such, I apprehend, was in general the fact. In many of the Christian bishops and teachers, there were various things reprehensible and defective, if we judge them by the strict rules of the divine law; and yet they appeared to be all excellent men, and patterns of virtue, if compared with those magistrates of cities and countries, who were opposed to Christianity; among whom examples of goodness and justice were very rare. And the same will hold true of the Christian common people.

(2) This scandalous practice of some Christian priests, in admitting females to be inmates of their dwellings, is professedly treated of by Henry *Dodwell*, in his *Dissertationes Cyprianicæ*, (Diss. iii.) and by Ludov. Anton. *Muratori*, in his *Disquisitio de Synisactis et Agapetis*, (thus these females were designated.) The *Disquis.* is to be found in his *Anecdota Græca*, (p. 218.) The former lets

his prejudices carry him too far: and the latter is quite too favorable to the views of the Romish church respecting the sanctity of celibacy. This shameful custom, doubtless, existed before the *third* century; and we meet some slight traces of it in *Hermas*, in *Tertullian*, and perhaps in others. But a clear and distinct mention of it, is made by no one before *Cyprian*, who severely inveighs against it in several of his epistles. But this and other questions relating to this subject, I pass over, as not pertinent to my present object; and I will confine myself to one fact, which learned men have either entirely omitted, or have treated only with much obscurity. All the priests did not assume this liberty of taking women into their houses and to their beds, but only those who had voluntarily renounced the right to marry, which all priests possessed in this century, or had made a solemn vow of perpetual chastity, for the sake of attaining to higher sanctity. For this custom of binding themselves by such vows was very common in those times. Neither were all females taken in such cohabitation, but only virgins: nor indeed all virgins, but those only, who had professed never to marry, but to preserve their bodies entirely consecrated to God. Those who mark these circumstances, will perceive the true nature and character of this most vile and perilous practice. These cohabitations, in fact, were a sort of sacred or divine marriages between persons bound, on both sides, by vows of perpetual chastity; marriages, I say, not of their bodies, but of their souls. For those early theologians, whose views most of the [p. 600.] moderns imperfectly understand, supposed that there was both an external marriage of bodies and also an internal marriage of souls; and that, as bodies are often united, while the souls are very discordant, so also, they supposed, souls might be united in marriage or become associated, without any consociation or marriage of the bodies. It is well known, that many married Christians in those days, by mutual consent, made vows of continence, and yet wished to be regarded as remaining married persons, and they were so regarded. Says *Tertullian* (ad Uxorem L. i. c. 6. p. 185.): Quot sunt, qui consensu pari inter se matrimonii debitum tollunt? voluntarii spadones pro cupiditate regni cœlestis. Quod si *salvo matrimonio* abstinentia toleratur, quanto magis adempto? In these married persons, the external marriage or that of their bodies was annulled, but the interior and more holy-marriage of their souls, not only continued, but was even strengthened. Now the radical principle of the cohabitations which we are considering, was the same with that just described; and the former differed from the latter merely in this, that the one had voluntarily taken vows of *abstinence* from a marriage of bodies, and the other had voluntarily taken vows for the *dissolution* of such marriage.

These observations, will, I think, enable us to understand why the unmarried cohabitants supposed their mode of life not liable to the reproaches cast upon it, and therefore complained of the injustice of the suspicions heaped upon them. Those married Christians, who voluntarily subjected themselves to the law of continence, could still live together, and sleep together, and no one took offence at it, or suspected them of secretly violating the rule of chastity which they imposed on themselves. On the contrary, most people considered the force of religious vows to be so great, that their voluntary vow was sufficient to keep them from any improper intercourse. And therefore, as our unmarried cohabitants were living together on the same principle, they supposed the same things to be lawful for them; and as both equally made solemn vows of chastity, so all, they supposed ought to conclude, that the force of *their* vow would make it impossible for them to violate the law of chastity. This at least we regard as certain, that many of the tenets and practices of the early Christians, which displease us, would appear more tolerable, and would assume a more becoming aspect, if they were tried by the opinions and customs of those times.

§ XXVI. **Christian Writers of this Century.** Among those who superintended and managed the affairs of the church, there were doubtless more learned and well-informed men than in the previous centuries. For many from the different sects of philosophers, especially from the Platonists, and also from among the rhetoricians, embraced Christianity; and they were honored for their [p. 601.] erudition and talents by being made bishops and presbyters. The Christians likewise perceived, that their cause needed the support of learning and human science, and therefore took pains to have the youth of the church instructed in sound learning and philosophy. And yet it is well attested, and not to be denied, that many illiterate and ignorant men presided over the churches, in numerous places, and that human learning was not yet considered as an indispensable qualification of a good bishop and teacher. For, not to mention the paucity of schools in which candidates for the sacred office might be educated, and the consequent scarcity of the learned men, the opinion was too deeply fixed in many minds to be at all eradicated, that learning and philosophy were prejudicial rather than advantageous to piety, and should therefore be excluded from the church.(¹) And hence, only a few Christians in this age obtained permanent notoriety, by their writings. Among those who wrote in Greek, the most eminent was *Origen*, who presided in the school of Alexandria, a man of indefatigable industry, and equalled by few in learning and genius, but of whose works the greatest and best part are lost, and a part are preserved only in Latin. Inferior to him in fame and reputation, but not, I think, in solid worth and genius, were *Julius Africanus*, *Dionysius* of Alexandria, and *Hippolytus*, most of whose writings have unfortunately not been preserved. Eminent among the disciples of Origen, was *Gregory*, bishop of Neocæsaria, more famous for the numerous miracles said to have been wrought by him, and from which he obtained the surname of *Thaumaturgus*, than for his writings.(²)—Among the Latins, only three deserve our notice: *Cyprian*, first a rhetorician, and then bishop of Carthage, a man, like most Africans, possessing eloquence, but at the same time tumid, and more splendid in his words and phrases than in his conceptions; *Minucius Felix*, from whose pen we have a neat and elegant dialogue, entitled *Octavius*, in which he skilfully recounts and nervously confutes the calumnies then charged upon Christians; and *Arnobius*, an African rhetorician, who strenuously defended the cause of Christianity against its opposers, and often with ingenuity, in his *Libri septem contra Gentes:* but he shows himself to be not well acquainted with the religion which he defends.(³)

(1) In the *Apostolic Constitutions*, falsely ascribed to Clemens [p. 602.] Romanus, there is a chapter, (Lib. i. c. 6., in the Patres Apostol. tom. 1. p. 204.) in which the reading of books on human learning is prohibited: and *Cotelier*, in a note on the chapter, has collected many passages of a similar nature from the early Christian writers. And it is well known, how much Origen was disliked by many, on account of his attachment to science and philosophy: and, while vindicating himself in an Epistle to Eusebius, he can mention only here and there an individual, who pursued a similar course.

(2) Those wishing to become acquainted with the Christian Greek writers of this and of every age, will find all they can desire, in the *Bibliotheca Græca* of Jo. Alb. *Fabricius*. The works of *Origen* explanatory of Scripture, were first published entire and correctly, and with valuable notes, by Peter Daniel Huet: to which he added a very learned work entitled *Origeniana*, containing elaborate discussions respecting the history and opinions of Origen; Rouen, 1668, fol., and reprinted in Germany. Afterwards Bern. de *Montfaucon*, a very learned Benedictine, published what remains of Origen's *Hexapla*, in two vols. fol., Paris, 1714. Lastly, *Charles* de la *Rue*, also a Benedictine monk, and distinguished for talents and learning, undertook to publish all the works of Origen which have escaped the ravages of time, from numerous manuscripts collected with great care and labor, accompanied with notes, a life of the author, and many dissertations. He divided the work into *five* volumes, the last of which was to contain Huet's *Originiana*, with notes, emendations, and additions, and also dissertations respecting Origen. The two first volumes were published at Paris, 1733, fol. The third appeared at Paris in 1740, after the editor's death, which occurred in 1739. There remains therefore the two last volumes, the first of which the learned author is said to have left nearly complete.—Of the writings of *Julius Africanus* and *Dionysius Alexandrianus*, only a few fragments are extant.—The reputation of *Hippolytus* is great: but his history is involved in obscurity, because several persons of this name became famous among Christians. The most elaborate account of the man is given by the Benedictine monks in the work they have commenced publishing, entitled

Histoire Litteraire de la France, tome i. p. 361. The meagre fragments that remain of this great man, though many of them are of doubtful genuineness, have been collected in two thin volumes, by Jo. Alb. *Fabricius*, designed, I suppose, as a collection for others to improve.—The few remains of ***Gregory*** of Neocaesarea, including his Panegyric on Origen, his preceptor, which is the best of his works, and a Greek biography of Gregory, were published by Gerh. ***Voss***, Mayence, 1604, 4to. The industry of Voss deserves commendation; but ***Gregory*** needs a more judicious and learned editor, who would inquire more sagaciously and freely, than any one has hitherto done, into the nature and certainty of [p. 603.] those miracles, by which Gregory is said to have excelled all the learned doctors of the church in all ages. Great suspicions of them have been awakened, among others by Anthony *Van Dale*, in the preface to his work ***de Oraculis***. These suspicions should be annihilated, if they can be; and if they can not, I wish to see them better elucidated and confirmed, so that the true may be distinguished from the false. For it is of vast importance to Christianity that hoary fables should be exploded, and no longer give nutriment to superstition: and it is equally important, that the attestations of divine power and interposition, actually exhibited in the early ages, should be placed beyond all doubt, so that they may sustain the majesty and dignity of our religion. Some of the miracles of Gregory bear manifest marks of spuriousness; and yet, perhaps, there was something true at the bottom of them, which the popular credulity, as usual, wrought upon, or rather perverted.

(3) Of the writings of *Cyprian* there are extant, first, *Epistles*, which shed much light on the ecclesiastical usages and the history of those times; and, secondly, various *Tracts*, in which he treats of practical duties, sometimes devoutly and eloquently, and sometimes with little solidity and correctness. All his works were published, near the close of the last century, in England, by John *Fell*, bishop of Chester, (Oxford, 1682, fol.), and with great dexterity and care; so that this edition was deemed worth reprinting in Holland and Germany. Afterwards Stephen *Baluze*, to whom other branches of divine and human learning are much indebted, spent many of the last years of his long life in laboriously correcting and elucidating the works of Cyprian; and having left his undertaking but partly accomplished, his associates, the Benedictine monks of St. Maur, added some dissertations, and published the whole, Paris, 1726, fol. But this edition lacks, not only the *dissertationes Cyprianicæ* of Henry Dodwell, which are very erudite, though abounding in doubtful opinions and conjectures, but also the *Annales Cyprianici* of John Pearson; so that it does not supercede the use of Fell's edition. After these labors of correction, we have the text of Cyprian sufficiently correct; and transcribers have committed fewer blunders with this author than with others: but it may be justly questioned, whether Cyprian has been adequately elucidated and explained. For he presents us with many passages, which no one can fully understand and comprehend, unless he is well acquainted with that antiquated theology which differed so much from the theology of any modern sect; yet we find the expounders of Cyprian ascribing modern views to him, because his words are still used by us to express *our* sentiments.—Very different is the fact with *Minucius Felix*, whose

ideas are sufficiently clear and intelligible, but his language is such as to create doubts whether we have his text correct. And hence, although eminent [p. 604.] men have labored intensely on the correction of his text, among whom the most noted were John *Davis*, an Englishman, and James *Gronovius*, who lived within our recollection; yet much still remains to tax the ingenuity of critics and grammarians.—Of *Arnobius*, (who is eloquent, but often very obscure, from the use of uncommon terms, and the vicious accumulation of figures and verbal ornaments,) the best editor is Desiderius *Heraldus*: yet he is not appreciated by the authors of the observations and emendations in the latest edition of Arnobius, Leyden, 1651, 4to. The friends of ancient literature will owe a debt of gratitude to the man who shall resolve to apply the aids of ingenuity and a knowledge of ancient authors to the elucidation of Arnobius, the explanation of his numerous difficult passages, and the correction of his many faults.

§ XXVII. **Philosophising Theologians. Origen.** The philosophising teachers of Christianity frequently resorted to what they regarded as the dictates of reason, in order to explain and elucidate those religious doctrines which appeared to lack precision and clearness, so that the harmony of human and divine wisdom might be manifest. The result was, that the ancient simplicity, which received without comment whatever was divinely inculcated, became less esteemed, the subtilties of human device became mixed up with the divine instructions, and contentions and disagreements arose respecting the nature of certain mysteries. In the western regions, indeed, this practice of commingling human and divine views made slower progress; and the Latin theologians of this century were still sufficiently cautious in their explications of the scriptural doctrines, except perhaps Arnobius, who began to write when but slightly acquainted with the principles of religion, and treated them rhetorically rather than philosophically. But among the theologians of Asia and Africa, we more frequently meet with such as ventured to explore the internal nature and the recondite grounds of scriptural doctrines, either for the gratification of curiosity, or for the purpose of confuting heretics and the opposers of Christianity. Among these the Alexandrian doctors of Egypt were preëminent, they having, in the preceding century, conceded to philosophy some authority in matters of religion. At the head of these doctors stood *Origen*, the master of the school at Alexandria, a man distinguished for genius, learning, virtue and usefulness. In his [p. 605.] *Libri de principiis*, still extant in a Latin translation, and in his

Stromata, which are lost, he attempted formally to demonstrate the harmony between philosophy and Christianity; and he endeavored to reconcile with the principles of reason whatever appeared strange and incredible in the Christian faith. And yet Origen himself,—and it greatly diminishes his fault,—treated this slippery and hazardous business with becoming prudence and modesty, and he repeatedly stated, that he timidly proposed *conjectures*, rather than inculcated and decided positively. But his disciples, who were very numerous, followed the speculations of their teacher, too confidently, and not unfrequently they put forth as certainties, what he had only stated as probabilities, and which he requested wise men to examine more profoundly.(1)

(1) Of Origen,—than whom, the church down to the times of Constantine, contained no greater man,—of his life, his virtues and his faults, his opinions and his errors, enough has been debated and written by Christians, during almost fourteen centuries, to fill out a volume of no small size. Great and excellent men, in former times, stood forth as his patrons and advocates; and they continue to do so still. But men equally great and excellent, to this day, have been his adversaries. And in fact, both to assail and to defend him, and with arguments of great apparent force, would not be difficult for an ingenious man, who would assume either office. In the life, labors, and opinions of Origen, there are many things of such excellence and worth, as must extort admiration from the most reluctant: and if a person regard these things only, he may easily persuade himself, that whatever appeared to conflict with such great excellencies must have been only slight faults, or perhaps were the fabrications and slanders of enemies, or the false constructions put upon allowable, or even upon correct opinions. On the other hand, there are among his opinions so many strangely divergent not only from our belief but also from the plainest dictates of reason, so many that are ridiculous and absurd, especially when viewed separately and apart from that system of doctrine to which he was attached, that they might excite our disgust, and induce the belief that this well meaning man was lacking in common sense: and if a person should fix his attention upon these things exclusively, he might easily be led to believe, that whatever appears great or illustrious in Origen may have arisen from slight or accidental causes, and be ascribable to the instincts of nature, or to his copying after others, rather than to the deliberate decisions of his own mind. And hence, although the long controversies respecting Origen, like most other controversies among men, arose in no small degree from passion and prejudice, yet the man [p. 606.] himself, who was so many times both attacked and defended, was, peculiarly, *in utramque partem disputabilis*, as Seneca expresses it; for he was a compound of contrarities, wise and unwise, acute and stupid, judicious and injudicious, the enemy of superstition and its patron, a strenuous defender of Christianity and its corrupter, energetic and irresolute, one to whom the Bible owes much, and from whom it has suffered much. Of the great number of facts in

regard to Origen, which have long been before the public, or which might have been brought forward, (for many have never been noticed.) I shall, for the sake of brevity, adduce only such as I deem necessary to account for the great changes he produced in the state of the church. For, although his bishop expelled him from the church, and he was afterwards assailed by numerous public and private condemnations, yet not only were many of his worst opinions suffered to go unrebuked, but his practice of explaining religious truths by means of philosophy, and of turning the inspired books into allegories, was very generally approved and adopted among Christians. Some institutions, likewise, which originated from his doctrines, took deep root and were at length regarded as sacred. It need not be stated that at all times there have been great men, and men of distinguished piety, who have esteemed Origen very highly, extolled his writings, and recommended their perusal by theologians, and have maintained that all the decisions against Origen were unjust. It would therefore be no mistake to say, that, as Constantine the Great imparted a new form to the civil state, so this Egyptian imparted a new form to the theology of Christians.

Among the writers concerning Origen, his opinions, and the contests they occasioned, the most eminent is undoubtedly Peter Daniel *Huet;* whose elaborate and very erudite work, in three books, entitled *Origeniana,* is the copious fountain from which all the more recent writers concerning Origen have drawn. Charles *de la Rue,* a Benedictine, the recent editor of Origen's works, designed to republish Huet's Origeniana, with additional notes and observations; but death frustrated the purpose of that learned man. Whoever may take up the design of de la Rue, and pursue it judiciously and impartially, will find the undertaking to be great and the materials abundant. For, great and excellent as the work of Huet is in its kind, it is not without faults and defects. In the first place, it is incomplete: for it does not state and explain all the peculiar doctrines of Origen, but only those which were publicly censured and condemned. I could easily show, to any man wishing to be informed, that Origen held many other opinions equally novel, false and pernicious with those charged upon him; which however, for diverse reasons, no person censured or condemned. Again, although no person can judge correctly of Origen's theology, [p. 607.] without well understanding his philosophy, which contained the grounds of his singular opinions on divine subjects, yet Huet neglects this whole subject, supposing that it was sufficient to say, generally, that Origen introduced the Academy almost entire into the church. The work of this very learned man is also badly arranged. For, in reviewing those doctrines of Origen which brought him into ill repute, he does not follow the order of nature, but that of the schools: nor does he show us how Origen's opinions stood connected with and dependent on each other, but he arranges them all under general heads without regard to their connexion. This mode of proceeding was quite favorable to his main purpose, which was simply to vindicate Origen; but it is embarrassing to those who wish to gain a correct knowledge and a just estimate of the errors of that great man. For it is not easy to judge of the importance of any error, without tracing it to its source and seeing its connexion with opinions to which it is related; because many sentiments, considered apart and by themselves, appear worthy of toleration or excuse, but if considered in connexion with their origin and consequences, they assume a different aspect, and become portentous. Lastly, throughout his work Huet labors to exhibit Origen as less censurable than his adversaries made him, and thus assumes the office of a patron and advocate, rather than that of a cautious guarded historian and a wise judge.

Among the arguments by which Huet thinks he can justify Origen, though not wholly, some are of considerable force, but others are quite weak and inefficient. Of the former character is the man's very great modesty; which also his early defender, Pamphilus, and among the moderns, Haloix, (in his Origines defensus, Lib. ii. c. 2.) have urged against his accusers. And it is true that, in many places, Origen professes not to decide positively, but only to bring forward, modestly and timidly, probable conjectures. Thus in his work *de Principiis*, Lib. i. c. 6. § 1. p. 69, when entering on a discussion respecting the end or consummation of the world, he deprecates all offence, by saying; Quæ quidem a nobis etiam cum magno metu et cautela dicuntur, discutientibus magis et pertractantibus, quam pro certo ac definito statuentibus. Indicatum namque a nobis in superioribus est, quæ sint de quibus manifesto dogmate terminandum sit. - - - - - Nunc autem disputandi specie magis, quam definiendi, prout possumus, exercemur. And he closes the chapter, (p. 71,) with a plain acknowledgment of his ignorance of the future condition of our bodies after the destruction of the world. Certius tamen qualiter se habitura sit res, scit solus Deus et si qui ejus per Christum et Spiritum sanctum amici sunt. In the passage on the incarnation of Christ, (*de Principiis*, Lib. ii. c. 6. § 2. p. 90,) he says: De quo nos non [p. 608.] temeritate aliqua, sed quoniam ordo loci deposcit ea magis, quae fides nostra continet, quam quæ humanæ rationis assertio vindicare solet, quam paucissimis proferemus, *suspiciones* potius *nostras* quam manifestas aliquas affirmationes in medium proferentes. And, lest any should misunderstand him, he closes the whole discussion with this sentence, (p. 92.): Haec interim nobis ad præsens de rebus tam difficilibus disputantibus, id est, de incarnatione et de deitate Christi occurrere potuerunt. Si quis sane melius aliquid poterit invenire et evidentioribus de Scripturis sanctis assertionibus confirmare quæ dicit, illa potius quam haec recipiantur. Similar protestations occur everywhere in his work *de Principiis*, and in his other writings. Sometimes he brings forward two or three explications of the same thing, and leaves it optional with his readers to select any one of them, or to reject the whole. *De Princip.* Lib. ii. c. 3. § 6. p. 83: His igitur tribus opinionibus de fine omnium et de summa beatitudine prout sentire potuimus adumbratis, unusquisque legentium apud semetipsum diligentius et scrupulosius judicet si potest aliqua harum probari vel eligi.——To this his commendable modesty, may be added his very great inconstancy in the explication of religious doctrines. For he does not always and everywhere advance the same sentiments, but, on the gravest subjects, he exhibits different views at different times and in different places: whence it is manifest, that the man changed his own views, and that he did not wish to prescribe laws for human thought. For example, if we compare the different statements he makes respecting the divine Trinity, or respecting Christ, and the Holy Spirit, we must be persuaded that to him, if to any one, the lines of Horace are applicable, (Epistles, Lib. i. ep. 1.)

> Quo teneam vultus mutantem Protea nodo?
> Quod petiit, spernit, repetit quod nuper omisit.
> Diruit, ædificat, mutat quadrata rotundis.

For, the Sabellians, the Arians, the Nicenists, and others, can all very plausibly lay claim to him. The cause of this modesty and instability, I will state presently. But those who wish correctly to understand what sort of a man Origen was, should remember, that he was not always and uniformly controlled by modesty and instability. His timidity and changeableness are apparent, when he offers *philosophical explanations* of those Christian doctrines which theologians call revealed truths, that is, of the doctrines which we learn exclusively from the Bible, such as the doctrine of three persons in the Godhead, the doctrine of Christ, of the Holy Spirit, and of the resurrection of our bodies. For while he assumes it as certain, that even these doctrines are accordant with the teachings of reason, or with the philosophy which is agreeable to reason, and that the former may be legitimately deduced from the latter; yet he does not pretend that he is one who can show infallibly how they stand connected, although he has no doubts that others, more intelligent than he, may be able to do it. But he is much more bold and confident, when expounding [p. 609.] the doctrines which lie within the sphere of human knowledge, or the doctrines of *natural religion*, such as those concerning God, the world, the soul, &c. For these he thinks should be explained,—and he himself confidently explains them, in accordance with the precepts of that philosophy which he embraced as true; and he sometimes ridiculed those who choose to hold these doctrines, simply, and according to the literal statement of the Scriptures, rather than to allow reason to explain and modify them. Take for example, what he says in the second book of his Principia, respecting the human soul of Christ, and the union of the divine with the human nature in our Savior. On this subject, having assumed that the soul of Christ was of the same nature with ours, he unhesitatingly applies to Christ's soul whatever he had learned respecting the human soul in the school of his master, Ammonius; and thus he produced a doctrine pregnant with dangerous consequences, and one altogether unknown in the Scriptures. Still it must be admitted, that although the modesty and inconstancy of Origen did not extend so far as his patrons and advocates wish us to believe, yet they do serve to vindicate him in a degree.—And of similar tendency is, what *Jerome* testifies of him, (Epist. lxv. c. 4.) that he wrote to Fabian, the Roman bishop, that his friend Ambrose had published some of his writings which he did not wish to have go abroad. And yet, in the works which he undoubtedly wished to see circulated unlimitedly, there are passages enough that may be censured.——If now, over and above these extenuations, we look at the apologies for Origen by Pamphilus, Haloix, Mirandula, Huet, and his many other advocates, we shall find little that can satisfy a sagacious and impartial mind. For example, it is true, as his friends assert, that the accusers of Origen disagree among themselves, and charge him with contrary errors; but the inference they would draw, that therefore Origen was innocent and was borne down by false accusations, will not follow. For they themselves admit, that Origen was not uniform in his belief, and that he uttered different sentiments at different times, according to the occasions, the persons he was combatting, and the particular state of his mind. And hence, he is not unfrequently at variance with himself, and the opinion he advanced at one time, he afterwards exchanged for another altogether different. And it may be added, that Origen is not the same man when calmly seated in the teacher's chair, as he is when, with heated feelings, he comes forth as a disputant and encounters an antagonist. As a teacher, he writes soberly, and as he really thinks; but when he is disputing, he does not state just what he believes or regards as true, but frequently such things, true or false, as are suited to embarrass his adversary. It would be easy to show, that he considered disputes as to be settled as wars are, or that it was not important, whether his antagonist was prostrated by guile and subtilty or by valor in combat. And hence, the positions he assumes [p. 610.] when confronting Celsus, or the Jews, or the heretics, are entirely different from those he lays down when calmly expounding Christian truth as a teacher.—No more account do I make of the argument, with which nearly all the patrons of Origen surfeit us, that many other doctors of the ancient church taught just as he did on many points of theology. For, not to insist on the principle that the multitude of those who embrace an error does not make it true, it was the fact, that most of those who agreed with Origen, lived after him, and they appear to have received their opinions from him, as being the common teacher of the church. Besides, these other doctors who teach and maintain the same doctrines with Origen, understood those doctrines differently from what he did, and they were led in a very different manner into the belief of them.——We will now take a nearer view of the man under consideration. And, *first*, we will speak of the man himself; *then*, of his philosophy; and *lastly*, of his theology, and his method of explaining religious subjects.

In the first place, Origen himself, if judged by his moral worth, was unquestionably a great and estimable man, and one who has had few equals in any age. Nor would it divest him of this praise, if it were perfectly true, (as stated by *Epiphanius*, Hæres. lxiv. c. 2.) that at Alexandria he was once brought to the alternative of either sacrificing to the gods, or yielding his body to be polluted by an Ethiopian; and that to avoid the infamy, he promised to offer sacrifice; yet he did not do so, for he retracted his promise, and the incense placed in his hands was shaken into the fire by the bystanders. Men of high character have maintained, and with pretty strong arguments, that this story should be classed among slanderous fables. But, suppose it true, and it will only prove that Origen, being suddenly arrested, and thrown off his guard, hastily concluded that he should sin less by sacrificing to the gods, than by yielding his body to be stained with eternal infamy by the Ethiopian; but that he presently recovered himself, and instantly reversed his determination. In this, I think, no one can find any great and wilful fault. For who among the holiest of mortals is so uniformly wise, that, in the most trying circumstances, he consents to no divergence from the strictest rule of duty? Yet, except this one thing, Origen possessed every excellence that can adorn the Christian character; uncommon piety, from his very childhood; astonishing devotedness to that most holy religion which he professed; unequalled perseverance in labors and toils for the advancement of the Christian cause; untiring zeal for the church, and for the extension of Christianity; an elevation of soul which placed him above all ordinary desires or fears; a most permanent contempt of wealth, honors, pleasures, and of death itself; the purest trust in the Lord Jesus, [p. 611.] for whose sake, when he was old and oppressed with ills of every kind, he patiently and perseveringly endured the severest sufferings. It is not strange, therefore, that he was held in so high estimation, both while he lived and after death. Certainly if any man deserves to stand first in the catalogue of saints and martyrs, and to be annually held up as an example to Christians, this is the man: for, except the apostles of Jesus Christ and their companions, I know of no one, among all those enrolled and honored as saints, who excelled him in holiness and virtue. He was censured indeed, by *Demetrius* and others, for having emasculated himself: and I will not acquit him of all fault in that matter. But the fault itself is such as demonstrates the strength of his resolution, and his devotedness to religion, nor could it be committed by an ordinary man.

But Origen does not appear equally great, when estimated by his native powers. Undoubtedly he possessed genius, had a very happy memory, great thirst for knowledge, a very fertile imagination, and uncommon eloquence and powers of teaching; and these caused both Christians and pagans to listen to him, with intense interest, when he taught philosophy and other divine and human sciences in the Christian school of Alexandria. But those who are capable of judging, and are familiar with his writings, will not rank him among geniuses of the highest order. Certainly he was not one who, as the saying is, could swim without his board; i. e. not one who, by the inherent powers of his own mind, could examine truth in its fundamental principles, and discover and judge what is accordant with those principles, and what is not. He was such a philosopher as many in this and every age, who can treasure up in their memory and well understand the systems of doctrine inculcated by their teachers, and can bring out their acquired knowledge, pertinently, when questions and occasions demand it; and if any obstruction is thrown in their path, they can swerve a little this way or that, yet always are sure that the truth lies wholly within the sphere of their received instructions. For it is very certain that Origen never travels, in thought or argument, beyond the bounds of that knowledge which he received in early life from his teachers; he never philosophises freely, and in the exercise of his own ingenuity, but regards the system he imbibed from Ammonius as the only rational and sound philosophy. And hence, so long as this philosophy, which was his sole reliance, supplies suitable matter for his discussions and compositions, he appears a valuable writer, and treats his subjects with acuteness and ingenuity; but when destitute of such aid, as is frequently the case, he is like a man travelling in a foreign country, who does understand how the roads run. This is no where more apparent than in his book against Celsus, the assailant of Christianity. In that work, so long as [p.612] he can draw from his philosophy, he appears forceable and methodical; but when this resource fails him, his arguments are weak, and sometimes futile. These remarks explain, *why* the man, who on many topics is a wise and acute reasoner, is on others puerile. Unassisted, he rarely produces anything of much importance; but when sustained by his master, or by the instructions of the Bible, he appears very respectable. The learning of Origen, for the age in which he lived, was abundant and excellent. He had read immensely, and was acquainted with the doctrines of all sects, both of philosophers and Christians. He had acquired from the Greeks their polite learning; and he was not ignorant of mathematics. In the philosophical department, dialectics, physics, astronomy, &c., he was well versed, in the way before stated, namely, whatever he had received from the lips of teachers or had learned from books, he retained well in memory, and had at command. In Hebrew learning he had some knowledge. In short, he had travelled through the whole encyclopædia of human knowledge in that age, and he was justly accounted a universal scholar, both by the Christians and by other people.

We now proceed to his philosophy. Besides *Clemens Alex.* rector of the Christian school at Alexandria, a follower of the eclectic mode of philosophizing, he had for his preceptor *Ammonius Saccas*, the celebrated founder of the new Platonic school, who, while he sought to bring all sects of philosophers to agreement, adopted the principle that the philosophers differed only on trivial points, and were agreed in matters of importance to virtue and happiness; and consequently, that there is but *one philosophy*, though under different forms, or differently stated. Now *that* philosophy, which Origen regarded as true, and as recognized by all the philosophers, was the Ammonian or the new Platonic, though slightly modified, that it might not conflict with Christian principles, with which it stood in the closest alliance. Of this philosophy I will give a brief summary, which it is easy to deduce from the writings of Origen: to state it fully, would be needless.

All things that exist, whether corporeal or void of gross matter, emanated eternally from God, the source of all things. This first principle of the new Platonic school, derived from Egyptian wisdom, as we have elsewhere shown, was the basis or foundation of Origen's philosophy. But the Christian scriptures reject this doctrine, taken in the sense in which the Platonists understood it. For the Platonists believed the world to be without beginning, and without end, or to have flowed forth from God eternally, and to be destined to continue for ever. The Christian's Bible, on the contrary, clearly teaches, that the world was created at a certain time, and that at a certain time it will perish. [p. 613.] Origen therefore thought it necessary to modify this doctrine, and adjust it to the instructions of Christianity; and so he introduced the idea of a perpetual succession or propagation of worlds. Innumerable worlds similar to this, existed and perished, before the present world was produced; and after this world shall end, innumerable others will exist in endless succession. (See de Principiis, lib. iii. c. 5. Opp. tom. i. p. 149.) Now admitting this doctrine, a person may believe the declarations of the Scriptures respecting the origin and the end of this world, and at the same time hold the Platonic dogma of the eternal efflux of the world from God, and its eternal duration. Yet this theory of an eternal series of worlds, successively springing up and falling to ruin, though not requiring any great powers of mind for its invention, did not originate with Origen. He simply adopted it from the Stoics and others, in compliance with the precept of the eclectic philosophy, that the truth is to be gathered from all sects.—We proceed: *Souls*, like all other finite things, emanated from the divine nature, long before the material world was formed; and they were originally all equal in their nature, in moral excellence, and in rank; and all, therefore, with no exception, had in them some combination or admixture of corporeal substance. For Origen uniformly inculcates, that only the divine Being is altogether free from corporeal matter and of a simple nature; that all the other beings endowed with reason, or all finite spirits, are enclosed in a sort of subtile and etherial vehicles, or a drapery of a corporeal nature. All souls moreover. possess free will, and equal power to do good or to do ill, or are able freely to do the one or the other. And this power or freedom of choice, is so inherent in them, that it can never become extinct and lost. Origen, (*de Principp.* lib. ii. c. 8. sec. 2. p. 94.) defines a soul to be *substantiam rationabiliter sensibilem et mobilem:* which definition may be understood from what has been said. On this freedom of volition, which is a property of all souls without exception, depend all the changes in human affairs whether past or future, all the changes in the universe, all the distinctions and differences among men and spirits, all the variations in the divine decrees and proceedings. For some souls, while in their celestial state, before this world was created, used their free will wisely and properly; but others abused it, in different ways, some more grievously, and others more lightly. And therefore divine justice demanded, that the souls which had misused their liberty should undergo some punishment. And hence came the present world, and the race of men. For God decreed, that the sinning souls should be clothed in grosser bodies, so that they might suffer in them the penalties of their temerity. And as there was great diversity in the offences committed by them, it became necessary for God to create bodies of different kinds or natures, so that he might assign to each a body suited to the magnitude and enormity of the sins which defiled it. [p. 614.] Some souls were therefore lodged in those splendid bodies, the sun, the moon, and the stars: for it was the belief of Origen, that all the stars have souls. Others were doomed to inhabit human bodies, which are vastly inferior in strength, healthiness, beauty, &c., because the souls to be imprisoned in them had in many ways deviated from the path of rectitude and virtue, and therefore deserved various kinds of chastisement for their ill deserts. Others, the demons for example, were attached to bodies more tenuous indeed than ours, but extremely ugly, and such as vehemently excite the soul to evil. By the wisdom of the supreme Being, all these bodies are skilfully located, and most fitly arranged, so as to produce the admirable fabric of the created world. But let us hear Origen explain his own views: (de *Principiis*, lib. ii. c. 9. sec. 6, p 99.) Deus æquales creavit omnes ac similes, quos creavit, quippe quum nulla ei caussa varietatis ac diversitatis existeret. Verum quoniam rationabiles ipsæ creaturæ - - arbitrii facultate donatæ sunt: libertas unumquemque voluntatis suæ vel ad profectum per imitationem Dei provocavit, vel ad defectum per negligentiam traxit. Et hæc exstitit caussa diversitatis inter rationabiles creaturas, non ex conditoris voluntate vel judicio originem trahens, sed propriæ libertatis arbitrio. Deus vero cui jam creaturam suam pro merito dispensare justum videbatur, diversitates mentium in unius mundi consonantiam traxit, quo velut unam domum, in qua inesse deberent non solum vasa aurea et argentea, sed et lignea et fictilia, ex istis diversis vasis vel animis vel mentibus ornaret. Et has caussas mundus iste suæ diversitatis accepit, dum unumquemque divina providentia pro varietate motuum suorum vel animorum propositique dispensat. And, after a few sentences, he thus recapitulates the whole statement: (sec. 8. p. 100.) Unumquodque vas (i. e. anima) secundum mensuram puritatis suæ aut impuritatis locum, vel regionem, vel conditionem nascendi vel explendi aliquid in hoc mundo accepit: quæ omnia Deus usque ad minimum virtute sapientiæ suæ providens ac dignoscens, moderamine judicii sui æquissima retributione universa disponit, quatenus unicuique pro merito vel succurri vel consuli deberet. Origen explains and inculcates this opnion often and largely; and not without reason: for he supposed it to be of vast importance, for the vindication of the divine wisdom and justice, and that it accounts for the endless diversities which exist among men and spirits. The souls, distributed through so many and such diversified bodies, do not change their essential nature; and of course they retain their native freedom of volition. And although they can not use their free will for good with the same success. as they did in their celestial state when disconnected with gross matter, yet they [p. 615.] are not by any means so oppressed and fettered by their bodies as to be unable, if they would but exert their rational powers, to improve slowly their condition, and gradually to recover their former beauty. Therefore such souls as exert their native powers, and by contemplation and other means sever themselves from the imagination and senses and from the concupiscence generated by the body, are thereby gradually purified; and, on becoming released from their bodies, they are again elevated to their former state. Yet they do not recover their primitive felicity, at once and in a moment, but they pass, by a slow process, through various changes up to God. And the souls which neglect this duty, will either migrate into other bodies, or will be subjected to some harsher modes of purgation, until they shall repent and begin to exert their liberty for good. And when all souls shall have returned to their primitive state and to God, then this material world will be dissolved. But because, from their very nature, souls can never lose their free will, nor, consequently, the power of abusing their freedom, the very souls that have overcome the evils of this life, as well as others, may and will again depart from duty and from God, and then again deserve punishment. And whenever their number shall be sufficiently large, God must again create bodies, and out of them frame a new world in which he can punish the violators of his eternal law, each according to his merits and the magnitude of his offence. And of this successive rise or worlds, there will be no end; because the liberty of the will, which naturally belongs to all souls, prevents their ever arriving at an unchangeable constancy in good. To judge correctly of the theology, which Origen based on this philosophy, we must keep in view his two preceptors, *Clement*, of Alexandria, and

Ammonius. The former of these, as we have already shown, held philosophy in very high estimation; and he maintained that philosophy correctly understood, and freed from the false notions of the sects, does not disagree with the religion of Christ. The latter, Ammonius, not only sought to reconcile the Christian religion with the precepts of his philosophy, but he also believed, as already shown, that Christianity could be reconciled with the Pagan religions, provided they were rightly explained and were divested of the fables and error brought into them by the vulgar and by the priests. Now Origen, treading in the footsteps of his teachers, regarded philosophy as a precious gift of God; and he supposed that the wisdom proclaimed by Christ, although more sublime and perfect than philosophy, was nevertheless based upon it; and that all Christian doctrines might be explained and vindicated by philosophy. Indeed, it is not to be concealed, that he coincided with Ammonius in the belief that the popular religions, if their fables and superstition were excluded, might in a measure be combined with Christianity. In order to reconcile the worship of one God, which Christianity requires, with paying homage to many gods, Ammonius assumed, that God had committed the administration and [p. 616.] government of the various parts of the universe to demons of great power and virtue; and that it was reasonable and proper that some honor and public reverence be paid to these powerful ministers of the divine Providence: because God, the supreme Lord, is honored in the person of his friends; just as the respect paid to the vicegerents and envoys of earthly kings and princes, redounds to the honor of the kings and princes whom they represent. Moreover, these legates and ministers of God have the power of conferring benefits on men, such as health, a salubrious atmosphere, fruitful seasons, and all the comforts of life; and on the other hand, they have power in various ways to harm those who despise them. And hence, the interests of mankind require, that some worship should be paid to them; and the people of the primitive ages were divinely instructed to do this; but, in process of time, a depraved human belief converted these ministers of God into imaginary deities, and introduced numerous errors and corrupt rites, and even caused the worship of the supreme Being to become almost extinct and lost. Now if these faults were corrected, and the worship of the demons restored to its pristine simplicity, there would be nothing to forbid men's paying supreme homage to the one supreme God, and at the same time, yielding reverence to the ministers of God, in the ancient manner, in certain places, at proper times, and with suitable rites. And to these views, for substance, Origen gave assent. He believed, that God has committed the care and government of the several provinces of his great empire, the universe, to angels of different orders, who are the guardians and protectors not only of nations, but of individual men, and also of animals, the fruits of the earth, &c. Whether prayers and worship should be offered to these angels, he does not explicitly state, in any of his works that have reached us: and yet, in a few passages, he does not disguise the fact that he leaned much towards an opinion but little diverse from that of Ammonius above stated, respecting the union of the worship of one God with the worship of demons. See Huet's *Origeniana*, Lib. ii. p. 89.

Origen's idea of the relation and connexion between Christianity and philosophy, may be learned distinctly from two passages in his writings still preserved. The first passage is in his *Philocalia*, taken from his epistle to Gregory Thaumaturgus, bishop of Neocæsarea, and exhibited in the edition of his works by Charles de la Rue, tom. i. p. 30. Here Origen asserts, that philosophy is as important to Christian theology, as geometry, music, grammar, rhetoric and astronomy are to philosophy: Ὅπερ φασὶ φιλοσόφων παῖδες περὶ γεωμετρίας - - - ὡς συνερίθων φιλοσοφίᾳ, τοῦθ' ἡμεῖς εἴπωμεν δὲ περὶ αὐτῆς φιλοσοφίας πρὸς χριστιανισμόν. This, he says, in reference to the *true* philosophy, or philosophy purified from the corruptions and figments of the sects: and such he believed to be the philosophy which he had learned from Ammonius, after correcting it in a few points [p. 617.] to make it harmonize with Christianity. Therefore, as astronomy, geometry, music, and the other sciences are useful to a philosopher for sharpening his acumen, strengthening his reasoning powers, and enabling him to comprehend and arrange more perfectly the precepts of philosophy; so, he supposed, philosophy is useful to a theologian, as helping him to acquire just views of Christian doctrines and to give just expositions of them. In the other passage, (which is in his xv. Homily on Genesis, sec. 3. Opp. tom. ii. 98.) he discourses more at large, and not only of what he considered the true philosophy, but also of the current philosophy of the day, whether true or false. He first lays down this proposition: Philosophia neque in omnibus legi Dei contraria est, neque in omnibus consona: and he then explains both parts of the proposition, adducing examples for illustration. On the agreement of philosophy with the divine law, he says: Multi enim philosophorum unum esse Deum, qui cuncta creaverit, scribunt. In hoc consentiunt legi Dei. Aliquanti etiam hoc addiderunt, quod Deus cuncta per verbum suum et fecerit et regat, et verbum Dei sit, quo cuncta moderentur. In hoc non solum legi, sed etiam Evangeliis consona scribunt. *Moralis* vero et *physica*, quæ dicitur, *philosophia*, pæne omnia quæ nostra sunt sentiunt. He then proceeds to the points of disagreement between the divine law and philosophy, thus: Dissident vero a nobis, cum Deo dicunt esse materiam coæternam. Dissident, cum Deum negant curare mortalia, sed providentiam ejus supra lunaris globi spatia cohiberi. Dissident a nobis, cum vitas nascentium ex stellarum cursibus pendunt. Dissident, cum sempiternum dicunt hunc mundum et nullo fine claudendum. Sed et alia plurima sunt, in quibus nobiscum vel dissident vel concordant. These statements of Origen will be better understood, if we consider his subdivisions of philosophy; namely, that philosophy was commonly divided into three parts, *logic*, *physics* and *ethics*, or into *rational*, *natural* and *moral*. Therefore, as he most explicitly affirms, that the philosophers agree perfectly with the Christians in physics and ethics, or in natural and moral philosophy, it is clear that the whole disagreement between philosophy and Christianity, in his opinion, related to *logic* or *rational philosophy*. But *his* rational philosophy is not that which we understand by the term; but it is *ontology*, or our *pneumatology*, *cosmogony*, and *natural theology*, as is manifest from the examples he adduces. This his rational philosophy, as taught by the philosophical sects, was, according to his judgment, in many things contrary to the Christian religion: but if freed from the errors and false opinions of the sects, and made to conform to the truth, it would contain nothing inconsistent with Christianity. And this *true* rational philosophy, he believed to be that which he had learned in the school of Ammonius. This was the philosophy, which he wished to associate with Christian truth, and to produce a system embracing both.

How large a place in theology, Origen would allow to what he [p. 618.] accounted true philosophy, and by what laws he would combine them together, we are now to show. In the first place, he affirmed, that all the things which must be believed in order to salvation, are most plainly set forth in the Scriptures: and these things, he would have men simply believe without subjecting them at all to the dominion of philosophy. Thus, in the introduction to his work *de Principiis* (sec. 3. p. 47.) he says: Illud autem scire oportet, quoniam sancti Apostoli fidem Christi prædicantes, de quibusdam quidem quæcunque necessaria (ad salutem) crediderunt, omnibus etiam his qui pigriores erga inquisitionem divinæ scientiæ videbantur, *manifestissime* tradiderunt. And of the doctrines which he supposed were taught in the clearest manner in the Bible, and which should be received without dubitation or criticism, he made out a sort of catalogue. It is this: (I) There is one God, the author and creator of all things. (II) In these last days, this God hath sent Christ to call first the Jews, and then other nations. (III) Jesus Christ was born of the Father, anterior to the creation (ante omnem creaturam), and was the minister of the Father in the creation of all things. (IV) The same Christ, although he was God, was made man, and became incarnate; and being made man, he remained God as he was before; he truly suffered, truly died, and truly rose again. (V) In honor and dignity, the Holy Spirit is an associate of the Father and the Son. (VI) Every soul possesses reason, and free volition and choice; and, when removed from the body, will be rewarded or punished according to its deserts. (VII) Our bodies will be raised in a state highly improved. (VIII) A devil and his angels exist; and they strive to immerse men in sins. (IX) This world will hereafter be dissolved. (X) The holy Scriptures were dictated by the Spirit of God; and they have a twofold sense, the one obvious, the other latent. (XI) There are good angels and powers, which minister to the salvation of men. These, he says, are specimens (*species*) of the things that are manifestly inculcated in the Apostolic annunciation. This language seems to imply, that Origen did not aim to make a complete enumeration of the doctrines clearly taught in the Bible and necessary to be known, but only to give a *specimen* of such a collection. Yet of this I am not entirely certain, and I leave others to decide.

But the inspired men, by whom the principal truths of religion are stated so intelligibly to all, have left other truths in some obscurity. In the first place, they have not clearly stated the *grounds and reasons* of the truths which they require us to believe: that is, they have not shown us how the revealed truths they teach stand related to the first principles of truth and reason. And again, the things themselves, they have indeed stated clearly enough; but of the *how, why* and *wherefore* they are so, they are silent. And here the industry of wise and perspicacious christians may find employment; first, in searching out and demonstrating, by the aids of philosophy, the *grounds and* [p. 619.] *reasons* of the doctrines divinely revealed; and secondly, in determining, on the principles of a true philosophy, the *modes and relations* of the things revealed in the Scriptures. Such, I suppose, were Origen's views: but let us hear his own words. In the preface to his work *de Principiis*, he says: *Rationem* assertionis eorum reliquerunt (Apostoli) ab his *inquirendam*, qui Spiritus dona excellentiora mererentur, et præcipue sermonis, sapientiæ et scientiæ gratiam per ipsum Spiritum Sanctum percepissent. Here we are taught, that the things at first obscure, afterwards become more clear. Again he says: De aliis vero dixerunt quidem, quia sint: *quomodo* autem, aut *unde* sint, siluerunt; profecto ut studiosiores quique ex posteris suis, qui amatores essent sapientiæ, exercitium habere possent, in quo ingenii sui fructum ostenderent, hi videlicet qui dignos se et capaces ad recipiendam sapientiam præpararent. These statements need exemplification; and Origen himself affords it. That the world at a certain time began to exist, and will at a certain time perish, is incontrovertible, and is most expressly affirmed in Scripture. But for what cause it was created, and why it will be destroyed, we are very obscurely informed. Therefore, these are things to be investigated by the aid of philosophy.—That men have apostatised, is clear; but the causes of their apostasy are not equally manifest, and therefore must be inquired after.—That the Holy Spirit, no less than the Son, proceeded from the Father, the Scriptures manifestly teach; but the mode of the procession, they do not define. He subjoins: In hoc non jam manifesto decernitur, utrum (Spiritus S.) natus an innatus, vel filius etiam Dei ipse habendus sit, nec ne. Sed inquirenda jam ista pro viribus sunt de sacra scriptura et sagaci perquisitione investiganda.—That the devil and his angels are real existences, and also the angels of an opposite character, no person who has read the Bible will deny. Of these he tells us; *Sunt quidem* hæc; *quæ* autem sint, aut *quomodo* sint, non satis clare exposuit. Here, therefore, he who seeks for knowledge, must labor for it.

On this subject it is especially to be noticed, that both here and elsewhere Origen teaches, that the Holy Scriptures are not entirely silent respecting the *causes* or *reasons* of the truths they assert, but as it were give us intimations of them; but respecting the *modes* or *forms* of the things, they are wholly silent. And hence, they who attempt, by the aid of philosophy, to explore the inmost recesses of theology, or in other words, to bring into the light what the Scriptures have left in the dark,—have not, in all cases, the same task to perform, and the same success to anticipate. Those who labor to explain the *causes* or *reasons* of the truths taught in the Bible, must not only call philosophy to their aid, but must also carefully search out the arcane senses of Holy Scripture. For Origen firmly believed, that under cover of the words, phrases, images, and narratives of the Scriptures, the Holy Spirit had concealed the internal reasons and grounds of things; or, as he himself expresses it, that in the *body* of holy writ, (so he denominates the *proper sense* of the words,) there was [p. 620.] a *soul*, (an arcane and recondite sense,) and that this *soul* exhibits, to careful contemplaters of it, as it were in a mirror, the causes, connections, and dependencies of both human and divine wisdom. In this he trod in the path of

Philo Judæus; whom he,—following the example and authority of *Clement*, his preceptor,—regarded as the wisest of all explorers of the true sense of Scripture, and therefore followed as his guide.—But when the *modes*, or *forms* of the things are to be examined, the philosophic theologian need not resort to the sacred Scriptures; because, as they say nothing of the *modes* of things, he must trust and follow his own ingenuity and the dictates of philosophy. A passage already cited is applicable here; but I will adduce another, equally explicit, and admirably illustrative of the character of Origen's system. He says, (p. 49): Oportet igitur, velut elementis ac fundamentis hujusmodi uti secundum mandatum quod dicit: *Illuminate vobis lumen scientiæ* (Hosea, x. 12, Septuag.) omnem, qui cupit seriem quamdam et corpus ex horum omnium ratione perficere, ut manifestis et necessariis assertionibus de singulis, quibusque quid sit in vero rimetur et unum (ut diximus) corpus efficiat exemplis et affirmationibus, vel his quas in sanctis Scripturis invenerit (i. e., he who would combine theology and philosophy, and from both frame one system, must endeavor to ascertain the grounds and reasons of the doctrines, by examining into the arcane sense of the sacred books.) vel quas ex consequentiæ ipsius indagine ac recti tenore repererit, (i. e. but if the *mode* is the thing sought for, of which the Scriptures say nothing, then it is sufficient to explain and define it in accordance with (*tenore recti*) the dictates of philosophy.)—These statements may enable us to understand why Origen, in explaining religious truths, generally betakes himself first to reason and philosophy, and then recurs to the sacred oracles, to elucidate by them his explanations, and to confirm his conjectures by some similitude; but sometimes, without consulting the Scriptures at all, he makes philosophy his sole guide. The former is his course, when he supposes the inquiry relates to the *causes* of things; and the latter when the *modes* or forms are discussed. Yet as these two things are intimately connected and often scarcely separable, he not unfrequently confounds them, and but seldom discriminates accurately between them.

The labor of investigating the *causes* or *reasons* of the revealed truths and doctrines by appeals to the Scriptures, is more arduous and difficult than the labor of exploring and defining the *modes* or *forms* of holy things. Because, for the former, the illumination and aid of the Holy Spirit are necessary; and none can succeed in it, (as he says,) "except those who have acquired the more excellent gifts of the Holy Spirit, and, especially, have obtained, through the Holy Spirit, the gift of language, of wisdom, and of knowledge." This he repeats often, both in his work de Principiis and elsewhere, declaring [p. 621.] that they only are competent to this work whom God deems worthy of his special friendship. He says, repeatedly: Certius sciunt, qui Dei per Christum et Spiritum Sanctum amici sunt. The full force of his declarations can be understood by those only who are familiar with the theology of the ancient Christians. It was an established opinion among them, one that prevailed long before the times of Origen, that the proper and natural sense of the words of the Bible is obvious to all readers who are not heedless and stupid; but that what Origen calls *spirtialem intelligentiam*—the remote sense, or that latent under the words and things,—is manifest only to those whom the Holy Spirit in-

structs and illuminates. And this gift of the Holy Spirit, which confers the power of discovering the mysteries hidden in the sacred books, they called *the gift of wisdom and knowledge*; and of this gift they understood *St. Paul* to speak, 1 Cor. xii. 8; "For to one is given by the Spirit the word of *wisdom* (σοφίας); to another the word of *knowledge* (γνώσεως) by the same Spirit." And hence they were accustomed to use the word *knowledge* (γνῶσις) to designate the mystical sense of the Bible. See Jo. Ern. Grabe's Spicil. Patr. et Hæreticor. Saec. i. p. 328; and the notes of the learned on the Epistle of *Barnabas*, § 6. Now, as Origen believed, that in the Scriptures the Holy Spirit teaches us—not indeed by the *words* but by the *things* which the words indicate, not openly but covertly, by allegories and enigmas—how the peculiar doctrines of Christianity harmonize with each other, and with the decisions of philosophy, it was natural for him to assert, that divine assistance is necessary for drawing this nut out of its envelope.—The other task, that of exploring the *modes* of things, was less difficult; because, in addition to a knowledge of true philosophy, it required only an earnest application of the powers of the human mind. And hence, as rational truth and revealed or heavenly truth do not disagree, a sagacious man, possessing sound reason, can easily discover their agreement. Yet he does not deny, but declares often and in various terms, that as divine things are more sublime and excellent than human, great care is necessary lest we misjudge in such matters; and that some parts of the Christian religion are so difficult, that they can scarcely, if at all, be adequately explained by human phrases and analogies. Of this nature, he gravely tells us, is the doctrine of the union of two natures in Christ, which, though he explains it according to the principles of his philosophy, yet he bids his hearers remember, can never be fully explained. Of this doctrine he says (de Princípp. L. ii. c. 6. § 2. p. 90): "I suppose that it is beyond the comprehension of even the holy Apostles; nay, perhaps, the explanation of this sacrament exceeds all created intelligence among the Angels."—From these statements, I think, we may learn the cause of the great modesty and timidity which Origen exhibits in his exposition of many topics in theology. He supposed no one, unless having familiar inter-
[p. 622.] course with God, and receiving the *gift of wisdom and knowledge*, could successfully explore the hidden meanings of the Bible; but whether he himself had obtained this gift from God, he dared not decide. He therefore always approached this species of discussion with timidity, and he left it timidly; he almost never affirmed positively, that he had ascertained the true import of the texts he discussed. He assumes more confidence, indeed, when he thinks the coincidence between theology and philosophy to be manifest; and he seems, sometimes, to know and be positive, rather than diffidently to utter his opinions. Yet, as he fully believed that many things in theology are beyond human comprehension, he seldom discusses what we call the mysteries of religion, in a manner that would imply the impossibility that anything more satisfactory can be said of them. On the contrary, he almost invariably declares himself ready to change his opinion, if any friend of God can offer more correct views of the subject.

It will now be seen, if I mistake not, of what nature and magnitude were those offences of Origen against Christianity, which occasioned so much controversy during so many ages. They all originated from this one principle, which he regarded as beyond all controversy, *that such affinity and congruity exist between Christianity and human reason, that not only the grounds but also the forms of all Christian doctrines may be explained by the dictates of philosophy.* Yet this error, though not small, might be considered only a slight stain upon that holy and extraordinary man, if it had not been carried beyond mere speculation. But he recommended to the preachers of Christianity, to carry what he taught into use and general practice; and he prescribed for their guidance the following maxim: *That it is vastly important to the honor and advantage of Christianity, that all its doctrines be traced back to the sources of all truth, or be shown to flow from the principles of philosophy; and consequently, that a Christian theologian should exert his ingenuity and industry primarily, to demonstrate the harmony between religion and reason, or to show that there is nothing taught in the Scriptures but what is founded in reason.* He himself, as we have seen, followed this his precept with some degree of moderation and prudence: but by laying down this principle, and also by his example, he gave to the more daring ample power and licence to do violence to revealed truth, and to strangely pervert the plainest doctrines of the Bible, so that they might appear in harmony with a true or false philosophy. His direction to make appeals to the Scriptures, might seem to counteract the evil, but, in reality, it increased and amplified it. For, by teaching that the philosophical reasons of all the Christian doctrines lie concealed in the narration and sentences of the Bible, and should be drawn forth by art and ingenuity, he prompted the indiscreet and those of exuberant imaginations, as it were, to put out the light of revelation, or obscure its simple wisdom, by their childish and silly allegories.—The foundation of all his faults was, that he fully believed nothing to be more true and certain than [p. 623.] what the philosophy he received from Ammonias taught him respecting God, the world, souls, demons, &c.; and therefore he in a measure recast and remodelled the doctrines of Christ, after the pattern of that philosophy, doing it indeed, for the most part, modestly and hesitatingly, but sometimes quite boldly, and in a style somewhat authoritative.

The entire system of philosophical religion which existed in the mind of Origen, no one has fully delineated: nor was Origen uniform and consistent in his statements of it; for he discards at one time what he affirms at another. A large part of his system, however, will be obvious to one who considers what we have already said of his philosophy, and especially what he held respecting the origination of all things from God, the free-will of souls, their transgressing in their primitive state, and before their union with bodies, and other kindred subjects; for, while he was undecided on many other topics, on these he had no doubts; and therefore he constantly applied these views to the explication of the Christian doctrines.—Specimens of his opinions on the most essential points in theology, are all we shall present for the gratification of those wishing to know these matters. In the first place, he supposed that all the declarations of the Scriptures respecting the Father, the Son, and the Holy Spirit, might be easily reconciled with his philosophy. For, believing that all things eternally emanated from the divine nature, he attributed to the Son and to the Holy Spirit the highest rank among these emanations from the divine nature. And he always and uniformly compares their origination from the Father, with the efflux of the solar rays from the sun; and teaches that these solar rays, although of the same nature with the sun from which they flow, are yet only minute particles of the solar light and heat issuing from the immense mass; and that they sustain the same relation to their source, as small streams issuing from great lakes, sustain to those lakes. In his opinion, therefore, the Father is the prime cause of all things, and the Son is a secondary cause, and, as it were, the instrument by which the Father created the world, and diffused widely his beneficence; just as a cloud, when fecundated by the sun's rays, scatters and spreads those rays over the earth. In evolving and expanding this doctrine, Origen is wonderfully variable; so that he sometimes seems to come very near the views of the Nicene fathers, at other times to incline towards the Sabellians, and at times to agree with the Arians. If we would judge him correctly and fairly, we must, I think, keep in view his first or fundamental principles.—Origen finds greater difficulty when he attempts to reconcile with his philosophy what the Scriptures teach respecting the union of two natures in Christ. For he thought it utterly impossible that God, a being entirely separate from matter, should ever assume a body, or be willing to associate himself with matter. He expressly tells us, (*de Princip.* L. ii. c. 6. p. 90.): Non enim *possibile* erat Dei naturam corpori sine mediatore misceri. That is, the divine nature, being [p. 624.] generically a different substance from matter, the two substances cannot possibly be commingled. To overcome this obstacle, and yet exclude from the divine nature all propension towards a body or matter, he conceived that God did not receive the man, but the man received God. Yet not the whole man did so, but only the *soul*, the principal part of man. That *soul*, which migrated into the body of Christ and inhabited it, exerted more perfectly than all the souls which emanated from God, its free-will, in the wisest and best manner, in its primitive state, and expended all its energies in the contemplation of the Son of God, the first emanation from the divine nature. This persevering and most intense consideration or contemplation of the Word or Son of God, procured for *this soul* the privilege that it received the entire Word of God into itself, or itself passed entire into the Son of God, (it is uncertain which.) and thus it became one person with the Son of God. Hear his own statement, (*de Princip.* L. ii. c. 6. p. 90.): Cum pro liberi arbitrii facultate varietas unumquemque ac diveritas animorum habuisset, ut alius ardentiore, alius tenuiore et exiliore erga auctorem suum amore teneretur, illa anima, de qua dixit Jesus: quia nemo auferet a me animam meam (Joh. x. 18,) ab initio creaturæ et deinceps inseparabiliter ei atque indissociabiliter inhærens, utpote sapientiæ et verbo Dei et veritati ac luci veræ, et tota totum recipiens, atque in ejus lucem splendoremque ipsa cedens, facta est cum ipso principaliter unus spiritus. - - - Unus spiritus esse cum Deo cui magis convenit, quam huic animæ quæ se ita Deo per dilectionem junxit, ut cum eo unus spiritus merito dicatur. What Origen here asserts of the soul of Christ, appears to us as a mere assumption; but he regarded it as accordant both with the dictates of reason and the declarations of Scripture. By reason, he thus supports his opinion: No one can be rewarded or punished by God, unless he merits it. Because God, being most wise and righteous, can do nothing inconsiderately or without good reason. And therefore he must distribute both happiness and misery, according to the merits of those who are susceptible of them. Hence it follows, that this supreme felicity which the *soul* of Christ received, was conferred upon it, solely because of its merits. And if so, then it follows that *this soul* excelled all others in its love to God, and in consequence of this love, became united to the Son of God.—As for scriptural evidence, he supposed the words of David, Ps. xlv. 8. [The sceptre of thy kingdom is a right sceptre,] were especially favorable to his opinion: and with that text, he connected others both from the Old Testament and the New.—By means of this union of the soul of Christ with the Word or Son of God, it became possible for God to be united to a human body: not indeed directly, and by itself, but indirectly, through the soul to which he was united. For, according to Origen's views, every finite spirit is clothed with a tenuous body or a subtile kind of matter, which subtile matter, without any difficulty, can coalesce with the grosser kind of matter of which our bodies are composed. And in a finite spirit, like the soul, the desire [p. 625.] may arise for greater happiness; and consequently, also a wish to possess a body. He says: Hac ergo substantia animæ inter Deum carnemque mediante, (non enim possibile erat Dei naturam corpori sine mediatore misceri) nascitur Deus homo, illa substantia media existente, cui utique contra naturam non erat corpus assumere. Sed neque rursus anima illa, utpote substantia rationabilis, contra naturam habuit capere Deum, in quem, uti superius diximus, velut in verbum et sapientiam et veritatem tota jam cesserat. Unde et merito etiam ipsa cum ea, quam assumserat, carne, Dei filius, et Dei virtus, Christus et sapientia appelatur: et rursum Dei filius, per quem omnia creata sunt, Jesus Christus et filius hominis nominatur.—But if these things were so, then most assuredly the *Son of God* did not connect himself with human flesh; but it was the *soul* of Christ that became incarnate. Nor did the Word or Son of God, though dwelling in a body, have any intercourse with that body, (according to Origen, that was impossible,) but only the *soul* with which the Word had some affinity, communicated with the body: that is, the soul, having so coalesced with the Son of God as to be one spirit, governed the body, and so regulated all its movements that they could not swerve from the rule of rectitude and duty. Moreover, the moving cause of the descent of the Son of God to this earth and of the incarnation, was not in God, in his good will towards mankind; but it was in the *soul* of Jesus Christ. For this soul first perseveringly longed after communion with the Word or Son of God, and, by the right use of its freedom of choice, obtained it; and afterwards, it desired to be joined with matter or to a body, which, according to Origen, the divine nature never could desire. And, therefore, in this whole matter, the Son of God had no concern, except that he became united with the soul of Christ, and then permitted that *soul* to follow its wishes and inclinations.

As to the object and consequences of the advent of the Son of God to our world, and of his sufferings and death, Origen nowhere fully and explicitly states his views; but that his opinions on this subject were very different from those of modern Christians, and from the faith taught in the Scriptures, his philosophical notions respecting the soul and other matters, will not allow us to doubt. And in various passages he does not disguise the fact, although he may seem to take much pains not to let his hearers fully understand him. One thing indeed he often states, namely, that Christ by his death made atonement, not for the sins committed by souls in their primitive state before they inhabited bodies, but for their sins in the body; and so far his opinions do not differ from the common views of Christians. But it is quite otherwise, if we carefully weigh what he abundantly inculcates. I will not dwell on his belief, that the sacrifice of Christ had a reference to the sun, the moon, and all the stars, and to demons and angels; for, while his philosophy taught him that sinning souls inhabited not only human bodies, but likewise other material [p. 626.] objects, and also the demons, both those wholly depraved and those but partially bereft of their native beauty, and that Christ proffers aid to all souls estranged from God; he could not possibly think otherwise. But, what is vastly more important, Origen was—if I am not wholly deceived—ignorant of the *vicarious* nature of Christ's atonement, or he did not hold that Christ, *in our stead*, paid to divine justice the penalty of our ill deserts. Nor will this appear strange, if we consider that he denied the communion of the Son of God with the body of Christ, and the union of the divine and human natures in Christ, or what we call the *hypostatic union;* and that he held, as we have before stated, that only the *soul* of Christ was connected with the Word or Son of God; from which it must indubitably follow, that the pangs and death of Christ's body were only those of the *man* Christ, and not also of *God* joined with human nature; and that the blood which Christ shed was only the blood of a man, and not the blood of God; or, what is the same thing, that Christ, not as both God AND man, but only as a *man*, expiated the sins of mankind. And if this be admitted, all that we teach respecting the vicarious satisfaction of Christ falls to the ground.—If now the inquiry be raised, in *what manner* he supposed the death of Christ to take away the sins of men? I answer, first: he is nowhere explicit on this subject. Yet I will add, that he seems to have held, that the effusion of Christ's blood was sufficient to *purify* men and to *appease* divine justice. He has a long passage on this subject, in his 24th *Homily*, on the book of Numbers, § 1. (Opp. tom. ii. p. 362, 363.) From this passage his views are more clearly learned than from any others. He first asserts: Omne peccatum propitiationem requirere; propitiationem autem non fieri, nisi per hostiam, *id est, per sanguinem victimæ Deo oblatæ;* eaque re necessarium fuisse, ut provideretur hostia pro peccatis hominum. All this seems well enough; but what he goes on to say, and the inferences he makes, clearly show, that he attached to this language a very different meaning from that common among Christians. For he asserts, that the blood of any righteous person can expiate the sins of a portion of mankind; and especially if the righteous person, at the time he dies and pours out his blood, prays God to pardon those for whom he dies. Between the sacrifice of Christ and those which holy and righteous men, such as Paul, Abel, and others, present to God by their death, there are two points of difference, viz.: first, the sacrifice of Christ was universal, or extended to the whole human race, while those of other righteous persons can benefit only a portion of mankind before God; secondly, the blood of righteous men derives its efficacy chiefly from the prayers of those men; while Christ, being God, can remit sins, solely by his power, on account of his death: Vide ergo, ne forte sicut Dominus et Salvator noster, quasi agnus ad occisionem ductus et in sacrificium altaris oblatus, peccatorum remissionem universo præstitit mundo: ita fortasse (a modest [p. 627.] statement, as usual with him, but in accordance with his real belief, as the whole context shows,) et cæterorum sanctorum ac justorum sanguis, qui effusus est a sanguine Abel justi usque ad sanguinem Zachariæ prophetæ, alterius quidem sanguis sicut vitulæ, alterius sicut hirci, aut capræ aut alicujus horum fusus est *ad expiandum pro aliqua parte populum.* And this, he thinks, can be proved from the law of Moses. For while the law required various kinds of animals, lambs, calves, goats, &c., to be immolated to God for sin, Origen supposed slain *lambs* to be emblems of Christ's death, but that the other animals represented the deaths of holy and righteous men. Hear him explicitly stating this strange doctrine: Quod *si agnus*, qui ad purificandum populum datus est, ad personam Domini et Salvatoris nostri refertur, consequens videtur, quod etiam cætera animalia, quæ eisdem purificativis usibus deputata sunt, referri dibeant similiter ad aliquas personas, quæ purificationis aliquid humano generi conferant. And he repeats the same thing a little after, adding that perhaps also some of the angels and celestial spirits may offer themselves to God, as victims to expiate the sins of men: Sic ergo fortassis et si quis angelorum, cœlestiumque virtutum, aut si quis justorum hominum, vel etiam sanctorum prophetarum atque apostolorum, qui enixius interveniat (i. e. *precetur*) pro peccatis hominum, hic pro repropitiatione divina, velut aries, aut vitulus, aut hircus oblatus esse in sacrificium ob purificationem populo impetrandam accipi potest. After elucidating this subject by the example of Paul, whose language (in Rom. ix. 3, I could wish myself accursed, &c.; and in 2 Tim. iv. 6, I am now ready to be offered, &c.) he cites in confirmation; and after fully explaining his views, he returns to the consideration of Christ's sacrifice, and its difference from human victims, and tells us: Talis hæc fuit (*Christi*) hostia ut una sola sufficeret pro totius mundi salute; *cæteri enim precibus peccata, hic solus potestate dimisit.* Strikingly coincident herewith are his remarks concerning martyrs and their blood, in his *Exhortatio ad Martyrium*, near the end: Forte, quemadmodum nos pretioso Christi sanguine redempti sumus; ita et quidam pretioso martyrum sanguine redimuntur: ὄυτως τῷ τιμίῳ ἅιματι τῶν μαρτύρων ἀγορασθήσονται τινὲς·——— Origen did not suppose, and, for various reasons, he could not suppose, that those holy and righteous men, the martyrs, who (as he believed,) expiated the sins of some men by their death or blood, were, either by God or by their own act, *substituted* in the place of the persons whose sins they expiated, and so endured the penalties due to God for other men's sins; and therefore, neither did he believe that Christ—whose death he regarded as not in itself differing from the sufferings of those holy and righteous persons—was a *substitute* for the human race, and endured our penalties. And, consequently, we must [p. 628.] believe that Origen thought the mere blood of an innocent person could, of itself, move God to pardon sinners; and that, for the remission of sins, divine justice does not require the penalties of them to be endured, either by the violaters of the law or by their substitutes.

What *we* most religiously believe, namely, that the Son of God satisfied the divine law *in our stead*, and, by his most perfect obedience, merited for us a title to eternal life,—all this was alien from the philosophical religion of Origen. According to his belief, there resides in the minds of all men a *free will*, a native power of obeying the divine commands, which, when excited by a knowledge of divine truth, and aided by the influences of the Holy Spirit, can so control and govern all the movements and actions of the man, as to make those actions perfectly harmonize with the divine will. Nor can God,—as Origen clearly states in several places,—bestow the rewards of law, or the forfeited eternal felicity, upon any souls except the meritorious; that is, such as exert wisely and properly their innate liberty. For as souls, by the depraved use of their liberty, have deservedly lost their happiness and been thrust into these human bodies, so also, by their own merits, and not by those of another, they must return to God, and regain their lost felicity.—I need not proceed further; enough has been stated to show what is the character of Origen's philosophical theology, which differed marvellously from that of Christians at the present day. Yet if any are desirous of examining the entire system of this celebrated man, and of judging correctly of the controversies of so many great men respecting his sentiments, (which, I can recognize no one hitherto as doing,) they must, first of all, investigate, methodically digest, and intelligibly explain that philosophy which Origen has given us by fragments in his writings; and this being done, it will be readily perceived, that *they* labor in vain who would persuade us that Origen had the same views of religion as most Christians of the present day. For example: distinguished men dispute, with great earnestness, what opinion did Origen hold in regard to the *resurrection*, or the return of souls to their bodies; and some accuse, and some defend him. I confess I am ignorant of his opinion; for on this subject, as on many others, he is variable and inconstant in the exposition of his views. But if I compare the Christian doctrine of the resurrection with his philosophical precepts, I readily see that he must have viewed the subject differently from us. For while he places the whole of man in his *soul*, and regards the concrete visible *body*, in which the soul lodges, as no part of human nature, but only the penitentiary or prison of the soul, it is evident that he could not suppose a soul, at the end of its period of exile, and when purged from its sins, would again become coupled with its body.—There is another thing generally overlooked by the disputants concerning Origen, which is of vast importance in their discussions. As Origen held to a two-fold religion, the one popular and the other philosophical; [p. 629.] so he treated religion in a two-fold manner, sometimes in a popular way and sometimes philosophically. Now, those who overlook this fact may often suppose him to disagree with himself, while, in reality, he is entirely consistent; and this is one cause of the endless disputes respecting his theology. They who plead his cause and defend his reputation, cite the passages in which he explains religious subjects as he would have them stated to the common people; and because, in these passages, he states divine truths just as the Scriptures and the common preachers of Christianity do, they think his bolder and more artificial statements should be amended so as to agree with the former; and they err greatly by confounding his exterior doctrines, suited to common apprehension, with his interior expositions, which he intended only for the ears of learned men. And those who accuse him of errors, argue from the passages in which he explains and accounts for the Christian doctrines on the principles of philosophy. This they have a right to do; yet they fall into two mistakes: *First*, they conclude from these passages that Origen drew away Christians from the ancient and simple religion of the earlier times, and plunged them in a sea of empty speculation; which was but partially true. For he did not aim to overthrow the ancient and simple religion of the previous ages, which he himself taught and recommended; but he wished the supervisors and doctors of the Christian church to have a more profound knowledge, and to be able, when occasion required it, to explain rationally that simple religion. *Secondly:* they suppose that the real views and opinions of Origen on religious subjects may be learned from the passages mentioned; which is sometimes actually the case, but not always. For he often gives us his conjectures, rather than his fixed opinions; and in several passages he proposes different opinions on the same subject. One thing indeed clearly appears; on many subjects he thought differently from other Christians; and the philosophy which he followed obliged him to think differently; but *how* he thought, is not, in many cases, equally clear; and, not unfrequently, he did not know himself how he ought to think.

§ XXVIII. **Origen's allegorical expositions.** Origen's new method of explaining and illustrating religious truths by means of philosophy, required also a new method of expounding the sacred Scriptures. For, meeting with many things in the Scriptures repugnant to the decisions of his philosophy, he deemed it necessary to devise some method of removing this disagreement. And as it would add confirmation to his opinions, if he could make it appear that they were supported by the authority of Scripture, some plausible way was to be devised which [p. 630.] should make his speculations appear to be taught in the holy oracles. Therefore, taking up the ancient doctrine of the Pharisees and Essenes, which also he had learned from his preceptor, *Clement*, namely, that of a double sense in holy Scripture, he amplified and adorned it so ingeniously that it afforded him ample means of bending the sense of Scripture to suit his purpose, and eliminating from the Bible whatever was repugnant to his favorite opinions.(¹) Yet strange as it may appear, this same Origen,—who had offered so much violence to the sacred books, and almost subverted their true meaning,—resolutely undertook and most patiently accomplished an incredible labor in aid of those who wish to investigate the literal sense of scripture, and thus produced an enduring monument of his industry, in what is called his *Hexapla.* And so, frequently, those who disagree with every body, also disagree with themselves; and having magnificently extolled something, are found tacitly disapproving and censuring it.([2])

(1) Those who wish to stigmatize the memory of Origen, represent him as the author and inventor of the *allegorical* mode of interpreting the Scriptures: and they account it one of his principal faults, and a great stain upon his character. His patrons, on the contrary, and particularly Huet, deny that he was the author of this mode of interpretation; and they demonstrate that not only Jews, but Christians also, before the days of Origen, recommended the study of allegories, both by precept and by their example: and they are angry at the ancient and modern assailants of Origen, who criminate him for following the example of his precursors; which was only a minor fault, and scarcely deserving much rebuke. In my opinion, both his accusers and his vindicators go too far. It is very certain that the Jews, and among them the Pharisees especially and Essenes, before the birth of our Saviour, believed that in the language of the Bible, besides the sense which is obvious to the reader, there is another more remote and recondite, concealed under the words of Scripture. And it is equally certain that *Aristobulus*, and others, and especially that celebrated Alexandrian Jew, *Philo*, many of whose works have come down to us,—did labor to deduce and to confirm the precepts of the philosophy they embraced, from and by the books of Moses and the prophets. And, finally, it is manifest that this mode of explaining the holy Scriptures was much approved and practised by the Christian teachers, before Origen was born; and those masters of the Alex- [p. 631.] andrian school, *Pantænus* and *Clement*, (the latter, Origen's preceptor) did tread in the steps of Philo; and they taught their disciples, according to his example, to believe that the elements of all philosophical truth are interwoven into the history and the laws of the sacred books. Origen therefore had for his precursors many men of high character; and he was not the first who brought into the church the study of either sacred allegories in general or philosophical allegories in particular. And this conduces not a little to diminish his fault. But, on the other hand, it is manifest that he did not keep himself within the bounds which his precursors had placed around this thing; but he allowed himself much greater liberties than the Christian doctors before him had deemed allowable. This he himself testifies. For he states repeatedly, that he had incurred the odium of many by his mystical interpretations, and that he was accused of violating the dignity of the holy Scriptures. In his *thirteenth Homily* on Genesis, sec. 3. (Opp, tom. ii. p. 95.) he maintains that Isaac,—who digged the wells which the Philistines filled up, (Gen. xxvi. 15.)—was an emblem of those interpreters who pass by the literal meaning and search for arcane senses in the sacred volume; and that the Philistines repre-

sented the persons who will never go beyond the historic sense of scripture. Qui sunt isti, (*Philistini*) qui terra puteos replent? Illi sine dubio, qui in lege terrenam et carnalem intelligentiam ponunt, et spiritalem ac mysticum claudunt, ut neque ipsi bibant, neque alios bibere permittant. From this exposition he takes occasion to inveigh severely against those who condemned his allegorical interpretations. Unusquisque nostrum, qui verbum Dei ministrat, puteum fodit, et aquam vivam quærit, ex qua reficiat auditores. Si ergo incipiam et ego veterum dicta discutere et sensum in eis quærere spiritalem, si conatus fuero velamen legis amovere, et ostendere allegorica esse quæ scripta sunt, fodio quidem puteos, sed statim mihi movebunt calumnias amici litteræ et insidiabuntur mihi, inimicitias continuo et persecutiones parabunt, veritatem negantes stare posse super terram. (By terram, he means the *literal sense.*) Sed nos si Isaac pueri sumus, puteos aquæ vivæ diligamus et fontes, a litigiosis et calumniatoribus recedamus, et relinquamus eos in terra, (i. e. in the *literal sense,*) quam diligant. Nos vero nunquam cessemus puteos aquæ vivæ fodiendo. (i. e. will never cease to follow after allegories.)—A passage not unlike this occurs in his *seventh Homily* on Levit. sec. 4. p. 223, 224. where he enters upon a discussion respecting clean and unclean animals and meats, with great caution, not to afford weapons to his opposers. De cibis qui per umbram dicuntur, ascendamus ad eos, qui per spiritum veri sunt cibi. Sed ad hæc investiganda scripturæ divinæ testimoniis indigemus, ne quis putet, (amant enim homines exacuere linguas suas ut gladium) ne quis, inquam, putet, quod ego vim faciam scripturis divinis, et ea, quæ de animalibus in lege referuntur, ad homines traham, [p. 632.] et de hominibus hæc dicta esse confingam. Fortassis enim dicat quis auditorum: cur vim facis Scripturæ? Animalia dicuntur, animalia intelligantur.—How came it, I ask, that Origen, by searching for mystical senses of scripture, incurred odium in an age when all the Christian doctors, either wholly overlooking or but slightly regarding the literal sense, fondly pursued allegories? Beyond a doubt it must have arisen from this, that Origen introduced many innovations into this mode of interpretation, and gave new and unheard of rules concerning it. Certainly, he would have had no enemies, if he had merely affirmed, what no one then called in question, that in addition to the sense which the *words* of Scripture convey, another sense latent in the *things* described, is to be diligently sought for. This will be manifest, if we consider who were the men that inveighed so bitterly against Origen's allegories after he was dead: I refer to *Eustatius*, *Epiphanius*, *Jerome*, *Augustine*, and many others. All these were themselves *Allegorists*, if I may use that term; and would undoubtedly have condemned any man, as a great errorist, who should have dared to impugn the arcane sense of Scripture, or to censure the deriving both doctrines and precepts, and the knowledge of future events, from the narratives and laws contained in the Bible. There must, therefore, necessarily, have been something new and unusual in Origen's exegetics, which appeared to them pernicious and very dangerous. Otherwise, they would have regarded his system of interpretation as beautiful and perfectly correct.

These things being so, it was not altogether wrong to call Origen the *author* of the allegoric interpretations: and it becomes an important inquiry, what were those additions made by him to the doctrine of allegories, which other believers in a double sense of scripture deemed altogether inadmissible. The first and chief was, that he pronounced a great part of the sacred books to be void of meaning if taken literally, and that only the *things* indicated by the words were the signs and emblems of higher objects. The Christians who had previously followed after mystic interpretations, let the truth of the sacred narratives and the proper sense of the divine laws and precepts remain in full force; but he turned much of the sacred history into moral fables, and no small part of the divine precepts into mere allegories. I would not say, that this corrupt mode of interpretation *originated* with Origen; I suppose rather, that before him, some among the Jews rejected the grammatical sense of their law, and followed only a moral and hidden sense of it. For I perceive that *Philo*, in his book *de Migratione Abrahami*, (Opp. tom. i. p. 450. ed. Angl.)—notwithstanding he himself sometimes seems to disregard almost wholly the literal sense, yet severely censures a certain class of men, who entirely disregarded the laws of Moses, and held only to a mystical interpretation of them: for example, they believed that all Moses' injunctions concerning circumcision, should be understood of the excision of our lusts and passions; and under this cover, they [p. 633.] spurned the *letter* of the law: but *Philo* admonishes them, distinctly, that the mystical interpretation of the law should be so pursued, as to leave inviolate the dignity and authority of the literal import of the word. He says; Ἔδει γὰρ ἀμφοτέρων ἐπιμεληθῆναι, ζητήσεώς τε τῶν ἀφανῶν ἀκριβεστέρας καὶ ταμίας τῶν φανερῶν ἀνεπιλήπτου. *They ought to regard both, searching critically for the non-apparent* (the remote sense), *and preserving the manifest unassailed.* Of the *Therapeutæ* I say nothing; because, what Philo tells us of their allegories, in his book *de Vita Theoretica*, does not appear to me sufficiently perspicuous, to justify a positive decision that they rejected the literal import of the law. But among Christians, there were none, before Origen, who adopted the opinion that many parts of the scriptures were destitute of any literal meaning. And hence it was, that when Origen ventured boldly to assert this doctrine, very many resisted it, and very justly feared, that the truth and authority of religion itself would be much endangered, if the people were told that many things narrated in the Bible never took place, and that many things were commanded which must be understood far otherwise than the words indicated. And it appears strange, that a man of so much discernment should not see, that those very heretics, the Gnostics, for instance, whom he sought to confute by this mode of interpretation, might very conveniently use it for overthrowing the entire history of the life and death of Christ, the truth of which they denied. But I suspect, that Origen became accustomed to this bold exegesis, in the same school in which he learned philosophy. For, those well informed on the subject, know that all the disciples of *Ammonius* interpreted *Homer*, *Hesiod*, and the entire history of the pagan deities, in the very same manner, in which Origen taught his followers to interpret a large part of the Bible. Nearly allied to this first fault, was another; namely, that he lauded immoderately the recondite and mystical sense of scripture, and unreasonably depreciated the grammatical or historical sense. The latter he compared to earth, mud, the body, and other things of little value;

but the former he compared to the soul, heaven, gold, and the most precious objects. By such representations he induced the expositors of scripture, to think little about the literal sense of passages, and to run enthusiastically after the sublimer interpretations. It was very different with the other Christian doctors who possessed good sense. Although they highly valued the mystical sense, yet they placed an equal value on the grammatical and historical: nay, they made the latter the foundation and basis of the former: whence it would follow, that no inquiry after the arcane and moral sense should be made, until the literal meaning is carefully and accurately ascertained. As the stability and authority of the Christian religion depend on the truth of the history given us in the Bible, and as the true forms and grounds both of its doctrines and precepts are to be learned from the proper sense of the words of scripture; it is manifest, that this religion is equally harmed, by him who makes no [p. 634.] account of the literal sense, and by him who considers the words to have no meaning.

Again, it was indeed not altogether a new thing, and yet it was a thing unusual and offensive to many, that Origen sought to derive from the scriptures by means of allegories, that philosophy which he had embraced; and that he believed, the philosophical grounds of the Christian doctrines were exhibited, though somewhat obscurely, by the sacred writers. Those who, up to that time, had sought for allegories in the scriptures, had found there only religious or sacred allegories; i. e. such as referred to Christ, to Antichrist, to the state of the church, and to the duties of Christians; but Origen, following the example of *Philo* Judæus, whom he was taught by his master *Clement* to follow as a guide, endeavored to make a large part of the Bible teach the dogmas of the philosophers. And this was the more offensive to Christians, because many of them still continued to regard philosophy as a pestilent thing, and to be for ever kept out of the church. Origen was led into this fault, not merely by the example of *Philo*, but also by the doctrine of his preceptor, *Ammonius*, respecting the harmony between philosophy and the Christian religion: the adoption of which doctrine, would necessarily lead him to carry philosophy into the holy scriptures. Among the dogmas of his acquired philosophy, one of the more considerable was, that noted one of the Platonic school respecting a two-fold world, a lower and an upper, or a visible and an invisible, a corporeal and a spiritual; and of the correspondences of things in this *visible world*, with the things of the *invisible* or *conceived world*. Considering this doctrine as most certain, he transferred it entire to the holy scriptures; and therefore he affirmed, that whatever the inspired writers tell us respecting changes and occurrences in this lower and visible world, relates also to the affairs and the history of the upper and invisible world. Of this doctrine we shall say more hereafter. But it being then altogether novel and strange to the ears of Christians, it could not fail to excite great complaints among those attached to the ancient Christian simplicity.—Now, as all the opinions we have mentioned, were displeasing to most Christian teachers, so the rules of interpretation introduced by Origen to advance them, could not but displease many, and be rejected not only as novel, but also as injurious to the scriptures and to their author. Before the times of Origen, the investigation of scriptural allegories was altogether unsettled, or regulated by almost no laws or fixed principles. And, therefore, when he attempted to subject it to fixed rules, founded on his own opinions, he might be accounted, and he actually was, an innovator.

As to the causes which induced Origen to amplify and to systematize the allegoric mode of interpreting scripture, it must be admitted, in the first place, that much was due to the excessively fecund genius of the man, to the customary practice among the Egyptians, to his education, to the instruction of his [p. 635.] preceptors, and to the example both of the philosophers whom he admired, and of the Jews, especially *Philo.* But in addition to these external and natural causes, as they may be called, there were others originating from his own deliberate judgment: and among the latter, some were not dishonorable, or unworthy of a religious teacher desirous of advancing the cause of Christianity. *First,* he hoped that the Jews would more readily be persuaded to embrace Christianity, if certain portions of the Old Testament were explained mystically and allegorically. For he supposed certain prophecies, which, if construed literally, would not refer to Christ, were an obstacle to the Jews' embracing Christ; but that if these prophecies were explained mystically, and no regard paid to the literal sense, the Jews might be more ready to believe that all that the ancient prophets foretold concerning the Messiah actually referred to Jesus of Nazareth.—*Secondly,* he supposed that the class of heretics called Gnostics, the Basilidians, the Valentinians and others, could not be completely put down and confuted, except by the admission of allegories in the Old Testament. For these sects, in order to prove that the supreme God, the Father of our Saviour, was a different being from him who created this world and caused the Old Testament to be written, cited many passages from the Mosaic laws, from the writings of the prophets, and from the historical books of the Old Testament, which they considered as unworthy of the majesty and holiness of the supreme God, and as indicative of a degree of weakness and wickedness. And as Origen despaired of solving these objections, he thought they must be avoided by resorting to allegories, and that all the passages with which the Gnostics reproached God and his friends and ministers, must be construed in a mystical sense worthy of the divine character. These two reasons, Origen himself repeatedly mentions; and especially in his book *de Principiis,* (Lib. ii. c. 8. p. 164. &c.) But if he had been influenced by no reasons besides these, his system of interpretation would have extended to only a very small portion of the scriptures; and it would not have greatly offended his fellow Christians. For others before him, in their disputes with the Jews and the Gnostics, had betaken themselves to allegories as their castle. There were therefore other reasons for the course he pursued, and reasons of a more exceptionable character. Among these the first undoubtedly was, his attachment to his system of philosophy. For, perceiving that many of the facts and declarations of the Bible conflicted with the principles of his philosophy, he felt the necessity of resorting to some means of escaping their force; and he could find none more easy and effectual than this assumption: Whatever in the sacred books conflicts with my philosophy, must not be taken literally, but must be converted into allegory. Safely posted behind this rule, he could easily resist whatever the scriptures might oppose to his opinions, and whatever the [p. 636.] philosophers might urge against Christianity. This we see exemplified in his book against *Celsus*.—Kindred with this was another reason, derived from the harmony between Christianity and philosophy. As we have before seen, he believed that the grounds of all the doctrines taught in the scriptures, might be deduced from the principles of philosophy. And closely connected with this opinion, was another, namely, that these philosophical grounds of Christian doctrines, were all taught in the scriptures, not indeed explicitly, but with some obscurity and as it were covertly; and, therefore, they can be discovered, and drawn forth by the sagacious, especially by those whom God favors with the gift of language, and of the so-called *knowledge*. Having assumed this, he was obliged to add, that those philosophical grounds of Christian doctrines, are wrapt up in figures, images, and facts, in the sacred volume: for if we adhere to the literal meaning, that harmony between religion and philosophy can not be found. To these two causes, a third may be added; namely, that Platonic dogma, which was firmly established in his mind, that there are two corresponding worlds, this visible world in which we dwell, and corresponding with it an upper or celestial world. And this dogma led him, in construing the Biblical history of nations and countries, besides the literal import of the words which refer to this visible world, to seek for another meaning applicable to the world above.—He held two other opinions, both false, yet in his view unquestionable. *First*, that it was greatly for the honor and glory of Christianity, that the holy scriptures, which are its source, should be accounted a book differing fundamentally from all human compositions, one full of various and recondite mysteries. And that if God is to be considered as the author of the book, there must necessarily be and appear in it, a portion, an effect, or some exhibition, of that manifold and arcane wisdom which is in God. To this purpose he frequently expresses himself distinctly. Thus in his *fifteenth Homily* on Genesis, (Opp. tom. ii. p. 99.) he says: Observandum est nobis scripturas sanctas legentibus - - - - scripturam divinam non (ut plurimis videtur) inerudito et agresti sermone compositam, (i. e. not in the manner in which men are accustomed to communicate their thoughts to one another,) sed secundum disciplinam divinæ eruditionis (i. e. sapientiæ) aptatam, neque tantum historicis narrationibus, quantum rebus et sensibus mysticis servientem. His *first Homily* on Exod. (Opp. tom. ii. p. 129.) commences thus: Videtur mihi unusquisque sermo divinæ scripturæ similis esse alicui seminum, cujus natura hæc est, ut cum jactum fuerit in terram, regeneratum in spicam, vel in quamcunque aliam sui generis speciem, multipliciter diffundatur, et tanto cumulatius, quanto vel peritus agricola plus seminibus laboris impenderit, vel beneficium terræ fœcundioris indulserit. - - Ita et hic sermo, qui nunc nobis ex divinis voluminibus recitatus est, si peritum inveniat et diligentem colonum, cum primo attactu videatur exiguus et brevis, ut cœperit excoli et spiritaliter tractari, crescit [p. 637.] in arborem, in ramos, et in virgulta diffunditur. - - Unus sermo ex his, quæ recitata sunt, in tantum posset longe, lateque diffundi, si tamen et auditorum capacitas sineret, ut vix nobis ad explicandum sufficeret dies. And, (*de Principiis*

L. iv. sec. 26. p. 189.) he says: Ad quam regulam etiam divinarum litterarum intelligentia retinenda est, quo scilicet ea, quæ dicuntur, non pro vilitate sermonis, sed pro divinitate sancti spiritus, qui eas conscribi inspiravit, censeantur.—*Secondly*, In the objections of the enemies of Christianity, there are not a few things which can in no way be fully cleared up and confuted, unless we abandon the historical and grammatical sense, and resort to allegories. Exemplifications will be given hereafter. Origen was, by his philosophy, disabled for answering satisfactorily all the objections adduced against Christianity by the pagan priests, the philosophers and the Jews. The pious man could have done it easily, if he had been willing to philosophise in a more liberal manner than the precepts of his masters allowed. And, therefore, to maintain the honor of that religion which he considered equally true with his philosophy, he went over to the side of the *Allegorists*; not perceiving, that in this way the objections of the adversaries were not confuted, but in reality were only eluded.

Peter Daniel Huet has written learnedly on Origen's doctrine of allegories, in his *Origeniana*, Lib. ii. Quæst xiii. p. 170.: but he writes confusedly, and not so much for the purpose of explaining and elucidating the subject, as for obscuring it, and for excusing and defending its author. He is therefore an unsafe guide to an inquirer on this subject. The system of Origen is much better stated and explained by a learned French writer whose name I have not learned, in a French work entitled, The Literal and the Mystical sense of holy Scripture, according to the views of the Fathers. Paris, 1727. 8vo. I have not been able to obtain the book; but *Charles de la Rue*, the editor of Origen, has given a lucid epitome of it, supported by citations from Origen, in his Preface to Origen's Works, vol. ii.—I will attempt to state Origen's views, more precisely than learned men have hitherto done, to correct their mistakes, to supply their deficiencies, and to exhibit this whole system of biblical interpretation, so far as it can be ascertained, in the most correct and intelligible manner within my power.

Origen's doctrine of allegories may be fitly divided into two parts; the *first*, embracing his opinions respecting the different senses of the holy scriptures; and the *second*, containing rules for distinguishing the different senses of scripture, and for determining in what passages the literal sense must be abandoned, and in what passages a mystical sense may be coupled with the literal sense. [p. 638.] The *first* part comprises the following PROPOSITIONS.

Prop. I. Holy scripture is like a man. As a man, according to Plato, consists of three parts, a body, a sensitive soul, and a rational soul; so also the sacred books have a threefold sense, a body or a historical and grammatical sense, a soul or a moral sense, and lastly a spirit or a mystical and spiritual sense. Origen's *fifth Homily* on Levit. sec. 5. (Opp. tom. ii. p. 209.): Triplicem in scripturis divinis intelligentiæ inveniri sæpe diximus modum, historicum, moralem, et mysticum. Unde et corpus inesse ei, et animam, ac spiritum intelleximus. *De Principiis* L. iv. sec. 2. (Opp. tom. i. p. 168.): Sicut homo constare dicitur ex corpore et anima et spiritu: ita etiam sancta scriptura, quæ ad hominum salutem divina largitione concessa est. Many more passages might be adduced from his writings; but these are sufficient.

Prop. II. As the flesh or body is the lowest and most ignoble part of man; so also the literal sense of scripture, which is like the body, is far below or inferior to the moral and the mystical senses. And as the body often induces even pious and good men to commit sin; so also the proper sense of the words of scripture may lead incautious readers into errors and faults. Origen's *Stromata* Lib. x. as quoted by Jerome, Lib. iii. Comm. in Galatas cap. v. (Hieronymi Opp. tom. i. p. 41.): Non valde eos juvat Historia Scripturæ, qui sic eam intelligunt, uti scripta est. Quis enim non docebitur servire luxuriæ, et fornicationem habere pro nihilo, quum Judam ad meretricem legerit ingredientem, et Patriarchas habuisse multas pariter uxores? Quomodo non ad idololatriam provocabitur, qui sanguinem taurorum et cæteras Levitici victimas non plus, quam quod in littera sonat, putaverit indicare? - - - Hæreses quoque magis de carnali scripturæ intelligentia, quam de opere carnis nostræ, ut plurimi æstimant, substiterunt. Nec non invidiam et ebrietatem per legis litteram discimus. Inebriatur Noe post diluvium, et Patriarchae apud fratrum Joseph in Ægypto. Sed in commessationes in Regnorum libro scriptæ sunt. - - - Multorum ergo malorum occasio est, si quis in scripturæ carne permaneat. Quæ qui fecerent, regnum Dei non consequentur. Quamobrem spiritum scripturæ fructusque quæramus, qui non dicuntur esse manifesti. - - - Quum hæc nobis aperta fuerint, *rationabiliorem habebimus fidem*, (Origen sought after a *rational religion*, i. e. one accordant with his philosophy, which he deemed to be accordant with reason,) et correctos mores temperantia comitabitur. *De Principiis* L. iv. sec. 8, 9. p. 165.: Simpliciores nonnulli, qui se de ecclesia esse gloriantur - - - de Deo suspicantur, quæ ne de homine quidem crudelissimo et injustissimo cogitare fas sit. Iis autem omnibus nulla falsarum opinionum, nulla impietatis et stolidorum de Deo sermonum caussa esse alia videtur, quam scriptura [p. 639.] non secundum sensum spiritualem intellecta. Many other passages might easily be collected.

Prop. III. Yet the literal sense is not altogether worthless; for to common people and the more ignorant, it may be of use to lead them to virtue and salvation. *De Principiis* L. iv. (sec. 12. p. 169.): Expositionem litteralem etiam per se utilem esse posse, testatur eorum multitudo, qui ingenue et simpliciter crediderunt. (sec. 14. p. 173.): Ipsum quoque spiritualium indumentum, id est, quod in scripturis corporeum est, in multis non est inutile, sed multos potest, quantum capaces sunt, meliores efficere.

Prop. IV. But those who possess a little more wisdom and intelligence than the vulgar, ought to seek after the *soul* of the sacred scriptures, passing beyond their body or literal sense: that is, they should search for the *moral* sense, which accompanies the grammatical; or, they should apply all they read to the mind and its moral improvement.

Prop. V. And those who have attained to perfection, or to the highest degree of piety, should ascend higher still, and pry with all their might into the *spirit* of the sacred books, or into their *spiritual* and *mystical sense*. These two last precepts, and also the one preceding, are placed beyond all doubt, by the following passage, (*De Principiis* L. iv. sec. 2. p. 168.): Tripliciter ergo describere oportet in anima sua unumquemque divinarum intelligentiam litterarum,

id est, (1) ut simpliciores quique aedificentur ab *ipso*, ut ita dixerim, *corpore scripturarum :* sic enim appellamus communem istum et historialem intellectum : (2) si qui vero aliquantum jam proficere cœperunt, et possunt amplius aliquid intueri, ab ipsa *scripturæ anima* aedificentur. (3) Qui vero perfecti sunt, ni tales ab ipsa spirituali lege, quæ umbram habet futurorum bonorum, tanquam *a spiritu* aedificentur. These are the rules which Origen invariably follows in his *Commentaries* and *Homilies* on the sacred books, yet extant. He either wholly omits, or but slightly touches on the historical or literal sense, and hastens on to the moral or mystical senses almost as soon as he names the passages.

Prop. VI. The *moral* sense of the Scriptures consists, partly, in doctrinal instructions, respecting those exercises or changes in the state of the mind of which both good and bad men may be the subjects; and partly in precepts, by which both the exterior and the interior life of a Christian man should be governed. Origen nowhere defines, (so far as I know,) what he means by the *moral sense of Scripture :* but the correctness of the definition above given is demonstrable from the numberless examples of this sense which he adduces. Thus Moses tells us, (Exod. i. 6, 7.) that after the death of Joseph, the Children of Israel multiplied exceedingly in Egypt. And to this statement Origen attaches *a moral sense*, (*First Homily* on Exod. § 4. Opp. tom. ii. p. 131.) : In te si moriatur Joseph, id est, si mortificationem Christi in corpore tuo suscipias et mortifices membra tua peccato (so in the printed copies; but I think it should read [p. 640.] *peccati*,) tunc in te multiplicabuntur filii Israel. Filii vero Israel *sensus boni* et *spirituales* accipiuntur. Si ergo sensus carnis mortificentur, sensus spiritus crescunt et quotidie emorientibus in te vitiis, virtutum numerus augetur. So the king of Egypt commanded the midwives to kill the Hebrew male children, but to let the females live. (Exod. i. 15, 16.) And, according to Origen, (*Homil.* ii. in Exod. § 1. p. 133.) the edict of Pharaoh contained this moral sense : Princeps hujus mundi seu cacodaemon vult sensum rationabilem, qui potest cœlestia sapere, necare ; quæcunque vero carnis sunt vivere, et quæ ad materiam pertinent corporalem augeri. Cum ergo videris homines in voluptatibus et deliciis vitam ducere, in istis scias quod rex Ægypti masculos necat et vivificat fœminas. In Matt. xv. 21, 22. our Saviour is said to have gone into the borders of Tyre and Sidon, where a Canaanitess of that country besought him to heal her daughter. According to Origen (tom. xi. in Matth. § 16. Opp. tom. iii. p. 503.) the moral sense of the story is this: Unusquisque nostrum dum peccat, versatur in finibus Tyri et Sidonis, migrans vero a vitio ad virtutem exit e finibus Tyri et Sidonis et ad fines partis Dei pervenit. Atque huic Christus, quemadmodum mulieri Chananaeæ, occurrit quasi in partes Tyri et Sidonis veniens.—These examples show that a large part of the philosophical instructions, which Origen supposed to be latent in the scriptures, are contained in the *moral* sense; while others of them are contained in the *mystical* sense, which we are next to consider.

Prop. VII. Of the *mystical* sense, Origen himself gives the following definition, (*de Principiis*, Lib. iv. § 13. p. 170.) : Spiritalis explanatio (πνευματικὴ διήγησις) est talis, si quis potest ostendere quorum cœlestium exemplaribus et umbræ

deserviunt hi, qui secundum carnem judaei sunt et quorum futurorum umbram lex habet et si qua hujusmodi in scripturis sanctis reperiuntur, vel cum requiritur quæ sit illa sapientia in mysterio abscondita (1 Cor. ii. 7.) et occasionem nobis præstat intelligentiæ, ut possimus advertere, quorum figuræ erant ista, quae illis (Judæis) accidebant. A part of this definition is perspicuous enough: he thinks emblems and predictions of things pertaining to Christ and the church are held up to view in the law of Moses and in the Old Testament history. Therefore, whoever refers to Christ, his acts and offices, and to the church, whatever in the literal sense refers to the Jewish affairs, discovers and follows the mystical or allegorical sense. Yet a part of this definition cannot be fully understood by those ignorant of Origen's peculiar opinions. Thus much indeed every attentive reader will perceive, that what Origen calls the *mystical* sense is twofold. For he says: (1) Judaeos secundum carnem cœlestium exemplaribus et umbræ deservire. The Greek is: ποίων ἐπουρανίων ὑποδείγματι καὶ [p. 641.] σκιᾶ οἱ κατὰ σάρκα Ἰουδαῖοι ἐλάτρευαν. (Heb. viii. 5.) Therefore the ceremonies of the law are shadows of heavenly things. He adds: (2) Legem tamen simul umbram futurorum habere: that is, the law is a shadow of Christ's deeds and of the events concerning him in this world. These two classes of things differ, just as the celestial and terrestrial, heavenly and earthly things differ. Again, he says (1) that in the scriptures a certain wisdom is hid in a mystery, as Paul tells us; and (2) that what things happened to the people of the Jews, were figures of certain future things; and these two classes of things also, he so clearly distinguishes, that they cannot be confounded. But all this is insufficient to make the views of Origen fully understood; and they must be more distinctly exhibited in the following more precise definition.

Prop. VIII. The *mystical* sense of scripture is that which presents to us the nature, state, and history of the spiritual or mystical world. Besides this corporeal or material world, there is another, a spiritual world, beyond the reach of our senses; and this other world is also twofold, celestial and terrestrial; and the terrestrial may also be called the *mystical* world. This *mystic* terrestrial world is the church of Christ on earth, the καινὴ κτίσις. See his Comm. on John, (tom. ix. vol. ii. Opp. p. 147, edit. Huetii. The recent Benedictine edition has not yet reached this commentary): Mundus autem et ornamentum mundi est ecclesia. And, after a few words: λεγέσθω τοινῦν ἡ ἐκκλησία κόσμος, ὅτε ὑπὸ τοῦ σωτῆρος φωτίζεται. Dicatur itaque ecclesia mundus, quando a Servatore illustratur. The other, the celestial or spiritual world, is in the upper regions: and it corresponds in all its parts with the lower or corporeal world. For the world in which we now dwell was fashioned after the model of the world above. See his Comm. on John, (tom. xix. vol. ii. Opp. edit. Huetii, p. 288. I give the Latin only, which agrees accurately with the Greek.): Est alius mundus præter hunc visibilem et sensibilem mundum (τὸν δεικνύμενον καὶ αἰσθητὸν κόσμον) constantem e cœlo et terra, vel e cœlis et terra, in quo sunt quae videntur: Et hoc totum est alius mundus, inaspectabilis mundus, qui non videtur, mundus intelligibilis (κόσμος ἀόρατος, κόσμος οὐ βλεπόμενος, καὶ νοητὸς κόσμος,) cujus visione et pulchritudine fruentur qui puro sunt corde, quo hujus mundi intelligibilis visione antea bene parati penetrant vel ad ipsum Deum videndum, qua-

tenus videri natura potest Deus. That world beyond our ken, which we can ontemplate only in thought, is, as before stated, perfectly like to this corporeal world; and of course it is divided into provinces, just as this world is. Therefore, as there is a terrestrial Palestine, Jerusalem, Tyre, Sidon, Arabia, [p. 642.] &c. so the upper or celestial world has similar places and provinces. The inhabitants of the celestial world are souls or spirits; its kings and magistrates are the angels, both the good and the bad. Whatever events occur in this world, the same occur in the world above; and there is a perfect similitude between these worlds. This doctrine he nowhere explains more fully than in his *Principia*, (L. iv. § 20, &c. p. 181, &c.) He there first demonstrates, as he supposes, that there is a celestial Judea, a celestial Jerusalem, a celestial Jewish people. Elevare quodammodo ex terra et erigere intelligentiam nostram volens sanctus Apostolus ait in quodam loco: *Videte Israel secundum carnem*, (1 Cor. x. 18.) Per quod significat utique quod alius Israel sit, qui non sit secundum carnem, sed secundum spiritum. - - - Si ergo sunt quædam animæ in hoc mundo (superiori) quæ Israel appellantur, et in cœlo civitas quædam, quæ Jerusalem nominatur, consequens est, ut hæ civitates, quæ gentis Israeliticæ esse dicuntur, Metropolia habeant Jerusalem cœlestem, et secundum haec de omni Judæa intelligamus, de qua putamus etiam prophetas mysticis quibusdam narrationibus loquutos. - - Quæcunque ergo vel narrantur vel prophetantur de Jerusalem - - utique de illa civitate, quam (Paulus) dicit Jerusalem cœlestem et de omnibus locis vel urbibus, quæ terræ sanctæ urbes esse dicuntur,—dicta esse intelligere debemus. Then dilating the idea, he extends it to the whole earth: Si ergo prophetiæ, quæ de Judea et Jerusalem et de Juda et Israel et Jacob prophetatæ sunt, dum non a nobis carnaliter intelliguntur, mysteria quædam divina significant: consequens utique est etiam illas prophetias, quæ vel de Ægypto vel de Ægyptiis, vel de Babylonia vel de Babyloniis, et Sidone ac Sidoniis prolatæ sunt, non de Ægypto ista, quæ in terris posita est, vel Babylone vel Tyro, vel de Sidone intelligi prophetatas. - - - - Sicut cœlestis est Jerusalem et Judæa, et gens sine dubio quæ habitat in ea, quæ dicitur Israel, ita possibile est etiam vicina his loca esse quædam, quæ vel Ægyptus, vel Babylon, vel Tyrus, vel Sidon appellari videantur, eorumque locorum principes, atque animæ si quæ in illis habitant locis, Ægyptii, Babylonii, Tyrii ac Sidonii appellantur. From this doctrine he infers, that whatever occurrences there are in this lower world, the same also exist in the world above; and the strange vagaries he indulges on this subject will be noticed hereafter.——This strange fiction is an exemplification of the degree in which Origen could accommodate his theology to his philosophy. For, although he would persuade his readers that he derived the doctrine of a twofold world, celestial and terrestrial, from Paul's writings, (e. g. 1 Cor. x. 18. Rom. ii. 28, 29. Gal. iv. 26. Heb. xii. 22, &c.); yet it is manifest that this doctrine is nothing more nor less than the opinion of *Plato* and the *Platonists*, respecting the eternal procession of the [p. 643.] images and patterns of all things from the divine intelligence, and of the formation of this visible world after the similitude of these so-called *ideas*. Captivated with this philosophy, his prolific fancy led him to amplify this doctrine, and apply it to the holy scriptures. Those acquainted with Platonism know, that the Platonic school, professedly following their master, maintained that from all eternity there issued forth from the divine intelligence the *images* of all things;—that these images were *substantial beings*, immutable in their nature, and distinct from the divine mind from which they issued;—that God looked on these eternal *ideas* while forming this corporeal world, just as a painter keeps his eyes constantly fixed on the objects he would represent in colors;—that therefore all corporeal and finite things are but copies of those eternal images;—that all truth and science reside in these images or ideas; that minds wrapped up in matter discover only the obscure shadows of them;—but yet, by reflection and study, they may gradually become able to look upon and contemplate the eternal ideas themselves; and this Plato supposed to be the perfection of all knowledge. All these notions Origen adopted as his own; and hence that fantastic dream of the resemblance of this world to the world above, and of the creation of the former after the pattern of the latter. But I do not know that any of the Platonists went so far as to declare, that all the things which occur among men, occur also in the heavenly world; that souls there live as men do on earth; that in heaven angels are rulers, and carry on wars, just as kings and princes do here below. At any rate this is clear, that Origen by holding these opinions was obliged to assert, that whatever the sacred books narrate respecting the countries, the nations, the kings, and the occurrences of this world, must be equally true of the heavenly world; so that the history of our world is also the history of the celestial world and of its inhabitants. And this he most distinctly asserts in his *Principia*, (L. iv. § 23. p. 186.): Unde consequens videbitur, etiam prophetias, quæ de singulis gentibus proferuntur, revocari magis ad animas debere, (because the celestial world is more excellent and noble than this our corporeal world,) et diversas mansiones earum cœlestes. Sed et historias rerum gestarum, quæ dicuntur vel genti Israel, vel Jerusalem, vel Judææ accidisse, - - - magis ista conveniebant illis gentibus animarum, quæ in cœlo isto, quod transire dicitur, habitant, vel etiam nunc habitare putandæ sunt. In his *eleventh Homily* on Numbers, (§ 4, Opp. tom. ii. p. 307.) he says: Puto, quia sicut quædam nomina vel gentium vel principum in Scripturis posita videmus, quæ absque ulla dubitatione ad malos angelos et ad virtutes contrarias referantur: ita etiam ea, quæ de sanctis viris et gente religiosa scribuntur, ad sanctos Angelos et ad benignas de- [p. 644.] bemus referre virtutes.

Prop. IX. As there is a *twofold* mystical world, the one here below, the church, and the other above, the examplar after which this material and corporeal world was created; so there is also a *twofold* mystical sense of scripture, the one relating to the church, and the other to the celestial world. That which relates to the kingdom of Christ, or the church, is called the *allegorical* sense; that which relates to the celestial world may be called the *anagogical* sense. Yet Origen does not always understand by the *allegorical* sense, that sense of the Bible which exhibits the transactions of Christ and his ambassadors in this lower world; he sometimes uses the term in a broader accepation; but still, of the great number of examples of the allegorical sense contained in his writings, most of the specimens we have adduced serve to illustrate the definition we have given.

Prop. X. The *mystical* sense pervades the entire scriptures; so that there is not a declaration, in the inspired books, in which there is not something latent that refers either to the church of Jesus Christ, or to the celestial world. See his *first Homily* on Exod. (§ 4. Opp. tom. ii. p. 131.): Ego credens verbis Domini mei Jesu Christi in lege et prophetis ieta quidem unum aut unum apicem non puto esse mysteriis vacuum, nec puto aliquid horum transire posse, nisi omnia fiant. He frequently inculcates this idea in various forms; and he extends it, not only to the Old Testament, but also to the New, which is of equal excellence and worth with the Old. See *Principia* L. vi. § 14, &c. (p. 171, 172.) In a passage § 16. (p. 174,) he most explicitly declares the New Testament to be equally spiritual and mystical with the Old Testament: Non solum autem de his, quæ usque ad adventum Christi scripta sunt, hæc Spiritus sanctus procuravit, sed utpote unus atque idem spiritus et ab uno Deo procedens, eadem similiter etiam in Evangelistis et Apostolis fecit. Nam ne illas quidem narrationes, quas per eos inspiravit absque hujuscemodi, quam supra exposuimus sapientiæ suæ arte contexuit. Hence, in his *eleventh Homily* on Num. § 1. (Opp. tom. ii. p. 305.) he thus expresses himself: Requiro, si sunt aliquæ (in scriptura sacra) quæ et secundum litteram quidem stare possint, necessario tamen in eis etiam allegoriam (here he used the word *allegoria* in the broader sense) requirendam. And a little after: Alia habent quidem secundum litteram veritatem sui, recipiunt tamen utiliter et *necessario* etiam allegoricum sensum.—It is therefore beyond all controversy, that those learned men err, who say that Origen believed many passages of the Bible to have no other than the literal sense: his opinion was quite otherwise. Nor must we assent to *Charles* de la *Rue*, and to the learned men whom he follows, in saying, (*Orig*. Opp. tom. ii. Praef. p. 11.): [p. 645.] "Sometimes only the literal sense is admissible, sometimes only the moral sense, and sometimes only the mystical." The man cannot have read Origen with due attention who can entertain such an opinion.

Prop. XI. Yet *both* the mystical senses are not found in all passages: some have only the allegorical sense, and some only the anagogical. That such was Origen's opinion his expositions clearly show; for from many passages of scripture explained by him, he deduces only a meaning applicable to the church of Christ on earth; but sometimes he rises to the celestial or upper world.

Prop. XII. In like manner the *moral* sense pervades the whole inspired volume; nor is there a single passage in which we have not some precept for regulating the mind and directing the conduct.

Prop. XIII. It is not so with the grammatical or historical sense. For there are many passages of the Bible in which the words are destitute of all literal meaning. Of his many declarations to this effect this one may suffice, *de Principiis*, L. iv. § 12. (Opp. tom. i. p. 169.) Ἐισὶ τίνες γραφαὶ τὸ σωματικὸν ὀυδαμῶς ἔχουσαι —— ἐστιν ὅπου οἱονεὶ τὴν ψυχὴν κὰι τὸ πνεῦμα τῆς γραφῆς μόνα χρὴ ζητεῖν Sunt scripturæ quædam, quæ nihil habent corporeum (i. e. no literal meaning): est ubi sola veluti anima (a moral sense,) et spiritus (a mystical sense) quærendus est.

Prop. XIV. Therefore all declarations of scripture are of *two* kinds; some have only *two* senses, a moral and a mystical, the latter either allegorical or anagogical; others have *three* senses, a grammatical or literal, a moral, and a mystical. But there is no passage whatever that has only *one* single meaning. In his ***Principia*** L. iv. sec. 12. (p. 169, &c.) Origen demonstrates this principle by a passage in John's Gospel (ch ii. 6.); presenting us at the same time with a specimen of allegorical interpretation. John tells us, that at the marriage in Cana, there were six water pots, set for the Jewish purification, containing two or three firkins each: and Origen gives this mystical interpretation of the passage: Quibus sub involucro designatur eos, qui apud Apostolum in occulto Judæi sunt, (Rom. ii.) purificari per scripturas, aliquando binas metretas capientes, id est, ut sic dicam, animam (the *moral* sense) et spiritum (the *mystical* sense): aliquando terras (trinas?) quum nonnullæ præter prædicta, (i. e. the moral and mystical; which are always present.) habeant etiam corpus (the literal sense) quod aedificare potest.

Prop. XV. The *literal* sense is obvious to all attentive readers. To discover the *moral* sense, some more intelligence is requisite; and yet it is not very recondite and difficult.

Prop. XVI. But the *mystical* sense, none but wise men, and such as are divinely instructed, can with certainty discover. Origen, agreeably to the custom of that age, considered the ability to interpret the holy scriptures mystically, to be one of those extraordinary gifts of the Holy Spirit which are conferred on but few Christians. And as he, from modesty, dared not lay claim to that gift, he generally brings forward his mystical expositions with diffidence [p. 646.] and caution: and sometimes he tells us, that he conjectures or supposes, rather than decides and pronounces confidently. In his *fifth Homily* on Levit. sec. 1. (Opp. tom. ii. p. 205.) he says: Sicut cognationem sui ad invicem gerunt visibila et invisibilia, terra et cœlum, anima et caro, corpus et spiritus, et ex horum conjunctionibus constat hic mundus; ita etiam sanctam Scripturam credendum est ex invisibilibus et visibilibus constare: veluti (1) ex *corpore* quodam, litteræ scilicet, quæ videtur: et (2) *animâ*, sensus intra ipsam deprehenditur; et (3) *spiritu*, secundum id quod quædam etiam in se cœlestia teneat; ut Apostolus, quia exemplari et umbræ deserviunt cœlestium. This passage, though not much connected with the point we are considering, I have thought fit to transcribe, because it not only exhibits clearly and distinctly his doctrine of a threefold sense of scripture, but it also shows, that he believed he had a philosophical reason for holding that doctrine, derived from the analogy of things. We will now accompany him as he proceeds: Quia ergo hæc ita se habent, invocantes Deum, qui fecit scripturæ *animam* et *corpus* et *spiritum*: *corpus* quidem iis, qui ante nos fuerunt, *animam* vero nobis, *spiritum* autem iis, qui in futuro hæreditatem vitæ æternæ consequentur, per quam, (I think it should read *per quem*, i. e. *spiritum*) perveniant ad regna cœlestia; eam nunc quam diximus legis animam requiramus, quantum ad præsens interim spectat. *Nescio autem si possumus etiam ad spiritum ejus ascendere* in his, quæ nobis de sacrificiis lecta sunt. This passage is very noticeable; because from it we learn, that Origen believed, (1) That a large portion at least of the ceremonial laws of Moses contained a *literal* meaning, pertaining, however, exclusively to the Jews; in which he was correct; (2) That in addition to this meaning, there was also in the Mosaic laws a *moral* sense, and that this sense is discoverable by all Christian teachers if they will give their attention to it: (3) But the *mystical* sense of these laws is not equally discoverable by all, but only by those who are chosen unto life eternal and are divinely illuminated. Therefore (4) he doubts, *whether he was qualified* to investigate this abstruse sense of scripture. After several other things which are not to our purpose, when he would exhibit the mystical import of certain things pertaining to the laws concerning sacrifices, he again acknowledges, explicitly, that without the Holy Spirit, he could effect nothing. He says, (sec. 5. p. 209.) Quia potius, secundum spiritalem sensum, *quem Spiritus donat ecclesiæ*, videamus, quod sit istud sacrificium, quod coquatur in clibano, vel quis iste clibanus intelligi debeat? Sed ubi inveniam? - - Dominum meum Jesum invocare me oportet, ut quaerentem me faciat invenire, et [p. 647.] pulsanti aperiat, ut inveniam in scripturis clibanum, ubi possum coquere sacrificium meum, ut suscipiat illud Deus. Thus he discourses with sufficient acumen and subtilty respecting this furnace. Yet, see how timidly and modestly he closes the discourse: Non dubito multa esse, quae nos lateant et sensum nostrum superent. *Non enim sumus illius meriti*, ut et nos dicere possimus: *Nos autem sensum Christi habemus.* (1 Cor. ii. 16.) Ipse enim solus est sensus, cui pateant universa, quae in legibus sacrificiorum intra litterae continentur arcanum. Si enim mererer, ut daretur mihi sensus Christi, etiam ego in his dicerem: *Ut sciamus quæ a deo donata sunt nobis, quæ et loquimur.* (1 Cor. ii. 12.) Similar passages abound in all his expository works on the sacred books. On the *moral* sense which he elicits, he is sufficiently positive; but his *mystical* interpretations, he obtrudes upon no one, always professing to be a learner, and ready to be taught better views by any one whom the Holy Spirit may enlighten.

Prop. XVII. Although a man may be divinely endued with the gift of interpreting the scriptures mystically, yet it will be presumption and folly for him to expect to understand *all* the arcane senses of the sacred volume. For the scriptures contain an immense treasury of divine truths, only a small part of which can be grasped by minds enclosed in material bodies. Even the Apostles of Jesus Christ were not able to understand *all* the mysteries of the sacred books. Origen discourses on this point, referring equally to the Old Testament and the New, in his *Principia*, L. iv. sec. 10. &c. He says: Evangeliorum accuratus sensus, utpote Christi sensus, eget gratia. - - Apostolorum autem epistolae cuinam sagaci et perito sermonum judici videantur apertae ac intellectu faciles, cum illic infinita prope sint, quae veluti per foramen maxima et quamplurima intelligendi materiam amplam praebeant? Quae cum ita se habeant et prope innumeri labantur, non sine periculo quis pronunciaverit, se legendo intelligere, quae indigent clavi intelligentiae, quam Salvator penes legisperitos esse ait. Passing over many other remarks, we will cite from sec. 26. p. 188. the passages in which he the most clearly expresses his views: Si quis curiosus explanationem singulorum requirat, veniat et nobiscum pariter audiat, quomodo Paulus Apostolus per Spiritum sanctum - - altitudinem divinae sapientiae ac scientiae scrutans, nec tamen ad finem, et, ut ita dixerim, ad intimam cognitionem praevalens pervenire, desperatione rei et stupore clamat et dicit. O altitudo divitiarum sapientiae et scientiae Dei. (Rom. xi. 33.) If this text appears to us irrelevant to the subject, it should be remembered, that Origen supposed Paul usually designates the *mystical sense* of scripture by the terms *wisdom* and *knowledge*. Quantumcunque enim quis in scrutando promoveat et studio intentiore proficiat, *gratia quoque Dei adjutus, sensusque* [p. 648.] *illuminatus*, ad perfectum finem eorum, quae requiruntur, pervenire non poterit nec omnis mens quae creata est. possibile habet ullo genere comprehendere sed ut invenerit quaedam ex his quae quaeruntur, iterum videt alia, quae quaerenda sunt. Quod etsi ad ipsa pervenerit, multo iterum plura ex illis, quae requiri debeant, pervidebit.

Prop. XVIII. Both diffidence and discretion are highly necessary, in searching after that mystical sense of scripture which relates to the celestial or upper world, or in applying what the scriptures relate of the people and the affairs of this world, to the inhabitants of the world above. Because this, the *anagogical* sense, God has very obscurely set forth in the sacred books, rather covering it up and concealing it than actually revealing it. In his *Principia*, (L. iv. sec. 23. p. 186,) he says: Si quis vero evidentes et satis manifestas assertiones horum de Scripturis sanctis exposcat a nobis, respondendum est, quia occultare magis haec Spiritui sancto in his quae videntur esse historiae rerum gestarum, et altius tegere consilium fuit, in quibus descendere dicuntur in Ægyptum, vel captivari in Babyloniam, vel in his ipsis regionibus, quidam quidem humiliari nimis et sub servitio effici dominorum, - - - quae omnia, ut diximus, abscondita et celata in Scripturae sanctae historiis conteguntur, quia regnum cœlorum simile est thesauro abscondito in agro. - - - Hi thesauri ut inveniri possint, *Dei adjutorio opus est*, qui solus potest portas aereas, quibus clausi sunt et absconditi, confringere et seras ferreas comminuere, quibus prohibetur ingressus perveniendi ad ea omnia, quae in Genesi de diversis animarum generibus scripta sunt et obtecta, &c. The passage is too long to be here transcribed.

I now proceed to the second part of Origen's doctrine of allegories.—As he maintained that the words of many passages of the Bible are altogether void of direct meaning, it became necessary for him to establish some rules for determining what passages of scripture have a direct or literal meaning, and what passages are destitute of such meaning, or have only a mystical and a moral sense. His first and most general rule is:

Rule I. When the words of any passage in either Testament afford a *good sense*, one worthy of God, useful to men, and accordant with truth and sound reason,—this must be considered a sure sign that the passage is to be taken in its literal and proper sense. But whenever any thing absurd, false, contrary to sound reason, useless, or unworthy of God, will follow from a literal interpretation, then that interpretation is to be abandoned, and only moral and mystical senses are to be sought for. This rule, Origen repeatedly attempts to confirm by the declaration of St. Paul, (2 Cor. iii. 6.) *For the letter killeth, but the spirit giveth life.* See his work against *Celsus*, Lib. vii. (sec. 20, 21. edit. Benedict.) By the *letter* in this text, Origen would have us understand the *literal sense*, and by the *spirit*, the *moral* and *mystical* sense; thus making the [p. 649.] import of the passage to be, that the literal sense of scripture often disturbs the human mind, and brings it into great difficulties; but the moral and mystical senses refresh the mind, and fill it with faith, hope, joy, and love to God and man. This general rule of Origen may therefore be thus expressed: Whenever the *letter* of holy scripture *killeth*, or disturbs the mind; then, disregarding the letter, a man should attend solely to the *spirit*, which *giveth life*.—In a general view, this rule appears not wholly unreasonable; for the wisest interpreters at the present day, both take the liberty, and also allow others, to give up the literal meaning of a passage, and to resort to a *metaphorical*, or, if you please, a *mystical* sense, whenever the language taken literally would give a sense clearly repugnant to reason, or contrary to plain passages of holy scripture. Yet between these expositors and Origen, there was a very wide difference; as the statement of his other rules will show.

Rule II. Consequently, that portion of sacred history, both in the Old Testament and the New, which narrates things probable, consonant to reason, commendable, honest, and useful, must be supposed to state facts, and of course must be understood literally. But that portion of sacred history which states actions or events that are either false, or absurd, or unbecoming in God and holy men, or useless and puerile, must be divested of all literal meaning, and be applied to moral and mystical things in both the spiritual worlds. Origen, for reasons hereafter stated, assumed it as certain, that the biblical history of both Testaments contained many false statements, statements of things that never did, and never could, take place. And he gives two reasons why God intermingled many fables with the true history in the Bible. The *first* is, that if people found nothing in the Bible but what is true, probable, beautiful and useful, they would never think of going beyond the literal meaning of the Bible, and thus would entirely neglect the *soul* and the *spirit* of it. But now, as they meet with things altogether incredible and absurd, these very impediments and stumbling blocks prompt them to search for the sublimer meaning. In his *Principia* L. ix. sec. 15. p. 173. (as translated by *Charles* de la *Rue;* for the ancient translation of *Ruffinus* is quite too free,) Origen thus expresses himself: Verum quoniam si legis utilitas et varietate oblectans historiae series ubique sese proderet, non utique credidissemus aliud quiddam praeter id, quod obvium est, in scripturis intelligi posse, idcirco Dei verbum in lege ac historia interponi curavit offendicula et impossibilia quaedam, ne dictione nihil praeter illecebram habenti deliniti, et nihil Deo dignum addiscentes, tandem a dogmatis recedamus, aut nudae literae penitus adhaerentes nihil divinius percipiamus. So then, if [p. 650.] we may believe Origen, when God caused the sacred books to be written, fearing lest the travellers should be so captivated with the beauty and comfort of a direct and smooth road, as to forget whither they were travelling, he placed in their path, here and there rocks, ditches, hills, and other obstructions, which should oblige them to swerve and deviate from the straight forward course.—His *second* reason is, that God wished to instruct men in *all* the doctrines and precepts necessary for their salvation, by means of sacred history. But this object could not always be effected by true history; and therefore, with the true, he interspersed here and there the false and fabulous, that men might learn what he wished them to know, by means of fictitious and imaginary examples. He says: Oportet autem et istud scire: cum eo praecipue spectet

Dei verbum, ut in rebus spiritalibus et gestis et gerendis seriem declaret: ubi secundum historiam invenit facta, quæ arcanis istis accommodari possent, illis usus est, multis occultans abstrusiorem sensum; ubi vero in explananda illa spiritalium connexione non sequebatur certarum quarundam rerum praxis, quæ propter arcaniora ante scripta fuerit, scripturæ subnexuit historiæ quod factum non erat, imo aliquando quod fieri non poterat, quandoque autem quod poterat quidem fieri, sed factum tamen non est. Accidit etiam aliquando, ut paucae interjectæ sint dictiones veritati, si ad corpus spectes non consentaneæ. The closing part of this passage shows, that Origen believed—(1) That many portions of the sacred history are mere fables: and that these fables are of two kinds; some have no semblance of truth, but are such fictions as could not have been facts; others have a verisimilitude, and might have been facts, yet were not so in reality. (2) Some portions of the sacred history are in the main true; yet among the things stated, there are some things inserted which are not true but fictitious. By the aid of this rule, Origen easily surmounts all difficulties in the historical parts of both Testaments. Whenever any fact occurs, which either conflicts with the principles of his philosopby, or seems to afford the enemies of Christianity a ground for cavilling, he boldly denies the fact, and converts it into either a moral or a mystical fable. All his Homilies and commentaries afford us examples: we will cite only one of them, from his ***Principia*** (L. iv. sec. 16. p. 174.) Quis sanæ mentis existimaverit primam et secundam et tertiam diem et vesperam et mane sine sole, luna et stellis, et eam quae veluti prima erat, diem sine cœlo fuisse? Quis adeo stolidus ut putet, Deum more hominis agricolæ plantasse hortum in Eden ad orientem, ubi lignum vitæ posuerit, quod sub oculos et sensus caderet, ut qui corporeis dentibus fructum gustasset, vitam inde reciperet, et rursus boni et mali particeps fieret, qui fructum ex hac arbore decerptum comedisset? Et cum Deus meridie in paradiso ambulare dicitur, et Adam sub arbore delitescere, neminem arbitror [p. 651.] dubitare his figurate per apparentem historiam, quæ taæen corporaliter non contigerit, quædam indicari mysteria.--Sed quid attinet plura dicere, cum innumera ejusmodi scripta quidem tanquam gesta sint, non gesta vero, ut littera sonat, quivis, modo non plane stipes, colligere possit. Respecting the New Testament history, he decides with equal assurance, discarding all the caution and reserve which he elsewhere rarely neglects. A large part of it he considers to be fables, by which the holy Spirit aims to instruct us in recondite mysteries. He says explicitly: Sexcenta ejus generis in evangeliis observare licet attentius legenti, unde colliget iis, quae secundum literam gesta sunt, alia adtexta esse, quae non contigerint. In his comment, on John, (tom. x. Opp. tom. ii. p. 150. edit: Huetianæ,) he openly acknowledges, that the whole history of the four Gospels is full of statements, either false, or contradictory to each other; and that there is no way left to defend the authority and the divine origin of these books, but by a recurrence to what he calls ἀναγωγήν. Λεῖ τὴν περὶ τούτων ἀλήθειαν ἀποκεῖσθαι ἐν τοῖς νοητοῖς. Veritatem harum rerum oportet repositam esse in his, quae animo cernuntur. He had just spoken of the forty days' conflict of Christ with the prince of hell, and he said: Λεῖ τὴν δοκοῦσαν διαφωνίαν λύεσθαι διὰ τῆς ἀναγωγῆς. Decet nos apparentem dissonantiam dissolvere per Anagogen;

i. e. by a mystical interpretation. I have already touched upon the causes which led him to adopt this very dangerous rule for interpreting sacred history. They are obvious to every attentive reader. The statements of the Bible respecting the creation of the world, the origin of man, &c. were contrary to the precepts of his philosophy; and, therefore, he would sooner deny the truth of a portion of sacred history, than give up his philosophy. Again, by the history of the Old Testament, the Gnostics endeavored to establish their doctrine, that the Creator of this world was a different being from the Father of Jesus Christ; and from the history in both Testaments, the philosophers drew arguments against Christianity; and Origen, not finding any other way to answer them, concluded to cut the knot he could not untie, by turning all the passages which his adversaries could use, into allegories.

Rule III. To the preceptive and didactic parts of scripture, the same principle is to be applied, as to the historical: namely, whatever occurs in them that is good, agreeable to reason, useful, and worthy of God, must, beyond all question, be construed literally. But whatever is absurd, useless, and unworthy of God, must not be taken literally; but must be referred to morals and to the mystical world. Origen believed, that the preceptive and didactic parts of the Bible contained some things, which, if taken literally, it was impossible to believe or to practice, and which were contradictory to sound reason and philoso-
[p. 652.] phy. That he explained a number of the Christian doctrines philosophically, is well known, and has been already stated. And such an explanation required him to maintain, that the passages thus explained have no literal meaning. Numerous examples for illustration, occur in his writings. We therefore will only remark briefly on the preceptive parts of the Bible. Respecting the laws of Moses, he utters himself very harshly, and in fact extravagantly, and almost impiously. In his seventh *Homily* on Levit. sec. 6. (Opp. tom. ii, p. 226.) he says: Si adsideamus literæ et secundum hoc vel quod Judaeis, vel id quod vulgo videtur, accipiamus quæ in lege scripta sunt, *erubesco dicere et confiteri, quia tales leges dederit Deus.* Videbuntur enim magis elegantes st rationabiles hominum leges, verbi gratia, vel Romanorum, vel Atheniensium, vel Lacedæmoniorum. Si vero secundum hanc intelligentiam, quam docet ecclesia, accipiatur Dei lex, tunc plane omnes humanas supereminet leges, et vere Dei lex, esse credetur. De *Principiis*, L. iv. (sec. 17. p. 176.): Si ad leges etiam Mosaicas veniamus, plurimæ si eas nude observari oporteat, *absardum*, aliæ *impossibile* præcipiunt. And this he endeavors to demonstrate by several examples, which we here omit. Respecting his mode of explaining the Mosaic laws, we shall presently speak particularly. The laws of the New Testament, he supposed indeed to be superior to those in the Old Testament, seeing they do not prescribe any rites and ceremonies; yet he supposed that many of these laws must be construed mystically and allegorically. Of this we have evidence in his *Principia*, L. iv. (sec. 18. p. 179.) where he says: Jam vero si ad Evangelium veniamus et similia requiramus, quid a ratione magis alienum, quam istud; *Neminem per viam salutaveritis*, (Lu. x. 4.) quod Apostolis præcepisse Salvatorem, simpliciores existimant? Et cum dextera maxilla percuti dicitur, res est a verisimili prorsus abhorrens, cum omnis qui percutit, nisi

natura mancus fuerit, dextera manu sinistram maxillam feriat. Neque potest ex Evangelio percipi quo pacto dexter oculus offensioni sit. After explaining these things at some length, he proceeds: Præterea Apostolus præcipit, dicens; *Circumcisus aliquis vocatus est? non adducat præputium.* (1 Cor. vii. 18.) Primum, quilibet haec abs re præterque propositum dicere Apostolum videbit. Nam quomodo de nuptiis et de castitate præcipiens, non videatur haec temere interposu isse? Secundo vero, quid obesset, si obscœnitatis vitandae caussa ejus, quæ ex circumcisione est, posset aliquis revocare praeputium? Tertio, quod certe fieri id omni genere impossibile est. Haec a nobis dicta sunt, ut ostendamus, quia hic prospectus est Spiritus sanctus - - non ut ex sola littera vel in omnibus ex ea aedificari possimus.

Rule IV. As to the Mosaic laws in particular, there are indeed many of them which have a literal meaning; and therefore are to be considered as direct rules for human life and conduct. But there are many others, the *words* of which convey no meaning whatever, and only the *things* indicated by [p. 653.] the words are of use to awaken moral and mystical thoughts in our minds. I will adduce some examples of both these classes of laws, in Origen's own words. Of the former class he speaks in his *Principia*, L. iv. (§ 19. p. 180.): Quis non affirmet mandatum hoc, quod præcipit: *Honora patrem tuum, et matrem tuam*, etiam sine ulla spiritale interpretatione sufficere, et esse observantibus necessarium? maxime cum et Paulus iisdem verbis repetens, confirmaverit ipsum mandatum. Quid attinet dicere de ceteris: *Non adulterabis, non occides, &c.* Rursus in Evangelio mandata quædam scripta sunt, de quibus non quæritur sintne ad litteram observanda, necne?—But it is not true as some learned men have believed, and among them Charles de la *Rue*, the editor of Origen,—that Origen excluded a mystical sense from those laws of Moses which he believed were to be obeyed in their literal interpretation. A little after the quotation just given, he adds these expressive words: Tametsi qui res altius scrutantur componere possint altitudinem sapientiæ Dei *cum litterali mandatorum sensu.* A *moral* allegory he could not indeed seek for in such laws; because their literal interpretation afforded a *moral* sense. But a *mystical* sense, as already observed, he would attach to every particle of the holy scriptures.—Of the latter class of laws we have examples in the same work, (§ 17. p. 176, &c.) as follows: In lege Moysi præcipitur exterminari quidem omne masculum, quod non fuerit octava die circumcisum: quod valde inconsequens est: cum oporteret utique, si lex secundum litteram servanda tradebatur, juberi, ut parentes punirentur, qui filios suos non circumciderunt. - - - Hæc verba: *Sedebitis domi vestræ singuli, nemo vestrum exeat e loco suo die septima,* (Exod. xvi. 29.) non videntur ad litteram posse servari, cum nullum animæ per totum diem immotum sedere queat.

Rule V. To determine what parts of the Mosaic law are to be understood literally, and what parts have no literal meaning, the following rule must be our guide; Whatever in the writings of Moses is called a *law*, admits of no literal interpretation; but whatever is denominated a *commandment*, a *precept*, a *statute*, a *testimony*, or a *judgment*, has a literal meaning which should not be disregarded. Many passages bearing these latter titles, in addition to their literal meaning, have also a moral sense, or are moral allegories.—This rule, so subtle, so obscure, and so difficult of application, Origen explains and inculcates at much length in his eleventh *Homily* on Numb. § 1. (Opp. tom. ii. p. 304.) To show how a *law* differs from commandments, precepts, testimonies, and judgments, he says: "A *law* has a *shadow of things to come:* but not so a commandment, or a statute, or a judgment; of which it is never written that they must be regarded as *shadows* of things to come; e. g., it is not written: This [p. 654.] is the *commandment* of the passover, but this is the *law* of the passover. And, because a law is a shadow of good things to come, the law of the passover is doubtless a shadow of good things to come: and, of course, its words have no direct meaning." - - "Of circumcision it is written: *This is the law of circumcision.* - - - Hence I inquire, Of what good things to come is circumcision the shadow." - - - "But when it is said: *Thou shalt not kill; thou shalt not commit adultery; thou shalt not steal,* and the like; you do not find the title of *laws* prefixed, for these are rather *commandments:* and thus that scripture is not made void among the disciples of the Gospel - - because not a commandment, but the *law,* is said to have a *shadow of things to come.* And a little after, (in § 2. p. 305.) he says: "Christ redeemed us from the *curse of the law,* (Gal. iii. 13.); he did not redeem us from the curse of the *commandment,* nor from the curse of the *testimony,* nor from the curse of *judgments,* but from the curse of the *law;* that is, that we might not be subject to circumcision in the flesh, nor to the observance of sabbaths, and other like things, which are not contained in *commandments,* but are to be considered as in the *law.*" By the *law,* in its stricter sense, Origen would have us understand the *ceremonial* law. Hence the import of his rule is, that the *ceremonial law* should be interpreted mystically, and not literally; but the *moral law* is to be first taken literally, before we proceed to any higher sense of it. Under the moral law, he also includes the civil or judicial code of the Jews; as many examples in his Homilies demonstrate. And yet Origen does not uniformly follow this rule. For he sometimes turns into allegories certain portions of the civil law; precepts which the heretics, and perhaps Origen himself, deemed too harsh, or which he could not explain satisfactorily. And, on the other hand, some of the ceremonial laws he forbids being construed only mystically. For instance, he enjoins on Christians the law of first fruits and of tithes. Thus, in his eleventh *Homily* on Numb. (§ 1. p. 303.): Hanc legem observari etiam secundum litteram, sicut et alia nonnulla (among the Jewish rites and institutions.) necessarium puto. Sunt enim aliquanta legis mandata (note—in the style of Origen, the *law* means the *ceremonial* law,) quæ etiam novi testamenti discipuli necessaria observatione custodiunt.

Rule VI. Although the ceremonial part of the Mosaic law has now only a mystical interpretation, or is not to be construed literally, yet we are not to understand that it always has been so. There are indeed some things in this part of the law which never had any literal meaning; but there are many other things, which, so long as the Jewish commonwealth existed, had a literal meaning for that people, and were to be observed by them accordingly. Since Christ's advent, however, the whole have lost their literal sense, and are either

to be construed as moral allegories, or to be referred to the two mystical worlds. All the learned men who have hitherto attempted to explain Origen's [p. 655.] system of interpretation, have judged that he considered the whole ceremonial law as purely mystical, and having no literal meaning. Thus Charles de la *Rue*, in his preface to Origen's works, (tom. ii. p. 14.) says, that "Each and every passage of scripture, which in any manner belonged to the *ceremonial law*, with no exception, had not a literal, but *only a mystical sense*." The falsehood of this assertion we have already shown: Origen *did* make exceptions. But I do not wonder that learned men should fall into this mistake. For, not being careful to make distinctions, and sometimes confounding things altogether different, Origen frequently talks as if he held such an opinion. But if we compare all his expositions, and carefully mark his expressions, it will be manifest, I think, that he could not have been so demented and destitute of common sense, as to suppose that *all* the ordinances of Moses respecting the tabernacle, sacrifices, the high priest, and other priests and Levites, and numerous other things, ought to have been mystically understood by the Jews; and that of course the *whole Levitical worship* was founded on a false exposition of the Mosaic law. It is indeed true, that he believed *some* of the ceremonial laws to be without meaning; and he accused the Jews of manifesting gross ignorance by scrupulously obeying them. Some examples have already been adduced, and more might easily be added. In his third *Homily* on Levit. (§ 3. Opp. tom. ii. p. 194.) he says, that the Jews very unsuitably and uselessly observed (indecenter satis et inutiliter observare) that law, which forbids touching a dead body or any unclean thing; and he maintains, that this law should be understood mystically. The same thing he repeats at large in his seventh *Homily*. And again in the third *Homily* on Levit. explaining that law (Levit. v. 15, 16.) which requires, in case of involuntary trespass, the offering of a ram, estimated by the shekel of the sanctuary, he says: Quod aperte secundum litteram quidem videtur absurdum, secundum spiritalem vero intelligentiam certum est, quod remissionem peccatorum nullus accipiat, nisi detulerit integram, probam et sanctam fidem, per quam mereari possit arietem (Jesum Christum.) In his fifth *Homily*, (§ 5. p. 209.) after citing the law in Levit. vii. 9: "And all the meat-offering that is baked in the oven, and all that is dressed in the frying-pan, and in the pan, shall be the priest's that offereth it,"—he expressly denies the literal interpretation of it, thus: Quid dicimus? Putamusque quod omnipotens Deus qui responsa Moysi cœlitus dabat, de clibano, et craticula et sartagine præciperit? - - Sed non ita ecclesiae pueri Christum didicerunt, nec ita in eum per Apostolos eruditi sunt, ut de Domino majestatis aliquid tam humile et tam vile suscipiant. Quin potius secundum spiritalem sensum, quem spiritus donat ecclesiæ, videamus, quod sit istud sacrificium, quod coquatur in clibano. More proof is not needed. Yet Origen did not venture to deny that the greatest part of the ritual law had a literal meaning, and that God by Moses [p. 656.] commanded that very worship which the Hebrews paid before Christ's advent: nay, he extols and lauds this same worship. To pass over many other examples, he thus commences his twenty-third *Homily* on Numb. (Opp. tom. ii. p. 356.): Si observatio sacrificiorum et instituta legalia quæ in typo data sunt

populo Israel, usque ad præsens tempus stare potuissent, exclusissent sine dubio Evangelii fidem. - - - Erat enim in illis, quæ tunc observabantur, magnifica quædem et totius reverentiæ plena religio, quæ ex ipso etiam primo aspectu obstupefaceret intuentes. Quis enim videns illud, quod appellabatur sanctuarium, et intuens altare, adstantes etiam sacerdotes sacrificia consummantes, omnemque ordinem, quo cuncta illa gerebantur, aspiciens, non putaret, plenissimum hunc esse ritum, quo Deus creator omnium ab humano genere coli deberet? See also the many expositions of the Mosaic laws in his *Homilies* on Exodus, Leviticus, and Numbers, in which he first inquires after the literal meaning and pronounces it useful, and then proceeds to the mysteries it contains. He however did maintain, that the Mosaic ritual law, which anciently had a literal or grammatical sense, entirely lost that sense after Christ's advent, and by Christians was to be understood only mystically. In his sixth *Homily* on Gen. § 3. (Opp. tom. ii. p. 77.) he says: Quod si edoceri vis, quomodo lex mortua sit, considera et vide, ubi nunc sacrificia, ubi nunc altare, ubi templum, ubi purificationes? nonne mortua est in his omnibus lex? Aut si possunt isti amici ac defensores litteræ, custodiant litteram legis. Origen pronounces the law *dead*, when it cannot and should not be observed; but it is *alive* when it can and should be obeyed according to its literal import. In his eleventh *Homily* on Exod. (§ 6. p. 171.) he says: Infirmatur lex in carne, id est, in littera, et nihil potest secundum litteram facere. - - Secundum autem consilium, quod nos afferimus ad legem, possunt omnia spiritaliter fieri. Possunt et sacrificia spiritaliter offerri, quæ modo carnaliter non possunt. - - - Quomodo nos sentimus et consilium damus, omnia facit lex: secundum literam autem non omnia, sed *admodum pauca.* Therefore there were *some*, at least, of the ritual laws, which he supposed, as before shown, can and should be observed at the present day. But by what marks we are to know what parts of the law never had any literal meaning, and what parts admitted of a threefold exposition before the advent of Christ, and now admit of only a twofold exposition,—a moral and a mystical, —I do not recollect that he has any where informed us. I make no question, however, that he appiied here that general rule already stated,—that whatever injunctions were unworthy of God, or absurd, or impossible to be executed, were to be regarded as having no literal meaning.

Rule VII. In the Biblical narrations and in the prophecies concerning nations, countries, and cities, in addition to the moral or spiritual sense, there is [p. 657.] also an *anagogical* sense, or one that relates to the celestial or upper world: but this sense must be explored cautiously and with diffidence, for it is extremely recondite. As we have shown, Origen believed that this lower world of ours resembles the world above, and therefore, whatever is narrated or predicted in the scriptures respecting the Jews, the Tyrians, the Sidonians, the Egyptians, and other nations,—all holds true also of the world of souls, in which the angels preside. In defending this fiction, he is extravagant enough to hazard the assertion, that even the sufferings and death of Christ in some sense took place also in the supersensible world. Thus, in his first *Homily* on Levit. (§ 3. p. 186, &c.): Recte ergo (Moses) secundo nominat altare, quod est ad ostium tabernaculi testimonii, quia non solum pro terrestribus sed etiam pro cœlestibus oblatus est hostia Jesus: Et hic quidem pro hominibus *ipsam corporalem materiam sanguinis sui* fudit, in cœlestibus vero ministrantibus (si qui illi inibi sunt) sacerdotibus, *vitalem corporis sui virtutem*, velut spiritale quoddam sacrificium immolavit. And this he very strangely endeavors to prove by Hebr. ix. 20. and Hebr. vii. 25. Concerning this opinion of Origen, *Huet* has a discussion in his *Origeniana*, (Lib. ii. Quæst. iii. p. 59, &c.); and he taxes all his ingenuity to screen the man, at least partially, if not wholly, from this charge. But this distinguished scholar effects nothing; and he did not, or would not, see that this fiction of Origen followed, necessarily, from his doctrine of the agreement and similitude existing between the celestial and terrestrial worlds.

(2) The learned have justly admired, and have extolled in the highest terms the untiring industry and perseverance of Origen, in compiling his *Tetrapla* and *Hexapla*, in which he brought together all the Greek translations of the Old Testament then extant, and compared them with the Hebrew text. What is called his *Tetrapla*, was an edition of the Old Testament, in which he combined with the Hebrew text the four celebrated Greek versions, those of the Seventy, of Aquila, of Symmachus, and of Theodotion; and so arranged the whole that they could easily be compared with each other, and with the Hebrew. The pages were divided into five columns; the first column contained the Hebrew text, first in Hebrew and then in Greek letters. The four other columns contained the four Greek versions above named, together with significant marks and critical notes. When three other Greek versions of the Old Testament were afterwards found at Jericho, Origen added these also to his work; which then acquired the name of *Hexapla*, because it contained *six* Greek versions of the Old Testament. They might have been called *seven*; but they were reckoned as only *six*, because the sixth and seventh, which perhaps differed but a little, were accounted but one, and occupied only one column, namely, the [p. 658.] seventh. Of this immortal work, *Bernard* de *Montfaucon* has treated largely, in the *Prolegomena* to his edition of the remains of the *Hexapla*, printed at Paris, 1713, 2 vols. folio. This immense labor Origen undertook, especially for the benefit of those who were either wholly ignorant of Hebrew, or had but a slight acquaintance with it, that they might obtain a better knowledge of the literal meaning of the Bible, by comparing so many different Greek versions. And yet this same Origen maintained that the words of scripture, in very many places, have no meaning at all; and he advised his pupils to disregard the literal sense of scripture, or what he calls the *body* of it, and to search only for its *marrow* and its *soul*, that is, for its mystical and moral interpretation. And his own practice as a commentator coincided with his precepts. And thus, frequently, very great men are inconsistent with themselves, or sometimes follow one principle, and sometimes another. It was certainly of no importance to have the means of arriving at the literal meaning, if that meaning is of no worth; and as for the mystical senses, they can be successfully explored, without the trouble of examining the numberless phrases and uses of words in the sacred volume. Origen, therefore, by that immense labor, produced a work of little utility, either to himself or to those who follow his mode of interpreting the scriptures; and he does not himself resort to his *Hexapla* for aid, in his *Commentaries* and *Homilies*, because it was little suited to his purpose.

§ XXIX. **Origen and Mystic Theology.** This Origen, who was the chief corrupter of Christianity by philosophical speculations, and who introduced the fictions of his own mind into the holy scriptures, did likewise, by his precepts respecting the origin of the soul, and its self-determination in action, give encouragement and support to that unsocial class of men who strive to withdraw their minds from all sensible and material objects, and to associate themselves with the divine nature by contemplation. At least, this is a fact, that after his writings began to circulate among Christians, and his opinions to be lauded, embraced, and propagated, far greater numbers than before gave up all worldly business and cares, to increase their piety; and, in order to behold God mentally, resolved to retire into solitary places, expecting, by concentrated meditation and by the mortification of their bodies, to obtain spiritual freedom and complete tranquillity of mind.(1) And, perhaps, the famous *Paul* of Thebais, who, to save his life during the Decian persecution, is reported to have fled into the deserts, and there to have lived to extreme old age, [p. 659.] and who was accounted the leader and father of the *Eremites*,—chose, on the termination of the persecution, not to return to social life, but to spend all his days among wild beasts, for this reason, that he might purge out of his mind all images of sensible things, and bind it to God by indissoluble ties.(2)

(1) Origen embraced and held all those principles which lie at the foundation of what is properly denominated *Mystic Theology*. In the first place, he believed that man has *two souls;* the one a rational soul, which is of divine origin; the other not rational, but capable of apprehending and of craving external objects, and of exciting various emotions in the man. He believed that the higher or rational soul originated out of the divine nature, and would return into it again; that it existed from eternity in the upper world, and was of a spotless character; that, for some fault committed, it was condemned to reside in its present concrete body; that it retains its innate perceptions of truth, goodness, and justice; that while inhabiting the body, it has a natural power of exciting the latent principles of truth and goodness inherent in it; that all its propenseness to evil and sin, arises from its connection with the sentient soul, and from the contagion of the body; and that there is no way for it to become perfect and happy, but by freeing itself from the ties which connect it with the animal soul, subduing the power of the senses, withdrawing itself from the objects which allure the senses, arousing its inherent perceptions (of virtue) by continued meditation, and by weakening and exhausting the activities of the body in which it is imprisoned. Now, the man who adopts all these notions, is a travel-

ler in the direct road to that system of doctrine which bears the name of Mystic Theology.—But, in addition to these notions, Origen held some opinions which give energy and force to those common notions of mystics, and prompt them more strongly and earnestly to desire solitude, and to indulge the hope of a mystical deification. The first of these opinions was his celebrated doctrine concerning the soul of Jesus Christ, which, he supposed, as we have before stated,—by intense and uninterrupted contemplation of the Word or Son of God, before his descent to our world, had become so absorbed in the divine Word, as to form but *one person* with him. For the soul of Christ is of the same nature with all other human souls. In his *Principia*, (L. ii. § 5. p. 91.) he says: Naturam quidem animæ Christi hanc fuisse, quæ est omnium animarum, non potest dubitari: alioquin nec dici anima potuit, si vere non fuit anima. Therefore, all the souls of men, though at present vastly inferior to that chief of all souls, and though living in exile and in prison houses,—have the power, by contemplating the Word of God, to withdraw themselves from the body and from the associated sentient soul, and to bring themselves into closer [p. 660.] communion with the Son of God. He says: Anima, quæ quasi ferrum in igne, sic semper in Verbo, semper in sapientia, semper in Deo posita est, omne quod agit, quod sentit, quod intelligit, Deus est. This indeed he says especially of Christ's soul; but he immediately adds, that he would not exclude entirely the souls of holy men from the same felicity. Ad omnes denique sanctos calor aliquis Verbi Dei putandus est pervenisse: in hac autem anima (Christi) ipse ignis divinus substantialiter requievisse credendus est, ex quo ad ceteros calor aliquis pervenerit. This then was Origen's belief: That every rational soul that follows the example of Christ's soul, and assiduously contemplates the Word of God, or Christ, becomes a participant of that Word, and, in a sense, receives the Word into itself. In another passage, (de *Principiis*, Lib. iii. c. iii. § 3.) he expresses the same sentiment thus: Sanctæ et immaculatæ animæ si cum omni affectu, omnique puritate se voverint Deo et alienas se ab omni daemonum contagione servaverint, et per multam abstinentiam purificaverint se et piis ac religiosis imbutæ fuerint disciplinis, *participium* per hoc *divinitatis* assumunt et prophetiæ ac ceterorum divinorum donorum gratiam merentur.—Whither these opinions lead, and how much they must strengthen the propensity and facilitate the progress of those naturally inclined to austerities, to holy idleness and to irrational devotion, all who are acquainted with human nature can easily perceive.

But I think it will not be unpleasant to many, to see this portion of Origen's system more fully developed, and to learn more clearly how the several parts stand connected, and by what arguments they are supported. I will therefore show, as briefly as I can, how Origen brings down souls, the daughters of the supreme Deity, from their state of blessedness in heaven, into this lower world: and what method he points out for their recovering their lost felicity. A knowledge of these things will be the more useful, the more numerous at the present day those are, who either altogether or in part agree with Origen, and the fewer those are, who treat of Origen with a full understanding of his views.

I. No one is prosperous and happy, no one is wretched and unhappy, and no one is either more happy or more miserable than other people, except in accordance with his own merits or demerits. For God, who rules and governs all things, is always and infinitely just; and therefore cannot allot to any creature, not meriting it, either reward or punishment. This is the great and fundamental principle, on which nearly the whole fabric of Origen's theology rests, and from which he deduces the greater part of his opinions.

II. All the souls or persons,—for Origen considered the *body* as no part of the man, so that with him *soul* and *person* were synonymous—all the souls inhabiting this world, are unhappy, or are encompassed with many evils and troubles, some with greater and some with less. Now as no one *can* be unhappy, [p. 661.] or be less happy than others, except by his own fault, we are compelled to believe that all the souls inhabiting bodies, have merited the evils they now suffer.

III. Hence we can not doubt that our rational souls, before they entered our bodies, used the powers God gave them, improperly, and for these their faults they were condemned to live in bodies; those guilty of greater offences were encompassed with greater evils, and those guilty of smaller offences were involved in lighter calamities. Unless this be admitted, we cannot account for the great difference in the conditions of men in this world; nor can we silence the objections of adversaries to the providence of God. These principles Origen inculcates in many parts of his writings: we will cite one of the principal passages, namely, *de Principiis* L. ii. c. 9. p. 97. where he says: Si hæc tanta rerum diversitas, nascendique conditio tam varia tamque diversa, in qua caussa utique facultas liberi arbitrii locum non habet (non enim quis ipse sibi eligit, vel ubi, vel apud quos, vel qua conditione nascatur.) Si ergo hoc non facit naturæ diversitas animarum, id est, ut mala natura animæ ad gentem malam distinetur, bona autem ad bonas, quid aliud superest, nisi ut fortuito ista agi putentur et casu? Quod utique si recipiatur, jam nec a Deo factus est mundus, nec a providentia ejus regi credetur, et consequenter nec Dei judicium de uniuscujusque gestis videbitur expectandum. To these objections of the heretics, he replies in the following words: Deus æquales creavit omnes ac similes quos creavit, quippe cum nulla ei caussa varietatis ac diversitatis existeret. Verum quoniam rationabiles ipsæ creaturæ—arbitrii facultate donatæ sunt, libertas unumquemque voluntatis suæ, vel ad profectum per imitationem Dei provocavit, vel ad defectum per negligentiam traxit. Et hæc exstitit caussa diversitatis inter rationabiles creaturas, non ex conditioris voluntate vel judicio originem trahens, sed propriæ libertatis arbitrio. Deus vero cui jam creaturam suam pro merito dispensare justum videbatur, diversitates mentium in unius mundi consonantiam traxit, quo velut unam domum - - ex istis diversis vasis, vel animis, vel mentibus, ornaret. Et has caussas mundus iste suæ diversitatis accepit, dum unumquemque divina providentia pro varietate motuum suorum vel animorum propositique dispensat. Qua ratione neque creator injustus videbitur, cum secundum præcedentes caussas pro merito unumquemque distribuit. And he attempts to prove these his assertions by scripture, especially by what is said of Jacob and Esau, Rom. ix. 11, 12. He closes his argument with these words; Justitia Dei demum lucidius ostendetur, si caussas diversitatis uniuscujusque vel cœlestium, vel terrestrium vel infernorum in semetipso *præcedentes nativitatem corpoream* habere credatur.

IV. God created all souls perfectly alike, and endued them all with the fullest power of employing their faculties well or ill, according to their pleasure; so that they might be able to look continually on the eternal Reason [p. 662.] of God or his Word and Son; and might, by this contemplation, increase in wisdom and virtue, and finally become united to God through the medium of his Son. This sentiment of Origen is most manifest from the passage just cited, and from many others.

V. These free souls, before they were enclosed in bodies, and before this world was created, were by God placed under the following law: Every soul that would be prosperous and happy, must look constantly upon the Son of God, his Wisdom, his Reason, just as he would upon a mirror or a pattern, and must imitate him. By so doing, that soul will increase in wisdom and virtue and in all blessedness, and will gradually become incapable of sinning, and will be united closely with the Son of God whose image it bears. But every soul that averts its attention from this only exemplar of wisdom and sanctity, and pleases itself with the contemplation of material things, by the righteous judgment of God, will forfeit its natural blessedness, and be punished for its offences in a material body.

VI. Of all souls no one obeyed this divine law more sacredly and earnestly, than that soul which became associated with Jesus Christ the Son of God. For, by a perpetual and most intense contemplation of the Word or Son of God, this soul attained to the highest point of sanctity, and merited to be made *one person* with the Word.

VII. But a vast multitude of souls disobeyed this divine law, and, disregarding the Son of God, the eternal divine Reason, slid into the contemplation of other inferior and more ignoble objects. The cause of this transgression may be traced partly to the very nature of the soul, which is finite and therefore mutable, and partly to that subtile body, with which all souls are clothed. For this tenuous, shadowy body, though it be etherial and very different from our gross bodies, nevertheless has some power, if the soul is off its guard, of withdrawing the mind from the contemplation of heavenly and divine things, and of inducing it to misdirect its movements. *De Principiis*, L. ii. (c. 9. sec. 2. p. 97.): Rationabiles istæ naturæ, quia esse cœperunt, necessario convertibiles et mutabiles substiterunt: quoniam quæcunque inerat substantiæ earum virtus, non naturaliter inerat, sed beneficio conditoris effecta. - - Omne (nempe) quod datum est, etiam auferri et recedere potest. Recedendi autem caussa in eo erit, si non recte et probabiliter dirigitur motus animorum. Voluntarios enim et liberos motus a se conditis mentibus creator indulsit, quo scilicet bonum in eis proprium fieret, cum id voluntate propria servaretur: sed desidia et laboris tædium in servando bono, et aversio ac negligentia meliorum initium dedit recedendi a bono. It is well known, that Origen assigned to all souls tenuous bodies.

VIII. So many souls having, by their own fault, become vicious, it was necessary for God to perform the duty of a judge, and execute his threat to connect them with material bodies and sentient souls. But as all had not sinned [p. 663.] in an equal degree, some having departed farther than others from goodness, divine justice required, that the punishment of each should be proportionate to his offence.

IX. Hence, God determined to create a world (or material universe,) admirably composed of innumerable bodies of divers kinds; so that each of the souls which had variously deviated from their duty in the upper world, might here severally find a prison corresponding with its crimes. From many passages, I select a few only. In his *Principia* (L. ii. c. 9. sec. 2. p. 97.) he says: Unaquæque mens pro motibus suis vel amplius, vel parcius bonum negligens, in contrarium boni, quod sine dubio malum est, trahebatur. Ex quo videtur semina quædam et caussas varietatis ac diversitatis ille omnium conditor accepisse, ut pro diversitate mentium, id est, rationabilium creaturarum—varium ac diversum mundum crearet. Ibid. (sec. 6. p. 99.): Deus cui creaturam suam pro merito dispensare justum videbatur, diversitates mentium in unius mundi consonantiam traxit. Ibid. (sec. 7. p. 100.): Unusquisque in eo quod mens creatus a Deo est vel rationabilis spiritus, pro motibus mentis et sensibus animorum, vel plus vel minus sibi meriti paravit, vel amabilis Deo, vel etiam odibilis extitit.—Nam justitia creatoris in omnibus debet apparere.

X. The cause, therefore, of God's creating this material world (or universe) was, the sins which souls committed before this world existed. Nor should we view this world otherwise than as a vast dwelling-place, comprising innumerable cottages of various classes, arranged with consummate art, in which souls, fallen into sin by their own fault, might be detained for a season, until they repent and return to their duty. In his *Principia*, L. ii. (c. 9. sec. 9. p. 100.) he says: Unumquodque vas secundum mensuram puritatis suæ aut impuritatis, locum, vel regionem, vel conditionem nascendi vel explendi aliquid in hoc mundo accepit: quæ omnia Deus usque ad minimum virtute sapientiæ suæ providens ac dignoscens, moderamine judicii sui aequissima retributione universa disponit, quatenus unicuique pro merito vel succurri vel consuli deberet. In quo profecto omnis ratio æquitatis offenditur, dum inaequalitas rerum retributionis meritorum servat aequitatem.

XI. Of the punishments endured by souls in their state of exile and captivity, besides the loss of their former felicity, the principal and the greatest is, that each is joined with an animated body; that is, with a mass of gross matter, in which lives a sentient soul, that now craves and desires, and now abhors and hates. For it results from this conjunction, that the rational soul feels little or no desire for heavenly and divine things, but on the contrary, craves and lusts after earthly and sensible objects, and is agitated and pained with desires that are sometimes vain and sometimes hurtful. And the society of the body not only increases this evil, and weakens the force and energy of the mind, but also causes the rational soul to participate in the pains and anguish of the body.

[p. 664.] XII. As all divine punishments are salutary and useful, so also that which divine justice has inflicted on vitiated souls, although it is a great evil, is nevertheless salutary in its tendency, and should conduct them to blessedness. For the tiresome conflict of opposite propensities, the onsets of the passions, the pains, the sorrows, and other evils arising from the connexion of the mind with the body and with a sentient soul, may and should excite the captive soul to long for the recovery of its lost happiness, and lead it to concentrate all its energies in order to escape from its misery. For God acts like a physician, who employs harsh and bitter remedies, not only to cure the diseased, but also to induce them to preserve their health and avoid whatever might impair it. *De Principiis*, L. ii. (c. 10. sec. 6. p. 102.): Si ad corporis sanitatem pro his vitiis, quae per escam potumque collegimus, necessariam habemus interdum austerioris ac mordacioris medicamenti curam: nonnunquam vero si id vitii qualitas depoposcerit, rigore ferri et sectionis asperitate indigemus: - - Quanto magis intelligendum est, et hunc medicum nostrum Deum volentem diluere vitia animarum nostrarum, quae ex peccatorum et scelerum diversitate collegerant, uti hujusscemodi pœnalibus curis, insuper etiam (apud inferos) ignis inferre supplicium his qui animae sanitatem perdiderunt. - - Furor vindictae Dei ad purgationem proficit animarum. - - Origen indeed here refers, more especially, to the pains and punishments which souls endure in hell; yet he states the nature of all the evils which God inflicts upon rational beings. And it is very clear, that Origen believed in no divine punishments but such as are useful and salutary (to the transgressors).

XIII. For the souls in whom the sorrows of their prison awakens a desire for their lost happiness, there is one and the same law, as for the souls destitute of bodies and resident with God. No soul *can* become happy, except by means of the eternal Reason and Wisdom of God, or his Word and Son; on whom they must fix their thoughts, and by persevering meditation and contemplation, must appropriate him, as it were, and make themselves one with him.

XIV. Innumerable souls, both among the Jews and among other nations, have performed this duty, and that before the advent of Christ. For exiled captive souls have not changed their natures, but retain still their inherent free will: and therefore they are able, although with difficulty, by their own inherent powers to elevate themselves again, and, by the use of correct reason, to gradually ascend to the eternal Reason or Son of God. And the more religiously and correctly a soul uses its reason, the nearer it approaches to God and to his Son. *De Principiis*, L. i. (c. 3. sec. 6. p. 62.): Participatio Dei patris pervenit in omnes tam justos, quam peccatores, et rationabiles atque irrationabiles. - - Ostendit sane et Apostolus Paulus, quod omnes habeant participium Christi. Rom. x. 6, 7, 8. Ex quo in corde omnium significat [p. 665.] esse Christum secundum id quod verbum vel ratio est, cujus participatione rationabiles sunt. See here the *Christ in us*, or the *Word within*, of which the Mystics talk so much.—And hence, there is good ground of hope for the salvation of the ancient philosophers, especially *Plato, Socrates*, and others, who averted their minds from the body and the senses.—Yet for souls oppressed with bodies, this is a very arduous and difficult task; and but few successfully accomplish it without divine aid.

XV. Therefore God, who is desirous of the salvation of souls, sent that Word of his, by communion with whom alone their recovery was possible, clothed in a human body, from heaven unto men, or unto the exiled souls enclosed in bodies; that he might distinctly teach them divine wisdom, by which the way of salvation is manifest, but to which they with difficulty attain when left to themselves; and that, while admonishing them of their duty, he might, by patiently enduring very great sufferings and even death, obtain from God a termination of their imprisonment and exile. What were Origen's views of the effects of Christ's death and sufferings it is very difficult to say: yet, unless I entirely misapprehend him, he did not believe with us, that Christ, by his death and sufferings, merited for us eternal life. This could not be admitted by the man who believed, that no one *can* become happy except by his own merits, and that even fallen souls must attain to happiness by the proper use of their own free will. This, therefore, was the great benefit, which he supposed the death of Christ procured for souls, his showing them that God can revoke his sentence against them and release them from prison and exile. The divine justice must, in some way, be moved to remit the punishment, which souls have merited by the abuse of their free will; and this requisite was supplied by the voluntary suffering to which Christ submitted. Christ, therefore, is like a wealthy and munificent citizen, who, by paying over an immense sum to the government, or by voluntarily performing some very difficult service for the public good, obtains from the injured sovereign permission for banished exiles to return to their country. But the malefactors who are permitted to return, are not thereby restored to their former happy state: this they must procure, either by their own virtue, or by the virtues of others.

XVI. There is now, since the advent of Christ, a plain and easy way for souls to recover that felicity from which they have fallen by their own fault. To walk in it, they must first, by faith, embrace the eternal Word of God, who has appeared on earth clothed in a human body; and they must constantly look on him as the only author and teacher of eternal salvation.

XVII. And then, to attain a closer union with Christ, and a more perfect knowledge of the divine wisdom residing in him, they must make it their first and great care, to free themselves from the contagion of the sentient soul. And therefore they must estrange themselves from their eyes and ears and other [p. 666.] senses, and with all their might must betake themselves to the contemplation of heavenly truth. Mortification must also be applied to the body, which greatly increases and strengthens the power of the sentient soul, especially, if it be luxuriously fed and greatly indulged. And finally, as the images of the things and persons about us or with which we are conversant are apt to rush into the mind through the senses, and greatly to excite and distract the mind, thereby inducing forgetfulness of the things beyond our senses, and great debility in our free will,—a man will best provide for the freedom and the fortitude of a mind altogether upright, by shunning as much as possible intercourse with men, conversation, business, and the bustle of the world, and retiring into solitude.

XVIII. The rational soul that will thus exercise itself, continually, and never remove its eyes from Christ, will, by a slow process, become what it was before it entered the body: that is, from being a soul propense towards corporeal things and seeking its pleasure in the senses, it will become pure and be elevated above all earthly and perishing objects. *De Principiis*, L. ii. (c. 8. sec. 3. p. 96.) : *Mens* (νοῦς), de statu suo ac dignitate declinans, effecta vel nuncupata est *anima* (ψυχη), et rursum *anima* instructa virtutibus *mens* fiet. Nay, as before stated, such a soul, by a perpetual contemplation of Christ, becomes transformed into Christ, according to its measure and capacity. See, among other passages, the *third* chapter of Book ii. of his *Principia;* where, in treating of Paul's words, 1 Cor. xv. 53. (For this mortal must put on immortality,) he says: Incorruptio et immortalitas quid aliud erit, nisi sapientia, et verbum, et justitia Dei, quae formant animam, et induunt, et exornant? Et ita fit, ut dicatur, quia corruptibile incorruptionem induet et mortale immortalitatem. *De Principiis* L. i. (c. 3. sec. 6. p. 62.) : Omnes qui rationabiles sunt, verbi, id est, Rationis participes sunt, et per hoc velut semina insita sibi gerunt sapientiae et Justitiae, quod est Christus. Ibid. c. ii. (sec. 7. p. 52.) : Propinquitas quaedam est menti ad Deum - - et per haec potest aliquid de divinitatis sentire natura, maxime si expurgatior et segregatior sit a materia corporali.

XIX. This whole work of purifying the soul and translating it into Christ, does not exceed the powers of man. For as the rational soul is allied to God, although it may lapse and go astray, it cannot lose its essential character or nature. If, therefore, the inherent energies of free will are called forth, the soul can, by its own power, wipe away its pollutions, and by a gradual process work its way out of its darkness. And as no one can become happy, but by his own merit, the soul will either never attain to happiness, or it will attain to it by its own powers.

XX. Yet those who properly use that power of free will which they possess, are assisted by the Holy Spirit; and this enables them to advance faster and reach the goal the sooner. For, as none can become sharers in the divine rewards and blessings, except they merit them, so the Holy Spirit aids no one, unless he merits that aid. *De Principiis*, L. i. (c. 3. p. 62.) : In illis [p. 667.] solis arbitror esse opus Spiritus sancti, qui jam se ad meliora convertunt, et per vias Christi Jesu incedunt, id est, qui sunt in bonis actibus, et in Deo permanent. And a little after, (in sec. 7. p. 63.) he more clearly states his views, thus: Est et alia quoque Spiritus sancti gratia, quae dignis praestatur, ministrata quidem per Christum, inoperata autem a Patre *secundum meritum eorum*, qui capaces ejus efficiuntur.

XXI. The gifts which the Holy Spirit imparts to the enlightened in order to facilitate their progress, are indeed various; but among them, two are prominent. *First*, the Holy Spirit lays open to them the mystical and spiritual sense of the holy Scriptures. *De Principiis*, L. ii. (c. 7. sec. 2. p. 93.) Per gratiam Spiritus sancti cum reliquis quampluriinis etiam illud magnificentissimum demonstratur, quod (ante Christum) vix unus ex omni populo superare poterat intellectum corporeum (legis et prophetarum) et majus aliquid, id est, spiritale quid poterat intelligere in lege vel prophetis: nunc autem innumerae sunt multitudines credentium, qui licet non omnes possint per ordinem atque ad liquidum spiritalis intellegentiae explanare consequentiam, tamen omnes persuasum habeant, quod neque circumcisio corporaliter intelligi debeat, neque otium sabbati, vel sanguinis effusio pecoris, neque quod de his Moysi responsa darentur a Deo: qui utique sensus dubium non est quod Spiritus sancti virtute omnibus suggeratur.—*Secondly*, to those striving after wisdom and virtue, the Holy Spirit explains the forms and the grounds and reasons of the doctrines taught in the Bible; and from these they derive great comfort and delight. Ibid. (sec. 4. p. 93.) De Spiritu sancto participare meruerit, cognitis ineffabilibus sacramentis consolationem sine dubio et laetitiam cordis assumit. Cum enim rationes omnium, quæ fiunt, quare vel qualiter fiant, Spiritu indicante cognoverit, in nullo utique conturbari ejus animus poterit: nec in aliquo terretur, cum verbo Dei et Sapientiae ejus inhaerens, Dominum Jesum dicit in Spiritu sancto. I omit what follows, for the sake of brevity.

(2) About the middle of this century, and during the Decian persecution, one *Paul* of Thebes, in Egypt, to preserve his life, fled into the deserts, and there lived till he died at an extreme age in the fourth century. And this Paul has generally been accounted the founder of the solitary or *Eremite* life; on the authority of *Jerome*, who composed his biography. (See the Acta Sanctor. Antwerp. Tom. i. Januarii ad diem x. p. 602.) But this opinion, as Jerome himself tells us in the Prologue to his Life of Paul, rests solely on the testimony of two disciple of St. Anthony, who are not witnesses above all exceptions; Amathas vero et Macarius, discipuli Antonii - - etiam nunc affirmant, Paulum [p. 668.] quemdam Thebaeum principem hujus rei fuisse. Thus much may be conceded to these men, that prior to St. *Anthony*, their master, this Paul resided in the desert parts of Egypt. But that no Christian anterior to Paul, either in Egypt or in any other country, retired from the society of men in order to acquire an extraordinary degree of holiness, can never be proved by the testimony of these illiterate men, who, like all the so-called *Eremites*, were ignorant of the history of the world. Nor was this opinion as to the origin of the eremite life, universally adopted in the age of Jerome: for he himself states various other opinions on the subject. He appears indeed to have believed the statement of the two eremites. And yet this is not altogether certain: for his words are not the same in the different copies of his work. *John Martianay*, in his edition of Jerome's Works, (tom. iv. P. ii. p. 89.) thus states them: Paulum quemdam principem istius rei fuisse, non nominis: quam opinionem nos quoque probamus. But *Erasmas* and the *Acta Sanctorum* read: Quod non tam nomine, quam opinione, nos quoque comprobamus; the meaning of which, it is difficult to make out. Other copies read differently. If Jerome did believe, what he says the two disciples of Anthony stated, that the eremite life originated with this *Paul*, he certainly erred. For it appears, both from examples and from testimony, that before this man, not a few of the class of Christians called *Ascetics*, especially in Egypt, a country abounding in persons naturally gloomy and averse from society, did retire from the cities and towns into the fields and the uncultivated regions, in order to deprive the sentient soul of its delights, to mortify the body, and to aid the divine mind toiling in its prison. And that very Anthony, whom some make the father of eremites, followed the example of an old man who had pursued this mode of life from his youth; as *Athanasius* expressly testifies in his Life of St. Anthony, (Opp. tom. ii. p. 453.) And before this old man, very many adopted the same mode of life, although they did not retire to perfectly secluded places and to the

haunts of wild beasts, but only erected for themselves a retired domicil not far from their villages. So *Athanasius*, in the passage just mentioned, says: Ἕκαστος δὲ τῶν βουλομένων ἑαυτῷ προσέχειν, οὐ μάκραν τῆς ἰδίας κώμης καταμόνας ἤσκειτο. Unusquisque eorum, qui animum curare volebat, solus non procul a pago suo exercebatur; that is, subdued the body by toil, and averted the mind from the senses by prayer, and by meditation on divine things. That so early as the second century, this mode of life was in Syria esteemed beautiful and acceptable to God, appears from the example of *Narcissus*, bishop of Jerusalem, as stated by *Eusebius*. (Histor. Eccles. L. vi. c. 9, 10. p. 210, 211.) This man, weary of the assaults of his enemies, and eager for a *philosophical life*, retired to unfrequented places: Ἐκ μακροῦ τὸν φιλόσοφον ἀσπαζόμενος βίον διαδρὰς [p. 669.] πᾶν τὸ τῆς ἐκκλησίας πλῆθος ἐν ἐρημίαις καὶ ἀφανέσιν ἀγροῖς λανθάνων, πλείστοις ἔτεσι διέτριβεν. Cum philosophicae vitae jam dudum amore teneretur, relicta ecclesiae plebe, in solitudine ac deviis agris plurimos annos delituit. After a long time he returned from solitude to his residence in Jerusalem, and was the admiration of every body and exceedingly courted by the people; τῆς τε ἀναχωρήσεως ἕνεκα καὶ τῆς φιλοσοφίας, cum ob secessum tum ob philosophiam (seu philosophicam vitæ formam.) Therefore, even *then*, the highest respect was paid to those who preferred solitude to society, and who, abandoning social life, retired into deserts. What Eusebius intended by the words *philosophy* and a *philosophical life*, those familiar with the customs of the ancient Christians need not to be informed. For they are aware, that the Christian *Ascetics*, who sought the health of their souls in prayer, meditation, forsaking all worldly business, and subduing and mortifying the body by a spare and simple diet, were classed with the philosophers and assumed the name and the garb of philosophers. And this high opinion of the influence of solitude in sanctifying the soul, like many others, passed over from the Pagans to the Christians. That such Egyptians as wished to excel in virtue, and to prepare their souls for the world of bliss, were accustomed from the earliest times, to resort to solitary places, can be shown by many proofs; among which, I think, one of peculiar value is found in *Herodotus*, Histor. L. ii. (sec. 36. p. 102. edit. Gronov.) where he mentions it as a trait distinguishing the Egyptians from all other nations, that while others shunned the society of wild beasts, the Egyptians thought it excellent to live among them: Τοῖσι μὲν ἄλλοισι ἀνθρώποισι χωρὶς θηρίων δίαιτα ἀποκέκριται, Αἰγυπτίοισι δὲ ὁμοῦ θηρίοισι ἡ δίαιτα ἐστί. Apud ceteros mortales victus a ferarum secretus est consortio: Ægyptii autem cum feris vivunt. Does not this language show, that many ages before our Saviour, there were in Egypt not a few Eremites, or persons choosing to live in deserts among the wild beasts? And at the present day the same customs prevail in Egypt, not only among Christians, but also among Mohammedans. The Platonic and Pythagorean philosophers, also, inspired their followers with the love of solitude; and especially those called New Platonists, the disciples of *Ammonius*, and the associates of that *Origen* of whom we are treating, were accustomed warmly to recommend retirement and seclusion from society to every one studious of wisdom. In *Porphyry*, the great ornament of this sect, there is a long passage on this subject, in his first book περὶ ἀποχῆς, *on Abstinence from flesh;* in which he speaks in perfect accordance with the sentiments of Origen and the leaders of the mystic school. For he recommends that a philosopher make it his great object to become, by contemplation, united with the really Existent, or [p. 670.] God, (§ 29. p. 24.) And to obtain this bliss, in his opinion, the senses must be repressed and restrained, food be withheld from the body, and society be abandoned, and all places where there is danger to the soul. He says, among other things, (§ 35. p. 30 edit. Cantabr.) : Ὅθεν ὅση δύναμις ἀποστατέον τῶν τοιούτων χωρίων, ἐν οἷς καὶ μὴ βουλόμενον ἐστὶ περιπίπτειν τῷ πλήθει. Unde quantum in nobis est, ab iis locis recedere par est, in quibus inviti forsan in hostile agmen incidemus. And this he confirms by the example of the early Pythagoreans, who τὰ ἐρημότατα χωρία κατῴκουν, loca desertissima incoluerunt; while others occupied τῶν πολέων τὰ ἱερὰ καὶ τὰ ἄλση, ἐξ ὧν ἡ πᾶσα ἀπελήλαται τύρβη, urbium templa et nemora, a quibus omnis turba et tumultus arcebatur. By comparing *Origen* with *Porphyry*, it is easy to see that they both belonged to the same school; for they lay down the same precepts in very nearly the same words. I will transcribe a passage from *Porphyry* in the Latin translation, (§ 30. p. 25.) in order to show the *Mystics* of the present day, whence came that doctrine which they deem so sacred, and which they suppose Christ taught. Oportet nos, si ad ea, quæ revera nostra sunt et homini propria reverti velimus, quæcunque ex mortali natura nobis adscivimus, una cum omni ad ea inclinatione, qua illectus animus ad illa descendit, deponere, recordari vero beatæ illius, ac æternæ essentiæ, et ad illud inaspectabile et immutabile properantes reditum hæc duo curare: unum, ut quidquid est mortale ac materiale exuamus, alterum, quomodo redeamus et salvi ascendamus, diversi jam cum ascendimus a nobis ipsis cum prius ad mortalia descenderamus. Intellectuales enim olim eramus. - - Sensibilibus vero complicati sumus.

§ XXX. **Origen's Controversies with his Bishop.** That the author of so many new and singular opinions should have been assailed and harassed by the criminations and reproaches of many, is not at all strange. And Origen himself, in his writings yet extant, complains bitterly of the malice, the machinations, and the abuse of his adversaries; some of whom condemned his philosophical explanations of Christian doctrines, and others assailed his rules for interpreting the scriptures. Yet his great merits, his blameless life, and the high reputation he had everywhere gained, might have overcome all this opposition, if he had not incurred the displeasure and hatred of his patron, *Demetrius*, the bishop of Alexandria. The cause of this enmity it is at this day difficult to trace; nor is the generally reported envy of Demetrius free from all doubts, while its effects are most manifest. [p. 671.] For Demetrius compelled Origen to flee his country, and in two councils convened at Alexandria in his absence, first removed him from his office of preceptor, and then deprived him of his standing among the priests! The great majority of Christian bishops approved the sentence; but the prelates of the churches in Achaia, Palestine, Phenicia, and Arabia, disapproved it.(1) He therefore passed the remainder of his very laborious life at Caesarea, and at other places; and at last died at Tyre, A. D. 253, an old man, exhausted by his heroic sufferings for Christ in the Decian persecution. But after his death he was the occasion of even greater disputes among polemics, some assailing and others defending his reputation and his correctness; of which long-protracted and unhappy contests, the history of the following centuries will exhibit abundant evidence.

(1) The contests of Demetrius, bishop of Alexandria, with Origen, which gave rise to long and fierce conflicts, greatly disquieting the church during several ages, have been much discussed; but the causes of the contention are involved in great obscurity, or, at least, are not so palpable as many suppose. For all our information must be drawn from a few not very perspicuous passages in the early writers; time having deprived us of the second part of Eusebius' Apology for Origen, which was expressly devoted to the consideration and illustration of this subject. See *Eusebius*, Hist. Eccles. (L. vi. c. 23. p. 224.) The same *Eusebius* tells us, (Hist. Eccles. L. vi. c. 8. p. 209.) that Demetrius was moved by *envy* at the great reputation which Origen had acquired, to persecute the man who had once been dear to him. So likewise *Jerome*, in his twenty-ninth Epistle, (Opp. tom. iv. P. ii. p. 68.) says: Damnatum esse Originem non propter hæresin, sed quia gloriam eloquentiæ ejus et scientiæ ferre non poterant, et illo dicente omnes muti putabantur. Relying on these very worthy authors, nearly all the writers on ecclesiastical history, and especially those favorably inclined towards Origen, confidently assert, that the unworthy controversy originated in the malevolence and envy of Demetrius; and they pity the hard fortune of Origen, whose only offence was his learning, his virtue, and his eloquence. But for my part,—to say nothing of the uncertainty of such judgments respecting the secret motives of human actions,—when I survey attentively and weigh the occurrences between Demetrius and Origen, I come to the conclusion, that Demetrius' ill-will towards Origen did not arise from *envy*, if by *envy* be meant *repining* at the prosperity or fame of another. For Demetrius placed Origen at the head of the Alexandrian school, when he was a youth but eighteen years old, and he afterwards favored and [p. 672.] befriended him in various ways; he gave him honorable testimonials and letters of introduction when visiting other countries; sent envoys to escort him home, after a long residence in Palestine; and after the disagreement between them commenced, he permitted him to continue in his office at Alexandria; and at last, did not command him to quit Alexandria, but after he had left the country voluntarily, called him to account. Do these things indicate a mind envious at

the reputation and virtues of Origen? Persons envious of the virtues or eloquence of others, do not bring them before the public and commend them; they do not invite them to return from abroad, do not confer favors on them; but rather, they depress them, treat them with neglect, and wish them away from their presence. Some other cause, therefore, in my opinion, must be sought for this conflict.—I will first state what appears to me the true history of the case: and then, as direct testimony is wanting, I will argue from the circumstances of the case. - - Demetrius cheerfully gave Origen employment and office; he was pleased with the honors and applause which Origen gained; he allowed him to visit other countries and churches which needed his aid, notwithstanding he knew that Origen would acquire fresh laurels by these journeys; and finally, he was unwilling that a man whom he knew to be so great an ornament and support to the church of Alexandria, should be removed or taken from him. No person can doubt any of these things, who shall even superficially examine the acts of Origen and Demetrius. But this same Demetrius wished Origen to remain in the station he was now in, and not to be raised higher, or be put in orders and take a place among the presbyters of the Alexandrian church. This fact is sufficiently obvious, the cause of it is not equally clear. Those favoring Demetrius may conjecture, either that the bishop supposed a man who had emasculated himself would be a dishonor to the sacred office, or that the bishop feared lest, if made a presbyter, Origen would neglect his duties in the school. Those who believe fully what the ancients say of the envy of Demetrius, may suppose that he was afraid that a man like Origen, long held in veneration, and superior to his bishop in many branches of learning, if made a presbyter, would acquire too much influence; or that, if authorized to preach in public, his eloquence would obscure the dignity and the fame of the bishop. On the other hand, Origen believed that his services and merits entitled him to promotion. Those who had presided over the catechetic school of Alexandria before him, *Pantænus*, *Clement*, and doubtless others, had been made presbyters; and therefore he, being in no respect inferior to them, thought himself worthy of the same honor. But when he could not obtain from Demetrius the honor to which he felt himself entitled, he went away to Palestine, and at Cæsarea imprudently obtained that honor from other hands. And hence those sad [p. 673.] scenes! Hence that wrath of Demetrius!—I will now show, from the circumstances of the case, as far as I can, that such were the facts.

In the year 215, or a little after, a severe persecution under Caracalla having arisen at Alexandria, Origen, at that time about forty years old, sought safety in flight, and proceeding to Palestine, he took residence at Cæsarea. There the bishops honored him, by allowing him to address the public assemblies, and in the presence of the bishops. This gave offence to Demetrius. But the Palestine bishops defended their proceeding, and told Demetrius, that it had long been customary among Christians for the bishops to invite those whom they knew to be fit persons to teach publicly, even if they had not been made presbyters. Whether Demetrius was satisfied with this excuse or not, is uncertain; but this is certain, he not only wrote to Origen requiring him to return home and attend to the duties of his public office in Alexandria, but, as Origen perhaps made some delay, he sent deacons to Palestine to bring him back. See *Eusebius*, (Hist. Eccles. L. vi. c. 19. p. 221, 222. These facts show, I. That Origen, at that time, notwithstanding his reputation for eloquence, was debarred from the pulpit, or from preaching in public, by his bishop. II. That Demetrius would not allow him to perform the functions of a public teacher, even among foreign churches; doubtless, from a fear that he would insist on doing the same at Alexandria, and would thus open his way to the rank of a presbyter. III. Yet he esteemed Origen very highly; and he considered his labors not only useful, but even necessary, to the church of Alexandria. This appears from his desire, and even great earnestness, to have the man return home. For, as Origen did not at once obey the letter of recall, the bishop sent envoys to Palestine, to press him with arguments and persuasives on the subject. It seems, that Origen manifested a disposition to remain in Palestine, where he received greater honor from the bishops than he received at Alexandria; but Demetrius thought the church of Alexandria could not part with so great a man without a serious loss. Perhaps also the deacons who were sent to Palestine, were instructed to watch Origen, lest on his way he should do as he had done in Palestine, and by his preaching draw forth the admiration and respect of the people. Hence, IV. we may conclude, that Demetrius felt no envy against Origen; for if the virtues and the learning of the man had been annoying to him, he would gladly have had him remain out of the country. Yet he was unwilling to enroll him among the presbyters of the Alexandrian church. And, undoubtedly, he did not follow the example of the Palestine bishops, and permit Origen to preach in public; but, as *Eusebius* clearly intimates, he required him to devote himself wholly to the school.

After a pretty long interval,—in the year 228, as learned men have supposed,—Origen again took a journey to Achaia; not without the [p. 674.] knowledge and consent of Demetrius his bishop, as *Photius* affirms, (Bibliotheca, Cod. cxviii. p. 298.) but, as *Jerome* testifies, (Catal. Scriptor. Eccles. c. 54 and 62.) with the consent of the bishop, and furnished by him with honorable testimonials, or an *Epistola ecclesiastica*. On this journey, as he was passing through Palestine, he was ordained a presbyter by his friends and admirers, *Theoctistus* bishop of Cæserea, and Alexander bishop of Jerusalem. (*Eusebius*, Hist. Eccles. L. vi. c. 8. p. 209; *Jerome*, Catal. Scriptor. Eccl. c. 54; *Photius*, Bibliotheca, Cod. cxviii. p. 298.)—On hearing this, the wrath of Demetrius burst forth; and he despatched letters through the Christian world, severely censuring both Origen and the bishops who ordained him. His allegation against Origen is stated by *Eusebius*. It was, that a man who had mutilated himself, though learned and of great merit, is unworthy of the priesthood; and therefore, Origen had grievously sinned, by consenting to become a teacher in the church, while conscious of the crime he had formerly committed. It appears that even then, voluntary eunuchs were excluded from the priesthood, if not by formal canons, (of which there is no certain evidence,) at least by common usage among Christians. For, unless we suppose this, we cannot understand how Demetrius, a man of high character and well versed in ecclesiastical law, should venture, on this ground, to pronounce Origen unworthy of the priesthood. But this stain upon the character of the pious and learned man, was not known by the bishops who ordained him. Therefore, as Demetrius assailed *them* also, accusing them of violating ecclesiastical law, we are obliged to suppose that *their* offence was of a different nature. What it was, no ancient writer has informed us; but it may be inferred from what Jerome says, (Catal. Script. Eccl. c. 62.) namely, that Alexander, the bishop of Jerusalem, in reply to the accusation of Demetrius, alleged the honorable testimonials given by Demetrius to Origen on his setting out for Achaia. From this it is manifest, if I do not mistake, that Demetrius criminated the ordaining bishops, for admitting Origen to the Presbytership, without the knowledge and consent of Demetrius his bishop, and without consulting him in the matter. Alexander replied, that he and his associates looked upon the splendid testimonials of Demetrius which Origen carried with him, as supplying the place of an express consent; and that they could not suppose a man so highly recommended by him, to be unworthy of the priesthood. How the business was conducted does not fully appear, on account of the silence of the ancient writers; yet a careful attention may clear up much of the obscurity of the transaction. In the first place, I will cheerfully concede, that Origen himself did not request ordination from the Palestine bishops; but only did not refuse it, when offered [p. 675.] by them. And I have little difficulty in assigning a reason why they should wish to ordain him. They wished that Origen might publicly instruct Christians, and expound to them the holy scriptures, as he had done with great approbation during his former journey. But he, recollecting the great indignation of Demetrius, when he had before allowed such functions to be assigned him, would not consent to their wishes, because he was not an ordained presbyter. To remove this obstacle out of his way, the bishops declared their willingness to ordain him; and Origen consented. I am led to judge thus favorably of Origen's motives, by the exemplary piety of the man, and by the knowledge of human conduct; both of which require us, in a case of doubt and uncertainty, to prefer the most favorable opinion. And yet I think it manifest, that Origen despaired of obtaining ordination from the hands of Demetrius, and at the same time desired, though modestly, to attain that honor. For, if he had either contemned the office of a presbyter, or had supposed he could obtain it from Demetrius, he would never, although urged to it, have consented to receive the office from these bishops. Being a sagacious man, he could easily foresee, that Demetrius would be offended with both him and the bishops, for the transaction was undoubtedly discourteous towards Demetrius. And the person who would incur the resentment of a powerful man, rather than not obtain a certain place, if he is not stupid or altogether thoughtless, shows that he has not a little desire for that place. As for Demetrius, though I admit that he showed neither prudence nor gentleness, nor a due regard for Origen's merits, yet I do not see how he can be charged with *envy*. From this vicious state of mind he is sufficiently exculpated, first, by the noble testimonial of his affection and esteem for Origen, given him when he set out for Achaia; and he is still more proved innocent by the fact that, although offended with Origen, and believing that he had just cause for resentment, he nevertheless was not at all opposed to his return to Alexandria, and to his resumption of his duties in the school. It is not usual for the envious to wish those, whose honors and fame they fear will injure them, to live by their side, and to fill respectable and important stations. Demetrius would have directed Origen to remain in Palestine, if he had supposed his new official standing would cause a diminution of his own authority and fame. Nor is it an indication of envy, that he publicly professed to wish only for more prudence in the ordaining bishops, and more modesty in Origen, who had not resisted the proposal of his admirers. For this declaration might have proceeded from other motives, either praiseworthy or censurable.

The commotions originating from Origen's elevation to the priesthood, did not prevent his completing his begun journey to Achaia; after [p. 676.] which he returned to Alexandria, and there resumed the duties of his office. Nor did Demetrius oppose his bearing the title and enjoying the rank of a presbyter; for if he had been so disposed, he could have degraded him. Nay, several learned men have thought, that Demetrius actually assigned him a place among the presbyters of his church. They conclude so, from the sentence pronounced against Origen by the emperor Justinian in the sixth century, in which he is expressly called a *Presbyter ecclesiæ Alexandrinæ.* It is at least very probable, that Demetrius, either expressly or tacitly, allowed him to sit among the presbyters, provided he would continue to fulfil the duties assigned him in the Alexandrian school.—On returning to Alexandria in 228, Origen not only resumed his former labors, but he also commenced an exposition of the Gospel of St. John, (*Origenes*, Comm. in Johann. Opp. tom. ii. p. 3. edit. Huetianæ.); and also wrote other books, among which *Eusebius* (Hist. Eccl. L. vi. c. 24. p. 225.) mentions his celebrated work *de Principiis.* But in the midst of these labors, a new storm burst upon him; at first, indeed, quite moderate and endurable; for, (in tom. vi. in Johann. p. 94.) he writes: *Jesus Christ rebuked the winds and the waves of the troubled sea;* and thus, even during the storm, he could carry forward his exposition of St. John as far as the fifth tome. Gradually, however, the storm increased in violence, and at last became so great, that in the year 231 he forsook Alexandria, leaving his school under the care of *Heraclas*, one of his earliest pupils, and retired to Cæsarea among his friends. (*Eusebius*, Hist. Eccl. L. vi. c. 26. p. 228.)—Respecting his presbytership, there was no longer any contention; so that there must have been some other cause of disagreement between him and Demetrius, which, unaccountably, neither his friends nor his enemies have stated, although they had abundant occasion to speak of it. For, what *Epiphanius* relates, (Hæres. lxiv. c. 2.) that Origen was so frightened by the threat of an atrocious insult to his person by an Ethiopian, that he consented to sacrifice to the Gods,—is very questionable; and, if true, could not have produced the new contest between Demetrius and him after his return. This new contest lasted more than two years, as we have already learned from Origen himself; and, being protracted through various vicissitudes, Origen was able, during its continuance, to compose *five* of his tomes on the Gospel of John, besides other works. But if Origen had, unwillingly, paid some worship to the gods, and his bishop had accounted him a criminal for it, the whole matter might have been speedily settled; for Demetrius had only to call a council, and debar the criminal from the sacred rites, which was the canonical punishment for those who sacrificed to the gods. But [p. 677.] the bishop, though he harassed Origen, yet still allowed him to perform his official duties, and even to retain the rank of a presbyter which he had acquired in Palestine. After surveying the whole case, and carefully weighing all the circumstances, I conclude the cause of disagreement was this: that Origen, as he was an ordained presbyter, wished to enjoy all the prerogatives of a presbyter, to preach in public, to sit in the council of the presbyters, and to be reckoned as one of them; but Demetrius was opposed to it. He admitted, indeed, that Origen was a presbyter, at least nominally, and he would give him the title, but he would not allow him to address the people from the pulpit. Perhaps, also, as his feelings were now alienated from Origen, he frequently criticised and assailed the opinions which Origen advanced in the school and elsewhere, and his expositions of the scriptures; while Origen defended those opinions and expositions against the bishop.

However this may be, Origen being weary of the perpetual reproofs or injuries he received from Demetrius, in order to enjoy more liberty and peace, relinquished his employment in the year 231, and secretly retired to Palestine; where he was very cordially received by the bishops, and obtained all that had been denied him at Alexandria. After this his flight, Demetrius commenced a prosecution against him; for previously he had not attempted, nor had been disposed to attempt, anything of the kind.—*Eusebius*, indeed, does not expressly say that Origen left Alexandria secretly, and without the knowledge of Demetrius; on the contrary, he clearly states that, on leaving, he surrendered his office to *Heraclas*. From both these circumstances learned men conclude, that Demetrius was neither ignorant of his design to leave Alexandria, nor dissatisfied at his going. For if he had either not known of his going, or had been displeased with it, would he have authorized him to transfer his school to another man, and one of his own selection?—But here, undoubtedly, there is misapprehension. The circumstance omitted by *Eusebius*, is indicated by *Origen* himself, (Comm. in Johann. tom. vi. p. 94.) where he compares his departure from Egypt with the Exodus of the Hebrews, and says: Deum, qui populum suum ex Ægypto eduxit, se quoque ex servitute extraxisse. But nothing could have been more inapposite than such a comparison, if he had gone away with the free consent of Demetrius. And as to what *Eusebius* says of his transferring the Alexandrian school to *Heraclas*, the language is pressed too far. For *Eusebius* does not say, that he *committed* or *transferred* his school to Heraclas, but that he *left* it to him: Ἡρακλᾶ διδασκαλεῖον καταλείπει. *Scholam Heraclæ reliquit*, (not, *tradidit.*) See *Eusebius*, (Hist. Eccles. L. vi. c. 26. p. 228.) *Heraclas* had been his colleague, and had taught the younger boys; and now Origen left the school to his sole management. Origen's departure was therefore clandestine; and his voluntary dereliction of an office which for so many years he had usefully filled, roused the ire of Demetrius to such a pitch, that he de- [p. 678.] termined to punish him. He acted, indeed, in a manner unbecoming a bishop, and yet not without some semblance of justice. For the man who abandons an office committed to him, without giving notice, or saying any thing to him from whom he received it, appears to injure his patron materially, and is quite culpable. Besides, this very indignation of Demetrius, though unjustifiable, proves him not guilty of that *envy* charged upon him. For it shows, that he was unwilling to part with the services of Origen, that he felt most sensibly the great loss, both to the church and the school; but such feelings could not find a place in an envious mind. Demetrius envied the Palestinians the possession of so great and so talented a man, but he did not envy Origen.

Therefore, as it was the only way in which he could punish Origen for the detriment to the church and the injury to himself, Demetrius summoned a council of bishops, with some presbyters. So *Photius* states, from *Pamphilus'* Apology for Origen, (Bibliotheca, Cod. cxviii. p. 298: *Synodum episcoporum et presbyterorum quorundam*). We may here notice, that *Pamphilus* applies the pronoun *some*, (*quorundam*, τινων,) to the *presbyters*, but not to the *bishops*. Hence, if I can judge, Demetrius summoned *all* the bishops under his jurisdiction. And this construction is confirmed by what will soon be said respecting his second council. The reason why he summoned *all* the bishops of Egypt, but only *some* of the presbyters of Alexandria, will be obvious. He well knew, that most of the presbyters were favorable to Origen, their preceptor and friend, whom they admired for his piety: and, therefore, he summoned only such of the presbyters, as he supposed were more attached to himself than to Origen. But the bishops had not been so intimate with Origen; and therefore, Demetrius hoped, with less difficulty, to bring the majority of them to vote according to his wishes. But he was disappointed. For the major part of the council decided, as *Photius* informs us from *Pamphilus*, in the passage just mentioned: *That Origen should be expelled from Alexandria,* (Alexandria quidem pellendum.) *and should not be permitted to reside or teach there; but that he should not be degraded from the priesthood.* Demetrius, who wished to have Origen degraded, had expected a severer sentence. But, either *Photius* or *Pamphilus*, I think, must have stated the decision incorrectly. How, I ask, could these Christian bishops, who were themselves scarcely tolerated in Alexandria and Egypt, and who had no influence or power whatever in the state—how could this despised and hated body of plebeians expel Origen from Alexandria, or send him into exile? If those honest men had attempted it, they would have acted just about as wisely as the Quakers of London, or the Mennonites of Amsterdam would if they should attempt to banish from their city some honorable and upright citizen: which all would regard as showing a lack of common sense. I [p. 679.] have, therefore, no doubt, that this council merely pronounced Origen unworthy of his post as a teacher in the school and church of Alexandria. And such a sentence, in my opinion, would not have been altogether wrong or unjust. For the man who abandons his post, without the consent or knowledge of the person who placed him in it, is not unsuitably cut off from all hope of regaining it. And, perhaps, Origen himself would not have complained, if such a decision had been satisfactory to his adversary. But Demetrius thought, that this deserter of his post ought to be more severely punished. He, therefore, summoned another council. As *Photius*, avowedly copying from the Apology of *Pamphilus*, writes:

Verum Demetrius una cum Ægypti episcopis aliquot, sacerdotio quoque ilium abjudicat, subscribentibus etiam edicto huic, quotquot antea suffragati ei fuissent. (But Demetrius, together with some bishops of Egypt, divested him also of the priesthood; and this decree, moreover, was subscribed by such as had before voted in his favor).—And here several things deserve notice, which learned men, in treating on the subject, pass by in silence. I. In this second council, only *some (aliquot)* of the Egyptian bishops were present. Therefore, in the former they *all* were present. That is, Demetrius excluded from the second council, those among the bishops who, in the first council, voted for the milder sentence, or were for sparing Origen. And hence it appears, that the decree of the first council was not passed unanimously, but only by a majority of the council. II. There were no presbyters present in the second council. Hence it is manifest, that *all* the presbyters were in favor of Origen, and their zeal in his behalf caused the milder sentence to pass the council. They, doubtless, expatiated on the great merits of Origen, in regard both to the church universal, and to the church of Alexandria in particular; and by such commendations they inclined the minds of a majority of the bishops to moderation. III. The bishops, who had voted for Origen in the first council, in acceding to the decree of the second council, changed their opinions, and came over to the decision of Demetrius and his associates. And this is proof, that in the second council Demetrius assailed Origen on new grounds, and thereby strengthened his cause: and that the dissenting bishops, in view of these new grounds, and being separated from the presbyters who had pleaded the cause of their preceptor and friend, concluded to yield the point. In the state of Christian affairs at that period, Demetrius could not have gained the votes of those bishops who favored Origen, by menaces and violence, nor by gifts and promises. It is, therefore, probable that Demetrius brought forward, and invidiously exposed the singular opinions of Origen, and his strange interpretations of Scripture; and against this new charge, which was much graver than the former, the bishops, most of whom were not learned, and perhaps were among those who opposed the modifying of theology by philosophy, were unable to make resistance. That Origen was actually accused and convicted of adulterating Christianity, at least in the second council, [p. 680.] is adequately proved, unless I greatly misjudge, from the single declaration of *Jerome*, (in his Tract against *Ruffinus*, L. ii. c. 5.) that Origen was not only degraded from the priesthood, but was also *excluded from the church*. For in that age, no Christian was excommunicated and debarred from the church, unless he was either guilty of criminal conduct, or had injured the cause of religion by his errors. Of any criminal conduct, neither Demetrius nor any other person ever accused Origen. Consequently, we must believe, that this punishment was inflicted on him because of his novel and noxious opinions. He had already composed his well-known work, *de Principiis*, yet extant in Latin, which is full of singular opinions, and of explanations of Christian doctrines never before heard of. Nor could that book have been unknown at that time in Alexandria, the place where it was written. From this book, therefore, it is not improbable, Demetrius derived his allegations.—Nearly all the Christian churches approved the sentence passed upon Origen; for Demetrius, by letters, excited them against his adversary. But the bishops of the fou Asiatic provinces, Palestine, Phenicia, Achaia, and Arabia, dissented; and not only permitted Origen to live among them highly respected, but also to have the liberty of teaching both publicly and privately. Nor is this very strange. For the bishops of Palestine, who were intimately connected with those of Phenicia, were the authors of *that* which brought upon the good man all his troubles: that is, they ordained him presbyter. As to the churches of Arabia and Achaia, Origen had laid them under great obligations to him, by settling disputes among them, and by other kind offices.—But this transaction, manifestly, contains a strong argument against those who maintain that, in this third century, all Christendom was submissive to the authority and decisions of the Romish prelate. If this had been the fact, those bishops who honored and patronised Origen, would have ceased from being in communion with all other churches. And yet it is certain, that they were not at all criminated for relying upon their own judgment, rather than on that pronounced at Alexandria, and approved by the Romish prelate.

§ XXXI. **Disputes in the Church respecting the Trinity and the person of Christ.** That authority, which Origen attributed to reason or philosophy—(for he held them to be the same thing)—over theology generally, was extended by others to certain parts of theology in particular, and especially to that part which distinguishes in the Divine Nature three persons, the Father, the Son, and the Holy Spirit. Closely connected with this doctrine is, that concerning the origin and the dignity of Jesus Christ. As this division of the Divine Nature, of which the Scriptures require a belief, may seem to disagree with what reason teaches [p. 681.] respecting the unity or oneness of God, various persons attempted to so explain it, as to remove all disagreement between theology and philosophy. Those who engaged in this business, pursued various methods; if, indeed, the ancients correctly apprehended their views, which I must confess is very doubtful. Wherefore, about *four* different opinions may be produced, respecting the Holy Trinity and the Saviour of mankind, advanced in this century. These opinions, all the prelates of the age strenuously resisted, casting their authors out of the church. But they did not so combat these opinions as to exterminate the roots of the evil, and prevent the future rise of similar opinions. For, although they determined what should *not* be believed, respecting God and Christ, and thus suppressed the rising errors; yet they did not determine, with equal care and clearness, what should be positively believed, and in what terms the Scriptural doctrine of three persons in one God should be expressed. And this enabled others, subsequently, and especially *Arius*, to disturb the church with new explications of this doctrine.([1])

(1) The prelates and councils condemned those who subverted the distinction of persons in the divine nature, and who maintained that God is altogether undivided. Thus they denied, that the Son and the holy Spirit are to be excluded from the number of the divine persons. Yet, to those who should acknowledge three persons in God, great liberty remained for disputing about the relations of these persons to each other, their origin, their dignity, and their parity or disparity; and for explaining differently the nature, the offices, and the acts of the several persons. This liberty produced a great variety of opinions, and afforded to those whose genius and inclination led them to subordinate revealed religion to reason, abundant opportunity for introducing their own fictions into the doctrine of the Trinity. Hence arose the rash attempts, not only of several individuals, whose efforts excited little attention, but especially of *Arius*, whose most unhappy contests are too well known. At length, under Constantine the Great, the Nicene council abolished that liberty, the dangers of which were not foreseen by the ancients, and defined precisely, how the three divine persons are to be viewed, and in what terms men should speak of them.

§ XXXII. **The Noëtian Controversy.** At the head of those in this century, who explained the scriptural doctrine of the Father, Son, and holy Spirit, by the precepts of reason, stands *Noëtus* of [p. 682.] Smyrna; a man little known, but who is reported by the ancients to have been cast out of the church by presbyters, (of whom no account is given,) to have opened a school, and to have formed a sect.([1]) It is stated, that being wholly unable to comprehend, how *that* God who is so often in Scripture declared to be *one*, and undivided, can, at the same time, be *manifold;* Noëtus concluded, that the undivided Father of all things, united himself with the man Christ, was born in him, and in him suffered and died.([2]) On account of this doctrine, his followers were called *Patripassians;* which name, though not perfectly correct and appropriate, yet appears to be not altogether unsuitable or inappropriate.([3]) That Noëtus and his followers believed as above stated, must be admitted, if we place more reliance on the positive testimony of the ancients, than upon mere conjecture, however plausible.

(1) All that can be said of Noëtus, must be derived from the three following writers: *Hippolytus*, (Sermo contra hæresin Noëti; first published by *Jo. Alb. Fabricius*, Opp. Hippolyti, tom. ii. p. 5. &c. It had before appeared in Latin:) *Epiphanius*, (Hæres. L. vii. tom. i. p. 479.) and *Theodoret*, (Hæret. Fabular. L. iii.

c. 3. Opp. tom. iv. p. 227.) All that the other fathers state, (e. g. *Augustine*, *Philaster*, *Damascenus*,) is either taken from the three above named, or is derived from those who resorted to these sources. *Theodoret* is very brief: *Hippolytus* and *Epiphanius* are more full: both however, treat only of the principal tenet of Noëtus, and that without method and clearness. They neither explain, accurately and distinctly, his erroneous sentiment; nor lucidly state either his conduct, or the proceedings of others against him. And hence, but little can be said, either of Noëtus or of his doctrine. That he lived in the third century, is certain; but in what part of the century he disturbed the peace of the church, is doubtful. *Hippolytus* and *Theodoret* say, he was a native of Smyrna; but *Epiphanius* calls him an Ephesian. Perhaps he was born at Smyrna, but taught at Ephesus. Whether he was a layman, or held some sacred office, no one has informed us. Both *Hippolytus* and *Epiphanius* tell us, he had a brother; and they both represent him as so delirious, that he declared himself to be Moses, [p. 683.] and his brother to be Aaron. But that he was under so great infatuation, is incredible; since these very men who tax him with it, show, by their discussions, that he was no very contemptible reasoner. I can believe, that after his exclusion from the church, and when laboring to establish his new sect, he compared himself with Moses, and his brother with Aaron; that is, he claimed, that God was using his and his brother's instrumentality, in the delivery of the Christian people from bondage to false religious principles, as he formerly employed the services of Moses and Aaron in rescuing the Hebrews from bondage in Egypt. And this really invidious and uncivil language, these his enemies perverted to a bad sense, thinking perhaps that he would gain few or no adherents, if he could be made to appear insane or crazy.—*The blessed presbyters* (οἱ μακάριοι πρεσβύτεροι) of the church to which he belonged, when they found that he taught differently from them respecting the person of Christ, required him to give account of himself in an assembly of the church. He dissembled concerning his views, which, at that time, only he and his brother cherished. But after a while, having gained a number of followers, he expressed his sentiments more boldly. And being again summoned before a council, together with those whom he had seduced into error, and refusing to obey the admonitions of the presbyters, he and his adherents were excluded from the communion of the church. Thus *Hippolytus* and *Epiphanius* both state. *Epiphanius* alone adds, that Noëtus and his brother both died, not long after this sentence upon them; and that no Christian would bury their bodies. In this there is nothing hard to be believed, nothing inconsistent with the common custom of Christians. But I wonder, they should not tell us *where* these things occurred; I also wonder, that only *the blessed presbyters* are named as the judges, and no mention made of a bishop. Some may, perhaps, infer that Noëtus himself was the bishop of the place where the business was transacted. But the usage of the ancient church did not give presbyters the power of trying and deposing their bishop. I would therefore suggest, that there may have been no bishop at that time in the place where Noëtus lived. This conjecture is not free from difficulties, I confess; but it has fewer than the former supposition.—Lastly, it should not be omitted, that *Theodoret*, and he only, states that Noëtus was not the original author of the doctrine for which he was punished; but that he only brought forward an error, which before him one *Epigonus* had broached, and one *Cleomenes* confirmed; and which, after the death of Noëtus, one *Callistus* continued to propagate.

(2) The ancients are agreed, that Noëtus, while he conceived that the doctrine taught by the Church could not be reconciled with those texts of Scripture, which deny that there are any gods beside the one God, the Parent of all things, (Exod. iii. 6. and xx. 3. Isa. xlv. 5. Baruch iii. 36. Isa. xlv. 14.—for both *Hippolytus* and *Epiphanius* distinctly tell us, that it was on these texts he based his doctrine,)—while Noëtus thus conceived, and yet could not doubt at all, that Christ is called God in the sacred Scriptures, he fell into the belief that the one [p. 684.] supreme God, who is called the Father of mankind and especially of Christ, took on himself human nature, in the person of Jesus of Nazareth, and, by his sufferings and death, made atonement for the sins of men. *Hippolytus* (Sermo in Noët. § 1.) says: Ἔφη τὸν χριστὸν αὐτὸν εἶναι τὸν πατέρα, καὶ αὐτὸν τὸν πατέρα γεγεννῆσθαι καὶ πεπονθέναι καὶ ἀποτεθνηκέναι. Dixit Christum eundem esse patrem, ipsumque patrem genitum esse, passum et mortuum. According to *Epiphanius*, Noëtus replied to the reproofs of the presbyters, by saying: Quid mali feci? Unum Deum veneror, unum novi, (καὶ οὐκ ἄλλον πλὴν αὐτοῦ, γεννηθέντα, πεπονθότα, ἀποθάνοντα,) nec praeter ipsum alterum natum, passum, mortuum. And a little after, he makes the Noëtians say: Οὐ πολλοὺς Θεοὺς λέγομεν, ἀλλ' ἕνα Θεὸν ἀπαθῆ, αὐτὸν πατέρα τοῦ υἱοῦ, αὐτὸν υἱὸν, καὶ πεπονθότα. Non plures Deos affirmamus, sed unum duntaxat Deum, qui et pati nihil possit, et idem filii pater sit, ac filius, qui passus est. But *Theodoret* the most explicitly of all expresses their dogma, (whose words I give only in Latin, for the sake of brevity,) thus: Unum dicunt Deum et patrem esse -- non apparentem illum, quando vult, et apparentem, cum voluerit -- genitum et ingenitum, ingenitum quidem ab initio, genitum vero, quando ex virgine nasci voluit; impassibilem et immortalem, rursusque patibilem et mortalem. Impassibilis enim cum esset, crucis passionem sua sponte sustinuit. (He adds:) Hunc et filium appellant et patrem, prout usus exegerit, hoc et illud nomen sortientem. What *Epiphanius* tells us, viz. that the Noëtians made *Christ to be both the Father and the Son;* or as *Theodoret* expresses it, They *called Christ both the Son and the Father, as the occasion required;*—This, both the ancients and the moderns have understood in a worse sense, than was necessary. For they tell us, that Noëtus believed the Father and the Son to be one and the same person; that this person bore the name of Father, before he connected himself with the man Christ; but took the title Son, after his union with the man Christ: so that he could be denominated both the Father and the Son, being the Father if viewed in himself and apart from Christ, but being the Son if viewed as coupled with the man Christ. From this exposition of his views, consequences are frequently drawn which are discreditable to the reputation and talents of Noëtus. But such were not the views of Noëtus; as an attentive reader may learn from the very confutations of them. He distinguished the *person* of the Father from that of the Son: the Father is that supreme God who created all things; the Son of God is the *man* Christ, whom he doubtless called the Son of God, emphatically, because of his miraculous procreation from the virgin Mary. The Father, when

joined to this Son, did not lose the name or the dignity of the Father; nor was he properly *made* the Son: rather, he *remained*, and will ever remain, the Father: nor can he change either his name or his nature. Yet, inasmuch [p. 685.] as the Father is most intimately joined to the Son, and become *one person* with him: therefore the Father, although his nature is distinct from the nature of the Son, can, in a certain sense, be called the Son. And thus Noëtus uttered nothing more absurd, than we do when we say, in accordance with the Holy Scriptures, *God is a man: a man is God: God became man: a man became God.* He only substituted the names *Father* and *Son*, in place of the terms *God* and *man.* And his propositions, *The Father is the Son*, and *the Father became the Son*, are equivalent with ours, *God is a man, God became man;* and they must be explained in the same manner in which ours are explained, namely, as the result of what we call the *hypostatic union.* The only difference between him and us, was, that he, by the *Father*, understood the whole divine nature, which he considered incapable of any division; we, by *God*, intend a divine *person* distinct from the person of the Father. The idea which he annexed to the word *Son*, was the same as that we annex to the word *man.* It is certainly altogether false, that Noëtus and all those called *Patripassians* believed, (what we find stated in so many books as unquestionable.) that the Father, the Son, and the Holy Spirit are only three designations of one and the same person. According to the apprehensions of this sect, the *Father* is the name of the *divine person* or God, the *Son* is the name of the *human person* or the man. As to the Holy Spirit, none of the ancients inform us, what were the views of Noëtus. Yet from his denying that God is distributed into three persons, it must be manifest, that he viewed the term Holy Spirit not as the name of a divine *person*, but as designating either a divine *energy*, or some *nature* distinct from God.

Therefore the system of Noëtus, so far as it can now be ascertained from the writings of the ancients, was this. I. Very explicit declarations of Scripture put it beyond all question, that, besides that God who is called the *Father* of all things, there are *no Gods.* II. But those who distinguish *three persons* in God, multiply Gods, or make more than one God. III. Therefore that distinction of *persons in God*, must be rejected as being false. IV. Yet the Holy Scriptures clearly teach, that *God was in Christ*, and that *Christ was the supreme God*, from whom all things originated. V. To bring the two representations into harmony, therefore, we must believe, that the God who is in Christ, is that supreme God whom the Scriptures call the *Father* of mankind. VI. This *Father*, in order to bring relief to fallen men, procreated from the virgin Mary, a *man* free from all sin, who in a peculiar sense is called the *Son of God.* VII. That *man.* the Father so united with himself, as to make of himself and the Son but *one person.* VIII. On account of this union, whatever befel or occurred to that *Son* or that divinely begotten *man*, may also be correctly predicated of the *Father*, who took him into society with his person. IX. Therefore the *Father*, being coupled with the Son, was born, suffered pains, and died. For although the Father, in himself [p. 686.] considered, can neither be born, nor die, nor suffer pains; yet, as he and the Son became one person, it may be said, that he was born and died. X. And for the same reason, the Father being present in the Son, although he remains still the Father, he may also be correctly called the Son.

This system subverts indeed the mystery of the Holy *Trinity*, but it does no injury to the person or to the offices of Christ the Saviour, and it is much preferable to the Socinian scheme and its kindred systems. Moreover, it is no more contrary to reason, than the system which supposes a divine *person* to have united himself with the man Christ; nay, in more consistency with reason, it seems to establish the perfect simplicity of the divine nature. But there are some men of high character, who can hardly persuade themselves, that Noëtus believed what I have stated: And they prefer the supposition, that Noëtus did not differ greatly from those commonly called *Unitarians*: that is, that he believed it was not the Father himself, but only some *virtue* from the Father, that entered into the man the Son. But I do not perceive that they adduce any arguments, which compel us to believe that the ancients did not understand his principles. What they tell us, that *Sabellius* was a disciple of Noëtus, and that therefore the system of the latter must be explained as coinciding with Sabellianism, is of no weight: for,—not to urge, that in regard to the real opinions of Sabellius there is very great debate,—only *Augustine* and *Philaster* tell us that Sabellius was a disciple of Noëtus; and the testimony of these men, who lived long after the times of Noëtus, and frequently made mistakes, is not worthy of as much confidence, as that of those Greeks who lived earlier, and who knew nothing of Sabellius' being a disciple of Noëtus.—Quite recently, an ingenious man, who is well read in Christian antiquities, *Isaac de Beausobre*, (Histoire de Manichée, vol. I. p. 534.) thinks he has found a strong argument against the common explanation of Noëtus' system, in the confutation of that system by *Epiphanius*, (Hæres. lvii. p. 481.) For *Epiphanius* there states, that *Noëtus* held God to be (ἀπαθῆ) *impassible* and *Beausobre* thence concludes, with much confidence, that *Noëtus* could not, without consummate folly, have at the same time believed that *God suffered* in the person of Christ: because, to *suffer* and to *be incapable of suffering*, are directly opposite and contradictory ideas.* But this objection is solved by the passage before cited from *Theodoret*, in which he says the Noëtians pronounced one and the same Father or God, to be *impassible* in one sense, namely, considered solely in his divine nature; but in another sense passible, on account of his union with the human nature of the Son. It is strange that this worthy man should not reflect, that this very thing, which he calls *consummate folly*, [p. 687.] the great body of Christians daily profess; namely, that God who from his nature cannot suffer, yet did, in Christ, suffer those penalties which men owed to God; that is the sufferings of Christ's human nature are predicable of God who was joined to that nature by an intimate and indissoluble union?—But what need is there of protracted arguments! If I do not wholly mistake, it is manifest from the texts of Scripture by which Noëtus supported his opinion, that the ancients did not misapprehend his views. In the first place, as we are told by *Hippolytus* and *Epiphanius*, he quoted the words of Paul, (Rom. ix. 5.)

---

* To show with what assurance this learned man expresses himself, I will subjoin his own words, (p. 534.) A moins que Noët et ses sectateurs ne fussent des foux a loger aux petites maisons, ils n'ont jamais dit, qu'un seul et même Dieu—est impassible et a souffert.

Whose are the fathers, and of whom as concerning the flesh Christ came, who is -- God blessed for ever. These words drive a man into difficulties, who maintains that only a certain divine *energy* was imparted to Christ; but they appear to aid those, who maintain that God the Father, personally, was in Christ. And Noetus thus argued from this passage: If Christ is *God blessed for ever*, then undoubtedly, *that God*, beside whom there is no other, and who is wholly indivisible, dwelt in Christ. He also applied to his own doctrine those words of Christ, (John x. 30.) *I and the Father are one:* and those addressed to Philip. (John xiv. 9. 10.) *He that hath seen me hath seen the Father. Believest thou not that I am in the Father, and the Father in me?* Both these passages stand much in the way of those, who believe that only some *energy*, emanating from the Father, animated Christ the ambassador of God: but they can be very serviceable to those who, with Noëtus, suppose that the *person* of God the Father became blended with the human nature of Christ so as to make but one person.

(3) The appellation *Patripassians*, which the early Christian writers applied to both the Noëtians and the Sabellians, is ambiguous, or does not express with sufficient precision the error which those sects are said to have embraced. For the term *Father*, as used in treating of God, had one meaning among orthodox Christians, and another among the Noëtians. The former understood by the term *Father*, the first person of the divine essence; but the latter, the Noëtians, who supposed that to admit of *persons* in God, would conflict with his unity, intended by the term *Father*, the supreme Deity who is altogether indivisible, or the whole divine nature. And, therefore, when a person hears them called *Patripassians*, he is liable, by taking the word *Father* (*Pater*) in its common acceptation among Christians, to fall into the belief, that they supposed it was not the Son, the second person of the divine nature, but the *first person*, who bore the penalties of our sins, which would be a mistake; yet it is a mistake into which many fall, being deceived by the ambiguity of the term. But if we affix to it the Noëtian sense of the word *Father*, then the appellation *Patripassians* will be a suitable one for the sect. The appellation was devised for the sake of exciting a prejudice against the Noëtians; and such is generally the fault in all such appellations.

§ XXXIII. **Sabellius and the Sabellians.** After the middle of this century, *Sabellius*, an African bishop, or presbyter, of Ptolemais, the capitol of the Pentapolitan province of Libya Cyrenaica, attempted to reconcile, in a manner somewhat different from that of *Noëtus*, the scriptural doctrine of Father, Son, and holy Spirit, with the doctrine of the unity of the divine nature. As the error of *Sabellius* infected several of the Pentapolitan bishops, and perhaps some others, *Dionysius*, the bishop of Alexandria, assailed it both orally and by writing; but he was not able to eradicate it entirely. For, from unquestionable testimony, it appears that, in the fourth and fifth centuries, there were Sabellians in various [p. 688.]

places.(¹) The doctrine of *Sabellius* was not identical with that of *Noëtus;* for the former did not hold, as the latter appears to have done, that the *person* of the supreme Deity, which he considered perfectly simple and indivisible, assumed the human nature of Christ into union with himself; but that only an *energy* or *virtue*, emitted from the Father of all, or, if you choose, a *particle* of the person or nature of the Father, became united with the man Christ. And such a *virtue* or *particle* of the Father, he also supposed, constituted the holy Spirit. Hence, when the ancients call *Sabellius* and his disciples *Patripassians*, the appellation must be understood differently from what it is when applied to *Noëtus* and his followers.(²)

(1) The name of *Sabellius* is of much more frequent and marked notice, in the writings of the ancients, than the name of *Noëtus*. Nor is he mentioned solely by those who treat expressly of the sects in the early ages, viz. *Epiphanius*, *Augustine*, *Theodoret*, *Damascenus*, *Philaster*, and the others; but there is frequent mention of him also, by those who contended with the Arians and the other corrupters of the doctrine of three persons in God, and by those who expounded the true doctrine concerning God and Christ. Nevertheless, the history of *Sabellius* is very brief: and his views of God and Christ are stated variously, both by the ancients and moderns.—The place where he lived can be fully ascertained from *Dionysius*, *Eusebius*, *Athanasius*, and many others; but of his station, his conflicts, and his death, we are left in ignorance. *Gregory Abulpharagius* (in his Arabic work, Historia Dynastiar. p. 81.) says that he was a *presbyter;* which, perhaps, was the fact: but what is added, that he held this office *at Byzantium*, is certainly false. *Zonaras*, (Interpretatio Canonum,) if my memory is correct, calls him a *bishop*. Which of these authorities is to be [p. 689.] believed, does not appear.—That his error spread widely, and not only in Pentapolis, but elsewhere, and particularly in Egypt; and that therefore, *Dionysius* of Alexandria elaborately confuted and repressed it, is fully stated by *Athanasius*, (in his work, de Sententia Dionysii, of which we shall speak hereafter,) and more concisely by *Eusebius*, (Hist. Eccles. L. vii. c. 6. p. 252). And it is no improbable supposition, that *Dionysius* held a council at Alexandria against Sabellius. The zeal of *Dionysius* may have driven the Sabellians from Libya and Egypt. But in the fourth century, according to *Epiphanius*, (Hæres. lxii. § 1. p. 513.) the Sabellians were considerably numerous in Mesopotamia, and at Rome. And in the fifth century, the abbot *Euthymius*, (as stated in his life, written by *Cyril* of Scytopolis, and published by *Jo. Bapt. Cotelier*, in his Monum. Ecclesiæ Græcæ, tom. iv. p. 52.) boldly assailed τοῦ Σαβελλίου συναίρεσιν, (*Sabellii conjunctionem*,) i. e. the Sabellian doctrine which confounds or *combines* the Father and the Son.—There is extant a Historia Sabelliana, by *Christian Wormius*, published at Leips. 1696, 8vo. It is a learned work, and useful

in researches into the early history of Christianity; but only a very small part of it relates to *Sabellius.*

(2) Respecting the real sentiments of *Sabellius*, there is great disagreement among learned men. The majority say: He taught that the Father, Son, and holy Spirit, are only three *names* of the one God, originating from the diversity of his acts and operations: that he is called the Father, when he performs the appropriate works of a Father, such as precreating, providing, cherishing, nourishing, and protecting; that he is called the Son, when operating in the Son, and thereby accomplishing what was necessary for the salvation of mankind; and that he is called the holy Spirit, when he is considered as the source of all virtue and sanctification. This exposition of his views, is supported by numerous passages from the ancients, who say that Sabellius taught that the Father himself bore the penalties of the sins of mankind; whence he and his disciples were denominated *Patripassians*. This opinion, *Christian Worm*, in his *Historia Sabelliana*, supports with all the arguments and authorities he can command. But others, relying chiefly on the authority of *Epiphanius*, maintain that the ancients misunderstood Sabellius; that he did not hold the Father, Son, and holy Spirit, to be only three *appellations* of the one God, as acting in different ways: but that he believed the Father to be truly God, in whom is no division; and the Son to be a divine *virtue*, descending from the Father upon the man Christ, so that he might be able to work miracles, and to point out correctly the way for men to be saved; and that he believed the holy Spirit to be another *ray* or *virtue* from the divine nature, moving the minds of men and elevating them to God. And on this ground, they conclude that there was a great difference between the doctrine of *Sabellius* and that of *Noëtus*, already described; and that the name of *Patripassians* was inapplicable to *Sabellius*, because he did not teach that the Father, or God, suffered penalties, but only some [p. 690.] *virtue*, proceeding from the Father, was present with the man Christ, and aided him when he bore our penalties. And they say that the doctrine of *Sabellius* did not differ greatly from that which is maintained by the Socinians.—Thus have thought, besides others of less fame, *Alexander Morus*, (in cap. liii. Esaiæ, p. 7, and in Observat. in N. T. pp. 81, 82. ed. Fabrici.) *Isaac* de *Beausobre*, (Histoire de Manichée, vol. i. p. 533, &c.) and *Simon* de *Vries*, (Dissert. de Priscillianistis, Traj. 1745, 4to. p. 35, 36). But de *Vries*, if I mistake not, has merely transcribed from *Beausobre*, without naming him.—After very carefully comparing and pondering the statements of the ancients, I have concluded, that those err who make the Sabellian doctrine and that of *Noëtus* to be the same; but those also are deceived, to some extent, who deny that the Sabellians could, with any propriety, be called *Patripassians* by the ancients, declaring that they were very much like the Socinians, and that if the statements of *Epiphanius* are compared with those of the earlier writers, the whole controversy will be settled.—I will now state, as carefully and perspicuously as I can, what appears to me true in regard to this subject.

I. That fear, lest God, who as both reason and the Scriptures teach is a perfectly simple unity, should be rent into a plurality of Gods, which influenced *Noëtus*, likewise induced *Sabellius* to deny the distinction of persons in the divine nature, and to maintain that there is only one divine person, or ὑπόστασις. And hence, according to *Epiphanius*, (Hæres. lxii. § 1, p. 504.) whenever the Sabellians fell in with unlearned persons, whom they hoped easily to convert, they proposed to them this one question: Τί οὖν εἴπωμεν, ἵνα Θεὸν ἔχομεν, ἢ τρεῖς Θεούς; *What then shall we say? Have we one God, or three Gods?*

II. But while *Sabellius* maintained that there was but one divine person, he still believed the distinction of Father, Son, and holy Spirit, described in the Scriptures, to be a *real* distinction, and not a mere *appellative* or *nominal* one. That is, he believed the one divine person whom he recognised, to have three distinct *forms*, which are *really different*, and which should not be confounded. This remark is of the greatest importance to a correct understanding of Sabellius' doctrine; and it ought, therefore, to be accurately substantiated. The first witness I adduce is *Arnobius*—not the elder *Arnobius*, who lived in this third century, and wrote the Libri vii. contra Gentes, but *Arnobius, junior*—a writer of the fifth century, whose work, entitled Conflictus de Deo uno et trino cum Serapione, was published by *Francis Feuardent*, subjoined to the works of Irenæus. Though he lived long after Sabellius, he is an author of much importance on this subject, because he gives us statements from a work of *Sabellius* himself, which he had before him. He makes *Serapion* say, (in *Feuardent's* edition of Irenæus, Paris, 1675, Fol. p. 520): Ego tibi Sabellium *lego*, (Serapion, therefore, must be considered as holding in his hand some book of *Sabellius*, [p. 691.] from which he *read*,) anathema dicentem his, qui Patrem, et Filium et Spiritum sanctum esse negarent, ad convincendam Trinitatem. *Serapion* had before said: In Sabellii me insaniam induxisti, qui unum Deum, Patrem et Filium et Spiritum sanctum confitetur. And when *Arnobius* had replied: Sabellium negare Filium et Spiritum sanctum; that is, that Sabellius taught that the Son and the holy Spirit are nothing different from the Father, Serapion produced an actual work of Sabellius, and showed from it that Sabellius *did not* maintain what *Arnobius* asserted, or did not confound the Son and holy Spirit with the Father, but clearly discriminated the two former from the latter. *Arnobius*, on hearing this, yields the point, or admits that it is so; but still he maintains, that there is a wide difference between the doctrine of Sabellius and that of other Christians; because the latter believed the Son to be *begotten* by the Father, which Sabellius denied: Nos autem Patrem dicimus et credimus, qui *genuit* Filium, et est Pater unici sui Filii ante tempora geniti. And this is a just representation: for although Sabellius made a distinction between the Father and the Son, yet he would not admit that the Son was a divine person, *begotten* by the Father. From this passage, therefore, it is manifest: (a) That Sabellius held to *a Trinity*. (b) That he anathematised those who denied the Father, Son, and holy Spirit, or a Trinity. Whence it follows, that (c) Sabellius held to a *real*, and not a mere *nominal* distinction between the Father, Son, and holy Spirit. Had he supposed the terms Father, Son, and holy Spirit, were three *names* of the one supreme Deity, there would have been no ground for his anathema. For there never was, and never can be, a single Christian who denies that these *terms* occur in the Bible, and are there applied to God. It is unquestionable, both from the course of the argument, and from the nature of the case, that Sabellius condemned those who commingled and confounded the Father, Son, and holy Spirit. But, most certainly, *they* do confound the Trinity, who make the Father, Son, and holy Spirit, to differ in nothing but in name. Therefore, it was such persons that *Sabellius* anathematised.—A second witness comes forward, viz. *Basil* the Great; who, although he sometimes seems to favor those who held that Sabellius taught a *nominal* distinction in the Trinity, yet, in two passages shows, not obscurely, that Sabellius held to some *real* distinction in God. One of the passages is, (Epist. ccx. Opp. tom. iii. p. 317. edit Benedict.): Ἀνυπόστατον τῶν προσώπων ἀναπλασμὸν, οὐ δὲ ὁ Σαβέλλιος παρῃτήσατο, εἰπὼν, τὸν αὐτὸν Θεὸν ἕνα τῷ ὑποκειμένῳ ὄντα, πρὸς τὰς ἑκάστοτε παραπιπτούσας χρείας μεταμορφούμενον, νῦν μὲν ὡς πατέρα, νῦν δὲ ὡς υἱὸν, νῦν δὲ ὡς πνεῦμα ἅγιον διαλέγεσθαι. Illud hypostasi carens personarum commentum ne Sabellius quidem rejecit, quippe cum dicat eundem Deum, cum subjecto unus sit, pro occurrentibus subinde occasionibus transformatum, modo ut Patrem, modo ut Filium, modo ut Spiritum sanctum loqui. The other passage is (Epist. ccxxxv. p. 364.): Σαβέλλιος πολλαχοῦ συγχέων την ἔννοιαν, ἐπιχειρεῖ διαιρεῖν τὰ πρόσωπα, την αὐτὴν ὑπόστασιν λέγων πρὸς ταν ἑκάστοτε παρεμπίπτουσαν χρείαν μετασχηματίζεσ- [p. 692.] θαι. Sabellius, tametsi confundit notionem (Dei), tamen sæpe conatur personas distinguere, dum hypostasin eamdem ait pro usu subinde occurrente varias personas induere. *Basil*, indeed, speaks less clearly than I could wish, on this very obscure subject. But this is plain enough, that the Trinity of Sabellius was not merely *nominal* or *verbal*. For while he maintained that there was but one *person* (ὑπόστασις) in God, he yet held that there are three (πρόσωπα) *forms*, or *aspects* of the one God, and that he assumes the one or the other of these forms, according to the state of things. But divers *forms* of one and the same being, however they may be considered, involve some *real* distinction, and cannot be confounded with different *appellations* for the same thing. But nothing will better elucidate and confirm my position, than the *comparison* by which the Sabellians were accustomed to illustrate their doctrine concerning the Father, Son, and holy Spirit, as it is stated by *Epiphanius*, (Hæres. lxii. p. 513). Having stated the Sabellian doctrine in the common form: εἶναι ἐν μιᾷ ὑποστάσει τρεῖς ὀνομασίας, *there are three appellations in one person*; he proceeds to show that this language must *not* be construed too rigidly, by saying: Ὡς ἐν ἀνθρώπῳ, σῶμα, καὶ ψυχὴ, καὶ πνεῦμα. Καὶ εἶναι μὲν τὸ σῶμα, ὡς εἰπεῖν τὸν πατέρα, ψυχὴν δὲ ὡς εἰπεῖν τὸν υἱὸν, τὸ πνεῦμα δὲ ὡς ἀνθρώπου, οὕτως καὶ τὸ ἅγιον πνεῦμα ἐν τῇ Θεότητι. Patrem, Filium, Spiritum sanctum sic se habere in Deo quemadmodum in homine corpus, animam et spiritum; corporis instar Patrem, animæ Filium, Spiritum denique sanctum in Divinitate instar spiritus se habere. Comparisons, undoubtedly, are not to be pressed too far; but this one would lose every shadow of likeness and similarity, and would become a dissimilarity rather than a similarity, if Sabellius had taught only a Trinity of *names* or words. If the difference between the Father, Son, and holy Spirit, is the same—I do not say *altogether*, but only *in part*—as that between the *body*, the *rational soul* or spirit, and the *sentient soul* in man; then, necessarily, the Father, Son, and holy Spirit, must differ *really* from each other. *Sabellius*, therefore, believed that, as a man is but *one person*, and yet in his one person *three* things may be discriminated, not in thought only, but as having a real existence, namely, the *body*, the *soul*, and the *spirit*, so, also, although there is but *one* undivided person in God, yet in that person, the Father, the Son, and the holy Spirit can be discriminated, not in thought only, but they must be *really* discriminated and kept distinct.—Other testimonies will occur as we proceed.

III. As Sabellius held to the *simple unity* of the person and nature of God, and yet supposed the Father, Son, and holy Spirit, to differ *really* from each other, and not to be three *names* of the one God, acting in different ways; we are obliged to believe, that he considered the Father, Son, and holy Spirit, as [p. 693.] being *three portions* of the divine nature, severed, as it were, from God, and differing from each other, yet not subsisting as three persons, but all dependent on the one individual divine nature. And therefore God, when about to create the universe, did not put his *whole* person in action, but he sent out *a portion* of his nature, by which he accomplished his design. And this *portion* of the Divinity is called the *Father;* because, by its agency, God has become the parent of all things, or procreates, sustains, cherishes, and governs all. This *Father* produced Christ in the womb of the virgin Mary, and for that reason is emphatically *Christ's Father;* and Christ is called the *Son of God*, because he holds the relation of a Son, in regard to this divine energy. Again, when the same God would reclaim to himself the human race by Christ, he sent forth *another portion* of himself, which, being united to Christ, is called *the Son;* because he resides in the Son of God, and by that Son teaches and works, and, in a certain sense, makes one person with the Son. Lastly, God sent out a *third particle* of his nature, perfectly separate from the two former, by which he animates the universe, and enlightens, excites, and regenerates the minds of men. This portion of God is called the *holy Spirit;* because, like a wind, he excites and produces holy movements in men. The three *forms*, or three πρόσωπα of God, therefore, according to Sabellius, were neither three *qualities* of the divine nature, (*existence, wisdom*, and *life;* as *Abulpharaius* supposed, Historia Dynast. p. 81.) nor three *modes of acting*, nor three *appellations* of the one God; but they were *parts or portions*, rent, indeed, in a sense from God, and yet in another sense connected with him.—This exposition is compatible with that celebrated comparison taken from the sun, which Epiphanius mentions, and which had led some worthy men to make the Sabellians agree with the Socinians. *Epiphanius* (Hæres. lxii. p. 513.) says, that the Sabellians were accustomed to explain their doctrine by a comparison with the sun, thus: In the sun there is but *one substance*, (μία ὑπόστασις,) but there are *three powers*, (ἐνέργειαι,) namely, (τὸ φωτιστικὸν, τὸ θάλπον, τὸ περιφερείας σχῆμα,) the *illuminating power*, the *warming power*, and the *circular form*. The warming power answers to the holy Spirit; the illuminating power, to the Son; and the form or figure, (τὸ εἶδος,) to the Father. This representation seems in itself to favor the opinions of those who make Sabellius discard all real distinctions in the divine nature. But *Epiphanius* explains the comparison in a manner that makes it apparent, that Sabellius did not intend, by this new comparison, to subvert his former comparison, taken from the *soul, body*, and *spirit* in a man. For he adds, that the Son was *sent out* like a yay from the Father, to perform what was requisite for the salvation of mankind, and, having accomplished the business, *returned* again to heaven; and that the holy Spirit also, in like manner, should be viewed as something *sent* into the world. Now, whatever is *sent forth* from God, and afterwards *returns* to God, must undoubtedly be something actually *separate* in some way from the divine nature: because, it could not possibly *return back* [p. 694.] to God, unless it had *departed* and been *separated* from God.—Let no one trouble himself with the difficulties which this dogma involves; for the question is, not how wisely Sabellius reasoned, but what distinction he made between the Father, the Son, and the holy Spirit.

IV. Therefore, although the ancients sometimes speak as if they would represent Sabellius to believe that the Father, Son, and holy Spirit, differ from each other only as three modes of acting, or three relations of the same man, yet their language is not to be pressed too much, but should be construed by what we have above stated. And they themselves, often correct what they have in certain passages stated less fitly and distinctly; and explain themselves in other passages, in accordance with our statements. One example we have already seen in *Epiphanius;* who seems to teach that the Trinity of Sabellius was only *nominal*, and yet he is with us. Another example is afforded by *Basil* the Great, who speaks (Epist. ccxiv. p. 322.) as if Sabellius denied any *real* distinction in the divine nature; and yet, in the two passages above cited, he admits that, while Sabellius rejected a *personal* distinction, he was not averse from admitting one that was *real* and true; and while denying that what was divine in Christ differed from God, in the same way that a son differs from a father, yet conceded that it might be viewed as a sort of separate (πρόσωπον) *person.* I will now add a third example, very striking, and well suited to our purpose, taken from *Theodoret.* In his Heretical Fables, (L. ii. c. 9, Opp. tom. iv. p. 223.) he explains the dogma of Sabellius in the usual way; viz. that he held to *one person under three names*, and called that person sometimes the Father, sometimes the Son, and sometimes the holy Spirit. But in his Eccles. History, (L. i. c. 4.) he gives us an Epistle of *Alexander*, bishop of Alexandria, to Alexander, the bishop of Constantinople; from which it appears, that Sabellius thought very differently. For he tells us (Opp. tom. iii. p. 533.) that Alexander wrote thus: πιστεύομεν εἰς ἕνα Κύριον, Ἰησοῦν Χριστὸν, τὸν υἱὸν τοῦ Θεοῦ μονογενῆ, γεννηθέντα· ἐκ τοῦ ὄντος Πατρὸς, οὐ κατὰ τὰς τῶν σωμάτων ὁμοιότητας, ταῖς τομαῖς ἢ ταῖς ἐκ διαιρέσεων ἀποῤῥοίαις, ὥσπερ Σαβελλίῳ, καὶ Βαλεντίνῳ δοκεῖ, ἀλλ' ἀῤῥήτως. Credimus in unum Dominum Jesum Christum, Filium Dei unigenitum, ex eo, qui Pater est genitum, non corporum ritu, per *incisiones*, divisionumque *fluxiones*, ut Sabellio et Valentino visum est, sed ineffabili modo. We may remark, that this is the statement of a man, than whom no one could better know the doctrine of Sabellius; for he lived in the country and city in which that doctrine originated, was propagated, and condemned: and he undoubtedly had in his possession the writings of *Dionysius*, his predecessor in the see of Alexandria, against Sabellius. This man, therefore, who is the very best authority in the case before us, *first*, states the doctrine of orthodox Christians respecting the generation of the Son of God; *secondly*, distinguishes [p. 695.] from it the error of Valentinus and Sabellius, in regard to the generation of the

Son ; and *thirdly*, tells us, that Sabellius and Valentinus held, that the Son was produced from the Father, in the manner of *material bodies*, either (ταῖς τομαῖς) by *sections*, or (ἐκ διαιρέσεων ἀποῤῥοίαις) by *emanation* or *effluxes of parts.* The latter of these two hypotheses, undoubtedly was that of *Valentinus ;* whose well known προβολὴ (*emission*), is here not unsuitably called an ἀποῤῥοία (*efflux*). The first hypothesis, therefore, beyond all controversy, was that of *Sabellius.* Consequently, *first*, Sabellius admitted a species of generation of the Son from the Father : not, indeed, a *personal* one, yet one of some sort. But, *secondly*, he described this generation very grossly, and in the manner of material bodies. *Thirdly*, he made the Son proceed from God, by (τόμην) a kind of *section.* Alexander, indeed, speaks of (τομαῖς) *sections*, in the plural ; but he appears to use the *plural* for the singular, as is common. For he also speaks of (ἀποῤῥοίαις) *fluxions*, in the plural ; and yet it is certain that *Valentinus* held to but one ἀποῤῥοίαν or προβολὴν of the Son from the Father. Hence, *fourthly*, it is manifest, that Sabellius considered that *divine thing*, which dwelt in the man Christ, as being a *part* or *portion* of God ; so that the Son differed from the Father, as a *part* differs from the *whole :* from whom he was severed by a *section.* I recollect, that *George Bull*, (in his Defensio Fidei Nicænæ, Sect. ii. c. 1, Opp. p. 33.) and perhaps others, explain this passage of Alexander differently, and maintain that Alexander does not here state the opinion of Sabellius, but only shows us how Sabellius explained the *common opinion* of Christians, respecting the generation of the Son of God ; viz. this heretic supposed, that a *division* of the essence of the Father would necessarily follow from the doctrine of the catholics. But a careful attention to the passage, will show that the learned man was deceived ; for the words will not bear his interpretation. The Sabellian and Valentinian opinions, respecting the nature of the divine generation, stand coupled together ; but the latter is certainly not the catholic opinion, as explained by Valentinian, but the opinion of Valentinian himself ; and, therefore, the Sabellian opinion coupled with it, is the opinion of Sabellius himself, and not that of the catholics, to whom he was opposed. *Bull* was led to his mistake by the full belief, that the common statement of Sabellius' doctrine is correct. He says : Norunt omnes, Sabellium docuisse, Deum esse μονοπρόσωπον, (a great mistake ! For we see clearly from *Basil*, that he acknowledged *three* πρόσωπα in God, but denied three ὑποστάσεις.) et nullam realem personarum *distinctionem* in divina essentia, nedum *divisionem* agnovisse. This is in the main false ! Sabellius denied any *personal* distinction in God, but not a *real and true* division.—But *Worm* (in his Historia Sabell. c. 1. p. 20.) blunders still worse. To elude the force of this passage, he would persuade us that the words τόμη and ἀποῤῥοία both refer to *Valentinian*, and neither of them to *Sabellius.* Strange that a [p. 696.] learned man should say this ! For who does not see that these two words express two different opinions ? And who, that has dipped into church history, can be so ignorant of it, as not to know that a τόμη, or *section*, can by no means be attributed to *Valentinus ?* But what need of discussion ?—We have another equally noticeable passage of an Egyptian of Alexandria, who must have been fully acquainted with the doctrine of Sabellius ; namely, *Arius* the heresiarch, the adversary of *Alexander*, who agrees with his enemy Alexander, and explains the doctrine of Sabellius in the same manner. His Epistle to Alexander, his bishop, is extant in *Epiphanius*. (Hæres. lxix. tom. i. p. 732). *Arius* there first condemns the opinion of *Valentinus*, respecting the divine generation, and says: προβολὴν τὸ γέννημα τοῦ Πατρὸς ἐδογμάτισεν: and then he rejects the opinion of *Sabellius*, in the following terms: οὐδ' ὡς Σαβέλλιος ὁ τὴν μονάδα διαιρῶν υἱοπάτορα εἶπεν. Nec ego doceo, ut Sabellius, qui unitatem *divisit* (here we have the τομάς of *Alexander*,) et Filium-Patrem appellavit. No language could better agree with our explanation. Sabellius *divided*, *cleaved* the unity of the divine nature; and he called that divine thing which dwelt in Christ, υἱοπάτορα, both *Father and Son:* and correctly, for a part of the Father was in Christ, and this part was at the same time the Son, being united with him; and therefore he might be called υἱοπάτωρ.

V. As Sabellius supposed the Son to be a *part* of God, or a portion of the divine nature, severed from it by section, the ancients were not altogether wrong in denominating him and his friends *Patripassians;* provided we understand by the *Father* the one supreme God, who, as Sabellius supposed, was not divisible into persons. For, whoever supposes that a certain *part* or portion of the eternal Father, taken in a certain sense out of him, and yet depending on him, and hereafter to return into him,—was in Christ when he suffered pains and died, and that it participated in the sufferings endured by the man Christ;—that man may not improperly be said to believe,—not that a divine *person*, but God the *Father* himself; not, indeed, in his *whole* nature, but so far forth as he was joined with Christ, actually suffered the penalties incurred by mankind. If any human being, Peter, for instance, could transfer a half or third *part of his soul* into another man, Paul, for example, and that Paul should be put to torture by some tyrant, might not that Peter be fitly said to have suffered torture in Paul?—I shall not cite here the testimonies of *Augustine*, *Eusebius*, and many others, who have told us either that Sabellius and his associates were called *Patripassians*, or that they truly merited that appellation; for such testimonies in great abundance have been already collected by *Worm*, *Tillemont*, and others: but I will add to those adduced, one witness of great value, and deserving the first rank, who has been omitted by all who have treated of the subject. He is *Dionysius* Alexandrinus, the first antagonist of *Sabellius*. The Arians of the fourth century, in their writings against Sabellius, affirm that this great and [p. 697.] excellent man professed exactly their sentiments concerning Christ. And to refute their assertion, *Athanasius* wrote a book, entitled *de Sententia Dionysii Alex. de Christo*, which has come down to us, and is in the Opp. Athanasii, (tom. i. P. i. p. 242, &c., edit. Benedict). In this book *Athanasius* shows, from the writings of *Dionysius*, that he demonstrated, against Sabellius, that the Father did not suffer; and, at the same time, he shows that the Sabellians *really* transferred to the Father those sufferings which Christ endured. In § 5. p. 246, he says: Τολμηρότερον ἐκεῖνοι τὸν υἱὸν ἠρνοῦντο, καὶ τὰ ἀνθρώπινα αὐτοῦ τῷ Πατρὶ ἀνετίθεσαν· δείξας ὅτι οὐχ' ὁ πατὴρ, ἀλλ' ὁ υἱός ἐστιν ὁ γενόμενος ὑπὲρ ἡμῶν ἄνθρωπος. Quum audacius illi (the followers of Sabellius in Pentapolis,) Filium negarent, (i. e. denied that the Son was a distinct person from the Father,) *et humana ejus* (his sufferings and death) *Patri adscriberent;* ostendit ipse (Dionysius) non

Patrem, sed Filium pro nobis hominem esse factum. And in § 26. p. 261, he cites from an Epistle of *Dionysius* to Euphranor and Ammonius, in confutation of the error of Sabellius: *προβάλλει τὰ ἀνθρωπίνας εἰρημένα περὶ τοῦ σωτῆρος, οἷά ἐστὶ τὸ πεινᾷν, τὸ κοπιᾷν - - ὅσα γὰρ ταῦτα ταπεινὰ λέγεται, τοσούτῳ δείκνυται μὴ ὁ πατὴρ γενόμενος ἄνθρωπος.* Prætermittit ea, quæ humano more de illo dicta habentur, cujusmodi sunt esurire, laborare: quanto enim hæc dictu sunt humiliora, tanto liquidius demonstratur Patrem non esse factum hominem. This renowned opponent of Sabellius, in the ardor of debate and zeal for victory, suffered himself to be carried so far, that, not without apparent justice, he was accused of error before *Dionysius*, bishop of Rome. For while *Sabellius* seemed to change the Son into the Father, or to confound him with the Father, *Dionysius* seemed to degrade the Son, or to rob him of his majesty. And hence it became necessary for him to explain his views more clearly, and he wrote two books in self vindication, namely, his *Elenchus* and his *Apologia*. On this subject *Athanasius* dwells much; and he clearly shows, by more than a sufficiency of citations from *Dionysius*, that he did not hold the error of the Arians respecting Christ. (See § 13. p. 252, &c.) But after all the diligence of Athanasius in defending Dionysius, and in wiping away every stain upon the character of a man, held in the highest veneration at Alexandria, it will be manifest, to a person carefully considering all that Athanasius has said in his defence, that there *was* something erroneous in *Dionysius*, and that his opinion of Christ. differed from the Nicene and the modern doctrine. The more effectually to confute *Sabellius*, who maintained that God himself, or the *Father* was born, suffered and died in Christ, *Dionysius* denied, (as *Athanasius* clearly shows, § 5. p. 246,) that the *passions of Christ* (humana Christi) *pertained to the God resident in Christ;* and he referred them exclusively to the Son. He therefore went to the opposite extreme. That is, *Dionysius* distinguished in Christ the *Word*, a *divine person* distinct from the Father, and also the *Son;* or rather, [p. 698.] he supposed *two Sons*, a human and divine. The *Word*, or the divine Son, he exempted from all the *passions* (*ἀνθρωπίνοις, humanis*) of Christ, or from all that Christ, as a man, did and suffered; and maintained, that all these *passions*, (*ἀνθρώπινα*)—his *being born, suffering, dying*, pertained solely to that Son of man who was born of Mary. Here he erred, and entered the direct road leading to the doctrine ascribed to *Nestorius*. For, if the *Son of God*, or the *Word*, which was united to the man Christ, had no part in the actions and sufferings of the *Son of man*, it is manifest, that there must have been both *two natures* and *two persons* in Christ, and that the *Son of God*, or the *Word*, only strengthened, enlightened, and aided the *Son of man*. And, therefore, not without reason, was *Dionysius* accused at Rome, although not with due accuracy and distinctness.—Yet, these mistakes of the pious and truth-loving *Dionysius*, serve admirably to elucidate the tenets of *Sabellius:* namely, that he supposed a *portion* of the divine nature was so united with the man Christ at his birth, as to be *born* with him, *suffer* and *die* with him, and participate in all the actions and sufferings of the man Christ, or the Son; and that *this portion* of the Deity, on account of its intimate union with the Son, is in Scripture called *the Son*, although, properly speaking, only the *man* Christ should be called the *Son.*

Either such were the views of *Sabellius*, or the entire argument of *Dionysius* against him is futile, irrelevant, and idle. That which we, following the Scriptures, denominate a *person* eternally begotten by the Father, *Sabellius* took to be a *part* of the Deity *separated* from him within a limited time. If he had only supposed the divine nature in Christ to be a *person*, he would have coincided with us, more exactly than *Dionysius* did.—But perhaps it will not be unacceptable, but rather agreeable to many, if I should discriminate with more exactness the Sabellian, the Dionysian, and our own opinions of Christ. We *all* hold to *two natures* in Christ, a divine and a human. And *we* hold that these two natures constituted *one person*, and we exclude the *personality* of the human nature, or place the personality in the divine nature. *Sabellius*, on the contrary, while he agreed with us in declaring that the two natures constituted but one person, excluded the *personality* of the divine nature, or made the personality to exist only in and by the human nature. And to confute him, *Dionysius* separated, not only the two natures in Christ, but also the persons, and held that the actions and passions of the human nature, were not predicable of the divine nature. Thus, in his zeal to confute one error, he fell into another equally great.

VI. But *Sabellius* and his disciples cannot be called *Patripassians*, in the same sense in which the *Noëtians* were; if the opinions of the latter are correctly stated by the ancients. For *Noëtus* thought the *whole person* of the Father, or the entire divine nature, associated itself with Christ: but *Sabellius* supposed, that only a *portion* of the divine nature descended into the man Christ. Hence, *Epiphanius* made no mistake when he said, in his *Anacephalæosis*, [p. 699.] (Opp. tom. ii. p. 146.): Sabellianos consentire in plerisque cum Noëtianis, hoc uno excepto, quod non ut Noëtiani Patrem passum esse doceant. This is perfectly correct, if it be explained as I have stated, that the Sabellians did not ascribe the sufferings of Christ to the Father, in the same sense in which the Noëtians did. And therefore, there was no ground for *Augustine*, (de Hæresibus,) and many others since him, to cast blame upon *Epiphanius*.

§ XXXIV. **Beryllus of Bostra, in Arabia.** About the same time a similar error, though a little worse, was broached by *Beryllus*, the bishop of Bostra, in Arabia, a man otherwise devout, grave, and erudite, who had long governed his congregation praiseworthily, and also acquired reputation by his writings. He likewise subverted the distinction of persons in God, and denied that Christ existed before Mary. He supposed that a soul, the offspring of God himself, and therefore, doubtless, superior to all human souls, was divinely implanted in Christ at his birth. This opinion of *Beryllus* was long opposed by many persons, but in vain. At length, *Origen*, being invited from Egypt for this purpose, confronted him in a council held at Bostra, with such force of argument, that *Beryllus* gave up his opinion, and was reconciled to the church.(¹)

(1) Nearly all that is now known of *Beryllus* and his doctrine, is derived from *Eusebius*, (Hist. Eccl. L. vi. c. 20. p. 222; and c. 33. p. 231.) and from *Jerome*, (Catal. Scriptor. Eccl. c. 60. edit. Fabricii). For all that others tell us, except a single passage in *Socrates*, scarcely deserves notice. *Eusebius* alone states distinctly the errors of the man: and yet the learned have found some obscurity in his language, and therefore have understood him differently. His words are these: Τολμῶν λέγειν μὴ προϋφεστάναι Χριστὸν κατ' ἰδίαν ὀυσίας περιγραφὴν πρὸ τῆς εἰς ἀνθρώπους ἐπιδημίας, μὴ δὲ μὲν Θεότητα ἰδίαν ἔχειν, ἀλλ' ἐμπολιτευομένην ἀυτῷ μόνην τὴν πατρικήν. I will subjoin the Latin translation of Henry de *Valois*, although it is not literal throughout, and is deemed faulty by some learned men. It is this: Ausus est asserere Christum antequam inter homines versaretur (more correctly: ante suum ad homines adventum, id est, antequam nasceretur. For a false inference may be drawn from the translation of de *Valois*,) non substitisse in propriæ personæ differentia, (the learned translator here departs from the *words*, but follows the *sense*; for he supposed ὀυσία to be here equivalent to ὑπόστασις. The literal rendering would be: secundum propriam essentiæ *circumscriptionem*,) nec propriam, sed paternam duntaxat di- [p. 700.] vinitatem in se residentem habere. Two propositions are here included: the *first*, relating to Christ previous to his birth, and the *second*, concerning him when clothed in a human body. In the first place, *Beryllus* denied that Christ, previously to his advent, so existed, that his *essence* or ὀυσία was *circumscribed*, (or *separated* from that of all other beings). Although most writers concerning *Beryllus* follow the translation of de *Valois*, yet learned men complain that he renders the words of Eusebius very badly. For ὀυσία among the Greeks is never synonymous with ὑπόστασις, and περιγραφὴ never signifies *difference*, but *circumscription*. So John le *Clerc*, (Ars Critica, Vol i. P. ii. sec. i. c. 14. p. 293, &c.) and the Nouveau Diction. Historique et Critique, (tom. i. Art. *Beryllus*, p. 268). The criticisms are correct: and yet I do not think de *Valois* guilty of any great fault. *Eusebius* aimed to express the very same thing, which de *Valois* has expressed in other words. *Beryllus* did not deny, that Christ existed in some manner, previous to his coming among men; but he did not admit that his *essence* (ὀυσία) was *circumscribed.* Now things are said to be *circumscribed*, or to have (περιγραφὴν) *circumscription*, when they are separated and secluded from other things by determinate limits or bounds. Therefore, *Beryllus* denied that Christ, before he was born of Mary, had a *separate existence*, or that he was distinct from the essence of the Father. To express this in our phraseology, would be to say: *Christ had no personality before he was born.* He, indeed, *existed* then, yet not as a *person*, but only *in the essence of the Father.* He existed, but undefined or *without boundaries*, if I may so express it; that is, he existed in *combination*, as it were, with the essence of the Father of all things. To use a homely illustration: thus the *wine*, now included in a glass, existed, indeed, previously in the *cask* from which it was drawn, but it had not then its own περιγραφὴν *circumscription*. In other words, Beryllus excluded from

the divine nature all divisions, and admitted no distinction of persons in God. *Jerome* expresses his conception, not erroneously, indeed, yet not with sufficient perspicuity, (Catal. Scriptor. Eccl. c. 60. p. 138.): *Christum ante incarnationem negabat.* He did not wholly deny the *existence* of Christ before his incarnation, but only his existence apart from the Father, or in our phraseology, his *personal existence.* That such was his opinion will, I think, be be very manifest from the second proposition of *Eusebius*, as follows: *Christ, after his nativity, had no independent divinity, but the divinity of the Father resided in him.* This proposition includes the three following positions: *First*, in the Son, or the man Christ, there was a *divine nature*, or a divinity, distinct from his human nature. Yet, *secondly*, this divinity was *exclusively Christ's* own. Those things are said to be a person's own, which he alone possesses, or does not hold in common with others. But, *thirdly*, the *divinity* in Christ was *that of the Father*; in other words, the divinity of the Father dwelt in him. This *third* proposition is not explicit; for it might be adopted by one holding, that the *entire divine* [p. 701.] nature was united with the man Christ, and by one who holds, that only a *part* of it was so united. But here *Socrates* comes opportunely to our aid, and exhibits clearly the views of *Beryllus*, (Hist. Eccl. L. iii. c. 7. pp. 174, 175). He tells us, that *Eusebius* and *Athanasius* assembled a council at Alexandria, in which it was decreed, *that Christ assumed, not only a body, but also a human soul.* He proceeds to say, that this same doctrine was taught by various of the holiest and most distinguished writers among the early Christians; and adds, that the council against *Beryllus*, bishop of *Philadelphia*,—(a slip of the memory, for *Bostra.*)—in Arabia, condemned the opposite doctrine of that bishop. Ἡ διὰ Βήρυλλον γενομένη σύνοδος γράφουσα Βηρύλλῳ τὰ αὐτὰ, (ἔμψυχον τὸν ἐνανθρωπήσαντα,) παραδέδωκεν. Synodus propter Beryllum facta scribens ad eum hæc eadem tradidit, Christum, qui homo factus est, anima præditum fuisse. Therefore, *Beryllus* must have believed, that Christ had *no human soul.* For how could the council have condemned this error in its Epistle to him, if he was entirely free from it? He, doubtless, admitted that Christ had a *sentient soul*, which the ancients distinguished from the *rational* soul; but the place of the latter, he supposed, was in Christ supplied by the *divinity* of the Father. But this divinity of the Father, which, according to *Beryllus*, supplied the place of a rational soul in Christ, was not the *whole* essence of the Father; nor was it a certain *influence* flowing from it; but it was a most wise, excellent, and immaculate *soul*, issuing from the very nature and essence of the Father, and therefore very like to the Father. I am led to this supposition by what *Beryllus* maintained, namely, that Christ, before his advent among men, had not a *distinct essence*, or περιγραφὴν οὐσίας. For, as it must follow from this, that after his advent he had a *circumscribed*, or distinct and definable *essence*. the opinion of *Beryllus* can be explained in no other way. And hence we may suppose, that *Beryllus* adopted the belief that God, the author of all things, in whom there is no natural distinction, formed the man Christ in the womb of the virgin Mary, and endowed him with a *sentient* soul; and then, to enable the man to perform the functions assigned him, united to him a most perfect *rational soul, derived from his own bosom.* And, therefore, when the fathers of the council attempted to reclaim him from his error, they contended that the *rational soul* of Christ must be distinguished from his *divine nature.*

§ XXXV. **Paul of Samosata.** Much more pertinacious, and producing far greater disturbance in Syria, was *Paul*, a native of Samosata, and bishop of the church at Antioch; a man not un- [p. 702.] learned, nor destitute of genius, but vain and proud, and, what was unusual, sustaining a civil office under the government.(¹) His opinion, respecting the divine nature and Jesus Christ the Saviour, is so variously and inconsistently stated by the ancients, that it is with difficulty ascertained. But by comparing the principal documents which have reached us, respecting the controversy with him, I think it will appear that *Paul* held these tenets: That the Father, Son, and holy Spirit, are not different persons: That the Son and the holy Spirit are *in God*, just as *reason*, or the reasoning faculty and *action*, or the operative power, are *in a man:* That the man Christ was born without any connection with the divine nature: That the Word or Reason of the Father descended into the man, and united itself with him; but not so as to make one *person* with him: That the Wisdom or Reason of the Father, merely dwelt in the man Christ, and taught and wrought miracles by him: On account of this connection of the divine Word with the man Christ, the latter is, though improperly, called God.(²)—*Dionysius* of Alexandria first wrote against him, and afterwards assembled some councils against him at Antioch. In the last of these councils, which appears to have met in the year 269, one *Malchion*, a rhetorician, an acute and eloquent man, so skilfully drew *Paul* out of the subterfuges in which he had before lurked, that his error became manifest to all. And, as he would not renounce his error, he was divested of the episcopal office, and excluded from the communion by common suffrage. This decision *Paul* resisted; and relying, perhaps, on the patronage of *Zenobia*, the queen of Palmyra, and on the favor of the people, he refused to give up the house in which the bishop resided, and in which the church was accustomed to assemble. But this queen, after governing the province of the East for a time, was conquered by the emperor *Aurelian*, in the year 272; and the contest being brought before the emperor, he did not, indeed, decide it, but referred it to the arbitrament of the Romish and Italian bishops, who decided against *Paul.*(3) He left behind him a sect, the *Paulians*, or *Paulianists*, which, however, was not numerous, and did not continue beyond the fourth century.

(1) All that has come down to us respecting the life and morals of [p. 703.] *Paul* of Samosata, is found in an Epistle composed by the bishops of the council of Antioch, in which he was condemned; a part of which Epistle is preserved by *Eusebius*, Hist. Eccles. L. vii. c. 30. p. 279, &c. *Paul* was faulty enough, and unworthy of a place among bishops, even if we suppose these bishops were excited by passion, and exaggerated his faults. I admit that in his case too much influence seems to have been allowed to personal dislike, partial feelings, rivalship and envy: and perhaps he would not have been even accused of any corrupt doctrine, if he had not been rich, honored, and powerful. And yet, in the charges against him, there are some things which could not have been fabrications; and these are a sufficient ground for entertaining an unfavorable opinion of his life and conduct.—I. Being born in indigent and needy circumstances, he suddenly acquired vast riches: and the bishops charge him with having accumulated his wealth by frauds, by deceptive promises, and base artifices.—This charge I can readily believe. For such was the condition of Christians in that age, that it was not possible the incomes of bishops should raise them to opulence, if they did nothing unbecoming their office, or repugnant to religion. I therefore must suppose, that the bishops state facts when they say, that *Paul* heard and decided causes according to the customs of the age, and suffered bribes to be tendered him by the litigants.—II. In the conventions of the clergy, he imitated the pomp of civil magistrates and judges. For he erected for himself a tribunal, and an elevated throne, from which he pronounced judgments; and he had a private audience room, like the Roman magistrates.—This also, I have no doubt, was true. For the whole history of Paul shows, that he was a proud, arrogant and vain man. Nor could one who was much at court, and high in favor there, relish the holy and devout modesty of the Christian bishops.—III. He loved to have his discourses received by the people, as the declamations of the rhetoricians and sophists were, with clappings and applauding acclamations: and he rebuked those who withheld from him this honor.—This perhaps is not perfectly true: and yet it is not altogether incredible. I suspect he was a sophist and rhetorician, before he became a Christian; and therefore was unwilling to forego that honor among Christians, which he had long been accustomed to receive from his pupils.—IV. He greatly lauded himself in his discourses, and spoke disparagingly of the ancient doctors.—Perhaps, he affirmed that certain religious doctrines were not explained and inculcated with sufficient clearness and accuracy by the ancients.—V. He abolished the use of the hymns in honor of Christ, to which the people had been accustomed.—There is no reason to doubt the truth of this charge. But I would direct attention to his reasons for discontinuing those hymns. The bishops, his accusers, do not say, that he discarded those hymns because they contained any errors, but *because they were recent, and com-* [p. 704.] *posed by modern persons.* They say nothing further: but I will state how I un-

derstand the matter. *Paul* discontinued the customary hymns, as being recent productions, and substituted in their place the ancient Psalms of David, which he wished to have used exclusively. For, being a shrewd man, and acquainted with the ways of the court, he wished in this matter to gratify the feelings of queen *Zenobia*, his patroness; who, as we learn from *Athanasius* and others, was attached to the Jewish mode of worship.—VI. He directed women to sing hymns to his praise, in a public assembly on the great festival of Easter, and caused the neighbouring bishops and presbyters to laud him in their sermons.—That such things occurred, namely, that *Paul* was publicly lauded by women and by neighbouring bishops and presbyters, I can believe without much difficulty; but that he was so infatuated, and so greedy of praise, as boldly to urge forward these proclaimers of his virtues, I cannot believe so easily. I suspect that *Paul*, after the controversy arising from his novel opinions had become warm, and the people had become divided into factions and parties, persuaded some bishops and presbyters to defend and support his cause in public discourses; and, through his satellites, he encouraged some women, on Easter day, when the people were all assembled, suddenly to shout forth his praise;—in order to conciliate popular favor to him, and to check the rising storm of opposition.—VII. He allowed his presbyters and deacons, among other wrong things, to keep the so-called *sub-introduced* (συνεισάκτας, *subintroductas*) *women:* and he himself kept *two* young women, and carried them with him when he travelled.—This was not contrary to the custom of the priests of that age: of which I have spoken elsewhere. But the bishops do not accuse *Paul* of any illicit intercourse with these women: whence it appears, that though a luxurious liver, he was not altogether regardless of the laws of chastity and decorum.

But it clearly was unusual and extraordinary, that while sustaining the office of a bishop among Christians, he held at the same time a high *civil office* under the government; for he was a *Ducenarius Procurator*. This kind of judges was instituted by Augustus; and they bore the title of *Ducenarii*, from the annual salary of two hundred sestertia allowed them. They are often mentioned in ancient books and inscriptions. That there were Ducenarii Procuratores in Syria, and particularly at Palmyra, where *Paul* was in favor, is put beyond all doubt by the inscriptions found at Palmyra, and published by *Abrah. Seller.* (See his Antiquities of Palmyra, p. 166. 167. Lond. 1696. 8.) But let us attend to the complaints of the bishops on this subject, in *Eusebius*, (L. vii. c. 30.); ὑψηλὰ φρονεῖ καὶ ὑπερῆρται κοσμικὰ ἀξιώματα ὑποδυόμενος. Καὶ δουκηνάριος μᾶλλον ἢ Ἐπίσκοπος θέλων καλεῖσθαι. Magna meditatur, et sæculares gerit dignitates; et Ducenarius vocari mavult, quam episcopus. Some learned [p. 705.] men, not able to believe that a bishop among the Christians, a people odious and condemned by the laws, was honored with so high an office among the Romans, try to construe the language of the bishops differently from the common rendering. Examples enough are found of *Christians* sustaining distinguished offices in the Roman commonwealth, but that a Christian *bishop* or *presbyter* should be enrolled among the Judges and Magistrates of the Roman empire, is without example, or any probability, nay, seems to be impossible. I formerly conjectured, that *Paul* of Samosata had been a *Ducenarius Procurator*, before his conversion to christianity: which, if it were the fact, would show how two so very different offices, the one sacred the other civil, came to be united in the man. But the language of the bishops above cited, will not comport with this supposition: for it could not have been regarded as criminal in *Paul*, to retain his civil office after his conversion; and the Christians who created a *Ducenarius* a bishop, would have been more criminal than *Paul*, who merely did not refuse the sacred office but superadded it to his civil office. Some learned men, therefore, feeling the difficulties of the case, would give a different sense to the language of the bishops. They say, the bishops do not state that Paul *was* in fact a Ducenarius, but that he would rather be *called* a Ducenarius than a bishop: and therefore they only show us, that he undervalued the title of bishop, and would have been glad, if he could, to exchange it for the more splendid title of *Ducenarius*. But, however specious this interpretation may seem to be, neither the words preceding nor those that follow, will permit it. For the bishops say, most explicitly, that he was κοσμικὰ ἀξιώματα ὑποδυόμενος, *clothed* with worldly honors, and not that he merely *coveted* them. And immediately after, they add that he *moved in state* through the forum, *read aloud and publicly* the letters (presented), *and dictated* (answers), and *appeared with a throng* (of attendants), *preceding and following* after him. Such things would not comport with the office of a Christian bishop, who, if he should act in such a manner, would undoubtedly be thought deranged or out of his senses; but they are perfectly in character and keeping for a Ducenary Judge or Magistrate; for such a man, clothed in the insignia of his office, and guarded by his attendants, at certain seasons presented himself before the people, in the forum, where causes were usually tried; with lictors going before him, and servants and ministers about him. And as he passed along, many petitioners, as was the custom, presented to him their petitions; and he, being the judge, read the petitions on the spot, gave his decision, and dictated it to the attending scribes.—But, say they, can it be believed, that the emperor would confer an office of so much importance on a Christian bishop?—I answer, it is not wholly incredible. This *Paul* was a very prosperous man, and possessed great wealth: and nothing is too high [p. 706.] to be reached by means of money. The Roman provincial governors often sold the public offices. But it is not necessary for us to suppose, that this bishop obtained the office of a Ducenarius from the *emperor*. It is known from the Roman history of those times, that *Zenobia*, the wife of Odenatus, a petty king of the Palmyrenians, a woman of great energy, and endowed with uncommon intellectual and executive powers, governed the East, directing all public affairs at her discretion, during the reign of the emperor Gallienus, from A. D. 263, to the year 272. Into the good graces of the queen, who was a great admirer of learning and learned men, *Paul*, being a man of learning, a rhetorician, and not ignorant of the fine arts, and of the ways of courts, had insinuated himself: as we are expressly told by *Athanasius*, (Epist. ad. Solitarios, Opp. tom. I. p. 386, &c. and in *Montfaucon's* Collectio Nova Patr. et Scriptor. Graecor. tom. II. p. 20.) and by *Theodoret*, *Chrysostom*, *Nicephorus*, (Hist. Eccl. L. vi. c. 27. p. 420.) and by others. From this queen, therefore, as others before me have conjectured, *Paul* obtained, perhaps, this office.—And yet to this queen also, whom he was most studious to please, he owed all those troubles, under which, after various contests, he succumbed. He was, as his conduct shows, not one of those who seek fame by means of religious controversies, but he was particularly eager for wealth and honor. Hence it is more than probable, that he would have left his people to believe what they pleased, had not his thirst for wealth and honors induced him to propose innovations. *Zenobia*, as is certain from the testimony of *Athanasius* and others, was either a Jewess, or at least exceedingly partial to the Jewish religion. Hence, like all the Jews, she was disgusted with the christian doctrines of three persons in one God, and of the generation of the Son of God. To abate her disgust, *Paul* accommodated his religion, as far as possible, to the taste of the queen, by discarding all that was particularly repugnant to the Jewish doctrine of one individual God. This is stated by *Theodoret*, (Hæret. Fabul. L. ii. c. 8. p. 222.) by *Chrysostom*, (Homil. viii. in Johann. Opp. tom. viii. p. 48. ed. Bened.) and by others. And as all his opinions concerning God and Christ, (as we shall soon see,) were manifestly suited to repress the cavils of the Jews, who contended that the Christians subverted the unity of the divine nature, and converted God into a man,—nothing, in my opinion, is more credible than the above statement. And the same desire to gratify the feelings of the queen, induced him, as before remarked, to order the discontinuance of the Hymns in common use among christians, and the substitution of the Psalms of David. For it was his aim, to make the christian [p. 707.] religion appear to differ as little as possible from that of the Jews.

(2) Respecting the impiety of *Paul* of Samosata, scarcely any writer since the third century, who has treated of the trinity of persons in God. and of Christ, either formally or incidentally, is silent; and the writers on heresies, one and all, place this man among the worst corrupters of revealed truth, and inveigh against him vehemently: so *Epiphanius*, *Theodoret*, *Augustine*, *Damascenus*, and the rest. Moreover, some of the public documents of the proceedings against him, have reached us; a circumstance which has not occurred in regard to most of the other heretics. For there is extant, I. a great part of the Epistle of the bishops, by whose decision he was condemned in the council at Antioch, addressed to all the bishops of christendom, to make it manifest that they had good reasons for what they had done: In *Eusebius*, (Hist. Eccl. L. vii. c. 30. p. 279, &c.) But it is to be regretted, that Eusebius has preserved only that part of the Epistle which recounts the vices and delinquencies of the man, omitting the part which stated his doctrines or errors. If the latter had been preserved, we could more confidently and more definitely determine what were his principles.—There is extant, II. a copy of one of the Epistles of the bishops of the council, addressed to *Paul*, relating to the controversy with him: in the Bibliotheca Patrum Parisiensis, (tom. xi. p. 302. ed. Paris. 1644. Fol.) In this Epistle, six of the bishops state their own opinions respecting God and Christ, and inquire of him, whether he disagrees with them.—There is extant, III. an Epistle of *Dionysius*, of Alexandria, to *Paul* of Samosata, in which the writer chides and confutes him; in the same Bibliotheca Patrum, (tom. xi. p. 273.) Some very erudite men, and for reasons worthy of consideration, deny indeed, that this Epistle was written by *Dionysius*. See *Henry de Valois* on

Eusebius, (p. 155.) The Epistle is unquestionably very ancient, and it was addressed to *Paul* by some bishop or presbyter, whose name being omitted in the early copy, some person, recollecting that *Dionysius* was an opposer of Paul, ascribed the Epistle to him. From Question x. and the Answer to it, (p. 298.) it seems to be inferable, that the writer of the Epistle, and of the Answers to the Questions, was a *presbyter:* for he is so styled by *Paul.*—There are extant, IV. ten Questions of *Paul* of Samosata, addressed to *Dionysius* of Alexandria, and the Answers of the latter to these Questions: in the same Bibliotheca Patrum, (tom. xi. p. 278.) Of these, my opinion is the same as of the Epistle above mentioned. That the Questions were composed by *Paul* himself, I do not hesitate to believe, because I see no ground for doubt. The Answers were not written by *Dionysius*, but by some one of those with whom Paul had discussion respecting his opinions.—But this unequalled abundance of documents relative to the heresy of Paul, has not prevented a great diversity in opinion, both among the ancients and the moderns, respecting his real sentiments. [p. 708.] For the ancients speak, sometimes obscurely, sometimes inconsistently, and sometimes they mistake, either from passion or prejudice; and hence the moderns differ widely, some criminating, and some vindicating the man. To find the truth, if possible, among these uncertainties, I will first collect together all that can be learned, respecting *Paul's* sentiments, from those Epistles and ancient documents just described; for they are certainly more veracious and trustworthy, than any others. And if we then compare with these statements, whatever has reached us from other ancient sources, we shall see what we ought to admit, and what we should reject. For whatever accords with those earliest testimonies, must doubtless be regarded as true; and whatever contradicts them, bears the marks of falsehood.

I. The bishops by whom Paul was condemned, in their Epistle, preserved by Eusebius, say:—*First,* That *he denied his God and Lord:* τὸν Θεὸν ἑαυτοῦ καὶ Κύριον ἀρνουμένου. (p. 280.)—*Secondly,* That before the bishops, assembled in council, he would not acknowledge *that the Son of God descended from heaven:* τὸν υἱὸν τοῦ Θεοῦ ἐξ οὐρανοῦ καταλεληλυθέναι.—*Thirdly,* That he distinctly said, *Jesus Christ originated on earth:* Λέγει Ἰησοῦν Χριστὸν κάτωθεν.—*Fourthly,* That he went over to the abominable heresy of *Artemas.* What the heresy of Artemas was, with which they tax Paul, is a question of doubt and uncertainty. I shall therefore pass by this charge, and consider only the others; in which, doubtless, the chief error of Paul was included, and that error which was the cause of so much odium against him.—From these charges it is evident, that he would not acknowledge *Jesus Christ* to be *both God and man;* or, he denied, that Jesus Christ was a person—if I may so say, *compounded* of God and man. For when he said, *the Son of God did not descend from heaven, but originated on the earth,* what could he mean, but that Christ was a *mere man,* though divinely begotten of the virgin Mary? And what could the bishops mean, when they taxed him with *denying his God and Lord,* but that he divested Christ of his *divinity,* or denied that a divine person received the man Christ into union with himself? From the same charges it also appears, that he called the *man* Christ the *Son of God;* and this, undoubtedly, because he was supernaturally produced from the virgin Mary. For he denied that the *Son of God descended from heaven;* and as this, most certainly, must be understood as referring to *Christ*, it is manifest that he applied the title *Son of God* to the *man Christ.* And this alone is a sufficient refutation of the error of those who believe, what *Marius Mercator* asserts, (de xii. Anathematismis Nestorii, in his Opp. tom. ii. p. 128.) that *Paul of Samosata represented Christ as being a man, born like other men of two parents.* Yet we have a better witness for confuting this error, in *Paul* himself, who distinctly says, (Quæstio v. in the Biblioth. Patr. tom. xi. p. 286.): Ἰησοῦς ὁ γεννηθεὶς ἐκ πνεύματος ἁγίου καὶ Μαρίας τῆς παρθένου. [p. 709.] Jesus ex Maria virgine et *Spiritu sancto* natus est.—That the bishops, whose charges we are considering, did him no injustice, he himself makes manifest. For all his *ten Questions* now extant, whether addressed to *Dionysius* or to another person, have one sole aim, namely, to evince, by means of various texts of scripture brought together, that Christ was a *mere man*, and destitute of any divinity; or, what amounts to the same thing, to confute the belief that the *divine* and *human* natures united in Christ produced *one person.* It is therefore not necessary to produce the testimony of others among the ancients to the same point. And yet I will add that of *Simeon* Betharsamensis, a celebrated Persian, near the beginning of the sixth century, whose testimony I regard as of more value than that of all the Greek and Latin fathers. In his Epistle on the heresy of the Nestorians, (in *Jos. Sim. Asseman's* Bibliotheca Oriental. Clement. Vatic. tom. i. p. 347.) he says: Paulus Samosatenus de beata Maria hæc dicebat: *Nudum hominem* genuit Maria, nec post partum virgo permansit. Christum autem appellavit *creatum*, *factum*, *mortalem* et *filium* (Dei) *ex gratia.* De se ipso vero dicebat: Ego quoque si voluero, Christus ero, quum *ego et Christus unius, ejusdemque simus naturæ.* These statements accord perfectly with the allegations of the bishops, and with the character of *Paul*, who was rash and extravagant. *Epiphanius* also, (Hæres. lxv. p. 617.) says of him: that *he gave himself the appellation of Christ:* a declaration which is elucidated by the quotation from the Persian *Simeon.*

II. The six bishops of the council of Antioch, in their letter to *Paul* before sentence was pronounced upon him, while they state their own doctrine respecting God and Christ, condemn some errors of their adversary. In the first place, they say, it could not be endured, that he should inculcate, υἱὸν τοῦ Θεοῦ Θεὸν μὴ εἶναι πρὸ καταβολῆς κόσμου. Filium Dei non esse Deum ante constitutionem mundi. And, δύο Θεοὺς καταγγέλλεσθαι, ἐὰν ὁ υἱὸς τοῦ Θεοῦ Θεὸς κηρύσσηται. Deos illos *duos* inducere, qui filium Dei prædicent Deum esse. (Bibliotheca Patr. tom. xi. p. 303.) The bishops speak less definitely than could be wished; in consequence, perhaps, of the studied obscurity of *Paul*, who did not wish his real sentiments to be distinctly known. And yet it is not difficult to see, whither tend the sentiments they attribute to him. First, he acknowledged, *that there is something in God, which the Scriptures call the Son of God.* He therefore supposed, that there are *two Sons of God;* the one *by grace*, the man Christ; the other *by nature*, who existed long before the other Son.—Secondly. *He denied, that the latter Son of God, was God anterior to the creation of the world.*—Thirdly. And consequently he held, *that this Son of God became God, at the time the world was created.*—These statements appear confused, and very different from the common apprehensions: but they will admit of elucidation. *Paul* meant to say, that the *energy*,—or, if any prefer it, the *Divine energy*, which he denominated the *Son of God*, was hidden in God, before the creation of the world; but that, in a sense, it issued out from God, and began to have some existence exterior to God, at the time God formed the created universe.—Fourthly. Hence, he inferred, *that* [p. 710.] *those profess two Gods*, (or speak of *two* as in the place of the *one God*,) *who proclaim the Son of God to be God:* but undoubtedly, considering what precedes, the limitation should be added: *before the creation of the world.* His belief was, that *they* divide the one God into two Gods, who make the Son of God to have existed as a *person*, distinct from the Father, before the foundation of the world. He did not deny, as we have seen, that the Son of God was, in some sense, made God, at the time the world was created.—From all this we learn, that *Paul* denied the *eternal generation* of the Son of God, and also his personal *distinctness* from the Father: and he supposed, that when God was about to create the world, he sent out from himself a certain *energy*, which is called the *Son of God*, and also *God*, although it is nothing distinct from God. These ideas may be further illustrated, by the subsequent charge of the bishops; in which they not obscurely tax *Paul*, with representing God the Father as creating the world by the *Word* (ὡς δι' ὀργάνου καὶ ἐπιστήμης ἀνυποστάτου) *as by an instrument, and by intelligence, having no separate existence or personality.* For it hence appears, that by the Son or *Word of God*, he understood the divine *wisdom* (ἐπιστήμην); which, before the world was created, had been at rest in God, and hidden during numberless ages; but now, when the supreme God formed the purpose of creating the world, it exhibited its powers, and as it were came out from the bosom of the Father; or in other words, it manifested its presence, by discriminating, acting, and operating. From that time onward, it is called, though figuratively, the *Son of God*, because it proceeded forth from God, just as a son does from his parents; and also *God*, because it is essentially God, and can be conceived of as separate from him only by an abstraction of the mind. In perfect accordance with these views, are the statements of other ancient writers. Thus *Epiphanius*, (Hæres. lxv. p. 608.) states the sentiments of *Paul: God the Father, Son and Spirit, are one God. The Word and Spirit are ever in God, as reason is in man: the Son of God has no separate existence, but he exists in God.* . . . . υἱὸς ἐν τῷ πατρὶ, ὡς λόγος ἐν ἀνθρώπῳ. *The Son is in the Father, as reason* (not *speech, sermo*, as Petavius rendered it: but ἐπιστήμη, as the bishops term it,) *is in man.* Epiphanius, who as an author, was not distinguished for his accuracy and research, has not stated all that *Paul* held, but what he has stated, is very well. I omit similar citations from *Athanasius* and others, that the discussion may not be too prolix.

III. *Dionysius*, or whoever wrote the epistle bearing his name, (in the Bibliotheca Patr. tom. xi. p. 273. 274.) says that *Paul* taught: δύο (esse) ὑποστάσεις καὶ δύο πρόσωπα τοῦ ἑνὸς ἡμῶν Χριστοῦ, καὶ δύο Χριστοὺς, καὶ δύο υἱοὺς, ἕνα φύσει τὸν υἱὸν τοῦ Θεοῦ προϋπάρχοντα, καὶ ἕνα κατ' ὁμωνυμίαν Χριστὸν καὶ υἱὸν τοῦ Δαβίδ. duas esse hypostases et duas formas (so I would render the word πρόσωπα, rather than by *personas*) unius Christi, et duos Christos, ac duos filios, [p. 711.] unum naturâ filium Dei, qui fuit ante sæcula, et unum homonyme Christum et filium David, qui secundum beneplacitum (κατ' εὐδοκίαν) Dei accepit nomen filii. Whether *Paul* so expressed himself, or whether *Dionysius* so inferred from the language of Paul, there is nothing here disagreeing with the opinions of Paul. For since he declared Christ to be a mere man, born of Mary; and denied that the Wisdom of God, combined with the man Christ, constituted one person; and yet asserted, that the eternal Son of God, by whom the world was created, dwelt in the man Christ; and as he also called the man Christ the Son of God, and applied the same appellation, Son of God, to that power of the divine Wisdom which projected the world;—it must necessarily be, that in some sense, he recognized *two* distinct and separate things in Christ, *two forms, two Sons, two Christs.* And here it should be noticed, that the word ὑπόστασις, in the language of *Dionysius,* is not to be understood in *our* sense of the term, but in a broader acceptation. And from the *Questions of Paul,* (Quæst. vii. p. 290.) it appears, that he used the word ὑπόστασις in a broad sense, as applicable to any thing that is or exists, whether it subsists by itself, or only in something else. The eternal Son of God, which *Paul* acknowledged to exist in Christ, he could not have regarded as truly an ὑπόστασις or *person.* For, if he had so regarded it, he would have admitted the very thing which he denied, namely, that the Son of God is a *person* distinct from the person of the Father.—In this same Epistle, (p. 274.) *Dionysius* blames Paul for saying: Hominem Christum magis Deo placuisse, quam omnes homines, ad habitandum in eo (ἄνευ τῆς ἀσκητικῆς καὶ ἐπιπόνου δικαιοσύνης) idque sine dura et laboriosa exercitatione justitiæ. He therefore admitted, that God, in the sense before explained, i. e. as being the *Wisdom of God,* dwelt in Christ.—But, he added, that God dwelt in Christ, *sine laboriosa justitiæ exercitatione.* This well explains the views of Paul, and in part confirms my former remarks. For *Paul's* meaning is, that *Christ,* while obeying the commands of the law, and suffering its penalties, acted and suffered *alone;* nor did *God,* as present with him, either act or suffer along with the man Christ. And hence it appears, that *Paul* rejected altogether the *union* of the divine and human natures in Christ. And in this manner, *Dionysius* correctly understood him; as appears from the confutation he subjoined, in which he endeavors to show, by many proofs, that God was *born* in Christ, and *suffered* the penalties, and *died.* More passages, of a similar character, might be drawn from this Epistle; but they are not needed.

IV. In the *ten Questions* proposed by *Paul* to *Dionysius,* the sole aim of *Paul* is, to prove that the *man* born of Mary had no *community of nature* or of *action* with *God* dwelling in him. Hence he brings forward the texts in which the soul of Christ is said to be *troubled* and *sorrowful.* (John, xii. 27. Matt. xxvi. 28.) And he then asks: Can the nature of *God* be sorrowful and troubled? [p. 712.] And he lays before his antagonist, the words of Christ to the Jews, *Destroy this temple,* &c. (John, ii. 19.) and then demands: Can *God* be dissolved? And this objection, so easy of solution, *Dionysius* answers miserably, by resorting to a mystical interpretation. For he would have Paul believe, that by the *temple* which Christ represents as to be *dissolved,* must be understood the *disciples* of Christ; because these the Jews actually *dissolved*, that is, dispersed and scattered. And some of the other answers are no better. In Question v. (p. 286.) *Paul* says: Luke tells us (ch. ii. 40.) that Christ *grew*. But can *God* grow? If, therefore, *Christ* grew, he was nothing but a *man*. With this argument, the good *Dionysius* is greatly puzzled. But at length he finds his way out, and says: The *boy* who, as Luke tells us, *grew and waxed strong*, is the *church; so* that Αὔξησις τοῦ Θεοῦ εἰς τὴν ἐκκλησίαν ἐστὶ, *the growth of God, relates to the church:* for it is recorded in the Acts, that the church increased daily and was enlarged; and that the word of God increased every day. How ingenious and beautiful! If all the bishops who opposed Paul, were like this *Dionysius* for acuteness and genius, I do not wonder they could not refute him. And lest this fine response should lose its force and beauty, *Dionysius* closes it with exquisite taunts.—But I will desist. *Paul*, undoubtedly, had wrong views, and views very different from those which the scriptures inculcate. But his adversaries also appear to have embraced more than one error, and they had not sufficiently precise and clear ideas on the subject they discussed.

These statements, derived from the best and most credable documents on the subject, if carefully examined and compared together, will give us easy access to the real sentiments of *Paul* of Samosata. The system he embraced, so far as it can be ascertained at the present day, is contained in the following propositions.—I. God is a perfectly *simple unit*, in whom there is no division into parts whatever!—II. Therefore, all that common christians teach, respecting different *persons* in God, an eternal Son of God, and his generation from eternity, is false, and should be corrected by the holy scriptures.—III. The scriptures speak indeed of the Father, the Son, and the holy Spirit. But those texts must be so understood, as not to militate with the clearest and most certain doctrine of both reason and scripture, respecting the *unity* of the divine nature.—IV. The Son of God mentioned in the scriptures, is merely the *Reason* (λόγος) and *Wisdom* (ἐπιστήμη) of God.—Those who have translated the Greek writers concerning Paul, into Latin,—*De Valois, Petavius*, and others,—commonly render the Greek word λόγος, by the Latin word *Verbum*. This is wrong. From the Epistle of the bishops at Antioch to *Paul*, it is clear, that *he* understood by λόγος the divine *Wisdom*. Hence this Greek word is equivalent to the Latin word *ratio*. Marius *Mercator*, whom many follow after, (de xii. Anathematismo Nestoriano, in his Opp. tom. ii. p. 128. edit. Garnerii) erroneously says: Verbum Dei Patris, non substantivum, sed *prolativum*, vel *imperativum*, sensit Samosatenus. But *Paul* did not recognize the word προφορικὸν (*prolativum*): and by the word λόγος, he intended the *Wisdom* or the *Reason* of God; as is manifest from *Epiphanius*, [p. 713.] who, it must be confessed, is not always sufficiently accurate; (Hæres. lxv. p. 609.): Λόγον νομίζουσι σοφίαν, οἷον ἐν ψυχῇ ἀνθρώπου ἕκαστος ἔχει λόγον. Vocant sapientiam, qualem quilibet homo in anima possidet divinitus acceptam.—V. This *Reason* of God was at rest in him, from eternity, and did not project or attempt any thing exterior to God. But when God determined to create the visible universe, this *Reason* in a sense *proceeded* out from God, and acted exteriorly to God. On this account, in the scriptures, it is metaphorically called the *Son of God.*—VI. The *Spirit* is that *power*, which God possesses, of producing and animating all things, at his pleasure. It first received the name of *Spirit*, when it manifested itself in the creation of the world; and it is so called, because it may be compared to the *wind* or the *breath*, which produces motions in the air. When it excites pious emotions in the souls of men, it is called the *holy Spirit.*—VII. And therefore, until God entered on the creation of the world, and operated externally, there was neither any Son of God, nor any holy Spirit. And yet both may, in a certain sense, be pronounced *eternal*, because they eternally existed in God.—VIII. When God would make known to men a way of salvation superior to that of Moses, he, by means of that eternal *power* of his, which gives life and motion to all things, and which is called the *holy Spirit*, begat, of the Jewish virgin Mary, that very holy and most perfect *man, Jesus:* and this *man*, because he was begotten by the power of God, without any intervening agency, is also called the *Son of God;* just as a house receives the name of its builder. (See *Dionysius*' Epistle to Paul, ubi Supr. p. 274.)—IX. This extraordinary *man*, though he was more holy and more noble than any other mortal, yet lived and acted in the way and manner of other men, and was subject to all the wants and frailties which are incident to our nature. And all the things which he either did or suffered, prove clearly that he was a *mere man.*—X. But to enable him to perform the functions of a *divine ambassador*, without failure, (for as a man, he was liable to errors and defects,) that same divine *Reason*, which proceeded forth as it were from God at the time the world was created, joined itself to his soul, and banished from it all ignorance on religious subjects and all liability to failure.—At what *time*, in the opinion of *Paul*, the divine Reason or Wisdom became associated with the soul of Christ, I do not find stated. I can suppose, that the advent of the Reason or Word of God to the man Christ, was delayed till the commencement of his public functions. Because, previously, the man Christ did not need the aid of this eternal Wisdom.—XI. This presence of the divine Wisdom, (which is nothing different from God himself,) in the man Christ, makes it proper that this man should be, and he is, called *God. Athanasius*, (de Synodis, Opp. tom. i. P. ii. p. 739,): Οἱ ἀπὸ Παύλου τοῦ Σαμωσατέως λέγονται, Χριστὸν ὕστερον [p. 714.] μετὰ τὴν ἐνανθρώπησιν ἐκ προκοπῆς τεθεοποιῆσθαι, τῷ τὴν φύσιν ψιλὸν ἄνθρωπον γεγονέναι. Pauli Samosateni discipuli dicunt Christum post incarnationem ex profectu (I am not sure, that *Montfaucon* here gives the true import of the Greek, ἐκ προκοπῆς.) Deum factum esse, naturâ vero nudum hominem factum esse.—XII. It will be no mistake, then, if we say, there are *two* Sons of God; and that there were in Christ two ὑποστάσεις, or two distinct separately existing things, two *forms* or πρόσωπα.—XIII. But we must be careful not to commingle and confound the acts of these two Sons of God. Each acts alone, and without the other. The *divine Reason*, with no coöperation of the man, speaks by Christ, instructs, discourses, sways the minds of the auditors, and performs the miracles. And on the other hand, the *man*, with no coöperation of the divine Reason dwelling in him, is begotten, is hungry, sleeps, walks, suffers pains, and dies.—XIV. At length, when the man

Christ had fulfilled his mission, the divine *Reason* left the *man*, and returned to God. *Epiphanius*, (Hæres. lxv. §. 1. p. 608.) · Φησὶ Παῦλος· Ἐλθὼν ὁ λόγος ἐνήργησε μόνος, καὶ ἀνῆλθε πρὸς τὸν πατέρα. This passage is miserably translated by Dion. *Petavius*, (as are many other passages in *Epiphanius.*) thus: Sed solum, inquit Paulus, adveniens verbum, totum illud administravit, et ad patrem revertit. The true meaning of the passage is: *The divine Reason came* (to the man Christ, long after his birth, and when in mature life,) *and solely* (without any community of action with the human nature,) *operated in him, and afterwards returned to God.*

I am aware, that learned men have made the system of *Paul* coincident with the commonly received doctrine of *Nestorius* concerning Christ. And it is easy to fall into such an opinion, if we take the words of the ancients in the sense ordinarily given to them. And indeed there is some affinity between the Nestorian and the Samosatean views. Nor is this coincidence a recent discovery; for in the council of Ephesus, in the fifth century, it was supposed that *Paul* prepared the way for *Nestorius*. (See *Harduin's* Concilia, tom. i. p. 1271.) And in the sixth century, *Simeon* Betharsamensis, (in *Asseman's* Biblioth. Orient. Clement. Vaticana, tom. i. p. 347.) tells us: Ex Paulo Samosateno orta est hæresis duarum naturarum (or rather, *personarum*) et proprietatum, operationumque earum. *Simeon* here refers to the Nestorian heresy.—Yet there really was a wide difference between *Nestorius* and *Paul.* The former admitted a plurality of *persons* in God; and he so coupled the second person of the divine nature, or the Son, with the person of the man born of Mary, that they continued to be *two* distinct persons. Neither of these positions was admitted by *Paul;* who denied any distinction of *persons* in God, and supposed that the mere *reason* or *wisdom* of God, was temporarily joined with the *man* Christ, and on this account, he acknowledged but *one person* in Christ.

(3) That more than one council was assembled at Antioch against Paul of Samosata, is certain, from *Eusebius*, (Hist. Eccles. L. vii. c. 28, p. 278) and from others. But how many councils were held, cannot easily be determined. [p. 715.] That the last was held in 269, has been proved by *Tillemont* and others, by arguments of the most satisfactory nature. (See *Tillemont*, Memoires pour - - - - l'Histore de l'Eglise, tome iv. p. 625.) In the preceding councils, as *Eusebius* says, Dogmatis suæ novitatem occultabat. (See also *Theodoret*, Hæret. Fabul. L. ii. p. 222, 223.) Being more crafty than his adversaries, *Paul* deceived the bishops with his ambiguous terms, so that they thought him free from error. This might easily be done, as may be inferred from what has been said respecting his sentiments; and especially before men who were, indeed, well disposed in regard to God and religion, but, as is quite evident, were without human learning, simple-hearted, and wholly unacquainted with the art of disputation. *Paul*, as we have seen, expressed his opinions in the very words and phrases used in the bible, and did not deny that Christ is *God*, and the *Son of God*, and that in God we must distinguish the Father, Son, and holy Spirit: but to these terms he affixed a different meaning, which the inexperienced would not perceive. There was need, therefore, of a more perspicacious disputant, who could draw the man out of his hiding-places, and strip him of his disguises,

by queries, interrogatories, and accurate distinctions. And such a man was at length found in *Malchion*, then a presbyter in the church at Antioch; who had once been a teacher of eloquence, and had presided over the school of the Sophists at Antioch, and, therefore, understood well all the artifices by which the rhetoricians of that age managed a bad cause. This man, by vanquishing Paul in argument, is a tacit witness to what I asserted, that the other persons engaged in this controversy, even the bishops, were men deficient in learning and talents, and inadequate arbiters in such subtle controversies. The records of this discussion, with few exceptions, have perished: but the point at issue between this Samosatean and *Malchion*, may be learned from *Theodoret;* who tells us, (Hæret. Fabul. L. ii. c. 8, Opp. tom. iv. p. 223,) that *Malchion* demonstrated: *That Paul considered Christ to be* ἄνθρωπον θείας χάριτος διαφερόντως ἠξιωμένον, *hominem insigniter divinâ gratiâ ornatum.* By artful and deceptive phraseology, therefore, *Paul* had endeavored to persuade the bishops, and perhaps had actually persuaded some of them, that he held Christ to be God; but *Malchion*, by his eloquence and skill, detected those artifices by which the good bishops had been beguiled. *Paul* was condemned and deposed, by the suffrages of the bishops. But, as *Eusebius* informs us, (ubi supr. p. 282,) he refused to vacate (τοῦ τῆς ἐκκλησίας οἴκου) *the house of the church.* This phraseology shows, as learned men have remarked, that the bishops of Antioch resided in the same house, in which the church ordinarily assembled. And *Paul* not only continued to occupy the house, but also to perform the functions of a bishop; as we are expressly told by *Theodoret*, (ubi supr. p. 223): Τὴν τῆς ἐκκλησίας κατεῖχεν [p. 716.] ἡγεμονίαν. Præfecturam ecclesiæ dimittere nolebat: notwithstanding the council (as *Eusebius* informs us) had appointed *Domnus* his successor. This however, would have been impossible, if the people of Antioch had regarded the decision of the council as obligatory. But, undoubtedly, the majority of the people chose to go with their bishop, rather than obey the council, although it was very large, and composed (as *Eusebius* says) *ex innumerabilibus* fere *episcopis.* This fact is confirmed by the bishops of the council in their epistle, (apud *Eusebium*, ubi supr. p. 281.) for they complain, that *Paul* not only allowed *Psalms to be sung in honor of himself*, in the church, *and his praises to be celebrated in the congregation*, (ἐν τῷ λαῷ,) but that he was also present in those assemblies, and did not rebuke persons who pronounced him to be *an angel from heaven, come among men*, i. e. a teacher of the true wisdom which is from heaven. The christian population of Antioch, therefore, or at least a large portion of them, rejected the new bishop; and remaining in communion with *Paul*, continued to resort to the house where he resided for the purpose of worship, and with willing ears listened to his praises publicly proclaimed from the pulpit. The bishops, in their Epistle, express their great displeasure at this: but when I consider carefully the whole case, I think they must themselves have caused the evil in part. For they disregarded the rights of the people, in the creation of a new bishop; and they do not conceal the fact, that *they alone*, without any regard to the judgment and authority of the people, placed *Domnus* over the church of Antioch, and ordered *Paul* to retire from his post. They say: Ἠναγκάσθημεν ἕτερον ἀντ' αὐτοῦ τῇ καθολικῇ ἐκκλησίᾳ καταστῆσαι. Nos episcopi coacti fuimus alium ejus loco episcopum ecclesiæ catholicæ præponere. They acted alone in the appointment; for they make no mention of the people, or of the church. And therefore, the people of Antioch stood up for their rights, and denied that it was lawful for the council, without their knowledge or consent, to undertake so great a matter, and substitute another man in place of their old bishop. And this shows us, how *Paul*, though condemned by so many bishops, was able for three years to hold a position, of which he had been pronounced unworthy. The people favored him: and if they had deserted him, the affair would have soon terminated. And yet I do not consider it an idle supposition of some, that queen *Zenobia*, the patroness of *Paul*, afforded him aid. But after her subjugation, in the year 272, the case was carried before the emperor *Aurelian*, (who had not then become hostile to the christians;) and he, after hearing the case, decided, (as *Eusebius* tells us): Τούτοις νεῖμαι τὸν οἶκον, οἷς ἂν οἱ κατὰ τὴν Ἰταλίαν κὰι τὴν Ῥωμαίων πόλιν Ἐπίσκοποι τοῦ δόγματος ἐπιστέλλοιεν. Iis domum tradi debere, quibus Italici christianæ religionis antistites et Romanus episcopus scriberent: or, that the building should be surrendered *to those whom the Italian bishops should by their letter approve.* This decision of the emperor deserves, I think, a more careful examination than is usually given it. In the first place, the emperor pays no regard to the decision of the council against Paul: nor does he order his ejectment from the church, as *Theodoret*, and after him many others, represent. The decision was not [p. 717.] in relation to *Paul* and *Domnus*; nor was the question, which of them was the true and lawful bishop of the church at Antioch: but the subject under consideration was, the possession of the *house*, and the rights of the parties who contended about it before the emperor's tribunal. Aurelian must have pronounced a very different sentence, if he approved the decree of the council, and decided that Paul was justly deprived of his office. It appears moreover, from this decision, that there were two *parties* at Antioch, who contended for the house of the church before the emperor. For the decree speaks of them in the plural number, (τούτοις νεῖμαι, κ. τ. λ.) If the Antiochians had been agreed, and had united in a petition against Paul on his refusing to vacate the church, undoubtedly, Aurelian would have decided in favor of the people against that single man: and he would not have referred the case to the judgment of the Italian bishops. But there was a division in the community at Antioch: no small part of the people—and perhaps also many of the neighboring bishops, (for among them, *Paul* had many friends; as the Epistle of the bishops, preserved by *Eusebius*, testifies,)—took sides with Paul: while others preferred *Domnus.* And both these parties contended for the possession of the house. Hence, thirdly, the emperor being in doubt, and, from his ignorance of the christian religion, unable to determine which party had the most valid claim, without pronouncing any judgment, he committed the case to the decision of foreign and disinterested bishops. And lastly, having learned that it was customary with the christians to submit all their religious controversies to the determination of councils, he thought the christian rule should be followed in this case; and therefore he directed the bishop of Rome to assemble the Italian bishops, to hear and judge the case; and he decreed that the decision of such a council should bind the parties. There are also, as I apprehended, some implications in this decree of the emperor, which throw light on the discipline of the christians in that age, and show us, that the bishop of Rome could decide nothing by himself, in the controversies referred to him, but was obliged to assemble the bishops of Italy in a council. It hence appears very manifest, unless I am greatly deceived, that the writers on ecclesiastical affairs wholly misrepresent this act of the emperor, and that the thing should be understood very differently. Fred. *Spanheim*, (in his Instit. Hist. Eccl. Opp. tom. I. p. 751,) says: Quum parere nollet, ac ædibus episcopalibus excedere Paulus, ab ipso Aureliano imperatore coërcendus fuit. In the same manner many others: and all of them wrong. Some tell us, more distinctly, that the whole congregation of Antioch went before the emperor, and besought him to expel the degenerate bishop whom the council had condemned from the house of the church; and that the emperor consented:—which is no nearer the truth. The fact was this. There were two parties at Antioch, the one adhered to *Paul*, and the other regarded *Domnus* as the true bishop; and [p. 718.] they litigated before the emperor, respecting the *house* of the church, and not—be it carefully noted—respecting the *bishop*. And this was wise. If they had carried their contest about the *bishop* before the emperor, they would have exposed to its enemies those evils in the church, which should be kept from public view; and they would undoubtedly have increased the odium under which they already lay. Besides, the question respecting the bishop, being a religious one, they considered it as not pertaining to the emperor's jurisdiction. But the controversy concerning the *house*, was purely of a civil nature, and therefore could be carried into the forum. Aurelian did not venture to adjudge the house in question to either of the litigating parties. For the Roman laws, as is manifest, could not be applied to the case. The emperor, therefore, permitted it to be tried by the christian ecclesiastical laws, and appointed for judges the bishop of Rome with the other bishops of Italy; because the oriental bishops, having sympathy with the parties, could not be safely trusted to decide the case. Such being the facts, I cannot agree with them who can see, in this transaction, evidence of the emperor's good will towards the christians. For nothing can be inferred from this decree of his, except that he would not at that time have the christians molested; and this, probably, for what we should call political reasons, or from motives of state policy. Neither can I accord with those, who suspect that Aurelian was influenced by hatred to *Zenobia*, whom he knew to be friendly to *Paul;* and that therefore he decided the case against him. For there was no controversy respecting *Paul*, before the emperor; nor is there any indication of ill-will towards *him*, in the edict of Aurelian.

§ XXXVI. **The Arabians reclaimed by Origen.** Seduced also by philosophy, beyond a doubt, were those Arabian followers of an unknown leader, who supposed the *soul* of man to *die with the body;* and that it would hereafter, along with the body, be *restored* by God to life. As the parent of this sect is unknown, they are denominated *Arabians*, from the country they inhabited. The disturbances produced by this sect in Arabia, under the emperor *Philip*, were quieted by *Origen;* who, being sent for, discussed the subject with so much eloquence, in a pretty numerous council, called for the purpose, that the friends of the error gave up their opinion.(1)

(1) All that we know of this sect,—which is very little,—is to be found in *Eusebius*, (Hist. Eccl. L. vi. c. 37. p. 233). Those adhering to it, believed—I. That the *soul* is only the *vital power*, pertaining to, and moving the human body.—II. Hence they concluded, that when the body dies, the soul also becomes extinct; as *Eusebius* says: συναποθνήσκειν τοῖς σώμασι καὶ συνδιαφθείρεσθαι. This language can have no other meaning than that above expressed. Those, therefore, are not to be regarded, who make this sect agree with the [p. 719.] so-called *Psychopannychians;* or, with those that believe human souls to be, indeed, distinct essences from the body, and that they continue to live or exist when the body dies, but that they are destitute of consciousness and perception, and, as it were, *sleep*, when separate from the body. For those Arabians supposed the soul, not only to die with the body, but also to *become extinct*. They, therefore, must have held the soul to be a constituent part of the body.—The author of this sect, I can suppose, was an *Epicurean* before he became a Christian. For there were, undoubtedly, in that age, adherents to the philosophy of Epicurus, both in Syria and Arabia. When he became a Christian, he attempted to combine with Christianity his philosophy respecting the soul; or rather, he would modify Christianity by his philosophy.—III. He therefore taught his followers to believe, that God will hereafter recall to life the whole man, or will restore to the body that vital power which it lost at death.

§ XXXVII. **Benefits to Christianity from Philosophy.** Yet, it must not be denied that Christianity received some advantages from this disposition to elucidate theology by means of philosophy. For, in the *first* place, certain doctrines, which had before been taught indistinctly and ambiguously, assumed a better form, and were better explained in the discussions with those who brought philosophy into the church. In the *next* place, the growth and progress of the Gnostic sects were more forcibly and more successfully resisted than before, by such as brought in the aids of reason. For if the philosophical light, which shone in *Origen* and others, was not great, yet it was sufficient to dissipate, and entirely to overthrow the absurd fictions of these sects. And therefore, from the time when Christians began to cultivate philosophical knowledge, the Gnostics were unable to entice so many from the Catholic ranks into their camp, and to found so many new associations, as in the preceding century, when they were assailed only with scriptural arguments.(1) *Lastly*, this light of human wisdom, though deceptive and dim, which some doctors wished to unite with the light of revelation, was useful in chasing from the church some opinions which the Christians had received from the Jewish schools, but which were thought by many to be of a holy and divine origin.

(1) Those who combated the Gnostics with scriptural arguments, were in general poor interpreters of the Bible, as we may see by *Irenæus*, and they [p. 720.] delighted more in allegories, than in the proper sense of scripture. And the Gnostics opposed allegories to allegories; for the greater part of them hunted immoderately after mysteries and recondite senses in the sacred books. But which party expounded scripture most correctly, it is hard to say, as neither of them adopted any fixed rules, but merely followed their fancy. Besides, the Gnostics had many other modes of evasion, so long as they were assailed only on scriptural grounds.

§ XXXVIII. **Chiliasm vanquished.** Among the Jewish opinions, to which, in this age, Philosophy proved detrimental, the most distinguished was that of the reign of Christ on earth, a thousand years, with the saints restored to their bodies. This opinion, I believe, was introduced into the church near the commencement of the Christian commonwealth. And down to the times of *Origen,* all the teachers who were so disposed, openly professed and taught it; although there were some who either denied it, or at least called it in question. But *Origen* assailed it fiercely; for it was repugnant to his philosophy: and, by the system of biblical interpretation which he discovered, he gave a different turn to those texts of scripture on which the patrons of this doctrine most relied. The consequence was, that this error lost its influence with most Christians. But, a little past the middle of this century, *Nepos*, an Egyptian bishop, endeavored to revive it and give it currency, by an appropriate treatise, which he called a *Confutatio Allegoristarum*. This book was admired by many in the district of Arsinoë, and was thought to confirm the visible reign of Christ on earth, by the most solid arguments. Hence great commotions arose in that part of Egypt, and many congregations gladly resumed their expectation of the future millennium. But these commotions were quieted by *Dionysius*, the bishop of Alexandria, a pupil of *Origen*, and inheriting his preceptor's learning, as well as his mildness of disposition. In the first place, he held a discussion with one *Coracion*, the head and leader of the controversy, and with his followers; in which, by his admonitions, arguments, and exhortations, he induced them to give up the opinion they had derived from the treatise of *Nepos:* and afterwards, to stop up the fountain of the evil, he wrote a confutation of *Nepos*, in two books, entitled *de Promissionibus divinis.* In the second book of this work he very discreetly treated particularly on the authority of the *Apocalypse of St. John;* from which *Nepos* had derived the chief support of his opinion.(1)

(1) The controversy respecting the reign of Christ on the earth, which [p. 721.] originated from the book of the Egyptian bishop, *Nepos*, against those he called *Allegorists*,—all the writers on ecclesiastical history, narrate to us from *Eusebius*, (Hist. Eccl. L. vii. c. 24, &c. p. 271, &c.) and from *Gennadius* of Marseilles, (de Dogmat. Eccles. cap. lv. p. 32.) for these are the only fathers, who make formal mention of it. Nor is there any great deficiency in their account, so far as the controversy itself is concerned, and aside from the causes which produced it: and yet their statements appear to me rather jejune, and do not embrace every thing important to a correct understanding of the controversy. I will therefore add some things, which I deem worthy of being known.—The doctrine of a future reign of Christ on the earth, a thousand years, with the saints, was undoubtedly of *Jewish* origin; and it was brought into the church, along with other Jewish notions, by those Jews who embraced Christianity. All Jews have not held one opinion, as to the termination of the Messiah's reign; and yet many among them, even at the present day, limit it to a thousand years. Among both the ancients and the moderns, many have supposed, that *Cerinthus* first propagated this error among the Christians. Few, however, will readily agree with them, if they consider, that this sentiment was embraced by many,—e. g. *Irenaeus*, *Tertullian*, and others,—who abhorred *Cerinthus*, and accounted him a pest to christianity. Nor do I think *Eusebius* is to be trusted, when he tells us, (Hist. Eccl. L. iii. c. 39. p. 112.) that the expectation of a millennium, flowed down to the subsequent doctors, from *Papias*, a bishop of Jerusalem in the second century. For, as *Papias* was not the first excogitator of the opinion, but received it from others, as *Eusebius* himself concedes, it is clear, that at least some Christians before *Papias*, had embraced this opinion; and therefore, those after him who received it, may have learned it from those who lived before him. And *Irenæus* (contra Hæreses L. v. c. 33. p. 333.) cites *Papias*, not as being the author of this opinion, but as bearing his testimony to it. It is most probable, that several of the Jewish Christians, to produce some agreement between the Jewish doctrine of an earthly kingdom of the Messiah, and the christian doctrine of our Saviour's kingdom of heaven, and to combine the Jewish expectation with that of Christians,—conceived in their minds, and also taught, that there is a twofold kingdom of Christ, and a twofold expectation of his disciples: and many of the christian teachers either approved this

device, or tolerated it, as they did many others, in order to facilitate the transition of Jews to the christian community. We know, how much inclined men are to combine the ideas they have received from their ancestors, with those which they are compelled by evidence to admit; nor are we ignorant how much was conceded, in the first ages of the church, to the weakness of the Jews. But, however this may be, it is certain that in the second century, the opinion that Christ would reign a thousand years on the earth, was diffused over a great [p. 722.] part of christendom; and that the most eminent doctors favored it; and no controversy with them was moved by those who thought otherwise. *Tertullian* (contra Marcionem, L. iii. c. 24. p. 299. edit. Rigalt.) speaks of it as the common doctrine of the whole church. He says: Confitemur, (Mark; he speaks without limitation; not a particle, to intimate that the sect of the Montanists, to which he belonged, differed from other christians on this subject,)—confitemur, in terra nobis regnum repromissum, sed ante coelum, sed alio statu (Then inserting some remarks on the nature of this kingdom, he proceeds:) Hæc ratio regni terreni, post cujus mille annos, intra quam aetatem concluditur sanctorum resurrectio, et quæ sequuntur.—As we learn from *Jerome*, (Catal. Scriptor. Eccl. c. 18.) and from the passage of Tertullian just quoted, *Tertullian* had written a book expressly on the subject, entitled de Spe Fidelium: but the book is lost. He errs, however, in attributing to the *whole* church, an opinion which was held only by a large part of it. Yet this is certain, from *Justin Martyr*, (Dial. cum Tryph. p. 243. 247. edit. Jebbii,) and others, that *very many*, and they men of great influence, thought as he did; nor were they, on that account, taxed with corrupt doctrine. One *Caius*, indeed, a Roman presbyter, in a dispute with Proclus, (as we learn from *Eusebius*, Hist. Eccl. L. iii. c. 28. p. 100.) criminates Cerinthus, for holding out the expectation of a terrestrial kingdom of Christ, abounding in all sorts of pleasures; but his phraseology puts it beyond controversy, that he censured, not so much that reign of Christ, as the corporeal pleasures in it which he supposed, truly or falsely, Cerinthus had promised. For there were, in that age, *two* opinions respecting this kingdom of Christ. Some supposed, that in it holy men would live in the same manner as men now do, and would freely indulge in all the pleasures which can be derived from the senses. Others, although they did not exclude all the sensual delights from that new kingdom of Christ, (which, for various reasons, was impossible,) yet they supposed its chief happiness to consist in the joys and pleasures of the mind. Says *Tertullian*, (in the passage before cited, p. 499.): Hanc novam civitatem dicimus excipiendis resurrectione sanctis et refovendis omnium *bonorum utique spiritualium copiâ* in compensationem eorum, quæ in saeculo vel despeximus, vel amisimus, a Deo prospectam. Si quidem et justum et Deo dignum, illic quoque exultare famulos ejus, ubi sunt et afflicti in nomine ipsius. Whoever reads this passage carefully, will clearly perceive, that the patrons of this opinion expected sensual enjoyments in that kingdom of Christ; for it says, *The saints will be refreshed*, in compensation for the pleasures, which in their former life they renounced for Christ's sake. But from these pleasures they excluded all lusts, and promised a higher delight in *spiritual* things. [p. 723.] Those who were addicted to the *former* opinion, were again divided into *two* classes, as we shall soon see; but both were considered as doing a great injury to Christ, and to the promises he has left us. On the other hand, the followers of the latter and more moderate opinion, were supposed to hold nothing very unbecoming in a Christian, and were accounted as brethren.

But in the *third* century, the reputation of this more moderate doctrine declined; and first in Egypt, through the influence especially of *Origen;* and afterwards in the other portions of the christian world, in which the opinions of Origen gradually acquired a high reputation. And yet it could not be exterminated in a moment; it still had, here and there, some respectable advocates. *Origen,* in various passages of his works still extant, censures and rebukes, vehemently, those who anticipated an earthly kingdom of Christ, and sensual pleasures in it. And in the eleventh chapter of the second Book of his work de Principiis, (Opp. tom. i. p. 104, &c.) he assails them expressly, both with philosophical arguments, and the exegetical principles which he had adopted. In this chapter, which is entitled *Of the Promises,* although he appears to assail only those patrons of a millennial kingdom, who promised themselves in it nuptials, festivities, offices, honors, palaces, &c. or, to use his own language, Secundum vitæ hujus conversationem per omnia similia fore putabant omnia quæ de repromissionibus expectantur, id est, ut iterum sit hoc, quod est; yet, by opposing his own doctrine concerning the divine Promises to theirs, he refutes also those who expressed themselves more refinedly and wisely, respecting the joys and felicities of this kingdom. For he utterly deprives souls, separated from the body, of all hope of receiving pleasure from the senses; destroys all expectation of any kingdom, to be established by Christ on this earth; and maintains, that God has promised nothing to souls, except an increase of knowledge, both natural and revealed. In this discussion, there are some things of which even modern philosophers need not be ashamed. For he infers from the boundless desire of knowledge natural to the mind, that God will satisfy that desire: and therefore, that the soul, if duly prepared in this life, and purified from its defilements, will, after its retirement from the body, mount on high, rove among the celestial orbs, discern clearly and manifestly, things which it only knew obscurely, while it resided in the body and was clogged by the senses, and will also comprehend the grounds and reasons of all the divine plans and operations.—But I am diverging from my subject.—*Origen* was more decidedly opposed to this doctrine of an earthly kingdom of Christ, affording pleasures, than others were, partly in consequence of the philosophy he embraced, and partly by the system of biblical interpretation which he exclusively approved. Agreeably to the system of philosophy which he adopted, human bodies are the penitentiaries of souls, which are doing penance for the sins they com- [p. 724.] mitted in a former life; the senses, and the use of the senses by the soul, are a great impediment to the celestial and rational soul: they prevent it from discerning and fully knowing the truth; sensitive pleasures and delights, even such as are lawful, allure to evil and poison the soul; the man, therefore, who is desirous of salvation, should withdraw his attention from the senses and from pleasures, and should nourish his soul with the contemplation of things altogether foreign from the senses; the comforts and conveniences of life should be avoided; and the body should be treated with rigor, and be divested of its natural energies. A man imbued with such sentiments, could by no means believe, that Christ will set up a kingdom on earth, in which his friends, clothed with new bodies, will enjoy the pleasures of sense. On the other hand, *Origen* was obliged to modify and debase the christian doctrine of the future resurrection of our bodies and of the reunion of our souls to them, so that it should contain nothing opposed to his opinion of the nature of a rational soul: and that he did so, is very well known.—And then, how much the method of interpreting the bible, which he prescribed, might dissuade him from admitting this millennial kingdom, the copious remarks already made upon it, will make manifest. For he wished to have the literal and obvious sense of the words disregarded, and an arcane sense, lying concealed in the invelop of the words, to be sought for. But the advocates of an earthly kingdom of Christ, rested their cause solely on the natural and proper sense of certain expressions in the bible; e. g. Matth. v. 6. and xxvi. 29. Luke xix. 17. and other similar passages, named by *Irenæus* and *Origen*. His mind, therefore, could not help revolting from their opinion; and he accounted it a great reproach to them, that they neglected what he considered the marrow of the sacred books, and dwelt only upon their exterior. He says, (de Principiis, L. ii. c. 11. § 2. p. 104.): Quidam laborem quodammodo intelligentiæ recusantes, et superficiem quandam legis literæ consectantes - - Apostoli Pauli de resurrectione corporis spiritali (Mark this language,) sententiam non sequentes. And having expatiated much on this censure, he closes with the following sentence: Hoc ita sentiunt, qui Christo quidem credentes, Judaico autem quodam sensu scripturas divinas intelligentes, nihil ex his dignum divinis pollicitationibus præsumpserunt. See also, what he says in his xviith tome on Matth. (Opp. tom. iii. p. 826. &c. of the new edit.) where he reckons it a great excellence of *Tropollogy*, (such is his term for the allegorical mode of interpretation,) that the defenders of a millennial kingdom cannot be confuted in any other manner. In the *Prologue* to his Commentary on the Canticles, (Opp. tom. iii. p. 28.) he promises a formal discussion, in another place, with such as anticipate sensual pleasures in a kingdom [p. 725.] of Christ: and perhaps he fulfilled his promise. Simpliciores quidam nescientes distinguere ac secernere, quæ sint quæ in scripturis divinis interiori homini, quæ vero exteriori deputanda sint, vocabulorum similitudinis falsi ad ineptas quasdam fabulas et figmenta inania se contulerint: ut etiam post resurrectionem cibis corporalibus utendum crederent. - - Sed de his alias videbimus. This bitter and censorious language shows, how odious this sect was to *Origen*.

The opinion which *Origen* resisted with so much resolution, *Nepos*, a bishop of some unascertained city in Egypt, endeavored to restore to its former credit, by a work written in defence of it, which he intitled ἔλεγχον Ἀλληγοριστῶν λόγον, *Confutationem Allegoristarum*. The opposers of this kingdom of Christ, he called *Allegorists;* because they maintained that the texts of scripture, on which the friends of the doctrine rested its defence, were *allegories* or mere metaphors. This appellation seems to have been given them in contempt by their antagonists, as early as the times of *Irenæus*. See his work (contra. Hæres. L. v. c. 35, p. 335.) Yet I can scarcely doubt, that *Nepos* had especially before his mind *Origen* and his disciples; who were spoken against by many on account of their excessive love of allegories, and who, by their principles of interpretation, pressed very hard upon the friends of a millennial kingdom. But *Nepos* was not one of those extravagant *Chiliasts*, of whom *Cerinthus* is said to have been the leader, and who taught that all kinds of corporeal pleasures are to be expected in the approaching kingdom of Christ: but he agreed with the other and more moderate class, who, although they did not exclude all sensual pleasures from the kingdom of Christ, yet circumscribed them within very narrow limits. For this we have the testimony of *Gennadius* of Marseilles; (de Eccles. Dogmatibus, cap. lv. p. 32,) who, while he leaves the doctrine of Nepos in much obscurity, yet says enough to show, that Nepos did not belong to the company of the Cerinthians. And his antagonist *Dionysius*, makes him to have been an estimable man, and among other commendable acts, ascribes to him the composition of very beautiful hymns. *Gennadius* says: In divinis promissionibus, nihil terrenum vel transitorium expectemus, sicut Melitani sperant. Non nuptiarum copulam, sicut Cerinthus et Marcion delirant. Non quod ad cibum vel ad potum pertinet, sicut Papia auctore, Irenæus et Tertullianus et Lactantius acquiescunt. Neque post mille annos (I suspect here is a corrupt reading, and that the word POST before *mille*, should be omitted. For Nepos did not teach that Christ's kingdom was to *commence* after a thousand years, but that it was to *continue* a thousand years) post resurrectionem regnum Christi in terra futurum, et sanctos cum illo in deliciis regnaturos speremus, sicut Nepos docuit, qui primam justorum resurrectionem et secundam impiorum confinxit. This passage is well framed for discriminating the various sects of the so called *Millenarians* of the early ages. For *Gennadius* enumerates *four* opinions among [p. 726.] them. The *first* is that of the *Melitani*, which is here obscurely stated, and, so far as I know, is not explained by any of the ancients. The *second* is that of Cerinthus and Marcion, who promised men pleasures of every kind, and especially those arising from the conjunction of the sexes, and therefore allowed a place for nuptials in the new Jerusalem. The *third* class was a little more decent. It included *Papias*, *Irenæus*, and others. These were indeed ashamed to admit of marriages in that kingdom; yet they did not hesitate to allow, that its citizens would enjoy the pleasures of eating and drinking. But the food admitted by them, was not to be like ours, gross, oppressive, and hard of digestion, but of a higher character, more excellent, and more subtile. Hence, it appears also, that the *bodies* they assigned to the just when recalled to life, would be more excellent, more sprightly, and more etherial than ours. The *fourth* opinion was that of *Nepos*, who taught in general, that *the saints will reign in delights*. The nature of these *delights* Gennadius does not explain. But as he distinctly represents Nepos as differing from all those before named, it is clear, that he did not include connubial pleasures, nor those of feasting and carousing, among the delights of the citizens of Christ. He doubtless conceded to them very splendid, convenient, and agreeable mansions, serene and pleasant skies, the delights of the eye, the ear, the smell, and perhaps also some new and etherial kind of aliment, suitable for bodies entirely different from ours and possessing almost the nature of spirits. But the greatest part of their happiness was to consist in mental pleasures, in continual intercourse with perfectly holy minds, in the contemplation of the providence and works of God, in their daily advance in the knowledge of divine and human things, in the exercise of the purest love, and in the joy arising from an increase of knowledge and intelligence.—The book, in which *Nepos* set forth his opinions, was admired especially by one *Coracion*, a presbyter doubtless in the province of Arsinoë, and also by many other citizens of that province. I suppose it was written in an eloquent and pleasing style, and on that account, more than from the force of its reasoning, it charmed the minds of the incautious. For as *Dionysius* (cited by Eusebius) tells us, *Nepos* was an elegant poet, and had composed very beautiful hymns, which were sung in all the churches of Egypt. And I therefore have no doubt, his work was written in a flowery style, such as poets usually adopt. That *Coracion* was a presbyter of some village in the province of Arsinoë, appears to me evident from the language used by *Dionysius* (in Eusebius p. 272.) For he says, that when he wished to confute publicly the opinion of *Nepos*, *he called together the presbyters and teachers who taught in single villages.* From this it appears, that no one of the *bishops* embraced the opinion of *Nepos*; nor did the doctrine find adherents in the cities, but only in the villages and hamlets. He [p. 727.] also informs us, that *Coracion*, when convinced of his error, promised no more *to preach* (διδάσκειν) that doctrine to the people. He therefore sustained the office of a preacher and presbyter in some village. But the opinion so highly approved by *Coracion* and many other, though it was quite moderate, and differed much from the fictions of the grosser Chiliasts, could by no means find approbation with *Dionysius*, who, as abundantly appears, was much attached to the principles of *Origen*. For, that souls once happily released from their prisons, should again become united to bodies possessing sensations and appetites, and susceptible of sensual pleasures, and should, during a thousand years, use the perishable good things of this life and the allurements to all evil, was wholly repugnant to the precepts taught by Origen to his followers. Therefore, first, in a public discussion of three days continuance, in the very province where the error prevailed, *Dionysius* confuted the arguments of *Nepos*; and then also, in two written tracts, he demonstrated that all the promises of Christ's kingdom had reference to the soul and to the celestial world. In the second tract he labored, not indeed to destroy, but to diminish, the credit of those divine visions of *St. John*, from which *Nepos* had drawn his principal arguments; by contending that the book called the *Apocalypse* was not the work of *St. John* the Apostle, but of some other person of the same name; a holy man, indeed, and one divinely inspired, yet inferior to an Apostle. This discussion respecting the Apocalypse of *St. John*, a part of which is preserved by Eusebius, contains several things both interesting and useful to be known: not the least of which is this, that *Dionysius* evidently supposed, there were different degrees of what is called divine inspiration; and that greater light and power were divinely imparted to the Apostles when they wrote, than to other writers who were influenced by the holy Spirit, but who had not the honor to be Apostles. For in the close of his discourse he tells us, that *St. John*, through the divine munificence, manifestly received not only the *gift of knowledge*, but also that of *utterance* or *eloquence.* Τὸ χάρισμα τῆς γνώσεως, καὶ τῆς φράσεως. But the writer of the Apocalypse, he thinks, received indeed from God γνῶσιν and προφητείαν, *the gift of knowledge and prophecy,* but not that τῆς φράσεως, or that *of utterance and eloquence.* Therefore his inspiration was less perfect than that of *John* and the other Apostles. What consequences may be drawn from this doctrine, I need not state. But it is very probable, that *Dionysius* supposed, the doctrines of religion can be fully proved only from the writings of *Apostles*, to whom, as he supposed, God granted *complete inspiration*, and not from the writings of those, to whom was given less full inspiration, or inspiration inferior to the *Apostolical.* For unless he supposed so, the object of his elaborate discussion respecting the author of the Apocalypse, cannot be discovered.—Perhaps the remark is worth adding, that it appears from the account *Dionysius* gives of his [p. 728.] conference with the followers of Nepos, that he pursued with them the Socratic and Platonic mode of discussion, that by questions and answers: which shows in what school he had been trained.

§ XXXIX. **Rise of Manichaeism.** Amid these efforts of the more sagacious Christian doctors, by means of philosophy, to arrest the progress of the Gnostic sects, and to purge Christianity from Jewish defilements, a little past the middle of the century, a new pest, worse than all that preceded, invaded the church from Persia; and, although the greatest and wisest men withstood it, both in oral discussion and in books, yet they could not prevent its spreading with surprising rapidity, almost throughout Christendom, and captivating a vast multitude of persons of moderate talents and judgment. Manes, a man of uncommon genius, eloquence, and boldness, and richly endowed with all the qualities which can easily move and inflame the popular mind,—either misled by some mental disease, or actuated by the love of fame, devised a new system of religion, which was a strange compound of the ancient Persian philosophy and Christianity; and boldly urged it upon the people, as being divinely communicated to men. The man himself experienced very adverse fortune, and died a miserable death; but the way of salvation which he proposed, though full of monstrous ideas and puerile conceptions, and in no respect superior to the Gnostic fables, and more absurd than most of them, obtained a wider circulation than any of the sects of the preceding times. Nor will this be strange to a person understanding its character. For, if we regard its doctrines, they are all popular, and explain whatever is abstruse and difficult of comprehension, in the manner best suited to vulgar apprehension; and if we regard its moral precepts, they are gloomy, and impress the beholder with a great show of sanctity, self-denial, and contempt for worldly things. Such systems of religion, though void of solidity, yet, through the weakness of human nature, generally find many friends and followers.(1)

(1) Of all the sects in the first ages of the church, none is more notorious, none was more difficult to be subdued and put down, none had a greater number of friends, than that founded by Manes; a prodigy of a man, and venerable [p. 729.] in a degree, even in the frenzy by which he was actuated. There is much similarity between him and *Mohammed;* for the former, like the latter, boasted of divine visions, proclaimed himself divinely commissioned to reform the corrupted religion of the Christians, and restore it to its original perfection; showed a book, which he falsely stated was dictated to him by God, and sought to obtrude it upon mankind; and finally, has left the succeeding ages in doubt, whether he should be classed among the delirious and fanatical, or among the artful impostors.—The number of the ancient documents, from which the history and the doctrines of *Manes* may be learned, is not inconsiderable. For, not to mention the well-known authors who wrote avowedly on the sects of the early times, namely, *Epiphanius, Augustine, Eusebius, Theodoret, Damascenus,* and *Philaster;* there are extant some of the writings of *Manes* himself, and his disciples, from which the opinions of the sect may be illustrated, and the false expositions of them be corrected. We have a large part of a tract of *Manes,* in a Latin translation from the original, whether Greek or Syriac, entitled *Epistola Fundamenti;* contained in a work of *Augustine,* in confutation of it. We have a small part of his *Sermo de Fide,* in *Epiphanius,* (Hæres. lxvi. 14. tom. i. p. 630.) We have his *Epistola ad Marcellum;* (in the *Archelai* Acta cum Manete, p. 6. edit. Zaccagnii.) We have some fragments of his Epistle to a certain woman, called *Menoch;* preserved by *Augustine* in his imperfect work adversus Julianum Pelagianum. We have, lastly, some fragments of his Epistles, extracted from a manuscript in the Jesuits' College at Paris, and published by Jo. Alb. *Fabricius,* (in his Bibliotheca Graeca, vol. v. p. 284.) In the next place, there are extant the *Acta disputationis Archelai, episcopi Mesopotamiæ, cum Manete,* first published by Laur. Alex. *Zaccagnius,* (in his Collectanea Monumentor. veteris Ecclesiæ Gr. et Latinæ, Rome, 1698, 4to.) and re-published by Jo. Alb. *Fabricius,* (in the second vol. of the Opera *Hippolyti.*) This is a very ancient work, and was known among Christians in the *fourth* century; as is manifest from *Cyril* of Jerusalem, and from *Epiphanius.* The credibility and authority of this tract are, indeed, learnedly impugned by Isaac de *Beausobre,* in his History of Manichæism, (vol. i. c. 12, 13. p. 129.) who thinks it a fable, composed by some Greek scribbler of the fourth century, about the year 330, and derived partly from hearsay, true or false, and partly from the ingenuity of the writer; and intended to exhibit the base character of the Manichæan errors. And he shows, plainly enough, that these acts contain some things, of the truth of which there is good reason to doubt. But, I think, he has not given evidence, that no such discussion ever occurred between Archelaus and Manes. This certainly cannot be legitimately inferred, from some few historical errors admitted, or

seeming to be admitted, by the writer; nor from the silence of some among the ancients and moderns respecting these Acts. Yet no better arguments [p. 730.] are offered by this very learned man, who possessed genius of a high order, but was too ready to question the credibility of the ancient Christian writers, and too often relied upon his own conjectures. But, be this as it may, these *Acts* are certainly of high antiquity; and as the depreciator will not deny, they contain many things, either extremely probable, or having the appearance of truth.—We have, moreover, at this day, a book of *Faustus*, a Manichæan bishop in Africa, in which he explains the doctrines of his sect, and defends them with all the eloquence and energy he possessed. This entire book, *Augustine* has very laudibly inserted in his confutation of it. To this work of *Faustus*, should be added two public disputes of *Augustine* with two Manichæan priests, *Felix* and *Fortunatus;* in both of which, the priests zealously plead the cause of their church, stating, at the same time, their sentiments.—Lastly, some of the early opposers of *Manes*, (of whom *Fabricius* has given a long list, in his Bibliotheca Græca, vol. v. p. 287.) have come down to us; and no competent and honest judge will accuse them of bad faith, in stating the opinions of the man they opposed, or of inability to confute those opinions. Preëminent among them is *Augustine*, the great doctor of the African church; whose writings against the Manichæans, seem entitled to more consideration than those of others on the same side, because he was for ten years, or from the nineteenth to the twenty-eighth year of his life, a member of the Manichæan community, and had imbibed all the principles of that sect. The learned *Beausobre*, just mentioned, objects, indeed, and denies that Augustine is one from whom the doctrines of the Manichæans can be ascertained with correctness; and he seeks to confirm this decision by examples. Nor is he wholly wrong; for it must be acknowledged, that *Augustine* sometimes deduces consequences from the language and opinions of the Manichæans, which they, his ancient associates, rejected; which is a common thing with all polemics. I will also willingly admit, that he slightly modifies some opinions of his adversaries, in order to assail them with more effect. And yet I deliberately affirm, after examining well the subject, that in most things, one who wishes to understand the mysteries of Manichæism, may follow *Augustine* without fear of being misled. Nor will the minor errors into which Augustine sometimes falls, prove injurious, since he quotes the very words of *Manes* and Manichæans, from which may be learned, without difficulty, whether he made a mistake or not.—Next to *Augustine*, among the antagonists of Manichæism who have escaped the ravages of time, the most worthy of notice is Titus, bishop of Bostra, in Phenicia, whose Libri tres contra Manichæos, together with the Argument of the fourth Book, (first published only in Latin,) are now extant, Greek and Latin, in the Lectiones antiquæ of [p. 731.] Henry *Canisius*, as re-published by Ja. *Basnage*, (tom. i. p. 156, &c.) This work is carefully and accurately written; although it does not embrace the whole system of *Manes*, but only a very material part of it, drawn from his book *de Mysteriis*. In the same Lectiones antiquæ, (tom. i. p. 197.) there is extant, Greek and Latin, the Liber contra Manichæos of *Didymus* of Alexandria; but it is brief, and does not adequately explain the views of the Manichæans.

More to be recommended, is the λόγος πρὸς τὰς Μανιχαίου δόξας, or Liber contra Manichæi opiniones, of *Alexander*, a philosopher of Lycopolis; published, Greek and Lat. by Francis *Combefis*, (in his Auctarium novissimum Bibliothecæ Patr. tom. ii. p. 260.) But it requires a sagacious reader, and one not ignorant of the new Platonic philosophy, to which the author was addicted, and the principles of which are made the basis of the argumentation. *Alexander* also passes over, or but slightly touches, many points very necessary to be known, in order to form a correct judgment of the controversy. Of other writers, inferior to these, and affording little aid to the investigator, I need not give account.—From the documents above described, yet without disregarding those which incidentally speak of the Manichæan doctrines, I will present to the view of my readers a brief, but faithful digest of the Manichæan system, methodically arranged, taking great care to state nothing as true, which is dubious and uncertain.

A catalogue of modern writers, concerning the Manichæans, is given by Jo. Alb. *Fabricius*, (in his Bibliotheca Græca, vol. v. p. 296.) but the best and most elaborate of them all, *Fabricius* could not mention, because his work was not then published. That writer is Isaac de *Beausobre*, a man of superior genius and of widely extended knowledge; whose *History of Manes and Manichæism*, written in French, was published at Amsterdam, 1734 and 1739, in two vols. 4to. This work will do honor to the author's name, in all future ages, wherever letters, genius, learning, and all good arts shall be held in estimation; for it admirably elucidates many points of Christian antiquities, and contributes not a little to a correct knowledge of the doctrines held by those who, in the first ages of Christianity, receded from the general church and formed separate communities. And yet, as in all human composition, so in this work of diversified learning and of vast labor, there are some things, which an impartial man, whose only aim is truth, could wish were otherwise. And first, in this history of Manes and of Manichæism, there are many things which do not relate to the subject. For the very learned author, who had read much, heard much, and treasured up much, upon every favorable occasion deviates from his subject, and pours forth abundance of matter, not at all necessary to our having a full knowledge of Manes and his followers. These frequent and long *digressions*, though all of them contain useful matter, often embarrass the reader, and may cause [p. 732.] him sometimes to misapprehend the author's meaning. For when things in some way connected, but in other respects wholly unlike, are associated and commingled, confusion may arise prejudical to the truth. Still, this superabundance, as it has its utility, we can the more easily overlook in this extraordinary man. But it is a matter of greater moment, that the author strains every nerve of his ingenuity, to make nearly all the heretics of the early ages, and especially the Manichæans, appear to be more wise, more holy, more excellent, than they are commonly held to be. In this matter, as may be easily shown, this excellent man is first carried too far by a kind of ill-will towards the doctors of the ancient church; and then, again, he is inconsistent with himself. For, frequently, when too much evidence presses upon him, he acknowledges, that among the heretics of the first ages there were men delirious and foolish; and that *Manes* himself, whom he favors the most, was a splendid trifler, and either aimed to beguile and deceive others, or was himself deceived by some vagary of his own mind: yet, at other times, he maintains that the very persons, whom he had before censured, were real philosophers, and not weak men; and he not only defends and vindicates *Manes*, but actually honors him, not merely with the splendid appellation of a *philosopher*, but of a philosopher *who reasons well*. Thus this erudite man fluctuates, and is borne in opposite directions, being urged on the one side by regard for truth, and on the other, by his partiality for the heretics, especially for *Manes*. And in order the more easily to defend Manes and the heretics generally, he either tacitly or expressly assumes as facts, some things which those who differ from him will not readily admit. Among these assumptions, the principal one is, that all the ancient doctors of the church, either from ignorance or from malice, calumniate the heretics, and misrepresent their sentiments. This is easily said; but it is far more difficult to prove it, than they imagine, who in our age adopt it in treating of the history of the heretics: and the number of such is well known to be great. Yet, relying on this maxim, this learned man, whenever he finds anything in favor of Manes or the other heretics, which seems not to accord with the decisions of his adversaries, confidently embraces it, as a thing not to be questioned at all, and applies it to overthrow the uniform statements of many other witnesses. And in such cases I never discover any want of learning and ingenuity, but I often see a deficiency of caution and fairness.—There is another of this learned man's rules, which is very dubious. It is, that whenever any doctrine attributed to the heretics contains things absurd, silly, futile, or contrary to common sense, then we must suppose that doctrine falsely attributed to those heretics. It is well, however, that the learned man himself does not always follow this rule; for he is sometimes compelled, reluctantly, to acknowledge, that Manes and others embraced not a few opinions wholly at variance with every appearance of rationality, the dreams of the delirious, rather than the judgments of men in their right minds. And yet he often resorts to that rule, although it is manifest that nothing could be more fallacious; and there are numberless examples of persons, not [p. 733.] wholly bereft of reason, yet most shamefully violating the first principles of reason, and debasing religion with the most silly fictions.—I will not mention other things, which might reasonably be censured, in a book otherwise most beautiful; things, however, which ought to be so censured, as not to detract from the great merits and reputation of the author.

§ XL. **The Life and Labors of Manes.** Respecting the life and labors of MANES, there is great disagreement between the Greek and the Oriental writers; and as this disagreement can in no way be reconciled, and both seem to have blended the true and the false, beyond the possibility of a separation at this late day, all that remains for us to do, is to state what they unitedly teach, and leave the rest to be discussed by the curious.(1) The things in which they all agree, are substantially as follows: MANES, or

MANICHÆUS, for he is called by both names, was a native of Persia, a man of a venerable aspect, of an exceedingly fecund genius, was educated in the schools of the Magi, and was master of all the arts and learning, which the Persians of those times considered as constituting human wisdom. Having become acquainted with the books of the Christians, and perceiving that the religion they contained agreed, in some respects, with his philosophy, but disagreed with it in other respects, he formed the purpose of combining them, correcting and enlarging the one by the other, and then of inculcating on mankind a new system of religion, compounded of the two. Adopting this plan, he first decided that *Jesus Christ* left his statement of the way of salvation imperfect; and in the next place, he ventured to declare himself to be either a divinely taught Apostle of Jesus Christ, or rather that very *Paraclete*, or Comforter, whom the retiring Saviour promised to his disciples.(²) With what sincerity he assumed such a character, it is not easy to say. Some tell us, that being by nature proud, excessively arrogant, and vain, his heated mind became deranged. Yet his insanity was not such as to prevent his digesting his system very well, and distinctly seeing [p. 734.] how it could be assailed, and how defended. Among other proofs of this, is the fact that he either wholly rejected, or essentially altered, whatever he found in the Christian scriptures apparently contrary to his doctrines and purposes; and in place of the discarded passages, he substituted others, especially such as he wished to have considered as written by him under a divine inspiration.(³)—The king of Persia, for some cause not ascertained, cast him into prison. Escaping from confinement, and calling to his aid twelve friends or Apostles, in imitation of Christ, he spread the religion he had devised, over a great part of Persia, persuading many to embrace it; and he sent out the most eloquent of his disciples into the adjacent countries, who were also successful. In the midst of these enterprises, by the command of the king of Persia, he was seized by soldiers and put to death. This was probably in the year 278, or a little later. As to the mode of his death, writers are not agreed. That he was put to death, is very certain. The memorial of it, the Manichæans annually celebrated in the month of March, by a festal day, which they called *Bema*.(⁴) This sad fate of the man strengthened his adherents, more than it terrified them. For such of them as had the most talent and eloquence, roamed over Syria, Persia, Egypt, Africa, and almost all countries of the civilized world, and everywhere converted many, by the gravity of their deportment, and by the rude simplicity of the religion they inculcated.

(1) The name of the man under consideration, was MANI; for so the Oriental writers call him, according to *Herbelot*. (Bibliotheca Orient. voce *Mani.*) Nor was this an uncommon name among the Persians. The Greek writers tell us, that he was at first called *Cubricus;* and that he dropped that, and assumed the name of *Manes. Beausobre* (tom. i. p. 67.) conjectures, that he was born in the city of *Carcoub*, and thence was called *Carcubius*, which became changed into *Cubricus.* There is nothing certain on this subject.—He is also called MANICHÆUS. According to *Augustine*, (de Hæres. c. 46. Opp. tom. viii. p. 10; and, contra Faustum, L. xix. c. 22. tom. viii. p. 231.) it was his disciples who gave him this name, in order to avoid a name which in Greek denotes *insanity.* For *Manes* (μάνης) in Greek, denotes a *mad* or *crazy man.* And therefore his enemies made his very name a reproach to him, and said: it was so ordered, in divine providence, that he should receive a name expressive of his insanity. To parry this weapon, of so little force, his adherents chose to name their master *Manichæus.*

All that the Greek and Latin writers state concerning him, with only [p. 735.] a few exceptions, is contained in the Contest of *Archelaus*, the bishop of Cascara, with *Manes*, first published by *Zaccagnius.*—These writers, however, deny that *Manes* was the author of the religion which he taught; and tell us that one *Scythianus*, a contemporary of the Apostles, who died in Judea, invented it, and committed it to writing in four Books. One of his disciples, named *Terebinthus*, who subsequently took the name of *Budda*, after the death of his preceptor, went to Assyria, and lived with a certain widow woman. He died a violent death: for, as he was praying on the roof of the house, an evil genius, by divine direction, precipitated him to the ground; which caused his death. The widow woman inherited the goods and the books of the unhappy man; and, with the money, she purchased a *boy* seven years old, whose name was *Cubricus;* and as he manifested fine native powers, she caused him to be instructed in the literature and arts of the Persians; and finally, at her death, five years after, she made him heir to all her fortune, including the books left by Terebinthus. *Cubricus*, after the death of his patroness, in order to efface all remembrance of his former servile condition, assumed the name of *Manes*, and devoted himself intensely to the study of the arts and sciences of the Persians, but especially to the understanding the books of Terebinthus. He was but twelve years old at the time he became his own master. When, from the books of Terebinthus, which he had always before him, he understood the whole system of *Terebinthus*, he not only embraced it himself, but also persuaded three others to embrace it, whose names were Thomas, Adda, and Hermas. When sixty years old, he translated the books of Terebinthus into the Persian language; adding, however, many silly and fabulous inventions of his own mind;

and therefore affixing his own name to the books, instead of that of the original author. After this, he sent out two of his disciples, one of them to Egypt, and the other to Scythia. About the same time, a son of the king of Persia became dangerously sick: and *Manes*, who had learned the medical art, went to the king, and promised to restore the child to health. But he could not conquer the disease; and the child died. The king therefore ordered the physician to be loaded with chains, and to be cast into prison. While he was a prisoner, *Manes* became acquainted with the Christian religion, of which he had before no knowledge. For his (two) disciples returning from their travels, told their master, that none resisted their teaching and exhortations so strenuously as the christians. Anxious, therefore, to acquaint himself with this subject, he directed his friends to procure for him the books of the christians. Having read them, and learning that Christ promised his followers to send them the *Paraclete*, he proclaimed himself to be that *Paraclete;* and he transferred into his own system, a portion of the christian religion, in an adulterated state. Then followed a new mission of his disciples into different countries, for the express purpose of [p. 736.] making proselytes. The king of Persia, on learning this new crime of *Manes*, purposed to kill him. But, by bribing his keepers, he escaped from prison, and concealed himself in a certain fortress called *Arabion.* Soon after, leaving this retreat, and taking with him his twelve Apostles or associates, he travelled over a part of Persia; and, among other efforts for the establishment of his sect, he held a public religious discussion with *Archelaus*, the prelate of Cascara. At last, the soldiers, whom the king commanded to pursue him, confined him in the fortress of Arabion: and the king ordered the unhappy man to be flayed, his skin to be stuffed and hung up before the city gate, and his body to be cast out and be food for the birds.—This story, *Beausobre* has illustrated in a long, copious, and very erudite Dissertation, introductory to his volume. But his chief aim is, to persuade us, that the greatest part of this narrative is a vile fable. And yet he adduces and inserts many things, which serve rather to protract and extend the discussion, than to confirm it; and which might be omitted, without any detriment to the cause espoused by the learned man.

We now proceed to the facts concerning this wonderful man, as stated by the Oriental writers, Persian, Syrian, and Arabian; which facts have been collected from various authors, by the well-informed Oriental scholars, Barthol. *Herbelot* (Bibliotheque Orientale, voce *Mani*, p. 548.) Thomas *Hyde*, (Historia Relig. veter. Persar. c. 21. p. 280.) Euseb. *Renaudot*, (Historia Patriarch. Alexandrinor. p. 42.) Edw. *Pocock*, (Specimen Hist. Arabum, p. 149, &c.) and a few others. These facts have been arranged in a certain order, and amplified with various observations, some more and some less necessary, by Ja. *Beausobre*, (Histoire de Manich. tome i. p. 155, &c.) They differ materially from the facts stated by the Greeks: and hence the question arises: Which statement is most worthy of credit? *Renaudot* (Hist. Patriarch. Alexandr. p. 48.) thinks the Greeks are the best authority: nor will this opinion meet strong opposition, from one who reflects, that the Greek authors are much more ancient than the Oriental; and that the latter, almost universally, are not distinguished for either accuracy, or method, or for their selection of facts, and moreover, that they delight in fables and marvellous stories. And yet *Beausobre* (p. 156.) deems the Oriental writers preferable to the Greeks; *first*, because the events occurred in their country; and *secondly*, because the facts which they state, are more according to nature (*plus naturelle*), than those stated by the Greeks. But I doubt whether there is so much strength in these two reasons, as the learned man supposed. For we know very well, that the Orientals recount very many occurrences in their country, which are exceedingly dubious and uncertain; as I could show by examples that are beyond all controversy, if it were necessary, and if this were a proper place. And, to say nothing of the superstition and habitual credulity of all the Oriental historians, it should be recollected, that it is only the *Persians*, and not like- [p. 737.] wise the Syrians and Arabians, who in this case can be said to relate occurrences in their own country.—Whether the things stated by the Greeks, or those stated by the Orientals, are in themselves the most probable, is a difficult question to determine; because the judgments of men, respecting the greater or less degree of probability, differ wonderfully. But I will not assume the functions of an arbiter in this controversy. Yet I think it proper to warn those who would assume those functions, that they should, in the very outset, determine which narrative of the Orientals is to be preferred to that of the Greeks. For, while the Greeks agree with each other very well, except only in some minute points, and perhaps all derived their information from one source; the Orientals differ exceedingly from each other, or do not all give the same account of the life, labors and death of Manes. This disagreement,—to speak plainly,—the learned *Beausobre* dissembles, and gives a history of Manes from the Oriental writers, in a manner that would lead the reader to believe, that all those writers accorded with each other, just as the Greeks do; and yet his history of Manes, which he calls that of the Orientals, and sets in opposition to that of the Greeks, is a tissue of various extracts taken from different writers. He states, for instance, that *Manes* was a presbyter among the Christians, before he formed his new religion; and he makes the statement, just as if all the Oriental writers testified to the fact. The thing stated is not incredible: and yet it is most certain, that no Oriental says it, except *Abulpharaius* only; who is indeed a respectable author, but a recent one, and far removed from the age of *Manes*, for he lived in the thirteenth century; he was, moreover, a Syrian, and not a Persian; and lastly, he was not exempt from all mistakes.—But let us hear what the Orientals can tell us about *Manes*.

In the first place, most of them agree that *Manes*, or rather *Mani*, (for that was his true name,) was a Magian by birth; and that he excelled in all the branches of learning, then held in estimation among the *Magi*. In particular, they tell us that he was very skilful in Music, Mathematics, Astronomy, Medicine, Geography, and finally in Painting; and the Persian *Condemir* tells us, that he ornamented his *Gospel* with admirable devices and imagery. All this is quite probable, nay, may be accounted nearly certain; for he was a man of exuberant genius, well fitted to acquire and to practise the arts in which the powers of genius and imagination predominate. The Greeks do not, indeed, expressly attribute to him all these acquisitions; yet they admit, in the general, that he was a very learned man; and, therefore, they do not in this matter contradict the Orientals. I can the most readily believe, what is reported of his ornamenting his *Ertung*, or *Gospel*, with beautiful imagery. For all the *Gnostic* systems of religion are of such a nature, as to be easily delineated, or [p. 738.] represented by drawings and colors in a picture; nay, they can be better understood from paintings, than from language and written books; and no one of them can be more easily delineated by the pencil, than the Manichæan; which consist almost wholly of fables or fictitious histories. And hence the Gnostic teachers, (as appears from the example of the *Ophites*, in *Origen* against *Celsus*,) were accustomed to put into the hands of the common people such pictorial systems of religion: that is, pictures, in which the principal topics of their religion were presented to the eye in diagrams, figures, and images. But what we are told of the exquisite skill of *Manes* in the above-named arts, must be understood and estimated, not according to our standard of excellence, but according to that of the Persians of that age. *Beausobre* seems not to have duly considered this; for he declares the man to have been, in general, an excellent Mathematician, Natural Philosopher, and Geographer. He might appear so to the Persians, but he was a small man, if compared with our Mathematicians, Philosophers, and Naturalists; nay, he was a rustic, and scarcely imbued with the rudiments of Mathematics, Geography, and Physical Science; and what is more, he embraced not a few errors, which even tyros among us can see through.

After embracing the Christian religion, *Manes* was made a priest, or presbyter, in the city *Ehwazi*, or in the province *Ahvas*, as *Herbelot* renders it. In this situation *he explained books, and disputed with Jews, with the Magi, and with Pagans.* Thus much, and no more, is transmitted by a single writer, *Gregory Abulpharaius*, (in his Historia Dynastarum, p. 82.) But the learned *Beausobre*, who is studious of honoring Manes all he can, not only relates the matter, as if it were supported by the united testimony of all the Oriental writers, but he adds to it several things supported by no authority. For he tells us,—I. That *Manes was learned in the scriptures; (Savant dans la Ecriture.)*—II. That he was very zealous in supporting the dignity and authority of christianity. (*Il avoit un grand zele pour la foi.*)—III. That these qualifications induced the Christians to raise him to a presbytership, *while but a youth*, and in a city of the first rank, (*une ville tres considerable.*)—IV. That in this station, he exhibited great proofs of zeal and virtue.—V. But that, at length, he apostatized from christianity; and, for this instance of bad faith, he was excluded from the communion of Christians.—I wonder how so great a man, one so acute and discriminating, one who severely censures and rebukes even the slight errors of great men, could boldly utter all this, when it has no authority whatever, but is drawn wholly from his own fancy. Surely! if another person had dared to do such a thing, this great man would have castigated him severely.

Manes,—it is uncertain on what occasion, or for what cause, went to the court of *Sapor*, the king of Persia, called *Shabour* by the Persians. And he so insinuated himself into the king's confidence, that he even drew him over to the religion he had devised. Emboldened by this success, he gathered [p. 739.] around him a number of disciples, and assailed publicly the ancient Persian religion, founded by Zoroaster. *Sapor*, either offended at this, or being prompted by the Magi and the priests, determined to put him to death. *Manes*, being informed of the design, fled into Turkestan. There he drew many to his party; and, among other things, (as Thos. *Hyde* states from one *Rustem*,) painted two Persian temples. Afterwards, finding a certain cave in which there was a fountain, he concealed himself in it during a year; having previously assured his disciples, that he should appear in a certain place after a year, and that in the meantime he should ascend to heaven. In that cave he composed his book, called by the Orientals *Azeng*, or *Arzenk*, i. e. a *Gospel;* and ornamented it with very beautiful pictures. At the end of the year, coming forth from the cave, he showed the book to his followers, as one which he received in heaven, and brought thence with him. These things are stated by a single Persian historian, *Condemir;* others know nothing of them. They are not incongruous with the genius of the man, but whether true or false, who can tell? In the meantime, Sapor, the king of Persia, died, and was succeeded by his son *Hormisdas*. On learning this, *Manes* returned from Turkestan to Persia, and presented to the new king his book, which he called divine and heavenly. *Hormisdas*, or *Hormouz*, not only received him kindly, but also embraced the religion contained in his book, and ordered a tower to be built for him, called *Dascarrah*, in which he might be safe from the plots of his enemies, who were very numerous. See *Herbelot's* Bibliotheque Orientale, (voce *Dascarrah*, p. 288. No authority is given.) This is the tower, as *Beausobre* conjectures, which the Greeks call *Arabion*. Those who may think this kindness of the king to *Manes* singular and strange, should consider that *Hormisdas*, previously, in the lifetime of his father, had favored *Manes* and his opinions. Nor is it supposable that, on merely hearing Manes speak, and seeing his book, he embraced his opinions. And here a conjecture arises, which, the more I consider it, the more probable it appears. I suspect, that what the Greeks tell us of the king's son's being consigned to the medical treatment of *Manes*, and dying in his hands, was an Oriental allegory, and was misunderstood by the Greeks. *Sapor* committed his son to the tuition of Manes, to be instructed in the precepts of his wisdom; but *Manes* seduced the prince from the religion of his ancestors, and initiated him in his new religion. This transaction, the Orientals, who delight in metaphors and allegories, wrapped up in similitudes, by comparing the ignorance of the prince with a disease, his instruction with the cure of the disease, and his defection from the religion of his ancestors with death; but the Greeks, [p. 740.] little accustomed to this species of discourse, supposed the things described to be real facts.—This prosperity of *Manes* was short. *Hormisdas* died at the end of two years; and his son *Varanes I.* whom the Persians call *Behram*, or *Baharam*, in the beginning of his reign, indeed, treated *Manes* with kindness; but soon his feelings were changed, and he determined to destroy him. He, therefore, allured *Manes* from the fortress in which he was concealed, under pretence of holding a discussion with the chiefs of the Magi, and then ordered him to be put to death, as a corrupter of religion. Some tell us he was cleaved asunder;

others, that he was crucified; and others, agreeing with the Greeks, that he was flayed. All, both Greeks and Orientals, agree that he was executed.—This short story, *Beausobre* has not only loaded with a mass of various observations, learned, indeed, but often having little connexion with the subject, but has also sometimes augmented, with conjectures wholly unsupported by any testimony.

(2.) *Manes* differed essentially from the other heretics. For they all professed to teach the religion which was inculcated by Jesus Christ publicly, or among his select friends; and they proved their doctrines by citations from the writings of his Apostles. But far otherwise *Manes;* as is put beyond doubt, by what he taught respecting himself. He acknowledged, that his religious system could not be proved, in all its parts, from the books left us by the Apostles: and he produced a new book, which, he said, was divinely dictated to him: and lastly, he maintained, that Christ set forth only a part of the knowledge of salvation; and left a part to be explained by the *Paraclete*, whom he promised to his followers. And he claimed to be himself that *Paraclete*, or that herald and expounder of divine truth, promised by Christ. How *Manes* and his disciples wished to have these subjects understood, must be explained accurately, and at some length; because both the ancients and the moderns are sometimes not uniform in their statements, and sometimes disagree with each other, respecting the character assumed by *Manes.* Nor has *Beausobre* brought forward all that is worth considering, although he says many things very learnedly, and demonstrates admirably the errors committed on this subject. (See his Histoire de Manichée, tome I. p. 252.) *Eusebius* (in his Historia Eccles. L. vii. c. 31, p. 283,) says: Manes *exhibited himself as Christ*, or *took the form of Christ* (Χριστὸν ἀυτὸν μορφόζεσθαι ἐπειρᾶτο.) And many repeat the same after him. The Orientals are more cautious, if *Herbelot* (Bibl. Orient. p. 549.) correctly expounds their meaning; namely, that he declared himself *another or second Christ or Messiah* (*un second Messie.*)—All these writers are undoubtedly mistaken. Nor have they any ground for their accusation, except in the number of associates whom *Manes* chose: for he took the same number of companions and friends as Christ took for his Apostles. The fallacy of such an [p. 741.] argument need not be pointed out. What the preceding writers expressly declare, *Augustine* only ventured to *suspect*, (contra Epistolam Manich. c. 8. Opp. tom. viii. p. 112;) Quid ergo aliud *suspicer*, nescio, nisi quia iste Manichæus, qui per Christi nomen ad imperitorum animos aditum quærit, pro Christo ipso se coli voluit? But he supports this conjecture by a very weak argument, not worth repeating and confuting.—Many others have told us, that *Manes* claimed to be the *Holy Spirit.* All these have a good excuse for making the mistake; and although in error, they do not deserve severe censure. For *Manes* did call himself the *Paraclete;* and all his disciples denominated him either simply the *Paracleti*, or the *Holy Spirit, the Paraclete:* nay, as *Augustine* repeatedly charges upon them, (in his work contra Faustum Manich.) they were accustomed to *swear by this Paraclete.* Now, when christians heard them take such oaths, without anything explanatory, and recollected that, in the scriptures, the Holy Spirit is called the *Paraclete*, and that no sane man swears by any other than God or some essence cognate with God;—who can wonder that they supposed the founder of this Manichæan sect arrogantly claimed to be the Holy Spirit? And those ancient doctors, who either said roundly, that *Manes* claimed to be the Holy Spirit, or else confessed, (as *Augustine* does, in his work contra Epistolam Manichæi, c. 17, and contra Faustum, Lib. xiii. and elsewhere,) that they did not *know*, what the Manichæans meant by applying this appellation to their master, whether they wished to indicate that *Manes* was himself the Holy Spirit, or only that the Holy Spirit resided in him ?—these writers, I say, in my judgment, committed no censurable offence. For, what rule of duty does he violate, who uses the very terms of a sect in stating their opinions, or who tells us, he does not know what meaning they affixed to their terms? They offend but slightly, who explain the appellation which *Manes* assumed, and either conjecture or report that the Manichæans supposed the Holy Spirit and Manes to be combined in one person. And the fault of this misrepresentation is chiefly chargeable on *Manes* and his followers, who, by obscure and ambiguous language, cause their meaning to be misunderstood. I see learned men of our day who endeavor to treat the history of christians more wisely than our fathers did, and become wonderfully copious, eloquent, and energetic, in exaggerating and castigating the errors, by which the ancient christian authors have marred their accounts of sects and heresies: but while they show themselves equitable towards heretics,—which is commendable,—they not unfrequently become unjust to the contenders against them, not reflecting that a great part, perhaps the greatest part, of the faults which deform the history of the early sects, originated from the obscurity, the ambiguity, and the foreign and unusual phraseology of the heretics themselves.—But let us pass on, and see what *Manes* [p. 742.] would have those think of him, whom he instructed.

In the first place, it is unquestionable that this Persian did not wish to be accounted *Christ* himself, but an *Apostle of Jesus Christ*, his Lord. For he commences that celebrated *Epistola Fundamenti*, against which *Augustine* wrote a Book, with these words: Manichæus Apostolus Jesu Christi providentiâ Dei Patris. Hæc sunt salubria verba de perenni et vivo fonte. (See *Augustine*, contra Epistolam Manich. c. 5. Opp. tom. viii. p. 111, and de Actis cum Felice Manichæo, L. I. p. 334, 335.) We have also the testimony of *Augustine*, (contra Epist. Manich. c. 6. p. 112, and contra Faustum, L. xiii. c. 4. p. 181.) that *Manes* assumed the same title, in all his Epistles.—But, as we shall soon see, *Manes* did not wish this title to be understood in its common and ordinary sense, when applied to himself, but in a sense much higher. For he placed himself far above the twelve Apostles of Christ, and proclaimed, that much greater wisdom was divinely imparted to him than to them. When, therefore, he styles himself an *Apostle*, he intended thereby that he was an extraordinary man, far superior to all the first Apostles, one whom Christ had sent to mankind, partly, to perfect his religion, and partly to free it from stains and corruptions.

In the next place, it is certain that *Manes* did not wish to be accounted the *Holy Spirit personally*; or to have his followers believe, that the entire Holy Spirit had descended into him, joined his person to him, and spoke and gave forth laws personally through him. They who attribute such insanity to *Manes* may be confuted by many proofs, and especially by the Manichæan doctrine concerning the Holy Spirit. Passing by all the arguments which have been adduced by *Beausobre*, we will demonstrate, solely from the Epistola Fundamenti of *Manes*, that he distinguished between the Holy Spirit and himself. For thus he speaks in that Epistle, (apud *Augustinum* de Actis cum Felice Manich. L. I. c. 16. p. 341.) Pax Dei invisibilis et veritatis notitia sit cum fratribus suis et carissimis, qui mandatis cœlestibus credunt pariter ac deserviunt: sed et dextera luminis tueatur et eripiat vos ab omni incursione maligna et a laqueo mundi: pietas vero *Spiritus Sancti* intima vestri pectoris adaperiat, ut ipsis oculis videatis animas vestras. Here *Manes* prays for, *first*, the peace of the supreme Deity, or the *Father*, and, *secondly*, for the aid and assistance of the *Son*. Because, by the *dextera luminis*, he means Christ, the Son of God. For, according to the Manichæan system, the *light* is God himself, the source of all light: whence, in Oriental phraseology, *dextera luminis* is *that*, by which the *light*, i. e. God, assists men, and manifests to them his kindness, his love, and his power; or that person who is nearest to God, and is the minister of his divine pleasure and govern- [p. 743.] ment. *Lastly*, he prays for the illumination of the *Holy Spirit*. For He it is, who must dispel the mental darkness, so that the *brethren might see their souls with their own eyes;* that is, that they might understand that in them was a *soul*, the offspring of eternal light, or of God; and that they might learn to distinguish it from the darkness, or from the body and the senses. Who does not readily see, on reading this passage, that Manes regarded the *Holy Spirit* as an essence cognate with God, and wholly different from himself? For he joins the Holy Spirit with the Son of God, and with the Father; and supposes his internal illumination to be necessary for men, to enable them to discover the truth and divine origin of his doctrines. A man could not so speak, who thought the Holy Spirit to be latent in himself, or that he was himself the Holy Spirit.

Although Manes did not wish to be considered as being the Holy Spirit, yet he declared himself to be that *Paraclete* whom the blessed Saviour, a little before his death, promised to his disciples. John xiv. 16 and xvi. 7, &c. This is apparently inconsistent with the previous statements. For how could a man, who dared not arrogate to himself the dignity and majesty of the Holy Spirit, and contented himself with the title of an *Apostle* of Christ,—how could he claim to be the *Paraclete* promised by Christ? But we shall soon see that these pretensions are easily reconcilable. I confess, indeed, that I once doubted whether it were true, that all the Greeks and Orientals really stated that *Manes* required men to believe him to be the *Paraclete*. Because, in the beginning of his Epistles, he called himself only an *Apostle of Jesus Christ*, and not the *Paraclete* I suspected that Manes probably thought more modestly of himself, and that the whole story of the mission of the *Paraclete* in the person of *Manes*, was, perhaps, got up by his disciples, who were eager to exalt their master, and to find evidence of his high dignity in the holy scriptures. For I said to myself, if *Manes* wished to be considered the *Paraclete*, why did he not assume that title in his Epistles? Why did he style himself only an *Apostle? Augustine* indeed (in his Liber contra Epist. Manichæi, c. 6. p. 112.) would convince us, that the astute and crafty man aimed tacitly to insinuate, even by the title *Apostle of Christ*, that he was the *Paraclete:* Quid hoc esse caussæ arbitramur, (viz. that he called himself an *Apostle of Christ*, and not of the *Paraclete*,) nisi quia illa superbia, mater omnium hæriticorum, impulit hominem, ut non missum se a Paracleto vellet videri, sed ita susceptum, ut ipse Paracletus diceretur. This indeed is not offering proof, but is indulging conjecture. Yet the same *Augustine*, in another manner, removed all doubt from my mind on this subject. For he clearly testifies, that *Manes* did refer the promise of the *Paraclete* to himself. He says, (ubi supra c. 7. p. 112.) Manichæus vester, sive missum, sive susceptum a Paracleto se affirmat. And a little after, (c. 8.) still more clearly: Spiritus sanctus nominatus non est, qui maxime debuit ab eo nominari, qui nobis Apostolatum suum *Paracleti promissione* commendat, ut evangelica auctoritate imperitos premat. These words merit careful attention. For it appears [p. 744.] from them, *first*, That Manes did not call himself the *Holy Spirit:* yet, *secondly*, That he *commended his Apostleship*, by applying to it *the promise of the Paraclete;* i. e. he would have the language of Christ concerning the Paraclete, to refer to *him*. From these declarations, I think it manifest, that the man distinguished the *Holy Spirit* from the *Paraclete*. For one who rejects the title of the Holy Spirit, yet calls himself the *Paraclete*, undoubtedly shows that he considers the *Holy Spirit* to be different from the *Paraclete*. This observation sheds great light on the subject; and it reveals the source of the error on this subject of the ancients. By the appellation *Paraclete* in the language of Christ, *Manes* supposed, was indicated, not the Holy Spirit personally, but *a man* whom Christ would send, *an Apostle of Jesus Christ*, as he expresses it; to whom the Holy Spirit (whose residence, he supposed, was in the air,) would communicate greater wisdom and illumination than to the first Apostles of Christ; whereby this *man* would be able to fill the blanks left by Christ in the science of salvation, and expunge the errors introduced by men. Perhaps, he confirmed this exposition by the language in John xvi. 15. *He shall not speak of himself; but whatsoever he shall hear, that shall he speak.* These words, considered by themselves, seem more applicable to a *man* taught by the Holy Spirit, than to a *divine* being or person. And previously to him, *Montanus*, who also called himself the Paraclete, and was so called by his followers, seems to have explained the term *Paraclete* in the promise of Christ, in the same manner. And it is certain that *Mohammed*, who, as before stated, in many points greatly resembled *Manes*, claimed nearly the same authority: and it is well known, that he wished to be accounted the *Paraclete*. And hence *Condemir*, the Persian historian, according to *Herbelot*, (Bibliotheque Orientale p. 549,) understanding the fact, was indignant that *Manes* should apply to himself Christ's language respecting the Paraclete, which, in his judgment, related to *Mohammed*. The disciples of *Manes*, to manifest this opinion of their master concerning the Paraclete, although they commonly call him simply *the Paraclete*, yet often add the words *Holy Spirit*, and call Manes *the Holy Spirit the Paraclete*. This we learn from *Augustine*, in his Disputatio cum Felice Manichæo, and in other places. The reason they assign for this double appellation, *Augustine*, (who is not always a favorable expositor for them,) has stated in his Book contra Epistolam Manichæi, (c. 8. p. 112.): Quod quum a vobis quæritur? (i. e. when you are asked, Why did *Manes* not call himself the Holy Spirit, but an Apostle of Jesus Christ?) respondetis, utique Manichæo Apostolo nominato, Spiritum sanctum Paracletum nominari, quia in ipso venire dignatus est. From this language it is manifest, *first:* That the Manichæans, in order to define the meaning of the title of *Paraclete*, with which they honored their master, called him also the *Holy Spirit the Paraclete.* And *secondly:* That they maintained, that this title had the same [p. 745.] force and meaning, with the title of *Apostle of Jesus Christ*, which he placed at the head of his Epistles. And hence, *thirdly:* According to the opinion of Manes and his disciples, the *Paraclete* is *a man* sent by Christ, in whom pre-eminently the *Holy Spirit* manifests his power and wisdom; or, in their own phraseology, *in whom the Holy Spirit* (venit) *comes to men.*—The Manichæan presbyter *Felix*, in his Discussion with Augustine, seems to modify or change this idea. For, although he calls his master *the Holy Spirit the Paraclete*, yet he gives the same appellation to the *Holy Spirit* itself; and he affirms, (p. 338.) that the Holy Spirit the Paraclete, among other things, *came* also *in St. Paul.* But this man, whom *Augustine* (Retractat. L. II. c. 8.) pronounces *ineruditum liberalibus litteris*,—was timid; and he acknowledges, that partly from fear of Augustine, whose authority he well knew, and partly from the terror of the imperial laws against the Manichæans, he did not bring out the whole system of his sect, but at times concealed some things, which would be particularly offensive to christians; and sometimes explained certain points differently from the common explanation of Manichæans, to make them appear less offensive. Thus he addresses his adversary, *Augustine*, (L. I. c. 12. p. 339.): Non tantum ego possum contra tuam virtutem, quia mira virtus est gradus episcopalis: (This language strikingly shows what power the christian bishops of that age possessed:) deinde contra leges Imperatorum, et superius petivi compendive, ut doceas me, quid sit veritas. This uneducated man expresses himself rudely, and violates the rules of grammar; but his meaning is sufficiently clear. When *Augustine* asked him to explain a passage in a certain book, which he called Thesaurus Manetis, he replied, (L. II. c. 19. p. 343.): Hanc tibi ego non possum interpretari scripturam et exponere quod ibi non est: ipsa sibi interpres est: ego non possum dicere, ne forte incurram in peccatum. This fear mars the whole discussion of *Felix*, and frequently leads him to modify the Manichæan opinions to meet the views of his adversaries. And therefore he can [not] always be regarded as an unbiased and safe witness.—The christian doctors, by the *Paraclete* mentioned by Christ in the Gospel of John, understood the Holy Spirit the third Person of the Deity; and indeed correctly: but they did not perceive that *Manes* gave another meaning to the term, and distinguished the *Paraclete*,—i. e. *a man* whom the Holy Spirit uses as his instrument,—from the *Holy Spirit* himself, who taught by that man. And hence, when they learned that *Manes* called himself the *Paraclete*, and was so called by his disciples, they easily fell into the error of supposing that *Manes* assumed to be personally the Holy Spirit, or would be thought to be a man whom the Holy Spirit had anointed with himself. Says *Eusebius*, (Hist. Eccl. L. vii. c. 31.) Τότε μὲν τὸν παράκλητον, καὶ αὐτὸ τὸ πνεῦμα ἅγιον, αὐτὸς ἑαυτὸν ἀνακηρύττων. Paracletum se, ipsumque Spiritum sanctum esse praedicabat.

The *office* of the *Paraclete* whom Christ promised, and consequently his own [p. 746.] office, according to his scheme, consisted principally in *two* things;

first, in restoring the religion of Christ to its original purity, or purging it from the corruptions brought into it by the base frauds or the ignorance of men; and *secondly*, in completing and perfecting the same religion, which, he maintained, Christ had left imperfect, or incomplete in its parts. For, as it was the design of *Manes* to combine the christian religion with the ancient Magian or Persian religion, which he imbibed in his youth, and many doctrines of Christianity were obstacles to his purpose, it became absolutely necessary, that he should, like *Mohammed*, consider the sacred books of the christians as corrupted, and should hold that not a few additions had been made to the christian system, which were foreign from the mind of Christ. Let us hear the language of *Faustus*, a man of note, and of no contemptible genius, among the followers of Manes: (in *Augustine*, contra Faustum Lib. xxxii. c. 1. 319.): Quid peregrinum hoc, aut quid mirum est, si ego de Testamento novo purissima quæque legens et meæ saluti convenientia, prætermitto quæ a vestris majoribus *inducta fallaciter* et majestatem ipsius et gratiam *decolorant?* A little after, the same eloquent and talented man thus addresses catholic christians: Soliusne Filii Testamentum putatis non potuisse corrumpi, solum non habere aliquid, quod in se debeat improbari? præsertim quod nec ab ipso (Christo) scriptum constat, nec ab ejus Apostolis, sed longo post tempore, a quibusdam incerti nominis viris, qui ne sibi non haberetur fides, scribentibus quæ nescirent, partim Apostolorum nomina, partim eorum, qui Apostolos secuti viderentur, scriptorum suorum frontibus indiderunt, asseverantes *secundum eos* se scripsisse, quæ scripserint. - - - Quæ quia nos legentes, animadvertimus cordis obtutu sanissimo, æquissimum judicavimus utilibus acceptis ex iisdem, id est, iis, quæ et finem nostram ædificent, et Christi Domini atque ejus Patris omnipotentis Dei propagent gloriam, cetera repudiare, quæ nec ipsorum majestati, nec fidei nostræ conveniant. These words, which certainly are lucid, teach us, among other things, that Manes denied those *Gospels*, which the Christians approved and accounted divine, to be the works of the Apostles; because they bore the superscriptions: (Κατὰ Ματθᾶιον, κατὰ Μάρκον,) *According to Matthew—Mark—Luke—John.* For he inferred from these superscriptions, that by them the writers meant to signify, that they wrote what was taught respectively by these Apostles. These blemishes, therefore, adhering to true christianity, according to Manes, the *Paraclete*, i. e. *Manes* himself, was commissioned by Christ to remove, and thus to separate the true from the false. Let us again hear *Faustus*, audaciously drawing a parallel between Jesus Christ and his master; (ubi supra, c. 6. p. 321.): Si Jesus docet, pauca veteris Testamenti accipienda esse, repudianda vero quamplurima: Et nobis Paraclitus ex novo Testamento promissus perinde docet, quid ex eodem accipere debeamus, et quid repudiare: de quo ultro Jesus, cum eum promitteret, dicit in Evangelio; *Ipse vos inducet in omnem veritatem, et ipse vobis annunciabit omnia et* [p. 747.] *commemorabit vos.* Quapropter liceat tantundem et nobis in Testamento novo per Paraclitum (i. e. *Manes*) quantum vobis in vetere licere ostenditis per Jesum. More of the like character is there added by *Faustus*, which we omit for the sake of brevity.—As to the other function of the *Paraclete*, there is abundant evidence. Let us consider this function. Manes wished to connect with christianity the fictions of the ancient Persians, respecting two first principles of all things, the origin of the world and of evil, the souls of men, &c. and to palm them on mankind as divine truths. And this design required him to teach, that Christ communicated to his Apostles only a *part* of the truth, necessary to the happiness of men in this and the future life, and left the other part to be taught and explained by the *Paraclete.* We will adduce but a single witness, yet an unexceptionable one, namely, *Felix*, who was one of the number of the *Elect*, as the Manichæans called them, i. e. one of those fully instructed in all the mysteries of the sect. Though he does not express himself very elegantly, yet he explains very well the views of his party. (Disput. cum Augustino, L. i. c. 9. in *Augustini* Opp. tom. viii. p. 338.): Paulus in altera Epistola (ss. 1 Cor. xiii. 9, 10.) dicit: *Ex parte scimus, et ex parte prophetamus: cum venerit autem, quod perfectum est, abolebuntur ea, quæ ex parte dicta sunt.* Nos audientes Paulum hoc dicere, venit Manichæus cum prædicatione sua, et suscepimus eum secundum quod Christus dixit: *Mitto vobis Spiritum sanctum:* et Paulus venit et dixit, quia et ipse venturus est et postea nemo venit: ideo suscepimus Manichæum. Et quia venit Manichæus, et per suam prædicationem docuit nos initium, medium, et finem: docuit nos de fabrica mundi, quare facta est, et unde facta est, et qui fecerunt: docuit nos quare dies et quare nox: docuit nos de cursu solis et lunæ: quia hoc in Paulo non audivimus, nec in ceterorum Apostolorum scripturis; hoc credimus, quia ipse est Paraclitus. Itaque illud iterum dico, quod superius dixi: Si audiero in altera Scriptura, ubi Paraclitus loquitur, de quo voluero interrogare, et docueris me, credo et renunico, (ss. Manichæo.)

We must now speak of the arguments, by which *Manes*, while he lived and when dead, induced so many persons to believe him to be the Paraclete, sent by Christ to reform and to perfect the christian religion. These arguments are manifest, from the passages just cited from *Felix*. Like his imitator *Mohammed*, Manes made no pretensions to miracles: nor did those who listened to him, demand signs of him. He simply bid men believe, that he was a messenger from God: and the doubting and such as asked for evidence, he pressed with this single argument; that Jesus Christ had promised the Paraclete, to perfect what he had begun, and to acquaint men with what was lacking in his [p. 748.] system. Since Christ left the world, until I came, no one adequate for this office has appeared; no one before me, has explained what Christ left unexplained—the origin of the world, the cause of all evils, &c.; but I have explained all these hitherto unknown things. Therefore, I am the Paraclete, whom Christ directed his followers to expect. And by this single argument the Manichæans defended themselves, when called on by the christian doctors to prove, that Manes was the chief Apostle of Christ, or the Paraclete. It appears, from the writings of *Augustine* against the Manichæans, and from other documents, that the christian disputants demonstrated, that the *Paraclete* whom Christ promised, in fact *came*, when the Holy Spirit descended upon the Apostles: Acts ii. The Manichæans denied that fact, on the ground that none of the Apostles had taught *all* the truths that are profitable and needful to men. *Felix* says, (in *Augustini* Disput. cum Felice, L. i. c. 6. p. 337.): Cum probatum mihi fuerit, quod Spiritus sanctus (*in Apostolos effusus*) docuerit veritatem, quam quæro, illam (*Manetis disciplinam*) respuo. Hoc enim sanctitas tua mihi legit, ubi Spiritum sanctum Apostoli acceperunt: et in ipsis Apostolis unum quæro, qui me doceat de initio, de medio et de fine: (i. e. the whole of religion or the whole science of salvation.) And he repeats the same things a little after, thus; Quia sanctitas tua hoc dicit, quod Apostoli ipsi acceperunt Spiritum sanctum Paracletum: iterum dico, de Apostolis ipsis quem volueris, doceat me quod me Manichæus docuit, aut ipsius doctrinam evacuet de duodecim quem volueris. All the pretensions of Manes, therefore, rested on this argument: He who explains the deficient topics in Christ's religion, is the Paraclete whom Christ promised: but *Manes* does this: therefore he is the Paraclete and Apostle of Christ. Nothing can be more fallacious, nothing more imbecile, than this argumentation; and yet many persons, and some of them neither simpletons nor unlearned, were persuaded by Manes and his disciples; and this single example shows, in what darkness the human mind is involved, and how easily popular schemes of religion, accommodated to vulgar apprehension, may entrap men.

(3) In the first place, Manes rejected the entire *Old Testament;* as did nearly all the Gnostic parties, who deformed the Christian religion by the precepts of the Oriental philosophy. The arguments with which the Manichæans assailed the Old Testament, are exhibited in a long array, by *Faustus*, the Manichæan, in *Augustine's* work against him; and still more fully and learnedly, by *Beausobre*, (in his Histoire de Manichée, vol. i. p. 269, &c.) The chief argument is this: The things, which the books of the O. Test. state concerning God, do not accord with the good Principle of the Manichæans, which they denominate *God.*—In the next place, they rejected the whole *New Testament*, as it is read by Christians. They did not indeed deny, that in most of the books of the N. Test., there are *some things* that are divine and came from Christ [p. 749.] and his Apostles: but among these things, they contended, are interwoven very many false things, and things wholly impious. Hence they inferred, that those things only in the N. Test. are intitled to belief, which are in accordance with the decisions of *Manes* their master, the reformer of christianity whom Christ has sent: every thing else is to be rejected.—But these ideas need a more full explanation, so that it may appear, in what sense we must understand the affirmation of *Beausobre*, (vol. i. p. 291.) that the Manichæans received our four Gospels and the Epistles of Paul. For here, too, this great man was influenced somewhat by his excessively kind feelings towards the Manichæans and towards all heretics.

First: As to our *four Gospels*, there were two opinions among the Manichæans, closely allied to each other, and practically, or in their effects, altogether alike. Sometimes they seem to admit, or rather do admit, these Gospels to be of divine origin; but they soon take back what they granted, and contradict it. For they add, that these Gospels are wretchedly corrupted, and interpolated, and enlarged and amplified with Jewish fables, by crafty and mendacious persons. Whence it would follow, that as they now are, they are of no use or value, and should be kept out of the hands of the pious, lest they should be imbued with noxious errors. At other times they deny, most explicitly, that the Apostles of Christ were their authors, or that they were written by those

Apostles whose names they bear. On the contrary, they contend that the authors of them were half-Jews, and credulous and mendacious persons. This I have already shown, from a passage of *Faustus;* and it may be shown by many other passages. I will adduce only one of them, embracing the substance of all, taken from *Augustine's* work against Faustus, (L. xxxiii. c. 3. p. 329.): Sæpe jam probatum a nobis est, nec ab ipso (*Christo*) hæc (*Evangelia*) sunt, nec ab ejus Apostolis scripta: sed multo post eorum assumptionem a nescio quibus et ipsis inter se non concordantibus semi-Judæis per famas, opinionesque comperta sunt: qui tamen omnia eadem in Apostolorum Domini conferentes nomina, vel eorum, qui secuti Apostolos viderentur, errores ac mendacia sua *secundum eos* se scripsisse mentiti sunt. Between these two opinions respecting the Gospels, the Manichæans fluctuated: and even *Faustus* is not uniform in his statements, but seems to incline, now to one opinion, and now to the other, as occasion offers. It was undoubtedly their real opinion, that the Gospels were fabricated by fallible men, and men unacquainted with true religion. But as this opinion was odious, they sometimes dissembled, and pretended not to repudiate those Gospels, which, in reality, they wholly despised. And with such conduct, several of the ancients reproach them. But both opinions lead to the same consequences; and both show, that the Manichæan sect was very far from receiving our Gospels. For how could those who thought so injuriously of the Gospels, or of their authors, recommend them, or even place them among [p. 750.]—I will not say, inspired books, but among the useful and profitable books? In particular, they considered the greatest part of the history of Jesus Christ, as contained in our four Gospels, to be false, imaginary, and wholly unworthy of the majesty of the Son of God. Let us again hear *Faustus*, lucidly explaining the views of his sect, in the work of *Augustine* against him: (L. xxxii. c. 7. p. 322.): De Testamento novo sola accepimus ea, quæ in honorem et laudem Filii majestatis vel ab ipso dicta comperimus, vel ab ejus Apostolis, sed jam perfectis ac fidelibus, dissimulavimus cetera, quæ aut simpliciter tunc et ignoranter a rudibus dicta, aut oblique et maligne ab inimicis objecta, aut imprudenter a scriptoribus affirmata sunt, et posteris tradita: dico autem (*mark these declarations*,) hoc ipsum natum ex fœmina turpiter, circumcisum Judaice, sacrificasse gentiliter, baptizatum humiliter, circumductum a diabolo per deserta, et ab eo tentatum quam miserrime. His igitur exceptis, et si quid ei ab scriptoribus ex Testamento vetere falsa sub testificatione injectum est, credimus cetera, præcipue crucis ejus mysticam fixionem, (from this language it appears, that the portion of Christ's history which they did receive, they did not understand literally, but mystically and allegorically,) qua nostræ animæ passionis monstrantur vulnera, tum præcepta salutaria ejus, tum parabolas cunctumque sermonem deificum, qui maxime duarum præferens naturarum discretionem (we shall misunderstand *Faustus*, if we suppose he here refers to the *two natures* in Christ, and the difference between them: the Manichæans assigned to Christ only one nature, viz. the divine: the human nature they wholly subtracted. The *two* natures, of which *Faustus* here speaks, are the two *Principles* of the Manichæans, *light* and *darkness*, the more subtile and the grosser kinds of matter,) ipsius esse non venit in dubium. Hence also they rejected the two *Gene-*

alogies of Christ, in Matthew and Luke: of which *Faustus* has much to say, (L. ii. c. 1. p. 133 &c.)—The Discourses of Jesus Christ recorded in our four Gospels, *Faustus* seems to approve: but beware, of supposing he really did so. *Manes* acknowledged, indeed, that in these discourses of Christ some things are true, divine, and useful; but he also contended, that in them the good is mixed up with the bad, the true with the false, and that prudence and judgment are necessary to discriminate them. This again, *Faustus* will tell us: (L. xxxiii. c. 3. p. 329.): Nec immerito nos ad hujusmodi scripturas (he speaks of the N. Testament) tam inconsonantes et varias nunquam sane sine judicio et ratione aures afferimus; sed contemplantes omnia et cum aliis alia conferentes, perpendimus utrum eorum quidque a Christo dici potuerit, necne. Multa enim a majoribus vestris eloquiis Domini nostri inserta verba sunt, quæ nomine signata ipsius cum ejus fide non congruant. To distinguish the true and the good from what they considered the false and fictitious in the Gospels, and in the [p. 751.] New Test. generally, the Manichæans adopted this universal rule: Whatever in the New Test. accords with the doctrine of our master, is to be accounted true; and whatever disagrees with it, (and there is very much that does so,) must be reckoned among the fictions and falsehoods of the writers. *Faustus* states this rule in the following terms, (L. xxxii. c. 6. p. 321.); *Paraclitus* ex novo Testamento promissus docet, quid accipere ex eodem debeamus, et quid repudiare.—These things being so, I can never persuade myself, that *Manes* placed a high value on our Gospels, or recommended their perusal to his followers. And yet the learned *Beausobre* would so persuade us: (vol. i. p. 291. Nos heretiques recevoient premierement les quatre Evangiles.) And this, he thinks, is manifest from the answer of *Faustus* to the question: *Accipis Evangelium?* The reply, as stated by *Augustine*, (contra *Faustum* L. ii. c. 1. p. 133.) is: *Maxime.* For *Beausobre* supposes the word *Evangelium* in this reply of *Faustus*, agreeably to its use in the Greek and Latin writers, means the four histories of Christ, which we call the Gospels: (Par l'Evangile on entend le *Volume*, qui contenoit les quatre Evangiles. C'est le style des Grecs et des Latins.) But the great man is certainly mistaken. I admit, that the adversary who asked the question, so understood the term: but *Faustus*, in his reply, affixed a very different meaning to it. Nor does he disguise the fact, but freely acknowledges it a little after, by saying: Scias me, ut dixi, accipere Evangelium, id est, *prædicationem Christi:* (of course, not the history.) In the same manner he explains the term in other passages. In L. v. (c. i. p. 139.) his adversary again asks: *Accipis Evangelium?* And *Faustus*, among other things which I omit, answers: Nescis, quid sit, quod Evangelium nuncupatur. Est enim nihil aliud, quam *prædicatio* et *mandatum* Christi. This Gospel, he says, he receives. The Manichæans, therefore, did not understand by the *Gospel* our volume of Gospels, but the *religion* taught by Christ: and as they believed this religion to be divinely communicated only to their master, it is evident, that they considered *the Gospel* to be nothing different from the religious system of *Manes.* And hence *Titus* of Bostra, (L. iii. contra Manichæos, in H. *Canisii* Lectt. Antiquis, tom. i. p. 139, edit. Basnagii,) very justly charges upon the Manichæans: Quod honorem tantum Evangeliorum simulent, ut esset simulatio invitamentum eorum, quos deciperent, quod lectionem Evangeliorum prætermittant: Ἐυαγγέλια ἀναγνώσει παραπέμπουσι, quod in locum Evangelii aliud eo nomine indignum substituant, &c. *Beausobre* censures this language of *Titus;* and maintains, that *the Manichæans did read the Gospels.* And this, he thinks, appears from their books still extant: (vol. i. p. 303. par le peu qui nous reste de leurs ouvrages.) And it certainly is clear, from these books, that [p. 752.] the Manichæan doctors did, privately, read and examine our Gospels, just as we read the religious books of the sects which go out from us: neither did *Titus* deny this, nor could he do so. But he did deny, that the Manichæans publicly read or expounded the Gospels in their assemblies, or that they read them religiously at home, for the sake of gaining instruction or support and consolation to their minds: and neither of these charges can be refuted by their books now extant. The Manichaean doctors would have been crazy and have contravened their own precepts, if they had either publicly read, or had directed their people to read those Gospels, the authors of which (as we have seen) they pronounced to be half-Jews, mendacious, rash and false assumers of Apostolic names, contradictory to one another, and destitute of divine illumination. But *Beausobre* promises to prove, from the language that *Augustine* puts into the mouth of *Faustus*, (par cette reponse que S. Augustin met dans la bouche de Fauste,) that our Gospels were read by the Manichaeans. But here this great man is somewhat in error. For *Augustine* does not repeat the words of *Faustus*, nor does he affirm that *Faustus* thought that which he attributes to him, but he only conjectures what he might say. His language is, (Lib. xiii. c. 18. p. 188.): Hic *forte* (he therefore states, not what Faustus or the Manichaeans *did* say, but what they *might perhaps* say) dicetis, sed Evangelium debet legere jam fidelis, ne obliviscatur quod credidit. I repeat, what I before said: The Manichaeans would have conflicted with themselves, and would have displayed consummate folly, if they had put into the hands of their people, books which they judged to be full of lies, and the productions of insane men.

I proceed to the *Acts of the Apostles;* to which the Manichæans were more hostile than to the Gospels. For while they could endure the Gospels, because they contained some things true and useful, they totally rejected the book of Acts. Thus *Augustine* testifies, (de Utilitate Credendi, c. 3. Opp. tom. viii. p. 36.): Si dicerent, Scripturas sive penitus abjiciendas putasse, tergiversatio eorum rectior, vel error humanior. Hoc enim de illo libro fecerunt, qui Actus Apostolorum inscribitur. *Augustine* wonders at this: Quod eorum consilium, cum mecum ipse pertracto, nequeo satis mirari. - - Tanta enim liber iste habet, quæ similia sint his, quæ accipiunt, ut magnæ stultitiæ mihi videatur, non et hunc accipere, et si quid ibi eos offendit, falsum atque immissum dicere. And he suspects, that their utter aversion to the book of Acts, arose from the declaration there of the descent of the Holy Spirit on the Apostles; they believing that the Holy Spirit came to mankind only in the person of their master. And he repeats the same conjecture, in his book against *Adimantus*, a Manichæan, (c. 17. p. 100.): Acta isti non accipiunt, quoniam manifeste continent Paracleti adventum. But they doubtless had other reasons also for wholly rejecting this book; which, however, it is not necessary here to investigate.

Of the *Epistles of Paul*, they thought more favorably than of the other books of the New Testament. When *Faustus* was asked by his adversary, [p. 753.] (apud *Augustinum* contra Faustum, L. xi. c. 1. p. 155.). *Accipis Apostolum?* He replied: *Maxime.* And there are other passages which show, that they did not question the fact, that *Paul* wrote those Epistles which we now read. But if any one pressed them with a passage from those Epistles, they instantly replied. that these sacred Epistles had been corrupted by nefarious men. What shall I do to you, says *Augustine*, (contra Faust. L. xxxiii. c. 6. p. 330.): quos contra testimonia Scripturarum ita obsurdefecit iniquitas, ut quidquid adversum vos inde prolatum fuerit, non esse dictum ab Apostolo, sed a nescio quo, falsario sub ejus nomine scriptum esse dicere audeatis? That *Augustine* here does them no injustice, is manifest from the reasoning of *Faustus;* who, when reduced to straits by citations from Paul, boldly replies, (L. xi. c. 1. p. 156.): Si fas non est, Paulum inemendatum dixisse aliquid unquam, *ipsius non est.* He had a little before said: Aliquid in Apostolo esse cauponatum. In another place, (L. xviii. c. 3. p. 221.) he says: Me quidem Manichæa fides reddidit tutum, quæ mihi non cunctis, quæ ex Salvatoris nomine scripta leguntur, passim credere persuasit, sed probare, si sint eadem vera, si sana, si incorrupta: (i. e. accordant with the opinions of *Manes;*) esse enim permulta Zizania, quæ in contagium boni seminis Scripturis pene omnibus noctivagus quidam seminator insperserit.—The opinions of the Manichæans, respecting the other books of the New Testament, are uncertain.

In place of our scriptures, the Manichæans substituted the books of their master, declaring them to be divinely inspired. *Beausobre*, having very fully and very learnedly discussed this subject, I will refer such as are eager for a knowledge of it to his work, vol. i. p. 305 &c. He might have despatched the whole subject in a few words; for very little has come down to us upon it. But the learned man very often digresses from the subject, and introduces topics altogether foreign, and dwells upon them longer than was necessary. He also advances many things concerning the sacred books of the Manichæans, which I would not venture to say, and which rest merely upon conjecture. *Manes* wrote many books, of which a list is given by Jo. Alb. *Fabricius*, (Biblioth. Græca, vol. v. p. 281 &c.) and by Wm. *Cave*, (Historia Literar. Scriptor. Eccl. tom. i. p. 139.): but both lists are imperfect; nor is that compiled by *Beausobre* without faults. That the Manichæans set a higher value on the writings of their master, than upon any other books named by them, no one can doubt, if he reflects that they considered him as the *Paraclete* promised by Christ. No one of the books of Manes was held by them in higher estimation than his *Epistola Fundamenti*, which *Augustine* has confuted in a single book; for this Epistle contained a sort of epitome of the whole doctrine of Manes. And hence *Felix* the Manichæan, when about to dispute with *Augustine*, requested this only of all the books taken from him by the order of government, to be re- [p. 754.] stored to him, (August. contra Felicem, L. i. c. 1. p. 345.): Ista enim Epistola Fundamenti est, quod et sanctitas tua bene scit, quod et ego dixi, quia ipsa continet initium, medium et finem, (i. e. the whole system of religion). Ipsa legatur. And (*August.* contra Epist. Fundamenti, c. 5. p. 111.): Potissimum illum consideremus librum, quem Fundamenti Epistolam dicitis, ubi totum pene, quod creditis, continetur. And hence, it was read to the people, in their assemblies, by the Manichæans: Ipsa enim nobis illo tempore miseris quando lecta est, *illuminati* dicebamur a vobis.

(4) The festal day, on which the Manichæans annually celebrated the memorial of their master's execution, was called Bema; from the *tribunal*, or elevated seat, which on that day was erected in their temples or places of worship. Says *Augustine*, (contra Epist. Fundam. c. 8. pp. 112, 113.): Vestrum *Bema*, id est, diem, quo Manichæus occisus est, quinque gradibus instructo tribunali et pretiosis linteis adornato, ac in promptu posito et objecto adorantibus prosequimini. And in his work against Faustus, (L. xviii. c. 5. p. 222.) he testifies, that this day was celebrated, with great festivity, in the month of March. The *tribunal* or pulpit, (βῆμα) a magnificent *chair*, hung with costly drapery, undoubtedly denoted that *Manes* was an inspired teacher, and greater and more excellent than all the other teachers sent of God to man; or, a man exalted above all other mortals. Βῆμα, among the Greeks, properly signifies *a step:* but it is also used of the elevated places, from which military commanders addressed their soldiers, teachers their disciples, and judges pronounced their decisions; for to all these the ascent was by steps. *Augustine* translates it *tribunal:* perhaps it might better be rendered *a chair, a pulpit.* Yet the term *tribunal* is admissable, because the Manichæans considered their master as not only a teacher, but also as a *judge* in matters of religion. Jac. *Tollius*, (Insign. Itinerarii Italici, p. 142.) translates it *an altar.* But he gives no reasons for this interpretation; which is manifestly opposed by *Augustine*, a very competent witness, who had been often present at this ceremony. *Beausobre* castigates *Tollius;* (vol. ii. p. 713.)—Why, the ascent to this tribunal or throne, representing the presence of their master, was by *five steps*, seems not very evident. But I conjecture, that the five steps correspond with the *five elements* of the Manichæans. For they distributed both the kingdom of darkness and the kingdom of light into five elements; and our world, they supposed, consisted of five compound elements, derived from both kingdoms. And, if I judge correctly, the Manichæans, by the five steps to the tribunal or pulpit of their master, intended to represent, that he alone fully understood the true nature of both kingdoms, [p. 755.] those of light and darkness, and of this our world; and had explained it all to mankind.—*Augustine*, moreover, speaks of the *tribunali in promptu posito;* i. e. so placed, that all present could see it, and have their eyes upon it; *et objecto adorantibus.* What does *adorantibus* here denote? *Beausobre* (ubi sup. p. 713.) thinks it equivalent to *precantibus:* and, of course, he supposes, that the Manichæans prayed to God, with their faces towards this tribunal. I would readily concede, that in the proper sense of the word, the Manichæans *adored* neither their master nor his pulpit. But as for the import of the word in this place, I dissent from him. Among the Latins, *adorare* was to show reverence, by bodily attitudes and motions, either to gods or to men; nor do I see any reason for believing, that *Augustine* used the word otherwise here. I therefore do not doubt, that he means to say, either that the Manichaeans *prostrated* themselves, in the Oriental manner, before this throne; or, that by some

other bodily act, they manifested their very great *reverence* for their master. The ceremony was similar to that of the Chinese; who salute, very respectfully, a tablet bearing the name of *Confucius;* in order to manifest publicly, that to that philosopher they are indebted for all their wisdom. This was not a religious *adoration*, but a manifestation of their feelings of gratitude and respect.

§ XLI. **Two Eternal Worlds, under Two Eternal Lords.** *Manes* affirmed *two* first principles of all things; namely, a subtile and a gross sort of matter, or *light* and *darkness*, separated from each other by a narrow space. And over each of these he placed an eternal King or *Lord;* the Lord over light, he called *God;* the Lord over darkness, he called *Hyle*, or *Demon.*(1) *The world of light* and *the world of darkness*, although different in their natures, have some things in common. For each is distributed into five opposing elements, and the same number of provinces: and both are equally eternal, and both, with their respective Lords, self-existent; both are unchangeable, and both to exist for ever; both are of vast extent, yet the *world of light* seems to fill more space than the *empire of darkness.*(2) The condition of the two *Lords*, presiding over the two kinds of matter, is equal; but they are totally unlike in their natures and dispositions. The *Lord of light*, being himself happy, is beneficient, a lover of peace and quietness, just and wise; the *Lord of darkness*, being himself very miserable, wishes to see others unhappy, is quarrelsome, unwise, unjust, irascible, and envious. Yet they are equal in the eternity of their existence, in their power to beget beings like themselves, in their unchangeableness, and in their power and knowledge; and yet the King of light, or God, excells the Prince of [p. 756.] darkness, or the Demon, in power and knowledge.(3)

(1) In substantiating the doctrines and opinions of the Manichaeans, I have determined to employ the very language of *Manes* and his disciples, as far as possible; and to cite the testimony of those only, who were well acquainted with the Manichaean system, and who had actually consulted the books of the sect, disregarding the writers of less authority and less accuracy; so that my statements may have unexceptionable credibility. In collecting the testimonies, I gratefully acknowledge myself indebted to the industry of *Beausobre*, that prince of the historians of Manichaeism. But this resource has failed me, in many cases; a fact which I mention, with no disrespect for that extraordinary man, who was my friend. For he not only omitted many things necessary to be known, and of use for a right understanding of the Manichaean religion; but also, being too favorably inclined both to *Manes*, whom he deemed no mean philoso-

pher, and to his followers, he taxes his genius and eloquence, to extenuate the baseness of the religion they professed. I shall sometimes mention, when the occasion shall seem to require it, that the best attested truth compels me to differ from this very learned man: yet often, to avoid wearying the reader, I shall silently deviate from him. Whoever shall take the trouble to compare his protracted and very copious work, with my slender and dry production, will see, I hope, a great difference between them; and will perceive, that I have examined with my own eyes, and not with those of another, this gloomy and obscure fable.

In the first place, it is beyond all controversy, that *Manes* affirmed the existence of *two first principles* of all things, and likewise of *two Lords* of the universe: in doing which, he followed the opinions of the ancient Persians and other Oriental nations. The Manichæans, when they would speak with precision and accuracy, applied the term *first principle* (*principium*) only to the *Rulers* or *Lords* over the two kinds of matter, the good and the evil, or light and darkness. *Faustus*, the most learned and eloquent of the Manichæans, says, (apud *Augustinum*, L. xx. c. 1. Opp. tom. viii. p. 237.): Pagani bona et mala unum *principium* habere dogmatizant. His ego valde contraria sentio, qui bonis omnibus *principium* fateor Deum, contrariis vero *Hylen:* sic enim mali *principium* ac naturam Theologus noster (Manes) appellat. And again, (L. xxi. c. 1. p. 249.): Duo *principia* confitemur, sed unum ex his *Deum* nominamus, alterum *Hylen* · aut, ut communiter et usitate dixerim, *Dæmonem*. - - - Duo *principia* doceo, *Deum* et *Hylen*. - - - Vim omnem maleficam Hylæ assignamus, et beneficam Deo, ut congruit. But to denote the *matter*, good and bad, or light and darkness, over which those first Principles had dominion, they used the terms *nature* and *substance*. So *Manes* himself, in his Epistola Fundamenti, [p. 757.] (apud *August.* contra Epist. Fundam. c. 12, 13, p. 115): Ausculta prius quæ fuerint ante constitutionem mundi, ut possis luminis sejungere *naturam* ac tenebrarum. Haec quippe in exordio fuerunt, *duæ substantiæ* a sese divisae. So also *Faustus*, and the rest of them, often. And *Augustine*, exactly according to the views of the sect, of which he had been a member, (de Haeres. c. 46. tom. viii. p. 11.) says: Ista duo *principia* inter se diversa et adversa, eademque aeterna ac coaeterna, hoc est, semper fuisse, composuit: duasque *naturas* ac *substantias*, boni scilicet et mali, opinatus est.—Yet examples occur in which this distinction is overlooked, and the term *first principle* is applied to matter, and the word *nature* applied to God and the Demon. I have just cited a passage from *Faustus*, (L. xx. c. 1. p. 237.) in which he uses both *principium* and *natura* in reference to the demon. He adds, (L. xxi. c. 1. p. 249.): Nec diffiteor, interdum nos adversam *naturam* nuncupare Deum. In a similar manner, they use the words *light* and *darkness*, which properly denoting the *matter* over which God and the Demon reign, yet sometimes denote the *Lords* of matter, or God and *Hyle*. This is a minute criticism, but it will help us to understand better some declarations of the Manichæans.

(2) *Manes* conceived, that in infinite space, there are *two* worlds, or two earths; the *one* shining, and overspread with light; the *other* very caliginous, or full of darkness and mists. In his Epistola Fundamenti, (apud *August.* c. 12. p. 115.) *Manes* calls the former: Lucidam et beatam terram; *and*, Illustrem et sanctam

terram. The latter he calls, (ibid. 15 .p. 116.) Terram tenebrarum: *and* Terram pestiferam. Both these worlds existed from eternity; neither of them had a beginning, or can have an end, or become extinct. Of the world of light or the empire of God, *Manes* also says, (ibid. p. 115.): Ita autem fundata sunt ejusdem (Dei) splendidissima regna supra lucidam et beatam terram, ut a nullo unquam aut moveri aut concuti possint. These passages prove the enduring stability of the world of *light*. That he believed the same stability characterized the world of *darkness*, is manifest from what he says of the destruction of our world, and the events that are to follow. For when God shall have conquered the Prince of darkness, he will not destroy his kingdom: *that* is beyond his power, since the world of darkness has an equally necessary existence, with the world of light. But, as the power of God is greater than that of the Ruler of darkness, he will shut up the latter in that realm of darkness of which he is Lord. On the eternity of the world of light there is a noted passage of *Felix* the Manichaean, in his Dispute with *Augustine*, (L. I. c. 17. 18. p. 342. 343.) *Augustine* asks him: Fecitne Deus, an genuit, terram illam lucis, an aequalis et coætanea illi erat? *Felix* at first replies evasively, and conceals his opinion. For he only proves that there *are* two worlds: Duae terrae mihi vindentur esse, secundum quod Manichaeus dicit duo regna. *Augustine* declares himself not satisfied, and repeats the question. But *Felix* still seeks concealment, and strives to elude the subject. For the unhappy man, then a prisoner, was afraid [p. 758.] of the imperial laws, and of the authority of *Augustine;* as he does not disguise. He supposed, he would be accused and punished as a blasphemer, if he should deny that heaven, the residence of God, was created by God. But, being pressed on every side, at last, laying aside fear, he stated clearly what he *did* believe: Dixisti de terra illa, in qua Deus habitat, an facta est ab illo, an generavit illam, an coaeterna illi est. Et ego dico, quia quomodo Deus aeternus est, et factura apud illum nulla est, *totum æternum est.* Augustine, not fully satisfied, asks again: Non illam ergo genuit, nec fecit? And *Felix* answers most distinctly: *Non*, sed *est illi coaeterna.* A little after, he assigns the reason why he does not believe that the world of light was produced by God: Quod nascitur, finem habet: quod innatum, non habet finem. It appears that from this principle he reasoned thus: As the world of light will have no end, it of course cannot have had a beginning: and, therfore, it was not made or generated by God. After a few remarks not pertaining to our enquiry, he is again interrogated by Augustine: Hujus ergo terrae (Deus) non est Pater, sed Inhabitator? And *Felix* answers promptly: Etiam. Augustine proceeds: Ergo duae jam erunt res ambae ingenitae, terra et Pater? To this *Felix* replies: *Immo tres sunt, Pater* ingenitus, *terra* ingenita, et *aër* ingenitus. Hence, it appears, that Manes assigned to the world of light an *atmosphere*, or supposed that world compassed with air, just as ours is. That Manes supposed the same thing true of the world of darkness, there can be no doubt. That world, therefore, together with its King or Lord, had existed from eternity. But, although both worlds have everlasting duration and permanence, and cannot be overthrown or demolished, yet it is possible that violence and injury should be done to them, or that some portion of either should be taken from it, and that world thus become diminished.

This is manifest beyond all doubt, from the war between the good and the malignant first Principles, or the Kings and Lords of the two worlds. For in this war, as we shall hereafter see, the King of darkness subjugated a portion of the elements of the world of light, and likewise not a few of its inhabitants. And of the same thing we have the best testimony, that of Manes himself, in his Epistola Fundamenti. (apud *August.* Disput. cum Felice, L. I. c. 19. p. 343. &c. and in other places,) : Lucis vero beatissimae Pater, sciens *labem magnam ac vastitatem*, quae ex tenebris surgeret, adversus sua sancta impendere Saecula, nisi quod eximium Numen opponat. The Demon therefore could *harm* the *sancta Sæcula*, or *the Æons* of God; and the danger from this source was to be resisted. The same was true, unquestionably, of the world of darkness. Such was the power of God, that although he could not subvert and annihilate the empire of the Demon, yet he could, if he chose, invade it and dismember it. But *this* he would not do; because, it would have been injurious to the tranquillity and happiness of his own kingdom, if he had brought a portion of [p. 759.] darkness into it.—Both worlds occupied very ample spaces, or were of very great extent. Of the world of darkness, Manes himself says, (Epist. Fundam. c. 15. p. 116. apud *Augustinum*,): Tenebrarum terra profunda et immensa magnitudine. But the world of light, the Manichaeans seem to have made rather more extensive than the realm of darkness. I gather this from the language of *Augustine*, (contra Epist Manichaei, c. 20. p. 118.) ; Dicant ergo, quid adjungebatur terrae lucis, si ex uno latere erat gens tenebrarum ? Non dicunt: sed cum premuntur, ut dicant, infinita dicunt esse alia latera terrae illius, quam lucem vocant, id est, per infinita spatia distendi et nullo fine cohiberi. *Manes* himself had not said this; for he spoke only in general terms, of the limits of the two worlds. But his disciples, when hard pressed, so explained their master's views: and, indeed, they had reason so to explain them. For he had said, (in Epist. Fund.): Juxta *unam* vero *partem* ac *latus* illustris illius ac sanctae terrae erat tenebrarum terra profunda. According to his idea, only *one side* of the world of light was bounded by the world of darkness. Therefore the Manichaeans inferred that the *other sides*, not being bounded, had no limits, but extended into infinite space. From this, it necessarily follows, that the world of light is more ample and extensive than the world of darkness. For that thing, which is contiguous to only *one part* or side of something, the other sides of which, being unbounded, are free and without limits;—that thing, undoubtedly, is smaller or less extensive than the thing to which it is contiguous; although it may, as *Manes* says, immensam profunditatem et magnitudinem habere, or, may extend over a very large and unbounded space.—In the world of light, eternal peace and uninterrupted happiness reign. For all its inhabitants being the progeny of the beneficent nature of God, there can be no place for discord and enmity among them: and as all are perfectly happy, in their respective spheres, they cannot be disquieted or moved by the desire of greater happiness. But far different is the state of the world of darkness. For there, all are continually at war with each other. Being naturally propense to broils, seditions, and discord, no solid and stable peace can exist among them. Says *Augustine*, (contra Faustum L. xxi. c. 14. p. 254, 255.) : Illa gens, inquiunt (Manichaei) excepto eo, quod vicinae luci mala erat, et apud se ipsam mala erat.--Vastabant se invicem, laedebant, occidebant, absumebant. (This must be understood of the animals living in the kingdom of darkness, of which we are soon to speak. For the progeny of the Prince of darkness, are equally immortal with the off-spring of the Lord of light.)

But the words *light* and *darkness*, used by Manes to denote the matter of his two worlds, or what they called the *two natures* or *substances*, have not the import commonly assigned them; namely, that one of these worlds was composed intirely of light, and the other wholly of darkness. This common misapprehension, which is found with some very learned men, is contrary to the clearest assertions and declarations of Manes and his disciples. *Light* [p. 760.] is only one *fifth* part of the world of light, and *darkness* is only one *fifth* part of the realm of darkness. But because *light*, from its very nature, is diffused throughout one of these worlds, and illumines the whole of it with its splendor, therefore, that whole happy region, inhabited by God himself, is called *light*, or the *world of light*. And moreover, *God* is *himself light*; and he undoubtedly diffuses the splendor of his nature throughout all the realm over which he reigns. On the other hand, as the *darkness* from its very nature, obscures the whole region of which it constitutes a fifth part, and spreads a sort of cloud over all the elements of it, that *terra pestifera*, (as Manes expresses it,) is called a *world* or *realm of darkness*. Not that there is no light at all in the world of darkness; for it contains *fire*, which of course must emit light. But the darkness in contact with this fire, causes it to emit very little light, and almost to assume the nature of darkness.

Manes distributed each of these worlds, from which he supposed all things were formed, into *five elements* and five *provinces*. Of the world of darkness, he has left us this full description, in his Epistola Fundamenti, (apud Augustinum c. 15. p. 116.): Juxta unam vero partem ac latus illustris illius ac sanctæ terræ erat tenebrarum terra profunda et immensa magnitudine, in qua habitabant ignea corpora, genera scilicit pestifera. (i. e. the Demons, with their Prince.) Hic infinitæ *tenebræ*, (Here is the *first element*,) ex eadem manantes natura inæstimabiles cum propriis fetibus: ultra quas erant aquæ *cænosæ* (the *second element*) ac turbidæ cum suis inhabitatoribus; quarum interius *venti* horribiles ac vehementes (the *third element*) cum suo Principe ac genitoribus. Rursum regio *ignea* ac corruptibilis (that is, which has power to corrupt, destroy, or consume; not that it is itself corruptible or consumable) cum suis ducibus et nationibus: (the *fourth element*.) Pari more introrsum *gens caliginis* ac fumi plena, (the *fifth element*,) in qua morabatur immanis Princeps omnium et dux, habens circa se innumerabiles Principes, quorum omnium ipse erat mens atque origo: hæque fuerunt *naturæ quinque* terræ pestiferæ. I will subjoin an extract from *Augustine*, (de Hæresibus c. 46. p. 11.) which throws light on some parts of this description; *quinque elementa*, quæ genuerunt principes proprios, genti tribuunt tenebrarum; eaque elementa his nominibus nuncupant, *fumum, tenebras, ignem, aquam, ventum*. (This is not accurately expressed, and does not clearly and fully exhibit the opinion of *Manes*. Augustine also changes the order of the elements.) In *fumo* nata animalia bipedia, unde homines ducere originem censent, in *tenebris* serpentia, in *igne* quadrupedia, in *aquis* natatilia, in *vento* volatilia. See also *Augustine* against Faustus, (L. ii. c. 3. pp. 133, 134.)—We will elucidate these whims a little.—The world of darkness is like an immense dwelling *house*, which is *five stories high*, and *each* [p. 761.] *story* having its own elementary matter, its Prince, its inhabitants, and its animals; the last all venimous and noxious, and resembling our noxious animals. In each story, therefore, we may distinguish *four* things: *first*, the elementary *matter; secondly*, the *Prince* who presides over the province; *thirdly*, the *subordinate rulers* who aid the Prince in the government; and *lastly*, the *animals* corresponding with the several elements. The elements themselves are fecund, or have the power of generation; for *Augustine* says: Suos sibi Principes genuerunt. Nor does he pervert the views of Manes; for we have a passage of his, which confirms what Augustine says, in *Titus* Bostrensis, (contra Manichæos, L. i. in *Canisii* Lectt. Antiquis, tom. i. p. 68.): Ἦν γὰρ ποτὰ φησὶν, ὅτε ἡ ὕλη ἠτάκτει, καὶ ἐγέννα καὶ ηὐξάνετο, καὶ διετέλει πολλὰς προβαλλομένη δυνάμεις. Erat, inquit Manichæus, (doubtless in his *Liber Mysteriorum*, which *Titus* had read;) tempus, cum materia sine ordine ferebatur, et generabat et crescebat, ac multas potestates producebat. Those Princes, therefore, or the *Governors of provinces* in the world of darkness, neither existed necessarily and from eternity, nor were they the offspring of the King of darkness. Whether the *inferior magistrates* also originated from the elements, or were the progeny of the Princes, seems to be doubtful. Yet, I suspect, they were begotten by the princes: for the supreme Lord of darkness generated his own subordinate commanders and ministers; and it is probable, that the Governors of provinces possessed the same powers. Besides, *Manes* makes express mention of *births* in the realm of darkness. The first *animals* that inhabited the several stories of the edifice, undoubtedly, were the product of the elements in which they lived. And these propagated their species, in the same manner that our animals do. This will very clearly appear from a passage soon to be cited. The inferior elements produce only the imperfect animals; and the more exalted the elements are, the more perfect are the beings they produce. The highest element produces the most perfect animals, namely, those most resembling human beings.—The *inhabitants* of all the stories are continually warring and fighting with each other; and *animals*, which are mortal, also devour and consume one another. *Manes* says, (apud *Titum* Bostrens. ubi supra, p. 70.): Ἤλαυνον καὶ κατήσθιον οἱ ἐξ αὐτῆς ἀλλήλοις, δεινὰ καὶ χαλεπὰ διατλαέντες. Qui ex malitia nati sunt, se mutuo insectati sunt et devoraverunt, dura et gravia passi. More might be said on these points, but it is not necessary. I proceed rather to a consideration of the *elements* themselves, on which some remarks may not be useless. *Augustine* has much to say of them, (contra Epist. Fundamenti, c. 28. p. 122.) but, as he too often is, he is more harsh and energetic than was necessary; nor did he understand the nature of these elements.

The lowest element, and that which produced reptile animals, was *tenebrae infinitæ;* that is, wide and infinitely extended *darkness*. But *Manes* did not, as commonly supposed, understand by the word darkness, what we do, the mere [p. 762.] absence of light; for, infatuated as he doubtless was, he was not so infatuated as to believe that *darkness*, in the proper sense of the word, can be ranked among elementary *substances*. And the Manichæans themselves, (apud *August.* loco citato, p. 124.) denied, that their darkness was the same as ours: Non tales erant illæ tenebræ quales hic nosti. *Manes* wrote in Syriac, as we learn from *Titus* Bostrensis; and perhaps his Latin translator did not adequately express his meaning. The *darkness* of Manes was, undoubtedly, *earth;* which, being opaque, and emitting no light, might be called *darkness*. This is not only manifest from the earthly and reptile animals generated from this darkness, but the thing itself shows it. For unless by *darkness* Manes meant *earth*, he excluded earth from among the elements; which is altogether incredible, and would be foreign from his views. For his superior world had the same number of elements, and of the same kinds, as our world has; and that *earth* is one of the elements of our world, *Manes* and all the Persians believed. Therefore, from this immense mass of earth, destitute of all light, arose, according to *Manes*, *inæstimabiles* (i. e. *innumerable*) *naturæ* (for thus doubtless it should read, instead of *natura*, as in the copies of Augustine,) and moreover, *fetus*, (i. e. the proper animals of the earth, serpents, vipers, worms, insects, and all that are destitute of feet and creep upon the ground.)—Adjacent to earth or darkness, was the element of *water;* filled, in like manner, with its appropriate inhabitants. But this *water* was not pure and limpid; it was polluted by the contiguous earth, and therefore turbid and dark-colored.—The *third* element, adjacent to the water, was *wind;* which likewise had its Prince, its generators, and its animals, namely, *birds;* yet not beautiful, harmless, and singing birds, but such as were savage and ferocious. Beware also of supposing that *Manes* understood by *wind*, what we understand by it, namely, a strong *motion* of the air. He was a senseless man, yet not so senseless as to account motion an elementary body, giving birth to various material beings. His wind was *air;* yet air obscured with clouds, and immensely and vehemently agitated. This appears from the thing itself, and also from the animals which lived in the *wind*, for they were all *aërial*.—Above the wind was the fourth region, which comprised *fire*, the fourth element. Here lived those quadrupeds whose natures most resembled *fire*, which destroys and consumes objects: namely, savage beasts, lions, tigers, elephants, bulls, and panthers. To the gentler animals, and those serviceable to mankind, such as sheep, cows, horses, &c. I suppose, he did not assign a place in the world of darkness. The Manichæans being asked, (apud *August.* loco cit. c. 32. pp. 124, 125.) why their master placed quadrupeds in the region of *fire*, replied: *Quod quadrupedes edaces sint;* (this, I suppose, means *rapacious*, *voracious*, inclined to bite,) *et in concubitum multum ferveant.*—The highest and most elevated of the elements, the fifth in number, but the first in rank, was *smoke;* in which resided the *Prince* of the whole world of darkness, [p. 763.] encompassed with a vast multitude of *princes* and *dukes*, who were *his offspring*. It appears strange, that *Manes* should place among the elements, and above all the others, *smoke*, which is merely a vapor, elicited and dislodged from burning bodies: and still more strange, that the King of the whole realm of darkness should dwell in *smoke;* and that the animals produced from smoke should be more perfect than any others; for they resembled men in form, were *bipeds*, and they generated men. Says *Augustine*, (contra Faustum, L. xxi. c. 14. p. 256.): Illi principi non tantum sui generis, id est, bipedes, quos parentes hominum dicitis, sed etiam cuncta animalia ceterorum generum subditi erant et ad ejus nutum convertebantur. And hence he ridicules this fifth element, (contra Epistolam Manich. c. 32. p. 125.) and says: Bipedes fumus offocat atque necat. - - At hic fumus bipedes suos—vitaliter atque indulgenter educaverat et continebat. But I can suppose there was no just cause for his ridicule. Perhaps, the Latin translator of the Epistola Fundamenti, did not understand the meaning of the Syriac word used by *Manes*. Those better acquainted with the Syriac language than am, can judge. But I may safely say, that such *smoke* as ours, was not intended by *Manes*, but a material substance more suitable for procreating animals superior to all others. The *smoke* of Manes was, undoubtedly, that element which was considered the *first* by the ancients, and which they called *ether*; or, as *Cicero* describes it, (de Natura Deor. L. ii. c. 36.): extrema ora atque determinatio mundi, complexus cœli omnia cingens et cœrcens, ardor cœlestis. This may be inferred from the fact, that it is contrasted with *air*; as we shall presently see. But this element, being in the world of darkness like the rest, was contaminated and corrupted; and having a resemblance to smoke, it might be called *smoke*. Pure genuine *ether* is thin and transparent; but this was dense, turbid, dark, and cloudy. These remarks go to show, why the malignant Lord of the dark world dwelt in this element as his home.

Correspondent with these five elements in the pestiferous world, there are five elements in the *world of light*, and arranged, doubtless, in the same order; yet they are salutary, beautiful, benign, and replete with happy and beneficent inhabitants. Says *Augustine*, (de Hæres. c. 46. p. 11.) the Manichæans teach: His quinque elementis malis debellandis alia quinque elementa de regno et substantia Dei (Here is some mistake. The *substance* of *God*, as we shall see, was the purest *light*, with no admixture of any other substance. Therefore, these elements are not composed of the *substance* of God, but only of the *empire of God*) missa esse, et in illa pugna permixta, fumo *aëra*, tenebris *lucem*, igni malo *ignem bonum*, aquæ malæ *aquam bonam*, vento malo *ventum bonum*. There is also much said by *Augustine* respecting these five celestial elements, in his work against Faustus, (L. xi. c. 3. and L. xx. c. 9.) But he does not arrange these [p. 764.] elements in their proper order. The last and lowest element in the kingdom of God, is *light*. And, as it is opposed to the *darkness* in the kingdom of darkness, it undoubtedly is a material substance, resembling earth, yet white and colorless, shining, pellucid, and thin. *Manes* calls it *Lucidam ac beatam terram*, (in his Epistola Fund. apud *August*. c. 13. p. 115.) And, because the splendor of this element is diffused through the whole realm of God, therefore this realm is pronounced *splendidissimum*.—Next came *good water*; that is, water pure and limpid, free from all earthly particles and feculency; for the *evil water* was, as *Manes* says, *cœnosa et turbida*.—The third element was *good wind*; that is, *air* moving gently and placidly, and tempering agreeably the heat produced by the inferior light and the superior fire.—This was followed by *good fire*; which, as it is opposed to *igni corruptibili*, i. e. to devouring and consuming fire, unquestionably, only warms, revives, and fecundates, like the fire of the sun, and does not consume and destroy.—The uppermost element, contrasted with the *smoke*, was *air ;* not that which is moved, and which Manes called *wind ;* but the purest and most refined *ether*, encompassing and embracing the whole realm of light.—Of the *Princes* and the *animals* of these five provinces of the world of light, I find no where a description. But as the world of light was the counterpart of the world of darkness, I doubt not, that Manes assigned to each of these elements its *Prince*, its *magistrates* and *inhabitants*, and also its *fœtus*, or animals.

You may say, these are whims, and more suitable for old women and children, than for a man of sense. I grant it: they are so. Yet they have their grounds and reasons in the first principles of the Manichæan doctrine; and therefore the man did not trifle, but reasoned consequentially from his premises. Like the Persians and many others among the ancients, (as appears from *Apuleius*, de Mundo, § 29.) *Manes* supposed this, *our world*, to be composed of *five* elements, *earth*, *water*, *fire*, *air*, and *ether*. And one of his fundamental doctrines was, that our world is a compound of the *commingled elements* of the *two* upper worlds, the good and the evil. For he despaired of accounting for the existence of evil, unless he admitted two first principles above us, from the commingling of which this our world originated. Hence, this reason,—if a necessity resulting from an assumed dogma may be called a reason,—this *reason*, I say, led him to suppose the worlds above to be composed of the same elements as ours is, and those elements arranged in much the same order as we here behold them. If he had assigned any other constitution, either to the world of light, or to the world of darkness, he could not have accounted for the condition of our world, and the changes which occur in it.

(3) That the founder of the Manichæan sect inculcated the belief of *two Deities* or *Gods*, is declared by most persons, both ancient and modern. But the erudite *Beausobre* is dissatisfied, and contends earnestly, that they [p. 765.] believed indeed in *two first Principles*, but by no means in *two Gods*. (See his Histoire de Manichée, tome i. p. 488.) He relies chiefly on the authority of *Faustus ;* (apud *August.* contra Faust. L. xxi. c. 1. p. 250.) who, being interrogated: *Unus Deus est, an Duo?* quickly replied: *Plane unus :* and then inveighed severely against those who explain otherwise the doctrine of his sect. He said: Nunquam in nostris quidem assertionibus duorum Deorum auditum est nomen. - - Est quidem quod duo *Principia* confitemur, sed *unum* ex his *Deum* vocamus. - - Quapropter inepta hæc et viribus satis effeta est argumentatio. *Augustine* strenuously confutes *Faustus :* but he fails to satisfy *Beausobre*, who affirms that in this controversy *Faustus* had the best of the argument: and proceeding still farther, he maintains that no one of the ancient heretics taught the existence of *two Deities*. I think otherwise; and I do not consider them in error, who declare that the Manichæans preached two Gods. This indeed, both *Faustus* and his learned patron have proved, that the Manichæans applied the name *God* to only the good Principle, and not also to the bad; and yet *Faustus* does not deny, that sometimes, the Prince of darkness is also called *God* by the Manichæans: Nec diffiteor, etiam interdum nos adversam naturam nuncupare *Deum*, sed non hoc secundum nostram fidem, verum juxta præsump-

tum jam in eam nomen a cultoribus suis. But the question is not about the *name*, but about the thing. We commonly designate by the name *God*, a being who is eternally self-existent, and subject to the authority and control of no other being. Now, of this character were both the good Principle and the evil Principle, according to the opinion of the Manichæans. And therefore, they truly held to *two Gods*, notwithstanding they, for distinction's sake, applied the name *God* only to the good Principle. And if one should change the definition, and say; God is not only an eternally self-existent being, but also one possessed of all conceivable perfections, and the cause of all things; this would not answer his purpose. For, according to this definition, the Manichæans held to no God at all; because they did not suppose their good Principle to be *absolutely perfect*, nor the *cause* of all things: so that he would not deserve the title of God, according to this definition. Yet I will grant, that in a certain sense, the Manichæans believed in but one God: namely, they supposed that only the good Principle was to be worshipped and honored. And, therefore, if it should be said, that the Being whom all men should religiously worship and adore, is God, then the Manichæans are free from the charge brought against them. And yet, in another sense, they may most justly be charged with what is called *Dualism*; that is, with holding to two Divinities.

Respecting the nature and attributes of the good Principle, I purpose to speak in the next section. Here I shall only make some remarks on the coinci-
[p. 766.] dences and the discrepancies between the good and the bad Principles, and on the character and conduct of the bad Principle.—And *first*, that the bad Principle was co-eternal with the good Principle, and equally self-existent, or dependent on no antecedent cause, is beyond all controversy. *Manes* himself says, (apud *Titum* Bostrens. L. i. p. 87.): Σατανᾶς ἦν πονερὸς, καὶ ὅυτε ποτὲ ὀυκ ἦν, ἀεὶ γὰρ ἦν. Καὶ ὀυκ ἀπό τινος ἦν, ἦν γὰρ. Καὶ ῥίζα ἦν, φησί, καὶ ἦν Κύριος, καὶ ἀυτὸς ἦν. I will translate this more clearly and accurately than Francis *Turrian* does, who is not always the best translator: Malus erat Satanas; neque tempus est, quo non erat: æternus enim est, neque originem ab aliquo accepit. Necessario enim et per se existebat. Et erat radix, inquit *Manes*, (who speaks in the Oriental style. *Radix* is equivalent to *pater* or *genitor*, one who begets a numerous offspring.) Et erat Dominus (i. e. he had an immense empire,) et idem erat (i. e. was immutable, and could not become extinct, nor change his nature.)—*Secondly*, the generative power of both Princes or their power of procreating beings like themselves, is immense. And therefore each of them has produced innumerable beings like himself. *Manes*, in his Epistola Fundamenti, (apud *August.* c. 13. p. 115.) expressly calls God *illustrem patrem ac genitorem (innumerabilium) beatorum et gloriosorum sæculorum*, (i. e. of *Æons*). More passages to the same effect, will occur hereafter. Of the evil Principle, he says, (ibid. c. 15. p. 116.): Habens circa se innumerabiles principes, quorum omnium erat mens atque origo. The Demon was the *mind* (*mens*) of all his children; because they received their *minds* or souls out of him, and had malignant minds, inclined, like his, to do evil.—*Lastly*, that the evil Principle possessed an immensely fertile genius, vast subtilty and sagacity, and consummate and amazing power, the plans which he devised, and actually

carried into effect, put beyond all question.—These are the particulars in which the two Divinities were alike. But in other respects they were very unlike.—1. The essential *natures* of the two Princes were totally different. For *God* was *light*, or his essence was light; as we shall show hereafter. But the *Demon* had a black opaque body, resembling *smoke*, i. e. *foul ether*; as we have before shown; and hence he bore the name of *darkness*. Augustine, when he was a Manichæan, doubted whether the Demon's substance was *earth*, or was air or ether. For thus he writes, (in his Confessions, L. v. c. 10. Opp. tom. i. p. 84.): Hinc enim et mali substantiam quandam credebam esse talem, et habere suam molem tetram ac deformem, sive crassam, quam *terram* dicebant, (It appears from this passage, that the Manichæans made *earth* to be one of the elements of the evil world: whence it follows, that what I before stated is true, viz. that the *darkness* of Manes was simply earth,) sive tenuem atque subtilem, sicut est aëris corpus, quam malignam mentem per illam terram (tene- [p. 767.] brarum) repentem imaginantur.—But II. the pious and ingenious man was unnecessarily in doubt: for *Manes* clearly taught, as we have seen, that the Prince of evils dwelt in *smoke* or corrupt ether, the counterpart to pure ether or air; whence, manifestly, his body was *etherial* or analagous to *smoke*. And when Augustine says, the Demon *creeps* (*repere*) through the whole world of darkness, according to the opinion of the Manichæans; he indicates, that the Demon's body was a *fluid*; which it might be, if it were *ether*, but not if it were earth.—III. God was not confined to any particular part of the world of light; but, like an immense luminary, he overspread and filled his whole empire. But the Prince of darkness resided in a single element of his realm; namely, the uppermost, which they called *smoke*: although his influence, as Augustine says, (*repit*) *creeps* or extends through that whole world. We had before learned the same thing, from *Manes* himself.—IV. God had no definite *form*; or at least, he had not the human form: as we learn from *Augustine*, (Confess. L. v. c. 10. p. 184.) For Augustine says, that he had formerly been pleased with the Manichæan doctrine, because it attributed to God no human form. But the Prince of darkness had a *body* altogether similar to a human body. Says *Augustine*, (contra Faustum L. xx. c. 14. p. 255.) Illi principi non tantum *sui generis*, id est, *bipedes*, quos parentes hominum dicitis, sed etiam cuncta animalium ceterorum genera subdita erant. The Demon was therefore a *biped*; and he also begat *bipeds of his own species*, that is, resembling men. Other proofs in confirmation of this point, the reader may easily collect out of the citations yet to be made. The Prince of darkness was, therefore, properly, as *Manes* says, *immanis dux*, a *monster*, a giant of immense bulk, like the *Micromegas* of an ingenious man, and like the *Typhæus* of ancient Greece. *Manes* wrote a book expressly on *Giants*, τὸν γιγάντειον βίβλον, as *Photius* says, (Bibliotheca Cod. 85. p. 204.) In that work he doubtless treated of the Prince of demons, and of his satellites and ministers; and applied what the ancients tell us of the war of the Giants against the Gods, to the conflict between the good Principle and the bad.—V. These Giants, procreated by the Prince of Giants, were of both sexes, male and female; and they propagated their race, just as men do, by their wives. This is manifest from a signal passage in the seventh book of the

Thesaurus ot *Manes*, which *Augustine* cites, (de natura boni contra Manichæos, c. 44. p. 365.): Potestates (malæ) quæ in singulis cœlorum tractibus ordinatæ sunt ex utroque sexu masculorum ac fœminarum consistunt. Another passage, proving clearly the same thing, will be cited further on. Augustine frequently touches upon this subject; e. g. (contra Faust. L. xxi. c. 10. p. 253.): Hinc etiam prolis fecunditas (among the inhabitants of the world of darkness) suppe-
[p.768.] tebat; nam et conjugia tribuunt eis. And the Prince of Darkness himself had a wife, as will appear further on; and, when a captive, he burned with lust, and even sought coition with a female being of another race, as we shall see in the proper place. But the citizens of the happy world, are not of different sexes; and of course do not beget and bring forth children.—VI. Although the realm of the Prince of darkness is vastly extensive, yet it is narrower and smaller than that over which God reigns. For the world of light is bounded only on one side. This I have before showed: and I now confirm it, by a very noted passage in *Augustine's* Confessions, (L. v. c. 10. p. 84.): Quia Deum bonum nullam malam naturam creasse, qualiscunque pietas me credere cogebat, constituebam (when a Manichæan) ex adverso sibi duas *moles*, (i. e. two *worlds*, of light and darkness,) *utramque infinitam, sed malam angustius, bonam grandius.* - - Et magis pius mihi videbar, si te, Deus meus, cui confitentur ex me miserationes tuæ, *vel ex ceteris partibus infinitum* crederem, quamvis ex *una*, qua tibi *moles mali* opponebatur, cogerer infinitum (so the Benedictine edition reads; but most corruptly. For it is clear as day, that for *infinitum*, it should read *finitum*) fateri, quam si ex omnibus partibus in corporis humani forma te opinarer finiri. But whether the Manichæans, when they said the realm of light was (*infinitum*) *unbounded* on all sides but one, and (*finitum*) *bounded* on that one side only, used the word *infinitum* absolutely, for that which has no limits whatever; or only in the sense of *indefinite*, or whose limits exceed human comprehension and measurement; I must leave undecided. The whole doctrine of the Manichæans respecting the boundaries of both kingdoms, is very difficult to be comprehended; nor could they themselves, when questioned, explain it.—VII. The Prince of darkness was wholly destitute of the moral virtues, justice, veracity, benevolence, &c.; for he vexed, afflicted and harrassed his subjects, and his own children. But God, on the contrary, cherished his subjects and his children in every way, and heaped upon them all the blessings he could.—VIII. The Demon undoubtedly possessed ingenuity, subtilty, and a knowledge of many things; but in this respect, God was superior to him: as may appear from the simple fact, that God had known the existence of the realm of darkness, but the Demon and his princes, for an infinite length of time, had no knowledge of the realm of light. *Manes* himself says, (apud *Titum* Bostrens. L. i. edit. Canisii tom. i. p. 70.): Ἐπαύσαντο ἀλλήλοις ἐπανιστάμενοι, μέχρι οὗ τὸ φῶς ὀψέποτε ἐφώρασαν - - ἀγνοοῦντες μὲν, κ. τ. λ. Principes tenebrarum non prius desierunt in se ipsos moveri, quam lumen *sero* tandem viderent, *quod antea ignorabant.* The Father of light himself confessed the *power* of the Prince of darkness; as *Manes* has informed us, in his Epistola Fundamenti, (apud *August.* de natura boni, c. 42. p. 364.): Lucis vero beatissimae Pater sciens labem magnam ac vastitatem, quae ex tenebris surgeret, adversus sua sancta impendere

saecula. The General of the race of darkness could therefore do much [p. 769.] harm,—not indeed to the realm of light, but to the *sancta Sæcula* of God, that is, to his holy *Æons*. Yet the victory of God over him, is indubitable evidence of the inferiority of the Demon in power.

§ XLII. **Nature and Attributes of the good God or Principle.** The God who governs the world of light, is, as it were, an immense *sun:* and consists wholly of the purest *light*, much more subtile than our light, wonderfully diffused through his whole realm. He has *twelve members*, equally bright and splendid; and an innumerable *family*, who abound in every species of good things. For he had begotten from himself an immense number of most happy *Sæcula;* that is, immutable and enduring Beings. But though the highest and greatest Being, yet he is finite, and limited to a certain space; and of course, is not omnipresent. His *natural powers* also have their limits. For he does not know all things, nor foresee future events, nor can he accomplish all his pleasure; and much less, can he effect his purposes solely by his volitions. But his *moral virtues*, his goodness, beneficence, justice, sanctity, and love of truth, can be confined within no bounds, nor be limited or restrained by anything.(1)

(1) As I am about to treat of the nature and attributes of that good Principle which *Manes* called *God*, and in accordance with his views, I will exhibit as my pattern and guide, that description of God, which *Manes* himself gave in his *Epistola Fundamenti;* and will illustrate it by testimonies from other sources. —In *Augustine's* Book against the Epistle of Manes, (c. 13. p. 115.) *Manes* says: Luminis quidem imperium tenebat Deus Pater, in sua sancta stirpe perpetuus, in virtute magnificus, naturâ ipsa verus, æternitate propria semper exsultans, continens apud se sapientiam et sensus vitales: per quos etiam duodecim membra luminis sui comprehendit, regni videlicet proprii divitias affluentes. In unoquoque autem membrorum ejus sunt recondita millia innumerabilium et immensorum thesaurorum. Ipse vero Pater in sua laude præcipuus magnitudine incomprehensibilis, copulata habet sibi beata et gloriosa Sæcula, neque numero, neque prolixitate æstimanda, cum quibus idem sanctus et illustris Pater et Genitor degit, nullo in regnis ejus insignibus aut indigente aut infirmo constituto. Ita autem fundata sunt ejusdem splendidissima regna supra lucidam et beatam terram, ut a nullo unquam aut moveri aut concuti possint. In this magnificent description of God, some things stand out clearly; namely the eternity of God, his sanctity or his *magnificentia virtutis*, as Manes speaks, his immutability, his love of truth, his wisdom, and his necessary existence. [p. 770.] These, therefore, I shall pass over, and confine myself to those things which are involved in some obscurity, or are stated too briefly.

I. *Manes* gives only a passing notice of that *light*, of which God is composed, by saying that the *Lumen Dei* has twelve members. But there are many other testimonies at hand, which put it beyond all doubt, that *Manes* made the essence of God to be the purest *light*. For he uniformly calls God φῶς, *lucem*, τὸ ἀνώτατον φῶς, *supremam lucem*, τὸ ἀΐδιον φῶς *lucem sempiternam*. See the fragments of his Epistles, in Jo. Alb. *Fabricius*' Bibliotheca Græca, (vol. v. p. 284, 285.) *Augustine*, in his Confessions, (L. v. c. 10. p. 84.) agreeably to the views of Manichaeans, whom he once followed, says: Ipsum quoque Salvatorem nostrum tanquam de massa *lucidissimæ molis tuæ* porrectum ad nostram salutem, (quum Manichaeus essem) putabam. Most accurately expressed! For *Manes* supposed God to be a *formless* but *splendid mass*; that is, *light* wholly without form, and spreading over infinite space. *Faustus*, (apud *August*. L. xx. p. 237.) says: Patrem quidem ipsum lucem incolere credimus summam ac principalem, quam Paulus alias inaccessibilem vocat.—These views of the nature of God, *Manes* held, in common with most ancient nations of the East, with the Gnostics also, and even with not a few christians, who were otherwise orthodox in regard to the Deity. Whoever, therefore, would form a conception of the happy world of *Manes*, must picture to himself a world just like our terraqueous globe, but larger, and one in which God supplies the place of the sun: for his heaven was like our earth, and was composed of the same elements as our world, though purer and nobler: and what the *sun* is in our world, *God* was in the world of light. And much the same idea is to be formed of his world of darkness, which was the counter part to the world of light. For that world also had the form of our world, and included the same elements, though deteriorated: and in the uppermost element, the ether, resided that most savage Giant, the Lord of that world.—But while *Manes* believed God to be *light*, he supposed this divine light to differ from the light which falls upon our visual organs. The light of God, as he supposed, is to be apprehended only by the mind in thinking, and not by our senses or bodily eyes. *Titus* Bostrensis, (contra Manichaeos L. i. p. 72.) quotes thus from *Manes*: Θεοῦ μὲν ἐστὶ φῶς αἰσθητὸν δημιούργημα, αὐτὸς δὲ ἂν εἴη νοητὸν, οὐκ αἰσθητόν. Lumen sub sensus cadens Dei quidem opus est, ipse vero Deus lumen est intelligibile, non sensibile. And *Augustine*, who assails the opinions of the Manichaeans with all his might, frankly owns, that they discriminated between the light which is the essence of God, and that grosser kind of light which meets our eyes: (contra Faustum L. xx. p. 238.): Quando enim discrevistis *lucem, qua cernimus*, ab ea *luce, qua intelligimus*, cum aliud nihil unquam putaveritis esse intelligere veritatem, nisi formas corporeas cogitare, &c.

[p. 771.] II. Although this lucid mass of God, which resembled the sun, had no form; yet, besides wisdom or the power of understanding and judging, according to *Manes*, it had *sensus vitales*. The import of this language, can be nothing but this; that, although God was destitute of a human form, and consequently, of eyes, ears, nose, and the other organs of sense, yet he had the faculty of *sensation* and perception; that is, he could see, hear, percieve, and know every object external to him.

III. God, by these *senses*, as Manes says: *Duodecim membra luminis sui comprehendit, regni videlicet proprii divitias affluentes.* Here he seems to present to us a great *enigma.* The light of God has *twelve members.* What are these members? *Beausobre* conjectures, (vol. i. p. 510.) that we are to understand by them the twelve *powers* of the divine nature, or in the language of philosophers, his *perfections*, which in Oriental phraseology Manes calls members. But this conjecture is, by the very language of *Manes*, divested of all semblance of truth. For he says, God *comprehends* these members, by his *sensus vitales.* But how could God, I ask, by his *sensus vitales*, that is, by the power of *sensation* and perception which was in him, comprehend the *perfections* inherent in his nature? How could he, for instance, by his faculty of (sensitive) perception, comprehend (or apprehend) his *wisdom* and *goodness?* Again; In each of these members: *Recodita sunt millia innumerabilium et immensorum thesaurorum.* How can this be said of the *perfections* of the divine nature? Take whichever of them you please, his power, his justice, his goodness; and see, if there can be conceived to be, innumerable and immense treasures in it? Lastly; To omit other arguments, *Manes* clearly distinguishes these *members* of God, from his *perfections* or attributes, from his authority, his truth, his eternity, his immensity.—I, indeed, have no doubt, that these twelve *members* are so many *lucid masses*, or *globes*, originating and proceeding from the divine Being; and either encompassing the happy world like *satellites*, or moving through its interior, illuminating and fecundating it. For *Manes* calls them members of the *light* of God, which God *comprehends* by his *sensus vitales;* that is, which, though separate and distinct from God, are yet seen, perceived, and governed by him. And in each of them are innumerable *treasures;* viz. multifarious specimens of the divine wisdom, power, and goodness; the riches of nature, of various kinds and uses. Finally there were *divitiæ affluentes*, not of God, but *proprii regni Dei;* that is, from these very splendid globes, various good things descended upon the whole kingdom of God, and on the inhabitants of all its elements. And the Prince of these divine members, I suppose, was *Christ;* whom the Manichæans regarded as a *light* of the second rank, proceeding from the most lucid mass of God. For *Manes*, in his Epistola Fundamenti, calls him the *right arm of light*, as if he were the principal member of the divine light: *Dextera luminis* tueatur et eripiat vos ab omni incursatione maligna. On the rest of the de- [p. 772.] scription, I have nothing to say.

IV. Copulata sibi Deus habet beata et *gloriosa sæcula*, quæ nec numero, nec prolixitate æstimari possunt. In the Syriac of *Manes*, undoubtedly, was the word *Holam*, for which the Latin translator used *Sæculum.* The Greeks express it by Ἀιών. By this word the Gnostics, and with them *Manes*, denoted beings of a divine origin, and therefore, etherial, immortal, and enduring. We, in scripture language, might call the *Sæcula* of Manes *Angels.* These *Æons* of Manes, like their Parents, lacked a human form, and must be conceived to be small shining masses or bodies. The *Æons* of the Gnostics were of both sexes, male and female. But *Manes* admitted of marriages only in the world of darkness; and therefore his *Sæcula* had no sexual distinctions. They were the offspring of God, or emanated from the divine nature. But what *Manes* meant when he said *Deum esse in sancta sua stirpe perpetuum*, I cannot satisfactorily determine. He seems to mean, that the progeny of God, or these Sæcula, were equally enduring and eternal with God himself, so that the eternity of God was imparted to his offspring. But his meaning may be, that God is always or for ever generating new Sæcula. In like manner, I do not understand what he means, when he says of those glorious and happy Sæcula: *Nec prolixitate æstimari possunt.* I can suppose he may mean, that the magnitude of the Sæcula is so great, that the human mind cannot estimate or comprehend it. Or can it be, that the *prolixitas* attributed to them, denotes abundance of gifts and virtues?

V. While *Manes* declares God to be *magnitudine incomprehensibilem*, he clearly denied his *infinity*. For he bounded the world of light by the world of darkness; so that infinity, immensity, or absolute omnipresence, could not be attributed to God. The world of darkness, also, was equally eternal and self-existent with the world of light; and, therefore, it could not be subject to God; who, if he were present in that miserable and wretched region, would change its nature, dispel its darkness, and bring joy and happiness to its inhabitants: all which, according to *Manes*, was impossible. But what need of arguments? *Faustus*, the most eloquent of the Manichæans, clearly states the views of his sect in the following words, (apud *August.* L. xxv. c. 1. p. 307.): Summus et verus Deus, utrum sit idem infinitus, necne, si quæritur, de hoc vero nos boni et mali contrarietas breviter poterit edocere. Quoniam quidem si non est malum, profecto infinitus est Deus: habet autem finem, si malum est: constat autem esse malum: *non igitur infinitus est Deus:* illinc enim esse mala accipiunt (I think, it should read: *incipiunt*) ubi bonorum est finis. Whether this passage is to be understood solely of the infinity of his *nature* or *essence*, or also of the [p. 773.] infinity of his *attributes* or *perfections*, appears doubtful. The very learned *Beausobre*, (vol. i. p. 503 &c.) who always defends the Manichæans, maintains, that they denied the infinity of the divine *nature*, by inclosing their God within local boundaries; but they admitted the infinity of his *attributes*, and particularly, they set no bounds to his *knowledge* and his *power*. Of this we shall see presently. We here only show, that *Faustus* intended, this infinity should be understood of both his nature and his attributes. For in the very discussion from which the extract is taken, he aims to prove, that the catholic Christians ascribed finite attributes to God, and therefore had the same views of God as the Manichæans. The Christians, he says, call God, the God of Abraham, of Isaac, of Jacob, and the God of the Hebrews; they therefore limit the power of God. He adds: Cujus autem finita potestas est, et ipse non caret fine. He subjoins other similar arguments, which are no better, and winds up by saying: Hic si est Deus (Abrahami, Isaaci, Jacobi) quem colitis, liquet ex hoc admodum, quod habeat finem. Si vero infinitum Deum esse vultis, hunc vos ante renunciare necesse est. His reasoning is ridiculous; yet, it puts it beyond all doubt, that he joined both the kinds of infinity together: and respecting both infinities, there was a discussion between orthodox Christians and Manichæans, when the question was put to Faustus: Deus finem habet aut infinitus est? For thus *Faustus* reasoned: Whoever is indued with finite attributes, is also finite in his nature: And conversely: Whoever is of a finite nature, must necessarily have finite attributes.

VI. The moral attributes of God, his love of truth, his goodness, his justice, his beneficence, were undoubtedly boundless, according to Manichæan principles. This is manifest from the language used by *Manes.* But his other attributes, and especially his *knowledge* and *power*, beyond all controversy, had limits. As to the limitation of the *knowledge* of the Manichæan God, I know not how any one can doubt it, who is acquainted with the history of the war between the good and the bad Principle. The Prince of the world of light knew not what was taking place in the world of darkness, although he knew that such a world existed. He did not foresee, that the Prince of darkness would make war upon him and his kingdom: for, had he foreseen it, he would have erected barriers against the assaults of the race of darkness, before the war commenced, as he did afterwards. He did not foresee, that the commander whom he first sent against the Demon, would be unsuccessful. He did not foresee, that in the conflict light would become mixed up with darkness. There are many other specimens of the ignorance of this God; and when I consider them, I cannot but wonder, that this perspicacious and extraordinary man should not have thought of them, but could bring himself to believe this Deity to be like the God of Christians. But love and hatred have a mighty influence.—As to the *power* of this God: in the first place, it is very certain, that it differed greatly from the power of the God whom we Christians worship. For our God can effect whatever he pleases, by his *fiat*, his volition, or word. Not so the Manichæan God. He was obliged to raise an army, in order to resist the troops [p. 774.] of the Prince of darkness, to array force against force, and wage a regular war. The same God could not, by his own power, rescue the light mixed with darkness; but had to resort to cunning, counsel, sagacity, in order to recover his property. Moreover, all that transpired between God and the Prince of darkness, shows his power to be finite; for he encountered many obstacles, which resisted the accomplishment of his wishes. The philosopher *Simplicius*, (in his Comment on *Epictetus*, p. 164.) has shown at some length, that the God of the Manichæans did not possess unlimited power.—But the very learned man (*Beausobre*) reminds us, that *Fortunatus* the Manichæan, (Disputatio cum *Augustino*, Opp. tom. viii. p. 73 &c.) calls God *omnipotent.* This is true: but it is also equally true, that the Manichæans used this word in a far more limited sense than the Christians do. In their view, indeed, God can do all things which are not contrary to nature; but these things are numerous. He cannot exterminate the Demon; he cannot destroy the kingdom of darkness; he cannot extirpate evil; he cannot restore to liberty the souls made captive by the Demon, solely by his word or volition, but he must employ some artifice for it; and finally, to pass by other things, he cannot produce *matter*, or create a thing, as we say, out of nothing. All things that exist, from a natural necessity, have existed from eternity. The God of the Manichæans, therefore, like the God of the Stoics, was obliged to yield to fate or necessity.—But, observes the same learned man, (pp. 505, 506.) God could punish the whole army of darkness, if he had been disposed; and he could so restrain them, that they could neither effect nor attempt any thing against him. But he would not, because this miserable race was unworthy of his regard. In proof, he cites *Augustine*, (contra *Adimantum* Manich. c. 7. p. 85.) who acknowledges that God, according to the belief of the Manichæans, *had prepared* (*præparasse*) an eternal prison for the race of darkness. But if this were so, it would not prove the power of God to be boundless. For it does not follow, that he can do everything he chooses, because he can hold a certain race in check, and prevent their doing harm to himself and others. But the fact was not, as the worthy man supposes. For if this God had possessed such power, he would have pursued a different course in his war with the Demon. We see him alarmed, and raising forces against the Prince of darkness. But his alarm and his army were needless, if he had power to repel, to coerce, and punish the Lord of darkness, by a mere volition or word. But our learned author does not quote truly the language of *Augustine*. That father did not write *præparasse*, but merely *præparare;* which makes the sense very different. The passage reads thus: Ipsi enim dicunt, Deum genti tenebrarum æternum carcerem *præparare*, quam dicunt inimicam esse Deo. From this statement, who can make out, that God could, if he [p. 775.] pleased, have prevented the race of darkness from issuing forth from their dark world, and invading the world of light, but that he despised the vile and imbecile rabble? The sense of the passage is this: God now holds captive the race of darkness, which he has vanquished, and in due time he will thrust them into prison. The prison is the world of darkness itself, into which God will, at the time appointed, compel them to return; as we shall see hereafter.—Yet, not to dissemble anything, there is a passage in the *Epistola Fundamenti*, which escaped the learned man's research, and from which it seems inferable, that *Manes* thought the power of God adequate to the destruction of the smoky race of darkness. For thus *Manes* speaks, (apud *August.* de natura boni, c. 42. tom. viii. p. 364.); Lucis vero beatissimæ Pater, sciens labem magnam et vastitatem, quæ ex tenebris surgeret, adversus sua sancta impendere Saecula, nisi aliquod eximium et praeclarum et virtute potens Numen opponat, quo *superet simul et destruat stirpem tenebrarum*, qua *extincta*, perpetua quies lucis incolis pararetur. But either *Manes* uttered this incautiously, and forgetting the principles of his system, or it must be understood merely of the *animals* in the world of darkness. Those *animals* spring up and die; so that the race of them might seem to be destructible. But, as for the Demon and his princes, although God vanquished them, yet he did not destroy and exterminate them; neither could he destroy and exterminate them, because they had a necessary existence, and were immortals. As, according to the views of the Manichaeans, God is unable to create a thing from nothing, so is he unable to reduce to nothing, any part or portion of eternal nature.

§ XLIII. **The Manichaean Trinity. Christ and the Holy Spirit.** The good God, the Lord of light, although he is one, simple, and immutable, yet, in a certain sense, is triple or threefold. For after the world was founded, he produced from himself two *Majesties*, that is, two Beings like himself; by whom he might both save the souls inclosed in bodies, and gradually extract the portion of light and of the good fire mixed with earth from it, and restore it to its original state.([1]) The one of these Beings is called *Christ;* the other the *Holy Spirit.* *Christ* is a splendid mass of the purest light of God, self-existent, animated, endued with wisdom and reason, and having his seat in the sun, yet communicating a portion of his influence to the moon. Hence prayers are to be directed to the sun and moon.([2]) Inferior to him, the *Holy Spirit* is also an animated and lucid mass, of the same nature with God himself, connected with and resident in the ether which encompasses our globe. He not only moves and illumi- [p. 776.] nates the minds of men, but he also fecundates the earth; that is, he excites the particles of the divine fire latent in the earth, and makes them shoot up in herbs, and shrubs, and trees, and yield fruits useful and convenient for men.([3]) This whole doctrine is derived from the ancient Persian system. And hence, all that the Manichæans teach respecting a divine Trinity, must be understood and explained, not in conformity with Christian views, but in accordance with the Persian principles respecting *Mithra* and the ether, to which *Manes* accommodated the Christian religion.

(1) That the Manichaeans believed in a species of Trinity, or held to two Beings of the same nature with God, subordinate to him, is unquestionable. *Manes* himself not obscurely acknowledges a Trinity, in his *Epistola Fundamenti*, (apud *August.* Disput. cum Felice, L. i. p. 341.) by saluting those to whom he wrote, thus: Pax (a) *Dei invisibilis* sit cum fratribus: - - sed et (b) *Dextra luminis* (his name for *Christ*) tueatur et eripiat vos ab omni incursione maligna - - pietas vero (c) *Spiritis sancti* intima vestri pectoris adaperiat. His disciples speak much more clearly. But they, as is manifest, prudently accommodate themselves to the phraseology of Christians, and especially to the decrees of the Nicene council, which was after the times of their master; in order not to appear differing too much from the common views of Christians. For when Constantine the Great, and so many emperors, had issued laws against their sect, the Manichaeans became very considerate and provident, and they clothed and concealed their sentiments under the usual phraseology of Christians, and in scripture language; in order to avoid odium as much as possible, and to show the coincidence of the Scriptures (which, however, they despised,) with their opinions. *Fortunatus*, who was peculiarly circumspect, and was well acquainted with the language of the Bible, which was always on his lips, says, (Apud *Augustinum* Disput. i. cum eo, p. 69.): Nostra professio est, quod incorruptibilis sit Deus, quod lucidus, quod inadibilis, quod intenibilis (i. e. cannot be *grasped* and *held fast*), impassibilis, aeternam lucem et propriam inhabitet: quod nihil ex sese corruptibile (and therefore no material bodies) proferat, nec

tenebras, nec daemones, nec Satanam, nec aliud adversum in regno ejus reperiri posse: Sui autem similem Salvatorem direxisse. - - - His rebus credimus et haec est ratio fidei nostrae, et pro viribus animi nostri mandatis ejus obtemperare, unam fidem sectantes *hujus Trinitatis, Patris et Filii et Spiritus sancti.* The cunning man says much about the office of the Son, which I omit here, but will cite in a proper place; while of the Holy Spirit he is wholly silent, till he comes to the end of his speech; and then he couples him with the Father and the Son, although he had not before been mentioned. The doctrine of the Ma-
[p. 777.] nichaeans respecting the Holy Spirit, he could not explain in the language of the Bible; and therefore he thought best to omit it and keep it out of sight. *Faustus,* of the same sect, a man of letters, courageous and self-confident, explains more boldly the nature of the Holy Spirit: his statements will be adduced shortly. At present, we only consider what he says of the Trinity. In his Discussion with *Augustine,* (L. xx. c. 1. p. 237.) he says: Igitur nos Patris quidem Dei omnipotentis, et Christi Filii ejus et Spiritus sancti unum idemque sub triplici appellatione Numen credimus. He seems here to accord with those who regard the three Persons in God, as only three names for one God, discarding any real distinction of the Persons. But, what follows acquits him of the error; for he very clearly inculcates, that the Son and the Holy Spirit are truly distinct from the Person of the Father. *Secundinus,* a very ingenious Manichaean, and apparently very modest, whose long and eloquent Epistle is extant in Augustine, (Opp. tom. viii. p. 369 &c.) commences thus: Habeo et ago gratias ineffabili ac sacratissimae Majestati, ejusque primogenito, omnium luminum (i. e. of all the splendid and happy *Sæcula* or *Æons*) Regi, Jesu Christo, habeo gratias et supplex Sancto refero Spiritui, quod dederint, praebuerintque occasionem, qua ego securus salutarem egregiam tuam sanctitatem. More proofs are not necessary.—But this Manichaean Trinity differed essentially from that which Christians profess; and a very learned man certainly lost his labor, when he attempted to prove that it was altogether the Catholic doctrine, except as to the manifest inequality of the Persons. This will appear further on. At present only one argument will be offered. It is, that neither the Son nor the Holy Spirit existed anterior to this our world. This is asserted most explicitly of the Son, by *Fortunatus,* a man generally cautious, as already remarked, and one who either dissembles or explains artfully what might be prejudicial to his sect. But in his Dispute with *Augustine* (i. p. 69.) he says: Nostra professio est - - Deum sui similem Servatorem direxisse (i. e. sent him unto men) *Verbum natum a constitutione mundi, cum mundum faceret,* post mundi fabricam inter homines venisse. *Secundinus,* indeed, in his Epistle to Augustine, (tom. viii. p. 369.) calls Christ the *first-born* (*primogenitus*) *of God:* which would seem to imply, that he existed before all the *Æons.* But the word is ambiguous, as *Augustine* observed in his reply, (c. 5. p. 377.) and might, as he says, denote the *superiority of his divinity.* For any one may be called the *first-born,* who is the chief and head of many of the same nature with himself, though he be posterior as to the order of births. If the Son did not exist before this world, but was born of God at the time the world was made; undoubtedly, the Holy Spirit, who was manifestly inferior to the Son in dignity

and greatness, was not superior in age. Besides, the offices sustained by the Son and the Holy Spirit,—not to mention also their residences, which were no older than the world,—remove all doubt in the case. For the sole [p. 778.] office of the Son was, to restore to freedom the good souls unfortunately immersed in gross muddy matter; and that of the Holy Spirit was, to aid intelligent minds in their upward aspirations, and to extract and separate the sparks of the good fire now mixed up with darkness or earth. Consequently, if that pernicious war between the Princes of light and of darkness had not occurred, producing the mixture of the good and the evil, there would have been no need of either the Son or the Holy Spirit. But a great number of souls being captured and carried off, and the light being commingled with darkness, it became necessary, that the Father of light should emit from himself and produce the two very powerful Beings, the Son and the Holy Spirit, by whom he might gradually recover the captured part of his realm, and restore it to its pristine felicity.

(2) Although Manes brought forward and used the appellation *Christ*, yet he deemed it unsuitable. It was Jewish, and was appropriate to that Messiah whom the Hebrew nation expected, who was materially different from the Son of God of whom he conceived. To this purpose, there is a striking passage in his Epistle to *Odas*, (apud Jo. Alb. *Fabricium*, Biblioth. Græca, vol. v. p. 285.): Ἡ δὲ τοῦ Χριστοῦ προσηγορία ὄνομα ἐστὶ καταχρηστικὸν, οὔτε εἴδους, οὔτε οὐσίας σημαντικόν. Appellatio Christi nomen est, quod per abusionem (as rhetoricians say) tantum adhibetur: (That is, it is a term unsuitable for the thing, yet one used because it is common;) nec enim vel *speciem* (i. e. the class of beings, to which the Son of God belongs,) vel *essentiam* ejus significat. We therefore see, why he chose, in his Epistola Fundamenti, (as we have before seen,) to call the Son of God *Dexteram Luminis.* For this appellation expressed the *nature* and dignity of the Son, according to his views. The *Christ* of the Manichæans was, as *Fortunatus* says, *like the Father*, and born of him. And therefore, as the Father was the *purest light*, a light which is conceivable by the mind, but not apprehensible by the senses, and is destitute of any form or shape; so Christ also must be a splendid or shining *mass*, and endued with the same attributes with his Parent, though inferior in degree, viz. wisdom, reason, goodness, munificence. Hence *Manes*, in his Epistles published by Jo. Alb. *Fabricius*, (Biblioth. Græc. vol. v. p. 284, 285.) calls him: Τοῦ ἀϊδίου φωτὸς υἱόν. *Sempiternæ Lucis Filium.* And he proves Christ to be *light*, by the narrative of his transfiguration on the mount. And that this *light* is most pure, and such as cannot be felt or seen by the eyes, he proves, (in his Epistle to *Cudarus*,) by the fact, that when the Jews attempted to stone Christ, *he passed through the midst of them, and was unseen.* Καὶ μέσος αὐτῶν διελθὼν οὐχ ὡράτο. And to this argument, he subjoins: Ἡ γὰρ ἄυλος μορφὴ – – ὁρατὴ μὲν οὐκ ἦν, ἐψηλαφᾶτο δὲ οὐδαμῶς, διὰ τὸ μηδεμίαν ἔχειν κοινωνίαν τὴν ὕλην πρὸς τὸ ἄυλον. Forma enim omnis expers materiæ neque videri poterat, neque tangebatur, quia materia nullam habet communionem cum eo, quod caret materia. Therefore, *Augustine*, while a Manichæan, agreeably to the views of his master, conceived of Christ as a broad and extended *light*, *projecting out* and issuing from the Father. [p. 779.]

He says, (Confessiones, L. v. c. 10. Opp. tom. i. p. 84.): Ipsum quoque Salvatorem nostrum unigenitum tuum tanquam de massa lucidissimae molis tuae *porrectum* ad nostram salutem, ita putabam, ut aliud de illo non crederem, nisi quod possem vanitate imaginari. Yet this *light* of the Son, though like that of the Father, and of course having, as *Manes* says (apud *Fabricium*): φύσιν ἁπλὴν καὶ ἀληθῆ, simplicem naturam et veram; yet could be so obscured and obstructed by matter, as not to put forth and exhibit all its energy. For, in his Epistle to *Zebena*, (apud *Fabricium* l. c. p. 284.) when assigning a reason why the Son of God assumed among men a human form, he says it was, ἵνα μὴ (φῶς) κρατηθῆ διὰ τῆς ουσίας τῆς σαρκὸς, καὶ πάθη, καὶ φθαρῆ, τῆς σκοτίας φθειρούσης αὐτοῦ τὴν ἐνέργειαν τὴν φωτεινήν. Ne lux comprehenderetur ab essentia carnis et pataretur ac corrumperetur, tenebris operationem lucis corrumpentibus. This is very explicit. There was, therefore, a great difference between the Father and the Son, although the latter had the like nature with the former. For, as the Manichaeans often inculcate, the *light* of the Father could not, in any degree, be contaminated, impaired, or weakened, by the darkness: but the light of the Son, if surrounded by matter or by material bodies, suffered some diminution, and was prevented from imparting all its efficacy to others. In whatever manner he explained this matter, it is certain that *Manes* considered the light of the Son as inferior to the light of the Father.

Christ or the Son, after he was born of the Father, established his seat or residence in the *sun;* yet in such a way, as to impart also a portion of his influence to the *moon*, and in some measure to reside in it. This is a well known dogma of the Manichæan school, and is attested by many writers. But no one has stated it more clearly than *Faustus; (apud August.* contra Faust. L. xx. c. 2. p. 237.) *Faustus* being asked: *Cur solem colitis, nisi quia estis paganni?* does not disown this worship of the sun and moon; but he denies, that these luminaries are Deities. He says: Nos Patrem quidem ipsum lucem incolere credimus summam ac principalem, quam Paulus alias inaccessibilem vocat: *Filium* vero *in hac secunda ac visibili luce* (ss. *the sun*) consistere, qui quoniam sit et ipse *geminus*, ut eum Apostolus novit, Christum dicens esse Dei *virtutem* et sapientiam: *virtutem* quidem ejus in *sole* habitare credimus, *sapientiam* vero in *luna*. From this passage, it is clear: *First;* That *Manes* supposed the Son of God not to be the *sun* itself, but to dwell in the *sun* as in a *palace*. The ancients indeed, and not a few of the moderns, think the Manichæans regarded the sun itself as Christ. But they are abundantly confuted by this passage of *Faustus:* who, besides other things, declares, that Christ *dwells in the second and visible light*. We have before seen, that the Son consists, not of the visible light which falls on our eyes, but of that light which constitutes the Father, which can neither be seen nor felt, and can be apprehended only by the mind. Therefore, that *second and visible light*, in which he *dwells*, must necessarily be distinct [p. 780.] from him. Besides, as *Augustine* has expressly stated, (Liber de Hæres. c. 46. p. 11.) the Manichæans denied, that the sun consists in what is properly denominated *light;* they supposed it to be made up of *good fire*, which is one of the elements of the world of light: Duo coeli luminaria ita distinguunt, ut lunam dicant factam ex bona aqua, *solem* vero *ex igne bono*. The good fire of the Manichaeans was of a different nature from the light. The rude and illiterate among the Manichaeans, or the flock of *Auditors* as they were called, doubtless confounded, as is usual, the sun with the Son of God who resided in it; and they supposed they worshipped Christ whenever they turned their faces to the sun. And hence arose the opinion of many among the ancients, that the *Manichaeans* considered the sun to be the Son of God.—The reason why *Manes* located the Son of God or Christ in the sun, it is not difficult to discover. It was necessary, as he supposed, that the inhabitants of this globe should have before their eyes an image of God, whom no mortal eye can see, or of that Son of God, whom God had produced from himself for the purpose of saving souls; in order that they might think the more constantly and intensely on the salvation to be obtained through him. But the Son of God could not be seen by the eyes of mortals, unless he were surrounded by a body, or by some appearance of a body. And besides, the pure *light* of which he was composed, would, as before noticed, be tarnished and obscured by material bodies, if it should present itself to them naked. As therefore Christ needed a *body*, in which he could be seen, and in which he could operate freely and strongly, he chose a body of a nature the nearest resembling light, in which to dwell. For *good fire*, which is very different from ours, could do no injury to the perfectly simple nature of the divine light. *Manes* says, (apud *Fabricium*, l. c. p. 285.): Τὸ δὲ ἀνώτατον φῶς ἔδειξεν ἑαυτῷ ἐν τοῖς ὑλακοῖς σώμασι σῶμα. Suprema lux (i. e. *Christ*, of whom he is speaking) ipsa sibi inter corpora ex materia constantia corpus demonstravit seu delegit: namely, such a body, as agreed the most perfectly with his nature.—*Secondly*; It appears from the passage in *Faustus*, that some of the energy of Christ resides in the *moon*, while his *virtus*, that is, (as I suppose,) his *essential nature* dwells in the sun. As we learn from the language of *Augustine*, recently quoted, the Manichaeans believed the moon to consist *ex aqua bona* (*of good water*); and therefore regarded it as a kind of sea. *Manes* himself, in the seventh Book of his *Thesaurus*, (from which *Augustine* gives a long extract, in his Tract de natura boni, c. 44. p. 366.) calls the moon *Navem vitalium aquarum*. Whence it appears, that they supposed the moon to have no light of its own, or to be an opaque body. But the splendor of the moon arises from the souls purified in it. For souls undergo a lustration in the moon, as we shall see in the proper place. Yet see *Simplicius* on Epictetus, p. 167. But, I must confess, I do not intirely understand what the Manichaeans mean, when they say, the *wisdom* of the Son of God appears especially in the moon, but his *virtus* (*virtue*, or *essence*) in the sun. All the ancients, as is well known, supposed the sun to be fed, sustained or nourished, by water. Perhaps the Manichaeans were [p. 781.] of the same opinion; and therefore they annexed the good water of the moon to the good fire of the sun, in order to afford it aliment. *Manes* discourses very largely respecting the sun, moon and stars, in his writings. Says *Augustine*, (Confessiones L. v. c. 7. p. 81.): Libri (sacri) eorum pleni sunt longissimis fabulis, de coelo et sideribus et *sole et luna*. Yet this part of the system of *Manes* must necessarily have been very obscure. For those of his disciples who lived in the fourth century, being called upon to give account of their master's precepts, either offered the merest nonsense, or, if more ingenuous, acknowledged that they did not understand them. *Augustine* requested *Faustus*, the most learned Manichaean of that age, to explain to him these mysteries : but *Faustus* frankly acknowledged his ignorance, and declined the task : Quæ tamen (i. e. the opinions of Manes respecting the sun, moon and stars) ubi consideranda et discutienda protuli, modeste sane ille (*Faustus*) nec ausus est subire ipsam (read, *istam*) sarcinam. Noverat enim se ista non nosse, nec eum puduit confiteri. Non erat de talibus, quales multos loquaces passus eram, *conantes ea me docere, et dicentes* (perhaps, *docentes*) *nihil*. - - Noluit se temere disputando in ea coartari, unde nec exitus ei esset ullus, nec facilis reditus. Of these fables respecting the sun, which *Faustus* could not explain, one was that which *Augustine* mentions, (contra Faust. L. xx. c. 6. p. 238.) viz. The Manichaeans denied, that the sun was *round ;* and maintained, on the contrary, that it presented a *triangular* form, or shone upon us through a sort of triangular window : Quum omnium oculis rotundus sol effulgeat, eaque, illi figura pro sui ordinis positione perfecta sit: vos eum triangulum perhibetis, id est, per quamdam triangulam coeli fenestram lucem istam mundo terrisque radiare. Ita fit, ut ad istum quidem solem dorsum, cervicemque curvetis ; non autem ipsum tam clara rotunditate conspicuum, sed nescio quam navim per foramen triangulum micantem atque lucentem—adoretis. If *Augustine* correctly apprehended the views of the Manichaeans, they supposed that we do not see the whole of the sun, because God has interposed between it and us a sort of triangular body, through which some portion of its splendor reaches the inhabitants of our world. But I doubt whether *Augustine* correctly understood the opinion of *Manes*.—The speculations of *Manes* respecting the sun, were not his own inventions, but were derived from the opinions of the Persians respecting *Mithra*. The Persians called *Mithra* τριπλάσιον (*triple*) : on which, I recollect to have made remarks formerly, (Notes on *Cudworth's* Intellectual System, tom. I. p. 333, &c.) They also called the moon *triformis* (*of three forms*) : as is stated by *Julius Firmicus*, (de errore profanar. religionum p. 413.) Perhaps *Manes*, being a Persian, said the same [p. 782.] thing ; but *Augustine* being unacquainted with Persian opinions, misapprehended, and supposed the form of a triangle to be mentioned.

As the Manichaeans supposed the Son of God to reside in the sun and moon, it is not strange that they should pay some honor to those luminaries; and it is abundantly testified, that they turned their eyes to them, when they prayed, *Augustine* says, (de Haeres. c. 46. p. 13.) : Orationes faciunt ad solem per diem, quaqua versum circuit: ad lunan per noctem, si apparet: si autem non apparet, ad Aquiloniam partem, qua sol cum occiderit ad Orientem revertitur, stant orantes. And in various passages, *Augustine* charges the Manichaeans with the worship of the sun and moon, as being a hateful crime. And so does the Platonic Philosopher *Simplicius*, (Comment. in Enchirid. Episteti, p. 167.) : Τῷ ἐκ πάντων τῶν ἐν τῷ ὀυρανῷ μόνους τούς δύο φωστῆρας τιμᾶν - - τῶν δὲ ἄλλων καταφρονεῖν, ὡς τῆς τοῦ κακοῦ μοίρας ὄντων. Sola totius cœli duo lumina honorant - - cetera vero ut quae ad malum pertineant, contemnunt. I know not whether it was true, as *Simplicius* here asserts, that the Manichaeans thought the other stars to be connected with evil ; indeed I can hardly believe it was true. But that they paid no honors to any celestial body, except the sun and moon, is beyond debate, and may be demonstrated by the testimonies of *Augustine* and *Faustus*. Nor will the reason of this distinction be deemed uncertain, if we consider, that they located the Son of God nowhere, except in the sun and moon. Moreover, the Manichæans do not disclaim all worship of the sun and moon; but only apologize for it. *Faustus*, cited by *Augustine*, (contra Faust. L. xx. c. 1. p. 237.) declares himself *not ashamed of the worship of the divine luminaries:* but he adds, that he holds to one God, and abhors all superstition: Ego a paganis multum diversus incedo: qui ipsum me—rationabile Dei templum puto: vivum vivæ majestatis simulacrum Filium ejus accipio - - honores divinos ac sacraficia in solis orationibus ac ipsis puris et simplicibus pono. As there is no doubt on this subject, the only inquiry is, whether the Manichæans addressed their prayers to the sun and moon themselves, or to God and his Son, as residing in the sun and moon. The ancient Christian doctors nearly all tell us, that this sect accounted the sun and moon among the Gods; and *Augustine* himself, when he becomes much heated with discussion, charges this crime upon them; although on other occasions, he explains their views more favorably. But this accusation may be refuted by strong arguments. *First*, as we learn from *Augustine*, the Manichæans supposed the sun to consist of *good fire*, and the moon of *good water*. But the Manichæans did not worship the celestial elements in place of God; it does not appear credible, therefore, that they should have worshipped the sun and moon as Gods. *Secondly*, *Alexander* of Lycopolis, an adversary of the Manichæans, (in his Tract against them, p. 5. in *Combefis'* Auctarium Biblioth. Patrum,) expressly says: Solem et lunam, non tanquam Deos revereri, verum tanquam *viam*, quæ ducit ad Deum: ὀυχ ὡς Θεοὺς, ἀλλ' ὡς ὁδὸν, δι' ἣν ἐστι πρὸς τὸν Θεὸν ἀφικέσθαι. This language does [p. 783.] not explain the *form* of the worship which the Manichæans paid to the sun and moon; for the phrase, *Naturam quandam ut viam ad Deum colere*, may be understood variously. Still, the passage acquits them of the crime commonly laid to their charge. Moreover, Augustine, a very competent witness, who had frequently been present at their worship, frankly owns, that he found nothing there contrary to the Christian religion: (Disput. cum Fortunato, p. 69.): Ego in oratione, in qua interfui, nihil turpe fieri vidi: sed solum contra fidem animadverti, quam postea didici et probavi, quod contra solem facitis orationem. Præter hoc in illa oratione vestra nihil novi comperi. The Manichæans, therefore, although they prayed publicly with their faces towards the sun, did not offer prayers to the sun, but to God himself. Yet this testimony of *Augustine* does not fully settle the question; for he adds, that he would have what he says to be understood of their common prayers, at which all Manichæans might be present; and that perhaps the prayers of the initiated, or those whom they called the *Elect*, were different: Utrum separatim vobiscum habeatis aliquam orationem, Deus solus potest nosse, et vos. - - Quisquis autem vobis opponit quæstionem aliquam de moribus, Electis vestris opponit. Quid autem inter vos agatis, qui Electi estis, ego scire non possum. To this suspicion, *Fortunatus* makes no reply. It appears, therefore, *first*, that the Manichæans did not place the sun and moon among Gods, for they worshipped only one God; and, *secondly*, that they addressed their prayers to God only, although they turned their faces to the sun.—It remains to enquire, whether the *Elect* among the Manichæans, who understood all the mysteries of the sect, made supplications in private to the sun and moon, not as being Gods, but as beneficient Beings. *Faustus*, a talented man, and one of the *Elect*, seems to settle this question; (in *Augustine*, L. xx. c. 1. p. 237.) Yet he does not settle it; for he equivocates, and avoids giving a clear and explicit answer. Thus much, indeed, we may learn from him, that *Augustine* had reason for the suspicion, that the *Elect* prayed differently from the common people, and paid a sort of worship to the sun and moon; but the nature of that worship, *Faustus* leaves dubious. One of his adversaries asked him: Cur solem colitis, nisi quia estis pagani et gentium Schisma, non secta? (i. e. not the *Christian* sect.) He answers very captiously. First, he concedes, that the Manichaeans do worship the sun and moon: Absit, ut divinorum luminum erubescam culturam. *Augustine* had witnessed, that the assembled people admitted nothing into their prayers that contravened the Christian religion, although they turned their faces to the sun. This confession of *Faustus* must therefore refer only to the *Elect*. *Faustus* then adds, that this worship of the luminaries *has nothing in common with paganism* (*nihil habere cum gentibus commune*). He therefore declared—what we also admit—that his sect did not [p. 784.] worship the sun and moon, as Gods. He proceeds to state, that the Father, the Son, and the Spirit, were invoked and adored by his people. Thus far well! But after speaking of the Holy Spirit, he returns to that worship, with which the Manichaeans were reproached; and he explains it, in a manner that shows plainly, the man would not disclose the nature of it: Quapropter et nobis circa universa, et vobis similiter erga panem et calicem par religio est, quamvis eorum acerrime oderitis auctores. That is: We worship and adore the universe, in the same manner in which you worship and adore the bread and the wine in the Lord's supper. This comparison seems to mean something; and yet it means nothing. And it was brought forward solely to darken the subject, and to elude the question. We learn from it, indeed, that the Christians of that age paid some external honor to the bread and wine of the sacred supper; but, what *Faustus* understood by this honor, does not appear. And therefore we cannot learn from this comparison, in what sense, or for what ends, the Manichaeans worshipped the sun and moon. And *Augustine*, in his reply to the passage, shuns the light as much as *Faustus*. He mentions, indeed, that the comparison is not to the point; but he does not tell us, what difference there was between the worship of the bread and wine by Christians, and the worship of the sun and moon by the Manichaeans. He first says, (c. 13. p. 243.): Noster panis et calix non quilibet, sed certa consecratione mysticus fit nobis, non nascitur. But this is nothing. For *Faustus* knew very well that the Christians consecrated the bread and the cup, and on that account, esteemed them mystical. *Augustine* proceeds: Quamvis sit panis et calix, alimentum est refectionis, non sacramentum religionis, nisi quod benedicimus, gratiasque agimus Domino in omni ejus munere, non solum spiritali, sed etiam corporali. This also is nothing to the purpose. For he changes the subject, and passes from the bread and wine of the sacred Supper, to ordinary or common bread and wine. concerning which there was no dispute: he denies that *a cup* and *wine* are a *religious sacrament:* and maintains, on the contray, that they are a *refreshing aliment.* This is true of common bread and wine; but not also of the bread and wine of the holy supper; for these are, not merely *refreshing aliment*, but a *religious sacrament;* as he had just before admitted, by saying they became *mystical* by consecration. And yet, after some cavils, as if he had triumphed, he closes the discussion thus: Quomodo ergo comparas panem et calicem nostrum et parem religionem dicis errorem a veritate longe discretum, pejus desipiens, quam nonnulli, qui nos propter panem et calicem Cererem et Liberum colere existimant. He therefore concedes, that the Christians worshipped the bread and wine; and he informs us, that on account of this worship, some persons believed, that the Christians adored Ceres and Bacchus. But he would not tell plainly, what was meant by this Christian adoration of the bread and wine, and how it differed from the Manichæan worship of the sun and moon. The crafty *Faustus*, perceiving the ulcer of his sect to be touched, led [p. 785.] his adversary into a snare by that comparison, and so escaped; and *Augustine* in like manner, looked around for a way of escape merely, and would not say, whether he approved or disapproved the Christian practice of adoring the bread and wine, nor disclose the true nature of it. At length, *Faustus* attempts to vindicate the practice of his sect in worshipping the sun and moon, by the example of all nations. He says: Tu vel quilibet alius rogatus, ubinam Deum suum credat habitare, respondere non dubitabit; In lumine: ex quo cultus hic meus (ss. *solis*) omnium testimonio confirmatur. But this is not clear. We are told, indeed, that the Manichæans venerate the sun or *light*, because it is the residence of God: but we wish to know the nature of this veneration or worship; and this the man dares not attempt to explain; but defers the subject to another time: De fide nostra si quærendum alias putaveris, audies. This was doubtless wise for *him;* but is unsatisfactory to *us.*—But however it was, the passage from *Faustus*, in which he compares the worship of the sun with the worship of bread and wine in the sacred supper, contains a suggestion, which, if it do not lead us to a full understanding of the subject, may enable us to approximate towards it. He says: Quapropter et nobis circa *universa* religio est: or, we religiously worship the *universe.* These words follow immediately after the above passage, and the word *quapropter* shows, that the ground for the worship in question, was implied in that passage. Now he had before said: Spiritum sanctum terram gravidare, eamque (foecundatam) gignere Jesum passibilem, omni suspensum ex ligno. He therefore gives this reason for the worship of the universe; viz. because the earth, on being impregnated by the Holy Spirit, brings forth the *passive Jesus.* This *passive Jesus* of the Manichæans, of which we shall speak elsewhere, is the *products* and *fruits* of the earth; in which, the Manichæans supposed, there were not only particles of celestial and divine matter, but also sensation and a soul. Consequently, they worshipped the *universe*, because all things are endued with a kind of divine sensation and a celestial soul. The *universe* (*universa*) denoted undoubtedly the five celestial elements of the Manichæans. Of course, they supposed these elements to be animated, (as appears also from other testimonies,) and full of a divine spirit; and therefore they paid them some worship. Consequently, the sun and the moon, being composed of *good fire* and *good water*, were intitled to worship. And, as they supposed good fire and good water to be animated, they doubtless believed the sun and moon to be endued with intelligence and sensation. This was an ancient and very common opinion, not only of the Oriental people, but also of many of the philosophers.—Putting all these things together, I think it probable, that the *Elect* among the Manichæans did invoke the sun and the moon; not indeed as Gods, but as excellent and benificent Beings, by whose influence they might become more happy, and better prepared for liberating their immortal souls from the bonds of the body.

[p. 786.] (3) Of the Holy Spirit, no one has spoken more fully than *Faustus*; (apud *Augustinum* L. xx. c. 2. p. 237.): Spiritus sancti, qui est majestas tertia (the third Person of the divine nature,) aëris hunc omnem ambitum sedem fatemur ac diversorium, cujus ex viribus et spiritali profusione, terram quoque concipientem, gignere patibilem Jesum, qui est vita ac salus hominum, omni suspensus ex ligno. The Holy Spirit, then, according to the views of the Manichæans, is a Being, produced from God the Father, when the world was formed. Hence it follows, that he is a lucid parcel or mass. His residence is the *air*; but not that gross air contiguous to us, for in that the Demon and his princes are confined as captives. Neither is this impure air, which is contaminated with the smoke that constitutes the fifth element of the world of darkness, a fit residence for a Being originating from the Father of lights. *Air*, in the Manichæan phraseology, is *ether*, *ex altissimis ignibus constans*, as *Cicero* says, surrounding and enclosing this our globe. Therefore, as the Manichæans located the Son of God in the *good fire* and *good water*, those elements of the world of light, so they located the Holy Spirit in the *ether*, which is also one of the celestial elements.—His *offices* are not all mentioned by *Faustus*, but only that one from which he could explain the ground for the worship of the sun and moon, then under discussion. Seated in the highest ether or heat encompassing our globe, the Holy Spirit, *first* warms, moves and instructs the minds of men, and raises them to the Father of lights; for, as the Manichæan school proclaimed, he imparted an extraordinary portion of his influence to *Manes*, a far greater than to the Apostles and other men. *Manes* himself says, in his *Epistola Fundamenti*: Intima pectoris humani adaperit, ut videant homines animas suas.—*Secondly*, He fecundates this our earth, and causes it to produce the *passive Jesus* (*Jesus patibilis*), that is, all kinds of *fruits* which men eat to sustain life. Of this *passive Jesus*, we shall treat, when we come to speak of the Manichæan doctrine respecting our earth: at present, I merely state, that the Manichæans supposed, there was in our earth a soul or vital force, which they called *Jesus*. That force, the Holy Spirit by his influence separates from the grosser matter, and conducts into plants and shrubs and trees, to make them bear fruit. And those *fruits*, because they contain a vital force or soul, are called *Jesus*; and, because they are masticated and crushed by the teeth of men, the *passive Jesus*. *Faustus* says of the *passive Jesus*: vita et salus est hominum; that is, it sustains human life, promotes health, and sometimes restores lost health. These are silly anile fables: but nothing better could be expected from a delirious old man, a rustic imbued with the Persian philosophy.—As to their praying to the Holy Spirit, I find nothing recorded. But as they professed to worship one God in three Persons, and considered [p. 787.] the Holy Spirit as a part of the divine nature, there can be no doubt, that they invoked him in connexion with the Father and the Son. Besides, *Manes*, in the beginning of his *Epistola Fundamenti*, prays for the *light of the Holy Spirit* to be shed on his people; and *Secundinus*, (in his Epistle to *Augustine*, Opp. tom. viii. p. 369, &c.) declares that he, *Spiritui sancto gratias habet et supplex refert.*

(4) *Manes*, being a Persian, estimated the Christian religion by the principles of the *Magi:* and what he teaches respecting the Son of God and the Holy Spirit, agrees entirely with the speculations of the ancient Persians respecting *Mithras* and the *ether*. Concerning that great Persian God *Mithras*, we have full commentaries by several learned men; viz. Phil. a *Turre*, (in his Monumenta veteris Antii,) Thomas *Hyde*, (Historia relig. vet. Persarum,) Jac. *Martini*, (de veterum Gallorum religione,) and others. What the Persians taught respecting *Mithras*, the very same taught *Manes* respecting *Christ*, or the Son of God. The vulgar among the Persians did not distinguish *Mithras* from the *sun:* but the wiser men did so, and held *Mithras* to be inferior to the supreme God, yet a great Deity, and resident in the sun. This I will not now stop to prove, lest I should turn aside too far; but it may be easily demonstrated from *Plutarch*.—*Mithras*, as *Plutarch* observes, (de Iside et Osiride, p. 369.) was a *middle* God, between the good Principle and the bad; and was therefore called by the Persians μεσίτης or *Mediator*. But beware of supposing, that *Mithras* possessed a middle *nature*, compounded some how of both light and darkness. This title of *Mediator* undoubtedly refered to his office, and denoted, that he withstood the efforts of *Arimanius*, the Prince of darkness, to enlarge his empire; and that he aided the souls abstracted from the light, in their return to God. Now the same title of *Mediator* being applied in the Scriptures to the Saviour of mankind, this alone might induce *Manes* to compare our Saviour with the Persian *Mithras*. The Persians also believed, of their *Mithras* as *Manes* did of *Christ*, that he was present not only in the sun, but likewise in the moon. And hence, in all the monuments of the worship of *Mithras* which have reached us, the moon always accompanies the sun. See Phil. a *Turre*, (Monum. veteris Antii, p. 157.) Anton. van *Dale*, (Dissertt. ad Antiquitates et Marmora p. 16.) and Jac. *Martin*, (Religion des Gaulois, L. ii. p. 421.) and others. They supposed *Mithras* possessed a twofold energy, the one male, the other female; and that the former resided in the sun, but the latter in the moon. Says Julius *Firmicus*, (de errore profanar. religionum p. 413, at the end of *Minucius Felix*, edit. Gronovii.): Persæ Jovem in duas dividunt potestates, naturam ejus ad utriusque sexus referentes et viri et foeminæ simulacra ignis substantiam deputantes. This doctrine the Manichaeans expressed in a Christian manner, and in Bible language (1 Cor. i. 24.) by saying, The *power* (*virtus*, δύναμις) *of Christ* dwells in the sun, but his *wisdom* in the moon. They dared not use the Persian terms and phras- [p. 788.] es, lest they should be thought to worship a God and Goddess, in the sun and moon, as the Persian vulgar did. *Firmicus*, whom I have just quoted, says a

little after, that the male Jupiter inhabiting the sun, was called *Mithras* by the Persians: nor is he in error. In my notes on *Cudworth*, (Intellectual System p. 327.) I have shown from *Herodotus*, that the word *Mithras* was also transferred to the moon, and while the dweller in the sun was called *Mithras*, the dweller in the moon was called *Mithra;* indicating that one and the same Being, though in a different manner, animated both the sun and the moon. It is therefore manifest, that *Mithras* and the Manichaean *Christ* actually differed in nothing, except in name. And perhaps also, the Persians hoped that *Mithras* would, at some future time, descend from the sun, assume a human form, and instruct mortals in the worship of the true God. But *Manes* would not have Christ worshipped in the way the Persians worshipped *Mithras;* for, in place of sacrifices, he substituted nothing but prayers and some external signs of reverence. This was the effect of christianity.—Respecting the worship of the *ether* by the Persians, we have not so many proofs as we have of their worship of the sun and moon, and of *Mithras* resident in those planets. Yet we have one striking passage in *Herodotus*, (Historia, L. I. § 131. p. 55. edit. Gronov.) which, while it affords confirmation to some other things that we have stated, shows, that the Persians located a Deity in the highest *ether*, and paid divine honors to it. He first tells us, that the Persians did not attribute a human form to their Gods: neither did *Manes;* as we have seen. He then says: Οἱ δὲ νομίζουσι Διῒ μὲν, ἐπὶ τὰ ὑψηλότατα τῶν ὀρέων ἀναβαίνοντες, θυσίας ἔρδειν, τὸν κύκλον πάντα τοῦ οὐρανοῦ Δία καλέοντες. Moris habent, editissismis conscensis montibus, Jovi (*Herodotus* uses the Greek appellation, to which the Persians were strangers,) facere sacra, omnem gyrum coeli (i. e. the *ether*, encompassing our earth,) Jovem (Deum) appellantes: or, supposing some God to reside in that *ether*. After this, he tells us, that the Persians likewise offer *sacrifices to the sun and the moon:* and hence, the worship of the *ether* was something different from the worship of the sun and moon. And he finally tells us, that they sacrificed to *the earth* (the *ground*,) *to fire, to water, to the wind.* Here we remark: *First;* The ancient Persians held to *five elements*, as *Manes* did: for, to the *ether*, which he had before mentioned, *Herodotus* adds four others.—*Secondly:* They *worshipped* the elements; whence it may be inferred that they supposed them *animated* as *Manes* believed.—*Thirdly: Wind* was ranked by them among the elements, as it was by *Manes.* But, by the *wind*, they undoubtedly did not mean the lower air or atmosphere.

§ XLIV. **War of the Prince of Darkness on the Prince of Light.** After a vast length of time, the race of darkness having become exceedingly numerous, an intestine war raged in that miserable [p. 789.] world, perhaps respecting boundaries and residences. In this war, while the victors pursued the vanquished, and the latter fled into the mountains on the frontiers of the province, suddenly, from these mountains, the sons of darkness descried the realm of light and its astonishing splendor, of which they before had no knowledge. On descrying the light they ceased fighting;

and, taking counsel together, they determined to invade that happy world they so much admired, and to bring it under their dominion. Without delay an army was raised and marched forth.—As the countless and infuriated host came near, the Lord of the world of light opposed to it a Being of his own nature, whom he had suddenly procreated, attended by the five celestial elements and a vast multitude of troops. This General of the world of light, who bore the name of *First Man*, conducted the war with valor and discretion, yet not very successfully. For the leaders of darkness not only plundered a considerable portion of the celestial elements, which they mixed up with their own depraved elements, but they also greedily devoured large quantities of the divine light, which was animated: nay, they nearly overpowered *First Man* himself, and stripped him of a part of his excellence. As therefore the hard pressed commander of the forces of light implored the aid of God, he sent forth another General, produced in like manner from himself, but more powerful than the former, and bearing the name of *Living Spirit.* This General rescued *First Man*, and conquered the Prince of darkness: but he could not restore to its pristine state the plunder taken from the world of light, because it had been commingled with vicious matter.(1)

(1) The fable of *Manes* respecting a war between the good and bad Principles, if estimated by our ideas of God and divine things, is impious and absurd; but if considered in relation to the objects of its author, and judged of by his fundamental principles, it is far less senseless: nay, it is necessary, and supported by good reasons. For, as *Manes* assumed it for a certainty, that good and evil arose from two separate causes, he could not show whence originated that intermixture of good and evil which is visible in our world, without imagining such a war; and adorning the fable with various circumstances suited to his purpose. I will endeavor to make the statements of this subject, as gathered from ancient writers, more intelligible than they are usually made: which will not only afford satisfaction to many minds, but also be useful for [p. 790.] illustrating the history of the church, and for correcting the errors of many.—As we have already seen, God knew that the world of darkness existed; but the people of darkness, as they were altogether wretched and miserable, so also were they ignorant and stupid, and knew nothing of God and of the world of light. *Manes* was obliged to suppose this ignorance in the Prince of darkness and his subjects, in order to account for their entering on the war. For if the King of darkness had known, that a most powerful Deity existed, and resided in the world of light, he would not have resolved to invade that happy land,

in order to subjugate it. *Titus* of Bostra tells us, from the Liber Mysteriorum of *Manes*, (contra Manichæos L. I. tom. I. p. 71. of *Canisius*' Collection,) Φησὶ τὸ γράμμα, ἀφ' οὗ τὰ παρὰ τοῦ Μάνεντος παρεθήκαμεν, ὡς οὐδ' ὅτι Θεὸς ἐν φωτὶ διητᾶτο ἐγίνωσκον, οὐδ' ὅτι τολμήσαντες κατὰ τοῦ οἰκητηρίου τοῦ Θεοῦ οὐκ ἔμελλον ἀθῷοι ποτὲ ἀπαλλαγῆναι. Scriptum est in libro (mysteriorum) Manetis unde hæc apposuimus, quod neque Deum in lumine habitare sciebant, neque se unquam impune laturos, si in Dei domicilium invadere auderent. Add p. 74. He well exhibits (p. 70.) the ground of this fiction. An unforeseen occurrence brought the inhabitants of the world of darkness to a knowledge of the world of light. A civil war having arisen in the world of darkness, where broils were unceasing, the vanquished party, on being chased by the conquerors from their homes. fled to the farthest boundaries of their country; and there both parties discovered the world of light. *Titus*, as recently quoted, states this from the books of *Manes* himself. See his work, (L. I. p. 74. and p. 71.) where he says: Φησὶν ἡ παρ' αὐτοῖς βίβλος, πρὸς ἀλλήλους στασιάζοντες ἐπεπόλασαν, καὶ μέχρι τῶν μεθορίων, καὶ τὸ φῶς εἶδον, θέαμα τι κάλλιστον καὶ εὐπρεπέστατον. Sic igitur est in libro quem habent (mysteriorum), seditione inter ipsos orta, prodierunt usque ad confinium et viderent lumen, spectaculum quoddam pulcherrimum et maxime decorum. After *Titus*, (who is more worthy of credit than all others,) the common writers on the Heresies, namely, *Epiphanius*, *Theodoret*, *Damascenus*, &c. relate the same thing. A more probable occasion of the discovery of the world of light by the inhabitants of darkness, *Manes* could scarcely have devised. To make this manifest, let it be considered, that the world of darkness was surrounded by lofty mountains, cliffs and eminences, which prevented the rays of light from falling upon it. For if it had been a level plane, the light of heaven, (which was over against the region of darkness,) being exceedingly bright, and shining to an immense distance, could not possibly have so long escaped the sight of the citizens of that region. In the farthest mountains and cliffs bounding the realm of darkness, therefore, the vanquished are supposed to have sought for safety. And the discovery of the light put an end to the battle. For the combattants stood amazed; and forgetting their hatred and fury, they feasted their eyes and their minds with the magnificent spectacle. On recovering themselves, they consulted together, how to get possession of that treasure; [p. 791.] and they resolved to seize upon it. Thus *Manes*, as quoted by *Titus*, (l. c. p. 71.):Οἱ δὲ ἠτάκτουν, φησὶ, καὶ ἠδίκουν ἀλλήλους, τὸ φῶς δὲ ἰδόντες ἐπαύσαντο. Illi vero, ait Manes, in perturbato erant, seque oppugnabant, viso vero lumine desierunt. And a little after: Τότε ὑπὸ τῆς ἐν αὐτοῖς κινήσεως ἐνθουσιῶντες κατὰ τοῦ φωτὸς ἐβουλεύσαντο, τι δὴ ποιήσαντες δύναιντο ἂν αὐτοὺς τῷ κρείττονι συγκεράσαι Tunc a motu illo, quem sentiebant, in furorem acti consultabant de lumine, quid faciendum esset, ut se cum eo, quod præstantius erat, miscerent.—It is manifest therefore, that those learned men entirely mistake, who represent *Manes* as believing, that the Prince of darkness deliberately made war upon God; and who compare this war with that which, as the Grecian fables state, the Giants waged against the Gods. The race of darkness, according to the views of *Manes*, were intirely ignorant of God, and could not possibly have resolved on a war against him.

When God perceived the host of darkness approaching his borders, he was aware that his subjects were in great peril from this furious enemy; and therefore he determined, that a valiant General with a numerous army, should go out to battle, in order to drive those smoky Giants beyond the limits of his kingdom. Thus *Manes* himself, in his *Epistola Fundamenti*, (apud *August.* de natura boni, c. 42. p. 364.): Lucis beatissimæ Pater sciens, labem magnam et vastitatem, quæ ex tenebris surgeret, adversus sua sancta impendere Sæcula, nisi aliquod eximium et præclarum et virtute potens Numen opponat. These words clearly show the weakness of God, or that his power was confined within narrow limits; and of course that those judge too favorably of the Manichæans, who make their God omnipotent. On this emergency, the Father of light first produced from himself a certain virtue or power, called *Mother of Life;* and she bore another Being, called *First Man;* and he with a great retinue, and armed with the five celestial elements, marched against the Prince of darkness. *Tyrbo*, (in the Acta Disput. *Archelai* cum *Manete*, p. 22. edit. Zaccagnii,) says in the language of *Manes:* Cum cognovisset bonus Pater, tenebras ad terram suam supervenisse, produxit ex se virtutem, quæ dicitur *Mater Vitæ*, qua virtute circumdedit *Primum Hominem* (so the ancient Latin translator renders it: but erroneously, as appears from the Greek, which is found in *Epiphanius*, and is: Καὶ αὐτὴν προβεβληκέναι τὸν πρῶτον ἄνθρωπον. Et illa *mater vitæ* produxit *Primum Hominem*) eumque circumdedit quinque elementis, quæ sunt ventus, lux, aqua, ignis et materia (so it is in the Latin, and in the Greek of *Epiphanius*. But it is evident, as *Beausobre* has said, that instead of ὕλη and *materia*, it should read *aër*. For ὕλη is a bad principle, and has no place among the elements of the world of light. The fifth element of the Manichæans was *air* or *either*,) quibus indutus tanquam ad paratum belli descendit deorsum, ad pugnandum versus tenebras. *Augustine* says, (contra Faustum, L. ii. c. 3. p. 133.) Profertis nobis ex armario vestro nescio quem *Primum Hominem*, qui ad gentem tenebrarum debellandum de lucis gente descendit, armatum aquis suis [p. 792.] contra inimicorum aquas, et igne suo contra inimicorun ignem, et ventis suis contra inimicorum ventos. Cur non ergo et fumo suo contra inimicorum fumum, et tenebris suis contra inimicorum tenebras, sed contra fumum *aere*, uti dicitis, armabatur, et contra tenebras *luce?* - - - Cur contra malum fumum non potuit afferre fumum bonum? These questions of *Augustine* are futile; and they show that he was ignorant of the nature of the elements of Manes. For the *smoke* was the bad either, the opposite of the good air; and *darkness* belonged to the misty world, the opposite of which was *light*, or the bright and splendid world. See also *Augustine*, (L. xi. c. 3. p. 157, and de Hæres, c. 42.) also *Titus* of Bostra, (L. I. p. 68.) and the other writers of less authority, who are well known. In these difficult conceits, there is still some discretion: for *Manes* is self-consistent, and dexterously adjusts all the parts of his system to his first or elementary principles: which shows that he exercised his reason in his wild vagaries. But it is difficult for us at this day, to discover the grounds of all his doctrines, because no small part of his system remains in the dark. The names he assigns to the persons he introduces, are not arbitrary, (as *Titus* of Bostra supposed, contra Manichæos L. I. p. 68.) but are derived from the nature of those persons, and therefore are appropriate to them. The *Mother of Life*, that Being whom God procreated from himself, when he saw the Prince of darkness approaching his borders, was undoubtedly a Deity, which had the power of transmitting life from herself to others, or of producing living beings. And for the son of this mother, no more fit name *could* be devised, than that of the *First Man.* For it is very certain, that he possessed the human form, because Adam was fashioned by the Demon after his likeness; as we shall see hereafter. Anterior to him, there had been no Being in the world of light, resembling men: and therefore, very correctly and properly, he could be called the *First Man,* namely, among celestials. For all the *Æons* or *Sæcula,* were merely lucid *masses,* like God their Parent, having no definite form. Nor was it suitable, that the inhabitants of the world of light should be like men, because the Prince of darkness and all his subordinate princes resembled men. And therefore that *First Man,* who warred against the Prince of darkness, was not received into the world of light, but resided with his mother in the smaller ship, or moon. And hence also, an answer may be given to the inquiry, why God did not himself produce that *First Man,* which he doubtless could have done, but produced another Being, the *Mother of Life* of whom he was born. For it was unbecoming the majesty and wisdom of God, to produce out of himself a Being resembling the Prince of darkness the Lord of evil; and therefore this function was transferred to an inferor Being. The purpose of God required, that a General of human form should march against the Lord of darkness; for it was the pleasure of God, that the [p. 793.] war should be conducted by artifice and stratagem rather than by force of arms, or that the fearful enemy should be entrapped and caught by blandishments, rather than vanquished in open war. Therefore, as the King of darkness was a *man,* or a giant of immense bulk, a hero of his form was to be sent against him; from whom he would expect no harm, supposing him to be of the same nature with himself, and would therefore fearlessly receive him to friendly intercourse. If the Lord of darkness had seen a Being unlike himself coming to meet him, he would doubtless have attacked him with all his forces, and very many ill consequences might have followed. That *First Man* of the Manichæans, therefore, was, we have no doubt, a giant of immense stature, and fully equal to his adversary in magnitude. The King of darkness, (in the Epistola Fundamenti of *Manes,* apud *August.* de natura boni c. 46. p. 366.) called him: *Magnum illum,* qui gloriosus apparuit. This could not refer to his *moral* greatness. His armour also, or his vestments, were the five celestial elements, by the efficacy of which the five evil elements were to be subdued. Many souls, likewise, or citizens of the world of light, were in his train.

I now come to the conflict between these giants.—As has been remarked, God, in his wisdom, would not have his General go into a pitched battle with the King of darkness; but he wished that the enemy might be circumvented, and artfully diverted from fighting against the light. And hence, as before observed, he opposed to him an amiable Commander, of the same form with the Demon, that so the Prince of darkness might take him to be one of his own race.—And he further bid him approach the adversary blandly and craftily; and using no violence, to inject and infuse the celestial elements, with which he was clad, into the elements of the adverse party. For pursuing this course, there were several reasons. *Frst*, God hoped, that the princes of darkness would become so intensely occupied and engrossed with these new and untried elements, that they would forget the war against the world of light. And *secondly*, he supposed that these elements, on being introduced into depraved matter, would subdue its virulence and rage, so that it could be managed. And *lastly*, he expected that the celestial matter, when joined with depraved matter, would gradually pervade and molify it, so that afterwards it might easily be driven back again, with its princes, into the wretched world from which it came. These things are well attested by the writings of Manes and his disciples, which have reached us. *Manes*, in his Book of Mysteries, (apud *Titum* Bostrens. L. i. p. 68.) says: Ὁ δὲ ἀγαθὸς δύναμιν ἀποστέλλει τινὰ, φυλάξασαν μὲν δῆθεν τοὺς ὅρους, τὸ δὲ ἀληθὲς δέλεαρ ἐσομένην εἰς ἀκούσιον τῇ ὕλῃ σωφρόνισμον. ὃ δὴ καὶ γέγονε. Francis *Turrianus* has badly translated this passage, as well as many others in *Titus*. I will therefore render it so as to make it intelligible. Bonus (Deus) potestatem quamdam mittit, tanquam fines (regni lucis) custodituram, revera vero ideo, ut materiæ incitamenti seu escæ loco esset, per quam, ad moderationem contra voluntatem suam seu invita etiam induceretur. A little after, *Titus* adds, that the Manichæans used to say: Materiam, tanquam feram belluam, missæ a [p. 794.] Deo potestatis cantione (i. e. by a magical charm) sopitam esse: Ὡς δι' ἐπῳδῆς τῆς ἀποσταλτίσης δυνάμεως ἐκοιμίσθη. The bishop does not mistake: for *Manes* himself, (in the acta Disput. cum Manete, § 25. p. 41. edit. Zaccag.) elucidates his doctrine by this very similitude taken from wild beasts: Similis est malignus leoni, qui irrepere vult gregi boni pastoris, (i. e. strives to invade the world of light, and to drive away the sheep of God, or the blessed *Æons*,) quod cum pastor viderit, fodit foveam ingentem, et de grege tulit unum hœdum (i. e. he exposes to him a small portion of the celestial matter,) et jactavit in foveam, quem leo invadere desiderans, cum ingenti indignatione voluit eam absorbere et accurrens ad foveam decidit in eam, ascendendi inde sursum non habens vires, quem pastor apprehensum pro prudentia sua in cavea concludit, atque hœdum, qui cum ipso fuerit in fovea, incolumem conservavit. Ex hoc ergo infirmatus est malignus, ultra jam leone non habente potestatem faciendi aliquid, et salvabitur omne animarum genus ac restituetur, quod perierat, proprio suo gregi. We shall soon see, that by this language *Manes* not badly explains his views. *Fortunatus*, the Manichæan, (in Disput. cum *Augustino II.* p. 78.) says: In contrariâ naturâ esse animam dicimus, ideo, ut contrariæ naturæ modum imponeret: modo imposito contrariæ naturæ, sumit eamdem Deus. And again, (l. c. p. 57.) *Fortunatus* says: Apparet - - missas esse animas contra contrariam naturam, ut eamdem sua passione subjicientes, victoria Deo redderetur. I omit the testimonies of *Augustine*, *Alexander* of Lycopolis, *Damascenus*, and others; because they are not needed.

The *First Man* followed exactly the pleasure of his Lord who sent him forth, and approached the enemy with guile and cunning. Says *Augustine*, (contra Faustum L. ii. c. 4. p. 134.) *Primum hominem* vestrum dicitis, secundum hostium voluntatem, *quo eos caperet*, elementa quæ portabat mutasse ac vertisse, ut regnum, quod dicitis, falsitatis, in sua naturâ manens, non fallaciter dimicaret, et substantia veritatis mutabilis appareret, *ut falleret*. - - Hunc *Pri-*

mum Hominem laudatis, quia mutabilibus et mendacibus formis cum adversa gente pugnavit. - - *Manichæus* annuntiat *Primum Hominem* nescio quibus fallacibus elementis quinque vestitum. Again, he says, (L. xi. c. 3. p. 157.): *Manes* annuntiat nescio quem *Primum Hominem*, nec de terra terrenum, nec factum in animam viventem, sed de substantia Dei, id ipsum existentem quod Deus est, membra sua, vel vestimenta sua, vel arma sua, id est, quinque elementa, cum et ipsa nihil aliud essent, quam substantia Dei, in tenebrarum gente mersisse, ut inquinata caperentur. The closing words in this passage, I suspect, have been corrupted. For, beyond all doubt, God did not wish the celestial elements to be received and become *defiled*, but to remain pure; and by [p. 795.] them to capture the princes of darkness. So *Augustine* expressly states in the previously cited passage. I therefore choose to read: Ut *per* inquinata (i. e. *by* the enemies) caperentur. Those who think the passage correct as it stands, must suppose, that *Augustine* illy expressed the views of *Manes*. The *First Man*, therefore, in order the more completely to deceive the race of darkness, did not present to them the celestial elements with which he was armed or clad, just as they were, but he changed their appearance. And, as he himself appeared like to the Prince of darkness, so he gave to his armor the appearance of the corrupt elements, or of the enemy's armor, so that he might not be shocked at it. And yet there is some obscurity here, which is not worth the pains of an explanation.

The artifice of the *First Man* was partially successful. The Prince of darkness, together with his friends and associates, greedily seized the celestial matter, liberally offered, and satiated himself with it. This calmed the Demon's furious passions, and checked his ardor for invading the world of light. It might fitly be called a carminative, which soothed his rage in spite of him, and subdued his inclination to evil; or, according to the simile of *Manes*, it operated like a magical charm, which has the effect of making wild beasts and serpents harmless. Says *Manes*, (apud *Titum* Bostrens. L. i. p. 68.): Θεασαμένη ἡ ὕλη τὴν ἀποσταλεῖσαν δύναμιν προσεπεκίσσησε μὲν ὡς ἐραϑεῖσα. Ὁρμῇ δὲ πλείονι λαβοῦσα ταύτην κατέπιε, καὶ ἔδηξε τρόπον τινὰ ὥσπερ ϑηρίον. Quum vidisset materia potestatem missam, (i. e. when the Demon saw the *First Man*, clothed in the five celestial elements, and pretending friendship,) amore capta concupivit eam, et ardentiore appetitu prehensam absorbuit, et quodammodo tanquam bellua ligata est. And thus the principal danger to the world of light was indeed averted: but another evil sprung up in place of it; and the issue of the scheme was not, in all respects, happy.—For, *First;* While the *First Man*, by injecting the celestial matter into the darkness, aimed to capture the Prince of evil and his associates; the latter, on the other hand, grasped the celestial elements and souls, and subjected them to his power. And four of the elements, namely, darkness, water, wind and good fire, he so combined with the depraved elements, that no force could possibly separate them. And no small part of the celestial matter, especially of the light or the souls, he and his officers devoured; and, as I may say, converted into their blood and juices. Says *Tyrbo*, (in the Acta Disput. *Archelai*, § 6. p. 10.): At vero tenebrarum principes, repugnantes ei, comederunt de armatura ejus, quod est anima. Tunc ibi vehementer afflictus est deorsum Primus Homo a tenebris. And, (§ 11. p. 20.) Deus non habet partem cum mundo, nec gaudet super eo, quod ab initio furtum passus sit a Principibus (tenebrarum) et aborta fuerit ei tribulatio. We shall hereafter cite the testimony of *Manes* himself, respecting this *light* which was devoured by the Princes of darkness. In the first of these passages, *Tyrbo* did not mistake, (as a very learned man supposes,) in saying, the *armor of the First* [p. 796.] *Man was soul.* It is indeed true, as that worthy man says, that the Manichæans considered souls as formed of light, or as particles of that eternal light which is invisible to our organs: but the armor of the First Man was not merely light, but also all the five celestial elements. And it escaped his recollection, that all the Manichæan elements were animated: and that mention is made in their schools, of various kinds of souls. Rational souls, which hold the highest rank, are the daughters of *light*, or particles from it. But, besides these nobler souls, others likewise, of an inferior order, proceed from the other elements. *Tyrbo* therefore could truly say, *the armor of the First Man was soul;* that is, all kinds of souls existed in the five elements with which he was invested. But I will subjoin a passage from *Augustine*, respecting the *souls* subdued and oppressed in that first conflict between light and darkness, (from his Liber de natura boni, c. 42. p. 363.) : Dicunt etiam nonnullas animas, quas volunt esse de substantia Dei et ejusdem omnino naturæ, quæ non sponte peccaverint, sed a gente tenebrarum, quam mali naturam dicunt, *ad quam debellandam, non ultro, sed Patris imperio descenderunt*, superatæ et oppressæ sint, affigi in æternum horribili globo animarum. This, *Augustine* confirms by the Epistola Fundamenti of *Manes;* in which, speaking of these souls, *Manes* says: Quod errare se a priori lucida sua naturâ passæ sint: unde, et adhærebunt iis rebus animæ eaedem, quas dilexerunt, relictæ in eodem tenebrarum globo, suis meritis id sibi conquirentes. The Princes of darkness, therefore, so connected with themselves a great number of souls, that those souls changed their nature, and voluntarily assumed the character of darkness; and therefore, they could not in any way be converted to God and recovered. And to this great evil, others were added. For,—*Secondly;* The Prince of darkness and his associates, devoured the *son* of the *First Man*, whose name was *Jesus.* This part of the Manichæan system is involved in much obscurity, and cannot be elucidated by clear and explicit testimonies. Yet I hope to make it intelligible. In the first place, it is certain that the *First Man*, the Being who encountered the Prince of darkness, had a son named *Jesus.* Deceived by this name, (as *Beausobre* has observed, vol. ii. p. 554.) *Augustine* confounds in many places this son of the First Man, with the Son of God our Savior; and therefore calls him not only *Jesus*, but also *Christ.* Thus, he says, (contra *Faustum* L. ii. c. 4. p. 134.) : Hujus Primi Hominis filium credi vultis Dominum Jesum Christum. Very faulty! The Manichæans had two *Jesuses*, an *impassive* and a *passive*, a Savior of souls and a Savior of bodies. The former, the Savior of souls, or the *impassive Jesus*, was the son of eternal light or of God, and was himself all light. The latter, the *passive Jesus*, who imparts health and strength to bodies, was the son of the *First Man.* The former was distinguished by the surname *Christ;* [p. 797.] which the Manichæans never applied to the latter. Hence, whenever *Augus-*

tine speaks of *Christ* as combined with fruits, herbs, products of the earth, and stars, and as being eaten by men, (and he speaks thus very often,) he blunders, through ignorance of the Manichæan doctrines. Thus he says, (l. c. p. 134.): Deliramenta vestra vos cogunt, non solum in cœlo atque in omnibus stellis, sed etiam in terra atque in omnibus, quæ nascuntur in ea, confixum et colligatum atque concretum Christum dicere, non jam Salvatorem vestrum, sed a vobis salvandum. Instead of *Christ* he should have said *Jesus.*—Whether the *First Man* begat this son, before he marched against the army of darkness, or in the heat of the contest, I do not find any where stated. But we may conjecture, that being reduced to straits by the enemy, he collected his energies, and produced from himself this potent Being, in order to have an associate in the fight. The reason for the name, is stated by *Faustus* the Manichæan, (apud *August.* L. xx. c. 2. p. 237.) where he says, that this *Jesus* is *the life* and *health of men.* It was the practice of the Manichæans, as we have before shown, to give names to the celestial Beings whom they mention, derived from the character and attributes of those Beings. As therefore, this son of the First Man afforded *health* (*sulutem*),—not indeed to souls,—but to bodies, which he nourished, strengthened and sustained, he was called *Jesus;* a name derived, as is well known, from the Syriac *Jeshua, servavit.* For *Manes* wrote in Syriac; and therefore he gave to this son of the First Man a Syriac or Hebrew name, indicative of his nature.—If now it be asked, What sort of a Being was this *Jesus?* I answer, without hesitation, He was a very large mass of celestial matter, in which resided vital power, or a living soul, and likewise ability to communicate of that living soul to others. When God saw the Prince of darkness invading his realm, he produced from himself a kind of *sixth element,* different from the other five; namely, the *Mother of Life,* that is, a Being endowed with the power of conferring life on things around her. And she produced the *First Man.* And he, having received from his mother that vital power, or if you choose, a sentient soul, poured it out in the conflict with the king of darkness, either by the command of God, or from his own choice. The Maichæans needed a sixth element of this character, in order to account for the production of fruits and useful plants and herbs; for these could not easily be deduced from the nature and powers of the five other elements. Moreover, this *Jesus,* the son of the *First Man,* is in the earth; from which he is drawn forth, by the Holy Spirit resident in the highest ether, and is diffused throughout the natural world. Hence *Faustus,* before quoted, (apud *August.* L. xx. c. 2. p. 237.) says: Terram ex Spiritus sancti profusione concipere, atque *Patibilem Jesum* gignere, omni suspensum ex ligno. It is very clear, that he means the fruits of trees; and these he calls *Jesus,* because they contain a portion of the sentient soul [p. 798.] generated by the First Man. For the Manichæans fully believed, that all fruits, pulse, plants, and whatever grows out of the earth, contained *Jesus,* or sensitive life. Thus *Augustine,* (de Hæres. c. 42. p. 12.) says: Herbas etiam atque arbores sic putant vivere, ut vitam, quæ illis inest, et sentire credant et dolere, cum læduntur: nec aliquid inde sine cruciatu eorum quemquam posse vellere aut carpere. These remarks, which might be confirmed by many other citations, make the *Passive Jesus,* if I mistake not, perfectly intelligible. *Au-*

gustine often debated with Manichæans on this subject, sometimes very correctly, but frequently not without some mistakes; for instance, when he represents, or falsely supposes, that this *living soul*, which the Manichæans honored with the name *Jesus*, was the same with Jesus our Savior. I will cite a passage, in which he avoids error, (de moribus Manichæorum, L. ii. c. 15, 16. Opp. tom. i. p. 554.): Quoniam, inquit (Manes), membrum Dei (i. e. *Jesus*, the son of the First Man) malorum substantiæ conmixtum est, ut eam refrenaret atque a summo furore comprimeret (sic enim dicitis), de commixta utraque naturá, id est, boni et mali, mundus est fabricatus. Pars autem illa divina ex omni parte mundi quotidie purgatur et in sua regna resumitur: *sed hæc per terram exhalans* et ad cœlum tendens *incurrit in stirpes*, quoniam radicibus terræ affiguntur, atque ita omnes herbas et arbusta omnia fecundat et vegetat. - - Primo quæro, unde doceatis in frumentis ac legumine et oleribus et floribus et pomis inesse istam, nescio quam, partem Dei. Ex ipso coloris nitore, inquiunt, et odoris jucunditate et saporis suavitate manifestum est. For much more of the like import, I refer the reader to *Augustine*'s works.—A large part of the mystery of the *Passive Jesus*, is now explained: and it remains, that we substantiate what we have said, that this *Jesus* was swallowed by the Prince of darkness, in the conflict with the First Man. And this we are able to do, from the declaration of *Manes* himself. Although this *Jesus* ascends from the earth in vegetables and trees and plants, yet he does not reside in the earth, but in the huge and monstrous bodies of the Prince of darkness and his compeers; and from their bodies he is expressed, by a wonderful artifice of God, descends into the earth, and is thence elicited by the influences of the Holy Spirit, and is distributed through the natural world. The artifice of God, by which the Demons are forced to eject the living soul descended from the First Man, will be explained elsewhere. We now merely show, from the declarations of *Manes*, that it does flow out from the body of the Demon upon the earth. The passage I quote, is in the seventh book of *Manes*' Thesaurus, (apud *August.* de natura boni, c. 44. p. 366.): Beatus Pater - - pro insita sibi elementia fert opem, qua exuitur et liberatur ab impiis retinaculis et angustiis atque angoribus *sua vitalis substantia.* - - Hoc enim viso decoro, (of this, hereafter,) illorum (Dæmonum) ardor et concu- [p. 799.] piscentia crescit, atque hoc modo vinculum pessimarum cogitationum earum solvitur, *vivaque anima* (not the *rational* soul,) *quæ eorundem membris* tenebatur, hac occasione laxata evadit. - - Id vero quod adhuc adversi generis maculas portat, per aestus atque calores particulatim descendit, *atque arboribus, ceterisque plantationibus ac satis omnibus miscetur.* - - Atque ex isto aspectu decoro vitae pars, quae in earundum membris habetur, laxata deducitur per calores in terram, &c. as hereafter will be cited.—Now, as it is manifest from this passage, that the living sensitive soul in plants, fruits and trees, descends into our earth from the bodies of the Demons, and as this soul is by the Manichaeans called the *Passive Jesus*, and the *son of the First Man;* it is certain, that the Demon and his associates must have devoured and swallowed this intire *Jesus.*—But I proceed: *Thirdly:* In that conflict, the *First Man* was reduced to the greatest extremities. For the King of darkness almost had him in his power; and, as the thing itself shows, he wished to return with all his plunder, to his own country, the

realm of darkness. And if he could have done so, that exquisite portion of the divine nature and of the celestial elements, which the Demon had made his own, would have been for ever miserable and unhappy. For God neither has any power over the world of darkness, which is equally eternal and abiding with the world of light; nor can he overthrow and destroy it. *Tyrbo* says, (in the Acta *Archelai*, § 7. p. 10.): Tunc ibi vehementer afflictus est deorsum Primus Homo a tenebris, et nisi orantem eum exaudisset Pater, et misisset alteram virtutem, quae processerat ex se, quae dicitur *Spiritus Vivens* (ζῶν πνεῦμα), et descendens porrexisset ei dexteram, et eduxisset eum de tenebris, (he was therefore already a prisoner of the King of darkness,) olim Primus Homo detentus periclitaretur. (That is, he would have been carried away, by the Lord of evil, into the world of darkness.)

When, therefore, victory was almost in the hands of the Prince of darkness, on the General's imploring succor, God sent a more powerful commander from the world of light, to renew the conflict, and to cut off the Demon's retreat with his plunder. The Manichæans tell us, that this new commander was procreated by God himself; whereas the former General had a mother, who was indeed of divine origin, but inferior to God. The name of the new General was, the *Living Spirit.* He was called *Spirit*, because he had not a human form, but was a lucid *mass*, like the Father. This we prove from the language of *Manes*, in his Epistola Fundamenti, (apud *August.* de natura boni, c. 46. p. 366.) where he represents the Demon as thus addressing his fellow-warriors, respecting this second General from the world of light: Quid vobis videtur *maximum hoc* [p. 800.] *Lumen* quod oritur? Intuemini, quemadmodum polum movet, concutit plurimas potestates. He was called *Living* Spirit, because he lives in and of himself, being the immediate offspring of God, and did not, like the *First Man*, derive his existence from a Being inferior to God. This second General did not proceed alone, but had three Virtues of immense power for his associates. Thus *Tyrbo*, (l. c. p. 11.): Tunc Vivens Spiritus—indutus alias tres virtutes, descendens eduxit (i. e. seized) Principes (tenebrarum), et crucifixit eos in firmamento. He therefore did not assail the foe, as his predecessor did, with artifice and stratagem, but with open combat; and he bound the vanquished, so that they could not retreat, and return with their rich plunder to their country. Yet, in this second campaign, although it was successful, there was an occurrence not anticipated, and adverse to the designs of God. The General of light had seized many of the *animals*, both male and female, which lived in the elements of darkness; and some of the females, being with young, were unable to bear the rapid motions of the heavens, and cast their young prematurely. These abortions afterwards fell from heaven upon this earth, and propagated themselves in our world, contrary to the pleasure of God. Hence arose our animals, especially the wild, noxious, and venimous, which cause so much trouble and danger to men. A fable of this sort was necessary for the Manichæans, to enable them to answer the inquiry, Whence originated the pernicious and hurtful animals, the serpents, insects, lions, tigers, &c. with which our world abounds. The fable is puerile; yet it harmonizes with the fundamental principles of the system. Says *Augustine*, (contra Faustum, L. vi. c. 8. p. 149.): Dicunt, in illa

pugna, quando Primus eorum Homo tenebrarum gentem elementis fallacibus irretivit, utriusque sexus Principibus indidem captis - - in quibus erant etiam fœminæ aliquæ prægnantes: quæ cum cœlum rotari cœpisset, eandem vertiginem ferre non valentes, conceptus suos abortu excussisse, eosdemque abortivos fœtus et masculos et fœminas de cœlo in terram cecidisse, vixisse, crevisse, concubuisse, genuisse. Hinc esse dicunt originem carnium omnium, quæ moventur in terra, in aqua, in aëre. Either this passage has been corrupted, which is very probable, or *Augustine* erred in stating the opinion of the Manichæans respecting the origin of our animals. For he speaks as if these animals were the offspring of the Princes of darkness, or rather of their wives; which was not true. For the chiefs of darkness begat beings like themselves, or having the human form. And in like manner, the animals of the world of darkness propagated their own genera and species. Besides, there is another passage of *Augustine*, (contra Faust. L. xxi. c. 12. p. 254.) in which he expressly tells us, our animals originated from the animals captured in that war: Itane in illa gente non erat sanitas corporum, in qua et nasci—et ita perdurare potuerunt illa *animalia*, ut quibusdam eorum gravidis, sicut desipiunt, captis, et in cœlo colligatis, nec saltim pleni temporis, sed abortivi fœtus de tam excelso in terram caden- [p. 801.] tes et vivere potuerint et crescere, et ista carnium, quæ nunc sunt innumerabilia, genera propagare? There is also another fault in that passage of *Augustine:* for he attributes the victory over the leaders of darkness, to the *First Man:* but that honor did not belong to him, as we have shown, but to the *Living Spirit*, the *First Man* having been vanquished.

It was necessary for *Manes* to suppose such an unfortunate battle of the first General of the world of light. For he had to show, whence it arose, that so many divine essences and particles of celestial matter became commingled with the corrupt elements and malignant bodies, and exposed in them to so great evils, sorrows, and sufferings, during so many ages. The blame could not be charged on God; for he, according to Manichæan views, is the kindest of Beings, and cannot hurt any one. They would have contradicted themselves, if they had said that it was God's will, that the souls descended from him should suffer numberless evils and sorrows during a very long period. They indeed taught, as we may learn from *Fortunatus* in his discussion with *Augustine*, that souls become intangled in matter, *not necessarily, but by the volition of God:* and this, in a certain sense, they could justly say, as appears from the account we have given of the warfare of the *First Man.* The adversaries of the Manichæans, including *Augustine*, (p. 78.) assailed this their doctrine, with the following interrogatory: Quid opus erat tanta mala animam pati per tantum tempus, donec mundus finiatur? (See *Titus* Bostrens. contra Manichæos, L I. p. 91. 92. &c.) To this question, *Fortunatus*, who was not master of the religion he professed, acknowledges, that he could give no answer: *Quid ergo dicturus sum!* But *Manes* had foreseen the question; and he furnished a sort of answer to it. The answer is: That it is not God's fault that souls are so long detained in matter, for he cannot possibly will evil to any being; but it was the fault of his General, the *First Man*, who, not being sufficiently on his guard, the celestial matter and the divine essence became completely intermixed with depraved matter in the battle, and therefore cannot now be separated from it, except by a long process. In this way, indeed, the difficulty which stumbled *Fortunatus* is solved, and God is made innocent of the many evils which good souls feel and perform in their long exile: but another blot, namely that of ignorance, is fastened upon him. For he is made to be ignorant of future events, or not to have foreseen, that the *First Man* would commit errors, and be overcome in the conflict with the Prince of darkness. This, however, the Manichæans readily conceded; for they denied to God other perfections besides that of foreknowledge. We may here remark,—what also suggests itself on other occasions, that *Manes*, although he may lack sagacity and wisdom, never lacks ingenuity. For he clearly perceived, that God would be judged imbecile and weak, if he taught that the evil Principle, contrary to the will and the efforts of God, got possession of souls [p. 802.] and the celestial matter; and unkind and cruel, if he taught, that it was according to the divine pleasure, that innocent souls for so many ages were in affliction and in conflict with depraved matter; and therefore, to escape these difficulties, he made him ignorant of the future. - - In this part of my discussion, several new views are advanced; but they are all based on reliable authorities. It is therefore unnecessary to weary the reader, by stating how far, and why, I deviate from other writers on Manichæism, and especially from *Beausobre*.

§ XLV. **Origin, composition and character of Man.** In the commencement of the new campaigne, the Prince of darkness, being terrified with the splendor of the *Living Spirit*, and foreseeing that the particles of divine light, or the rational souls devoured by him and his companions, would be wrested from them, formed a cunning device for avoiding, in a measure, so great a loss. For he persuaded his chiefs to transfer into their wives by coition those portions of light which were in them: and the children thus produced, he himself devoured, and of course with them all the souls: and they being thus incorporated with his blood and fluids, he embraced his wife, and so begat the first man *Adam*, in part resembling the celestial *First Man* whom he had seen, and in part like himself.(1) When all the souls which the Princes of darkness had captured, were in this manner inclosed in the body of *Adam* only, and thus placed beyond the power of the *Living Spirit*, the King of darkness gave to Adam a wife, namely *Eve;* and Adam, being allured by her beauty, copulated with her contrary to the will of God: and thus the miserable race of mortals peopling our globe, began to exist and to be propagated.(2) These unhappy children of Adam consist of a *body* and *two souls.* Their body is composed of *depraved matter*, and belongs wholly to the King of darkness, the father of Adam; and consequently, when a man dies it returns to its original source. Of their two souls, the *one* is animal, sentient, and concupiscent, and was derived from the same Prince of evil; but *the other*, which possesses reason, and is alone immortal, is a *particle* of that divine *light* which was captured by the race of darkness in the contest with the *First Man*, and was afterwards by their Prince infused wholly into the body of Adam, and thence distributed among all his offspring, male and female. It hence appears, whence arose that mixture of good and evil in indivi- [p. 803.] dual men, and the perpetual conflict between reason and concupiscence.(³)

(1) That the first human beings were formed by the Prince of evil, and consequently, that the whole race of men are his descendants; and also that marriages, by which the race is propagated, were his device; all the ancient writers declare, and on this subject there can be no doubt among such as keep in sight the origin of the Manichæan system. But as to the manner in which the first human beings were formed, there is some disagreement among those on whose testimony we must here rely. It is fortunate, however, that a long extract from the Epistola Fundamenti of *Manes*, which treated of this very subject, has been preserved by *Augustine*, and gives a clear and perspicuous account of Adam's origin. This, therefore, is to be especially consulted, and to be exclusively followed; while the divergent and contrary statements of later authors, *Theodoret* for instance, and others, must be wholly rejected, as proceeding from impure sources. *Beausobre*, who is particularly solicitous to make out that *Manes* was not a fool but a philosopher, exerts all the powers of his superior genius, (vol. II. p. 401 &c.) to turn the fable of Manes, which we are considering, into an allegory; the import of which shall be, that the Prince of darkness did not beget the first man and woman, but formed them out of matter, which, as he thinks, was called the Demon's wife. But *Manes* does not afford him the slightest countenance; nor let drop one word on which a conjecture can be fastened, that he purposed to enlighten the friend he was addressing by any sort of fiction. On the contrary, the Exordium of the Epistle, (preserved by *Augustine*, Epistola Fundamenti, p. 114.) clearly shows, that *Manes* uttered himself seriously, and according to his real belief, aiming to give Paticius whom he addressed a naked and simple statement of facts. He says: Hæc sunt salubria verba ex perenni et vivo fonte, quæ qui audierit, et eisdem primum crediderit, deinde quæ insinuant custodierit, nunquam erit morti obnoxius, verum æterna et gloriosa vitâ fruetur. Nam profecto beatus est judicandus, qui hac divina instructus cognitione fuerit, per quam liberatus in sempiterna vitâ permanebit. Can we believe a man would write so, if he aimed to lead his friend into error by some allegory, or to elude his curiosity by an obscure *fable?* But Manes goes on to say: De eo igitur, frater dilectissime, Patici, de quo mihi significasti, dicens, nosse te

cupere, utrum verbo (by command of God) iidem sunt prolati, an primogeniti ex corpore, (i. e. begotten of the Demon's body,) respondebitur tibi ut congruit. Namque de his a plerisque in variis scripturis, relationibusque dissimili modo insertum atque commemoratum est. (Various opinions therefore, relating to [p. 804.] the origin of the first men, were afloat in the East in various books. Quapropter veritas istius rei ut sese habet ab universis fere gentibus ignoratur, et ab omnibus, qui etiam de hoc diu multumque disputarunt. (He therefore proposes to give a new opinion, not before heard of.) Si enim illis super Adæ et Evæ generatione provenisset manifesto cognoscere, nunquam corruptioni et morti subjacerent. The salvation of men and eternal life, therefore, depend on a correct knowledge of the origin of Adam and Eve! And would *Manes* involve a doctrine of such moment in a ludicrous and silly *fable?* But there are other proofs, which intirely overthrow the officious opinion of *Beausobre;* among which the strongest is, that according to *Manes*, no living and animated being *can* be produced, either in the world of light or in the world of darkness, except by generation. Yet the ingenious man has one argument in his favor. He observes, that no one except *Manes* only, has said that Adam and Eve were the fruits of the Demon's intercourse with his wife. This, however, is not perfectly true; nor if it were true, would it effect anything. For *Manes* alone, when *his* opinions are concerned, is of higher and greater authority than all others. Besides, the others do not speak so fully and distinctly on this subject as *Manes* does, they aiming to express summarily what he had expressed more fully and minutely, so that they, as we shall see, treat the subject more concisely and indistinctly. Let us therefore hear *Manes* himself; and let us not hesitate to take his statements in their literal sense. I will cite the entire passage from *Augustine*, (de natura boni c. 46. p. 366. 367.) It will give us a vivid idea of the man's singular genius. He recites what the Prince of darkness said to his compeers, thus: Iniquis igitur commentis ad eos, qui aderant, ait: Quid vobis videtur maximum hoc lumen, quod oritur? (He refers to the *Living Spirit*, who came down from heaven to renew the contest.) Intuemini, quemadmodum polum movet, concutit plurimas potestates. Quapropter mihi vos potius æquum est, id quod in vestris viribus habetis luminis, (namely, the *light*, which the several leaders of the army of darkness had devoured in the first conflict,) prærogare: Sic quippe illius magni, qui gloriosus (i. e. *lucid*,) apparuit, imaginem fingam: (The *Great One* here, whose image the King of the land of darkness would copy, is not the *Living Spirit;* for he was merely a splendid *mass*, without any form: it was therefore the *First Man*, after whose likeness Adam was formed, according to *Manes*:) per quam regnare poterimus, tenebrarum aliquando conversatione liberati. Hæc audientes (duces et proceres terræ tenebrarum,) ac diu sêcum deliberantes, justissimum putaverunt, id, quod postulabantur, præbere. Nec enim fidebant, se idem lumen jugiter retenturos: unde melius rati sunt Principi suo id offerre, nequaquam desperantes, eodem se pacto regnaturos. Quo igitur modo lumen illud, quod habebant, præbuerint, considerandum est. [p. 805.] Nam hoc etiam divinis scripturis, arcanisque cœlestibus adspersum est? (That is, the sacred books touch indeed upon this subject, but it is only briefly and summarily,) sapientibus vero, (to men divinely taught, as *Manes* himself pretended to be,) quomodo sit datum scire. minime est difficile: nam coram aperteque cognoscitur ab eo, qui vere ac fideliter intueri voluerit. Quoniam eorum, qui convenerant, frequentia promiscua erat, fœminarum scilicet ac masculorum, impulit eos, ut inter se coirent: in quo coitu alii seminarunt, aliæ gravidæ effectæ sunt. Erant autum partus iis, qui genuerunt similes, vires plurimas parentum, uti *Primi* (ss. *Hominis*,) obtinentes. Hæc sumens eorum Princeps uti præcipuum donum gavisus est. Et sicuti etiam nunc fieri videmus, corporum formatricem naturam mali inde vires sumentem figurare: ita etiam ante dictus Princeps sodalium prolem accipiens, habentem parentum sensus, prudentiam, lucem, (i. e. a rational soul, which is a particle of light,) simul secum in generatione procreatam, comedit: ac plerisque viribus sumptis ex istiusmodi escâ, in qua non modo inerat fortitudo, sed multo magis astutiæ et pravi, sensus ex fera genitorum gente, propriam ad se conjugem evocavit, ex ea, qua ipse erat stirpe manantem: et facto cum ea coitu, seminavit, ut ceteri, abundantiam malorum, quæ devoraverat: nonnihil etiam ipse adjiciens ex sua cogitatione et virtute, ut esset sensus ejus omnium eorum, quæ profuderat formator, atque descriptor: ejus compar excipiebat hæc, ut semen consuevit culta optime terra percipere. In eadem enim construebantur et contexebantur omnium imagines, coelestium ac terrenarum virtutum, ut pleni videlicet orbis, id quod formabatur similitudinem obtineret. Most of the things here narrated are plain and very unlike an allegory. *Augustine* states the whole matter more briefly, (de Hæres. c. 42. p. 13.) thus: Adam et Evam ex Prinipibus fumi asserunt natos, cum Pater eorum nomine *Saclas* sociorum suorum fetus omnium devorasset, et quidquid inde commixtum divinæ subtantiæ ceperat, cum uxore concumbens, in carne prolis tanquam tenacissimo vinculo colligasset.—The name of *Saclas* here given by *Augustine* to the Prince of evil, as it is also by *Theodoret*, (Hæret. Fabul. L. i. c. 26. p. 213.) and by others,—was a common appellation both among the Manichæans and the Gnostics, as *Epiphanius* informs us, (Haeres. xxvi. § 10. tom. i. p. 91.) and hence it is manifest, that this was the usual name for the Demon among the Orientals. His wife's name, as preserved by *Theodoret*, was *Nebrod*. Of the origin of these names, I offer no discussion. For what certainty or utility can such discussions promise us? It will be more profitable to elucidate certain parts of *Manes*' statements, and confirm them by other testimonies, so that we may more clearly see what *Manes* dreamed, or, if you choose, adopted from the Magian system, respecting the origin of mankind.

In the *first* place, the time of the formation of the first men by the Prince of evil, must be noticed. In the beginning of the passage just quoted, [p. 806.] *Manes* clearly shows, that *Saclas* formed the purpose of producing man, when he beheld the new Luminary from heaven appearing, and causing his princes to tremble; that is, when he saw the *Living Spirit* coming to succeed the *First Man*, and to renew the war. He did not greatly fear the *First Man*, who was of his own form, and operated more by craftiness and deception, than by prowess: but on seeing this new General, he lost all confidence in his own power and that of his associates; and, from the first movements of the new captain, he could foresee, that he and his companions would have to give up the light which they had captured. To prevent the loss of this plunder, he deemed it necessary to collect it together, and to place it in safety; and this, he thought, could not be better accomplished, than by withdrawing it all from the warriors, and, after getting it into his own body, to commingle it perfectly with matter. It may therefore be assumed as certain, that the first human beings were formed, at the very commencement of the second war, and before the *Living Spirit* had obtained the victory; and consequently, they, or at least one of them, Adam, existed before the world was framed: and this world was certainly formed by the *Living Spirit*, after the subjugation of the Prince of darkness. This is a new thought. For all the writers on the subject, whom I have consulted, say, that according to *Manes*, this earth of ours is older than man; and that man was generated for the sake of the earth. And for the support of their opinion, they have the respectable testimony of *Tyrbo*, (in the Acta Disput. *Archelai*, § 7. p. 12.) besides others, who might be mentioned. But they most certainly err, if reliance can be placed on *Manes*. Man was prior to our world; and the previous generation of man was, undoubtedly, the cause of the formation of our world; and God would not have given orders for its formation, had not the crafty foe, by generating man, frustrated the divine plans, by shutting up the souls which God wished to rescue, in a body as their prison. In confirmation of these facts, several passages might be adduced from *Titus* of Bostra; but I will content myself with citing only one, from a Manichæan who wrote a book περὶ τῆς ἀνθρωπίνης πρωτοπλασίας, de prima hominis formatione; inserted by *Titus* in the Preface to his third Book, (tom. I. p. 137. edit. *Canisii*,): "Εκαστος αὐτῶν τῶν τῆς ὕλης ἀρχόντων τῆς γενομένης κινήσεως ἕνεκεν καὶ τοῦ φανέντος πρῶτον ἐπὶ τὴν λύτρωσιν τῆς ψυχῆς, τῆς θύρας πρῶτον ἀνοιγείσης, ὑπ' ἐκπλήξεως ἄκων καταπέμψας τὴν ἐν αὐτῷ δύναμιν, ἐμόρφωσεν ἑαυτὸν εἰς θήραμα τῆς ψυχῆς καὶ μίμημα ἔπλασεν ἐπὶ τῆς γῆς, οὗ δυσαποψάστως ἠνάγκασεν τὰς ψυχὰς κατακηλουμένας. Καὶ πλάσμα αὐτῶν ἐστὶ πρῶτον ὁ 'Αδὰμ, κ. τ. λ. Unusquisque procerum materiæ, simulatque motus factus erat, isque apparebat, qui liberare jussus erat animas, simulatque janua (cœlorum) aperiebatur, præ terrore invitus virtutem, quæ in eo erat, dimittebat et formavit se ipsum ad venandam animam. Et imitationem sui finxit (This, doubtless, must not be understood of all the princes of darkness, but only of their King; whom all Manichæans, as well as the founder of the sect, [p. 807.] represented as the father of the first human beings,) in terra, (Beware of hence inferring, that our earth then existed; for this writer had previously denied it clearly,) cœgitque animas delinitas, ut in eam ingrederentur. Ac primum quidem eorum specimen Adamus est. What *Manes* himself had stated clearly, and at full length, his disciple here states more briefly and indistinctly. Yet, in the main points, he agrees fully with his master. For he manifestly teaches:—1st, That great terror seized the princes of darkness, when they saw the gates of heaven open, and the *Living Spirit* issuing forth with a mighty movement. The cause of their trouble was, the fear that the light they had plundered, would be wrested from them, and that they should fall back into their former wretchedness and misery. For thus the writer had before stated: Quia cognoverunt magistratus materiæ, quod si omnino pars luminis, quod in eos incidit, auferretur, mors (by *mors*, he means some *dire calamity;* for the princes of darkness could not *die*,) eis adventura esset, machinati sunt descensum animæ in corpora.—2dly, He teaches, that God purposed to rescue the captured light or souls, by means of the *Living Spirit.*—3dly, That the princes of darkness, to frustrate the designs of God, determined on the formation of a man, or a material body, and inclosing the captured souls in it.—4thly, That for this purpose, they gave up all the particles of light which they had seized, reluctantly, indeed, yet prefering this as the least of two evils.—5thly, And hence it was, that Adam was formed, and all the souls thrust into him. Therefore, what we have stated cannot be denied; namely, that at the commencement of the new campaign, and as soon as the *Living Spirit* made his appearance, the Prince of evil determined to generate man; so that truly, man was born, before that most powerful Spirit founded this terraqueous globe.

The *second* thing demanding attention in the passage cited from *Manes*, is, the objects proposed by the Prince of darkness in the formation of man. The first or immediate object, had reference to the light. For the Lord of evil wished to retain dominion over that light which he and his associates had seized, and to prevent its recovery by the *Living Spirit.* The other, or more remote object, is not so manifest. *Manes* thus describes it: Fingam imaginem, per quam regnare poterimus, conversatione tenebrarum liberati. He therefore promised himself and friends a *kingdom*, as the result of the formation of man: and his captains and co-warriors relied upon this promise. A little reflection will make this expectation intelligible. The King of darkness anticipated, that Adam, when he should generate him, would propagate his species by means of Eve: and thus all the souls collected together in him, would gradually become distributed into as many bodies. And he had no doubt, that these souls, when intangled in bodies, would follow their senses and their pleasures, rather than their reason: and all who yield to lust and to the instincts of depraved matter, are under the power and dominion of the Prince of evil. In this ex- [p. 808.] pectation, the Lord of evil was not disappointed. He therefore actually prepared for himself a kingdom, when he generated the first man.

The *third* thing requiring illustration in the passage from *Manes*, is as follows: The King of darkness says, that he *imaginem Magni illius, qui gloriosus apparuit, ficturum esse;* that is, that he would form a man, like to the *First Man.* So *Manes* and all his sect believed, that *Adam* was a copy of that *First Man* whom God sent against the army of darkness. *Tyrbo*, (in the Acta *Archelai*, § 7. p. 12.) says: Convocavit (Princeps malorum) omnes principes primarios, et sumpsit ab eis singulas virtutes, et fecit hominem hunc secundum speciem Primi Hominis illius, et junxit animam (i. e. all the souls) in eo. It is well known, and yet is worth repeating, that Adam also bore the image of his father, the Prince of darkness. Thus *Tyrbo*, (l. c. p. 19.): De Adam vero quomodo creatus sit, ita dicit (Manes), quia qui dicit: *Venite, faciamus hominem ad imaginem et similitudinem nostram*, secundum eam, quam videmus, formam Princeps est, qui hoc dicit ad collegas suos principes, id est, venite, date mihi de lumine, quod accepimus, et faciamus secundum *nostram*, qui principes sumus, *formam et secundum eam*, quam videmus, quod est Primus Homo, et ita hominem creaverunt. Adam therefore, in one sense, resembled the *First Man*, but in another sense he resembled his father, the King of evil. As to his external *form*, he was like his father; for we have before showed, that the Lord of darkness was a giant in a human form. In his figure, therefore, we must not seek for the resemblance of Adam to the *First Man.* That he was equal to his father in stature and magnitude, and much taller and larger than his posterity, cannot be doubted. The likeness of Adam to the *First Man,* I therefore suppose, was placed by *Manes* in his attributes of light and power. For, as his father had imparted to him all the souls, those particles of light, he could not fail of being resplendent, and possessed of great power and strength; just as the *First Man* was. Most of the Orientals, and many of the Jews likewise, were persuaded that Adam was a giant, and was clothed with a very luminous body. This Oriental opinion, *Manes* doubtless embraced, and incorporated in his religion.

Lastly, passing over things so plain as not to need a comment, there remains to be noticed, the opinion expressed by *Manes* in the passage, concerning the origin and nature of the *soul.* The Prince of darkness committed the whole *mass of souls* under his control, to the vast and gigantic body of his single son *Adam.* And therefore, whatever exists anywhere on our globe, having the nature of soul, proceeded wholly from Adam by natural generation, and has thus reached his posterity. Notwithstanding souls had existed in the world of light long before bodies were formed, yet souls were not thrust into bodies by God on account of their sins, as *Plato* thought; nor did they, as others supposed, [p. 809.] voluntarily enter into bodies, from a love of voluptuous indulgence; but involuntarily, and contrary to the pleasure of God, they were intangled in the bonds of material bodies, by the Lord of darkness; and they are propagated from parents to their children, by a law of nature, in the same manner as bodies are. This I could confirm abundantly, from *Augustine* and others, if it were necessary. But I only refer to the testimony of *Manes* himself, which is hereafter to be cited.—His opinion respecting souls, obliged our Persian to profess what is called the *Metempsychosis,* or the migration of souls through different bodies. For he supposed, only a limited and definite number of souls were thrust into material bodies; and they who think so, must suppose that when souls go out of their bodies, they pass into new ones.

Respecting the generation of *Eve,* nothing has reached us in the writings of *Manes.* But *Tyrbo,* (in the Acta *Archelai,* § 10. p. 20.) repeats as his, the following words: Evam quoque similiter fecerunt, dantes ei de concupiscientia sua ad decipiendum Adam. From this declaration it is manifest, that *Eve* was of a worse character, and had more depraved matter in her composition, than her husband. For in Adam, into whom his father had infused the greatest part of the light, there was, as we shall soon show, more of light and goodness than of darkness and evil matter: but in *Eve* there was a less quantity of light, and a far greater quantity of darkness or propension to pleasures. This *Tyrbo* indicates, by the words: Dantes ei de concupiscentiâ sua. And such a character was necessary to her; as it was by her, that the cause and author of all evil, wished his son to be induced to apostatize from right reason. *Theodoret* tells us, (Hæret. Fabul. L. i. c. 26. p. 213.) that *Eve* had no rational soul, when she was born; but that a certain male virgin, named *Joël* and *Daughter of Light,* afterwards imbued her with light or a rational soul. And it may be, that *Manes* so taught.

For, as the Prince of evil had exhausted the whole mass of light in generating Adam, he could impart nothing to *Eve*, except a sentient soul. But this part of the fable, from the want of documents to elucidate it, must be left very much in the dark. Yet the longer I ponder and consider the fable of *Manes*, the more certain I become, that Eve was born long after Adam, and after our world was established. And I hope those will agree with me, in this point, who may peruse what I am about to say respecting *Manes'* views of Adam's sin.

(2) What all Christians believe, on the authority of the inspired writer Moses, that Adam apostatized from God, and was enticed into sin by the Prince of hell,—*Manes* also confessed; yet he explained the matter very differently from other Christians. What the ancients state, and among them *Augustine* who had read Manichæan books, respecting the opinions of *Manes* in regard to the sin of the first man, are so various and so discordant, that the most ingenious cannot reconcile them. Some of them listened too much to rumors, others confounded certain Gnostic notions with the opinions of *Manes*, and [p. 810.] others appear to have misrepresented the truth, from their hatred of the sect. Therefore laying aside and disregarding the dubious, the uncertain, the false and the contradictory, I will first bring forward the testimonies which have most authority; and then from these will endeavor, as far as possible, to elicit the true sentiments of *Manes* and arrange them methodically. Three passages embrace the whole subject. The *first* is from *Tyrbo*, (in the Acta Disput. *Archelai*, § 10. p. 17.) who tells us, that *Manes* converted the Mosaic account of Adam's transgression into an *allegory:* Paradisus autem, qui vocatur mundus, et arbores, quae in ipso sunt, concupiscentiae sunt: (An incorrect statement, as appears from what is said afterwards:) et ceterae seductiones corrumpentes cogitationes hominum. *Concupiscencies*, then, are not inordinate emotions of the human mind or will, but real *things*, which stir up and excite those emotions or lusts of the man. *Tyrbo* adds: Arborem scientiae boni et mali esse ipsum Jesum, quo duce ac magistro homines bonum malo secernere discunt. This manifestly contradicts what he had before said. For, if the trees of Paradise were sensible objects, which the man craved and desired, how could the tree of knowledge of good and evil be Jesus? I suppose, *Manes* likened Jesus to that tree, and that *Tyrbo* converted the metaphor into a dogma.—The *second*, a very noticeable passage, is from *Manes* himself, (Epistola ad filiam *Menoch*, which is preserved in the unfinished work of *Augustine*, contra Julianum Pelagianum, L. iii. Opp. tom. x. p. 832.): Operae pretium est advertere, quia prima anima, quae a Deo luminis manavit, accepit fabricam istam corporis, ut eam fraeno suo regeret. Venit mandatum, peccatum revixit, quod videbatur captivum: invenit articulos suos Diabolus (i. e. an occasion, suited to his purpose,) materiam concupiscentiae in eam seduxit et per illam occidit. Lex quidem sancta, sed sancta sanctae, et mandatum et justum et bonum, sed justae et bonae. I will here subjoin an extract from *Augustine's* reply to Julian, which affords light on this subject. *Augustine*, aiming to convict *Julian* of coinciding with *Manes*, by means of this Epistle, says: Manichaeus non hoc de homine, sed de animâ bona dicit, quam Dei partem atque naturam—opinatur - - in homine per concupiscentiam decipi. Quam concupiscentiam non vitium substantiae bonae, sed malam vult esse substantiam. Mala

non vacuum fuisse dicit Adam, *sed ejus minus habuisse, multoque plus lucis.* The *third* passage is from *Augustine*, (de moribus ecclesiae Catholicae et Manichaeorum, L. ii. c. 19. Opp. tom. i. p. 552.) : Talis apud vos opinio de Adam et Eva: longa fabula est, sed ex ea id attingam, quod in praesentia satis est. Adam dicitis, sic a parentibus suis genitum, abortivis illis principibus tenebrarum, ut *maximam partem lucis* haberet in anima et perexiguam gentis adversae. Qui cum sancte viveret propter exsuperantem copiam boni, commotam tamen in eo fuisse [p. 811.] adversam illam partem, ut ad concubitum declinaretur: ita eum lapsum esse atque peccasse, sed vixisse postea sanctiorem. A Manichaean, whom *Augustine* had previously mentioned for exemplification, when he was severely bastinadoed for deflowering a virgin, relying upon this doctrine, clamabat, ut sibi ex auctoritate Manichaei parceretur, Adam primum heroëm (so all the copies read; but I think it should read *hominem*. For in what sense could Adam, the son of the evil Demon, be called a *hero* by the Manichaeans ?) peccavisse, et post peccatum fuisse sanctiorem.—Whoever will carefully consider the things above stated in these passages, some of them clearly and others obscurely, and will compare with them what has been already proved, and particularly what we have said respecting *Eve*, the mother of the human race; unless I greatly misjudge, will be able to form no other conception of *Manes'* opinion in regard to the sin of the first man, than as follows:—*First*, When the Prince of evil had placed in safety those souls or particles of divine light, which the *Living Spirit* had been commissioned by God to recover, and they were now all enclosed in the single body of Adam, the offspring of the Prince of darkness; the first care of God was, to prevent Adam from neglecting, and dissipating by carnal copulation, that immense treasure of light which was stored up in him.—*Secondly*, He therefore placed him in some part of that world, which the *Living Spirit* had been instructed to fabricate; and commanded him to watch carefully, lest what was of a divine nature in him should be overcome by the assaults of the body and of the evil soul or concupiscence. The fact that God gave a law to Adam, is most clearly stated by Manes; who says, that the substance of the law was: *Ut Adamus, freno animæ divinæ, corpus* (naturally inclined to lust) *regeret.* I therefore wonder that *Faustus*, a disciple of *Manes*, (apud *August.* L. xxii. c. 4. p. 258.) should censure the Mosaic history of the first human beings, because, (as he says): Deus in ea fingatur ignarus futuri, ut præceptum illud, quod non esset servaturus Adam, ei mandaret. When uttering this he must have forgotten the written statements of *Manes*. It is certain, as we have before put beyond controversy, that the God of the Manichaeans was *ignorant of the future;* and he did give a law to Adam, which he was not to keep.—*Thirdly*, Adam could, with a little pains, have kept the law which God gave him. For although the collection of souls or the mass of light, which his father had committed to him, was resident in a malignant body, and also connected with a turbulent and vicious soul; yet the portion of the divine nature which he possessed was far greater and more abundant, than the portion of depraved matter with which it was surrounded. Nor is this unaccountable: for the whole mass of light, which the entire race of darkness had seized upon, was collected and deposited in him: so that he had only *one* evil and vicious soul, but good ones innumerable.—*Fourthly*, Therefore, Adam, for some time, being mindful of the divine law, lived a holy life, and curbed the emotions of desire, by sound reason.—*Fifthly*, But this continence portended great danger to the wishes of the Prince of evil. For if Adam should persevere in it, the [p. 812.] whole band of souls latent in him, on the extinction of his body, would soar aloft to the world of light, and deprive the Demon of all hope of founding for himself a kingdom.—*Sixthly* The Prince of darkness perceiving this, generated a most beautiful woman, who was to allure Adam to sin, or to enkindle in him that desire which was kept in subjection by the divine souls. She at first had only a sentient and vicious soul, because her father had previously divested himself of all light. But God, wishing to make her better, and to prevent Adam's sinning, added to her sentient soul a divine and good soul, by means of a celestial Being named the *Daughter of Light*. But this good soul was too weak, to subdue and hold in subjection that mass of depraved matter, of which Eve was composed.—*Seventhly*, The result therefore was as the Prince of evil wished. For Eve, in whom desire was more powerful than reason, kindled a flame in Adam. And, overcome by her blandishments, he yielded to her solicitations, and lay with her. And thus the tree of knowledge of good and evil, the fruit of which ruined man, was *Eve:* and the sin of Adam was, intercouse with the wife provided for him by the Prince of evil.

(3) What *Manes* thought of *man*, cannot be unintelligible to those who have read with moderate care the preceding discussions. And yet this subject demands some attention, especially in regard to the *soul*. Manes constituted man with *two* souls, the one good and the other evil, and a *body* altogether evil. And not only was the body propagated from the parents, but likewise both souls, though in a different manner. For the body is begotten by a body, and the soul by or from a soul. *Manes* will explain this shortly.—To begin with the body: It is clear, that the body consists wholly of depraved and vicious matter. For when all the celestial matter, now mixed with the depraved matter, shall have escaped and evaporated, the impure residuum and malignant dregs constitute the human body. *Augustine* is eloquent in explaining this doctrine, (de moribus Manichæorum, L. ii. c. 15. Opp. tom. i. p. 543.): Carnes jam de ipsis sordibus dicitis esse concretas. Fugit enim aliquid partis illius divinæ, ut perhibetis, dum fruges et poma carpuntur; fugit, cum affliguntur vel terendo, vel molendo, vel coquendo, vel etiam mordendo atque mandendo. Fugit etiam in omnibus motibus animalium vel cum gestiunt, vel cum exercentur, vel cum laborant. - - Fugit etiam in ipsa quiete nostra dum in corpore illa, quæ appellatur digestio, interiore calore conficitur. Atque ita tot occasionibus fugiente divina naturâ, quiddam sordidissimum remanet, unde per concubitum caro formetur. - - Quo circa cum anima etiam carnem deseruerit, nimias sordes reliquas fieri. Hence all bodies belong, not to God, but to his adversary, the Prince of darkness; who forms and fabricates them by means of lust, which comes from him. In his Epistle to *Menoch*, (in *Augustine's* unfinished work against *Julian*, L. iii. Opp. tom. x. p. 828.) *Manes* says: Sicut auctor [p. 813.] animarum Deus est, ita corporum auctor per concupiscentiam (which passed from him into the evil soul,) Diabolus est, ut in viscatorio Diaboli per concupis-

centiam mulieris. (Here seems to be something wrong in the language, but the sense is clear. *Manes* (I suppose) would say, that women now, as formerly Eve, is the bird-lime of the Prince of evil, by which he enkindles lust in men, and entraps them.) Unde Diabolus aucupatur non animas, sed corpora sive per visum, sive per tactum, sive per auditum, sive per odoratum, sive per gustum. (Good souls, being of a celestial nature, and free from all emotions and desires, cannot possibly be *ensnared*, or have lustful feelings excited in them. But bodies, in which evil and concupiscent souls reside, can be insnared or stimulated to sin, by means of the five bodily senses.) Tolle denique malignæ hujus stirpis radicem, et statim te ipsam spiritalem contemplaris.

That *Manes* assigned two souls to men, is most certain. See *Augustine's* unfinished work against Julian, (L. iii. p. 828.): Duas simul animas in uno homine esse delirant, unam malam, alteram bonam, de suis diversis Principiis emanantes. And there is extant a Tract of *Augustine*, (Opp. tom. viii. p. 55 &c.) intitled: Libellus de duabus animabus contra Manichæos. But whoever shall expect to gain from it a full and accurate knowledge of the Manichæan doctrine, concerning the soul, will find his expectations disappointed in the perusal. For the author disputes against the doctrine in a general way, and without defining and explaining it. Indeed, *Augustine* confesses, though obscurely, in his unfinished work, (L. iii. p. 828.) that he did not fully and intirely understand the doctrine of his antagonist concerning the soul. I can believe, that both *Manes* and his disciples expressed themselves differently at different times, on this as on many other subjects. I will state what can be ascertained in regard to it.—The evil soul comes from the Prince of evil, and is the seat of all the passions, lusts, appetites, and desires, by which men are agitated and led astray; but the good soul is a daughter of light, and of a divine nature, and cannot become excited, nor crave any of the external objects that meet the senses. This depraved soul is attached to the body, and is excited and impelled to concupiscence, by the objects presented to the five senses. This, I think, is clear, from the passage of *Manes* before cited, in which he says: *Diabolus aucupatur non animas* (i. e. not the good souls,) *sed corpora*, (in which the vicious soul resides,) by means of the five senses. This soul is propagated, with the body, from the parent to the child. Says *Manes*, in his Epistle to *Menoch*, (apud *August.* Operis imperf. L. iii. p. 829.): Caro (i. e. the *body*, in which resides the soul that is evil by nature,) adversatur spiritui, quia filia concupiscentiæ est, et spiritus carni, quia filius animæ est. Quare vide, quam stulti sint, qui dicunt, hoc figmentum (the animated body) a Deo bono esse conditum, quod certi sunt a spiritu concupis- [p. 814.] centiæ gigni. Parents obtain those souls, which they impart to their children, through the aliments they use. For all matter, and all the five elements of it, the Manichæans supposed to be animated or full of souls; and this they supposed, not only of bad matter, but also of good matter. Therefore, whenever people nourish their bodies with flesh, wine, and other nutritious substances, they take therewith into their bodies, the turbulent and vicious soul latent in those substances. And consequently, it must be, that the children procreated from their bodies, receive also that root of all evils.—If now it be asked, to which of the five elements, of which all things are composed, the evil soul belonged?—(for the Manichæans recognized no Beings as simple essences, and void of matter,) I suppose, it was a portion of *smoke*, or the *bad ether*. For the Prince of darkness lives and dwells in smoke, or in the thick murkey ether; and he consists of smoke or malignant ether, just as God does of light. And as evil souls are descended from him, it is to be supposed, that they will possess the same nature with their parent. Therefore, the depraved soul of the Manichæans, was a portion of smoke or bad ether, which is diffused through all matter, and from it is transfused into all human bodies.

Its opposite, the good soul, is a particle of celestial light. Of this, there can be no doubt. But whether it is a portion of that divine nature or light, of which God himself consists, or whether it belongs to that celestial element, which the Manichæans denominated light, is not equally certain. The ancient adversaries of the Manichæans, *Titus*, *Augustine*, and the others, affirm in many places, that the good soul of the Manichæans was a part of God himself. Read merely the Tract of *Augustine* de duabus animabus, in the beginning of which, he several times declares the good soul of the Manichæans to be *de substantiâ Dei*. But *Beausobre* takes great pains to prove, that the ancients erred in this matter, and that the good soul is only a portion of the celestial elements. To me the point appears doubtful: because the doctrine of the Manichæans respecting the soul is nowhere explained with sufficient clearness. *Manes*, in a passage soon to be adduced, calls the soul *divinæ stirpis fructum:* but this is ambiguous, and may be understood either way. The good soul is propagated: but in what manner, *Manes* himself seems not to know; and, if I mistake not, he is not self-consistent in regard to the soul. But let us hear him descanting on the subject, in his Epistle to his daughter *Menoch*, (apud *August.* Operis imperf. L. iii. p. 828.) where he thus addresses the lady: Gratia tibi, et salus a Deo nostro, qui est revera verus Deus, tribuatur, ipseque tuam mentem illustret et justitiam suam tibimet revelet, quia es divinæ stirpis fructus. - - - Per quos et tu splendida reddita es, agnoscendo qualiter prius fueris, ex quo genere animarum emanaveris, quod est confusum omnibus corporibus et saporibus [p. 815.] et speciebus variis cohæret. Nam sicut *animæ gignuntur animabus*, ita figmentum corporis a corporis naturâ digeritur. Quod ergo nascitur de carne, caro est, et quod de spiritu, spiritus est: spiritum autem animam intellige, anima de animâ, caro de carne. - - Caro enim adversatur spiritui, quia filia concupiscentiæ est: et spiritus carni, quia filius animæ est. *Manes* here seems explicitly to support the opinion of those who make souls originate from souls. And hence *Julian* the Pelagian, who wished to prove *Augustine* to be a Manichæan in his doctrine of the soul, says: Cognoscis nempe, quomodo signatissime Manichæus traducem confirmet animarum, et quo testimonio utatur ad vituperationem carnis, illo videlicet, quod in ore vestro versatur, id est, Quod nascitur de carne, caro est, et quod de spiritu, spiritus est. *Augustine* here hesitates, and knows not what reply to make. He first says: Nescire se hanc epistolam Manichæi. This perhaps was true; but it was nothing to the purpose. He then adds, That if *Manes* wrote so, he contradicted himself: Si hoc dixit Manichæus, quid mirum est, quod se ipse destruxit? This is no mistake: for the opinion, which *Manes* here seems to profess, in regard to the propagation of souls, evidently disagrees with his other opinions respecting the generation of man, the world, and other subjects. Finally, he says he does not know the opinion of *Manes* respecting the soul; and he is not disposed to inquire into it: Quomodo dicat Manichaeus animas nasci, ad nos quid pertinet? But I wonder, the acute *Augustine* should not perceive, that the very words of *Manes* before us, contain enough to overthrow this opinion of the generation of souls by souls. For *Manes* says to his daughter, whom he is addressing: Animam emanasse de illo animarum genere, quod est confusum omnibus corporibus et saporibus et speciebus variis cohaeret. If *Manes* said this in reference to the *good* soul of his daughter, then that soul was not born of the soul of her parents; but it came into their bodies with their food and drink, and thence passed into their daughter. That *Manes* had reference to the *evil* soul, I see no reason at all to believe. And hence, either the doctrine of *Manes* concerning the soul, was incoherent and a compound of contradictions,—which perhaps was the fact; or we must suppose, that when he said, *Souls are the daughters of souls*, he only meant, that all good souls descended from that mass of light or souls, which the Prince of darkness had got into his power. Yet no small portion of those souls resides in herbs and trees and animals; because the souls of men which are not purgated, migrate at death into various kinds of bodies, from which in process of time they return into men. And thus *Augustine* himself explains the Manichæan doctrine, in another place, (contra duas Epistolas Pelagianorum, L. iv. c. [p. 816.] 4. Opp. tom. x. p. 310.): Dicunt Manichæi animan bonam, partem scilicet Dei, pro meritis inquinationis suae per cibum et potum, in quibus antea colligata est, venire in hominem atque ita per concubitum carnis vinculo colligari.—Let us proceed to other points. This good soul, being of celestial origin, and nothing celestial being able to put off or change its nature, must be holy and just and good, and it cannot lose its holiness even in the body. It may indeed become debilitated, or its natural energy and power may be impeded, by the body to which it is joined, and by the evil soul its associate; but it is absolutely impossible for it to become corrupted or vitiated, or to harbor lusts and passions. Whatever enormities and crimes, therefore, are committed by men, they all pertain to the evil soul and the body; and when they are committed, the good soul dissents, is unwilling, and reluctating. Says *Augustine*, (Operis imperf. L. iii. p. 829.): Spiritum concupiscentiae Manichaei substantiam dicunt esse malam, non vitium substantiae bonae, quo caro concupiscit adversus Spiritum. But let us hear *Manes* himself. In his Epistle to *Menoch*, (l. c. p. 828, 829.) he warmly contends that the good soul cannot do wrong or sin: Cum *animo nolente* coëunt et secretis pudoribus gerunt, quo tempore odio habent lucem, uti ne manifestentur opera eorum. Cujus rei gratiâ ait Apostolus: Non est volentis: ut subaudiatur, hoc opus. Sive enim bonum geramus, non est carnis: quia manifesta sunt opera carnis, quae sunt fornicatio, &c. *Sive malum geramus, non est animæ:* quia fructus Spiritus pax, gaudium est. Denique clamat et ad Romanos Apostolus: Non bonum, quod volo, ago, sed malum operor, quod exhorreo. Videtis vocem animae contumacis, contra concupiscentiam defendentem libertatem animae. Dolebat enim, quia peccatum, id est, Diabolus operaretur in se omnem concupiscentiam. Legalis auctoritas indicat malum ejus, cum omnes ejus usus vituperat, quos caro miratur et laudat: omnis enim amaritudo concupiscentiae suavis est animae, per quam nutritur anima et ad vigorem accitur. Denique coërcentis se ab omni usu concupiscentiae animus vigilat, ditatur et crescit: per usum autem concupiscentiae consuevit decrescere. He adds other things of the same nature; but I omit them, because these are sufficient to exhibit his opinion.—Yet, in a certain way, all the sins of the depraved and vicious soul, pertain also to the good soul. For this soul is required to repress the passions and lusts of the evil soul, and to keep it in subjection: and it has ability to fulfil this divine command. If, therefore, it is neglectful of its duty, and suffers the lust of the evil soul to predominate, it is not only weakened thereby, but it contracts guilt, and, in a sense, sins through the evil soul, which it ought to restrain. That *Manes* so thought, is manifest from his commending penitence, and promising forgiveness of sins to the penitent. See [p. 817.] *Augustine's* Tract de duabus animabus, (c. 12. p. 64.): nunquam negaverunt, dari veniam peccatorum, cum fuerit ad Deum quisque conversus: nunquam dixerunt (ut alia multa) quod Scripturis divinis hoc quispiam corruptor inseruerit. And (ch. 14. p. 65.): Inter omnes sanos constat, et quod ipsi Manichaei non solum fatentur, sed et praecipiunt, utile esse poenitere peccati. *Augustine*, in this place, slily asks the Manichaeans, Whether it is the good soul or the bad one that repents? And he says: Si animam tenebrarum peccati pœnitet, non est de substantia summi mali: (Well said!) Si animam lucis, non est de substantiâ summi boni. (This argument, the Manichaeans would easily answer. For they would say, The good soul does not itself sin, but by permitting the sins of the evil soul, it becomes guilty.) But there was no need of *Augustine's* asking the question, since it is manifest, that repentance is the act of the good soul and not of the bad one. For if the latter could feel sorrow for its sins, it would not be wholly evil. These doctrines of *Manes*, in regard to the duty and the powers of the good soul, and the utility of repentance, show, that *Manes* attributed to the good soul not merely intelligence, but also a will, feelings, and emotions; notwithstanding he seems to exclude from it all inclination, desire, and passion. And yet, to tell the truth, the opinions of the Manichæans respecting the two-fold soul of man, are not altogether clear: and hence they, as well as their founder, appear to have doubted how they ought to think, and to have expressed their opinions in dubious and equivocal terms. Still, from what they have said, it is evident, I think, that those are mistaken, who once held, or now hold, that the Manichæans considered the soul to be tied down by fate and necessity. The evil soul indeed is enslaved, and, by its very nature, is borne on to all kinds of concupiscence and wickedness. But the good soul, although somewhat weakened and fettered by its evil associate, yet possesses free volition, even in the body; and it *can*, according to its pleasure, either authoritatively restrain and curb its associate, or suffer it to be guided by its depraved instincts. And whenever it does the first of these, it advances its own interests, gains strength, and becomes more fit for a return to the world of light; but when it does the last, it incurs salutary chastisement at the hands of God.

§ XLVI. **Formation of this our World. Its structure and design.** Man having been formed by the Prince of darkness, and the souls, those daughters of light, inclosed in his body, and the celestial elements combined with matter or with the elements of the world of darkness; nothing remained for God, who was desirous of rescuing those souls and the celestial elements, except, to form from the vitiated matter an intermediate world, between [p. 818.] the world of light and that of darkness, and compounded of both; which should afford to men a domicile, and to God a suitable opportunity for carrying out his purpose of gradually extracting the souls from the bodies, and separating the good matter from the bad, and restoring both to the world of light.(1) Therefore, by God's command, the *Living Spirit*, who had already conquered the Prince of darkness, constructed this our world. In doing so, he first fabricated the sun and moon, from matter that had not been corrupted; then, from that which was but little contaminated, he formed the ether, and the stars which revolve in the ether; and lastly, from that which was entirely pervaded by depraved matter, he constructed this our earth.(2) And, as the son of the *First Man*, whose name was *Jesus*, was still detained a captive in the bodies of the Prince of darkness and his associates, those miserable Beings were to be confined, lest they should abscond with their plunder: and therefore the *Living Spirit* chained them to the stars. This measure was necessary and wise, and on many accounts exceedingly useful; and yet it was a source of troubles and dangers. For these Princes of evil, from the stars where they dwell, not only lay snares for good minds, but also send down upon our world hosts of evils, pestilences, thunders, lightnings, tempests, war, &c.(3) And lest so vast a world should fall and come to pieces, a very powerful Being from the world of light, by divine command, props it up and sustains it. His name is *Omophorus*, significant of the very onerous task he has to perform. And lest he should succumb under such a burden, an assistant is given him, to hold the suspended orb steady. He is a Being equally strong and robust, and bears the name of Splenditenens.(4)

(1) That our world was created, according to *Manes*, not only with the knowledge and consent of God, but also by his command, there can be no doubt. And, therefore, those do him injustice, who tell us that the Prince of

darkness was the former of the material universe: unless, possibly, they mean no more than that the Cause of all evil produced the occasion, or, if you choose, the necessity for God to construct the world. Says *Augustine*, (de Haeres. c. 42. p. 11.): Mundum a naturâ boni, hoc est, a naturâ Dei (He means *that Being* or nature, born of God, which the Manichaeans called the *Living Spirit.*) factum, confitentur quidem, sed de commixtione boni et mali, quae facta est, quando inter se utraque natura pugnavit. And so *Augustine* explains his views in other passages. Thus, (contra Faustum, L. xx. c. 9. p. 240.): Vos [p. 819.] primum hominem cum quinque elementis belligerantem et *Spiritum potentem* (who is also called *virens*) de captivis corporibus gentis tenebrarum, an potius de membris Dei vestri victis atque subjectis *mumdum fabricantem* creditis. See also the Exordium of his first Dispute with Fortunatus, p. 67. And *Fortunatus* himself, (in this first dispute, p. 72.) says: Constat, non esse unam substantiam, licet ex *unius* (bonae) *jussione* eadem ad compositionem hujus mundi et faciem venerint. Although *Fortunatus* here, as *Augustine* himself often, says that God formed the world; yet we must understand it to have been only by the direction or command of God. For it would not be suitable for God himself, a most pure and holy Being, to put his own hand to the work: so that, what God is said to have done, he only caused to be done by his minister, the *Living Spirit;* whom *Alexander* of Lycopolis (contra Manichaeos p. 4.) calls δημιουργον. —The causes which induced God to order a world formed, from impure and defiled matter, may be understood from what has been stated. The first and principal cause was the human race, which, as God could easily foresee, would be born and propagated. For the crafty Prince of evil had collected the whole mass of souls that he had captured, and placed them beyond the reach of the *Living Spirit*, by depositing them all in the single body of Adam: and then he gave him Eve for a wife, and Adam overcome by her blandishments had begun to procreate children. By this artifice the liberation of souls, for which God was solicitous, was rendered a long and tedious process; and during its continuance, some place was to be prepared in which Adam and his posterity might reside. This cause for creating the world, of which we have heretofore treated, is expressly mentioned by *Tyrbo*, (in the Acta Disput. *Archelai* § 10. p. 20.) where, having spoken of the formation of the first human beings by the Prince of evil, he closes the passage with these words: Καὶ διὰ τούτων γέγονεν ἡ πλάσις τοῦ κόσμου, ἐκ τῆς τοῦ Ἄρχοντος δημιουργίας. Et propter haec (on account of Adam and Eve,) factum est figmentum (the fabric) mundi, propter fabricationem nimirum Principis (malorum), who had made the first man. In addition to this first cause, there was another. In the conflict of the Prince of darkness with the *First Man*, celestial matter had become completely commingled and coherent with malignant matter; and to separate it from the evil elements, and restore it to its primitive state, which was the wish of God, would be a vast undertaking, and would require a very long time, if that matter remained in a confused and chaotic state. But if assorted and arranged in proper order, the good and divine might with greater ease be severed from the evil and the vicious; and thus in a shorter time, that complete separation which God desired, might be effected. See *Theodoret*, (Hæret. Fabul. [p. 820.]

L. i. c. 26. p. 213.) Lastly, the matter which the *Living Spirit* had wrested from the grasp of the Lord of evil, was not all of one kind : some portions of it were better, purer and more holy than others ; for some portions had contracted more, and others less vitiosity and malignity in that contest. And this diversity in the condition of the matter, rendered a separation and distribution necessary.—The pattern for the new world he was about to form, the *Living Spirit* undoubtedly borrowed from the world of light. Our world contains the same elements as the world of light, although our elements are polluted ; and they are arranged in the same order, as in the kingdom of God. Our world, therefore, is a sort of picture or image of that blessed world, where God and the innumerable host of his Æons dwell. It was a common opinion among the people of the East, and one prevalent among the Gnostics, that this our world was formed after the model of the upper or celestial world. Moreover the Manichaeans divided this material universe into two parts, the heavens and the earth. The Heavens they reckoned to be *ten* in number, if we may believe *Augustine ;* but of earths, they reckoned but eight. Thus *Augustine* says to Faustus, (L. xxii. c. 19. p 327.): Unde scis, octo esse terras et decem coelos, quod Atlas mundum ferat, Splenditenensque suspendat, et innumerabilia talia, unde scis hæc ? Plane, inquis, Manichæus me docuit. Sed infelix credidisti, neque enim vidisti. As to the number of heavens, I make no question : but as to the earths, I have abundant reasons for doubt, since I no where find the Manichaeans speaking of more than one earth, as being laid upon the shoulders of their *Omophorus.* There is indeed a passage in the Latin version of the Acta *Archelai.* (§ 7. p. 11.) which resembles that of *Augustine* ; Et iterum (Spiritus vivens) creavit terram, et *sunt octo.* But in the Greek of *Epiphanius*, it reads : Ε'ις εἴδη ὀκτὼ. Creavit terram octupli formâ, seu specie. And this reading certainly accords better with the preceding noun, *terram*, of the singular number ; and also with the whole narration of *Tyrbo*, who uniformly speaks of but one earth, than it does with the words of the Latin translator, who seems to have read Ε'ισὶ δὲ, instead of εἰς εἴδη. Neither will the Manichaean notion of a single world-bearer or *Omophorus*, admit of more earths than one. For how, I pray, could that one *Omophorus* carry eight worlds, in whatever manner you arrange them? I therefore suppose that Augustine was deceived, either by the ambiguity of the words, or perhaps by the mistake of the Latin traslator of *Archelaus*, and believed the Manichaeans' earth to be an *octagon.* That the Manichaeans assigned to the heavens a round or spherical form, *Cosmas* Indicopleustes alone informs us, (in his Topographia Chistiana, published by *Montfaucon* in his Nova Collectio Patrum Græcor. tom. ii. L. vi. p. 270, 271.) : Μανιχαῖοι τὸν τε οὐρανὸν σφαιροειδῆ νομίζοντες. Manichaei æstimant coelum sphaericum esse. This passage offers occasion to correct a striking error of the learned *Beausobre* (vol. 2. p. 374.) [p. 821.] He asserts, that *Cosmas* above cited, tells us that *Manes* was an excellent *mathematician :* and this testimony of Cosmas, he thinks, is a strong proof that *Manes* possessed much genius and learning. For he supposes *Cosmas* to be speaking of *Manes*, (L. vi. as above, p. 264.) where he says: Μεχανικοῦ ἀνδρὸς καὶ λογίου καὶ ὑπὲρ πολλῶν ἐμπείρου. Vir mechanicus et doctus, multos peritiâ rerum superans. But this eulogium is not bestowed by *Cos-*

mas on our *Manes*, but on a certain Egyptian mathematician, whose name was *Anastasius*. I suppose it was an error of the eye, and that the learned man read Μανιχαίου, instead of Μηχανικοῦ, which is the word used by Cosmas.

(2) The matter, from which the *Living Spirit* had to form the world which God commanded, was of different kinds. Some of it was perfectly pure, having remained uncontaminated. Another portion was slightly contaminated with base matter; and another was wholly immersed in bad matter. Interspersed with these was a portion of the depraved elements, or evil fire, left behind by the flying leaders of darkness, and not at all modified by the celestial elements. To this very different condition of the materials to be used, the builder of the world had to pay attention in the execution of his work. *Manes*, or the Magians, from whom he learned his doctrine, had to so imagine things, as to be able to account for the great dissimilarity in the different parts of this material universe. The whole system, as I have already said, was absurd and futile, and especially if tested by the precepts of the bible and of sound reason; but if tried by the opinions and conceptions of the Persians and other Oriental nations, it will appear more tolerable; and there really was genius and ingenuity in its conception and plan, and in the nice adjustment of its parts.—The founder of the world, therefore, first collected and arranged that celestial matter, which was not defiled with the contagion of evil, and had remained pure and uncontaminated by the war. Of the good fire and the light, he constructed the sun; and of the good water, he formed the moon. Thus *Tyrbo*, (in the Acta Disput. *Archelai*, § 7. p. 11.): Tunc vivens Spiritus creavit mundum, et indutus alias tres virtutes descendens creavit luminaria (τοὺς φωστῆρας, the sun and moon,) quæ sunt reliquiæ animæ, ἅ ἐστι τῆς ψυχῆς λείψανα (we have already remarked, that *Tyrbo* calls all the celestial elements ψυχὴν, *animam;* for they were all animated,) et fecit ea firmamentum (τὸ στερέωμα) circumire. *Augustine*, (de Hæres. c. 46. p. 11.) says: Quas itidem naves (we shall see in the proper place, that the Manichæans called the sun and moon *ships*, or compared them to ships,) de *substantiâ Dei purâ* perhibent fabricatas. Lucemque istam corpoream - - in his navibus *purissimam* credunt. And not inconsistent with this, is the declaration, (L. xxi. c. 4. p. 251.): Solem tam magnum bonum putatis, ut nec factum (created from nothing.) a Deo putatis, sed prolatum vel missum esse credatis; i. e. consists of celestial matter, which emanated from the essence of God. Compare, besides [p. 822.] others, *Simplicius*, (on Epictetus, p. 167.) and *Titus* of Bostra, (contra Manichæos, p. 99.) who says: Solem Manichaeus decernit non habere mixtionem mali. And hence the Son of God himself, and many other celestial Beings of the highest dignity and power, have fixed their residence in the sun and moon. Whence *Faustus*, (apud August. L. xx. c. 1. p. 237.) calls the sun and moon *divina Lumina*.—Of the good air or ether that remained unpolluted, I find nothing said. But, since the Holy Spirit, as we have heretofore remarked, dwells in the ether that encompasses our earth, and he cannot possibly have intercourse with corrupt matter; we are obliged to believe, that a good part of the celestial ether, in the battle with the Prince of darkness, escaped the contamination of the smoke or bad ether, and was collected together by the *Living Spirit*.—The pure matter being properly located, the framer of the world pro-

ceeded to that which had only a small portion of depraved matter mixed witn it. Out of this slightly defiled matter, he formed the heavens and the stars. For the stars emit light, though less in quantity and more obscure than the sun and moon. And therefore, it must have been concluded, that a considerable portion of light is in the heavens and the stars, though they are not intirely free from defilement. Says *Alexander* of Lycopolis, (contra Manichaeos, p. 5 and 15.): Τὸ δὲ ἐν μετρίᾳ γέγονος κακίᾳ ἀστέρας καὶ τὸν οὐρανὸν σύμπαντα. Ex partibus autem materiae mediocri a pravitate pollutis fecit sidera et universum cœlum. Hence *Simplicius* (in Epictetus, p. 167.) says, The Manichaeans worshipped only the sun and moon, τῆς τοῦ ἀγαθοῦ μοίρας λέγοντες αὐτούς, quae sidera dicunt boni (id est, Dei) partem esse; but the other heavenly bodies, they despise, ὡς τῆς τοῦ κακοῦ μοίρας ὄντων, quae ad malum (Daemonem) pertineant. Yet these declarations properly refer, not to the *matter* of the heavenly bodies, but to the *inhabitants* of those bodies. For, as we shall soon show, the Demons dwell in them. Says *Augustine*, (Confessiones, L. xiii. c. 30. Opp. tom. I. p. 181.): Dicunt te fecisse fabricas coelorum et compositiones siderum, et haec non *de tuo*, (that is, not from matter altogether pure and celestial) sed jam fuisse alibi creata, quae tu contraheres et compaginares atque contexeres, cum de hostibus victis mundana mœnia molireris.—After the heavens and the stars, the world-builder framed this earth; as *Tyrbo* clearly asserts, (in the Acta Disput. *Archelai*, p. 11.): Καὶ πάλιν ἔκτισε τὴν γῆν. Et denuo (after making the heavens and the stars,) terram conficiebat. The earth is composed of that portion of matter, which contained more evil than good, or into which the elements of darkness had completely insinuated themselves. Says *Tyrbo*, (l. c. § 8. p. 18.): Mundus autem ex parte materiae (τῆς ὕλης, so the Manichaeans call the evil principle,) plasmatus est, et ideo omnia exterminabuntur, or will be destroyed.—Lastly, such matter as had not come in contact with any portion of the celestial matter,—as the bad fire, wind, air, and water, which the vanquished princes of [p. 823.] darkness had left behind, he cast intirely out of the world, and erected strong walls to keep it from entering and destroying it before the appointed time. *Tyrbo*, (l. c. p. 22.) mentions: τὸ τεῖχος τοῦ μεγάλου πυρὸς, murum magni ignis, murum item venti, aëris et aquae: So that each sort of evil matter excluded from our world, had its own separate wall, to keep it out. *Augustine* likewise occasionally mentions the *mounds* (*aggeres*), by which God excludes vicious matter from our world. (See his Confessiones, L. xiii. c. 30. and elsewhere.) But at the end of the world, this evil and devouring fire will issue from its prison, the mounds being removed; and then it will consume and destroy the whole fabric of our world.

(3) Before he commenced fabricating the world, the *Living Spirit* imprisoned the Prince of darkness, and his associates and captains, in the air. *Tyrbo*, (in the Acta Disput. *Archelai*, p. 11.) says: Tunc Spiritus vivens descendens eduxit principes (tenebrarum) et crucifixit eos in firmamento, quod est eorum corpus, (Greek, ὅ ἐστιν αὐτῶν σῶμα,) *sive* sphaera. On this passage, we may remark, first, that the word *crucifixit* must not be construed too rigorously. For, as we shall soon see, the princes of evil were held in quite free custody, and, at their pleasure, could do many things contrary to the will of God. Hence

crucifixit must mean no more than *he stationed, required them to reside.* Besides, the Greek of *Epiphanius* has not the word ἐσταύρωσε, but ἐστηρίωσε, that is, he so *stationed* them, that they could not change their residence, he assigned them a fixed and constant abode. Perhaps this reading is more correct than that which the Latin translator of the Acta *Archelai* had before him: and yet the latter is supported by *Epiphanius* and *Damascenus*, who retain it. What follows, namely, that the firmament is the *corpus* (σῶμα) of the Demons, is so contrary to the views of the Manichaeans, that it must be regarded as spurious. It should undoubtedly read δῶμα, *domus*, or *domicilium.* The heavens are the seat or house, in which the *Living Spirit* commanded the princes of darkness to abide, until the time when God should order them to return to their ancient abode. This heaven, it is added, is a *sphere* or *globe.* Here, therefore, is another passage, beside that of *Cosmas*, adduced while treating of the heavens, from which I now again learn that the Manichaeans assigned a globular form to the heavens.—This passage of *Tyrbo*, and others of the ancients which accord with it, only indicate in general the place where the authors of all evils are detained. But *Beausobre*, (vol. II. p. 353.) wishes to determine precisely, in what part of the air or heavens they are located; and he thinks he proves, by the authority of *Theodoret*, and Simplicius, that they were confined in the southern regions of the sky. But vain are the efforts of the ingenious man. For Simplicius, (comment. in Epictet. p. 2. 12.) and Theodoret (Haeret. Fabul. L. I. c. 26. Opp. tom. iv. p. 212.) merely say, that *Manes* assigned three parts to God or the world of light, the East, the West, and the North; and only one, the South, to the Demon or the [p. 824.] world of darkness. Says *Theodoret*, and with him *Simplicius* agrees perfectly: Σχεῖν τὸν μὲν Θεὸν τάτε ἀρκτῶα μέρη, καὶ τὰ ἑῷα, καὶ τὰ ἑσπέρια, τὴν δὲ ὕλην τὰ νότια. Tenuisse Deum (before the war with the Prince of darkness,) partes Septentrionales, Orientales et Occidentales, materiam vero Meridionales. Thus, by these authorities, the position of the world of darkness is indeed defined; but not the residence of the Demons, beyond our earth, since they were vanquished by the *Living Spirit.* We will adduce something from *Augustine*, which is better and more certain. The conquered Demons were stationed by the *Living Spirit* in the stars. And the more celestial matter any of them had in his body, the higher and loftier place he obtained. *Augustine*, (contra Faustum, L. vi. c. 8. p. 149.) says: Dicunt isti vaniloqui et mentis seductores, in illa pugna, quando primus eorum homo tenebrarum gentem elementis fallacibus irretivit, utriusque sexus principibus indidem captis, cum ex eis mundus construeretur, plerosque eorum *in cœlestibus fabricis* (thus *Augustine* frequently designates the *stars.*) colligatos esse. - - In ipsa structura mundi eosdem principes tenebrarum ita per omnes contextiones (ss. the *stars*,) a summis usque ad ima colligatos dicunt, ut quanto quisque amplius haberent commixti boni (of the celestial elements and a sentient soul,) tanto sublimius collocari mererentur. The stars, as before observed, are composed of matter, for the most part good, yet slightly tinctured with evil. Yet the stars are not all of one character; some are more pure and sound than others. Those nearest to the earth, contain more depraved matter, than those higher or farther off. Therefore, the *Living Spirit*, according to the rules of equity, stationed those Demons who possessed the smallest portion of celestial matter, in the lower stars which are less pure; while to those possessing a greater portion of the celestial elements, he assigned a residence in the higher and purer stars. In what place the Prince of evil himself resides, whether, as may be supposed, in the highest and loftiest of the moving stars or planets, or beyond all the stars in the open heavens, no one, so far as I know, has informed us. But as he contains in his immense body more celestial matter than all his fellow-warriors, it can scarcely be doubted, that *Saturn*, the highest of the planets, is his residence; and there also the Gnostic multitude located their *Jaldabaoth*, or Prince of the aërial Demons.

But the Princes of evil are not so confined and tied to the stars, that they cannot accomplish or plot anything. They cannot, indeed, leave their places; but in other respects they are most busy and active, and they bring to pass numerous things adverse to the kingdom and purposes of God. In the first place, they hold a sort of dominion over the stars which they inhabit. For they are not solitary beings there, as *Augustine* clearly intimates in the passage just quoted, but, together with their wives, and the animals of the world of darkness captured in the war, they live there, and beget and bring forth offspring. [p. 825.] Of course there is, undoubtedly, in each star, a sort of commonwealth or state, which some one, more potent than the rest, governs. In the next place, they strive to establish and confirm that empire, which, contrary to the will of God, they founded on the earth, by the generation and propagation of mankind; and they guard and defend it, against the efforts of God for its subversion. The manner in which they do this, may be easily understood. *Augustine* expressly states, that all the leaders of darkness are not confined in the stars, but only the major part of them. Many of them, therefore, roam freely through the air, far from the stars. And these, doubtless, the Prince of evil and his associates employ as their satellites and ministers, in accomplishing among men their plans for advancing the interests of their empire on the earth. The great solicitude of the Prince of evil is, to withdraw the inhabitants of the earth from the knowledge of the true God, and to induce them to adore and worship himself instead of God. For this purpose, he introduces false religions, by means of his legates and prophets; that is, by men actuated and impelled by himself. Of this nature was the Jewish religion, which Moses brought forward under the influence of the Demon: and such were the pagan religions, prevailing over the world. *Tyrbo*, (in the Acta *Archelai*, p. 18.) repeats from the lips of *Manes*, thus: De prophetis autem hæc dicit: Spiritus esse impietatis sive iniquitatis tenebrarum illarum, quæ ab initio ascenderunt, a quibus decepti, non sunt locuti in veritate: excæcavit enim Princeps ille mentes ipsorum, et si quis sequitur verba ipsorum, morietur in sæcula, devinctus intra massam (εἰς τὴν βῶλον. i. e. the world of darkness, to which, as we shall see, those souls that cannot in any way be reclaimed, will be confined,) quoniam non didicit scientiam Paracliti. And again, (§ 11. p. 20.): Illum vero, qui locutus est cum Mose, et Judæis et sacerdotibus, Principem esse dicit tenebrarum; Et ideo unum atque idem sunt Christiani et Judæi et gentes eundem Deum colentes: in concupiscentiis enim suis seducit eos, quia non est Deus veritatis. Propter hoc ergo quicumque in illum Deum sperant, qui cum Moyse locutus est et prophetis, cum ipso habent vinculis tradi, quia non speraverunt in Deum veritatis: ille enim secundum concupiscentias suas locutus est cum eis. And these severe censures, which *Faustus* the Manichæan, in many passages occurring in *Augustine*, casts upon the Mosaic law, clearly show, that the sect believed the intire Jewish law and religion, to be an invention of the Prince of darkness for deceiving the Jews. What this audacious *Faustus* thought of the Old Testament prophets, appears from his own words, (L. xii. c. 1. p. 162.): Exempla vitæ honestæ et prudentiam ac virtutem in prophetis quærimus: quorum nihil in Judæorum fuisse vatibus, quia te non latuerit sentio. He also assails Moses with very great reproaches, (in several places, one of them is L. xiv. c. 1. p. 187.) Some of these I will mention: Mosen, quanquam humanorum nulli unquam, divinorumque pepercerit blasphemando, plus tamen hinc *execramur*, quod Christum Filium Dei diro convitio lacessivit: utrum volens, an casu, tu (*Augustine*) videris. [p. 826.] - - Ait enim maledictum esse omnem, qui pendet in ligno. He also most contumeliously assails the God of the Hebrews, (L. xv. c. 1. p. 193, 194.): Sordent ecclesiæ nostræ Testamenti veteris et *ejus auctoris* munera. - - Amator vester et pudoris corruptor, Hebræorum Deus, diptychio lapideo suo (referring to the two tables of the law,) aurum vobis promittit et argentum, ventris saturitatem et terram Cananæorum. - - Pauper est, egens est, nec ea quidem præstare potest, quæ promittit. Hebraeorum Dei et nostra admodum diversa conditio est: quia nec ipse, quae promittit, implere potest, et nos ea fastidimus accipere. Superbos nos adversus blanditias ejus, Christi liberalitas fecit. And he expressly says, that the God of the Jews is the Demon, (L. xviii. c. 1. p. 220.): Placet ad ingluviem Judaeorum Daemonis (neque enim Dei) nunc tauros, nunc arietes cultris sternere? But I forbear.—So far as I can make out by probable conjecture, *Manes* supposed the God of the Jews to be the Prince of evil himself, and the Deities of other nations to be his chiefs and captains resident in the stars; all of whom, being excessively proud by nature, used various arts and impositions to procure for themselves divine worship among mortals.

Not content with these evils relating to the whole human race, the King of darkness and his associates prevent, as far as they can, the good souls of individual men from performing their duty. For, by the five bodily senses, and by the body itself, they excite and strengthen the evil soul, which in all men is associated with the good soul, so that, burning and inflamed with lust, it overcomes and weakens and oppresses the good soul. In explaining this topic, *Secundinus* the Manichaean is copious and eloquent, in an Epistle to *Augustine*, (in the Opp. *Augustini*, tom. viii. p. 370.) and he strongly urges *Augustine* to beware of the snares of the most crafty and deceptive Prince of evil: Illumque (divinae personae) a nobis repellant atrocem spiritum, qui hominibus timorem immittit: et perfidiam, ut animas avertat ab angusto tramite Salvatoris, cujus omnis impetus per illos principes funditur, contra quos se Apostolus in Ephesiorum epistola certamen subiisse fatetur. - - Ipse enim non ignoras, quam pessimus sit, quamque malignus, quique etiam tanta calliditate adversus fideles et summos viros militat, ut et Petrum coëgerit sub una nocte tertio Dominum negare. The King of darkness is so laborious, because he wishes not to have his empire overthrown or destroyed.

Lastly, whatever calamities befall our world or its inhabitants, except only the earthquakes,—as the excessive rains, the tempests, the thunders, the pestilences, the wars,—all proceed from the Prince of evil, and his associates, residing in the air and the stars. Thus *Titus* of Bostra, (contra Manichaeos, L. ii. p. 109.) I quote only the Latin, which exactly represents the Greek: Rursus [p. 827.] est aliud genus eorum, quae Manichaeus dementissimus accusat, terrae motum dico (Here *Titus* errs; for earthquakes do not proceed from the King of evil, but from *Omophorus*, as we shall soon show,) pestem, famem ex sterilitate, ex locustis, et aliis hujusmodi, tanquam a principio contrario haec proficiscantur. He had a little before (p. 107.) said: Bella etiam assignant et attribuunt nequitiae: (τῇ κακίᾳ, that is, to the evil principle.) And *Tyrbo*, (in the Acta *Archelai*, § 8. p. 14.): Princeps ille magnus producit nebulas ex se ipso, uti obscuret in irâ sua omnem mundum, qui cum tribulatus fuerit (this clause needs illustration, and will receive it further on,) sicut homo sudat post laborem, ita et hic Princeps sudat ex tribulatione sua, cujus sudor pluviae sunt. Sed et messis princeps (one of the Demons, who mows down men, when he procures their death by sending diseases and pestilence,) effundit pestem super terram, ita, ut morte afficiat homines - - incipit excidere radices hominum, et cum excisae fuerint radices eorum, efficitur pestilentia, et ita moriuntur. Among those evils, which the Prince of darkness, from his prison or residence, prepares for men, is *wine*. For often, kindling into rage and fury, he lets out a part of his bile; which falls on the earth, and produces vines and grapes. *Augustine*, (de moribus Manichaeorum, L. ii. § 44. tom. i. p. 545.): Quae tanta perversio est vinum putare *fel Principis tenebrarum*, et uvis comedendis non parcere! (See also his Book de Haeres. c. 46. p. 11, &c.) And therefore, the more perfect among the disciples of *Manes*, or those called the *Elect*, are bound to abstain from wine altogether. Of this we shall speak in the proper place.

(4) How great and acute a philosopher and investigator of nature, *Manes* was, can scarcely be learned more clearly, from anything, than from his doctrine concerning the props of our world; which was entirely accordant with the fancies of the Persians and other Orientals, and was derived, I suppose, from the schools of the Magi. This discerning man thought the world would tumble down, if it were not propped up. He therefore placed this enormous load upon the shoulders of an immensely great angel, whom he named *Omophorus*, on account of the office which God assigned him: And, lest he should become exhausted, and should stagger under his immense burden, he assigns him an assistant, called *Splenditenens*, to take part in his toil: and he, weeping and groaning, holds the suspended world steady. Says *Augustine*, (contra Faustum, L. xx. c. 9. p. 240.): Vos autem primum hominem cum quinque elementis belligerentem, et *Spiritum potentem* de captivis corporibus gentis tenebrarum, an potius de membris Dei vestri victis atque subjectis mundum fabricantem, et *Splenditenentem*, reliquias eorundem membrorum Dei vestri in manu habentem, et cetera omnia capta, oppressa, inquinata plangentem, et *Atlantem* maximum subter humeris suis cum eo ferentem, ne totum ille fatigatus abjiciat—creditis et colitis. Also, (L. xv. c. 5. p. 196.): Ostende nobis moechos tuos, *Splendi-* [p. 828.] *tenentem* ponderatorem et *Atlantem* laturarium. Illum enim dicis ca-

pita elementorum tenere, mundumque suspendere, istum autem genu fixo, scapulis validis, subbajulare tantam molem, utique ne ille deficiat. Ubi sunt isti? And *Tyrbo*, (in the Acta *Archelai*, p. 11.): Est autem *Omophorus* (*Augustine* translates the name: *Laturarius* in Latin,) deorsum, id est, qui eam (terram) portat in humeris. But *Omophorus*, as we might naturally expect, sometimes becomes impatient with his immense burden, and therefore trembles under it: And this is the cause of earthquakes. Thus proceeds *Tyrbo:* Et cum laboraverit portans intremiscit, et hæc est caussa terræ motus præter constitutum tempus. - - Quotiens enim efficitur terræ motus, tremente eo ex labore, vel de humero in humerum transferrente pondus, efficitur. A perspicacious interpreter truly, of the mysteries of nature, and one admirably instructed by his Magian teachers! And hence God sent his Son down into the lower parts of the earth, to either solace or reprimand the groaning, sweating Atlas or *Omophorus:* Hac de caussà Filium suum misit benignus Pater de finibus suis in cor terræ, et in interiores ejus partes, quo illum, ut par est, coërceret, ὅπως αὐτῷ τὴν προσήκουσαν ἐπιτιμίαν δῷ, as it is in the Greek of *Epiphanius*. These are memorable expressions! For it appears from them how *Manes* understood the descent of Christ into hell. He supposed, as other Christians did, that the Son of God actually descended into the infernal regions. But by that language he understood the interior or lower parts of our earth; and the object of this descent was, he supposed, to reprimand the huge carrier on whose shoulders the earth rested.—These two pillars of earth the Manichaeans religiously honored with hymns, venerating them as Deities. According to *Augustine*, (contra Faustum, L. xv. c. 5. 6. 7. p. 197, 198.) they had a public sacred hymn, in the tumid and inflated style of the Persians, composed by *Manes* himself, and called *amatorium*. In it they first praised God: An non recordaris *amatorium* canticum tuum, ubi describis maximum regnantem regem, sceptrigerum perennem, floreis coronis cinctum et facie rutilantem? Next followed the twelve Æons; for that was their number, according to the Manichaeans: Sequeris cantando et adjungis duodecim Sœcula floribus convestita et canoribus plena et in faciem Patris flores suos jactantia:—Duodecim magnos quosdam Deos profiteris, ternos per quatuor tractus, quibus ille unus circumcingitur. Then followed the other citizens of heaven, the angels, inferior to the Æons: Adjungis etiam innumerabiles regnicolas—et angelorum cohortes; quae omnia non condidisse dicis Deum, sed de sua substantia genuisse. Lastly, the hymn extolled, with very high praises, the heroes of the supreme Deity, and among them *Splenditenens* and *Omophorus:* Et *Splenditenentem* magnum, sex vultus et ora ferentem, micantemque lumine (from this light or splendor, he doubtless derived his name; q. d. *Splendidus* Angelus, qui terram *tenet*,) et alterum regem honoris, Angelorum ex- [p. 829.] ercitibus circumdatum (this, perhaps, is Christ) et alterum adamantem heroam belligerum, dextra hastem tenentem et sinistra clypeum (this undoubtedly is the *Living Spirit*, who conquered and imprisoned the Prince of darkness,) et alterum gloriosum Regem tres rotas impellentem ignis, aquae et venti: et *maximum Atlantem*, mundum ferentem humeris et eum genu fixo, brachiis utrinque secus fulcientem.—This worship, paid by the Manichaeans to their *Omophorus* and *Splenditenens*, is a sufficient confutation of the ingenious *Beausobre*; who, perceiving this fable of a world-bearer, to be too silly to come from a philosopher of even moderate abilities, and esteeming *Manes* a great philosopher,—maintains that it is an allegory. (Vol. ii. p. 370.) And it is the custom of this erudite man, whenever he cannot otherwise excuse or justify *Manes*, to depart from the literal interpretation, and direct his readers to believe, that *Manes* wrapped up plain and sober truths in the vestments of figures and metaphors. He therefore thinks, *Omophorus* must be an Angel holding up the world, not with his shoulders, but by some unknown force; and *Splenditenens*, he supposes, to be the air which encompasses the earth. But who can believe that the Manichaeans sang the praises of the air in their assemblies; not to mention many other things, which will occur to the reader without my stating them? And if *Omophorus*' carrying the world on his shoulders is a mere metaphor, what becomes of the cause of earthquakes, as taught by the Manichaeans? I may add, that the Manichaeans deny that their master concealed the truth under images and fables; and they place it among his chief excellencies, that he gives us the knowledge of divine things nakedly and in simple language. Says *Augustine*, (contra Faustum, L. xv. c. 5. p. 197,): Tibi præcipue laudari Manichaeus non ob aliud solet, nisi quod romotis figurarum integumentis, ipse tibi veritatem nudam et propriam loqueretur. And (c. 6. p. 197.): Tu vero praecipue Manichaeum ob hoc praedicas - - quod figuris antiquorum apertis et suis narrationibus ac disputationibus evidenti luce prolatis, nullo se occultaret aenigmate. Addis eam praesumptionis hujus causam, quod videlicet antiqui, ut figuras hujusmodi dicerint, sciebant, istum postea venturum, per quem cuncta manifestarentur, iste autem, qui sciret, post se neminem adfuturum, sententias suas nullis allegoricis ambagibus texeret. The Manichaean community were instructed, therefore, to understand all the doctrines of their master according to the literal and proper sense of the words.

§ XLVII. **The Mission and Offices of Christ.** The world being framed and adjusted, the grand aim of the supreme Deity was, *first*, to liberate from bondage, and restore to the world of light, those particles of his own nature, or of eternal light, that is, [p. 830.] the rational souls, which had become inclosed in bodies; and *then*, gradually to extract from depraved matter, and recover to their former happy state, those shreds of the celestial elements which were dispersed among all the depraved matter; and *lastly*, to press out and set free, the living and sentient soul, the son of the *First Man*, which was absorbed in the bodies of the Prince of darkness and his fellow warriors. To hasten the return of *souls* to the world of light, as much as possible, their heavenly Father had frequently sent among mankind angels and very holy men, actuated by himself, to instruct men both orally and by writings, and to show them the way of return to God when released from the body. But the work went on too slowly; for the Prince of darkness, by his ministers and satellites, by the body and its senses, and by the depraved soul, impeded the divine plans, and ensnared the good souls. And, in the meantime, *Omophorus* became weary of his burden, and earnestly importuned for an end of his toil. And, therefore, to accelerate the recovery of the numerous souls unhappily inclosed in bodies, God directed Christ, his Son, to descend from his residence in the sun to this lower world. And he, having assumed a human form, but without uniting himself to a body or to human nature, appeared among the Jews; and he, by his words and deeds, made known to the captive intelligences the way of escape from their thraldom: and, lest mortals should not place confidence in him, he demonstrated his divinity by the most signal miracles. But the Prince of darkness, fearing the subversion of his empire, excited the Jews, his most loyal subjects, to seize and crucify him. Yet Christ did not really endure that punishment, but only seemed to men to do so. For, as he had no body, and only assumed the appearance of a man, he could neither be seized, nor crucified, nor die at all. Yet Christ feigned death, in order that, by this seeming example, he might teach men, or the good souls lodged in bodies, that the body and the evil soul resident in the body, should be tortured, chastised, and mortified, if they would obtain freedom and salvation. When he had accomplished his mission, Christ returned to his residence in the sun, having directed his Apostles to diffuse his religion among mankind. These ambassadors of Christ, although they did immense good to men, and [p. 831.] greatly weakened the empire of the Prince of darkness, yet did not make known that full and perfect wisdom which is necessary for the souls that long for salvation; for Christ did not impart to them the full knowledge of the truth. But, as he was departing, he promised to send forth in due time a greater and more holy Apostle, whom he named the *Paraclete;* who should add to his precepts such things as men at that time were not able to receive and digest, and should dissipate all errors in regard to divine things. That *Paraclete* came, in the person of *Manes* the Persian; and he, by command of Christ, expounded clearly and perfectly, and without figures and enigmas, the whole way of salvation for toiling and suffering souls.(1)

(1) Some things here stated, have already been sufficiently elucidated and

confirmed, and they are here repeated only to make the connection of the whole system the more evident. Therefore, passing by these, I shall now explain and demonstrate only those things which need confirmation.—I begin with the *causes* of Christ's mission to men. According to the opinion of the Manichæans, there were two causes of his advent: the *first* was, the acceleration of the deliverance of the souls shut up in material bodies by the Prince of darkness: and the *second* was, the impatience of *Omophorus*, who propped up the world: for he, finding himself oppressed by the immense load, longed for the termination of his toil, and often besought God for relief. Both these causes are mentioned by *Tyrbo*, (in the Acta *Archelai*, § 8. p. 12.): Cum autem vidisset Pater vivens affligi animam in corpore, quia est miserator et misericors, misit Filium suum dilectum ad salutem: hac enim caussâ, *et propter Omophorum* (here you see the *second* cause,) misit eum. Of the *first* cause, the Manichæans often speak magnificently, and very nearly in the language of the Catholics: which might induce one not familiar with these matters, to suppose there was little difference of opinion between Christians and Manichæans, as to the object of Christ's advent among men; whereas, there was a vast difference, as will be hereafter shown. For the causes above stated, therefore, the Son of God descended from the sun into our world, inclosed indeed in the form and appearance of a human body, but intirely separate and removed from any kind of body or matter. *Manes* could not possibly have assigned to the Son of God a real body, or one composed of matter: for he supposed the matter of all bodies to belong to the world of darkness, and to be the seat and source of all wickedness and lust. Says *Tyrbo*, (l. c. p. 12.): Et veniens Filius transformavit se in *speciem* hominis, et apparebat quidem hominibus ut homo, cum *non esset homo*, et homines putaverunt eum natum esse. But we will let *Manes* himself speak. [p. 832.] In his Epistle to *Zebena*, (in *Fabricius*' Biblioth. Græca, vol. v. p. 284.) I cite only the Latin: Lux (Christus) non attigit carnis essentiam, sed *similitudine* et *figura* carnis (ὁμοιώματι καὶ σχήματι σαρκὸς ἐσκιάσθη) ne comprehenderetur et corrumperetur. Quomodo ergo passa esset? In his Epistle to *Odda*, (l. c. p. 285.): Quomoda Galilaei (i. e. the Catholic Christians) duas naturas nominant atque in Christo esse affirmant, effuse rideamus: nesciunt enim naturam lucis materiae alii non misceri, (ἡ οὐσία τοῦ φωτὸς ἑτέρᾳ οὐ μίγνυται ὕλῃ,) sed sincera est ac simplex, neque uniri alteri naturae potest, licet illi conjungi videatur. Nothing could be more evident!—Therefore, if some minor parties among the Manichaeans, as some of the ancients have stated, assigned to Christ either a body like ours, or an etherial one, they departed entirely from the opinions of their master, and abandoned the first principles of his system. Holding this opinion of Christ the Manichaeans of course rejected and denied all that the sacred history tells us of his birth from Mary, of his genealogy and descent from David, and of his childhood and education. They declared these to be mere fables, tacked on to the history of Jesus Christ by some Jews. They said, it would be altogether unbecoming the majesty of the Son of God, to come into the world from the womb of a virgin; and that his divine and celestial nature would absolutely resist an assumption of humanity. *Manes* himself, (in the Acta *Archelai*, § 47. p. 85. of the edition of *Zaccagni*, which we always use,) says: Absit ut Dominum nostrum Josum Christum per naturalia pudenda mulieris descendisse confitear: ipse enim testimonium dat, quia de sinibus Patris descendit. - - Sunt innumera testimonia hujuscemodi, quae indicant, eum venisse et non natum esse. Then follows a discussion of *Manes*, which is too long to be conveniently transcribed, in which he tries to prove from various expressions in the New Testament, that Christ was not born, and that he had not a body. But I will trascribe another passage, which will show, that *Manes* did not believe the *baptism* of Christ; (§ 50. p. 91.): Mihi pium videtur dicere, quod nihil eguerit Filius Dei in eo, quod adventus ejus procuratur ad terras, neque opus habuerit columbâ, neque *baptismate*, neque matre, neque fratribus, fortasse neque patre (what follows shows, that *pater* here does not mean a natural father, but a step-father or a foster-father,) qui ei secundum te (*Archelaë*) fuit Joseph, sed totus ille ipse descendens, semetipsum in quocunque voluit transformavit in hominem, eo pacto, quo Paulus dicit, quia (σχήματι,) habitu repertus est ut homo. - - Quando voluit hunc hominem rursum transformavit in speciem solis ac vultum: (as on mount Tabor.) All Manichaean writers, whose works have reached us, uniformly repeat the opinions and arguments of their master on this subject. *Fortunatus*, (in his first Dispute with *Augustine*, in the Opp. *August.* tom. viii. p. 73.) says: Salvatorem Christum credimus de cœlo venisse. Vos secundum carmen asseritis ex semine David, cum praedicetur ex virgine [p. 833.] natus esse, et Filius Dei magnificetur. Fieri autem non potest, nisi ut quod de spiritu est, spiritus habeatur, et quod de carne est, caro intelligatur. Contra quod est ipsa auctoritas Evangelii, qua dicitur, quod caro et sanguis regnum Dei non possibebunt. *Faustus*, the Manichaean, in many passages, disputes largely and fiercely, against those who think that Christ was born and had a body. See Lib. ii. iii. vii. xi. xxiii. xxix. Among many other things, he says, (L. xxiii. c. 2 p. 300.): Symbolum vestrum ita se habet, ut credatis in Jesum Christum, Filium Dei, qui sit natus ex Maria virgine: vestrum ergo de Maria accipere Filium Dei, nostrum ex Deo. - - De hac sententia nemo nos prorsus dejiciet ex Deo accipiendi Filium Dei, non ex utero mulieris natum. *Secundinus*, a Manichaean not destitute of genius, in his Epistle to *Augustine*, (p. 372.) says: Desine quæso utero claudere Christum, ne ipse rursum utero concludaris. Desine duas naturas facere unam, quia appropinquat Domini judicium. Those Gnostics, who having similar views of the nature of matter with *Manes*, likewise denied to Christ a body and humanity, still admitted, that in the opinion of men, or in appearance, he was born of Mary. But the Manichæans had such abhorrence of the idea that Christ was *born*, that they would not even concede so much. *Faustus*, indeed, (L. xxix. c. 1. p. 313.) seems not very averse from the opinion, which makes Christ to have been apparently born. He says: Vos pro certo puerperium fuisse (Christum) creditis et utero muliebri portatum. Aut si ita non est, fateamini vos quia hoc etiam imaginarie sit factum, *ut videretur natus*, et omnis nobis erit profligata contentio. But *he only*, among the Manichæans, so thought: the rest thought very differently. For thus *Augustine* replies to *Faustus:* Quaero ab eis, si nostra contentio terminatur, cum hoc dixerimus, cur hoc ipsi non dicunt? Cur ipsi mortem non veram, sed imaginariam Christi affirmant: nativitatem autem non saltem talem, sed *prorsus nullam* dicere delegerunt? - - An quia mortem simulare honestum est, nativitatem autem etiam simulare turpe est? Cur ergo nos hortatur hoc confiteri, quo possit nostra contentio profligari? And again, (contra Faustum L. xxxi. c. 6. p. 318.) *Augustine* says: Mors Christi visa vobis est vel fallax et simulata prædicanda: at non etiam nativitas. - - In nativitate enim quia ligari Deum vestrum creditis, hanc nec saltem fallaciter imaginatum Christum creditis: *Manes* therefore would say, that Christ descending suddenly from heaven, appeared among the Jews, in the form of a man; but he was without father, without mother, without relatives, without brethren, without a body; and all that occurs in the Gospels contradictory to these assertions, as also the history of his baptism, he would place among Jewish fables. Says *Faustus*, (L. xxxii. c. 7. p. 322.): Nos de Testamento novo sola accipimus ea, quæ in honorem et laudem Filii majestatis dicta comperimus, dissimulamus cetera - - - dico autem hoc ipsum (a) [p. 834.] natum ex fœminâ turpiter, (b) circumcisum Judaice, (c) sacrificasse gentiliter, (d) baptizatum humiliter, (e) circumductum a Diabolo per deserta et ab eo tentatum quam miserrime. His igitur exceptis, et si quid ei ab scriptoribus ex Testamento vetere falsâ sub testificatione injectum est: credimus cetera.—The reason why Christ showed himself among the Jews especially, and not among other nations, was, undoubtedly, that the Jews, as *Manes* supposed, worshipped the Prince of darkness himself instead of God, while the other nations only served his captains and fellow warriors. The King of darkness, therefore, had established the seat of his empire in Palestine.

He who is destitute of a body, has no need of food or drink, or of sleep and rest. *Manes*, therefore, could not believe, that Christ really ate, drank, slept, and rested: but all these he pretended to do, that the Jews might not doubt his humanity. Says *Faustus*, (L. xxvi. c. 1. p. 307.): Jesus ab initio sumptâ hominis similitudine, *omnes humanæ conditionis simulavit affectus:* Sic ab re non erat, si in fine quoque consignandæ œconomiæ gratia fuit visus et mori. But the miracles ascribed to him, *Faustus* admitted to be real, (L. xxv. c. 2. p. 307.): Nam et cœcum a nativitate lumen videre natura non sinit, quod tamen Jesus potenter operatus videtur erga hujus generis cœcos - - manum aridam sanasse, vocem ac verbum privatis his per naturam redonasse, mortuis et in tabem jam resolutis corporibus compage reddita vitalem redintegrasse spiritum, quem non ad stuporem adducat? - - Quæ tamen omnia *nos* communiter facta ab eodem *credimus* Christiani, non consideratione jam naturæ, sed potestatis tantum et virtutis Dei. It is strange, that the Manichæans could believe these miracles real. For they were all wrought upon bodies: and bodies, in their estimation, are the fabrications of the evil Demon; and they belong to the world of darkness, because they consist of gross concrete matter. And therefore, the Son of God, who had come to destroy bodies, those works of the Prince of darkness, and to liberate souls from their prisons, actually restored and healed these vicious bodies, so that the unhappy souls might be the longer detained in them; and thus the Light bestowed labor on the darkness, and renewed, arranged, and preserved from destruction evil matter, the possession of his enemy. Who that embraces Manichæan views, could easily believe this? And still more incredible should it be, to a Manichæan, that Christ restored the dead to life. For death, according to the opinion of *Manes*, was the release of a soul or a particle of the divine nature, from its gloomy and severe imprisonment. There is an Epistle of *Augustine* to a certain Manichæan presbyter, (Epist. lxxix. Opp. tom. ii. p. 141. edit. Benedict.) from which it appears, that the Manichæans despised death. He says: Bene, quia non times mortem. And he subjoins the cause they assigned, for this their contempt of death: Quia mors est, quod adjungis de vestro, separatio boni a malo. This Ma- [p. 835.] nichæan reasoned most correctly, from the opinions of his master. Now who could easily persuade himself, that the Son of God would, by recalling the dead to life, again connect *the good* and divine when *separated from the evil*, with the evil work of his enemy? This is so incongruous with the object for which the Son of God came among men, that nothing could be more so. And yet the Manichæans, as *Faustus* states most explicitly, did believe the miracles of Christ; that is, although at the first rise of the sect, they disagreed on this as well as other points.—In like manner, the Manichæans believed, that the discourses ascribed to Christ by his biographers, were really uttered by him: and in those discourses, they thought they discovered their own primary doctrine of two first principles of all things. Thus *Faustus*, (L. xxxii. c. 7. p. 322.) says: Præcepta salutaria Christi, tum parabolas, cunctumque sermonem deificum, qui maxime duarum præferens naturarum (i. e. of two first principles) discretionem, ipsius esse non venit in dubium.

Now, when the Prince of darkness saw those miracles of Christ, and heard his discourses, and perceived that Christ intended to subvert his empire, and to abolish the law which the Prince had enacted through Moses, he formed the purpose of destroying him. He therefore instigated the Jews, the most faithful subjects over whom he reigned, to seize Christ and nail him to the cross. *Secundinus*, a Manichaean, (in his Epistle to *Augustine*, § 4. p. 370.) says: Ipse non ignoras, quam audacter (the Lord of the world of darkness) illud molitus sit, ut Domino - - Iscariotem rapuerit, et ut ad ultimum crucis supplicium veniretur: in perniciem ipsius Scribas, Pharisaeosque accenderit, ut Barrabam dimitti clamarent et Jesum crucifigi. The Son of God was therefore seized by the Jews, subjected to punishment, nailed to a cross, and at length died; yet none of these things actually occurred, but the whole was feigned. For the divine Light, being destitute of a body and of all matter, could not be seized, nor could he die; only the shadow of a body of Christ, therefore, appeared to endure all these things. Says *Manes*, (Epistle to *Zebena*, in the Biblioth. Graeca of *Fabricius*, vol. v. p. 284.): Ἁπλῆ φύσις ὀυκ ἀποθνήσκει κὰι σκιὰ σαρκὸς ὀυ σταυροῦται. Μίαν ὀῦν ἔμεινε τὴν φύσιν κὰι ἐνέργειαν τὸ φῶς μηδὲν παθοῦσαν τῷ ἐπισκιάσματι τῆς σαρκὸς ὀυκ ἔχοντι φύσιν κρατουμένην. Simplex natura non moritur, et umbra carnis non crucifigitur. Perpetuo igitur unam naturam et unam operationem Lux (the Son of God, consisting of a mass of divine light) habere perseveravit nihil patientem ab umbra carnis, quae naturam (simplicem) nentiquam comprehensam tenet. So, also, in his Epistola fundamenti, (apud *Euodium*, Libro de fide, c. 28. in Opp. *Augustini*, tom viii. Append. p. 29.) *Manes* says: Inimicus quippe, qui eundem Salvatorem justorum patrem crucifixisse se speravit, ipse est crucifixus, (metaphorically, not literally): quo tempore aliud actum est, atque aliud ostensum. And *Faustus*, (L. xiv. c. 1. p. 187.) says: [p. 836.] Mosen execramur, quod Christum, Filium Dei, qui nostrae salutis caussâ pependit in ligno, diro devotionis convicio lacessivit—dicens maladictum esse omnem, qui pendet in ligno. (His reasoning is very silly, and inconsistent with his own doctrines; and it is brought forward only to calumniate Moses. For *Faustus* himself did not believe that Christ hung on the tree, but only his shadow.) So, also, (L. xxix. c. 1. p. 313.) he says expressly: Denique et nos *specietenus* passum, nec vere mortuum confitemur. And, (L. xxvi. c. 2. p. 308.): Nobis nec Jesus mortuus est, nec immortalis Elias. See also *Alexander* of Lycopolis, (contra Manichæos, p. 19.) where he says: Ὁ Μανιχαῖος διδάσκει περὶ τούτου ὥσπερ ἀδυνάτου ὄντος ἐκείνου τοῦτο ποιεῖν, id est, παθεῖν. Manichæus docet, fieri id nullo modo posse, ut Christus vere patiatur. *Augustine*, (contra Faustum, L. xxix. c. 2. p. 314.): Passionem mortemque ejus specietenus factam et fallaciter dicitis adumbratum, ut mori videretur, qui non moriebatur.—Christ had weighty reasons for feigning death, and the sufferings and trials that preceded it. The *first* was, to teach men the wretched state of souls inclosed in bodies. For a soul bound to a body, is, as it were, nailed to a cross, and dreadfully wounded. *Fortunatus*, (in his first dispute with *Augustine*, p. 69, 70,): Hoc ergo sentimus de nobis, quod et de Christo, qui cum in forma Dei esset constitutus, factus est subditus usque ad mortem, ut *similitudinem animarum nostrarum* ostenderet. - - Si fuit Christus in passione et morte, et nos: si voluntate Patris descendit in passionem et mortem, et nos. And *Faustus*, (L. xxxii. c. 7. p. 322.): Credimus præcipue crucis Christi fixionem mysticam, qua nostræ animæ passionis monstrantur vulnera. *Alexander* of Lycopolis, (contra Manichæos, p. 19.) quoting from a book of *Manes* on this subject, says, that Christ was crucified, to exhibit to men: τὴν δύναμιν τὴν θείαν ἐνήρμοσθαι, ἐνεσταύρωσθαι τῇ ὕλῃ. divinam virtutem, id est, animam in materiam immersam et in materia crucifixam esse.—The *second* reason for Christ's feigning death, was, to teach men to despise death, or to show them that death is no evil, but a boon, and therefore should be endured with firmness. *Augustine*, (contra Faustum, L. xxx. c. 6. p. 318.): Mortem tanquam separationem animæ, id est, naturae Dei vestri a corpore inimicorum ejus, hoc est, a figmento Diaboli, praedicatis atque laudatis: ac per hoc rem dignam fuisse credidistis, quam Christus etsi non moriens, tamen mortem simulans, commendaret.—*Lastly*, by feigning death, Christ designed to admonish souls, that they must not spare the body, if they wish to be saved; but must crucify the flesh and all its lusts, or wholly extirpate and slay them. *Alexander* of Lycopolis, (contra Manichaeos, p. 19.) says: *Manes* wrote, that Christ suffered crucifixion, εἰς ἐπίδειγμα, to *set men an example* [p. 837.] *for their imitation*. These reasons for Christ's feigning death, are manifestly futile; and, I believe, *Manes* would as readily have denied the death of Christ, as he did his birth, if he could have done it: but there was so much evidence of his death and resurrection, that he dared not deny them; and therefore, he must resort to some fanciful explanation, that he might not appear to avoid the subject. *Faustus* himself, (L. xxix. c. 1. p. 313.) seems to place little reliance on these reasons: Nos passionis Christi rationem *aliquam* reddimus *et probabilem:* (and therefore not solid, sufficient, and satisfactory.) Manes could not possibly deny either the death or the resurrection of Christ. He therefore taught, that Christ was laid in the grave, returned from the tomb to his disciples, showed them the scars on his body, and perhaps ascended to heaven before their eyes. But all these, as well as his death, were only imaginary, and emblematic of the return of a soul to its primeval state. Says *Fortunatus* the Manichæan, (in his first Dispute with *Augustine*, p. 70.): Quemadmodum Christus in se mortis similitudinem ostendit, et se a Patre esse de medio mortuorum resuscitatum: eo modo sentimus et de animis nostris futurum, quod per ipsum poterimus ab hac morte liberari. And *Augustine*, (de Hæres. c. 46. p. 13.): Affirmant (Manichæi) Christum non fuisse in carne vera, sed simulatam speciem carnis ludificandis humanis sensibus præbuisse, uti non solum mortem, verum etiam resurrectionem similiter mentiretur. And, (contra Faustum, L. xxix. c. 2. p. 313.): Ex quo fit, ut ejus quoque resurrectionem umbraticam, imaginariam, fallacemque dicatis: neque enim ejus, qui non vere mortuus est, vera esse resurrectio potest. Ita fit, ut et cicatrices discipulis dubitantibus falsas ostenderit, nec Thomas veritate confirmatus, sed fallaciâ deceptus clamarit, Dominus meus, et Deus meus: et tamen persuadere conamini, linquâ vos loqui verum, cum Christum dicatis toto corpore fuisse mentitum.—This pious fraud of Christ, in exhibiting to men the appearance of a body instead of a real body, had reference not only to the Jews, but also to his own Apostles; for they had no doubt, that Christ really died, and actually arose from the dead. And *Manes*, by the command and inspiration of God, first brought the truth to light.

As the Manichæans held the opinions described, respecting Christ, they could not possibly observe all the festal days consecrated by Christians to the memory of the Savior; and those, which their principles allowed them to observe, they of necessity celebrated in a different manner from other Christians. In the first place, the day commemorative of the *nativity* of Christ, they absolutely could not observe. For they so strenuously denied the birth of Christ, as not even to concede to him an apparent birth. Neither could they consecrate the day, on which the Oriental Christians commemorated his *baptism*. For they denied that Christ was baptized. But as they believed that Christ was apparently crucified and died, they could celebrate the time of his *death*; [p. 838.] and they actually did religiously observe it, though with little display or solemnity. The anniversary of the execution of *Manes* their master, as already stated, they celebrated with considerable display; but in celebrating Christ's death, they were quite lukewarm. And for this difference, they offered the following reason: *Manes* really died; Christ only appeared to die. Thus *Augustine*, (in his Liber contra Epistolam Manichæi, c. 8. p. 112.) says: Cum saepe a vobis quaererem illo tempore, quo vos audiebam, quae caussa esset, quod Pascha Domini (We may observe, that *Augustine* here uses the word *pascha*, as the ancient church did, as denoting, not the day commemorative of Christ's resurrection, but the day commemorative of his death.) plerumque nullâ, interdum a paucis tepidissimâ celebritate frequentaretur, nullis vigiliis, nullo prolixiore jejunio auditoribus indicto, nullo denique festiviore apparatu, quum vestrum Bema, id est, diem, quo Manichaeus occisus est - - magnis honoribus prosequamini. Hoc ergo quum quaererem, respondebatur, ejus diem passionis celebrandum esse, qui vere passus esset; Christum autem, qui natus non esset, neque veram sed simulatam carnem humanis oculis ostendisset, non pertulisse, sed finxisse passionem. Whether they likewise observed the day of Christ's resurrection, that other *pascha* of Christians, called ἀναστάσιμον, cannot be determined from this passage of *Augustine*, nor from any other source. Perhaps they did not deem this necessary, because, like other Christians, they observed, every week, Sunday, as the day on which Christ rose from the dead. But there was this singularity among them, that while the laws of the church forbid fasting on the day called the *Lord's Day*, the Manichaeans passed the day without food. The cause of this custom, *Leo* the Great tells us, was their reverence for the sun; *Leonis* Sermo xli. c. 5. Opp. tom. i. p. 106. edit. Quesnellii): Manichaei in honorem solis et lunae die Dominico et secundâ feriâ deprehensi fuerunt jejunare: uno perversitatis suae opere bis impii, bis profani sunt, qui jejunium suum et ad siderum cultum, et ad resurrectionis Christi instituere contemtum. - - Ob hoc diem salutis et laetitiae nostrae sui jejunii moerore condemnant. *Leo* repeats the same thing, (Epist. xv. ad Turibium, p. 228.): Manichaei, sicut in nostro examine detecti ac convicti sunt, Dominicum diem, quem nobis Salvatoris nostri resurrectio consecravit, exigunt in moerore jejunii: Solis, ut proditum est, reverentiæ hanc continentiam devoventes. But a very different reason for this practice, is adduced by *Hebed Jesu*, an Armeno-Nestorian bishop, on the Canons, (apud *Jo. Sim. Assemanum*, Biblioth. Oriental. Clement. Vatic. tom. iii. pars ii. p. 361.) For he tells us, that the Manichæans abstained from food and drink on Sunday, because they supposed the world would be dissolved [p. 839.] on that day, and therefore looked for the destruction of it every Sunday: Manichæi resurrectionem abnegantes contra Christianos jejunium, luctamque in die Dominico faciunt, aientes, in isto die fore, ut hoc sæculum habeat interitum dissolutionemque omnem. But this reason is intirely inconsistent with the opinions of Manichaeans respecting the world; and therefore, is doubtless untrue. For, according to the views of Manichæans, the destruction of our world is to be the end of all evils, the separation of light from darkness, and the termination of the empire of the Prince of darkness; and therefore it presented to them ground for rejoicing, rather than for sorrow. Besides, if we believe them, this world will not be destroyed, until the greatest part of the souls in it are recovered to God: and therefore they had no reason to fear its speedy dissolution. Whether the reason offered by *Leo* was more true, I very much doubt. I know the Manichæans paid some honor to the sun and moon; and I have already stated the fact. But that they consecrated certain days to the sun and moon, and considered fasting as a part of the worship to be paid to these heavenly bodies, no one, acquainted with the principles of the sect, will easily believe. I will state, what has occurred to my mind, while thinking on the subject. The Manichæans had little regard for the festal days of Christians; and not without reason. For they denied the reality of the facts, in commemoration of which those days were kept. Yet, that they might not appear to differ too much from other Christians, they observed as many of these days as they could consistently. And they said, that on those days they expressed by action, the things symbolized by the apparent actions and sufferings of Christ. *Au-*

gustine is authority for this opinion, in his Tract against *Adimantus*, a celebrated Manichæan, (c. 16. § 3. p. 98.) where he says: Nos et Dominicum diem et Pascha solemniter celebramus, et quaslibet alias Christianas dierum festivitates. - - Manichæi autem sic ea reprehendunt, quasi nullos dies et tempora observent. (You see, the Manichæans had little attachment to these festival days; and they declared, that in the celebration of them, they differed from other Christians:) Sed cum de his interrogantur secundum opinionem sectæ suæ, omnia conantur exponere, ut non ipsa tempora, sed *res, quarum illa signa sunt*, observare videantur. And therefore, on the day kept in memory of Christ's death, they did not direct their thoughts to his *death*, which they regarded as only fictitious; but they meditated on, and in a sense performed, the thing signified by that imaginary death. The death of Christ was a figurative representation of the calamity and misery, in which souls were involved, when they were inclosed in bodies. They therefore fixed their thoughts on the sad condition of their souls, and endeavored to restore the soul in some measure to life, or to abstract it from the body. And, I can suppose, they did the same thing on Sundays. The feigned resurrection of Christ, they supposed, was emblematic of the deliverance of souls from the bondage of their bodies. And therefore, on Sundays they solaced themselves with the hope of such deliverance, and also prepared the way for it. Among the effective means of freeing a soul from its prison, and fitting it for its celestial journey, abstinence [p. 840.] from food was not the least: and therefore, on Sundays, they denied the body food, to advance the liberty of the soul.

§ XLVIII. **Christ as the Saviour of Men.** Christ the Son of God, therefore, came to restore lost happiness to souls: but he did not, by his sufferings and death, make expiation for the sins of intelligent beings; nor did he, in their stead, satisfy the divine law. For, good souls, because they are parts of the divine nature, and God is unchangeable, cannot become polluted and corrupt; and, of course, they cannot really commit sin. They remain pure, holy, and innocent, even in the most impure body; and, by their native energy, if they would exert it, they can pave and prepare for themselves a way of return to their celestial country.(1) Christ therefore came down to men, *first*, to destroy the kingdom of the Prince of darkness; that is, to withdraw men from the worship of the evil Principle, and his captains, and fellow warriors, and draw them to the worship and religion of the true God. And, *secondly*, he came down to teach men in what ways the evil soul, together with the body in which it resides, should be overcome and subdued; so that the good mind may be purged from all its contagion, and gradually become fitted and prepared for a return to the world of light from which it came. Christ therefore taught a severe moral discipline, and prohibited all desires after external and sensible objects, and all bodily and sensual pleasures whatever. For as the body is composed of matter that is evil by nature, and the soul living in it is a part of the nature of the Prince of darkness; and as in these, consequently, the root of all evil is located; all the motions of the sentient and craving soul are to be most studiously repressed; and the body, which excites those motions, must be weakened and enervated.(²)

(1) The Manichaeans so talk of the object of Christ's advent to men, that if one were to regard only their language, and not estimate its import by their other doctrines, he might easily suppose that there was little or no difference of opinion on this subject between them and other Christians. For they say, that Christ, by his advent, procured life and salvation for souls; that without him, there was no way to eternal life; that he is the only Saviour of mankind; and that his death was beneficial to men, by procuring eternal life. In place of all, hear how *Fortunatus*, a Manichaean presbyter, speaks, (in his first Dispute with [p. 841.] *Augustine*, p. 69.): Nostra professio est - - Deum sui similem Salvatorem direxisse - - ipso ductore hinc iterum animas ad regnum Dei reversuras esse, secundum sanctam ipsius pollicitationem, qui dixit: Ego sum via, veritas et janua. Et: Nemo potest ad Patrem pervenire, nisi per me. His rebus nos credimus, quia alias animae, id est, alio mediante non poterunt ad regnum Dei reverti, nisi ipsum repererint viam, veritatem et januam. Ipse enim dixit: Qui me vidit, vidit et Patrem meum. Et: Qui in me crediderit, mortem non gustabit in æternum, sed transitum facit de morte ad vitam, et in judicium non veniet. His rebus credimus, et hæc est ratio fidei nostræ. And, after a few other remarks, he says, (p. 70.): Nos fatemur et ostendimus ex Salvatoris adventu, ex ipsius sancta prædicatione, ex ipsius electione, dum animis miseretur, - - ut eamdem animam de morte liberaret, et perduceret eam ad æternam gloriam, et restitueret Patri. And near the end of the discussion, (p. 73.): Animæ substantiam ostendit (Paulus; whom he had just quoted,) quod sit ex Deo, et animam aliter non posse reconciliari Deo, nisi per magistrum, qui est Chistus Jesus, - - Salvatorem Christum credimus de cœlo venisse, voluntatem Patris complere. Quæ voluntas Patris hæc erat, animas nostras de eadem inimicitiâ (Dei) liberare, interfectâ eadem inimicitiâ. And, a little after: Virtute Dei contrariam naturam vinci confiteor et ad meum regressum Salvatorum esse Christum missum. These declarations appear sound and beautiful, if considered in the gross: but if compared with the Manichaean doctrines concerning Christ and the soul, they differ immensely from the sentiments of other Christians, as to the objects of Christ's advent. For, in the first place, the Manichaeans supposed Christ had no flesh and blood, and that he died only in appearance. Of course, they could not possibly believe, that he endured punishment in the stead of mankind, and that he expiated our sins by his death and blood. In the next place, they denied, that our souls are infected and defiled with any stain originating from the first human pair: for, as souls are portions of the divine nature, which never

can be corrupted, vitiated, or deprived of its sanctity, so also souls cannot in any degree lose their integrity and purity. And hence, souls never do properly sin; but, contrary to their will, they are driven by an opposing nature, which is connected with them while they reside in bodies, to permit the criminal deeds of the depraved soul. I have already substantiated this, by the declarations of *Manes* in his Epistle to his daughter *Menoch*; and I will now adduce some other testimonies. *Fortunatus* discoursed much on the subject with *Augustine*; and I will cite some portions of that discussion. In the first Dispute, (p. 70.) *Fortunatus* says. Negasti (Augustine.) animam ex Deo esse, quamdiu peccatis ac vitiis deservit, - - quod fieri non potest, ut aut Deus hoc patiatur (that a soul should serve sin,) aut substantia ejus, (the soul.) Est enim Deus incorruptibilis, et substantia ejus immaculata est et sancta. He goes on to enlarge upon the subject, constantly inculcating, that the soul is of divine origin, [p. 842.] and therefore can neither think nor do anything that is evil. In the second Dispute, (p. 73.) he says: Dico, quod nihil mali ex se proferat Deus omnipotens, et quod quae sua sunt incorrupta maneant, uno ex fonte inviolabili orta et genita: cetera vero quae in hoc mundo versantur contraria, non ex Deo manare. And therefore in the soul, which originated from God, sinful emotions and vicious desires cannot arise; they are exterior to the soul, and arise from the body and the evil soul. Hence, both *Manes* and all his disceples most positively deny *free will*, or the power of the soul to incline itself to either good or evil. Because the soul, being an offshoot from God, is most constantly, and by its own nature, borne towards the good, and cannot possibly choose what is evil. The same *Fortunatus*, strenuously arguing against free will, says: Si mala (if our evil thoughts and emotions) ex Deo essent, aut daret licentiam peccandi, quod dicis liberum arbitrium dedisse Deum, consensor jam inveniebatur delicti mei—aut ignorans, quid futurus essem, delinqueret. - - Quae ab ipso diximus facta esse, uti ab opifice Deo, uti ab ipso creata et genita incorruptibilia haberi—fides Evangelica docet. - - *Inviti peccamus et cogimur* a contrariâ et inimicâ nobis substantiâ. And (p. 75.): Dicimus, quod a contrariâ naturâ anima cogatur delinquere. - - Constat, hoc, quod in nobis versatur, malum, ex auctore malo descendere et portiunculum esse mali hanc radicem. *Secundinus* the Manichaean, in his Epistle to Augustine, (§ 2. p. 369.) says: Si anima a spiritu vitiorum incipiat trahi—ac pœnitudinem gerat, habebat harum sordium indulgentiæ fontem. *Carnis enim commixtione ducitur, non propriâ voluntate.* And hence *Augustine*, (Disput. II. cum Felice, c. 8. p. 348.) shrewdly remarks: Secundum vos (Manichæos) nulla peccata sunt. Gens enim tenebrarum non peccat, quia suam naturam facit: *Natura lucis* non peccat, quia quod facit, facere cogitur. Nullum ergo invenis peccatum, quod damnat Deus.—These things being so, as the good soul cannot change its divine nature, nor commit any sin, it is manifest, that such a soul has no need of a Saviour, to wash away and remove its sins, by his death and sufferings. Yet *Augustine* went too far, in saying that there were no sins whatever, which God could punish, on Manichaean principles. For according to their views, a soul sins, especially if it has received a knowledge of the truth, whenever it does not use its intelligence to suppress the emotions and desires of the body and of the malignant soul. It sins by its negligence and inaction. For it is required to subdue the body and the inclination to sin; and this it can do, partly by its natural energy, partly by the aid of the truth, and partly by the assistance of God and the Holy Spirit. It therefore sins whenever it neglects this duty, notwithstanding the offences of the body and of the evil soul, do not properly belong to it. *Fortunatus*, (Disput. II. cum August. p. 75.) says explicitly: Id est peccatum animæ, si post commonitionem [p. 843.] Salvatoris nostri et sanam doctrinam ejus, a contrariâ et inimicâ sui stirpe se non segregaverit anima, et prioribus se non adornans anima: aliter enim non potest substantiæ suæ reddi. Dictum est enim: Si non venissem et locutus eis fuissem, peccatum non haberent. And yet this sin of negligence and inaction, is not voluntary, but is constrained and coerced against the will of the soul. For *Fortunatus* immediately subjoins: Patet igitur, (he had just cited Rom. viii. 7.) his rebus, quod anima bona, factione illius, quæ legi Dei non est subjecta, peccare videtur, *non sua sponte*. And in proof of this doctrine, he cites Galat. v. 17. and Rom. vii, 23. The Manichaeans, indeed, sometimes speak, as if the soul sinned voluntarily; and, by its assent, approved the lusting of the evil soul. Thus *Secundinus*, (Epist. ad August. § 2. p. 370.) Si vero anima a spiritu vitiorum incipiat trahi et *consentiat* ac post *consensum* pœnitudinem gerat. - - At si cum seipsam cognoverit, *consentiat malo* et non se armet contra inimicum, *voluntate sua* peccavit. Hence *Euodius*, (de fide contra Manichaeos, c. 5. in Opp. August. tom. I. Append. p. 25.) says; Ipse etiam Manichæus non potuit nisi fateri animas, etiam quas dicit ad substantiam Dei pertinere, *propriâ voluntate peccare*. And this he attempts to prove, by some passages in the *Thesaurus* of Manes, and from his *Epistola Fundamenti*. But whoever will compare together all the things said in these passages, will easily see, that the Manichaeans use terms improperly, when they say, the good soul sins voluntarily, and consents to the lustings of the evil soul. The soul, the offspring of the divine nature, cannot possibly will or approve evil; and therefore its consent is not real. Yet the soul is said to consent to the evil deeds of the bad soul, when it suffers its perceptions to be obscured by the flesh and the evil soul, and its energies to become so impaired and weakened, as not to resist them; it consents, when it allows itself to be overcome and compelled by the evil mind, so as not to prevent what it abhors. This consent is like that of a man, who does not shut up his house at night, nor keep a guard, and by such negligence affords thieves an opportunity to plunder some portion of his goods. Therefore this, the only sin which the soul can commit, is in one sense involuntary, and in another sense voluntary. It is involuntary, in as much as the pure mind cannot but abhor the purposes and actions of the evil soul, and is unwillingly over come and compelled not to arrest those purposes and actions; and it is voluntary, in as much as it does not brace itself against them, when it is blinded and overcome. This sin, whatever it may be, is not so great and heinous, that God cannot let it pass unpunished; nor does it require any Saviour. All the criminality of it may be washed away by repentance, because it was not voluntary. So the Manichaeans invariably teach. Thus *Secundinus*, (Epist. ad August. § 2. p. 369.); Si anima post consensum pœnitudinem gerat, habebit harum sordium indulgentiæ fontem. Carnis enim commixtione ducitur, non propria voluntate.

- - Quam si iterum pudeat errasse, paratum inveniet misericordiarum [p. 844.] auctorem. Non enim punitur, quia peccavit, sed quia de peccato non doluit. And *Fortunatus*, (Disput. ii. cum Augustino, p. 75.); Unde patet, recte esse pœnitentiam datam post adventum Servatoris et post hanc scientiam rerum, qua possit anima, acsi divino fonte lota, de sordibus et vitiis tam mundi totius, quam corporum, in quibus eadem anima versatur, regno Dei, unde progressa est, repræsentari.—This doctrine of the Manichaeans respecting the sins of the good soul, as likewise all that they teach respecting both the good soul and the bad one, is, I admit, a compound of incongruities, and appears not well put together. But I will not go into any discussion, as I am merely acting the historian.

(2) According to *Manes*, Christ's advent had two objects. In the *first* place, it brought to men the knowledge of the truth. Before the advent the greatest part of mankind, through the wiles of the Prince of darkness, followed the grossest errors, and were alike ignorant of their own nature, and of the nature of God. The Jews, instead of worshipping God, worshipped the Prince of darkness himself; and obeyed his law given by Moses, as if it were divine. The other nations served the prefects of the world of darkness resident in the stars, and supposed them to be Deities. The Son of God, therefore, came to overthrow this kingdom of darkness among men, which was based on ignorance and error; or to teach mortals, whence came evil, what was the origin of souls, and what is the cause of the perpetual conflict in man between reason and inclination, &c. Says *Fortunatus*, (Disput. I. cum August. p. 74.): Quia inviti peccamus —idcirco sequimur scientiam rerum. Qua scientiâ admonita anima et memoriae pristinæ reddita (for the soul resident in the body, forgets the truth which it before understood) recognoscit, ex quo originem trahat, in quo malo versetur, quibus bonis iterum emendans, quod *nolens* peccavit, possit per emendationem delictorum suorum, bonorum operum gratiâ, meritum sibi reconciliationis apud Deum collocare, auctore Salvatore nostro, qui nos docet et bona exercere et mala fugere.—In the *second* place, Jesus Christ, both by precept and by example, showed men, how the good soul dwelling in an evil body, and associated with an evil soul, must be purgated, in order to become worthy to return to its celestial country. He therefore prescribed an austere system of moral discipline. That code of morals, which *Manes* says was taught by Christ, and which *Manes* expounded in his Epistola Fundamenti, (as *Augustine* testifies, in his work de moribus Manichæorum, L. ii. c. 20. Opp. tom. i. p. 554.) was most gloomy, and repulsive to human nature. The principal parts of it are recounted with much complacency, by *Faustus*, an eloquent disciple of *Manes*, (L. v. c. 1. 2. p. 140.) thus: Ego patrem dimisi, et matrem, uxorem, filios, et cetera, quæ Evangelium jubet, et interrogas, utrum accipiam Evangelium? Nisi adhuc nescis, quid sit, quod Evangelium nuncupatur. Est enim hihil aliud, quam prædicatio et mandatum Christi. (So then the Manichæans affirmed, that the *Gospel* [p. 845.] consisted principally in the rules of life enjoined by Christ.) Ego argentum et aurum rejeci, et æs in zonis habere destiti, quotidiano contentus cibo, nec de crastino curans. - - Vides in me Christi beatitudines illas, vides pauperem, vides mitem, vides pacificum, puro corde, lugentem, esurientem, sitientem, (*Faustus* omits the words *for righteousness*, in order to find his *fasting*, or the hungering

and thirsting practised by his sect, among the precepts of Christ;) persecutiones et odia sustinentem. - - Omnia mea dimisi, patrem, matrem, uxorem, filios, aurum, argentum, manducare, bibere, delicias, voluptates. *Faustus*, a man of ingenuity and fluency, pursues the subject at considerable length; and, among other things, he says: Age, interrogemus Christum, unde potissimum nobis salutis oriatur occasio. Quis hominum in regnum tuum intrabit, Christe? Qui fecerit, inquit, voluntatem Patris mei, qui in cœlis est. Non dixit, qui me professus fuerit natum: (for the Manichæans pertinaciously denied, that Christ was ever born.) Et alibi dixit ad discipulos, Ite, docete omnes gentes—docentes eos servare omnia, quæ mandavi vobis. Non Dixit: docentes eos, quia sum natus. Nec non in monte quum doceret: Beati pauperes - - nusquam dixit: Beati, qui me confessi fuerint natum. - - Diviti quaerenti vitam aeternam: Vade, inquit, vende omnia, quae habes, et sequere me. Non dixit: Crede me natum, ut in aeternum vivas. And thus, whatever precepts Christ gave to his Apostles, or to individual men, are all converted into general rules of life, and, solely by performing them, souls become prepared, as they supposed, for salvation. Says *Secundinus*, (Epist. ad August. p. 369.): Ut hominum corpora arma peccati sunt, ita salutaria (Christi) praecepta arma justitiae.—As the whole religious system of *Manes*, is nothing but the religion of the Persian *Magi*, tinctured with some portions of Christianity; so, also, this severe code of morals, is Persian, and derived from the schools of the Magi, in which *Manes* was educated. For this assertion, I have the authority of *Diogenes Laërtius*, and likewise of *Eubulus*, whom *Jerome*, (contra Jovinianum, L. ii. Opp. tom. iv. p. 206. edit. Benedict.) thus cites: Eubulus, qui Historiam Mithrae multis voluminibus explicuit, narrat apud Persas tria genera Magorum, quorum primos, qui sint doctissimi et eloquentissimi, excepta farinâ et olere, nihil amplius in cibo sumere. I add *Clemens* Alexandrinus, (Stromat. L. iii. p. 533. edit. Paris.) who says: Ἀμέλει διὰ φροντίδος ἐστὶ καὶ τοῖς Μάγοις, οἴνου τε ὁμοῦ, καὶ ἐμψύχων καὶ ἀφροδισίων ἀπέχεσθαι, λατρεύουσιν ἀγγέλοις καὶ δαίμοσιν. Certe Magis quoque curae est, qui angelos et daemones colunt, simul a vino et animatis et rebus venereis abstinere. No two things could be more perfectly alike, than the Manichaeans and these Magi. According to our feelings, most of the duties which *Manes*, in imitation of the Magi, enjoined on his followers, are exceedingly unpleasant; but they [p. 846.] were, undoubtedly, less annoying to the Persians; whose bodies, like those of all the Orientals, do not require so much nutriment as ours, and who can dispense with flesh and solid food without much inconvenience, and neither crave nor relish wine. The modern Persians have no fondness for wine or flesh, and can live very comfortably on fruits, herbs, and melons. I have no doubt, therefore, that both *Manes* and his early followers observed the precepts he set forth, and led a sober and apparently an austere life. This, *Manes* could the more easily do, because he had been accustomed to those rules from early life among the Magi. But this discipline, which in Asia was but slightly repulsive and painful, when transferred to Europe and other regions, was very annoying and painful, and it exhausted and emaciated the body. Hence the Manichæans who lived at Rome, and in Italy, and Africa, were most of them pale, lean, and emaciated, with gloom and anguish visible in their countenances. This appearance of excessive abstinence and self-denial, is conceded to them by their most virulent opposers, notwithstanding they give intimations that the private habits of the sect were not very sober and chaste. *Augustine*, in his work de utilitate credendi, addressed to *Honoratus*, whom he wished to recover from Manichæism, (c. 18. Opp. tom. i. p. 51.) thus writes: Alia multa me docuit ecclesia catholica, quo illi homines (Manichæi) *exsanques corporibus*, sed crassi mentibus adspirare non possunt. And *Leo* the Great, (Sermo xxxiii. c. 4. Opp. tom. i. p. 93.) says: Neminem fallant (Manichæi) discretionibus ciborum, sordibus vestium, *vultuumque palloribus*. Non sunt casta jejunia, quæ non de ratione veniunt continentiæ, sed de arte fallaciæ. *Leo* would persuade his hearers, that the lean and emaciated form, and the pallidness of the Manichæans, which could not be denied, were the result of some imposition, and not of abstinence: but I know not, whether he had good evidence to support him. The pallidnes of the Manichaeans became proverbial at Rome; so that persons meeting a young woman with a pallid countenance, would call her a Manichaean. Thus *Jerome* tells us, (Epist. xviii. ad Eustochium de custodia virginitatis, Opp. tom. iv. Pars II. p. 32.): Et quam viderint pallentem atque tristem, miseram, Monacham et *Manichæam* vocant. And yet these colorless, lean, and sorrowful Manichaeans, who dwelt at Rome and in Italy in the fourth and fifth centuries, were not genuine followers of *Manes*, but had departed in many respects from the strict rules of their master. For the Manichaean discipline had been relaxed in the countries of the West; nor were even their bishops able to endure the discipline, which *Manes* imposed in his Epistola Fundamenti. A striking example in point, is narrated by *Augustine*, (de moribus Manichaeorum, L. ii. c. 20. tom. i. p. 553, 554. and, contra Faustum, L. v. c. 7. tom. viii. p. 142.) One *Constantius*, a Manichaean of the class called *Auditors*, a man of great wealth, and peculiarly devoted to the intersts of his sect, was much troubled, at hearing that the dispersed and vagrant Manichaeans often lived quite otherwise than the [p. 847.] law of *Manes* required. And, to put an end to this disgrace, he wished to collect them together in his own house, where they could conveniently live according to the precepts of their master. At first, the bishops of the sect, knowing the intollerable severity of their rules, resisted his purpose; and *he complained, that his so important efforts were foiled, by the laxness of the bishops*, (who, nevertheless, were pallid and colorless,) *by whose assistance those efforts ought to be carried into effect.* But, by good fortune, one of the bishops favored his project. *Therefore all the Elect, who could be collected, were assembled at Rome. The rule of life in the Epistle of Manes was proposed. Many deemed it intollerable, and retired; but a considerable number, from modesty, remained. These commenced living, as Constantius wished, and as was prescribed by so high authority.* But their zeal was of short duration. First, broils arose among them; then, *they muttered, that these mandates could not be endured; and thence sedition.* Constantius, the founder of the company, showed them clearly, *that, either all these precepts are to be followed, or the man must be deemed a consumate fool, who gave precepts which no one can follow.* But he could effect nothing. First the bishop eloped; and many followed his example. Yet, a few remained, who had separated from the rest. And these, the other Manichaeans contemptuously called

Mattarii, because they slept on *mattæ* (mats), a sort of rude beds without frames.—This shows, how great was the severity of the moral discipline of *Manes;* which could not be endured, even by those who otherwise lived abstemiously and harshly, or by persons who manifested by their countenances, and by the leanness and emaciation of their bodies, how much they shunned all indulgences.—But, let us come more directly to our subject.

As the body, according to *Manes*, is itself evil, and is the work of the Prince of darkness, or a prison in which good souls are held captive, it was necessary that he should teach, that the body is to be attenuated, tortured, and deprived of all comforts. And as he further held, that the good soul is influenced by no cravings and no desires, and maintained that all appetites and lusts are seated in the evil soul, which dwells in the body; he could not avoid inculcating, that all appetence whatever of things without us, is not merely to be restrained and allayed, but to be wholly extirpated; that all emotions and affections of the mind, being in their very nature evil, are to be slain, and no inclination is to be gratified. For, the more liberty is allowed to the evil soul of desiring and hankering, the more langor and weakness befall the good soul; so that it becomes less able to purge itself, and to repel the defilements with which it is beset on every side. And, on the contrary, the more rigidly the good mind binds down and confines the body and the evil soul, the more easily it forces its way out of the darkness. The true Manichæan, therefore, will not suffer himself to be influenced by any desire whatever of any sensible object; he must neither sorrow nor rejoice, neither fear nor hope, every pleasure must be shunned, and the drama of this world must be contemplated with a stable, unmoved, and tranquil [p. 848.] mind. Those only who obey this law, can hope to return to the world of light when they leave the body.—But, as *Manes* could foresee, that if he prescribed to all his followers this very stringent law so revolting to human nature, he could have but few adherents, and be the head of only a small sect; he prescribed a more indulgent rule for the multitude or the common people. And thus, following the example of the Magi, from whom he derived the greatest part of his regulations, he divided his commonwealth into the *Elect* and the *Auditors;* the former, bound to observe most sacredly all the irksome precepts soon to be described, and the latter, allowed to follow the instincts of nature. Of this distinction among Manichæans, we shall treat in the proper place; we now consider only the rule of life for the *Elect*, and which is the only way to salvation.

The Manichæans arranged their whole system of moral discipline under three heads, which they called *Signacula*, or Seals; namely, the *signaculum of the mouth*, *of the hands*, and *of the bosom.* Thus *Augustine*, (de Moribus Manichæor. L. ii. c. 10. p. 538.): Videamus tria illa *signacula*, quæ in vestris moribus magna laude ac prædicatione jactatis. Quæ sunt tandem ista *signacula?* Oris certe, et manuum ac sinus. Ut ore, et manibus, et sinu, castus et innocens sit homo. I have no doubt that *Manes* derived this distribution of duties from the Persian Magi.. *Augustine* contends that it is clumsy and imperfect; which we readily grant: but if the system was in other respects correct, we could put up with the imperfection of the distribution. Before we arrange the duties enjoined by Manichæans under these three heads, let us hear their own explanation of the distinction they make. *Augustine* thus states the views of the doctors of the sect: Quum os nomino, omnes sensus, qui sunt in capite, intelligi volo; quum autem manum, omnem operationem; quum sinum, omnem libidinem seminalem. Therefore, all duties and faults, which can be referred to the eyes, the ears, the tongue, the mouth, the taste, or the smell, belong to the first *signaculum*, that of the *mouth*. All actions, whether commanded or forbidden, are comprehended under the second *signaculum*, that of the *hands*. The third *signaculum*, that of the *bosom*, prohibits all venereal desires whatever.—Among the duties of the signaculum of the *mouth*, the first was, (as *Augustine* tells us, l. c. c. 11. p. 538.) *to refrain from all blasphemy*. This precept, in accordance with their views, they so explained as to declare those *blasphemers*, who professed but *one* first cause of all things, who taught that the bodies of men and animals were created by God, who inculcated that the law of Moses proceeded from God, who declared that the Son of God was born and actually died; and, on the contrary, those had holy thoughts of God, and were believed to eschew all *blasphemy*, who embraced and professed the religion taught by *Manes*. This precept is therefore very broad, and requires the adoption of the intire system of the Manichæans.—In the next place, to the *signaculum oris* belongs, the rigid and austere abstinence of the Manichæans. This required them, first, [p. 849.] to abstain from all *flesh*. See *Augustine;* (de Hæres. c. 46. and, de Moribus Manichæor. L. ii. c. 13, &c. p. 540.) *Faustus*, also, (L. vi. c. 1 p. 145.) says: Omnem ego carnem immundum existimo. The principal reason for this precept undoubtedly was, that the use of flesh as food, strengthened the body, which should be weakened and attenuated; and excited and inflamed animal passions, which should be wholly extinguished. But there were other reasons. Animals, while alive, contain light or celestial soul commingled with matter; but when dead, their flesh is wholly without soul, and consequently is a mere mass of matter, belonging entirely to the kingdom of darkness: and therefore, those who eat it, augment and enlarge the quantity of evil which is in them. Says *Augustine*, (de Moribus Manich. L. ii. c. 15. p. 543.): Aiunt, cum anima carnem deseruerit, nimias sordes reliquas fieri, et ideo eorum, qui carnibus vescuntur, animam coinquinari. That no portion of light or celestial matter remained in the flesh, they proved from this, that flesh when burned emitted no light. Says *Augustine*, (l. c. c. 16. p. 544.): Dicitis, olivæ folia cum incenduntur, ignem emittere, in quo præsentia lucis apparet; carnes autem cum incenduntur non idem facere. I pass by other reasons.—From the same causes, undoubtedly, they reckoned *eggs* and *milk* among forbidden aliments. Says *Augustine*, (de Hæres. c. 46. p. 12.): Nec ova saltem sumunt, quasi et ipsa cum franguntur expirent, nec oporteat ullis mortuis corporibus vesci - - Sed nec alimoniâ lactis utuntur, quamvis de corpore animantis vivente mulgeatur sive sugatur, non quia putant divinæ substantiæ nihil ibi esse permixtum, sed quia sibi error ipse non constat. *Augustine* here thinks, they had no reason for prohibiting the use of milk; but it is sufficiently clear, that they had a reason.—*Fish*, they abominated, even more than flesh; and they would rather starve than eat it. *Augustine*, (contra Faustum, L. xvi. c. 9. p. 205.): Cur ita piscem vos noxium prædicatis, ut si alia esca non occurrat, prius fame consumamini, quam pisce vescamini. Perhaps, as often elsewhere, *Augustine* here exaggerates, in regard to the Manichæan abhorrence of fish. But if his statement is true, I confess I can assign no reason for this abhorrence.—As the Manichæans prohibited the use of all animal food, they were obliged to repel hunger, with bread, salads, herbs, pulse, fruits, and the products of the earth and trees. They therefore used, first, *bread;* both ordinary bread, and also cakes. Of their bread *Augustine* speaks, (contra Faustum, L. xx. c. 23. p. 248.): Eo pane vescimini, quo ceteri homines, et fructibus vivitis et fontibus. Of their cakes he often speaks, and particularly, (de Moribus Manichæor. L. ii. c. 16. p. 547.): In Electis vestris esse non potest, qui proditus fuerit, non concupiscendo, sed medendo (for [p. 850.] the recovery of health,) partem aliquam coenasse gallinae: esse autem in iis potest, qui vehementer cumiphas (a species of cakes,) et alia placenta desiderasse se ipse providerit. I cite this passage in preference to others of the kind, because it shows, that flesh was so strictly prohibited by them, that even the sick could not use it without offending. They also preferred potherbs and the products of trees and the ground, before bread and cakes; because the former, they supposed, contained a greater portion of the celestial elements than the other kinds of food. Says *Augustine*, (de Moribus Manichæor. L. ii. c. 16. p. 543.): Quaero, unde doceatis, in frumentis ac legumine, et oleribus, et floribus et pomis inesse istam nescio quam partem Dei. Ex ipso coloris nitore, inquiunt, et odoris jucunditate, et saporis suavitate manifestum est: quae dum non habent putria, eodem bono sese deserta esse significant. A little before, (c. 13. p. 541.) he had given a list, though an imperfect one of the Manichaean eatables, thus: Quid porro insanius dici aut cogitari potest, hominem boletos, orizam, tubera, placentas, caroenum, piper, laser, distento ventre cum gratulatione ructantem et quotidie talia requirentem, non inveniri, quemadmodum a tribus signaculis, id est, a regula sanctitatis excidisse videatur, aliam vero fruges vilissimas fumoso obsonio (*lard*, he supposes,) condientem certo supplicio praeparari. But of no food were the Manichaeans more fond, than of *melons.* For their master had a predilection for them; which is not strange, he being a Persian, and the Persians to this day making great use of melons, which their country produces of the most delicious kind. Says *Augustine*, (de Moribus Manichaeor. L. ii. c. 15. p. 544.): De thesauris Dei melonem putatis aureum esse. And, (c. 18. p. 550.): Melonibus quam hominibus estis amiciores. Next to melons, they preferred *potherbs* and *olives.* Says *Augustine*, (l. citato, p. 544.): Cur nitorem atque fulgorem olei clamare copiam coadmixti boni arbitramini, et ad id purgandum fauces et ventrem paratis. The first Manichaeans, like their founder, ate their fruits, potherbs and salads, simple, or undressed and unseasoned; and this was required by the law of *Manes;* which condemned all gratifications of the bodily senses, lest the evil soul should become excited by them. But in this particular, as in many others, the European and African Manichaeans departed widely from the rule of their master; for they seasoned their potherbs and pulse, with pepper and other things. Hence *Augustine*, (l. citato, c. 13. p. 541.) charges upon them that: Exquisitas et peregrinas fruges multis ferculis variatas et largo pipere adspersas nonâ horâ libenter assumant, noctis etiam principio talia coenent. And, (c. 16. p. 541.) he says to them: Quae ratio est, vel potius amentia, de numero Electorum hominem pellere, qui forte carnem valetudinis caussâ gustaverit: Si autem *piperata tubera* voraciter edere concupierit, immodestià tantum forte possitis reprehendere, non autem ut corruptorem damnare signaculi? And yet *Augustine* admits, [p. 851.] that there were some among them, though few, so zealous for the ancient and rigid customs, that they blamed these too luxurious brethren; (l. citato, p. 541.): Electus vester tribus signaculis prædicatus, si ita, uti dixi, vivat, ab uno et fortasse duobus gravioribus reprehendi potest, damnari autem tanquam signaculi dissignator non potest. Si autem semel frusto pernae vel rancido labra unxerit et vappa udaverit, solutor signaculi vestri auctoris sententia judicabitur.—From their food, I pass to their *drink*. The law of Manes most strictly prohibited all use of wine; and, undoubtedly, all other intoxicating drinks. *Wine*, as already stated, Manes declared to be the gall of the Prince of darkness, poured upon the earth. Yet his Italian and African disciples, in the times of *Augustine*, had no hesitation to eat grapes. Says Augustine, (l. citato, c. 16. p. 545.): Quæ tanta perversio est, vinum putare fel principum tenebrarum, et uvis comedendis non parcere? Magisne inerit illud fel cum in cupa, quam cum in acinis fuerit? But, I suppose, these Manichæans took greater liberties, than the very severe and troublesome law of their master allowed. And these later Manichæans differed also from the more ancient, in other things pertaining to this part of their discipline. The primitive Manichaeans drank either pure water, or as *Cyrill* of Jerusalem says, (Catechcs. vi. § 31. p. 108.) water with an infusion of wheat or barley straw: τοῖς ἀχύρων ὕδασι, *palearum aquis*. But the Augustinian Manichaeans were more indulgent to the palate; although it was displeasing to the graver and more austere brethren. For *Augustine* says, (l. citato, c. 13. p. 541.): Bibebant mulsum, carœnum passum, et nonnullorum pomorum expressos succos, vini speciem satis imitantes, atque id etiam suavitate vincentes. What *Augustine* here calls *carœnum passum*, he had just before called *coctum vinum*, (c. 16. p. 546.): Carœnum, quod bibitis, nihil aliud quam coctum vinum est, quod vino deberet esse sordidius. *Beausobre*, (vol. II. p. 775.) well conjectures, that this *carœnum* was water in which bruised grapes had been boiled. Undoubtedly, it was some kind of liquor, produced from bruised grapes, by boiling; and one which the Latins called *passum*, a name also used by *Augustine*. But I do not suppose this caroenum, to be that *species of sweet factitious wine*, called *carenum*, mentioned by *Palladius*. And yet I have doubts, whether the two words *carœnum passum* should be joined together, as they are in the printed editions of *Augustine;* or should be disjoined, so as to make them denote two kinds of liquor. Some of the Manichaeans also used *hordei succo;* that is, as I apprehend, *beer* or *ale*. Says *Augustine*, (c. 16. p. 546.): Hordei quidam succo vinum imitantur.—Hoc genus potus citissime inebriat: nec tamen unquam succum hordei fel principum dixistis.—I proceed to other things. As the *signaculum oris* extended to all the senses, and condemned all indulgence of them, I suppose we must refer to it;—*First*, That the Manichaeans were [p. 852.] required by their master to sleep, not on couches, but on the ground, or on *matts* or coarse rags. *Epiphanius*, (Haeres. lxvi. § 12. p. 629.) says, they slept ἐπὶ καλάμοις, *on rushes.* Of this, I have already spoken; and I may here observe, that *Manes* borrowed this part of his discipline also from the Magi. For *Sotion*, as quoted by *Diogenes Lærtius*, (Proem. de dictis et factis Philosophor. p. 6.) says of the Magi: Τούτων δὲ ἐσθὴς μὲν λευκὴ, στιβὰς δὲ εὐνὴ, καὶ λάχανον τροφὴ, τυρὸς τε καὶ ἄρτος εὐτελής. His vestis candida, lectus humus, esca olus, caseus, panisque cibarius est. If you except from this list the *cheese*, which, as well as milk, the Manichaeans abhorred; you have here, the mode of living prescribed by *Manes* to his disciples.—*Secondly*, That they were to be clad in plain, and even sordid garments, entirely without ornament; and to wear their beards and hair long, after the example of their master. We have already cited a passage from *Leo* the Great. As for the clothing and beard of *Manes*, see *Archelaus'* Dispute with him, (p. 23.): Habebat calceamenti genus, quod quadrisole vulgo appellari solet, (high and troublesome:) pallium autem varium, tanquam aërina specie, (old and much worn, I suppose, so that its color could hardly be determined:) in manu vero validissimum baculum tenebat, (as was usual with the Magi,) ex ligno ebelino; crura etiam braccis obtexerat colore diverso, quarum una rufa, alia velut prasini choris erat, (that is, to indicate his poverty, he wore trowsers of various pieces of different colored cloth sewed together; such as beggars wore.) Vultus vero ut senis Persæ artificis et bellorum ducis (that is, grave and venerable,) erat. *Archelaus* thus addressed him, (§ 36. p. 23.): Barba (i. e. long-bearded) Sacerdos Mithræ et collusor.—*Thirdly*, That they were required to shun the baths, the shows, and the theatres. *Augustine*, (in his last Book de Moribus Manichæorum, p. 551, 552,) specifying in what respects the Manichæans had abandoned the unconfortable rule of their master, among other things, says: Multi in vino et carnibus, multi lavantes in balneis inventi sunt. In theatris Electos et aetate et moribus graves cum sene presbytero saepissime invenimus. Omitto juvenes, quos etiam rixantes pro scenicis et aurigis deprehendere solebamus. Baths, therefore, and theatres and shows, were utterly forbidden them. *Tyrbo*, likewise, (in the Acta Archelai, § 10. p. 16.) testifies to the strict prohibition of the baths.—To all these duties, comprised under the *signaculum* of the *mouth*, were added *fasts*, both annual and on certain days of each week, obligatory on Manichaeans. As to their annual fasts, I find nothing specific on record: yet that they held such fasts, cannot be doubted. *Jerome* tells us, (Comment on Amos. c. 3. Opp. tom. iii. p. 1396.) that, just like *Tatian:* Manichaeum laborare continentiâ et jejuniis, xerophagiis, chamaecuniis. Many suppose the last word to denote *vigils;* but I doubt it. [*Du Cange*, Glossar. mediae et imf. Latinit. tom. i. p. 1042, thinks *chameunæ* (χαμευνίαι) to be *matts spread on the ground* for sleeping.] Yet it is certain, [p. 853.] that the Manichaeans kept vigils, and held them at stated times: *Augustine* occasionally mentions them. *Jerome*, in another passage, (Comment on Joel, tom. iii. p. 1345.) says: Jejunat Manichaeus: sed hoc jejunium saturitate et ebrietate deterius est. Two days in every week, Sundays and Mondays, the Manichaeans devoted to fasting: of this we have before given evidence. One of these fasts, that on what we call the Lord's day, or Sunday, was observed both by the *Elect* and the *Auditors;* and, of course, was a fast of the whole church. To this *Augustine* testifies, (Epist. ccxxxvi. tom. ii. p. 643.): Auditores die quoque Dominico cum Electis jejunant, et omnes blasphemias cum illis credunt. From this it is inferred, that the fast of the second day of the week, or Monday, was confined to the *Elect.* That these fasts were very strict, and restrained the Manichaeans from all food and drink, the precepts of the sect put beyond all controversy. And hence, they accounted it among the best proofs of their sanctity. Said *Faustus*, (L. v. c. 1. p. 140.): Vides me esurientem et sitientem: et interrogas, utrum accipiam Evangelium? Hunger and thirst, therefore, according to the Manichaeans, were not the smallest part of that Gospel which the Son of God proclaimed to men: and to prove it, they mutilated the words of the Savior, Matth. v. 6. by omitting the word, δικαιοσύνην, *righteousness;* so that their copies read simply; *Blessed are they that hunger and thirst.*—Of all the pleasures of sense, the *signaculum oris* tolerated but *one*, that derived from *music.* For they supposed music to be of divine origin; as *Augustine* informs us, (de moribus Manichaeor. L. ii. c. 16. p. 546.): Dulcedo musica, quam de divinis regnis venisse contenditis, nobis mortuarum carnium sordibus exhibetur. *Beausobre*, (in the Preface to his Histoire de Manicheé, p. xxxi.) adds the pleasure, which the mind derives through the nostrils from perfumes and burning incense. Where he learned this, I do not know; but it is quite credible; for the Persians, like all the people of the East, are exceedingly fond of sweet odors. Besides, that the pleasures of smell were not deemed unlawful by the Manichaeans, is sufficiently manifest from the fact, before mentioned, that they concluded *ex odoris* jucunditate emitted by fruits and flowers, that these contained more celestial matter than other objects. See *Augustine*, (de moribus Manichaeor. L. ii. c. 16. p. 543.)

I pass to the *signaculum* of the *hands;* which prohibited all actions inconsistent with the tranquillity of the soul, or proceeding from any desire. For, if we except the single desire of returning to the celestial country after leaving the body, which the divine and good mind ought to cherish, all other desires, instincts, and appetites, according to the opinion of the Manichaeans, originate from the body and the evil soul, and are therefore vicious and impure. *Augustine*, (de moribus Manichaeor. L. ii. c. 17 &c.) treats of this *signaculum manuum*, as if it required nothing but to abstain from killing animals and lacerating vegetables. But it required many other things, which *Augustine* seems [p. 854.] to have omitted, lest he should be obliged to acknowledge something good and commendable in the Manichaean discipline; and so he named only that, which would afford opportunity for most censure and vituperation.—*First*, The perfect Manichaean, therefore, following the example of Christ's Apostles, ought to divest himself intirely of all natural affection towards parents, children, brothers, and relatives; and also to suppress the love of life, health, and comfort. For the love of kindred originates from flesh and blood, and of course from evil; and the end of life is the liberation of the soul from its prison, which the wise should rather desire than fear. Said *Faustus*, (L. v. c. 1. 2. p. 140.): Ego patrem dimisi et matrem, uxorem, filios et cetera, quae Evangelium (so he calls the system of moral discipline,) jubet. - - Omnia mea dimisi, patrem, matrem, uxorem, filios, aurum, argentum, manducare, bibere, delicias, voluptales. Other proofs may be gathered from the testimonies heretofore adduced.—*Secondly*,

The perfect Manichaean ought to live in extreme poverty, and neither to possess nor desire any worldly goods, neither gold, nor silver, nor furniture, nor home, nor anything whatever; and to live contentedly on a slender, sparing, daily amount of food, supplied him by those called *Auditors.* Said *Faustus*, (L. v. c. 1. 2. p. 140.): Ego argentum et aurum rejeci (when I became a Manichæan,) et aes in zonis habere destiti, quotidiano cibo, nec de crastino curans.—Vides in me Christi beatitudines illas, vides pauperem. And a little after: Christus dixit: Beati pauperes; et, diviti quaerenti vitam aeternam, Vade, vende omnia quae habes, et sequere me. We may here remark that the Manichæans, in order to prove that Christ required this absolute penury of all things, read the language of the Saviour, Matt. v. 3. simply, Μακάριοι οἱ πτωχοὶ, (*Blessed are the poor;*) omitting the words τῷ πνεῦματι, (*in spirit.*) And *Tyrbo*, (in the Acta Archelai, § 9. p. 16.) says: Si quis dives est in hoc mundo, cum exierit de corpore suo, necesse est, eum in corpus pauperis injici. - - - Qui aedificaverit sibi domum, dispergetur in omnia corpora. I am aware, that this *Tyrbo* erred in some things; but in reporting the precepts of the Manichæans, he did not mistake. *Augustine*, (de moribus ecclesiae et Manich. L. i. c. 35. p. 531.) says: Quid calumniamini, quod fideles jam baptismate renovati procreare filios, et agros ac domos, pecuniamque ullam possidere non debeant. - - Dicitis catechumenis licere habere pecuniam, fidelibus non licere.—*Thirdly*, The perfect Manichaean should refrain from all labor, and from all business whatever; and should spend his life in uninterrupted repose and contemplation. He should therefore not build up, nor pull down; not bake bread, nor grind in the mill; not till the ground, nor reap the grain, nor engage in any manual labor whatever. *Tyrbo*, (in the Acta Archelai, § 9. p. 16, 17.) having said, that it is not lawful for Mani-
[p. 855.] chaeans, (he means, the *Elect*,) to plant, build, reap, put grain into the mill. or bake bread, adds: Διὰ τοῦτο ἀπείρηταί αὐτοῖς ἔργον ποιῆσαι. Propter hoc illicitum est apud eos opus quoddam facere. And hence *Augustine*, (de utilitate credendi, c. 1. p. 34.) says, that he refused to pass from the class of *Auditors* to that of the *Elect* among the Manichaeans, Ne hujus mundi spem atque negotia dimitteret. And a little after, he says that he, while a Manichaean, Spem gessisse de pulchritudine uxoris, de pompa divitiarum, de inanitate honorum, ceterisque voluptatibus. Haec omnia, (he says,) cum studiose illos audirem, cupere et sperare non desistebam. Sed *fateor, illos sedulo monere, ut ista caveantur.* The reason of the precept is obvious. All manual labors proceed from solicitude, and are subservient to the desires of men; but all solicitudes are evil; and therefore, a holy man should neither obey them nor harbor them.—*Fourthly*, In particular, it was not lawful for a true and perfect Manichaean, to pluck the fruit from trees, to strip trees of leaves, to pull up plants, shrubs, and herbs, or to do violence to any part of nature. Of this obligation, *Augustine* treats in many places, and formally, in his work de moribus Manichaeorum, (L. ii. c. 17 &c.) where, among other things, he says: Poma ipsi non decerpitis, herbamque non vellitis, sed tamen ab Auditoribus vestris decerpi et evelli atque afferri vobis jubetis. He had just before said: Si quis non imprudentiâ, sed sciens pomum, foliumve de arbore decerpat, signaculi corruptor sine ulla dubitatione damnabitur, sed omnino (damnabitur) si arborem radicitus eruat. And

(de Haeres. c. 46. p. 12.): Agrum spinis purgare, nefas habent.—Electi nihil in agris operantes, nec poma carpentes, nec saltim folia ulla vellentes, expectant haec afferri usibus suis ab Auditoribus suis. And, (contra Faustum, L. xvi. c. 28. p. 214.): A vobis quisquis vulserit spicas, ex traditione Manichaei homicida deputatur. This puerile precept will not appear very strange to one well acquainted with the principles of their system. The Manichaeans supposed all nature to be animated. or that, in all its parts, there was a commixture of the celestial elements with matter. Thus *Manes* himself, (Epist. ad filiam Menoch, apud *August.* Opus imperf. L. iii. in a passage already quoted,) says: Animam confusam esse omnibus corporibus et saporibus, et speciebus variis cohaerere. And, as quoted by *Alexander* of Lycopolis, (contra Manichaeos, p. 19.) he says: Πάντα νοῦς ἐστὶ. *Omnia sunt anima.* *Augustine*, (de Haeres. c. 46. p. 11, 12.) says: Herbas atque arbores sic putant vivere, ut vitam, quae illis inest, et sentire credant, et dolere, cum laeduntur, nec aliquid inde sine cruciatu eorum quemquam posse vellere aut carpere. Therefore, in the opinion of this sect, whoever plucked off or pulled up herbs, apples, leaves, or any fruits, not only offered violence and gave pain to some soul, but also dislodged it from its place or habitation. There was also another and a graver reason. The Manichaeans were persuaded, that rational human souls, portions of the divine light, [p. 856.] if not sufficiently purgated, migrated into other bodies, and also into trees, herbs, and plants: of this we shall treat hereafter. *Augustine*, (de Haeres. c. 46. p. 12.) says: Animas et in pecora redire putant et in omnia, quae radicibus fixa sunt, et aluntur in terra. Hence it might be, that he who plucked leaves, or an apple, or a fig, or pulled up an herb, might be equally culpable with one who slew a man. And, as I have before shown, it was common for Manichaeans to compare the laceration of shrubs, and violence done to trees and ears of corn, with the crime of homicide.—*Fifthly*, Manes had the same reasons for strictly forbidding his more *perfect* disciples, from pursuing agriculture, or anything auxiliary to it; although he allowed the *Auditors* a liberty to cultivate the ground. Says *Augustine*, (de Haeres. c. 46. p. 12.): Agriculturam, quae omnium artium est innocentissima, tanquam plurium homicidiorum ream dementer accusant. And *Tyrbo*, (in the Acta Archelai, § 9. p. 16.) tells us, that they held agriculture in such abhorrence, that they said of usurers, those bloodsuckers of the unfortunate, that they sin less than husbandmen. And *Augustine*, (de moribus Manichaeor. L. ii. c. 17. p. 550.) after saying, that the founder of the sect allowed the *Auditors* to pursue agriculture, proceeds thus: Quanquam saepe etiam dicere audeatis fœneratorem innocentiorem esse, quam rusticum. *Manes* supposed the whole earth to be full of souls; so that whoever disturbs their repose, commits an offence, as it were, against God himself, the parent of those souls.—*Sixthly*, But it was a much greater violation of the *signaculum manuum*, to slay animals of any species whatever. This was not allowable even for the *Auditors;* although they might eat the flesh of animals killed by others. See *Augustine*, (de Haeres. c. 46. p. 12. and, de moribus Manichaeor. L. ii. c. 17. p. 549. and many other places.) For this prohibition, *Manes* himself gave a special reason. Animals came into this world from the kingdom of darkness, or, as was shown in a proper place, they fell down from the stars where the demons reside. Therefore the princes of darkness are attached to these animals, and inflict punishments on such as kill them. *Augustine*, (de moribus Manichaeor. L. ii. c. 17. p. 549.): Non deest homini callido (*Maneti*) adversus indoctos in naturæ obscuritate perfugium. Cœlestes enim, ait, principes, qui de gente tenebrarum capti atque vincti, a conditore mundi in illis ordinati sunt locis, sua quisque possidet in terra animalia, de suo scilicet genere ac stirpe venientia: qui peremptores eorum reos tenent, nec de hoc mundo exire permittunt, pœnisque illos quibus possunt et cruciatibus adterunt. But from this prohibition of killing, they excepted the insects which annoy men's bodies, fleas, &c.; for they denied that these animals came from the skies, and accounted them the filth of our bodies. *Augustine*, (l. citato, p. 550.): Quid quod a nece animalium nec vos ipsi in pe- [p. 857.] diculis, in pulicibus et cimicibus temperatis. Magnamque hujus rei defensionem putatis, quod has esse sordes nostrorum corporum dicitis. Against this opinion, *Augustine* argues with shrewdness.—*Lastly;* strange as it may appear in men professing to be strict imitators of Christ, they forbid the giving of bread and other things, to the poor, who were not Manichæans. But, for this inhumanity, if so it may be called, they had their reasons, derived from the internal principles of their religion. *Augustine*, (de moribus Manichæor. L. ii. c. 15. p. 543.): Hinc est, quod mendicanti homini, qui Manichæus non sit, panem, vel aliquid frugum, vel aquam ipsam, quæ omnibus vilis est, dari prohibetis, ne membrum Dei (i. e. good and celestial matter,) quod his rebus admixtum est, suis peccatis sordidatum a reditu (ad terram lucis) impediat. But to free themselves in some measure from the odium they incurred by this custom, they allowed *money*, instead of bread, to be given to the needy. *Augustine*, (l. cit. c. 16. p. 547.): Quæ cum ita sint, etiam panem mendicanti dare prohibetis: censetis tamen propter misericordiam, vel potius propter invidiam, nummos dari. Quid hic prius arguam, crudelitatem an vecordiam? *Beausobre*, (vol. ii. p. 786, &c.) as he is always officious in behalf of the Manichæans, so he labors hard to wipe from them this stain, which he erroneously thinks to be worse (*plus surprenante*) than all others. But this excellent man, in the explication of this matter, commits mistakes which show that even great men may err; and he adduces no proof, on which even a suspicion can be raised, that *Augustine*, whohad lived nine years among the Manichæans, voluntarily misstated and calumniated them. Nor is *Augustine* the only writer, as this learned man supposes, that accuses the Manichæans of this crime. To pass over others, *Theodoret*, (Hæret. Fabul. L. i. c. 26. tom. iv. p. 213.) says: Την δὲ εις πένητας γινομένην διαβάλλουσι φιλανθρωπίαν, τῆς ὕλης ἐιναι λέγοντες θεραπείαν. Benignitatem quæ exercetur erga pauperes reprehendunt, dicentes, eam esse cultum materiæ. By ὕλη or *materia*, as has been shown, and as *Theodoret* had just before stated, the Manichæans were accustomed to designate the *Lord* of matter, or the Prince of darkness himself. They therefore supposed, that to give food to a poor man, not a Manichæan, (this limitation is omitted by *Theodoret*,) would be to render some honor or service to the demon. This reason appears to differ from that assigned by *Augustine;* but both may be made to harmonize. Those who were not Manichæans, were the servants and subjects of the Prince of darkness: but he who aids and assists the servants of God's enemy, in a sense serves that enemy.

Moreover, in every part of nature, during that first conflict between the good and the evil Principles, some portion of celestial matter became intermixed; and it must be gradually separated and restored to its original state. Such a separation is happily effected in the bodies of Manichaeans, whose souls, mindful of their duty, withdraw the celestial in their food from pollution. [p. 858.] Says *Augustine*, (l. cit. p. 543.): Cibi, qui de frugibus et pomis parantur, (for *flesh* is altogether evil, and contains nothing divine,) si ad sanctos, id est, ad Manichæos veniant, per eorum castitatem, et orationem, et psalmos, quicquid in eis est luculentum et divinum purgatur, id est, ex omni parte perficitur, ut ad regna propria sine ulla sordium difficultate referatur. But in the bodies of servants of the Prince of darkness, in which the evil soul has the ascendancy, such a separation is hindered. For the evil soul appropiates to itself all the food they take, and retains the particles of celestial matter in bondage. And hence, a holy man cannot give food to such men. Says *Athandsius*, (Historia Arianor. ad Monachos, Opp. tom. i. p. 381.): Παρὰ Μανιχαίοις ἔλεος ὀυκ ἐστὶν, ἀλλὰ καὶ ἐχθρὸν ἐστὶ παρ' ἀυτοῖς τὸ ἐλεεῖν πένητα. Apud Manichæos nulla est commiseratio, resque illis odiosa est pauperem (He should add: *non Manichaeum*) miserari. This was apparently very criminal in them: but it was less so, than it appeared to be; and it was rather superstitious, than criminal, if duly considered. For *first*, the Manichæans were kind and liberal to the poor of their sect. They wholly maintained the ***Elect*** among them, as will be shown hereafter; and they undoubtedly succoured those of the *Auditors* who were needy. But, *secondly*, their Auditors were forbidden to give to the indigent of other sects, bread, water, and those aliments which spring from the earth, with which they supposed some portion of celestial matter to be mixed. Yet, *thirdly*, they might, to such baggars give *flesh*. For, as flesh belonged wholly to the world of darkness, and was intirely destitute of celestial matter, after the soul left it at the death of the animals, there was nothing to hinder their giving it to them. Moreover, *fourthly*, it was lawful to give such persons *money*, with which they could buy food if they wished. As I have said, there was *superstition* in this regulation; and I will add, foolish and ridiculous superstition: but as for that great *sin*, which their enemies found here, and also learned men of this age, I do not see it. For it is substantially the same, to give a person *money* with which he can buy food, as to give the food itself.—I have placed this prohibition among the rules of the severe discipline of the Manichæans, but in reality it was only a part of the laxer discipline, or a rule of duty for those called *Auditors*. For the ***Elect*** or more perfect, were absolute paupers, and lived entirely on the gratuities of the *Auditors*. They had neither money, nor bread, nor houses, nor barns, nor fields, nor anything superfluous; and therefore, they could not give either bread, or flesh, or money to mendicants.

The *signaculum of the bosom* required perfect chastity, and forbid all lust, unchastity, and even marriage. For the distinction of sexes and the procreation of children, as it is well known, the Manichæans believed to be a cunning device of the Prince of darkness, by which souls are bound up in bodies, [p. 859.] the empire of darkness in this world extended, and the return of the light, or the celestial matter, to God, impeded. And, therefore, they enjoined upon all their disciples all possible continence and virginity, and upon the *Elect* they imposed perfect celibacy. According to their views, whoever procreates a body, begets a prison for a celestial soul; and, by the gratification of lust, he serves the Prince of all evil. Hence, married persons, wishing to be admitted to the rank of the *Elect*, were required forthwith to put away their wives and husbands. *Faustus*, (apud *August.* L. v. c. 1. p. 140.) says: Omnia mea dimisi, patrem, matrem, uxorem, liberos. This point does not need elaborate proof, being so perfectly well known, that no one doubts it. In place of all, see the passage in *Faustus*, (L. xxx. c. 4. p. 316.) Some one objecting to him, that the Manichæans were the persons prophetically foretold by St. Paul, 1 Timo. iv. i: Discedunt a fide, intendentes doctrinis dæmoniorum, prohibentes nubere; *Faustus* discusses the subject largely, and denies that his sect prohibited marriage; because, so strong is the force of nature, that to attempt to suppress it, would border on madness. He says: Demens profecto ille, non tantum stultus putandus est, qui id existimet lege privatâ prohiberi posse, quod sit publicâ concessum; dico autem hoc ipsum nubere. Yet he confesses, that they exhorted the people to avoid matrimony: Nos hortamur quidem volentes, ut permaneant (coelibes,) non tamen cogimus invitos, ut accedant. Novimus enim, quantum voluntas, quantum et naturæ ipsius vis etiam contra legem publicam valeat, nedum adversus privatam, cui respondere sit liberum: Nolo. Nor does he deny, that absolute chastity was required of the *Elect*. And this regulation he defends, by the words of Christ, Matth, xix. 12, at the same time calling Christ, Professionis puellarum coelibem sponsum. He says: Quid de magistro ipso dicemus ac sanctimonii totius auctore Jesu, qui tria genera taxans spadonum, eis palmam attribuit, qui se ipsos spadones fecerunt propter regnum coelorum, significans virgines et pueros, qui nubendi ipsa a cordibus suis exsectâ cupiditate, spadonum vice in ejus ecclesiâ semper, tanquam in domo regia conversentur. Et hoc vobis doctrina videtur dæmoniorum? From this difficult part of his discipline, *Manes* exempted the common people, who were called *Auditors*. Respecting the milder discipline appointed for the *Auditors*, we shall speak when we come to treat of that order of persons. Some parts of it, however, have already been cursorily noticed.

§ XLIX. **The Return of holy Souls to the World of Light.** So many souls as receive *Jesus Christ* for the Son of God and Savior, and, forsaking the worship of the Prince of darkness and his associates, serve only the Father of Light, and obey with all their [p. 860.] might the perfectly holy law enacted by Christ, and constantly resist the desires of the evil soul; are becoming gradually purged from the pollutions of vicious matter. This process, indeed, the Prince of darkness, both personally and by his ministers and satellites, strives with all his power to retard: But the Holy Spirit, resident in the ether, aids the struggling souls, that they may more easily escape his snares and overcome the perpetual temptations.(¹) And to those souls which occasionally succumb and give the reins to the evil soul, as is not uncommon, the gate of sorrow and repentance is open, by which the pardon of their offences may be obtained from God.(²) Yet the entire purgation of souls cannot be effected in the body. Therefore, these souls, when released from the body, must undergo a two-fold lustration after death; the first by pure water, and the second by fire. That is, they are first elevated by the sun's rays, and pass into the moon, which is composed of good water: in that they are purified during fifteen days, and then they proceed to the sun, the good fire of which entirely takes away what defilement remains; and thence they go perfectly clean and bright to their native country.(³) And the body, which they left on the earth, being composed of evil matter, returns to its original state, and will never be resuscitated.(⁴)

(1) That the Manichæans believed the Holy Spirit, resident in the air, and God in general, to aid and assist souls conflicting with the Prince of darkness, the body and the evil soul, in order to their victory, there can be no doubt. *Faustus*, (L. xx. c. 1. p. 237.) mentions: Vires ac spiritalem profusionem Spiritus Sancti, quam (dicit) tertiam Majestatem. And *Manes* himself, in the beginning of his Epistola Fundamenti, (apud *August.* Disput. i. cum Felice, p. 341.) says: Pietas Spiritus Sancti intima vestri pectoris adaperiat, ut ipsis oculis videatis animas vestras. And *Secundinus*, a Manichæan, (in his Epist. ad *August.* § 1. p. 260.) says much about the aid, which all the three divine Persons afford to good souls, against the efforts and the machinations of the Prince of evil. After giving thanks to the Father, the Son, and the Holy Spirit, for affording him an opportunity for a discussion with Augustine, he proceeds thus: Nec mirum: Sunt enim (Pater, Filius, Spiritus Sanctus) ad omnia bona præstanda et ad omnia mala arcenda satis aptissimi, quique tuam benevolentiam suis defendant propugnaculis, eripiantque ab illo malo—quod paratum est, ut veniat. - - Nam dignus es, qui ab iisdem talia munera consequaris, iidemque veritatis tuæ nutritores efficiantur, vere lucerna, quam in cordis tui can- [p. 861.] delabro dextra posuit veritatis, ne furis adventu thesauri tui dilapidetur patrimonium, - - illumque a nobis repellant atrocem spiritum, qui hominibus timorem immittit et perfidiam, ut animas avertat ab angusto tramite Salvatoris: cujus omnis impetus per illos principes funditur, contra quos se Apostolus, in Ephesiorum Epistola (Ephes. vi. 12.) certamen subiisse fatetur. - - Hoc Paulus, hoc *ipse testatur Manichæus.* Non ergo armorum pugna est, sed spirituum, qui iisdem utuntur. Pugnant autem animarum gratiâ. Horum in medio posita est anima, cui a principio natura sua dedit victoriam. Hæc si *una cum Spiritu* virtutem fecerct (—The Manichæans, therefore, did not suppose the saints alone and unaided, repressed the instincts of nature and the motions of the evil soul, but they had the Holy Spirit assisting them—) habebit cum eo vitam perpetuam,

illudque possidebit regnum, ad quod Dominus noster invitat. Nor does *Augustine* deny, that the Manichæans had no doubts of the grace afforded to men in conflict with the evil Principle, strengthening, assisting, and confirming them. For, in repelling the calumny of the Pelagians, who charged catholic Christians with having the same views of human nature with the Manichæans, (contra duas *Epistolas* Pelagianor. L. ii. c. 2. Opp. tom. x. p. 286.) he says: Manichæi meritis naturæ bonæ, Pelagiani autem meritis voluntatis bonæ, perhibent divinitus subveniri: Illi dicunt: Debet hoc Deus laboribus membrorum suorum; isti dicunt: Debet hoc Deus virtutibus servorum suorum. *Augustine* apprehended the sentiments of the Manichaeans correctly. For, as they supposed that the good soul did not come voluntarily into this world and into these bodies, but involuntarily, and by a sad misfortune; and as they moreover believed the rational soul to be a portion of the divine nature, or of eternal light, and therefore ever remaining entire, and neither vitiated nor capable of vitiation; consistency required them to maintain, that God was compelled by justice, to aid these holy souls toiling in bodies and combatting with vile matter. It is therefore certain, that the Manichaeans promised divine grace and the assistance of the Holy Spirit to their people. But in what way and manner the Holy Spirit aids souls, or with what energy he illumines them, and by what means he moves them, I do not find anywhere explained; and perhaps, the Manichaeans gave no explanations. They were ignorant of *spiritual* substances, and supposed both the human soul and the Holy Spirit to consist of a subtile kind of *matter* or of light. And therefore, in a manner very different from what we believe, they must have supposed the Holy Spirit operates on minds, or moves and guides them.

(2) The Manichæans ascribed great efficacy to repentance, in restoring souls accidentally lapsing, and in averting the retributions of the divine Judge. This has been already demonstrated from some passages in *Augustine.* I will now explain the subject more fully, and confirm it by a splendid passage from a celebrated and ingenious Manichæan.—*Manes* made repentance [p. 862.] to consist in sorrow for sins unintentionally committed. For, as we have showed, the soul, which is a portion of eternal light, or of the divine nature, and absolutely unchangeable,—cannot sin in the proper and true sense. But it is said to sin, when it suffers the evil soul to follow and obey its lusts and instincts: and whenever it does so, it increases and confirms its own filthiness and servitude. And this negligence is regarded by God, just as if it had consented to the criminal deeds of the evil soul; which, however, was impossible from its nature. Moreover, what is said of the soul's sinning, must be understood especially of enlightened souls; that is, of such as have attained a knowledge of the truth, or, as the Manichæans speak, such as *have a knowledge of themselves;* such as have learned, either from the instruction and books of *Manes*, or in some other way, the origin of this world, the distinctness of good and evil, the source of evil, their own divine nature, &c. For, souls remaining in darkness, and in ignorance of these things, go astray, indeed, and have no prospect of salvation after death; yet they do not properly commit sin, because no one can transgress a law, of which he has no knowledge. Therefore peni-

tence, with Manichæans, was *the sorrow of an enlightened soul, arising from a consciousness of negligence in repressing the desires of the evil soul.* The effect of this sorrow is, that it exempts from those punishments in hell, which souls merit, by consenting to the desires of the evil soul, after they have received a knowledge of the truth. Repentance, therefore, does not purgate the soul, and open the way for its salvation or return to heaven; nor does it free the soul from the discomfort of a migration into another body: but it removes the fear of hell, or induces God to remit the penalty of hell-fire to the sinner. Says *Secundinus*, (in his Epist. ad *August.* § 2. p. 369.): Si anima a spiritu vitiorum (so he called *the evil soul*, in which all the desires and appetites reside,) incipiat trahi et consentiat, ac post consensum pœnitudinem gerat, habebit harum sordium indulgentiæ fontem. Carnis enim commixtione ducitur, non propria voluntate. At si cum seipsam cognoverit, consentiat malo, et non se armet contra inimicum, voluntate sua peccavit. Quam si iterum pudeat errasse, paratum inveniet misericordiarum Auctorem. Non enim punitur, quia peccavit, sed quia de peccato non doluit. At si cum eodem peccato sine veniâ recedat, tunc excludetur - - tunc ibit cum diabolo ad ignem originis ipsius.

(3) Of the return of the souls purgated in the body, to the world of light, *Augustine* and the other adversaries of the Manichæans, treat only briefly and generally. *Augustine*, for instance, (de Hæres. c. 46. p. 11.) says: Quidquid undique purgatur luminis per quasdam naves, quas esse lunam et solem volunt, regno Dei, tanquam propriis sedibus, reddi putant. Quas itidem naves de substantiâ Dei purâ perhibent fabricatas. - - Naves autem illas, id est, duo coeli luminaria, ita distinguunt, ut lunam dicant factam ex aquâ bona, solem vero ex igne bono. And very nearly the same statement is given, not only by [p. 863.] *Augustine* in several other places, but also by the other writers, both historians and disputants. The Manichaeans, therefore, supposed the sun and moon to be two *ships*, in which souls purgated from their filth, were transported to their country: the sun they called the greater ship, and the moon the lesser. But in both ships, the disembodied souls had to undergo a severe lustration, before they were restored to their former happy state, or were borne to their desired haven. For, although the soul while in the body should spare no efforts or diligence in expelling and ejecting the filth of depraved matter, it will never depart pure and luminous out of this dark and filthy body. Its grosser filth is therefore washed off in the good water, of which the moon is composed. But its interior filth, or the minuter particles of malignant matter, which have penetrated deeper into the soul and have vitiated, so to speak, its very marrow, requires a severer lustration by the good fire, of which the sun is composed: and this fire, being kindred with that light of which the soul consists, permeates and pervades it perfectly, and consumes what there is remaining of the evil elements within. And thus the mind, being first washed, and then roasted, becomes bright and shining, and therefore worthy to return to its pristine glory. And as Christ dwells in the sun and in the moon, as we have before showed, hence it is manifest that He, since his departure out of our world, is a Saviour of souls; He perfects their purgation begun in this life, after they leave the body.

What the ancient writers state generally, in regard to the return of souls to the world of light, *Tyrbo* describes more particularly and minutely, in the Acta Disputationis Archelai cum Manete. But these Acta, as published in Latin by Laur. Alex. *Zaccagni*, and by Jo. Alb. *Fabricius*, (in the Opp. *Hippolyti*, tom. ii.) are much corrupted, and greatly deformed by numerous blemishes. And hence, *Epiphanius*, who had access to earlier and purer Greek copies of these Acts, should be consulted and compared, in order to a better understanding of this amusing fable of *Manes*, or rather of the Magi, his master. *Tyrbo*, (§ 8. p. 12. &c.) thus begins: Cum venisset Filius Dei, machinam quandam concinnavit ad salutem animarum, id est, rotam statuit habentem duodecim urceos, quae rota per hanc sphæram vertitur hauriens animas morientium, quasque luminare majus, id est, sol radiis suis adimens (in the Greek of *Epiphanius*, λαβὼν, *sumens, attrahens*,) purgat et lunæ tradit, et ita adimpletur lunæ discus. Naves enim vel translatorias cymbas esse dicit (*Manes*) duo ista luminaria. *Tyrbo* tells wonders! For, what, pray, is that *wheel*, furnished with twelve water-pots, and whirled and turned about by a sphere, which the Son of God constructed? But *Epiphanius*, (Hæres. lxvi. § 10. p. 626.) partially explains the enigma, and corrects the errors of *Tyrbo*, or perhaps, of his translator and transcribers. I [p. 864.] will give only *Petavius*' Latin version of *Epiphanius*, which is sufficiently faithful: Sapientia illa sidera in cœlo collocavit - - et illam duodecim elementis, ut Græcis placet, constantem machinam produxit. (μηχανὴν διὰ τῶν δώδεκα στοιχείων.) Quibus ab elementis affirmat mortuorum hominum et aliorum animalium animas in altum splendidas et collucentes evehi, unde in scapham ferantur. Solem quippe et lunam navigia quædam esse existimat. We here remark:—*First*, The erection of the machine in question, is not here ascribed to the Son of God, as it is by *Tyrbo*, but to the wisdom of the Being who placed the stars in the sky, or the Being called the *Living Spirit* by the Manichaeans; a very different personage from the Son of God.—*Secondly*, There is no mention of a *wheel*, nor of twelve water-pots, but only of a *machine* composed of twelve *elements*. The words *rota* and *urceus* were metaphorical terms, here used by the Manichaeans in the manner of the Persians. In place of them *Epiphanius* gives the proper terms.—*Thirdly*, The *machine* is the same that the Greeks mention. This leads us to believe it to be *the heavens;* which the Manichaeans compared to a wheel, because the heavens rotate or turn around like a wheel. And this being admitted, it is at once evident, that the twelve *elements* (στοιχεία) must be the *twelve celestial signs*, which the Manichaeans compared to water-pots. This conjecture was before made by *Beausobre*, (vol. ii. p. 503.) but upon other grounds: for he did not call in *Epiphanius* to aid him, who, as I suppose, establishes the point. If there were room for it, and my plan would allow it, I could show from the Greek writers, that the celestial signs were by them called στοιχεία or *elements*.—*Fourthly*, These twelve elements take up the purified souls, as they leave the body, and bear them to the moon, there to be purgated. This then was the opinion of the Manichaeans: That the better souls, which had carefully attended to their purgation while in the body, were borne by the orb of signs, the *Zodiac*, as the Greeks named it, up to the moon: and, to enable them more easily and expeditiously to perform the journey, they were aided by the light and influence of the stars. Nor was *Manes* alone in this belief: For some philosophers, and some sects of Gnostics, believed that souls returned to God, or to their celestial country, along the orb of signs. See *Clemens* Alexand. (Stromat. L. v. p. 538.) who thinks *Plato* was of this opinion: and *Macrobius*, (in Somnium Scipionis, L. i. c. 12. p. 60. 61.)—Let us now follow the souls escaping from the body. Their first station was in the moon: which, being a sea of celestial *water*, was admirably fitted to wash off the external filth of souls. Fifteen days the souls swam in this celestial ocean: and when these days terminated, the moon emptied itself, by transferring the well washed souls to the sun, to be more perfectly lustrated. On this subject, *Tyrbo* is not sufficiently explicit: but *Epiphanius*, (l. cit. § 10. p. 626.) happily explains it, thus: Navigium minus pro lunae crescentis spatio onus quindecim diebus vehit, idque demum, confecto post xv. diem cursu, majus in navigium, [p. 865.] solem videlicet, exponit.—This puerile fable was invented by the Magi, or by *Manes*, to explain the cause of the waxing and waning of the moon. These subtle philosophers, observing that the moon was sometimes luminous and sometimes dark, that it increased and decreased; and, from their consummate ignorance of astronomy, being unable to ascertain the cause of these changes in the moon's appearance,—explained this great mystery to their disciples, by ascribing it to the return of souls to the world of light. The moon in creases and becomes luminous, according to these acute men, when souls, those particles of light, are congregated there in great numbers; and it decreases and loses its light, when it transfers to the sun these shining souls, which illumined its waves. Says *Tyrbo*, (l. cit. p. 13.): Cum repleta fuerit Luna, transfretare animas ad subsolanam partem, et ita Apocrysin detrimentum (luna) patitur, cum onere fuerit relevata, et iterum repleri cymbam et rursus exonerari, dum hauriuntur per urceos animae. The moon was said, by the Greek Astronomers, to make its *Apocrysin*, when it became old or waned. *Epiphanius* states the same thing, (l. cit. c. 22. p. 639.): Plena est alias luna, alias luce privatur, quod eam animae repleant. Also *Alexander* of Lycopolis, (contra Manichaeos, p. 15.) and *Simplicius*, (comment. in Epictet. p. 167.) and many others.—Were these persons worthy of high commendation from learned men, for their knowledge of philosophy and their acumen, and to be placed above the ancient Christians in intelligence?—After fifteen days spent in the moon, the moon approached the sun; and then the souls passed from the lesser ship into the greater, the sun, where they sustained a new and more thorough purgation. How long a time was required for this second lustration, I do not find any where stated. The tediousness of it was relieved by the agreeable society which they enjoyed in the sun. For Christ himself, the Saviour of souls, was present in the sun; and besides him, many celestial beings, eminent for their virtues. I shall hereafter cite a splendid passage from the seventh Book of *Manes'* Thesaurus, which will confirm a large part of these statements. The allotted time having passed, the sun transferred the souls to their native country, the world of light. Says *Tyrbo* (in the Acta Archelai, p. 13.): Cum igitur luna (here is an error of *Tyrbo* or the transcriber: it should read: *Sol*, the *sun*,) onus quod gerit, animarum saeculis (τοῖς Ἀιῶσι, the *Æons*, as the Gnostics called them, agreeing in many things with *Manes*,) tradiderit Patris, permanent illæ in columnâ gloriæ (ἐν τῷ στύλῳ τῆς δόξης,) quod vocatur aër perfectus. Hic autem aër (—The Latin translator, who often blunders, here incorrectly read: ἀνήρ. and therefore translated it: *Vir perfectus;* which makes no sense. In *Epiphanius*, the reading is ἀήρ—) est columna lucis, repleta est enim mundarum animarum. By this *air*, in which the happy souls dwell, undoubtedly, must be understood, that which *Photius*, (Bibliotheca Cod. clxxix. p. 405. 406.) from *Agapius* a Manichaean, thus describes: [p. 866.] Θεολογεῖ δὲ καὶ τὸν ἀέρα κίονα αὐτὸν καὶ ἄνθρωπον ἐξυμνῶν. Aerem vero (*Agapius*) tanquam Deum praedicat, columnam eum et hominem cum laude vocans. *Epiphanius* expresses the views of *Tyrbo*, or rather of *Manes*, more concisely and more exactly, thus: Solem vero sive majorem illam navim in aeternam vitam (—In the Greek it is: εἰς τὸν τῆς ζωῆς αἰῶνα. that is: *in aeonem vitae.* For the Gnostics and the Manichaeans apply the name of *Æons*, not only to the eternal and unchangeable *Beings* descended from God, but sometimes also to their residence or habitation. This *Æon vitae*, therefore, is the *region* where is true and never ending *life*—) et terram beatorum animas transmittere putant. In another passage, (§ 22. p. 640.) *Epiphanius* neatly and vivaciously expresses the thing thus: A lunâ tanquam minori navigio animas exonerari putat et intra solem recipi atque in ævum beatorum (—So *Petavius* translates the Greek: εἰς τὸν τῶν μακάρων αἰῶνα,) exponi. What is here called *aeon vitae* and *aevum beatorum*, we have found *Tyrbo* calling στύλον, *columna gloriæ et lucis*, and *aërem perfectum. Beausobre* supposes this pillar to be the *milky way:* in which, as we learn from the Somnium Scipionis of *Cicero*, and its expositor *Macrobius*, many of the ancients supposed the happy souls to reside. But I do not attribute much weight to this conjecture. *Manes* himself, (in the seventh Book of his Thesaurus, from which *Augustine* gives a long extract, in his treatise de natura boni, c. 44. p. 366. 367.) describes the sun and moon: Naves esse lucidas, quæ ad evectationem animarum atque ad *suæ patriæ* transfretationem sunt præparatæ. Therefore, according to the founder of the sect, souls return to their *native country*. But that is the *world of light*, from which they came down, by command of God, to combat with the Prince of darkness; and it is not the *milky way*, to which the description of the world of light is altogether inapplicable.

(4) That God will resuscitate human bodies, the Manichaeans could not possibly believe. For bodies are works of the Prince of darkness, composed of depraved base matter, and the prison-houses of good souls; and if God should restore them to the purgated and liberated souls, he would strengthen the empire of his enemy, and involve good minds in new perils, calamities and toils. Says *Theodoret*, (Haeret. Fabul. L. i. c. 26. p. 214.): Τὴν τῶν σωμάτων ἀνάστασιν ὡς μύθον ἐκβάλλουσιν. Mortuorum vero corporum resurrectionem tanquam fabulam rejiciunt. And *Augustine*, (de Haeres. c. 46. p. 13.): Christum novissimis temporibus venisse dicunt ad animas, non ad corpora liberanda. The same testimony is given by all writers concerning the Manichaeans and their affairs. And to avoid the force of the declarations of holy Scripture respecting the resurrection of the body, they either pronounced those declarations interpolations by imposters, or explained them mystically, of the renovation of souls by means of divine truth. *Augustine*, (contra Faustum, L. iv. c. 2. p. 140.): Dicitis, [p. 867.] nunc esse resurrectionem tantummodo animarum per praedicationem veri-

tatis, corporum autem, quam praedicaverunt Apostoli, futuram negatis. (Compare L. x. c. 3. p. 157.) See also the extract from *Agapius* a Manichaean, in *Photius*, Bibliotheca Cod. clxxix. p. 404.)

§ L. **Condition of unpurgated Souls after Death.** The Souls that were ignorant of the saving truth, or that neglected their purgation while in the body, or that committed certain great crimes, would, after their exit from their former bodies, pass into other bodies, either of animals, or trees, or plants, or of something else; until they shall fully expiate their guilt, and become prepared to enter on their celestial journey. In this matter, divine justice will regard the different merits of individuals, and will assign purer and better bodies to the more innocent, and more uncomfortable and filthy habitations to the more polluted and deformed.(1) Heavier punishments will fall on the souls which either contemptuously rejected the truth when presented to them, or persecuted its friends and professors, or defiled themselves with crimes of the higher order. For, on leaving the body, such souls will be delivered over to the princes of darkness dwelling in the stars, to be tortured and punished by them, in proportion to their offences, in the bad fire situated beyond our earth. And yet these punishments of hell are to have an end. For, after a certain time, determined by God, has been spent in hell, these souls will be sent again into this our world, and be put into other bodies, to commence as it were a new course, and to resume with more fervor the purgation which they neglected in their former life.(2)

(1) The migration of souls into other bodies, is one of the principal dogmas of *Manes:* and it is a doctrine indispensable to his system. For as God is extremely desirous that all the particles of light, or all the souls, which by a sad misfortune have become connected with material bodies, may be restored to their original state; and as the greatest part of these souls neglect the purgation prescribed by Christ, and give way to the lusts of the body and of the evil soul; it is necessary that divine goodness should afford them opportunity to awake and become vigilant, and should in various ways attempt to reform them. This doctrine, moreover, as well as many others, *Manes* received from the Magi, his instructors; for they all, as *Porphyry* informs us, (de abstinentia a carnibus, L. iv. § 16. p. 165, from *Eubuli* Historia Mithrae,) held the doctrine of the transmigration of souls as most sacred: Δόγμα πάντων ἐστὶ τῶν πρώτων τὴν μετεμψύχωσιν εἶναι. Omnibus Magis (though divided into various classes,) primum hoc et maxime ratum dogma est, dari animarum transmigrationem. But from this brief statement, it cannot be determined whether *Manes* agreed in all respects, or only in part, with the views of the Magi. As we have seen, *Manes* [p. 868.]

exempted a large portion of human souls from the discomforts of a migration into new bodies. Whether the Magi did the same, or whether they doomed all souls without exception, to this process, is not sufficiently known.—The different state of souls on leaving the body, according to the views of *Manes*, as likewise his whole religious system, was professedly expounded by *Agapius*, a shrewd and crafty Manichaean, who, for the sake of concealment, used the common words and phrases of Christians, but affixed to them meanings accordant with the opinions of his master. His work was sufficiently extended and copious, for it consisted of xxiii. Books, and 102 Chapters. From it *Photius* has given us some extracts, (in his Bibliotheca, Cod. clxxix. p. 402.) which are not indeed useless, and may be serviceable to help us understand the subtilty of the later Manichæans in concealing their doctrines; and yet they are more brief than could be wished. Among them, however, is the following neat epitome of the doctrine of the Manichæans, respecting the state of souls when released from the body: Κρατύνει δὲ καὶ τὰς μετεμψυχώσεις, τοὺς μὲν εἰς ἄκρον ἀρετῆς ἐληλυκότας, εἰς Θεὸν ἀναλύων. Τοὺς δὲ εἰς ἄκρον κακίας πυρὶ διδοὺς καὶ σκότῳ. Τοὺς δε μέσως πῶς πολιτευσαμένους, πάλιν εἰς σώματα κατάγων. Probat praeterea animarum migrationes: alios quidem, qui summum virtutis gradum attigerunt, ad Deum facit reverti: alios vero, qui ad fastigium malitiæ pervenerunt, igni tradit et tenebris: inter hos vero, qui medio quodam modo hic vixerunt, eos in corpora iterum detrudit. *Manes*, therefore, distributed departing souls into *three* classes, the *pure*, the *impure*, and the *partially pure*. The *pure*, which had kept the whole law of Christ, went directly to God, and regained their primeval seats: Such were the souls of the perfect Manichæans, whom they called the *Elect*. The *impure*, which had wholly disregarded the law of Christ, were delivered over to the princes of darkness, to suffer the just penalty of their wickedness. The *partially pure*, who had fulfilled their duty in part, were obliged to migrate into other bodies; Such were the souls of those called *Auditors*, who in many things obeyed the body and the instincts of nature. Of the return of purer souls to God, by means of the moon and the sun, we have already spoken; so that it now remains only to speak of the *impure* and the *partially pure*.

Such souls as are *partially pure*, pass into other bodies, until they shall have completed their purgation; and they pass not only into the bodies of men [p. 869.] and animals, but also into those of trees, plants, herbs, &c. For the whole world of nature, as *Manes* most expressly asserts, is full of souls. I will cite only a single passage from Augustine, (de Hæres. c. 46. p. 12.): Animas *Auditorum* suorum (—he means, such of them as live up to their duty,) in *Electos* revolvi arbitrantur, aut feliciore compendio in *escas Electorum*, (melons, cucumbers, herbs, fruits,) ut jam inde purgatæ in nulla corpora revertantur. Ceteras autem animas et in pecora redire putant et in omnia, quæ radicibus fixa sunt, atque aluntur in terra. But from the animals into whose bodies souls may migrate, the Manichæans excepted the very small animals, and particularly fleas, lice, gnats, and other insects; which, they said, were not animals, but the filth of human bodies; and the reason, I suppose, was, that their bodies were thought too small to contain human souls. Says *Augustine*, (contra Adiman-

tum, c. 12. tom. viii. p. 90.): Negant (Manichæi) usque ad ista minutissima animantia revolvi animas humanas posse. Hoc negant, ne tam multarum interfectionum rei teneantur, aut cogantur parcere pediculis et pulicibus et cimicibus, et tantas ab eis molestias sine ulla cædis eorum licentiâ sustinere. Nam vehementer urgentur, cur in vulpeculam revolvi anima humana possit, et non in mustelam, cum catulus vulpeculae fortasse etiam minor sit, quam magna mustela. Deinde si in mustelam potest, cur in murem non potest? Et si in istum potest, (The Manichaeans certainly did admit, that a soul might migrate into a *mouse;* as will be shown.) cur in stellionem non potest? Et si in eum potest, cur in locustam non potest? Deinde in apem, deinde in muscam, deinde in cimicem, atque inde usque in pulicem, et si quid est aliud multo minutius pervenire. Ubi enim terminum constituant, non inveniunt. On this subject *Augustine* reasons in the same manner, (de moribus Manichaeor. L. ii. c. 17. tom. i. p. 550.) where, among other things, he says: Huc accedit illa gradatio, quae, cum vos audirem, nos saepe turbavit. Nulla enim caussa est, cur propter parvum corporis modulum pulex necandus sit (because, not containing a soul. For this was the reason why a flea might be killed.) non etiam musca, quae in faba gignitur. Et si haec, cur non etiam ista paullo amplior, cujus certe fetus minor est, quam illa. - - Ne lonqum faciam, nonne videtis his gradibus ad elephantum perveniri? I know not whether the Manichaeans also excepted from among animals into which souls migrate any of those that are noxious and troublesome to mankind. But I think it quite probable; because we learn from *Augustine* (de moribus Manichaeor. L. ii. c. 17. p. 550.) that they thought some of these animals are not genuine animals, but originated from the dead bodies of men: Impunius ergo occiditur vel anguis, vel sorex, vel scorpio, quos de humanis cadaveribus nasci, a vobis potissimum solemus audire. Perhaps, also, there were some species of trees, plants, and herbs, which they supposed incapable of receiving human souls. But I find nothing written [p. 870.] on the subject.

These transmigrations of the imperfectly purgated souls, are ordered of God in perfect equity, according to the merits of individuals. For as each, while in the body, conducted himself well, or ill, or indifferently, so his new habitation will be either noble or ignoble, either wretched or tolerable. *Tyrbo,* in the Disputation of Archelaus, has said much respecting this doctrine, but very confusedly; and he is apparently not free from errors. I will attempt to systematize the subject. In itself, it is indeed of little importance; yet it may be of use for elucidating some passages in the ancient writers, and for explaining the internal principles of this sect.—*First,* the souls of the *Auditors,* which came the nearest to the virtue practised by the Elect, who neither cultivated the ground, nor slew animals, nor begat children, nor busied themselves with building houses or accumulating wealth, although they pursued other kinds of worldly business, married wives, and ate flesh;—these souls, I say, being purer than others, passed either into the bodies of the *Elect,* or into t e kinds of food most used by the *Elect,* such as melons, cucumbers, olives, potherbs, &c. From such bodies there is direct access to heaven. For, as the Elect live in celibacy, they cannot again infuse souls into new bodies, as others do, by cohabitation. Moreover, the food eaten by the *Elect*, is so purified by their prayers and sanctity, that the souls latent in it, can freely ascend to the world of light. A passage which substantiates this, has just been cited from *Augustine*. I will now add two others of similar import. The first is, (contra Faustum, L. v. c. 10. p. 144.): Fallitis Auditores vestros, qui cum suis uxoribus, et filiis et familiis et domibus et agris vobis serviunt.—Nam eis non resurrectionem, sed revolutionem ad istam mortalitatem promittitis, ut rursus nascantur et vita Electorum vestrorum vivant—aut si melioris meriti sunt, in melones et cucumeres, vel in alios aliquos cibos veniant, quos vos manducaturi estis, ut vestris ructatibus cito purgentur. The other passage is, (de Hæres. c. 46. p. 11.): Ipsam boni a malo purgationem non solum virtutes Dei facere dicunt, verum etiam Electos suos per alimenta, quæ sumunt. Eis quippe alimentis Dei substantiam perhibent esse commixtam, quam purgari putant in Electis suis eo genere vitæ, quo vivunt Electi. A harder lot awaited those (*Auditors*) who pursued agriculture, and especially reapers. Plowmen were promised impunity; if *Augustine* has correctly stated the views of the sect, (de Hæres. c. 46. p. 12.): Auditoribus suis ideo agriculturam (by which, however, many homicides were committed,) arbitrantur ignosci, quia præbent inde alimenta Electis suis, ut divina illa substantia in eorum ventre purgata impetret eis veniam, quorum traditur oblatione purganda. But those who cut down wheat, herbs, potherbs, grass, &c. would, after death, pass into stalks of [p. 871.] grain, grass, or herbs, that they might suffer the same pangs which they had inflicted on grass and herbs. *Tyrbo*, (in Acta Archelai, § 9. p. 15.) says: Messores necesse est transfundi in fœnum, aut in faseolum, aut in hordeum, aut in olera, ut et ipsi desecentur et demetantur. *Tyrbo* adds: Qui manducant panem, necesse est, ut et ipsi manducentur, panem effecti. Yet this cannot be entirely true; for the *Elect* themselves, whose souls go immediately to God at the death of their bodies. ate bread. I therefore suppose, that this is to be understood of such as ate bread, without obtaining a license from the *Elect*. For, the *Auditors* who consulted the interests of their souls, went before the *Elect*, and commended themselves to their prayers, that so they might fearlessly eat their food, and especially bread. Such *Auditors* as slew animals, which was a thing absolutely forbidden, migrated into the bodies of such animals as they had slain. *Tyrbo*, (l. cit. p. 16.): Qui occiderit pullum, et ipse pullus erit, qui murem, mus etiam ipse erit. A heavier punishment was to be endured by those, who had labored to accumulate riches, or had built for themselves convenient houses: Si quis vero est dives in hoc mundo, cum exierit de corpore suo, necesse est eum in corpus pauperis injici, ita, ut ambulet et mendicet. - - Qui autem ædificaverit sibi domum, dispergetur per omnia corpora; that is, he will wander through various bodies. For, as he wished to prepare himself a permanent seat or constant home in this life, his just punishment will be, when released from the body, to have no fixed residence, but to dwell sometimes in one body, and sometimes in another. It was allowed to Manichæan *Auditors*, (but not to the *Elect*, of whom absolute poverty was required,) to hold property of all kinds descending to them from their ancestors; and there were examples of wealthy men among them: such was that *Constantius* of Rome, mentioned a few times by *Augustine*, who was very wealthy and prosperous. But it was criminal to eagerly heap up riches, or to build houses: for all such as indulged their desires and lusts, serve the evil soul and the Prince of evil. Those who committed any great crime, would be punished by divine justice, in proportion to the magnitude and atrocity of their offences. A *homicide*, for instance, as *Tyrbo* says: In elephantiacorum corpora transferetur: that is, will pass into human bodies infected with some species of leprosy, the most loathsome and filthy of diseases. And he who shall have planted a *persea*, (a tree, but of what species I know not.* It was held in the greatest abhorrence by the Manichæans, probably, because its fruit was thought to excite lascivious desires,) necesse est eum transire per multa corpora, usque quo persea illa, quam plantaverat, concidat. Other crimes, doubtless, had also their specific penalties. The *Elect*, as already remarked, if they should swerve from duty, could wash out the stain thus contracted, by repentance. Souls not belonging to the Manichæan community, and destitute of a knowledge of what they called the truth, when life ended, roamed through the bodies of five animals; and, if they became somewhat purgated in these, [p. 872.] they passed into the bodies of Manichæans; but if they wholly neglected their purgation in the five bodies, they were sent to hell. Says *Tyrbo*, (§ 9. p. 15.): Animæ (doubtless, meaning the souls destitute of the light of truth,) in alia quinque (—In the Gr. of *Epiphanius*, πέντε. The Latin translator erroneously says, *quoque.*—) corpora transfunduntur. In horum primo purgatur aliquid ex ea parum, deinde transfunditur in canem, aut in camelum, aut in alterius animalis corpus.

(2) The transmigration of souls into other bodies, was rather a paternal chastisement, or a salutary admonition, than a judicial penalty; or, if you please, it was the penalty for negligence. But there were souls, which either sinned enormously, or contemned God's gentle and wise coercion of the erring, and in a degree added malignity to negligence; and to these divine justice allotted a heavier punishment, and they were therefore sent to hell to be tormented by the demons. For the Manichæans had their hell, though very different from ours. When the *Living Spirit* arranged the material substances, so as to frame our world, he found a mass of *evil fire*, with no mixture of good fire in it, which the vanquished and flying princes of darkness had left behind. And that mass he cast out of this world, shutting it up in a place without our world, I know not where, but probably in the air, lest it should injure this terrestrial globe; and this is the Manichæan hell. Over this noxious fire, which is a portion of the world of darkness, the princes of darkness and their king preside: and as they are stationed in the stars or the regions above us, that fire must be situated in their vicinity. Such souls, therefore, as are distinguished for the magnitude of their crimes, are delivered over to the enemies of God, not indeed to perish, for this the divine goodness cannot permit; but that they may be roasted, as it were, in that fierce and terrible fire, and thus become freed in good measure from the depraved matter which they have absorbed. Some of these souls are sent, immediately on leaving the body, into this fire; but others, after a fruitless peregrination in certain bodies. Of the former of these two classes, besides some perhaps not mentioned by the ancient writers, are:—1st. Those

* Du *Cange*, (Glossar. med. et inf. Latinitatis, tom. iii. p. 277.) supposes it was a *peach tree*, the *malus Persica* of the Latins, which the Greeks called περσέα. *Tr.*

which spurn divine truth, or the religion of *Manes*, and wilfully persevere in their errors. *Tyrbo*, (in the Acta Archelai, § 10. p. 18.) says: Si exierit anima, quæ non cognoverit veritatem, traditur dæmonibus, ut eam doment in gehenna ignis. And, a little after: Si quis sequitur verba ipsorum (Moses and the Jewish prophets,) morietur in sæcula (εις τοὺς αιῶνας, *in longum* ævum,) devinctus intra massam (εις τὴν βωλὸν, namely, *of evil fire*,) quoniam non didicit scientiam Paracliti, (that is, of *Manes*.) Beware of understanding this, of the souls unavoidably ignorant of the truth; these pass into the bodies of various animals, as we have before shown. The souls here intended, were undoubtedly such as [p. 873.] rejected the light of divine truth, and obstinately preferred darkness to light.—2dly. The souls which apostatize from the Manichæan religion, after having embraced it. The Manichæans called deserters from their sect, men destitute of light, or men wholly forsaken by the light. Says *Augustine*, (de utilitate credendi, c. 1. tom. i. p. 35.): Desinant dicere illud, quod in ore habent tanquam necessarium, cum eos quisque deseruerit, qui diutius audisset: Lumen per illum transitum fecit; that is, as *Augustine* himself immediately explains it: A lumine plane desertus est. For those who have cast away the truth, have lost all claim to divine favors, and deserve to be delivered over to the rulers of darkness for chastisement.—3dly. Still more worthy of such punishment, were the souls which obstructed the progress of the religion of *Manes*, and reviled and abused its professors. *Manes* himself, in his Epistola Fundamenti, (apud *Euodium*, de fide, c. 1. in Append. Opp. *August.* tom. i. p. 25.) says: Quæ inimicæ lumini sancto extiterunt, aperteque in perniciem sanctorum elementorum se armarunt, et igneo spiritui (the Demon) obsequutae sunt, infesta etiam persecutione sua sanctam ecclesiam, atque Electos in eadem constitutos cœlestium praeceptorum observatores afflixerunt, a beatitudine et gloria terrae sanctae arcentur—et configentur in praedicto horribili globo.—4thly. Into the evil fire will be sent, the souls which left the body without penitence and sorrow for the sins they may have committed. Says *Secundinus*, (Epistola ad August. § 2. p. 369.): Si cum eodem peccato (anima) sine venia recedat, tunc excludetur, tunc virgini stultae comparabitur, tunc heres erit sinistrae manus, tunc a Domino pelletur ex convivio nuptiarum, nigrarum caussa vestium, ubi fletus erit et stridor dentium, ibitque cum diabolo ad ignem originis ipsius. Non punitur, quia peccavit, sed quia de peccato non doluit.—5thly. The souls which would not supply the *Elect* with food. The *Elect*, as before shown, spent their lives in leisure amid prayer and meditations, and could neither engage in or perform any worldly business whatever; they were also absolute paupers, and wholly destitute of either money or goods. Hence the *Auditors* were required to afford them support. Nor was this any great burden, or an onerous duty, because the *Elect* lived upon bread, water, fruit, herbs, and melons; and also macerated their bodies with frequent fasts. Therefore, such *Auditors* as refused sustenance to these very holy persons, involved themselves in an atrocious sin. Says *Tyrbo*, (in the Acta Archelai, § 9. p. 16.): Qui non præstiterit Electis ejus alimenta, pœnis subdetur gehennæ, et transformatur (after enduring this punishment,) in catechumenorum corpora, usque quo faciat misericordias multas. Consequently, these hard and inhumane *Auditors*, before they passed into other bodies, were subjected to severe punishments in hell.—Of the other class of souls, (on which transmigration was first tried, and then hell-fire,) were:—(a) Such as retained their desires for wealth and riches, even in the bodies of paupers and mendicants, into which they had been sent. Says *Tyrbo*, (in the Acta Archelai, p. 16.): Dives in hoc mundo cum exierit de corpore suo, necesse est [p. 874.] eum in corpus pauperis injici, ita ut ambulet et mendicet, et post hæc (namely, if in this body he did not overcome his thirst for wealth,) eat in pœnas aeternas. (i. e. in the style of the Manichaeans, in pœnas *diuturnas*.)—(b) The souls which, after migrating through the five bodies, retained all their vitiosity. The Manichaeans supposed, that in general souls pass through five bodies of animals in each of which they ought to drop some portion of their filth; but if they did not, they deserved the punishment of hell. For more forceable and energetic medicines are necessary when moderate and gentle ones fail.

But these punishments in hell, to which God sends the more perverse souls have their termination, doubtless, according to the offences of the individuals; and they are salutary to souls. For by that fierce fire a large part of the filthiness which hindered their purgation in the former life, is consumed; and, this being as it were roasted out of them, they are again sent into other bodies, for a new probation, in which they are to conflict again with the body and the evil soul. Says *Tyrbo*, (in the Acta Archelai, p. 18.): Si exierit anima, quae non cognoverit veritatem, traditur daemonibus, ut eam doment in gehenna ignis, et posteaquam correcta fuerit, (μετὰ τὴν παίδευσιν. See here, the salutary influence of these punishments.) transfunditur in alia corpora, ut dometur, (to be purgated.) et ita injicitur in magnum illum ignem usque ad consummationem. He here expresses himself concisely, as he usually does; but it is manifest, that he intended to say: If a soul, after punishment by fire, is sent into other bodies, and still perseveres in its negligence, and follows its lusts, just as in the former life, it loses all hope of salvation, and is again cast into the bad fire, over which the princes of darkness have control; and it will remain in that fire until the end of the world. What will become of it at the end of the world, we shall soon show.—The Manichaeans therefore believed, as other Christians did, though for different reasons, and in a different way, that many souls of sinful men are now in hell, and are tormented by evil demons. What *Tyrbo* states on this subject, is also stated by *Epiphanius*, and by other more modern writers, whose testimonies I need not cite.

§ LI. **The Liberation of the Passive Jesus.** Besides the rational and intelligent souls, those particles of the divine light, there are portions of the celestial elements scattered throughout the natural world, and mixed up with base matter; and these, in various ways, but especially by the heat and influence of the sun, are detached from base matter, and drawn upwards; and, being purgated in the moon and sun, they return to the world of light.(¹) But the son of the First Man, the *Passive Jesus*, whom [p. 875.] the Prince of darkness and his warriors devoured during the first war, and still hold in durance, is gradually liberated by a singular artifice of God. For at certain times God presents to the view of the demon some of the celestial Beings resident in the sun and moon, clothed in the form of very beautiful boys and girls; and on seeing them, the lusts of the demons are so inflamed that they sweat most profusely, and the celestial matter oozing out with the sweat from their huge bodies, falls upon our earth. This celestial matter, thus expressed from the princes of darkness and falling upon the earth, fecundates it and causes it to produce or send forth trees, fruits, plants, salads, potherbs, &c.; and when these are eaten, that which is divine in them, the sentient soul, is detached from depraved matter and escapes, and, being purgated in the moon and sun, ascends to the world of light. And this accounts for the clouds, the rains, the storms, the showers, the lightnings and the thunder. For the Prince of darkness and his associates, becoming enraged and agitated when God frustrates their lustful desires, disturb both heaven and earth, and frequently produce terrible commotions in nature; which, however, are in some respects useful and salutary.(2)

(1) These statements will be easily understood, from what has been said and repeated more than once. Souls pertain to the element *light;* and consequently, they are nearly allied to the nature of God, or rather, they are his offspring. But besides this light, there are four other elements; and innumerable particles of all these elements, in the war of the First Man with the Prince of darkness, became mixed up and joined with the depraved elements. And therefore, previously to the destruction of this world, it is necessary that so much of the celestial elements as adheres to the vicious elements, should be disengaged, and be restored to the kingdom of God. And this God effects in various ways, but especially by means of the heat and rays of the sun. For instance, the sun, by its influences, gradually extracts the particles of good water joined with the bad water in our world, and transmits them when purgated to their native country. And so of all the elements. Our fire is principally evil fire; yet it contains many particles of good fire, and these gradually escape, being elicited by the air which agitates the fire. *Augustine*, (de natura boni, c. 44. p. 365.): Ipsam partem naturae Dei dicunt, ubique permixtam in coelis, in terris, sub terris - - solvi vero, liberari, purgarique non solum per discursum solis et lunae, et virtutes lucis (Beings living in the sun and moon,) verum etiam per Electos suos.

[p. 876.] (2) We now come to that portion of the Manichæan system which, although not destitute of ingenuity, exceeds all the rest in senselessness and folly, according to our apprehensions: I say, according to our apprehensions, for to the people of the East, especially to the Persians, who philosophized more grossly than we do, it was undoubtedly less insipid, and perhaps appeared wise. By the commixture of good with evil, *Manes* would account for all occurrences in the physical world and in human nature. And in many particulars, his plan seemed to succeed pretty well. But in the midst of his course, a great difficulty met him; namely, whence originated the clouds, the showers, the tempests, the soaking rains, the thunders, &c? From God they undoubtedly do not come; for he is perfectly and exclusively good. Although the rains are of some use in fertilizing the earth and causing it to produce fruits and plants and trees, the food of the Elect; yet they also cause many evils and inconveniences to men. But the storms, tempests, thunders, and fogs, appear simply evil and hurtful. Therefore, the Princes of darkness residing in the air or the upper regions, undoubtedly, are the cause of these occurrences in nature. But the rain, though often hurtful, is yet beneficial both to the earth and to its inhabitants: and nothing useful or good can come from the rulers of darkness, who are evil by nature. This difficulty compelled *Manes* again to resort to his commixture of good and evil, and to suppose that a considerable portion of celestial matter still remained in the bodies of the evil demons, notwithstanding the principal part of it, the *light*, had been forced out of them. Still the difficulty was not wholly removed; for it might be asked, What induces the Prince of darkness and his associates to give up the celestial matter contained in their bodies, and to suffer it to descend upon this our earth? That they would do it spontaneously, cannot be believed. It must then be that they are compelled, unwillingly, to relax their hold on the celestial matter. But who can, either by force or by artifice, bring them to relinquish so great a treasure? To free himself from this difficulty, the fertile genius of *Manes* invented a fable, in itself monstrous and void of all reason, yet coinciding very well with his other opinions. He supposed, 1st, That during the first conflict between the good and evil Principles the general of the army of light produced a son:—2dly, That the Prince of darkness and his warriors devoured that son:—3dly, That God, in order to extract gradually from the bodies of the demons and liberate this son of the First Man, (who is a mass of celestial matter, endowed with a sentient soul.) excites the natural lusts of those demons;—4thly, And then suddenly withdraws the spectacle, by which he had inflamed their lustful desires;—5thly, And then the demons, being much agitated, are thrown into violent perspiration, and pour out with their sweat the vital matter contained in ther members.—6thly, This sweat is our rain:—7thly, And the thunders, high winds, tempests [p. 877.] and tornadoes, which often accompany rain, are indications of the rage of the demons when deluded by God with fictitious images.—For the sun and moon, those two divine ships, are full of celestial Beings, or, as *Manes* himself calls them, Angels. And God, as often as he sees fit, transforms some of these Angels into very beautiful boys and girls, and bids them exhibit themselves to the princes of darkness. The boys show themselves to the female demons, and the girls to the male demons. And those extremely libidinous giants, on seeing these very beautiful images, rush to embrace them, eager for coition. But the beautiful Angels flee; and by their flight elude the hopes of their lovers: and hence the amazing heats and violent commotions in their bodies. Their lust first raises a very copious perspiration; and with their sweat, as God intended, they let out the vital and celestial matter: a part of which, mixed with the rain, falls upon our earth, and makes it productive of plants and trees; and a part becomes mixed with the air, and flows into the sun and moon, where it is purgated, and then is transmitted into the realm of light. The sweating princes of darkness meanwhile exhibit terrific evidence of their rage and fury, on account of the flight of the beautiful young men and maidens. Their Lord manifests his rage by terrific roaring, and by darting the malignant fire, of which he has abundance: and these are the thunders and lightning which frighten mortals. He and his associates violently agitate the air, and produce whirlwinds, hale, tornadoes and tempests, and emit dense vapors, which form clouds, obscure the sky, and intercept the rays of the sun; and thus they often put all nature into commotion. *Tyrbo*, (in the Acta Archelai,) relates this absurd fable, though not very accurately or perspicuously, from the oral teaching of *Manes* himself: and *Cyrill* of Jerusalem, (Catecbes. vi. § 34. p. 110.) tells us, he had read it in the books of Manichaeans. *Augustine* and others often mention it, and reproach the Manichaeans with it. (See *Augustine*, contra Faust. L. xx. c. 6. p. 238. and, de Hæres. c. 46. p. 18. and elsewhere.) *Felix*, the Manichaean, tacitly admits and acknowledges it, (in his second Dispute with August. c. 7. 8. p. 348.) Says *Augustine* to him: Dicitis, Deum virtutes suas convertere in masculos ad irritandum concupiscentias dæmonum fœminarum, et eosdem rursus convertere in fœminas ad irritandum concupiscentias dæmonum masculorum, ut cum dæmoniis injiciunt libidinem, accensis in formas confictas a Deo, relaxentur membra eorum et sic evadat pars Dei, quæ ibi fuerat colligata. Hoc tantum opprobrium, hoc tantum sacrilegium credere ausi estis et prædicare non dubitatis. And what reply does *Felix* make? Does he deny the facts? Or assert that the whole is a calumny of their adversaries? Or does he strive to extenuate and explain [p. 878.] away the turpitude of the thing? Nothing of these. He is silent. Silent, did I say? He acknowledges that this fable was taught by his master; and maintains, that Christ taught what equally grates on human ears, respecting the punishments of the wicked in hell: Crudelem asseritis Manichæum hoc dicentem? de Christo quid dicimus, qui dixit: Ite in ignem æternum!—But these many and credible witnesses have not induced the very learned *Beausobre*, to believe that so foolish and absurd a fable could come from *Manes*, whom he regards as no contemptible philosopher: (Histoire critique du Manichée, vol. ii. p. 388 &c.) Manichée n'a jamais porte l'egarement jusque-là. He does not indeed venture to deny, that *Manes* considered the rain to be the sweat of the Prince of darkness, and thunder to be his angry voice: but the rest of the fable he boldly denies, placing it among the false criminations maliciously invented, to bring dishonor upon a man who erred indeed, yet was not wholly infatuated. *Manes*, he supposes, taught his followers that God, whenever he thinks rain to be needed by mankind, exhibits to the princes of darkness a species of *virgin light*, i. e. the purest kind of light, perfectly chaste and spotless; and that they are so charmed and captivated with this delightful spectacle that the sweat flows from them; and when they are deprived of it, they manifest their strong indignation by lightning, clouds, and thunder. The other things were idle whims,

originating in the brains of enemies to the good Persian; and who, from ignorance of the highly figurative Oriental style, transformed *virgin light*, or the most perfect light, into a beautiful virgin.—But *Manes* himself rejects this erudite patron; and demands liberty to retain and assert the opinion, which this worthy man would abstract from him. *Beausobre*, a man of immense reading, and at other times of an excellent memory, was so carried away by his strange eagerness to exculpate and make respectable the ancient heretics, that he could not recollect a long and noted passage, still extant, from the seventh Book of the Thesaurus of *Manes*, in which he not only states but expounds, in a copious and eloquent discourse, that whole fable, concerning which *Beausobre* says, Nothing could be more stupid. The passage is not only in *Augustine*, (de natura boni, c. 44. p. 364, 365.) but likewise, in the same words, in *Euodius*, (de fide, c. 16, p. 26, 27.) That there may be no ground for a suspicion of any misrepresentation, I will cite the passage entire. It will conduce much to a just estimate of the genius of *Manes*; and it will show that the Christians of those times did not deceive posterity by declaring his system folly, and the man himself absurdly ingenious. It reads thus: Tunc beatus ille Pater (God, the Lord of the world of Light,) qui lucidas naves (the sun and the moon,) habet diversoria et habitacula seu magnitudines, (i. e. who has placed in the sun and moon, as their homes, many Angels and celestial Beings,) pro insita sibi clementiâ fert opem, qua exuitur et liberatur ab impiis retinaculis et angustiis atque angoribus (from the bodies of the princes of darkness,) sua vita- [p. 879.] lis substantia: (the son of the First Man, the *Jesus passibilis*, of whom we have already spoken.) Itaque invisibili suo nutu illas suas virtutes, quæ in clarissimâ hac navi (the sun) habentur, transfigurat, (for the Angels, like God himself, are mere lucid matter without form,) easque parere (i. e. *apparere*) facit adversis potestatibus (to the demons,) quæ in singulis cœlorum tractibus ordinatæ sunt. Quæ quoniam ex utroque sexu, masculorum et fœminarum, consistunt, ideo praedictas virtutes partim specie puerorum investium (beardless,) parere jubet generi adverso foeminarum, partim virginum lucidarum formâ generi contrario masculorum; sciens eas omnes hostiles potestates propter ingenitam sibi lethalem et spurcissimam concupiscentiam facillime capi, atque iisdem speciebus pulcherrimis, quae apparent, mancipari, hocque modo dissolvi. Sciatis autem, hunc eundem nostrum beatum Patrem hoc idem esse, quod etiam suae virtutes (that is, these Beings or Angels are of the same nature with God, and were begotten of him,) quas ob necessariam caussam transformat in puerorum et virginum intemeratam similitudinem. Utitur autem his tanquam propriis armis atque per eas suam complet voluntatem. (Behold, the moral character of this stupid fable!) Harum vero virtutum divinarum, quae ad instar conjugii contra inferna genera statuuntur, quaeque alacriaate ac falicitate id, quod cogitaverint, momento eodem efficiunt, plaenae sunt lucidae naves: (the sun and moon.) Itaque cum ratio posceret, ut masculis (daemonibus) appareant eaedem sanctae virtutes, illico etiam suam effigiem virginum pulcherrimarum habitu demonstrant. Rursus cum ad foeminas ventum fuerit, postponentes species virginum, puerorum investium speciem ostendunt. Hoc autem visu decoro illarum ardor et concupiscentia crescit, atque hoc modo vinculum pessimarum earum cogitationum solvitur, (For the princes of darkness

have resolved, never to part with that celestial matter which they have devoured: it doubtless temperates and alleviates their misery. But God so beguiles them with images of youths and virgins, that they forget themselves, and disregard their pernicious plans and purposes;) vivaque anima, (not endowed with reason, but only with life and sensation,) quae eorundem membris tenebatur, hac occasione laxata evadit, et suo purissimo aëri miscetur, ubi penitus ablutae animae ad lucidas naves, (the sun and moon,) quae sibi ad evectationem atque ad suae patriae transfretationem sunt praeparatae. Id vero quod adhuc adversi generis maculas portat, per aestus atque calores particulatim descendit, (namely, by the rain,) atque arboribus, ceterisque plantationibus ac satis omnibus miscetur et caloribus diversis inficitur. Et quo pacto ex ista magna et clarissama nave, (the sun,) figuræ puerorum ac virginum apparent contrariis potestatibus, quæ in [p. 880.] cœlis degunt, quæque igneam habent naturam atque ex isto aspectu decoro vitae pars, quae in earumdem membris habetur, laxata deducitur per calores in terram: eodem modo etiam illa altissima virtus, quae in navi vitalium aquarum habitat, (*Christ* is here intended, whom the Manichaeans made resident in the moon,) in similitudine puerorum ac virginum sanctarum per suos angelos apparet his potestatibus, quarum natura frigida est atque humida, quaeque in coelis ordinatae sunt. Et quidem his quae foeminae sunt, in ipsis formâ puerorum apparet, masculis vero virginum. Hac vero mutatione et diversitate divinarum personarum ac pulcherrimarum, humidae frigidaeque stirpis principes masculi sive foeminae solvuntur, atque id, quod in ipsis est vitale, fugit; quod vero resederit, laxatum deducitur in terram per frigora et cunctis terrae generibus admiscetur. After reading these declarations attentively, can we say, that the ancient Christians did injustice to Manes?—The demons or princes of darkness dispersed about in the upper regions and resident in the stars, are not all of the same nature, nor of the same sex. Some are of a fiery nature, and others of a cold and humid nature: And some are males, and others females. But they all carry in their bodies no small quantity of celestial matter, or of *vital soul*, as Manes calls it. They are all full of unbridled lust; and this they have most unfortunately propagated among mankind through their bodies. And God very sagaciously employs this their innate vitiosity, to extort from them the *vital soul.* The princes of a fiery nature, God excites to let out the celestial matter, by the igneous Beings resident in the sun, clothed in the forms of young men and virgins. The princes of a cold and humid nature, Christ, residing in the moon, moves by means of the lunar Beings. The celestial matter or vital soul, elicited by such deceptions from the huge giants of both sexes in sweat and otherwise, is in part pure and uncontaminated, and in part defiled with the stains contracted in those foul bodies. That which is pure, mingles at once with the virgin air, and mounts aloft to the world of light. But that which has stains, descends with the rains, frosts and showers, to the earth, becomes connected with plants and trees, and causes the *passive Jesus* to shoot forth, which, as *Faustus* says, hangs on all the trees. A ludicrous and amusing philosophy truly, and not unworthy of Persian ingenuity!—This fable, which *Manes* himself announces rhetorically and pompously, others explaim more briefly, in accordance with the oral teaching of Manes, and with the books of

Manichæans. Among these, are *Tyrbo*, (in the Acta Archelai, p. 13, 14.) and *Cyrill* of Jerusalem. *Tyrbo* says: Virgo quædam decora et exornata, elegans valde, furto appetit Principes (masculos,) qui sunt in firmamento a vivente Spiritu educti et crucifixi, quæ, cum apparuerit, maribus foemina decora apparet: foeminis vero adolescentem speciosum et concupiscibilem demonstrat. Sed principes quidem (masculi) cum eam viderint exornatam, amore ejus in libidinem moventur: (All this, we have heard *Manes* himself say: what [p. 881.] follows, is not so clearly stated by him.) et quia eam apprehendere non possunt, vehementer instigantur amoris incendiis excitati: rapti sunt enim libidinis calore: cum enim currentibus post eam anxii effecti fuissent, virgo subito nusquam comparuit. Tunc princeps ille magnus producit nebulas ex semetipso, uti obscuret in irâ sua omnem mundum, qui cum tribulatus fuerit plurimum, sicut homo sudat post laborem, ita et hic Princeps sudat ex tribulatione sua, cujus sudor pluviae sunt: (which are often preceded by thunders and lightnings.) *Cyrill* also, (Catecheses. vi. § 34. p. 110.) more concisely: Imbres ex amatorio æstu oriri statuunt, audentque dicere, esse quamdam in coelo speciosam virginem cum juvene formoso - - illam (virginem) fugere aiunt, istum persequi, atque inde sudorem emittere, quo ex sudore imbrem exsistere. Hæc in Manichæorum libris scripta sunt. Ea nos legimus, dum narrantibus nolumus fidem habere. These absurd notions of the origin of rain, lightning and thunder, induced the Manichæans, when it thundered and lightened, not like other Christians to implore the divine clemency by prayers, but to curse the Prince of darkness, whose voice they supposed they heard. This we learn from *Cyrill*, (l. cit. p. 110.): Tonat Deus et contremiscimus omnes: isti autem in blasphemas voces erumpunt: (That is, they curse the author of the thunder.) Fulgurat Deus, omnesque nos in terram procumbimus: illi autem de coelis con vicia jactant: περὶ οὐρανῶν τὰς δυσφήμας ἔχουσι γλώσσας.

§ LII. Destruction of the World and Consummation of all things.

When the greatest part of souls shall have been recalled to the world of light, and of course the human race be reduced to a few persons, when the celestial matter dispersed through our world shall in various ways have been extracted, and no souls remain on earth, except such as can in no way be purgated and reformed; then will God remove the walls and ramparts by which the evil fire is inclosed; and that fire, bursting from its caverns, will burn up and destroy the fabric of the world. At the same time *Omophorus* will withdraw his shoulders from it, and will suffer this dirty, depraved mass, now divested of all life, to be consumed. After this, the Princes of darkness, being deprived of all celestial matter or light, will be compelled to return to their own wretched country: and in that dreary world they will forever remain.(1) And to prevent their again invading the world of light, God will guard the orb of darkness with a very strong [p. 882.] force: for those souls, whose reformation and salvation are despaired of, like a cordon of soldiers, will surround the world of darkness and guard its frontiers, lest its wretched inhabitants should again issue forth and invade the realm of light.([2])

(1) Our world was created of God, only that the good matter mixed with evil might be gradually detached; and especially, that the souls, those daughters of eternal light, which by the crafty Prince of Darkness had been inclosed in bodies, might be liberated from their prison. This arduous business being completed, and the greatest part of the good matter being restored to its original state, nothing will remain but a deformed mass, filthy, vile and sterile, which ought to be thrown back whence it came. Therefore, when God shall have accomplished his object and recovered his treasures plundered by the evil Principle, a conflagration of this world will ensue. That immensely great Angel, *Omophorus*, who sustains the world on his shoulders, being notified by God that the consummation of all things is at hand, will cast down his burden, the evil fire will burst its barriers, and will consume the whole fabric; and all things will return to their original state. God, with the Beings begotten of him, will lead a life of blessedness in the world of light: and the Prince of darkness, with his associates and friends, will lead a life of wretchedness in the world of darkness. Says *Tyrbo*, (in the Acta Disput. Archelai, § 11. p. 21.): Post hæc omnia, ad ultimum *Senior* cum manifestam fecerit ejus imaginem, tunc ipse *Omophorus* extra se terram derelinquit, et ita dimittitur magnus ille ignis (that evil fire, which the Living Spirit cast out of this world, when he formed the earth, and inclosed within strong ramparts or mounds, and in which the very wicked souls that would not be reformed have been for a time tormented,) qui mundum consumat universum. - - Tunc autem hæc fient, cum statuta venerit dies. What is here said of an Elder's exhibiting his image, is very obscure. But this much is obvious, that by this *Elder*, whoever he may be, God will signify to the world-bearing Atlas, called *Omophorus*, that the end of the world has come. And on learning this, the huge giant will quit his position, and throw down his load, as he had long and ardently wished to do. *Tyrbo*, soon after, proceeds: Post hæc restitutio erit duarum naturarum, (the Latin version has: *duorum luminarium*, i. e. of the *sun* and *moon:* Extremely erroneous. In the Greek of *Epiphanius*, we correctly read: Ἀποκατάστασις τῶν δύο φύσεων The sun and the moon need no restoration. The *duæ naturæ*, in the style of Manichæans, are the *two first principles* of all things, good and evil. The import of the passage therefore is: Those two natures (or substances) will then return to their original state, or that in which they were before the war between the good and evil Principles:) et Principes habitabunt in inferioribus partibus suis: (in the world of darkness, where they dwelt before the war:) Pater autem (God) in superioribus, (in the world of light,) quæ sua sunt recipiens: [p. 883.] (i. e. after all the celestial matter which the princes of darkness had seized, shall have returned to him.)—The burning of our world will be slow and of long continuance. For *Tyrbo* says, that all those celestial Beings, who were concerned in the government of our world, and also the Living Spirit, the

framer of the world, will reside in the sun and moon, until the whole fabric is consumed. And he adds, that he had not learned from *Manes*, how many years the burning would continue. Majori in navi (the sun,) vivens Spiritus (the world-builder,) adhibetur, et Murus illius ignis magni (the *Angel*, the guardian of hell fire, who keeps watch lest this evil fire should burst from its caverns before the appointed time,) et Murus venti (the *Angel*, who guards the winds) et aëris, et aquae, et interioris ignis vivi (i. e. *boni.* Each of the elements had its superintending Angel, or keeper and governor.—) quæ omnia in luná habitabunt, usque quo totum mundum ignis absumat; in quot autem annis, numerum non didici. And I suppose, *Manes* himself did not know the number of these years.—This whole statement of *Tyrbo* is confirmed by nearly all the ancient writers. *Alexander* of Lycopolis, (contra Manichæos, p. 5.) adds moreover, that this fire which is to consume the world, will also consume itself; which it is difficult to conceive: Ἀναχωρισθείσης τῆς θείας δυνάμεως τὸ ἔξω πῦρ, φασί, συμπεσὸν ἑαυτὸ καὶ ἄλλο σύμπαν, ὅ τι δὲ ἂν λείπεται τῆς ὕλης, συγκαταφλέξειν. Segregatâ vero à materiâ omni virtute cœlesti, erumpet ignis externus, et semetipsum una cum omni, quæ restat, materiâ, consumet. The same thing appears to be stated, though less distinctly, by *Titus* of Bostra, (Contra Manichæos, L. ii.) But I omit this passage, to avoid needless prolixity.—The time or day of this conflagration of the world and restoration of all things, none of the ancient writers has indicated. But a modern writer, *Hebed Jesu*, an Armenian, (apud *Assemanum*, Biblioth. Orient. Clement. Vatic. Tom. iii. P. ii. p. 361.) affirms, that the Manichæans believed: Fore, ut in die Dominico hoc sæculum habeat interitum, dissolutionemque omnem post circulum novem mille annorum. But as this statement is neither confirmed nor contradicted by any other writer, it must be held doubtful.

(2) The God of the Manichaeans was cautious and provident, but imbecile, or of moderate power. And he had reason to fear, lest the Prince of darkness, although once vanquished, would again venture to invade the world of light; and if he should do so, the same tragedy as in the former war, would undoubtedly recur. To prevent this great and terrible evil, he enrolled a powerful army of guards, from among the souls which would not be purgated, and therefore could not return to the world of light, and yet could not be given over to the kingdom of darkness because possessed of a divine nature,—of these souls, I say, he formed an army, which should valiantly resist the counsels and machinations of the inhabitants of the world of darkness, and prevent their passing beyond their frontiers. As before shown, the souls which have twice passed through five successive bodies without being reclaimed, are sent to hell, to be tor- [p. 884.] mented in the evil fire until the end of the world. When the world is about to be destroyed, they will be drawn forth from hell, and be made garrison soldiers for the supreme God, or guards of the world of darkness. To these will be added the souls, which the last day will find still resident in the bodies of men, animals, and other things; for these also are such, that their salvation is hopeless. Says *Manes*, in the second Book of his Thesaurus, and in his Epistola Fundamenti, (apud *Euodium*, de fide contra Manichaeos, c. 4. p. 25.): Animae quae negligentiâ sua a labe praedictorum (malorum) spirituum purgari se minime

permiserint, mandatisque divinis ex intergo parum obtemperaverint, legemque sibi a suo liberatore (Christ,) datam servare plenius noluerint, neque ut docebat sese gubernaverint, quae mundi amore errare se a priori sua lucida naturâ passae sunt, atque inimicae lumini sancto extiterunt - - a beatitudine atque gloriâ terrae sanctae arceantur. Et quia a malo se superari passae sunt, in eadem mali stirpe perseverabunt, pacifica illa terrâ et regionibus immortalibus sibimet interdictis. Quod ideo illis eveniet, quia ita iniquis operibus se obstrinxerunt, ut a vita et libertate sanctae lucis alieniantur. Non igitur poterunt recipi in regna illa pacifica, sed configentur in praedicto horribili globo, *cui etiam necesse est custodiam adhiberi.* Unde adhaerebunt his rebus animae eaedem, quas dilexerunt, relictae in eodem tenebrarum globo, suis meritis id sibi acquirentes. When *Augustine*, in his second Dispute with *Felix* the Manichaean, (c. 15. p. 351.) had said, that according to the opinion of *Manes*, many portions of the divine nature would be damned; his antagonist denied the fact, and replied in these words: Hoc, quod dixit sanctitas tua, quia pars, quae se non mundavit ab coinquinatione gentis tenebrarum: et sic dicit Manichaeus, quia non sunt missi in regnum Dei. Hoc enim asseris tu, quia damnati sunt: Sed Manichaeus non hoc dicit, quia damnati sunt, sed ad custodiam positi sunt illius gentis tenebrarum. Yet *Augustine* did correctly apprehend the sentiment of *Manes;* as appears from several passages, but especially from this very lucid one, (de Haeres. c. 46. p. 13.): The Manichaeans say, In nobis sanatum hoc vitium (of lust) nunquam futurum: sed a nobis sejunctam atque seclusam substantiam istam mali, et finito isto saeculo post conflagrationem mundi in globo quodam, tanquam in carcere sempiterno, esse victuram. Cui globo affirmant accessurum semper et adhaesurum quasi coopertorium atque tectorium ex animabus, naturâ quidem bonis, sed quae tamen non potuerint a naturae malae cogitatione mundari. If we estimate the doctrine of *Manes* by these passages, the souls whose filthiness prevents their being received into the world of light, will be stationed within the sphere of darkness, or on its exterior, and will cover the whole sphere like a [p. 885.] garment or outer covering, so as to leave no crevice through which the inhabitants can escape. But *Tyrbo*, (in the Acta Archelai, p. 21.) seems to indicate, that those impure and slothful souls will have their station or camp, not within the world of darkness, but on the intervening space between the world of bliss and the world of misery. He says: Deinde (in the end of the world,) iterum (dæmones) dimittunt animam, (or rather *animas*, which were detained in the evil fire,) quæ objicitur (is opposed to the demons,) inter medium novi sæculi (the world of light,) ut omnes animæ peccatorum vinciantur in æternum. But the two opinions are not so different, as to be utterly irreconcilable.

I have bestowed much labor on the explanation of the Manichaean system, for more reasons than one. None of all the sects that arose among Christians, was more difficult to be suppressed than this; and it still exists, notwithstanding it is regarded as vile and hateful by the Mohammedans as well as Christians. Perhaps also the books of *Manes* are preserved to the present day, and read by his many followers in the eastern countries. There have also been, and still are numerous discussions among learned men, respecting this singular form of religion. Some regard it as not altogether nonsense and folly, but as very dexterously solving all difficulties respecting the origin of evil; while others look upon it as perfectly absurd, and more worthy of brute animals than of men. The candid man will acknowledge, that the system as a whole, and in a general view, displays ingenuity, that it deduces all its doctrines from a very few principles, which have a great appearance of plausibility, and that all the parts of the system are harmoniously consistent. But if we examine it minutely, we shall find in it much that is silly, trifling, and fabulous. For *Manes*, finding that he could not well explain all the changes and operations in nature from the few principles he had admitted, was compelled to tax his ingenuity to invent and devise fables, in order to solve by means of the imagination, what could not be solved by reason. Moreover, the most discerning and ingenious of the Manichæans themselves have admitted, that some of their master's dogmas could not be explained and demonstrated satisfactorily. And among these dogmas, they name in particular, that of *two first principles* of all things, or, as they call them, *two natures;* and the doctrine of the new age or world, (de novo sæculo,) and some others. Yet they contended, that these dogmas, although above human reason, were to be simply believed, because revealed to us by God. Thus *Secundinus* writes to Augustine, (p. 371.): Illud tamen notum facio tuæ sagacissimæ bonitati, quia sunt quædam res, quæ sic exponi non possunt, ut intelligantur: excedit enim divina ratio mortalium pectora: ut puta hoc ipsum, quomodo sint duæ naturæ, aut quare pugnaverit (Deus) qui nihil poterat pati, nec non etiam de sæculo novo, quod idem memorat. What *Manes* taught respecting a new age or world, like several other things pertaining to his system, is at this day almost wholly unknown.

§ LIII. **Public Worship among Manichæans.** The mode [p. 886.] of public worship among the Manichæans was very simple. They had no temples or houses dedicated to God, no altars, no images, no love-feasts, nor any of the ceremonies usually practised by other Christians. When assembled they prayed to God with becoming devoutness, but with their faces turned towards the sun. They sung hymns in praise of God, of the sun and moon, and of the principal Æons; read the books of *Manes*, especially his Epistola Fundamenti; and heard exhortations from their teachers, enjoining the renunciation and subjugation of sinful desires. They observed Sunday as a sacred day, but abstained wholly from food on that day. Among their annual holy days, the most noted was the *Bema*, the day on which they honored with great solemnity the memory of their master, who was cruelly slain by the king of Persia. The Christian festivals commemorative of the birth and baptism of the Saviour, they did not observe; because they denied that Christ was either born or baptized. Easter they observed with other Christians, but with little, or rather with no ceremony. For, believing that Christ only feigned death and a return to life, they supposed that short services were all that the day required.(1)

(1) Of the simple manner in which the Manichaeans worshipped God, *Faustus* the Manichaean discourses exultingly, (apud *Augustinum*, L. xx. c. 1. tom. viii. p. 238 &c.); and as *Augustine* in his reply charges him with no misrepresentation, his statements are undoubtedly correct. Some one had objected, that the Manichaeans *were a sect of Pagans and Gentiles*. This charge *Faustus* first answers, by showing that there was a very wide difference between Manichaeans and the Gentiles. He says; Mea opinio et cultus longe alia sunt, quam paganorum. - - Pagani aris, delubris, simulacris, victimis atque incenso Deum colendum putant. Ego ab his multum diversus incedo, qui ipsum me, si modo sum dignus, rationabile Dei templum puto: vivum vivae majestatis simulacrum Christum filium ejus accipio: aram, mentem bonis artibus et disciplinis imbutam, honores quoque divinos ac sacrificia in solis orationibus, et ipsis puris et simplicibus, pono. The Manichaeans, therefore, had no temples or houses consecrated to God; and no images either of God or saints: Christ to them was in place of all visible representations. Neither had they altars. And lastly, the principal [p. 887.] part of their worship consisted in prayers to God, and those prayers *pure and simple*. If this last clause is true,—and that it is so I will presently show by other testimony,—then it is manifest, that all rites and ceremonies were excluded from their worshipping assemblies, except only the custom of turning the face towards the sun in prayer. In this matter, as in many others, *Manes* followed the example of his countrymen the Persians. For it appears from the testimonies of *Herodotus* and others, collected by Barnabas *Brissonius*, (de regio principatu Persarum, L. ii. § 28. p. 360 &c.) that the Persians deemed it next to insanity, to dedicate temples, images, and altars to the gods.—Having vindicated his sect from this calumny, he turns his artillery in another direction, and endeavors to prove that the Christians were more truly *a sect of Pagans*. In doing this, he again testifies that the Manichaeans disregarded and despised the ceremonies usual among other Christians in that age, and were studious of simplicity in the worship of God. He says: Vos sacrificia (gentium) mutastis in agapas: (The Manichaeans therefore omitted altogether those feasts of love, which the other Christians celebrated.) Vos vertistis idola in martyres, quos votis similibus colitis: (The Manichaeans therefore paid no honors or worship to martyrs, they kept no images of them, and they did not observe their *Natalitia*, or the days consecrated to their memory.) Vos defunctorum umbras vino placatis et dapibus: (This cuts the Christians of those times, who carried wine and food on certain days to the sepulchres of the martyrs, and there held feasts.) Vos solennes gentium dies cum ipsis celebratis, ut kalendas et solstitia: (Therefore the Manichaeans abhorred the practice of the Christians, after the time of Constantine the Great, of annexing the Christian rites, and in a sense giving consecration, to the festal days of the Pagans.) De vitâ certe mutastis nihil. All these things *Augustine* endeavors to excuse; but he denies nothing.—As the Manichaean worship consisted chiefly in prayers, they called their wor-

shipping assemblies *the prayer.* This we learn from *Fortunatus*, a Manichaean, (in his first Dispute with *Augustine*, p. 69.) who inquired of Augustine: Interfuisti (nostrae) orationi? And Augustine replied: Interfui. The subsequent remarks plainly show, that Manichaean assemblies for public worship were intended. And it is worthy of special notice, that *Augustine* confesses that nothing reprehensible occurred in their worshipping assemblies. He disapproves of only one thing, namely, their turning their faces to the sun in prayer. He says: Quamvis orationi vestrae interfuerim, utrum separatim vobiscum habeatis aliam orationem, (They certainly had other worship, as *Augustine* himself informs us soon after; nor does *Fortunatus* deny it,) Deus solus potest nosse et vos. Ego tamen in oratione, in qua interfui, nihil turpe fieri vidi, sed solum contra fidem animadverti, - - quod contra solem facitis orationem. Praeter hoc in illa oratione vestra nihil novi comperi. On other points here stated, we have heretofore treated, so that we need not again remark upon them.

§ LIV. **The exclusive Worship of the Elect. Baptism and** [p. 888.] **the sacred Supper.** Besides the public assemblies, in which the *Elect* or perfect and the *Auditors* or imperfect met together, other and more private conventions for religious objects were held exclusively by the little band of the *Elect.* What was done in these private conventions, or in what manner God was there worshipped, is not known at the present day; the books of the sect being lost, or at least not being known.(1) To the arcane or private worship of the Manichæans, pertained *baptism* and the *sacred Supper.* Baptism, the Manichæans held to be a mere ceremony, which conveyed no benefit whatever to the soul. They did not admit that Christ was baptized; and their fundamental principles forbid their believing that any efficacy existed in water for purifying the divine soul, the offspring of God. Hence they did not require their people to receive baptism: but if any of the *Elect* desired a lustration by water, the leaders of the sect did not oppose their wishes.(2) Of the *sacred Supper* of the Elect, nothing scarcely is known at the present day: for the horrid and obscene rites of it, reported by many of the ancients, lack authority, credibility, and probability; and the genuine followers of *Manes* cannot be taxed with them, without extreme injustice.(3)

(1) Says *Augustine*, (Disput. I. cum Fortunato, Opp. tom. viii. p. 68.): De moribus vestris plene scire possunt, qui Electi vestri sunt. Nosti autem, me non Electum vestrum, sed Auditorem fuisse. - - Quisquis autem vobis opponit quæstionem aliquam de moribus, Electis vestris opponit. Quid autem inter vos agatis, qui Electi estis, ego scire non possum. Nam et Eucharistiam audivi a vobis saepe, quod accipiatis: (It is manifest from this language that the Eu

charist pertained to the arcane mysteries of the *Elect*, and that the *Auditors* were not admitted to it,) tempus autem accipiendi cum me lateret, quid accipiatis, unde nosse potui? All these remarks *Fortunatus* passes by, and therefore approves, or tacitly acknowledges them to be true. Moreover, there is other evidence which puts it beyond controversy, that the *Elect* held secret meetings, from which the *Auditors* were excluded.

(2) Respecting *baptism* among Manichaeans, learned men have disagreed; some affirm that they practised it, others deny it, and others combine the two opinions in some way. The cause of this disagreement is in *Augustine;* who seems in some places to teach, that the Manichaeans despised baptism, while other passages are extant, and some of them in *Augustine*, which bid us believe the contrary. *Tillemonte*, (in his Memoires pour servir a l'Histoire de [p. 889.] l'Eglise, tom. iv. p. 948.) thinks the difficulty cannot be surmounted, except by supposing that the Manichaeans, sometimes, and inconsiderately, (*par fantaisie*) when the bishops happened to take it into their heads, practised baptism; but at other times, when their leaders deemed it expedient, they neglected baptism. But it is wholly incredible, that a thing of this nature should be regulated by no rules among them, and should be left altogether to the caprice of the bishops. *Beausobre*, (in his Histoire du Manichée, tom. ii. p. 715, &c.)—if I do not mistake,—inconsiderately cuts the knot, which he would gently untie. For he tells us, that *Augustine* has deceived us: and he contends, that the Manichaeans not only baptized, but attributed to baptism a purifying influence on the soul, and for that reason they also baptized infants. This extraordinary man would have judged differently, I apprehend, if he had more carefully considered the passages of *Augustine* and others on the subject, and had compared them with each other.—*Augustine* no where says, what learned men consider him as saying.—I will try, if I can disentangle this subject, and lay open the true character of Manichæan baptism.

First: Baptism was undoubtedly practised among the Manichæans. The first witness to this fact is *Cyrill* of Jerusalem, (Cateches. VI. § 33. p. 109.) He says: Ὀυ τολμῶ ἐπὶ ἀνδρῶν καὶ γυναικῶν τὸ λυτρὸν ἀυτῶν διηγήσασθαι. Lavacrum eorum coram viris et mulieribus enarrare non audeo. Seeing that the common bathing was prohibited among the Manichæans, as we have already shewed, the word λυτρὸν must here necessarily mean *baptism*. Besides, *Cyrill* connects this λυτρὸν with the sacred Supper. He therefore here criminates the Manichæans for immersing males and females entirely naked, in the presence of both men and women. If this were the fact, which for many reasons I doubt, they certainly offended against the laws of decency and modesty.—The second witness is *Felix* the Manichæan, who, in his first Dispute with Augustine, (c. 19. p. 344.) derives an argument from baptism, in proof of the existence of an evil Principle opposed to a good one: Si adversarius nullus contra Deum est, ut quid (perhaps it should read: *ad quid*) baptizati sumus? Ut quid Eucharistia, ut quid Christianitas, si nihil contra Deum est.—The third witness is *Augustine*, (de moribus eccles. et Manichæor. L. i. c. 35.) The passage will be cited hereafter.—The fourth witness is *Jerome*, who bitterly inveighs against *Hilary*, a Roman deacon, because he had received into the church persons baptized by

Manichæans; (Dialogo contra Luciferianos, Opp. tom. iv. p. 305.): Diaconus eras, O Hilari, et a Manichæis baptizatos recipiebas?—To these are to be added the testimonies, which will be cited to prove, that baptized Manichæans when received into the Romish and other churches, were not re-baptized.

Secondly: Yet the Manichaeans attributed to baptism no salutary influence on the soul; and, for that reason, they did not require any of their people to receive baptism. With this, *Augustine* sometimes reproaches them; [p. 890.] and whoever understands the opinions of the sect, will readily admit his charge. He says: (de Haeres. c. 46. tom. viii. p. 13.): Baptismum in aqua nihil cuiquam perhibent salutis afferre: nec quemquam eorum, quos decipiunt, baptizandum putant. And (contra duas Epistt. Pelagianor. L. ii. c. 2. tom. x. p. 286.): Manichaei lavacrum regenerationis, id est, aquam ipsam dicunt esse superfluam, nec prodesse aliquid profano corde contendunt. And, (same work, L. iv. c. 4. p. 310.): Quid eis (Pelagianis) prodest Baptismum omnibus aetatibus necessarium confiteri, quod Manichaei dicunt in omni aetate superfluum. And, (contra litteras Petiliani, L. iii. c. 17. tom. ix. p. 208, 209.) *Petelian* having supposed, that baptism was conferred on the Manichaean Auditors, *Augustine* confutes him thus: Petilianus, quod ei placet de illorum (Manichaeorum) baptismo dicat et siribat, nesciens, aut nescire se fingens, non illic ita appellari catechumenos, tanquam eis baptismus quandoque debeatur. Those learned men, who infer from these and some similar passages, that the Manichaeans held all baptism in abhorrence, see in the passages more than they really contain. *Augustine* merely says, that the Manichaeans did not baptize those who came over to their church, and that they accounted baptism to be a mere ceremony. And this may be substantiated, not only from *Augustine*, but from the language of *Manes* himself, (in the Acta Disput. Archelai, § 50. p. 94.) In a discussion respecting the baptism of Christ, *Archelaus* uses this language to *Manes:* Baptisma si non est, nec erit remissio peccatorum, sed in suis peccatis unusquisque morietur. *Manes*, on hearing this, is surprised, and asks with astonishment: Ergo baptisma propter remissionem peccatorum datur? This was as much as to say: You tell me something new and unheard of; that sins are forgiven through the medium of baptism. He therefore disbelieved the saving influence of baptism. *Archelaus* replied to his question: *Etiam:* this *is* my opinion. And *Manes* craftily uses this answer, to disprove the baptism of Christ, and says: Ergo peccavit Christus, si baptizatus est?—*Felix* the Manichaean, in the passage recently quoted, seems, indeed, to admit, that there is some virtue in baptism against the Prince of evil. But learned men have long since remarked, that *Felix* was not perfectly acquainted with the religion he professed: and the testimony of the master is doubtless of more weight than that of the disciple.

Thirdly: But if any of the *Elect* wished to be baptized, it was conceded to them. But no *Auditor* could receive baptism. These propositions will be clear and beyond all controversy, if it can be shown,—I. that, among Manichæans, infants were not received into the church by baptism:—II. that the *Auditors* were not admitted to baptism:—and III. that all the *Elect* were not baptized, but it was left optional with each of them, to receive baptism or not.—I. *Beausobre*, among others, (vol. ii. p. 718 &c.) maintains, that *all* Manichæans, indis- [p. 891.]

criminately, and infants in particular, were baptized with water. In proof of this opinion, a certain passage of *Augustine* is adduced, and then the language of *Manes* himself is appealed to. *Augustine*, in his work opposed to two Epistles of Pelagius, (L. iv. c. 3. Opp. tom. x. p. 309.) seems to say, that *Manes* believed infants to need a Saviour. He says: Quapropter utrosque (the Pelagians and Manichæans) damnat atque devitat, quisquis secundum regulam catholicæ fidei sic in hominibus nascentibus, de bona creaturâ carnis et animæ glorificat Creatorem, quod non vult Manichæus: ut tamen propter vitium, quod in eos per peccatum primi hominis pertransiit, fateatur et parvulis necessarium Salvatorem, quod non vult Pelagius. In the last clause of this passage, some of the learned think, *Augustine* expounds the opinion of the Manichæans. But this is much to be doubted. For, from what *Pelagius* denied, that infants need a Saviour, it never can be inferred that the Manichæans believed the contrary. But, suppose it was as learned men think, and that *Manes*, according to the testimony of *Augustine*, believed that infants need a Saviour, (which, however, for several reasons, is not credible,) what inference can be drawn from it? Can we reason thus: *Manes* believed infants to need a Saviour, and therefore *Manes* required infants to be baptized? I think not. For the first proposition may be true, and yet the second be false.—A stronger argument for their purpose, seems to be found in the language of *Manes* in his Epistle to his daughter Menoch, (apud *Augustinum*, Opere imperf. contra Julianum, L. iii. § 187. tom. ii. p. 833.): Qui (the Catholic Christians) his verbis mihi interrogandi sunt: Si omne malum actuale est; ante quam malum quispiam agat, quare accipit purificationem aquæ, cum nullum malum egerit per se? Aut si necdum egit et purificandus est, licet eos naturaliter malæ stirpis pullulationem ostendere, illos ipsos quos amentia non sinit intelligere neque quæ dicunt, neque de quibus affirmant. A person, on reading this passage cursorily, might easily fall into the belief, that *Manes* here supposes (*purificationem aquæ*) *baptism*, to be needful and salutary to infants; but on a closer inspection, he will change his opinion. *Manes* here argues *ad hominem*, κατ' ἄνθρωπον, as logicians say, from the belief of his adversaries, and not from his own belief; and his argument is this: You Catholics unwillingly establish what I teach, namely, that evil is not, as you say, a negative thing, or *nothing*, (*nihil;* as *Secundinus*, in his Epistle to Augustine, p. 369. explains his opinion of original sin,) but something actually existing and present in mankind. For, you baptize infants, before they have done anything evil, in order, as you say, to purify them. And thereby, you admit that evil really ex- [p. 892.] ists in infants, before they have acted any evil, and that they are (*malæ stirpis pullulatio*) *the sprout of an evil root*, or in a certain sense belong to the Prince of darkness, and are the work of his hands. And in this manner *Julian*, a Pelagian, who was opposing Augustine, understood this passage of *Manes*. He says: Audis (Augustine,) quomodo convinciatur nobis (Manes)? Amentes vocat, nec intelligentes vel quæ dicamus, vel quæ affirmemus, qui malæ stirpis pullulationem negemus, cum baptizemus etiam eos purificante aquâ, qui nullum malum egerint, id est, parvulos. *Manes*, therefore, was laboring to confute the Catholics on their own principles, and not on his!—II. That the *Auditors*, or the imperfect among the Manichæans, were not admitted to baptism, is clearly taught by *Augustine;* who was one of their *Auditors* nine years, and therefore a most competent witness. In his work, contra Epistolam Petiliani, (c. 17. tom. ix. p. 208, 209.) he most explicitly teaches, that *Auditors* among the Manichaeans were not admissible to baptism, or that it was not their custom to baptize them. And the same thing is manifest from the very ancient work entitled, Commonitorium, quomodo agendum sit cum Manichæis qui convertuntur, usually ascribed to *Augustine*, and printed with his works, (tom. viii. Appendix, p. 34.) For we clearly learn from it, that Manichæan *Auditors*, when they went over to the Orthodox Christians, were admitted to the rank of *Catechumens*, that is, such as had not yet been baptized; but if any of their *Elect*, who had received baptism among the Manichæans, were converted, they were enrolled among the *Penitents*, or such as did not need baptism. Unusquisque (of the converted Manichæans,) det (to the bishop) libellum confessionis et pœnitentiæ suæ atque anathematis, petens in ecclesia vel *Catechumini*, (that is, if he had been an *Auditor* among the Manichæans; as appears incontrovertibly by what follows:) vel *Pœnitentis*, (that is, if he had been one of the *baptized Elect;* which also will be put beyond all doubt, by what I shall presently quote,) locum. - - - Nec facile admittantur ad baptismum, si Catechumeni sunt, (Therefore the *Auditors* were unbaptized persons, whose place among Christians was that of *Catechumens*,) nec ad reconciliationem, si pœnitentiæ locum acceperint, (For to the *Elect* who had been baptized among the Manichæans, the church did not deem baptism to be necessary, but only *reconciliation* or admission to fellowship,) nisi periculo mortis, urgent vel si eos aliquanto tempore probatos esse, cognoverit episcopus.—III. *All the Elect* among Manichæans did not receive baptism, but only such as requested it. This also is demonstrated by the same Commonitorium, which manifestly discriminates between the baptized and the unbaptized Elect: Electis vero eorum, qui se converti dicunt ad Catholicam fidem, etiamsi et ipsi hæresim anathemaverint, non facile dandæ sunt litteræ, sed cum Dei servis esse debebunt, sive Clericis, sive Laicis in monasterio, donec appareant penitus ipsa superstitione caruisse: et tunc vel baptizentur, *si non fuerint baptizati* (Therefore, all the Elect were not baptized,) vel reconcilientur, si (being already baptized) pœnitentiæ locum acceperint.

Fourthly: Such of the *Elect* as chose to be baptized, must remain in [p. 893.] the class of the *Elect*, and might not change their manner of life. The mode of life prescribed to the Elect, was, as we have seen, exceedingly severe and disagreeable; and those who found by experience, that they could not endure its rigors, might pass over to the class of *Auditors*, who were subjected to a much milder law. But those who received baptism, deprived themselves of this privilege, and might in no case recede from their adopted rule of life. This, if I do not wholly misapprehend, is confirmed by *Augustine*, (de moribus ecclesiæ et Manichæor. L. i. c. 35. tom. i. p. 531, 532.): Quid calumniamini (vos Manichæi), quod fideles jam baptismate renovati procreare filios, et agros ac domos, pecuniamque ullam posidere non debeant? Permittit hoc Paulus. According to the Manichaean principles, baptized persons were perpetually bound exclusively to the rigorous rules of the *Elect*, which forbid their procreating children, or possessing any property whatever. But we have shown, that all the *Elect* did not receive baptism: we must therefore conclude, that such ones might relinquish that rule of life. And this, doubtless, was the reason why *all* the Elect did not desire baptism.

With what forms and rites the Manichaeans baptized their *Elect*, who were doubtless esteemed holier and better than other people, no one of the ancients has informed us: for this was a part of the sacred arcana of the sect. But learned men very justly suppose, they baptized with water, and in the name of the Father, Son and Holy Spirit. We have already seen, from the *Commonitorium* ascribed to Augustine, that the baptized Elect were admitted, by the Latin church, among *Penitents*, and were not to be again baptized. And this is confirmed by an Epistle of *Leo* the Great, (Epist. viii. ad episcopos per Italiam, tom. i. p. 215.) in which he writes that he, de voragine impietatis suae confessos, pœnitentiam concedendo, levasse certain Manichaean doctors, whom he found at Rome: and he makes no mention whatever of a renewed baptism. It is also confirmed more distinctly, by the prayers of *Augustine*, at the close of his book de natura boni, (c. 28. p. 368.) where he says: Dona nobis, Deus, ut per nostrum ministerium, sicut jam multi (Manichaeorum) liberati sunt, et alii liberentur, *et sive per sacramentum sancti baptismi tui*, sive per sacrificium contribulati spiritus et cordis contriti et humiliati in dolore *pœnitentiæ*, remissionem peccatorum accipere mereantur. These sentiments accord exactly with the *Commonitorium.* Some Manichaeans were received into the church, by baptism; and others, without baptism, by mere penitence. Now, if this was the fact, the two following things were undoubtedly true: *first*, that not all, but only some Manichaeans had been baptized: and *secondly*, that the Manichaeans who had received Manichaean baptism, were not again baptized, but were merely [p. 894.] purified by penitence. The Latin church accounted Manichaean baptism legitimate and valid. But how could they so esteem it, if the Manichaeans baptized in a way and manner different from that prescribed by Christ to his followers? For the Latins accounted all baptisms vain and useless, in which any other substance than water was employed, or in which the names of the Father, Son and Holy Spirit were not used. I therefore suppose, *Turibius*, (a Spanish bishop of Astorga,) must have been misled by rumor or misapprehension, when, in an Epistle published among the Epistles of *Leo* the Great, (tom. i. p. 232.) he states that the Manichæans baptized with oil.

(3) The passages from *Felix* the Manichæan, and *Augustine*, which I recently quoted, when treating of baptism and the sacred rites of the Elect, demonstrate that the *Elect*, and they only, among the Manichæans, celebrated the holy supper. *Augustine*, who had been only an *Auditor*, did not know, what the *Elect* might receive in the holy supper, or in what manner the supper was administered. This portion of the secret worship of the Manichæans, therefore, lies wholly in the dark. Some learned men have conjectured, that they used water instead of wine; because it was not lawful for the *Elect* to drink wine: but they might also use oil, in which they supposed much celestial matter to be latent. Among the ancients there were men of high authority, such as *Cyrill* of Jerusalem, *Augustine*, and *Leo* the Great, not to mention several of less character and fame, who report that, in the sacred supper, flour or figs sprinkled

with human semen was presented to the Elect to be swallowed. Says *Augustine*, (de hæres. c. 46. p. 11.): Qua occasione vel potius execrabilis cujusdam superstitionis necessitate, coguntur Electi eorum velut Eucharistiam (the flour: which *Cyrill* calls a *fig*, or a *dried fig*, Catechės. vi. p. 110.) conspersam cum semine humano sumere, ut etiam inde, sicut de aliis cibis, quos accipiunt, substantia illa divina purgetur. There are other passages of *Augustine*, in which he states this grave charge more fully: but they need not be cited. The very learned patron of the Manichæans, *Beausobre*, (in the close of the second volume of his History of the Manichæans,) inquires very fully, and with much zeal and ingenuity, into the truth of this accusation; and, after weighing with great care all the arguments and testimonies, he pronounces it to be a fabricated falsehood. I think the business may be accomplished in a more summary manner. In the first place, the Manichæans do not deny, that there was an infamous and filthy set of people, who defiled themselves with such a ceremony; but they most strenuously repel the base charge from their sect. *Augustine* (loco cit.) says: Sed hoc se facere negant, et alios nescio quos sub nomine Manichæorum facere affirmant. And a little after, he says, that a certain Manichæan, named *Viator*, declared before a judicial court, that *they who did those things, were called Catharistæ;* that they originated from the Manichæans, and used Manichæan books, yet were a distinct people from the genuine [p. 895.] Manichæans. In another place, (de natura boni, c. 47. p. 367.) he says: Isti autem cum hoc eis objicitur, solent respondere, nescio quem inimicum suum de numero suo, hoc est, Electorum suorum, descivisse et schisma fecisse, atque hujusmodi spurcissimam hæresin infecisse. In my judgment, confidence in this matter is to be reposed in the Manichæans, who best understood their own affairs. Some one may say: What the Manichæans admit, namely, that some among them, bearing the name of Manichaeans, were guilty of that obscene conduct, may be believed; because no reason can be assigned, why they should fabricate such a story. But the other part, that true Manichaeans abhorred such conduct, cannot with equal safety be believed. I, however, maintain, that the latter also may be received as true; and this, on the authority of *Augustine* himself. For he, although he labors in several passages to make it appear, by arguments and testimony, that the Manichaeans were not so innocent in this matter, as they wished to be accounted, yet in other places, he hesitates, fluctuates, and shows plainly, that he had nothing certain to guide him. And this, in my judgment, is sufficient to establish the testimony of the Manichaeans respecting themselves. *Fortunatus* the Manichaean, publicly demanded of *Augustine*, either to prove the truth of the stories in circulation respecting the sacred supper of the Manichaeans, or to admit their falsehood. He says, (tom. viii. p. 68.): Falsis criminibus pulsamur. Ex te ergo praesentes audiant boni viri, utrum sint vera, super quibus criminamur et appetimur, an sint falsa. Etenim ex tua doctrinâ, et ex tua expositione et ostensione poterunt verius scire nostram conversationem, si a te fuerit prodita. *Augustine* showed foresight and caution by declining the task assigned him by the Manichaean: and his first reply is, that the question before them did not relate to the morals of the Manichaeans, but to their faith. But *Fortunatus* still persists, and says, that it is necessary, before discussing the creed of the Manichaeans, to investigate their moral character, which appeared to many to be most base. When driven to extremity, *Augustine* acknowledges, that he has no certain knowledge of the morals of the Manichaean Elect. He knew, indeed, that the Elect attended the sacred supper; but what they received there, he did not know: Eucharistiam audivi quod accipiatis: quid vero accipiatis, unde nosse potui? This ingenuous acknowledgment of his ignorance, destroys all the force of those passages, in which he boldly and confidently charges the Manichaeans with the shameful conduct above mentioned. In another place, where he is professedly inquiring what there is reprehensible in the morals and usages of the Manichaeans, (de moribus Manichaeorum, L. ii. c. 19. tom. 1. p. 551.) he again very timidly and cautiously touches this subject: Quia non possunt ab Auditoribus vestris talia semina (hominum et animalium) vobis purganda offerri, quis non *suspicetur*, (So the whole thing rests on *suspicion!*) secretam de vobis ipsis [p. 896.] inter vos fieri talem purgationem, et ideo illis ne vos deserant, occultari? Quae si non facitis, *quod utinam ita sit.* (Who can suppose the man who so speaks, is stating well ascertained facts?) Videtis tamen quantae *suspicioni* vestra superstitio pateat, et quam non sit hominibus succensendum id opinantibus, quod de vestra professione colligitur, cum vos animam per escam et potum de corporibus et sensibus liberare praedicatis. Nolo hic diutius immorari: et videtis, quantus sit invectionis locus. Sed res talis est, ut eam potius reformidet quam insectetur, oratio. Thus wrote *Augustine*, in a calm and tranquil state of mind. When warmed by passion, he speaks more confidently. But the utterance of the sober mind, refutes the declarations of the impassioned mind.

§ LV. **Constitution of the Manichæan Church.** The organization of the community established by *Manes*, was peculiar. Over the whole community an individual presided, who represented Jesus Christ. Next to him were twelve *Magistri*, representing the twelve Apostles. After them came seventy-two *Bishops*, corresponding with the seventy-two disciples of Christ. To the several Bishops were subject the *Presbyters* and *Deacons*. All these belonged to the class of the *Elect*, and were the head men of the sect.(1) The members of the community were divided into two classes, the *Elect* or *Perfect*, and the *Auditors*, who were also called *Catechumens*. The *Elect* were subjected to a severe and uncomfortable rule of life, and consequently were held in very high veneration. They were of two descriptions, the *baptized* and the *unbaptized*. The baptized could never change their condition; but the unbaptized, if they found themselves utterly unable to endure the rigorous discipline of the *Elect*, might descend to the rank of *Auditors*, who were allowed to live and act with greater freedom.(2)

(1) On the constitution of the Manichæan church, there is only one passage to be cited from *Augustine*, (de Hæres. c. 46. p. 13.): Ipse Manichaeus duodecim discipulos habuit, ad instar Apostolici numeri, quem numerum Manichæi hodieque custodiunt. Nam ex Electis suis habent duodecim, quos appellant *Magistros* et tertium decimum principem ipsorum: *episcopos* autem septuaginta duos, qui ordinantur a Magistris: Et *presbyteros*, qui ordinantur ab episcopis. Habent etiam episcopi *diaconos*. I could wish *Augustine* had described with more particularity the constitution of the Manichaean community, had named the place where the head of the sect and the Magistri resided, and had informed us what were the powers and duties of the several orders of the clergy, [p. 897.] how they were inducted into office, &c. But I suppose that, being only an *Auditor*, he did not himself know these things, as they pertained to the sacred arcana of the sect, and to the interior discipline of the *Elect.* It is probable, that the head of the sect and the college of the *Magistri* resided in some city of *Persia;* for the sect originated in Persia, and its founder was a Persian. But in the times of *Augustine*, the severe laws of the emperors, which are now extant in the *Codex Theodosianus*, were in force against the Manichaeans; and therefore, undoubtedly, they concealed the residence of their chief, and the other things from which the internal state of the sect might be known.—The Manichaeans, then, had a supreme *Pontiff;* though by what title he was designated, is not known; for the term *Princeps* used by Augustine, was not probably his true title. I conjecture that, as *Manes* himself assumed the appellation of *Apostle* of Jesus Christ, the same appellation was transmitted to his successors. With the Pontiff was associated a college of twelve *Magistri:* but whether they were dispersed in various places, or all resided near the Pontiff, does not appear. The Pontiff, I suppose, was elected and consecrated by the *Magistri;* and he, in return, appointed and consecrated the Magistri. In what way the *Bishops* were created, does not appear: but they could be installed only by the *Magistri;* and afterwards they installed the *Presbyters.* The Bishops seem to have selected the Deacons, and to have inducted them into office. Diverse from all these, yet doubtless belonging to the sacred order, were the *Evangelists*, as we may call them, or those whose office it was to extend and propagate the sect; but what title the Manichaeans gave to them, I do not know. They were the more distinguished among the *Elect* for talents, ability, and zeal. Says *Augustine*, (loc. cit. p. 13.): Mittuntur etiam ipsi, qui videntur idonei ad hunc errorem, vel ubi est, sustentandum et augendum, vel ubi non est, etiam seminandum. The electing and commissioning of them, undoubtedly belonged to the head of the sect.

(2) That *Manes* divided the members of his community into two classes, the *Elect* and the *Auditors*, is a fact well known. Says *Augustine*, (de Haeres. c. 46. p. 11.): Electi Manichaeorum sanctius vivunt et excellentius Auditoribus suis. Nam his duabus professionibus, hoc est, Electorum et Auditorum, ecclesiam suam constare voluerunt. Some suppose, that *Manes* borrowed this classification from the Pythagorean school; which was composed of the *Mathematici* and the *Acusmatici* (ἀκουσματικοί), the former corresponding with the *Elect*, and the latter with the *Auditors.* I am persuaded that this Persian, who was doubt-

less ignorant of *Pythagoras*, followed in this matter his instructers, the *Magi*. *Eubulus*, in his history of Mithra, (apud *Porphyrium* de abstinentia a carnibus, L. iv. § 16. p. 165.) besides others, testifies that the *Magi* were distributed into [p. 898.] *three* classes: Primi et doctissimi neque edebant animalia, neque necabant: These were very similar to the *Elect* among the Manichaeans. Secundi ordinis Magi animantes interficiebant quidem, sed nullas cicures: That is, they slew the noxious animals, or such as were injurious to mankind, but spared the useful animals. Nor was it wholly unlawful for the Manichaean *Auditors* to slay those animals which endanger the lives of men, such as serpents, field-mice, and scorpions: these, however, according to the testimony of *Augustine*, (de moribus Manichaeor. L. ii. c. 18. tom. i. p. 550.) they supposed not to be real animals, but to originate from the dead bodies of men. Tertii generis *Manichæi* (*Magi?*) quaedam quidem animalia edebant, sed non omnia. There are several things which go to show, that the Manichaean *Auditors* were also forbidden to eat certain animals.

The *Elect*, as *Theodoret* testifies, (Haeret. Fabul. L. i. c. 26.) were likewise called *τέλειοι*, the *Perfect;* because they appeared to obey the whole of the law which was considered as enjoined by Christ. And, although they were not all *priests*, yet they were all compared to the Jewish priests, and were generally called priests, and the priestly order. Thus *Faustus*, (L. xxx. c. 1. p. 316.): Nos quidem solum in plebe sacerdotale hominum genus censemus a carnibus abstinere debere. Perhaps *Faustus* likewise used the word *Fidelium;* for *Augustine* often calls them *fideles:* e. g. (de morib. ecclesiae cathol. L. i. c. 35. p. 532.): Nolite dicere catechumenis uti licere conjugibus, *fidelibus* autem non licere: catechumenis licere habere pecuniam, *fidelibus* autem non licere.—*Tyrbo*, (in the Acta Archelai, § 9. p. 16.) is the first that gives the appellation *Catechumens* to the *Auditors*. After him, *Epiphanius* several times designates them by this appellation. But some learned men disapprove the term: they think that the term *Catechumens*, which was appropriate to Catholic Christians, is indiscreetly applied to a class of persons very different from *Catechumens*. But *Tyrbo*, and those who followed him, committed no mistake. For *Augustine*, once himself an *Auditor*, and therefore a very competent witness, informs us that the title of *Catechumens* was applied, even among the Manichaeans, to the Auditors. I have just cited from him a passage which proves it. But I will add one still clearer and more irrefragable, (contra litteras Petiliani, L. iii. c. 17. p. 208, 209.): Nescit (Petilianus,) non illic, (among Manichaeans,) ita appellari Catechumenos, tanquam eis baptismus quandoque debeatur, (for Petilian had supposed, that the Manichaean Catechumens, like those of other Christians, were to be baptized,) sed eos hoc vocari, *qui etiam Auditores vocantur*, quod videlicet tanquam meliora et majora praecepta observare non possint, quae observantur ab eis, quos Electorum nomine discernendos et honorandos putant.—They were also called *Seculars;* because they might engage in secular business. [p. 899.] *Faustus*, (L. xvi. c. 6. p. 204.): Judaei Christo credere non poterant, indifferentiam docenti ciborum, et a suis quidem discipulis (the Elect,) omnia penitus removenti, sæcularibus vero (to the *Auditors*,) vulgo concedenti omnia quae possent edi.

The number of the *Elect* was small. It would appear from the *Acta Archelai*, (§ 10. p. 19.) that *Manes* was attended by only *seven:* Præcipit Electis suis solis, qui non sunt amplius, quam *septem* numero. But I must confess, this testimony appears to me doubtful. For in the same *Acta*, a little after, (§ 12. p. 23.) *Manes* is said to have arrived, adducens secum juvenes et virgines electos ad viginti duo simul. Besides, it is beyond all controversy that *Manes*, after the example of Christ, had twelve disciples of the highest order, or twelve Apostles; and these were undoubtedly of the class of the *Elect*. I suspect that the seven, whom *Tyrbo* calls *Elect*, were *Magistri;* and that *Manes*, at that time, could find no more of the *Elect* worthy of being thus promoted. The smallness of the number of the *Elect* will not appear strange, to one who considers what we have frequently shown, that the *Elect* were obliged to lead a very uncomfortable and cheerless life. For as they must live in perfect inactivity, and must so refrain from all labor and business as not even to pull up an herb or pluck an apple, without sinning; this very inactivity was more painful and disagreeable than the most busy and active life. They were prohibited from everything that can delight the senses, exhilarate the mind, or give pleasure to the body, except only music. In part, these disagreeables were relieved by the high veneration in which they were held. For they were addressed, as Deities are, on bended knees. Thus *Augustine*, (Epist. ccxxxvii. ad Deuterium, tom. ii. p. 643.): Auditores qui appellantur apud eos et carnibes vescuntur, et agros colunt, et, si voluerint, uxores habent, quorum nihil faciunt qui vocantur Electi. Sed ipsi Auditores ante Electos genua figunt, ut eis manus supplicibus imponantur, non a solis presbyteris, vel episcopis aut diaconibus eorum, sed a quibuslibet Electis. Therefore, although the bishops, presbyters, and deacons, were higher in rank or dignity, yet all the *Elect* were supposed to possess equal sanctity, and the power of conferring celestial gifts on the *Auditors*. As they were entirely penniless, and could neither possess anything nor supply their wants by labor, it was necessary that the *Auditors* should furnish them with salads, potherbs, fruits, melons, bread, &c. for their sustenance; and whoever neglected this duty, was deemed guilty of atrocious sin, and deserving the flames of hell. And hence the *Auditors* were always ready and willing to present to the *Elect* whatever they needed; and frequently they brought to them more than they wanted. Says *Tyrbo*, (in the Acta Archelai, p. 16.): Si quid optimum est in escis (those, namely, which the *Elect* might lawfully eat,) offerunt illud Electis. But this very liberality of the *Auditors* frequently became onerous to the Elect: for, whatever the *Auditors* presented to them, was considered as consecrated, [p. 900.] And therefore could neither be eaten by any other persons, nor be thrown away. And hence the *Elect* had to load their stomachs immoderately, whenever a large quantity of food was offered them; or the boys whom they had under instruction, were compelled to eat what their masters were unable to consume. *Augustine*, (de moribus eccles. et Manichæor. L. ii. c. 16. p. 527.): Quae vobis quasi purganda afferuntur, (*Manes* supposed some portion of the divine and celestial substance was combined with all natural objects; and that the continence, the chastity, and the sanctity of the *Elect*, caused all that was celestial and divine in the things they ate, to be at once separated from sordid matter, and so to return to the world of light. Therefore *Augustine* says:) Quod ea, quæ vobis quasi purganda afferuntur ad epulas, nefas putatis, si quis alius, præter Electos, ad cibandum tetigerit, quantae turpitudinis et aliquando sceleris plenum est? Si quidem saepe tam multa dantur, ut consumi facile a paucis non possint. Et quoniam sacrilegium putatur, vel aliis dare quod redundat, vel certe abjicere, in magnas contrudimini cruditates, totum quod datum est quasi purgare cupientes. Jam vero distenti et prope crepantes, eos, qui sub vestra disciplinâ sunt, pueros ad devorandum reliqua crudeli dominatione compellitis: ita, ut cuidam sit Romæ objectum, quod miseros parvulos cogendo ad vescendum tali superstitione necaverit. Quod non crederem, nisi scirem, quantum nefas esse arbitremini, vel aliis haec dare, qui Electi non sunt, vel certa projicienda curare. Unde illa vescendi necessitas restat, quae ad turpissimam cruditatem paene quotidie, aliquando tamen potest et usque ad homicidium pervenire. This is a memorable passage on several accounts, and particularly as teaching us, what we nowhere else learn, that the *Elect* occupied themselves to some extent in teaching and training up boys. These boys, undoubtedly, were devoted by their parents to the mode of life prescribed to the *Elect.* For the sanctity of the *Elect* being held in the highest estimation, and their souls being supposed to go directly to the celestial world on leaving the body, it was a common thing for parents, influenced by affection and superstition, to commit their children to the training of the *Elect*, so that they might become habituated to their harsh and cheerless mode of life, and be imbued with sound religious knowledge. And if any one ask, how we know that these boys were consecrated to the life of the *Elect;* I answer, we may infer it from the nature of the case. These boys were compelled to eat the surplus food of the *Elect:* but no one of the profane or the *Auditors* might touch the food that had been presented to the *Elect:* therefore these boys must have been of the class of the *Elect*, or were destined to belong to that order. The instruction and education of boys not aspiring to the highest degree of sanctity, was deemed beneath the dignity of such very great men, and was therefore intrusted to the *Auditors.*—Before the *Elect* ate the bread presented to them, (and, I suppose, it was the same if other food was offered them,) they called both God and men to witness, that they had no concern with the sins committed in the production of that bread. For the Mani-[p. 901.] chæans believed, that those who till the ground, reap the corn, grind it, or bake the bread, commit a sin not unlike homicide; because, as they supposed, this whole material universe is full of celestial and animated matter. The *Elect* also added prayers for the *Auditors* who presented the bread, that God would pardon the sin committed in making the bread. This custom is mentioned by *Cyrill* of Jerusalem, (Catechcs. vi. § 32. p. 108. edit. Bened.) But he speaks in too invidious a manner: for he tells us, the *Elect* imprecated curses instead of blessings, on the *Auditors* who presented to them the bread; nay that they blasphemed God himself. Now this is in itself incredible, and it is at variance with the fundamental precepts of the Manichæan religion. I choose, therefore, to explain the subject by the language of *Tyrbo*, (in the Acta Archelai, § 9. p. 16.) with whom *Epiphanius* and *Titus* of Bostra agree: Cum voluerint manducare panem, orant primo, ista dicentes ad panem: Neque ego te messui, neque molui, neque tribulavi, nec in clibanum te misi, alius te fecit et detulit te mihi, ego innocenter te manduco. Et cum intra semetipsum haec dixerit, respondit ad eum, qui ei detulit: Oravi pro te, et ille discedit ita. These things were superstitions; but they will be readily credited, by one acquainted with the Manichæan system. After eating, the *Elect* again prayed; and then anointed their head with consecrated oil, for the purpose, I suppose, of expelling or enervating the virus of the evil matter combined with the celestial in the food. Says *Tyrbo*, (loc. cit. p. 19.): Praecipit autem (Manes) Electis suis solis, ut cum desinerint manducantes, orarent, et mitterent oleum super caput exorcidiatum, invocatis nominibus plurimis (either of *Æons*, the good spirits, or of the bad ones,) ad confirmationem fidei hujus. But all this pertained to the arcane discipline: hence, *Tyrbo* adds: Nomina tamen mihi non manifestavit, (*Tyrbo* being only an *Auditor*,) soli enim Electi his utuntur nominibus.

The *Auditors* had little that was peculiar in their mode of living. Says *Augustine*, (contra Faust. L. xx. c. 23. p. 248.): Cum Auditores vestri et uxores habeant, et filios, quamvis inviti, suscipiant, eisque patrimonia congerant vel custodiant, carne vescantur, vinum bibant, lavent, metant, vindemient, negotientur, honores publicos administrent, vobiscum tamen eos, non cum gentibus, computatis. But this liberty was circumscribed by some limitations; neither was everything lawful for Manichaean *Auditors*, which was permitted by other Christians.—*First:* Although they might possess houses and lands, which they received by inheritance or by gift; yet, to build houses, or to labor for the acquisition or increase of property, was accounted a great iniquity. This has been already shown. The poorer a person was, and the less he cared about wealth, the more happy was he considered.—*Secondly:* It was lawful for them to eat the flesh of animals, though doubtless, with moderation: but to kill or slaughter animals, was criminal. The reason has been already stated.—[p. 902.] *Thirdly:* They were not forbidden to marry: but they were instructed by their teachers, to avoid as far as possible the begetting of children. Nearly all writers on their affairs, tax them with this. Thus *Titus* of Bostra, *Epiphanius*, *Theodoret*, and others; but no one more frequently, or more expressly and vehemently, than *Augustine*. I will cite some of his most noticeable passages; and they will show us, what precepts they gave for avoiding the procreation of children. The first is, (de Haeres. c. 46. p. 12, 13.): Monent Auditores suos, si utuntur conjugibus, conceptum tamen generationemque devitent, ne divina substantia vinculis carneis ligetur in prole. Another is, (contra Faustum, L. xxx. c. 6. p. 318.): Vos cum praecipue concubitum detestamini, qui solus honestus et conjugalis est, et quem matrimoniales quoque tabulae prae se gerunt, liberorum procreandorum caussâ: unde vere non tam concumbere, quam nubere prohibetis. Concumbitur enim etiam caussâ libidinum, nubitur autem non nisi filiorum. A third passage is, (contra Faust. L. xxii. c. 30. p. 270.): Perversa lex Manichaeorum, ne Deus eorum, quem ligatum in omnibus seminibus plangunt (that is, *souls*, those particles of the divine light or nature,) in conceptu feminae arctius colligetur, prolem ante omnia devitari a concumbentibus jubet, ut Deus eorum turpi lapsu potius effundatur, quam crudeli nexu vinciatur. There is a passage still more full and explicit, (de moribus Manichaeor. L. ii. c. 18. p. 551.):

Nonne vos estis, (Manichaei,) qui filios gignere, eo quod animae ligentur in carne, gravius putatis esse peccatum, quam ipsum concubitum? Nonne vos estis, qui nos (Auditores) solebatis monere, ut, quantum fieri posset, observaremus tempus, quo ad conceptum mulier post genitalium viscerum purgationem apta esset; eoque tempore a concubitu temperaremus, ne carni anima implicaretur? Ex quo illud sequitur, ut non liberorum procreandorum caussâ, sed satiandae libidinis habere conjugem censeatis. Whatever some learned men, the advocates of the Manichaeans, may say on this subject, I can never persuade myself that *Augustine* has fabriated all these charges unjustly; and especially, as he is supported by other writers, and by the primary doctrines of the sect. Yet *Augustine* himself acknowledges, that the procreation of children was tolerated among the Manichaeans, and that no penalties were inflicted on the fathers and mothers: but still he maintains, that it was necessity that directed this lenity, and that their doctrines condemned it. He says, (contra Faust. L. xxx. c. 6. p. 318.): Nec ideo vos dicatis prohibere (*legitimate marriage;* which *Augustine* had charged upon them,) quia multos vestros Auditores in hoc (in avoiding the procreation of children,) obedire nolentes vel non valentes salvâ amicitiâ toleratis. Illud enim habetis in doctrina vestri erroris, hoc in necessitate societatis.—*Fourthly:* The *Auditors* were not required to observe so many fasts and vigils as the *Elect:* only on Sundays or Lord's Days, all food and drink were strictly forbidden, to them as well as to the *Elect.* I have already cited a passage from [p. 903.] *Augustine* on this subject: and I will now add another, which has not been noticed, (Epistle xxxv. c. 12. tom. ii. p. 60.) From this we learn, first, the *severity* of this fast: Toto (enim) die Dominico usque ad medium noctis, vel etiam usque ad diluculum, reficere corpora non curabant: and then also the *sanctity* of this fast: Impiissimi Manichaei jejunia diei Dominicae non aliqua necessitate occurrente peragere, sed quasi sacra solennitate statuta dogmatizare coeperunt, et innotuerunt populis Christianis.—None of the ancients has acquainted us with any other rules obligatory on the *Auditors*, except those of kneeling before the *Elect*, feeding them, and paying them reverence.

§ LVI. **The Sect of the Hieracites.** The Manichaeans were early divided into several sects: which is by no means strange, considering how many of their doctrines were vaguely stated. Among these sects, many esteem that to be *one*, which was successfully founded in Egypt by *Hierax* or *Hieracas*, an Egyptian of Leonto, a learned man and a great writer, near the close of the century. But this opinion is not supported by competent testimony, nor by valid arguments. For although *Hierax*, equally with *Manes*, opposed marriages, and enjoined on his followers a severe code of morals, and perhaps also believed that the source of all evil propensities and sins is to be found in mat ter or the body; yet in other respects he differed widely from *Manes;* nor is there any testimony that he approved the fundamental principles which are the basis of the Manichaean religion. (1)

(1) *Hierax*, or as some call him *Hieracas*, was not the least among those who, in this century, disquieted the church with new opinions. For, near the close of the century, he founded a very considerable sect in Egypt, which continued after his death; yet, as *Epiphanius* expressly states, (§ 3. p. 714.) it gradually receded, as is common, from the severity prescribed by the founder. Nearly all we know, at this day, respecting the man or his opinions, is derived from *Epiphanius;* whose *Haeresis LXVII.* is that of the *Hieracites.* From him, *Augustine* and the other historians of the sects, derive all that they recount to us respecting the *Hieracites.* What we can learn from others, adds very little to our knowledge, and perhaps does not all relate to this *Hierax.* The man was a native Egyptian of the town of Leonto: he was well versed in the Grecian sciences, especially in medicine, and was well acquainted with the polite learning and literature of both the Greeks aud the Egyptians: and his life and habits, as *Epiphanius*, his adversary, testifies, (§ 1. p. 710.) was *plane* [p. 904.] *admirabilis:* ἀνὴρ ἐμπληκτὸς τῇ ἀσκήσει. The sanctity of his life so captivated the Egyptian Monks, that many of them joined his sect. By occupation, he was a book maker; that is, he wrote elegantly in both the Grecian and the Egyptian characters, and obtained his living by transcribing books. Says *Epiphanius*, (loc. cit. § 3. p. 712.): Ἑως τῆς ἡμέρας, ἧς ἐτελεύτα ἐκαλλιγράφει. Καλλιγράφος γὰρ ἦν. Ad obitum usque libros descripsit; calligraphus enim seu librarius erat. He lived to a great age, and was vigorous when over ninety years old. He wrote many books, especially commentaries on the books of the Bible, and in particular a History of the Creation of the World, or of the six day's work of God. He also composed and published some hymns.

Venerable as he was for his mode of life, his temperance, his chastity, and his piety, he nevertheless deviated in many things from other christians, as *Epiphanius* expressly states. Yet *Epiphanius* mentions and refutes only a few of his opinions; and he is wholly silent as to the sources from which those very base doctrines, as he terms them, flowed. Yet that the errors assailed by *Epiphanius*, were only consequences from other and more general notions or principles, is manifest. It is very embarrassing, that the early writers on the affairs of christians, state only some portion of the doctrines advanced by the religious innovaters; and that they give no account of the coherency of those doctrines, and of the sources from which they originated. And hence the true import of the errors mentioned, cannot be accurately determined or estimated; and learned men may, with no little plausibility, either censure or excuse the authors of those errors. And hence the writers who treat of the *Hieracites* are, one and all, sterile and dry. Most of them merely state, that *Hierax* condemned marriages, and denied the resurrection of our bodies. And as *Manes* also held these errors, some confidentially affirm, that *Hierax* was one of the early disciples of *Manes.* But I apprehend, something more may be said, and that the alledged Manichaeism of the *Hieracites* may be completely disproved.

I. Those books of the Old and New Testament, which Christians regarded divine, *Hierax* also received; and on some of them he wrote expositions. This is expressly stated by his adversary, *Epiphanius;* who adds, that he was well acquainted with both Testaments. But his regard for the sacred books was tarnished by *two* errors. For, *first*, in addition to the sacred volume which all Christians revere, he appears to have regarded some other books also as divine, and books written by fallible men. For this we have the testimony of *Epiphanius*, a competent witness in the case. He not only tells us that *Hierax*, in support of his error concerning the Holy Spirit, (of which we shall speak hereafter,) placed special reliance on a passage from a book called the *Ascension of* [p. 905.] *Isaiah;* but also quotes the passage of that book, (§ 3. p. 712.) which is evidence, among other facts, that *Epiphanius* actually saw and read the books of *Hierax*. Of this book, the Ascension of Isaiah, Jo. Alb. *Fabricius* treats, (in his Codex Pseudepigraphus Vet. Test. tom. I. p. 1086, &c.)—*Secondly*, abandoning the literal sense of the holy scriptures, and following the example of Origen, *Hierax* converted the historical narrations into moral fables and allegories. See *Epiphanius*, (loc. cit. § 3. p. 712.) This method of interpreting or rather perverting the sacred books, doubtless afforded him a very convenient refuge against all the texts and arguments from the scriptures, in opposition to his views: and perhaps also, it gave rise to some of his errors. He may have been a disciple of *Origen*.—As *Hierax* held the Old Testament to be equally inspired with the New, it is evident that he had nothing in common with *Manes;* who maintained that the entire Old Testament was the work of the Prince of darkness, and Moses a legate of the evil demon; while *Hierax* venerated Moses as a prophet of the most high God, according to *Epiphanius*, (loc. cit. § 1. p. 710.) *Manes* also taught that the New Testament is either falsely ascribed to the Apostles of Jesus Christ, or is entirely corrupted and vitiated. But here some learned men bring forward *Athanasius*, who wrote, they say, (in his Sermo contra omnes hæreses, §. 9. Opp. tom. ii. p. 233. Edit. Bened.) that *Hierax*, equally with *Manes*, discarded the Old Testament. For, disputing with *Hierax* respecting marriage, he introduces *Hierax* as saying: Ἀλλὰ τι λέγεις; ὅτι οὐ δέχομαι τὴν παλαιὰν (διαθήκην). Quid vero dicis? Vetus testamentum non admitto. But these learned men here err, through ignorance of the system of *Hierax*. The sense of the passage is; I do not admit the arguments or dicta of the Old Testament, in this debate about marriage. *Athanasius* had proved the divine origin of marriage from the Old Testament, and particularly from the history of Adam and Eve. But *Hierax* conceded, as we shall soon learn, that under the Old Testament, marriage was allowed to all; but he contended, that Jesus Christ, the giver of a more perfect law, had abolished this liberty of marriage. He therefore replied to his antagonist: Your arguments from the Old Testament, in this matter, prove nothing. But there are other proofs, besides those already stated, from which it appears that *Hierax* detracted nothing from the divinity of the Old Testament. He wrote expositions of some of the books of the Old Testament, and in particular, a very copious explanation of the history of the creation, or of the six day's work. And who will believe, that a man would voluntarily expend so much labor in explaining a book which he despised and rejected? Moreover he taught, that Melchizedek was the Holy Spirit. He therefore did not deny the divine inspiration of that book of Moses which contains the history of Melchizedek.

II. Respecting God, and the three persons in one God, *Hierax* was sound and orthodox; as *Epiphanius* clearly teaches, (§ 2. p. 721.): De Patre, [p. 906.] Filio et Spiritu sancto non eadem, quæ Origenes, sentit: quin potius et a Patre Filium revere genitum, et Spiritum sanctum credit a Patre procedere.—But here again some learned men think to detract from his fame. For they find, (apud *Epiphanium*, Hæres. lxix. Arianor. § 7. p. 733: and, apud *Athanasium* de duabus Synodis, § 15. Opp. tom, i. P. ii. p. 728: and, apud *Hilarium* de Trinitate L. vi. § 5. Opp. p. 881.) an Epistle of *Arius* to Alexander the bishop of Alexandria, in which he says that *Hierax* maintained, that the Son of God is, as it were, lucernam e lucernâ: λύχνον ἀπὸ λύχνου. aut lampadem in duas partes divisam: ὡς λαμπάδα εἰς δύο. And he adds, that this idea of the generation of Christ was publicly refuted and condemned by Alexander. And hence these learned men do not hesitate, to place *Hierax* among those who debased the doctrine of the eternal generation of the Son from the Father, by unsuitable and improper comparisons. But, as no other one of the ancients has accused *Hierax* of any error, in regard to the doctrine of three persons in one God; and, on the contrary, as *Epiphanius* declares his opinions concerning God to have been sound; it appears to me doubtful, whether it was our *Hierax*, or another of the same name, that believed as Arius states, respecting the generation of the Son of God. The name *Hierax* or *Hieracas* was very common in Egypt, as might be shown from *Athanasius* and others: and therefore, it might be, that some presbyter at Alexandria bearing this name, used the above comparison.

III. However this may be, it appears, that *Hierax* deviated somewhat from the common opinions of Christians respecting the Holy Spirit. *Epiphanius*, (loc. cit. § 3. p. 711,) says, that *Hierax*, de Spiritu sancto fusissimam disputationem instituere, multasque nugas proferre: πολλὰ φλυαρῶν περὶ τοῦ ἁγίου πνεύματος. From this it may be inferred that he erred in more than one respect, in regard to the doctrine of the Holy Spirit. And yet *Epiphanius*, (both here, and Hæres. lv. Melchisedecianor. § 5. p. 472.) mentions only one of his false notions: namely, that *Melchizedek* the king of Salem, who blessed Abraham, was the Holy Spirit. This opinion *Hierax* proved, or rather, stupidly attempted to prove, from Rom. viii. 26. Hebr. vii. 3. and from the *Ascension of Isaiah*. It was easy for *Epiphanius* to refute these arguments: and yet the chief proof he employs, in regard to both passages, appears to me not entirely unexceptionable. If, says he, Melchizedek was the Holy Spirit, then the Holy Spirit undoubtedly assumed human nature; for Melchizedek was a man. But how absurd is such a supposition: for where was the mother of the Holy Spirit? It is therefore false, that Melchizedek was the Holy Spirit. In reasoning in this manner, *Epiphanius* forgets what he had before told us, that *Hierax*, after the example of Origen, disregarding the literal sense, changed the sacred history into an allegory. Undoubtedly, therefore, he maintained that the history of Melchizedek, [p. 907.] is not an account of actual occurrences, but only a sort of picture of the blessings with which the Holy Spirit enriches men; and that Abraham represents all saints and devout persons.

IV. The office of Christ, he placed especially in the promulgation of a new *law*, more strict and more perfect than that of Moses. This, perhaps, was the greatest of all his errors. *Epiphanius*, (loc. cit. § 1. p. 710.) clearly shows us, that he so thought; as we shall soon demonstrate. Nor will it be unreasonable to suppose, especially if we consider his doctrine respecting the salvation of infants, which will soon be brought forward, that he wholly denied the expiation of our sins by the death and obedience of the Saviour; and that he made the endeavors of men to repress the evil instincts of nature, the ground of eternal salvation. How widely such opinions differ from those taught in the New Testament, is manifest. And yet no one either of the ancients or the moderns has noticed this the worst of all the errors of *Hierax*.

V. Regarding this opinion as true and undeniable, he concluded that Jesus Christ interdicted to his followers marriages, flesh and wine, and enjoined a life void of all pleasures. According to *Epiphanius*, (§ 1. p. 710.) he thus reasoned; Jesus Christ introduced a new and more perfect *law*. But, if we except continence only, every thing that Christ commands, was also required in the Old Testament. Therefore, unless we would believe that Christ introduced nothing new, we must believe that he prohibited marriage, &c.: Quid verbum novi prædicare, aut quod egregium facinus moliri voluit (Christus)? Si Dei timorem dixeris, hoc jam lex ipsa continebat. Si invidiam, avaritiam, injustitiam damnasse dicas; hæc omnia Veteri Testamento comprehensa sunt. Superest ergo, id ut unum efficere voluerit, ut continentiam prædicaret in mundo, ac sibi ipsi castimoniam deligeret.—Here again, we perceive a wide difference between *Manes* and *Hierax*. For the latter conceded, that the law of Moses was divine and full of good precepts, although in a few things less perfect than the law of Christ; but the former declared the law of Moses to have been ordained by the Prince of darkness. Moreover, it was for very far different reasons that *Manes* prohibited marriage, and the use of flesh and wine.

VI. So then, *Hierax* taught, that *marriage* was abolished by Jesus Christ. He admitted, that marriages were lawful under the Old Testament; as *Epiphanius* expressly states repeatedly, (§ 1 and 6. p. 710. 714.) But he tells us, that Jesus Christ, the author of a holier and better law, has abrogated the liberty to marry. And hence, as *Epiphanius* says, (§ 2. p. 711.): Neminem in gregem suum admittebat, nisi virgo esset, aut Monachus, aut continens (ἐγκράτης,) aut vidua. But his followers, whether by his permission and authority, or from their own choice, I know not; Mulieres contubernales (συνεισάκτους γυναῖκας) [p. 908.] secum habebant, quas ad quotidianum duntaxat ministerium se adhibere gloriabantur. See *Epiphanius*, (loc. cit. § 8. p. 716.)—Did *Hierax* then teach, that our Saviour absolutely forbid marriage? And did he therefore believe, that no married person can attain eternal salvation? Thus all, I perceive, explain his views. And it must be confessed, that the ancient writers, especially *Epiphanius* and *Athanasius*, speak as if this were true. Says *Athanasius*, (Oratio contra omnes haereses, § 9. tom. ii. p. 255.): Τὸν ἀνόητον καὶ ἀτυχέστατον Ἱερακᾶν ἀθετεῖν τὸν γάμον. Insanum et infelicissimum Hieracam virginitatem extollere, nuptiasque aspernari. And *Epiphanius*, (loc. cit. § 1. p. 710.) says, that *Hierax* denied: Hominem conjugio vinctum cœleste regnum consequi posse.—But I suppose, that no one of the ancient heretics, who were hostile to marriages, was so infatuated as to maintain, that marriages are absolutely prohibited: I imagine rather, that they all merely recommended celibacy, as a state more perfect and more pleasing to God. No one ever entertained a worse or a more degrading opinion of matrimony than *Manes;* for he pronounced it a device of the Prince of darkness, for detaining wretched souls in the prison of bodies. And yet he could see, that nature is more powerful than regulations and comminations; and therefore he permitted the common people to marry. And that our *Hierax* did the same thing, and that the reports of his abhorrence of matrimony must not be understood strictly, I am led to believe, by the very *Epiphanius* whom those follow, who tell us that *Hierax* excluded all married persons from the kingdom of heaven. For *Epiphanius* tells us, (§ 2. p. 710, 711.) that when some persons quoted the language of Paul, 1 Cor. vii. 2. (*To avoid fornication, let every man have his own wife,*) in opposition to the opinion of *Hierax* respecting marriage, *Hierax* replied: 'Ουκ ἐπαινῶν φησὶ γάμον μετὰ τὴν παρουσίαν, ἀλλὰ συμβαστάζων, ἵνα μὴ εἰς περιττὸν ὄλεθρον ἐμπέσωσιν. Non laudat Paulus post adventum Domini conjugium, sed tollerandum putat, ne majus in exitium praecipites ruant homines. Now what can be plainer? *Hierax* did not condemn matrimony absolutely; but, on the authority of Paul, he supposed it should be tolerated, on account of the infirmity of nature. His company therefore was, perhaps, in this respect, like the Manichæan community. Those who aimed at the highest degree of sanctity, and wished their souls to go to heaven immediately on leaving the body, lived in celibacy; while others, whom the fear of purgation after death did not so much terrify, were allowed to obey the instincts of nature. Perhaps also,—and this is the more probable supposition,—*Hierax* did not so much aim to found a *sect*, as to establish a religious *association* or order, like those of our *Monks*, into which he received none but unmarried persons. Other Christians he accounted, indeed, as brethren, and allowed to live in their own way; but he considered them farther removed from eternal felicity. Yet, whatever may have been his institution, it appears that [p. 909.] those err, who suppose he absolutely cut off from everlasting bliss, all married persons.

VII. This error of *Hierax*, respecting marriage, if I do not mistake, produced that opinion respecting Paradise, which *Epiphanius* thus censures in him, (§ 2. p. 711.): 'Ου πιστεύει δὲ οὗτος παράδεισον εἶναι αἰσθητόν. Paradisum porro sensibilem esse non putat. This is obscure: but as he adds, that *Origen* held the same opinion, the meaning must be, that *Hierax* considered as mystical, or turned into a sacred allegorical fable, the narrative of Moses respecting our first parents, Paradise, and the state of innocence. From the reasoning of *Athanasius* against him, (contra omnes Christianos, § 9. p. 235.) I perceive, that his opposers urged the history of our first parents, in refutation of his error respecting the excellence and sanctity of celibacy. *Hierax* believed, that marriage was allowed, indiscriminately, under the Old Testament; but that it was otherwise under the New Testament, that Jesus Christ did not sanction marriage, but only tolerated it in the more imbecile; that he forbid it to such as wished to be ad-admitted to the inheritance of the life to come, immediately after death. To confute this opinion of *Hierax*, the Christians of more correct views derived an argument from the history of our first parents in Paradise. God himself joined the first human beings in the bonds of marriage in Paradise. And can you then suppose, that Christ has prohibited, what God himself approved and instituted? To parry this argument, *Hierax* denied that the account given of Paradise was truly a history. And as, like *Origen*, he was very fond of allegories, and therefore obscured the history of the creation, or of the six days work, with very *flimsy allegories* (*vanissimis allegoriis*,) as *Epiphanius* expressly states, (§ 3. p. 712.) can any think it strange, that he should treat the history of Paradise in the same manner?

VIII. He not only exhibited a severe mode of life, abstaining from all animal food and from wine, but he also directed his followers to live in the same austere manner. See *Epiphanius*, (loc. cit. § 3. p. 712.)—But that this mode of life, like his rule respecting marriage, was not imposed on all his disciples, but only on the more perfect, I think we may learn from *Epiphanius*, who says: Ἐμψύχων τὲ πολλοὶ ἐξ ἀυτῶν ὀυ μετέχουσι τῶν ἀληθινῶν ἀυτῶν τοῦ δόγματος *Multi* eorum, qui sectam illius vere et ex animo profitentur, ab animatis abstinent. If only *many* of his true disciples lived on herbs, fruits, and pulse: the inference is, that the rigid abstinence from all flesh and wine, was prescribed only for those who could endure it.

IX. He denied the resurrection of the *bodies* of the dead: and to elude the force of the passages of Holy Scripture, which promise a renewed life to deceased bodies, he maintained that those texts referred to the soul. Says [p. 910.] *Epiphanius*, (§ 2. p. 711.) he affirmed: Solas animas resurgere, et spiritualem nescio quam fabulam contexit: Ἀνάστασιν νεκρῶν λέγει ἀνάστασιν τὲ τῶν ψυχῶν, καὶ πνευματικὴν τίνα φάσκων μυθολογίαν. He, therefore, undoubtedly, supposed the resurrection to be the illumination and renovation of souls; which the sacred writers often compare with a restoration to life. Nor is such an opinion surprising, in a man inflamed with the love of allegories, and disregarding the proper import of scripture language.—How *Hierax* was lead into this error, *Epiphanius* has not told us. Perhaps his fondness for allegories produced it: but more probably, he believed, with *Manes* and others, that *matter* is in itself evil, and that the fountain of all depravity is situated in the *body;* whence it would follow, that the body is the prison of the soul.

X. *Hierax* excluded from the kingdom of heaven, all *infants* dying before they came to the use of reason, on the ground that rewards are due only to those who have combatted legitimately against their bodies and the force of their lusts. See *Epiphanius*, (§ 2. p. 711. and § 4. p. 713.)—This dogma of *Hierax*, and the ground of it, afford strong and just suspicion, that he embraced corrupt opinions respecting the redemption and satisfaction for sin by Jesus Christ; and that he supposed, eternal life is to be obtained, not so much by faith in Jesus Christ, as by one's own efforts to overcome the depravity of nature, or the commotions of the body and the senses. For, if children, dying before the use of reason, fail of salvation, *because* they have not conflicted, or have not, by reason, overcome the incitements to sin;

it follows, that those who attain to salvation, are crowned solely because they resisted strenuously their natural propensities. But the sterility and indiscretion of *Epiphanius*, who expatiates largely upon doctrines imperfectly and cloudily explained, prevent our forming a just estimate of this opinion of *Hierax*.

END OF THE THIRD CENTURY.

THE

ECCLESIASTICAL HISTORY

OF THE

FOURTH CENTURY.

---

§ I. **Attempts of the Pagan Priests to get up a new persecution.** At the commencement of the fourth century after the birth of the Savior of mankind, the Roman empire was under the government of four sovereigns; of whom the two highest in rank, *Diocletian* and *Maximianus Herculius*, were called *Augusti*, and the two lower in rank, *Constantius Chlorus* and *Maximianus Galerius*, were called *Cesars;* but each of them had supreme power over the province allotted to him. Under these four Emperors, the state of the christian community, as well as that of the commonwealth, was quite flourishing. For the chief of the Augusti, *Diocletian*, although superstitious and an assiduous worshipper of the Gods, yet harbored no ill will against the Christians; and the first of the Cesars, *Constantius Chlorus*, was averse to the pagan religion, followed reason as his religious guide, was friendly to the Christians, and preferred them before the idolaters. Nor did the future portend any worse condition of the church: but rather, it was to be expected, that Christianity would soon gain the ascendancy in the Roman empire, or at least obtain as much influence and reputation as the old superstition. The friends of paganism, particularly the priests, perceiving the danger, exerted themselves to the utmost to raise a new persecution against the Christians, who then felt themselves too secure: and, by fictitious oracles and other frauds, they labored especially to excite *Diocletian*, whom they knew to be timid and credulous, to enact laws against the Christians.(1)

(1) *Eusebius* (Hist. Eccles. L. viii. c. 1. p. 291.) eloquently describes the flourishing state of the christian community, at the beginning of this century

before the rise of the Diocletian persecution; and also the security felt [p. 912.] by the christians in consequence of their prosperity, and their vices and contentions. The palaces of the Emperors were full of Christians, and no one hindered their freely professing and worshipping Christ without any fear. Some of them were selected for confidential friends of the Emperors, the governors of provinces, magistrates, and military commanders. And the bishops and ministers of religion were treated with great respect, even by those who preferred the ancient religion before that of Christ. A vast multitude of people, continually, every where, abandoning the Gods, made profession of Christianity. And hence, in all the cities, large and spacious buildings were erected, in which the people publicly assembled for religious worship. So that there remained but one thing to be desired by the Christians, namely, that one or more of the Emperors might embrace their religion; of which the consequence would undoubtedly be, that the worship of the Gods would become prostrate, in a great part of the Roman empire, and the Christian religion might contest with the pagan for the preëminence. And the state of the empire at that time, afforded the observing not a little hope, that the desires of Christians would not be disappointed. *Diocletian*, although timid and immoderately addicted to superstition, was yet averse from blood and slaughter; and he had Christians among his familiar friends, who, understanding well the genius and character of the man, might perhaps, if no obstacle was raised, withdraw the manageable man from his idolatry. Besides, *Prisca* the Emperor's wife, had renounced the worship of the Gods, and privately joined the Christian church. And *Constantius Chlorus*, his colleague, who ruled over Spain, Gaul and Britain, was a semi-Christian, and favored the Christians to the utmost of his power. And his son *Constantine*, who afterwards obtained the appellation of the *Great*, a youth endowed with extraordinary powers of mind and genius, and admired equally by the people and the soldiers, was living very honorably in the court of *Diocletian*, with the highest and most certain prospect of attaining to the rank of an Emperor. Being the child of a father, who was the worshipper of the one God, and the friend of Christians, and of a Christian mother, *Helena*, he had undoubtedly received from his parents a hatred of superstition, and kind feelings towards Christians and Christian worship; and although he did not publicly profess Christ, he doubtless showed by his conduct, what would take place if he obtained supreme power. I have pronounced *Helena*, the mother of Constantine the Great, a *Christian:* for I do not hesitate to admit as true, what *Theodoret* states, (Hist. Eccles. L. i. c. 17.) that she instilled into her son the elements of piety. From this opinion I am not induced to recede, by a passage in *Eusebius*, (de vita Constantini, L. iii. c. 47. p. 506.) from which learned men would prove, that *he* converted *her* from the worship of the Gods to the Christian religion. For that passage may very suitably be understood of his inspiring her with a desire to manifest, by actions and various works, her piety towards God. *Maximianus Galerius*, the last of the Emperors, was indeed unfriendly to the Christians; but, being the son-in-law of *Diocletian*, he [p. 913.] had a wife, *Valeria*, who followed the pious example of her mother *Prisca*, and was averse from the worship of imaginary Deities. The state of the Roman

commonwealth, at the commencement of this century, was therefore such, as to indicate a great religious change, and vast accessions to the Christian cause, as near at hand. Situated as the three imperial courts then were, a slight unforeseen occurrence might divest the priests and worshippers of the Gods of a large part of their honors and emoluments, and place the Christian religion on the throne. As this danger was much better understood by the pontiffs of the Gods and the friends of the ancient religion, than it can be by us with the few and dubious monuments before us, who can wonder, that they exerted all their diligence and cunning to avert that danger? But, for their own preservation and that of their Deities, it was necessary, that a persecution more violent than any of the preceding and more pernicious to the Christians, should be got up by the authority not merely of one but of all the Emperors, and should extend through all the Roman provinces: for the persecutions under the former Emperors were only partial tempests, of short continuance or limited extent; or they were so obstructed in various ways, that, though not a little afflictive to the Christian cause, they did not destroy its vital energies. Yet it was a very difficult business, which necessity compelled the patrons of the Gods to undertake. For they had to act upon a man sluggish, timid, encompassed by Christians, and of a disposition by no means cruel, averse from shedding blood, and fond of peace and quietude: for, that such was *Diocletian*, both his actions and the testimony of the ancients show. But as he was both credulous and superstitious, they concluded to terrify him with fictitious oracles, omens, and other artifices; and thus to obtain from him by *fear*, what they could not accomplish by arguments. History acquaints us with two of their artifices; which demonstrate the fears of the priests as well as their malice and cunning. One of them is stated by a very distinguished and trust-worthy witness, the Emperor *Constantine* the Great, in his public letter to the provincials of the East, (apud *Eusebium* de vita Constantini L. ii. c. 50, 51. p. 467.) It was reported to the Emperor, that Apollo had complained,—not through the priest by whom he usually gave forth his oracles, but personally, by a mournful voice issuing from a cavern, Obstare sibi justos viros in terra degentes, quo minus vera praediceret, atque idcirco falsa ex tripode oracula reddi. *Diocletian*, when informed of this oracle, at once anxiously enquired of the courtiers about him, who were those *just persons*, whom Apollo accused. And some of the sacrificers or priests of the Gods, being present, instantly replied, that they were the Christians. On hearing this, the Emperor was in a rage, and forthwith decided, that severe laws should be issued against the Christians, and that their religion should be extir-
[p. 914.] pated. But soon after, being an unstable man, and perhaps being pacified by his wife and christian friends, he abandoned his designs and returned again to a state of tranquillity.—Of the reality of the occurrence, there can be no doubt; for *Constantine* was himself present at the time, and he affirms on oath, or calls God to witness, that he speaks the truth: Te testem appello, Deus altisime.—This oracle, it is manifest, was a fabrication of the priests of Apollo: and it obviously had a twofold object. In the first place, the Christians, in order to convert the idol worshippers to wisdom, demonstrated the falsehood and equivocation of the oracles uttered by the Gods; and thence they

inferred, that the Deities worshipped by the pagans, were unreal beings. And it is well known, that the priests defended the truth and sanctity of the pagan religion by divination; and therefore, if this argument were overthrown, the chief prop and support of the popular religion was removed. And perhaps the Christians who were the ministers and friends of the Emperor, had assailed the superstition of *Diocletian* himself by arguments from the vanity and falsity of divination and oracles. The fact alleged, the priests could not deny: for they were daily confounded by examples of the flexible, false, and dubious oracles. And hence they only attempted to account for the fact, that the Gods no longer relieved, as formerly, the anxieties of those who consulted them, with clear and certain responses. And honest *Apollo* himself acknowledged, that being hard pressed by the Christians, his oracles had failed of late: but he charged the blame on the *just* or the Christians, who withstood his power of divination.—But whatever construction we put upon it, the response was not only a stupid but a hazardous one: for the Emperor might infer from it, that the Christians' God, and Christians themselves, were more powerful than Apollo. Yet with such a man as Diocletian, imbecile, sluggish, and superstitious, this was a grave and important matter.—The epithet *just*, given by Apollo to Christians in the oracle, was not a commendation, as some learned men have supposed. For who ever praises his enemies? It was rather a reproach. And Apollo denominates those the *just*, who vainly and falsely boast of their justice, who without any reason pretend to be more just than others, and who maintained that the whole worship of God is summed up in righteousness, and therefore contemned the sacrifices, the ceremonies of their ancestors, and the public religious rites.—With this first object of the oracle under consideration, another was very closely connected. By this oracle, the priests wished to stimulate the Emperor to put an end to the peace of the Christians, and to induce him to enact severe laws against them.—This event occurred, undoubtedly, in the year 302, or the year before the persecution.

A little afterward, another plot of the same character, occurred in the East. Of this we have an account in *Lactantius*, (Institut. divinar. L. iv. c. 27. p. 393. edit. Heumann.) and in the work generally ascribed to *Lactantius*, (de mortibus persequutor. c. 10. p. 943.) In the year 302, while *Diocletian* was in the [p. 915.] East, as his fears led him to inquire into future events, he sacrificed sheep, and searched in their livers for indications of coming events, according to the rules of haruspicy. The haruspices, cunning and crafty men, pretended not to find the usual signs in the entrails, and frequently repeated their sacrifices. After several fruitless researches, the master of the haruspices said: Ideirco non respondere sacra, (that is, the reason why future events could not be divined by the entrails of the sheep, was) quod rebus divinis profani homines (thus the impostor designated the christians,) interessent. For among the ministers and friends of the Emperor, who, according to the rules of their station, followed him into the temple, and attended him while sacrificing, there were many Christians. *Lactantius* believed, that here was a miracle; for the Christians who attended on the sacrificing Emperor, he says: Immortale signum (the sign of the cross,) frontibus suis imposuisse: hoc facto, daemones fugatos et sacra turbata esse. Many of the moderns follow the judgment of *Lactantius*. And that *he* should attribute to the cross the power of chasing away demons, and should consider haruspicy an invention of the Devil for deluding mortals, I do not much wonder: but when I see men of our own age, and not destitute of learning, agreeing with him, and entertaining no doubts that the haruspices did foretell future occurrences by the entrails of sacrificed animals, and that the sign of the cross could frustrate this sort of divination, I am at a loss what to say. It is very manifest, that the haruspices wished to terrify the timid and superstitious Emperor, who was continually surrounded by Christians; and they pretended, that the business of divination failed of success, as Apollo had already declared, because Christians were present; and their aim was, to stimulate the Emperor, who was eager to know future events, to drive Christians from his court, and subject them to persecution. Besides, the soothsayers, the diviners, the augurs and the haruspices, as appears from many examples, could not easily practice their futile arts in the presence of Christians, who, as they were aware, could see through their tricks, and were ready to expose them.—This new fraud of the priests was more successful than the former: for *Diocletian*, boiling with indignation, as *Latantius* states: Non eos (tantum,) qui sacris ministrabant, sed (etiam) universos, qui in palatio erant, sacrificare jubebat, et in eos, si detrectassent, verberibus animadverti, etiam milites cogi ad sacrificia, datis ad praepositos litteris, praecipiebat, ut qui non paruissent, militia solverentur. But, as the Emperor was unstable, and not of a cruel character, this fit of rage also soon cooled down.

§ II. **Maximianus Galerius moves Diocletian to commence Persecution, A. D. 303.** As these artifices produced little effect, the priests used *Maximianus Galerius*, a man naturally cruel, pround, superstitious, barbarous, and hostile to the Christians, for inflaming the mind of his father-in-law against the Christians. And [p. 916.] this high patron of the sinking cause of the Gods, seems to have been found ready at hand, rather than sought for, by the anxious ministers of the Gods. For his own rough and furious temperament, which delighted in nothing but war, and his mother's extravagant devotion to the Gods and to the priests, and that lust of power with which he burned, sufficiently prompted him to extirpate a class of people opposed to his desires and purposes. He therefore did not cease to urge and importune *Diocletian*, then residing at Nicomedia, till he finally obtained from him, in the year 303, an edict, by which the temples of the Christians throughout the Roman empire were to be demolished, their sacred books to be burned, and Christians themselves to be deprived of all their civil privileges and honors.(1) This first edict, although it spared the lives of the Christians, yet caused the destruction of many, who refused to deliver up to the magistrates the sacred books, the furniture of the temples and the treasures (of the churches,) as the imperial law demanded. And yet many, even among the bishops and clergy, to save their lives obeyed the commands of the Emperor, and gave up the books in their hands and the sacred utensils; and these persons, who supposed themselves guilty of only a slight fault, were considered by the more resolute Christians as having committed sacrilege, and were therefore reproachfully denominated *Traditors*.(2)

(1) This most bloody of all the persecutions against the Christians, a persecution of ten years continuance, has been called the persecution of *Diocletian;* but it might more properly be called the persecution of *Maximian*. For although Diocletian, being deceived by the frauds of the priests, inflicted some injuries on the Christians resident at court, or attached to the camps, and also subsequently enacted laws adverse to them; yet it is certain, that the principal author of this calamity was his son-in-law, *Maximianus Galerius*,—a man of low birth, agrestic, distinguished for nothing but military bravery, and friendly to none but soldiers,—who extorted from his unwilling and reluctating father-in-law the edicts destructive to the Christians. It is true that Diocletian, on occasion of two conflagrations in the palace at Nicomedia, came down upon the Christians of that city, in his first law against Christians. But those who attentively inspect this furious attack upon them by the personal direction of the Emperor, will perceive that the Christians were arraigned before a court and punished as *incendiaries*, or not on religious grounds, but as perpetrators of an alledged crime. And hence this calamity, though interwoven with the great tragedy, should be considered as a distinct and separate act. I may add, that in less than two years from the commencement of the persecution, *Diocletian* relinquished the imperial power, and retired to private life; whence it [p. 917.] is clear that the greatest part of the persecution, or that decreed and inflicted on Christians during the eight following years, is not attributable to him. And lastly, *Maximian* himself, in the edict by which, a little before his death, he restored peace to the Christians, confesses that he himself moved the persecution. See *Eusebius*, (Histor. Eccles. L. viii. c. 17. p. 315.) and *Lactantius*, (de mortibus persequutor. c. 34. p. 984. edit Heumann.)

There can be no doubt that the pagan priests, who had in vain attempted to stimulate Diocletian to attack the Christians, were the principal authors and instigators of this bloody persecution by *Maximian*, a barbarous man, and ignorant of everything except military affairs, and of course both superstitious and cruel. And men like him, attached to nothing but lust and war, usually care little about religion and sacred things. Yet such persons, chiefly occupied with lust and war, if their passions are roused by cunning men, can readily engage in the most unjust and cruel projects; and can persevere in prosecuting them, if there are causes which confirm and strengthen their unrighteous plans and purposes. *Maximian* himself, in his edict in favor of the Christians just mentioned, states, that attachment to the religion handed down from the ancients, was a reason why he assailed the Christians, the followers of a new religion. He says: Volueramus antehac juxta leges veteres et publicam disciplinam Romanorum cuncta corrigere, atque id providere, ut etiam Christiani, qui parentum suorum reliquerant sectam, ad bonas mentes redirent. I have no doubt, that he wrote this in sincerity: but undoubtedly, this zeal for the Romish superstition, in a man caring only for the body and disregarding the soul, would have been sluggish and inefficient, if it had not been excited and inflamed by the priests.—But the priests were aided by the querulousness of his mother, *Romulia*, whose influence with her son was very great. She was, mulier admodum superstitiosa, as *Lactantias* says, (de mortibus persequutor. c. 11. p. 944.) and when she had conceived hatred against the Christians, Filium non minus superstitiosum querelis muliebribus ad tollendos homines incitabat. The cause of her hatred to the Christians, *Lactantius* tells us, was this: She offered sacrifices almost every day, and then held feasts upon the meats sacrificed and presented to the Gods. But the Christians would not attend those feasts; nor could they do it, consistently with their principles. It is presumeable, that this undoubtedly proud woman regarded this conduct as disrespectful to herself. But besides this reason, I apprehend, another may be gathered out of *Lactantius*, although it is not expressly stated. He tells us that Romulia, Deorum montium cultricem fuisse; i. e. that she worshipped the Deities supposed by the Romans to preside over mountains. Now the Christians of that age, as much as possible, chose to erect their sacred edifices on mountains and elevated places. [p. 918.] The Christian temple at Nicomedia, on which the persecution first commenced and which was destroyed by command of the Emperor before it was completed, was situated on a mountain: In alto constituta ecclesia, ex palatio (Imperatoris) videbatur; says *Lactantius*, (loc. cit. c. 12. p. 947.) And at Carthage also, as we have seen in another place, there was a christian church built on a mountain. I therefore suspect, that this woman regarded the christian temple on the mountain as highly injurious to those Gods whom she honored; and on this account, she besought her son with tears and entreaties to suppress this reproach to the Gods. This conjecture is strengthened by the consideration, that she and her son were undoubtedly then living at Nicomedia, in the imperial palace, and of course had the Christians' temple continually before their eyes.—This ground for persecuting the Christians, is dishonorable to *Maximian*; but in the edict already twice mentioned, he states another reason rather more honorable and not improbable; which it is strange that no one has mentioned when treating on this subject. For he says, that he assailed the Christians because they had departed from the religion of their ancestors, and had become split into various sects and parties, differing in opinion and practice. Siquidem quadam ratione tanta eosdem Christianos voluntas invasisset, et tanta stultitia occupasset, ut non illa veterum instituta sequerentur, quæ forsitan primi parentes eorundem constituerant, sed pro arbitrio suo, atque ut hisdem erat libitum, ita sibimet leges facerent, quas observarent, et per diversa (loca) varios populos congregarent: (i. e. and formed various sects and churches in divers places. *Eusebius* correctly apprehended the meaning of the Emperor, and expressed it in his Greek version of the edict; (Hist. Eccles. L. viii. c. 17.) *Maximian* therefore distinctly charged upon the Christians:—I. That the religion of Christians in that age differed essentially from the first or primitive christianity, established by their progenitors.—II. That in the primitive religion of Christians, the institutions of the Romans and other nations were undoubtedly retained and approved: that is, that the worship of inferior Deities or Gods, to whom the supreme Deity committed the government of the world, was not rejected or disapproved by the author and head of this religion.—III. But that the later Christians had abandoned that first law of their religion, and had substituted in place of it new regulations.—IV. And hence various sects, holding very different opinions, had arisen among them, in the several provinces of the Roman empire. This reason for the persecution was unquestionably suggested to the Emperor, who was wholly ignorant of such matters, by those Platonic philosophers, hostile to the Christians, some of whom were called to that council at the court of Nicomedia, which deliberated on the subject of crushing and destroying the Christians. For these philosophers, as appears from credible testimony elsewhere adduced, wished to make out, that the later Christians had corrupted the religion taught by Christ, and had swerved from the injunctions of their master: That Jesus Christ sought indeed to correct certain faults [p. 919.] and imperfections in the ancient religions, to restore the knowledge and worship of the supreme Deity, which had been obscured and almost extinguished by the worship of the Gods, and to abrogate some useless and superstitious ceremonies; but he by no means wished to subvert the most ancient religion, or the worship and honors of the ministers of divine providence, that is, of the inferior Deities who presided over nations and departments of nature: for nature itself and right reason taught us, that some honor or worship, though much less than to the supreme Deity, ought to be paid to those exalted Beings whom God employed in the government of human affairs: And although the priests and the people went too far in this matter, and transferred the ministers of God into Gods, yet the thing itself, if restored to its primitive integrity, could by no means be condemned or disapproved: And that the Christians, as they had departed from the intentions and precepts of their master in this as well as other things, so they sought wholly to subvert all the institutions of the ancients and the worship of the Gods, and even wished to have Christ worshipped as a God, although he never arrogated to himself divine honors: That having thus changed the original laws of Christ, it followed as a necessary consequence, that the Christians became divided into various mutually hostile sects. Such were the common sentiments of *Ammonius* and most of his followers: and they undoubtedly brought them forward, to fix the fluctuating and hesitating mind of Diocletian, and to induce him to enact laws against the Christians. And they said it was right, that the Christians, who, as *Maximanian* says, Parentum suorum sectam reliquerant, should be compelled—not indeed by capital punishments, yet by severe laws,—to return back to their ancient religion: which if they should do, all disputes respecting the Gods and religious subjects would be at an end.—Lastly, it can scarcely be doubted, if we consider the conduct of *Maximian* and the state of the republic at that time, that *political reasons* also conduced to recommend the war upon the Christians: and these, perhaps, had more influence on the mind of *Maximian*, than the exhortations of the priests, the entreaties of his mother, or the reasonings of the philosophers. Being inflated with pride and the lust of dominion,—for he ridiculously wished to be thought procreated by the God *Mars;* (See *Lactantius*, loc. cit. c. 9. p. 942: *Victor*, Epitome c. 35.) —he could brook neither a superior nor an equal, but wished to dethrone the other Emperors, and to rule the Roman empire alone. It is well known that two years after the persecution commenced, he deprived both his father-in-law and *Maximianus Herculeus* of the imperial dignity. But the Christians appeared to stand in the way of his ambition. For they were completely devoted to *Constantius Chlorus* and his very promising son *Constantine*, both of whom greatly favored the Christian worship and cared little for the Gods; and under *their* government, the Christians hoped to enjoy happy times. And hence it was easily foreseen, that the Christians would take arms, and would vigorously [p. 920.] defend their protectors if any attempt were made either to exclude them from the throne or to crush them by war. But *Maximian*, the youngest of the Emperors, could not hope to become lord of the whole empire, except by the extermination of *Constantius* and his son. And, therefore, to prevent the occurrence of a dubious civil war, in which the Christians would combat for *Constantius* and his son, and the worshippers of the Gods for *Maximian*, it seemed necessary to weaken the very considerable power and resources of the Christians, and, if possible, to exterminate their religion, before the contest for supremacy in the republic was commenced.

Moved by such considerations, in the year 303, *Maximian* proceeded to Nicomedia, the capitol of Bithynia, whither *Diocletian* had retired on coming from the East, for the purpose of persuading his father-in-law to enter into a public and formal war against the Christians. On this subject, there was, between the father-in-law and the son-in-law, strong opposition both of feelings and opinions. Diocletian, indeed, conceded to his son-in-law, that Christians might be excluded from the palace and the army, and that all the attendants on the palace and the soldiers should be compelled to sacrifice to the Gods; but he refused to issue public laws against the Christians, and especially to inflict on them capital punishments. Says *Lactantius*, (loc. cit. c. 11. p. 945.): Ostendebat quam perniciosum esset, inquietari orbem terræ, fundi sanguinem multorum. Satis esse, si palatinos tantum et milites ab ea religione prohiberet. But this moderation would not comport at all with the designs of *Maximian*. He wished to reign sole Emperor; and of this he could have no hopes, if the Christians were spared. He therefore urged, that public laws should be enacted against all Christians throughout the Roman empire; and that they, who—sacrificio repugnassent, vivos cremandos esse. The sooner to accomplish his designs, and wholly overthrow the Christian community at once, he was disposed to proceed, not as in the former persecutions, which sought gradually to overcome the minds of Christians by exhortations, menaces, imprisonments, tortures, confiscations of goods, banishments, &c. but to adopt a more summary process, and decree that those who refused to offer sacrifices, should forthwith be put to death, with all manner of tortures. If this cruel counsel had prevailed, a very grievous wound would unquestionably have been inflicted on the Christian cause. But *Diocletian* could not be induced to assent to it. After various discussions, it was determined to refer the very important matter to the advice of friends, or to a few prudent men of approved fidelity. A few persons, therefore, were selected, partly from the jurists and partly from the military officers, who were to judge which mode of proceeding would be best and most salutary to the republic. *Maximian*, being exceedingly attached to soldiers and military affairs, undoubtedly thought military officers would be the best counsellors; but Diocletian had more confidence in jurists, on a subject relating to the interests of the republic. Says *Lactantius*, (loc. cit. p. 945.): Admissi ergo judi- [p. 921.] ces pauci, et pauci militares, ut dignitate antecedebant, interrogabantur. But *Lactantius*, who often does injustice, if I can judge, to the Emperors that persecuted the Christians, misrepresents the design of Diocletian in referring this question to the judgment of men of experience and intelligence. For he says, it was Diocletian's custom, Cum malum facere vellet, multos in consilium advocare, ut aliorum culpæ adscriberetur, quicquid ipse deliquerat. But *Lactantius*' own statements show, that this censure is unjust. For it is clear, from the facts recorded, that Diocletian was averse from doing the *evil*, and he wished to hear the opinion of eminent men, in order to avert from the Christians much of the evil which his son-in-law was plotting. The Emperor's intentions are also vindicated by the fact, that when the more rigorous course was approved by the arbiters mutually chosen, he was utterly unwilling to follow it. In this council of friends or wise men, the harsh plan of *Maximian* received the preference. For some, from personal hatred of the Christians, others from fear of offending *Maximian*, and others to gain his favor, Inimicos Deorum et hostes religionum publicarum tollendos esse censebant. Among the jurists or judges called to decide this question, was *Hierocles*, the vicar-governor of Bithynia; whom *Lactantius*, (loc. cit. p. 952.) pronounces, Auctorem et consiliarium ad faciendam persecutionem fuisse: and he says, (Instit. divinar. L. v. c. 2. p. 417.): Auctor in primis faciendæ persecutionis fuit. This man, afterwards in the midst of the persecution, addressed two short treatises to the Christians, whom he called (φιλαληθεῖς) *lovers of truth*. And in these treatises, he loads with much abuse and injustice the Christian Scriptures, which he shows himself to have read attentively; and Jesus Christ, whom he has the audacity to compare with Apollonius Tyanæus, yet without denying his miracles; and especially Peter and Paul, the Apostles of Christ. *Lactantius*, in the latter of the passages just quoted, states pretty fully the argument of this treatise against the Christians. This *Hierocles*, as learned men have long agreed, was a different person from the Platonic philosopher of the same name, whose respectable Commentary on the Golden Verses of Pythagoras, has been often published. Yet, from the extracts which *Lactantius* makes from his book, it is apparent, that he also was a follower of Ammonius Saccas, or one of those philosophers called the younger Platonists. For, although he would have the gods to be worshipped, yet he makes them to be not gods, but merely the ministers of the one supreme God. Says *Lactantius*, addressing him: Ademisti Jovi tuo regnum, eumque summa potestate depulsum in ministrorum (Dei) numerum redegisti. - - Affirmas Deos esse, et illos tamen subjicis et mancipas ei Deo, cujus religionem conaris evertere. He had just before said; Assertor Deorum, eos ipsos ad ultimum prodidisti. For *Hierocles*, at the end of his book, composed a splendid eulogy on the [p. 922.] supreme God, in order to show, that he was far from approving the superstition of the people and the priests, and that he would have the ancestral Deities so honored, that God should still be exalted greatly above them all, and should receive the supreme homage. Says *Lactantius:* Prosecutus es summi Dei laudes, quem Regem, quem maximum, quem opificem rerum, quem fontem bonorum, quem parentem omnium, quem factorem, altoremque viventium confessus es.—Epilogus itaque te tuus arguit stultitiæ, vanitatis, erroris.—When contemplating this subject, it appears to me exceedingly probable, that from this *Hierocles* especially, originated the charge against the Christians in the edict of *Maximian*, that they had changed the religion taught by their fathers; and also the project of burning the sacred books of the Christians, against which he inveighs so violently in his work, taxing them with many errors.

Although the opinion of *Maximian*, that the Christians should be extirpated, was approved by the arbiters chosen by the two Emperors, yet *Diocletian* still refused his consent. Men, he said, were fallible: and therefore, that nothing might be done preposterously and imprudently, he would have the matter referred to the Gods, and particularly to the Miletian Apollo. And, as *Lactantius* says, Apollo when consulted, answered, ut divinae religionis inimicus; that is, he took sides with Maximian, and ordered the Christians to be exterminated. Therefore, to satisfy his son-in-law and friends, and likewise Apollo, and yet follow his own timid disposition and aversion to blood, he adopted a sort of middle course; viz. he would allow public laws to be enacted against the Christians, which he had before refused; but he would have the business accomplished without bloodshed: (rem sine sanguine transigi volebat.)—From the facts now faithfully stated, is it not evident that Diocletian was reluctantly, and most unwillingly, brought to disturb and persecute the Christians? and that the cause of the many evils endured by the Christians for ten years, was rather in *Maximian*, who was inflamed with superstition and lust for power, and was instigated by the priests and his mother? And hence, in my judgment, large deductions should be made from the reproaches and complaints, which both the ancients and the moderns have heaped upon *Diocletian.* I acknowledge that he was in fault, from his instability, superstition, and timidity; but he was much less in fault, than is commonly supposed.

This long and cruel persecution commenced in the month of February or April, A.D. 303 as has been shown by learned men, *Tillemonte*, *Noris*, (Histor. Donatistar. P. 1. c. 2. Opp. tom. iv. p. 9, 14, 15.) and many others: and it was introduced by the destruction of the spacious Christian temple at Nicomedia, and the burning of the books found in it. See *Lactantius*, (de mortibus persequutor. c. 12. p. 946, 947.) The Emperor's edict was published the day following. Strange as it may appear, its specific injunctions are not stated, collectively and methodically, by any of the ancients: and therefore we collect them from diverse sources.—I. The Emperor's edict required all the sacred edi- [p. 923.] fices of the Christians to be levelled with the ground. See *Eusebius*, (Hist. Eccles. L. viii. c. 2. p. 293, 294: and Oratio in laudem Constant. c. 9.

p. 629.) It added, that the thrones of the bishops in those edifices, and the doors, should be publicly burned. See the Gesta purgationis Felicis Aptungani, (apud Steph. *Baluzium*, Miscellan. L. ii. p. 84.): Galatius perrexit ad locum, ubi orationes celebrare (Christiani) consueti fuerant. Inde cathredram tulimus et epistolas salutatorias, et ostia omnia combusta sunt, *secundum sacrum praeceptum*. Whatever was of stone, was to be pulled down; and what was of wood was to be burned.—II. The decree commanded that the sacred books should be delivered up, by the Christians, and especially by the bishops and clergy, to the magistrates. See the Passio S. Felicis, (apud *Baluz*. Miscell. tom. ii. p. 77, 78.): Magnilianus curator dixit: Libros deificos habetis? Januarius presbyter respondit: Habemus. Magnilianus dixit: Date illos igni aduri. The same Magnilianus thus addressed Felix the bishop: Da libros vel membranas qualescunque penes te habes. Felix episcopus dixit: Habeo, sed non trado legem Domini mei. Magnilianus dixit: Primum est *quod Imperatores jusserunt*, quia nihil est quod loqueris. Other examples may be seen in the citations hereafter made.—And the penalty of *death* was decreed, both against the magistrates who should be negligent in executing the decree, and against the Christians who should refuse to give up the sacred books. Of the penalty incurred by the Christians refusiug to surrender their religious books, when demanded by the governors or their officials, we shall soon speak: at present, we speak only of the magistrates who were remiss or lenient in the requisition of the Christian books. That they were to be punished with *death*, appears from two passages in *Augustine*, (Breviculum collationis cum Donatistis, c. 15. et 17. Opp. tom. ix. p. 387. et 390.) One Secundus had boasted, that when ordered by the magistrate to deliver up the books, he declared he would not. It was replied, This is incredible. For a magistrate would endanger his life, if he should let such a man go unpunished. Secundus Centurioni et Beneficiario respondit, se omnino non tradere Scripturas. Quod illi auditum quomodo illo dimisso renuntiare potuerint *sine suo exitio* non apparet. Death (*exitium*) was therefore the penalty incurred by a magistrate, who should hesitate to obey the decree of the Emperor. The second passage expresses the same thing more clearly: Ordo et Curator et Centurio et Beneficiarius *ad discrimen capitis* pervenissent, qui Secundum tradere nolentem impunitum dimisisse prodebantur. Hence the more cautious magistrates did not send their centurions or other subordinates, to bring the sacred books from the temples and bishops' houses, but contrary to custom, they went themselves to the churches and clergymen's houses; and whatever books or other articles they found there, they caused to be carefully collected, inventoried, and taken away. A striking example of this, we find in the Gesta purgationis Caeciliani, (apud *Baluzium*, Miscell. tom. [p. 924.] ii. p. 92 &c.) For Munatius Felix, a flamen, and the chief magistrate and curator of the colony of the Cirtensians, went in person, first to the Christian temple, and then to the dwellings of the bishop, the lectors, the subdeacons, and even of the private Christians, and every where demanded the books and papers: Proferte scripturas legis, et si quid aliud hic habetis (in the temple, the vestments, the chalices, the lamps, the candlesticks,) ut praecepto et jussioni parere possitis. III. The imperial edict decreed, that all the Christian books

given up or found, should be publicly *burned* in the forum. *Eusebius*, (Hist. Eccles. L. viii. c. 2. p. 293, 294. See also p. 318.) Here should be read the Acta passionis Philippi, episcopi Adrianopolitani, (apud *Mabillonium*, Analector. tom. iv. p. 189 &c. of the new edit.) Bassus the governor, there addresses Philip thus: Legem Imperatoris audistis, jubentis nusquam colligere Christianos. - - Vasa ergo quaecunque vobiscum sunt aurea, vel argentea: Scripturas etiam, per quas vel legitis, vel docetis, obtutibus nostrae potestatis ingerite. This Bassus, as I have said was usual with the more cautious magistrates, went in person to the temple of the Christians: and the bishop with his assistants standing at the doors, immediately gave up the vessels. Vasa, quae postulas, mox accipe. Ista contemnimus. Non pretioso metallo Deum colimus, sed timore. But the books he refused to give up. Bassus therefore snatched them from the place where they were kept, carried them into the forum, and, according to the Emperor's command, *burned* them all. Igne subposito, adstantibus etiam peregrinis, civibusque collectis, scripturas omnes divinas in medium misit incendium.—By the Christian books ordered to be burned, the Emperor seems to have understood merely their divine books, or the holy scripture, *libros deificos, scripturas legis*, as it is expressed in the passages just quoted from *Baluze*, or γραφὰς, as Eusebius calls them. But as he knew not what books the Christians accounted divine, and what human, he used general terms; and as those who were entrusted with the execution of the law were equally ignorant, and supposed that the Christians accounted *all* as divine, that were religiously kept either in the churches or in the dwellings of the bishops and presbyters; therefore all papers, letters, documents, and Acts of martyrs were indiscriminately drawn from their repositories and cast into the flames. Bassus of Heraclea, as we have before seen, demanded of Philip *all* the *scripturas, per quas vel legerent, vel docerent*; and whatever he found in the temple, he ordered to be burned. From the Acta purgationis Felicis, (apud *Baluz.* Miscel. tom. ii. p. 84.) it appears that even the *Epistolae Salutatoriae*, which the bishops wrote to one another on various occasions, were burned. For these were commonly deposited in the churches. And hence the history of Christianity suffered an immense loss in this Diocletian persecution. For all that had come down from the ear-
[p. 925.] lier ages of the Church, the documents, the papers, the epistles, the laws, the Acts of the martyrs and of councils,—from which the early history of the Christian community might be happily illustrated,—*al'*, or at least very many of them, perished in these commotions.—And I have little doubt, that the *Hiercoles* already mentioned, and such other philosophers of the Platonic school as may have sitten among the arbiters chosen by the two Emperors, instilled into those Emperors this malignant purpose of destroying by fire the sacred books of the Christians. This project certainly could not have originated from uninformed men, who had no knowledge of Christianity, or such men as *Maximian* and his father-in-law; but it must have come from men of learning, men acquainted with the sacred volume, men who had themselves seen what is there inculcated, and knew from their own perusal, what influence the scriptures have to fortify the mind of Christians against pagan worship and superstition. And just such a man, was *Hierocles*; who, in his work against the Christians,

as *Lactantius* says, (Instit. divinar. L. v. c. 2. p. 417, 418.) : Adeo multa, adeo intima (ex sacro codice) enumerabat, ut aliquando Christianus fuisse videretur. —IV. The imperial edict decreed, that such as resolved to remain Christians, and refused to sacrifice to the Gods, should forfeit all their honors, offices, rank, and all civil rights and privileges, and if servants they should be incapable of manumission. *Eusebius* has briefly and imperfectly described this part of the law, (Hist. Eccles. L. viii. c. 2. p. 294.) He says: *Ut honorati quidem* (τιμῆς ἐπειλημμένοι. He doubtless means those in public stations, or holding some office or post of honor,) *infamia notarentur* (ἀτίμους. which, I think, *Valesius* here translates in language too strong. I should suppose the sense to be, *That they shall be divested of all their honors and distinctions* :) Τοὺς δὲ ἐν οἰκετίαις ἐλευθερίας στερεῖσθαι. As to the meaning of these words, learned men are not agreed. Henry *Valesius*, with whom many agree, renders them : *Plebeii vero libertate spoliarentur.* This very learned man supposes the Emperor decreed, that if men holding posts of honor ad distinction, would not return to the religion of their ancestors, they should be reduced to the rank of plebeians, and be deprived of all honor and distinction ; but if they were plebeians, they should lose their freedom, and become servants or slaves. But, in the first place, the natural import of the phrase, οἱ ἐν οἰκετίαις, is inconsistent with this interpretation : for it almost invariably denotes *servants* and not plebeians. Again, history is opposed to it : for no example can be produced of plebeian Christians being made slaves ; while many examples occur of persons retaining their liberty who merely gave up the sacred books. Hence, very many, and I go with them, prefer the Latin translation of the passage in Eusebius by *Rufinus*, a very competent authority in this case. *Rufinus* renders it : *Si quis servorum permansisset Christianus, libertatem consequi* [non] *posset.* Some punishment, undoubtedly, was to be inflicted on servants who refused to sacrifice to the Gods : yet the Emperor wished no blood to be shed in this transaction : and therefore servants could not be punished, except by the loss of all prospect of obtaining freedom ; and no more grievous punishment [p. 926.] could be inflicted on servants sighing for liberty. *Eusebius* therefore speaks only of the penalties decreed by the Emperor against men of distinction and slaves ; of plebeians he says nothing.—*Lactantius*, (de mortibus persequutor. c. 13. p. 947.) states more at large, and yet not very distinctly, the penalties of the Diocletian edict, thus : Postridie prospositum est edictum, quo cavebatur, ut religionis illius homines cararent omni honore et dignitate, (this manifestly refers exclusively to the men holding offices and honors ;) tormentis subjecti essent, ex quocunque gradu et ordine venirent, (this reaches all classes, or both gentlemen and plebeians ; yet the former rather than the latter ;) adversus eos omnis actio valeret, ipsi non de injuriâ, non de adulterio, non de rebus ablatis agere possent, (this, I suppose, was intended for the plebeians. They might be accused by any body, but could accuse no one ;) libertatem denique ac vocem non haberent. This last clause I refer, with *Baluze*, to servants : and I assign it this meaning. Such servants as refuse to abandon the Christian religion shall forfeit all hopes of becoming free, and they shall not be allowed *vocem*, or have a right to petition or pray for liberty.—V. Moreover, the decree of the Emperor severely prohibited all religious *assemblages.* This we learn from the edict of the Emperor *Maximin* in favor of the Christians, extant in *Eusebius,* (Hist. Eccles. L. ix. c. 10. p. 364.) which says: Compertum nobis fuit, occasione *legis* a Diocletiano et Maximiano parentibus nostris latæ, ut Christianorum *conventus* penitus abolerentur, (τὰς συνόδους τῶν χριστιανῶν ἐξηρῆσθαι,) multas concussiones factas. These words of *Maximin* likewise informs us, that the edict was promulgated, not in the name of Diocletian only, but in the name of both Diocletian and Maximian. It appears also, that *death* was the penalty for holding religious meetings. There are extant, in *Baluze's* Miscellanea, (tom. ii. p. 56, &c.) the Acta martyrum Saturnini Presbyteri, Felicis, Dativi, and others, who were put to death for holding meetings (*collectas,*) or, in the words of the Acta, Quia ex more dominica sacramenta celebraverant. This was their chief, nay, their only crime: Cum Proconsuli offerrentur, suggererenturque, quod transmissi essent Christiani, qui contra interdictum Imperatorum et Cæsarum collectam dominicam celebrassent, primum Proconsul Dativum interrogat, utrum collectam fecisset: qui se Christianum in collecta fuisse profitebatur.—VI. Finally, it appears from the edict of *Maximin* just quoted, (apud *Euseb.* Hist. Eccles. L. ix. c. 10. p. 364.) that, (ἐκ τῆς κελεύσεως) by the decree of the Emperors, the houses and grounds, which had belonged to the Christians, were confiscated, seized upon by the cities, and either sold or given away.

(2) That many of the Christians were put to death, immediately after the promulgation of the imperial edict, is placed beyond all controversy by *Eusebi-* [p. 927.] *us, Lactantius,* and others of the ancients. And yet Diocletian had ordered the business to be conducted without bloodshed, and he would not allow persons to be punished capitally, who should refuse to sacrifice to the gods. I have therefore no doubt, that the persons slain, were put to death because they would not surrender the sacred books. By the edict of the Emperor, this was a capital offence. In the Passio Felicis Tubizacensis, published by *Baluze,* (Miscellanea, tom. ii. p. 77 &c.) the judge thus addresses Felix: Si Scripturas deificas (I suppose the word *deificas,* so often repeated in these and other *Acta,* was used in the very edict of the Emperors,) tradere nolueris, *capite* plecteris. Felix episcopus dixit: Plus paratus sum plecti *capite,* quam *libros* dominicos sacrilegio tradere. The *Cognitor,* on hearing this reply, and before pronouncing sentence, ordered the imperial edict to be read: Tunc memoratus Cognitor jussit, ut sacra Imperatorum (edicta) recitarentur. Cumque a Vincentio scriba quæ constituta fuerant legerentur, Cognitor dixit: Quoniam iste homo tantum in eadem confessione duravit, *secundum præceptum* hunc eundem Felicem episcopum *gladio* animadverti constituo. In the imperial decree, therefore, it was explicitly stated and ordered, that those who persisted in refusing to give up the sacred books, should be capitally punished. The fact is confirmed by numerous examples on record, of persons of various classes being tortured and slain, for no other cause, than that they deemed it sinful to surrender the sacred books, when they knew they were to be burned. *Augustine* (Breviculum collationis cum Donatistis, L. iii. c. 13. p. 386. et c. 15. p. 387.) tells us, that Secundus Tigisitanus, in an Epistle to Mensurius; Commemorasse multos martyres, qui cum tradere noluissent, excruciati et occisi sint: and that Secundus added: Non

quoslibet infimos, sed etiam patresfamilias, cum persecutoribus respondissent, habere se quidem sacros codices, sed omnino tradere nolle, crudelissimis mortibus occisos esse.—And hence, as *Augustine* reports, from an Epistle of Mensurius to Secundus, (loc. cit. c. 13. tom. ix. p. 386.) some Christians, either from weariness of life, or from the hope that their sins would be expiated by a glorious death, voluntarily went before the magistrates, and declared that they had sacred books, but would not surrender them: Quidam in eadem epistolâ (Mensurii) arguebantur et fisci debitores, qui occasione persecutionis vel *carere* vellent onerosâ multis debitis *vitâ*, vel purgare se putarent et quasi abluere facinora sua. For it was supposed, that shedding one's blood for Christ, took away all sins. To these may be added the full testimony of *Optatus Milevitanus*, who explicitly says, that the *Traditors* wished to escape *death*, (de schismate Donatistarum, L. i. § 13. p. 13, 14. edit. du Pin.): Quid commemorem laicos,—quid ministros plurimos, quid diaconos,—quid presbyteros? Ipsi apices et principes omnium, aliqui episcopi, illis temporibus, ut damno æternæ vitæ, *istius incertæ lucis moras brevissimas compararent*, instrumenta divinæ legis [p. 928.] impie tradiderunt. The Emperors, therefore, ordered a severer procedure against those who should refuse to bring forth and surrender the sacred books, than against those who should refuse to sacrifice to the gods. The latter would only forfeit their civil rights and privileges, but the former would forfeit their lives. And, consequently, it is not strictly true, as *Lactantius* affirms, that *Diocletian* commanded the business to be done without bloodshed. Yet, undoubtedly, the philosophers summoned to the council, and especially *Hierocles*, assured the Emperor that if the sacred books of Christians were burned, the whole Christian religion would fall to the ground; and they added, that the Christians, if made liable to capital punishment, would all surrender their books: for they had such a horror of sacrifices, that they would rather die than make an oblation to the gods; but to deliver up their sacred books, was not prohibited by their law, and therefore, undoubtedly, they would all redeem their lives by surrendering their books. Influenced by these arguments, *Diocletian*, who would otherwise have commanded the sparing of blood, permitted the penalty of death to be decreed against refusers to surrender the books. But the result was not as the Emperor anticipated: for multitudes, as we have seen, would sooner die than surrender the divine books. And yet many prized life more than the books; and they were regarded as *apostates*, and were branded with the opprobrious name of *Traditors*. See *Augustine*, de baptismo contra Donatistas, (L. vii. c. 2. tom. ix. p. 126.) The term, however, is ambiguous, for it may denote simply one who delivers up something: or it may, in a more restricted sense, denote a flagitious *betrayer*. Of the vast number of these *Traditors* in Africa, we shall have occasion to speak hereafter. Out of Africa, there arose no controversy respecting *Traditors*, although there can be no doubt, that in all the provinces, there were persons who deemed life more precious than their books. And hence it is highly probable, that the offence of the *Traditors* was esteemed a lighter matter in most parts of the Christian world, than among the Africans, who were naturally ardent.

§ III. **First Year of the Persecution. Occurrences at Nicomedia. New Edicts.** The hatred of *Diocletian* against Christians became more violent a little after the promulgation of his first decree, when two fires occurred in the palace at Nicomedia; for the enemies of Christianity persuaded the credulous and timid old man that the Christians were the authors of those fires. Therefore the Emperor commanded that the Christians of Nicomedia, of all classes and descriptions, should be put to *torture;* and many were burned at the stake as incendiaries.(1) About the same time, se-
[p. 929.] ditions occurred in Armenia and Syria; and as the enemies of Christianity charged the blame of these also upon the Christian pastors and teachers, the emperor issued a *new edict*, requiring all bishops and clergymen to be thrown into prison. This decree was soon afterwards followed by a *third*, in which the Emperor ordered that all the imprisoned clergymen, who refused to worship the Gods, should be compelled to offer sacrifices by tortures and extreme penalties. For the timid Emperor, terrified by the priests and their friends, had come to believe that neither he nor the republic could be safe so long as the Christians remained; and he hoped, that if the bishops and teachers were subdued, their flocks would follow their example. And thus a great multitude of holy and excellent persons, in all the provinces of the Roman empire, were put to death by various kinds of the most cruel executions: and others, mutilated and deprived of their bodily members, were condemned to the mines.(2) *Gaul* alone escaped this calamity; for there *Constantius Chlorus*, although he did not prevent the Christian temples from being demolished, forbid the infliction of personal injuries on the Christians.(3)

(1) *Lactantius*, (de mortibus persequutor. c. 14. p. 948.) mentions *two* conflagrations in the palace at Nicomedia soon after the first edict against the Christians: *Eusebius*, (Hist. Eccles. L. viii. c. 6. p. 297.) mentions only *one;* and *Constantine* the Great, who tells us he was in Nicomedia at the time, (Oratio ad sanctor. cœtum, c. 25. p. 601.) also mentions but *one*. But the second fire, which was fifteen days after the first, was early discovered, and therefore, doubtless, promptly extinguished. And this, I suppose, is the reason why *Eusebius* and *Constantine* take no notice of it.—But respecting the first fire, or rather, respecting its *cause*, there is ground for no little dubitation. For the three witnesses to the occurrence, entirely disagree. *Constantine*, an eyewitness, being then resident at the court of Diocletian, declares that the palace

was struck by lightning and that the *celestial fire* destroyed the *Emperor's bed-chamber:* and he adds, that the Emperor was so terrified by this thunder-clap, that he was all his life after afraid lest he should be struck with lightning. As to any accusation against the Christians, as authors of the fire, he is silent. But *Eusebius*, who published this very Oration of Constantine, annexing it to his history, although he tells us this conflagration was attributed to the Christians, and describes minutely their sufferings in consequence of the [p. 930.] charge, yet declares (ὀυκ οἶδ' ὅπως) that he *did not know the cause* of the fire. And lastly, *Lactantius* says, that *Maximian* himself, in order to obtain severer edicts against the Christians from his father-in-law, Occultis ministris palatio subjecisse incendium; and afterwards caused a rumor among the vulgar, that, Christianos, consilio cum eunuchis habito, de extinguendis principibus cogitasse, et duos Imperatores domi suæ pæne vivos esse combustos. And he states that the second fire, fifteen days after, was contrived by the same *Maximian.*—Now, which of these authors shall we follow? Those learned men, who have written since *Baluze* published the tract of *Lactantius*, one and all place reliance on *Lactantius:* but whether, with due consideration, is a question. Whence did the honest *Lactantius* learn, that *Maximian*, by his servants, fired the palace, in order to excite odium against the Christians? Certainly not from *Maximian* himself, nor from the servants he employed in the business. All who have any knowledge of human affairs, are aware how studiously powerful men and princes, who resort to such crimes, conceal their own agency in them. And *Lactantius* himself acknowledges, that the authors of the fire were (*occulti*) *concealed*, and never (*apparuisse*) *became known.* He therefore undoubtedly derived his statement from the belief, or rather from the *suspicion* of certain Christians; who, knowing that *Maximian* was very malignant against the Christians, *suspected* that this tragedy was artfully contrived by him; and what they thus suspected, they reported to their brethren as a fact. But that this suspicion was not universal, or was only of some few Christians, the silence of *Eusebius* and *Constantine*, I think, places beyond all controversy. For if it had been the common opinion of the Nicomedian Christians, it would certainly have been known by *Constantine* and his friend *Eusebius;* and they, being exceedingly incensed against *Maximian*, would certainly not have omitted a matter so reproachful to the man they hated. Besides, as on the authority of *Constantine*, who cannot possibly be discredited, the palace of Nicomedia was set on fire by *lightning*, I do not see how *Maximian* could have been the author of the conflagration. And lastly, in *Lactantius* himself, there is something which tends to absolve *Maximian*, if not altogether, yet at least in part. For it appears from his statement, that the Christians were not supposed by Diocletian, to have been the authors of the first fire; this we shall soon show more clearly. But if *Maximian* had fired the palace by his servants, in order to enkindle the rage of his father-in-law against the Christians, he would undoubtedly, immediately after the first fire, have accused the Christians of it, either himself or by others. It appears, therefore, that *Constantine* the Great, the spectator of this sad event, is the most worthy to be credited; and he tells us, that *lightning* struck the palace, and even the bed-chamber of the Emperor; and that he considered the [p. 931.] fire, as evidence of the divine wrath against Diocletian, for his persecuting edict against the Christians. And yet *Eusebius* and *Lactantius* exhibit objections to an exclusive adherence to the statement of Constantine. For they inform us at much length, that severe inquisition, attended by tortures, was instituted against the authors of the conflagration; and that afterwards, immense sufferings were brought upon the Christians, in consequence of that fire. How, I would ask, could the authors of this occurrence be sought after, with so much eagerness? or how could the Christians be suspected of firing the palace, if it were, as *Constantine* states, not by the fault of men, but by a flash of lightning, that the palace took fire? What tyrant is so senseless and cruel, that when he knows some evil came upon him, accidentally, or from natural causes, yet tortures and torments innocent men, to find out the author of it? Neither the testimony of *Constantine*, confirmed, as it is, by that strong proof, the mental disease of Diocletian, produced by the sudden thunder-clap, can be rejected; nor can the statements of *Lactantius* and *Eusebius*, also resting on many fact proofs, be denied. What then are we to understand? I, indeed, after long considering the subject, find no other way of reconciling the disagreement of these witnesses of the highest credibility, than by supposing that *two fires* broke out in the palace on the same occasion, the one caused by lightning, and the other by the villany or fault of persons unknown. Nor is this supposition incredible. For it might easily occur, that while one part of the palace was burning in consequence of the lightning, and all were rushing forward to extinguish that fire, some evil disposed persons might at the same time set fire to another part of it, in order to have a safer and better opportunity for plundering. Who does not know, that such villanies at all times have occurred among mankind?

The first fire being subdued, the affrighted Emperor commanded the most vigorous inquisition to be made respecting the authors of so great a crime. Says *Lactantius*, (de mortibus persequutor. c. 14. p. 949.): Irâ inflammatus excarnificari omnes suos protinus praecepit. Sedebat ipse atque innocentes igne torrebat: item judices universi, omnes denique qui erant in palatio magistri, data potestate torquebant. (viz. to find out the author of the fire.) Erant certantes, quis prior aliquid inveniret. Nihil usquam reperiebatur: quippe quum familiam Caesaris (i. e. of Maximian,) nemo torqueret. For *Lactantius* supposed, the author of the fire was in the family or among the servants of *Maximian*. From this statement, I think, three things appear. *First:* The Christians were not supposed to be the authors of the first fire. For Diocletian ordered (*omnes suos*) *all his own* servants, (the greatest part of whom, it is manifest, were pagans,) to be subjected to torture. But if the false rumour, that the Christians sought to burn up the Emperors in the palace, had been then current, manifestly not all the waiters and servants of the palace, but solely the Christians, would have been subjected to the rack.—*Secondly:* The author of the fire [p. 932.] was sought for among the inmates of the palace and the Emperor's own servants; and no one out of the palace was suspected of the high crime. —*Thirdly:* In this first onset, no one was put to death; and as nothing could be ascertained by means of torture, the inquisition after a short time was discontinued. To these conclusions, we may add, with great probability, that only persons of inferior rank, and especially servants, were subjected to this inquisition: this is easily inferred from the language of *Lactantius*.

But another fire broke out fifteen days afterwards. And although it was soon extinguished, yet *Maximian* fled away, contestans, fugere se, ne vivus arderet. And then it was, the fatal calumny was spread abroad, Christianos, consilio cum eunuchis (the eunuchs who were Christians, and lived in the palace,) habito, de extinguendis principibus cogitasse. And as the weak and credulous *Diocletian* gave full credit to this calumny, he vented his rage against the Christians only, yet both against those in the palace and those out of it: The worshippers of the Gods were unmolested. Believing fully, that the Christians had set fire to the palace, he first commanded all persons residing in it, to offer sacrifice to the Gods; intending in this way, to rid his house of those noxious people. And first of all, he required his daughter *Valeria*, and his wife *Prisca*, *sacrificio se polluere.* This mandate shows, that those women abhorred the worship of the Gods, and had secretly professed the Christian religion. They however obeyed the command of their father and husband. But when the eunuchs and officers of the bed-chamber, who were also Christians, were addressed, a different scene arose. For they most resolutely declared, that the religion which they professed, would not allow them to pay honors to the Gods. And therefore the chief of them, after long and exquisite tortures, were put to death. *Lactantius* says: Potentissimi quondam eunuchi necati, per quos palatium et ipse ante constabat. *Eusebius*, (Hist. Eccles. L. viii. c. 6. p. 296.) more fully describes their glorious deaths.—Having destroyed those whom he regarded as his household enemies, the Emperor next attacked the Christians of the city; very many of whom, especially the clergy, he ordered to be put to death with the most cruel tortures, without any regard to legal forms of proceeding. This he did, not so much on religious grounds, (for he had not yet decreed capital punishment against such as refused to worship the Gods,) as because he fully believed, what certain impious men had told him, that the Christians living without the palace had conspired with the eunuchs in the palace, and had produced both the fires. Says *Lactantius :* comprehensi presbyteri ac ministri (or the *deacons,*) et sine ulla probatione ad confessionem damnati, cum omnibus suis deducebantur (ad supplicium.) Some learned men, not comprehending the meaning of the words *ad confessionem damnati*, have supposed the passage corrupted, and have attempted to amend it. But the passage is correct, and needs no amendment. The sense is, that these Christian priests, when liable to no just suspicion, were nevertheless subjected to torture to make them confess, that either they or their brethren and friends were the authors of the [p. 933.] fire; and when they would not so confess, and nothing could be drawn from them by torture, they were still accounted guilty, and were put to death in the usual manner. The most distinguished of those who were so unjustly slain in this storm, was *Anthimus*, the bishop of Nicomedia. This, *Eusebius* attests, (loc. cit. p. 297.) agreeing perfectly with *Lactantius*, yet amplifying and illustrating his more concise account. *Lactantius* thus proceeds: Omnis sexus et aetatis homines ad exustionem rapti (as *incendiaries*): nec singuli (quoniam tanta erat multitudo) sed gregatim circumdato igni ambiebantur. *Eusebius* adds, that many men and women, under strong excitement, leaped into the burning fire. The punishment of the servants was lighter: Domestici alligatis ad collum molaribus mergebantur.

This terrible inquisition, although interwoven with the persecution raised by Diocletian, should nevertheless be regarded as a separate transaction. For it was not properly decreed on account of religion, but on account of the conflagration: neither did it extend to the whole Christian community, but only to the people of Nicomedia, and to the Emperor's domestics. And hence, after a short period, it ceased altogether: nor did the Emperor take occasion from it, to issue other and more severe edicts against the Christians; as will appear further on. *Lactantius* indeed, after describing the sufferings and calamities of the Christians occasioned by the conflagration, subjoins: Et jam literae ad Maximianum atque Constantium commeaverant, ut eadem facerent. From which it seems to follow, that Diocletian wished the other Emperors to harrass and afflict the Christians of their provinces, in the same manner that he had the Nicomedians. But here, as also in some other particulars, *Lactantius* is not perfectly correct. It is demonstrable, from the order of events in this persecution, and from the authority of *Eusebius*, that during this first year of these troubles, besides the bishops and clergy, none but those who refused to surrender the sacred books, were exposed to penalties and tortures. And the subsequent edicts, of which we shall soon speak, place this beyond all controversy. And therefore the words of *Lactantius* above quoted, should be referred, not to the storm at Nicomedia produced by the burning of the palace, but to things more remote, namely, the edicts first issued by Diocletian and his son-in-law; which edicts were undoubtedly sent also to the other Emperors. It is evident, that *Lactantius* is rather unjust towards all the enemies of the Christians, and of course towards Diocletian and Maximian; whom he assails with bitter reproaches, in a manner not very christian.

(2) Like other weak and timorous men fond of ease, *Diocletian* was easily thrown into a violent passion; but he could not long retain anger. Hence, as his fright at the conflagration subdued, his rage ceased. But soon afterwards, a new cause of fear arose. Some persons, I know not who, disturbed the peace in [p.934.] Syria and Armenia, by attempted insurrections: and the enemies of Christianity easily persuaded the Emperor, that the Christians had excited these civil commotions. He therefore, this same year, A. D. 303, published a new edict, not against the Christians, but against their presiding officers and teachers. For, as he supposed the Christian people to be guided entirely by *their* authority, views, and example, he ordered all their *teachers* of every grade to be thrown into prison; anticipating, that the irksomeness and discomforts of imprisonment would induce them to abandon Christianity. Says *Eusebius*, (Hist. Eccles. L. viii. c. 7. p. 298.): Cum alii in Melitina, Armeniae rigione, alii in Syria imperium arripere conati essent, promulgatum est Imperatoris edictum, ut omnes ubique ecclesiarum *antistites* in carcerem truderentur. And therefore, in a short time, as *Eusebius* adds: Omnes carceres *Episcopis, Presbyteris, Diaconis, Lectoribus, et Exorcistis* pleni erant. I may here remark in passing, that it appears from this representation, that in the beginning of the fourth century, the whole

Christian clergy were distributed into *five* classes, at least in the East; or, that to the three ancient orders of bishops, presbyters and deacons, two others, *Lectors* and *Exorcists*, had been added in the preceding century.—There could be no clearer and stronger proof than this new decree presents, that *Diocletian* long persevered in his purpose of accomplishing the business without blood or slaughter; and that the inquisition which he ordered at Nicomedia, in consequence of the fire, did not extend to all Christians. The cause of this edict, which assailed only the Christian *clergy*, was the rise of the civil commotions in Armenia and Syria; as is manifest from the declaration of *Eusebius*. These commotions, the enemies of the Christians undoubtedly, persuaded the Emperor to believe, originated from the secret machinations of the Christian clergy. But he found his expectation, that bonds and imprisonment would overcome the resolution of the clergy, to be fallacious: for the majority of them remained immovable in their religion. And therefore, near the close of the year, as I suppose, a *third edict* was issued; according to which, the imprisoned clergy, if they would offer sacrifices, were to be released: but if they refused to sacrifice, they were to be compelled by tortures to worship the Gods. See *Eusebius*, (loc. cit. p. 298.) From this edict, began the *bloody persecution*. For an innumerable multitude of clergymen, through all the provinces of the Roman Empire, were subjected to the most cruel tortures and sufferings, and many of them most painfully and heroically expired amidst those tortures. In recounting these events, *Eusebius* is much more full and exact than *Lactantius*. In his Eccles. History, (L. viii. c. 7. &c.) he describes the cruel sufferings of the Christians in Egypt, in Thebais, in Phenicia, and in Phrygia. On the *Martyrs of Palestine* he has left us a separate treatise, annexed to the Eighth Book of his Eccles. History, which is full of examples of a cruelty almost exceeding belief. Yet in his Eccles. History, *Eusebius* seems not to have followed the due order of events in his narrative, but to have intermingled events consequent on the *fourth* edict, with those which befell only the clergy, in consequence [p. 935.] of the *third* edict. For the second and third edicts did not embrace the *people*, but only the *pastors* of the people. And *Eusebius* himself, (de martyribus Palæstinae, c. ii.. p. 320.) expressly says, that in the first year of the persecution, the cruelty of the enemies of the Christians spent itself upon—μόνων τῶν τῆς ἐκκλησίας προέδρων—*only the officers of the Church.* And yet, in his history, he relates many instances of both men and women among the common *people*, who, after the *third* edict, were in several provinces put to death by different modes of torture and execution. And therefore, either he confounds dates in his narrative, which is the most probable supposition; or, what might also occur, the governors and judges in many places, went beyond the limits prescribed in the edict, and tortured the people, either from superstition, or cruelty, or avarice. This indeed is indubitable, that the governors and magistrates did not confine their proceedings within the limits of the imperial edicts; but either from their savage dispositions, or from a desire to please *Maximian*, who, they well knew, wished the Christians exterminated, or from some other causes, they proceeded against the Christians in most of the provinces, more rigorously than they were commanded to do. Although Diocletian, in his first edict, sanctioned the capital punishment of such as refused to surrender the sacred books, and afterwards showed himself incensed against the Nicomedian Christians, on account of the fire of which they were accused: yet in no edict (of this year,) did he command those to be put to death who would not renounce the Christian religion. I will prove this by *Eusebius*, when we came to the fourth edict. And therefore, the very considerable number of Christians, who were put to death by the magistrates during the two first years of the persecution, perished contrary to the will of the Emperor. And I wonder, that so many learned men, and men well read in ancient history, should write, that *Diocletian* condemned to death, the Christians who would not worship the Gods.

(3) *Maximianus Herculius*, the other Emperor, who ruled in *Italy*, readily obeyed the commands of Diocletian and Maximian (Galerius.) But the other Cesar, *Constantius Chlorus*, being a man of a mild disposition, and a follower of the religion of nature and reason, was friendly to the Christians in the provinces under his control, and aided their cause so far as he could. He governed *Gaul, Spain*, and *Britain*. But he could not effect all he wished, lest he should seem to despise the authority of the First Emperor, and violate the terms of association in the government. In *Spain* many Christians were exposed to violence, and even death, under his dominion; as appears from many testimonies: and *Eusebius*, (de martyr. Palæstinae c. 13. p. 345.) clearly states the fact. What occurred in *Britain*, we are not informed. But in *Gaul*, where *Constantius* was present in person, he caused the Christians to be exempt from any great evils, and even to live quietly and comfortably. If he had been able, he would also have spared their temples and property: but something was to be conceded to the authority of the Emperor, to the wishes of the superstitious populace, and to the official station of the magistrates and governors. He [p. 936.] therefore did not *command* the Christian temples in Gaul to be demolished; yet he did not *prohibit* the magistrates and the people from either demolishing them or shutting them up. Says *Lactantius*, (de mortibus perseq. c. 15. p. 951.): Constantius, ne dissentire a majorum (Augustorum) praeceptis videretur, conventicula, id est, parietes, qui restitui poterant, dirui *passus* est, verum autem Dei templum, quod est in hominibus, incolume servavit. *Eusebius* states the same, (Hist. Eccles. L. viii. c. 13. p. 309. and c. 18. p. 317.) I omit other passages in which *Eusebius* praises the clemency and justice of *Constantius* towards the Christians. But I suspect, and not groundlessly, that *Eusebius* and *Lactantius* do not tell us *all*, that *Constantius* permitted to take place in Gaul lest he should seem to despise the edict of Diocletian; but they extenuate, as much as possible, the injuries which he suffered to light upon the Christians of his provinces, in order to please his son, the Emperor *Constantine*. First, *Eusebius* himself, (de martyr. Palæst. c. 13. p. 345.) expressly places, not only *Spain*, but also *Gaul*, among those provinces which, in the two first years of the persecution, *belli furorem expertae sunt*, but afterwards obtained peace: which certainly would be false, if only the sacred edifices were demolished in the life time of *Constantius*. Again, the same *Eusebius*, (de vita Constant. L. 1. c. 17. p. 416.) states, that the Christians living in the palace of *Constantius*, could freely worship God; and that among them also there were λειτουργοὺς

Θεοῦ—*the ministers of God*, i. e. priests or presbyters: but he adds, beyond the palace, (παρὰ τοῖς πολλοῖς—*among the common people.*) it was not allowed even to utter the name of Christians. Now, if these things were so,—and no one can well doubt them, then, certainly, the edicts of Diocletian were proclaimed in *Gaul;* and there was a severe prohibition of all public profession of Christianity, and of assemblies for Christian worship. And it was to remedy this evil in a measure, that *Constantius* took some Christian priests into his own palace, so that *there*, and under these priests, the Christians might enjoy religious worship which they could not have elsewhere. And lastly, the same edict which ordered the temples to be demolished, also commanded the sacred books of Christians to be given up and burned. And therefore I have no doubt, that the sacred books were taken by the magistrates from the Christian temples in *Gaul*, and perhaps they were here and there burned. Yet this one commendation is due to *Constantius*, that he forbid the publication and execution of those later edicts of the Emperor, which commanded all clergymen to be imprisoned and then compelled to offer sacrifices. In this, *Constantius* followed not only his own mild disposition, but also the dictates of his religion. For he was averse from the pagan worship, and therefore could not, without feelings of repugnance and self-condemnation, permit any person to be driven by fear or penalties, to worship the Gods.—Yet the Gauls speak of some martyrs slain under *Constantius:* but the accounts we have of them, are of doubtful authority.

§ IV. **Fourth Edict of Diocletian.—Maximian Emperor of the East.** [p. 937.] When the enemies of Christianity found these laws against the Christian pastors and ministers less effective than they anticipated, they induced Diocletian, in the second year of the persecution, A. D. 304, to issue a *fourth edict*, more cruel than the preceding, in which he required all Christians, without exception, to be *compelled* to worship the gods, by all the methods of torture and punishment which ingenuity could devise. Yet, even this edict, sanguinary and most iniquitous as it was, did not *command* the capital punishment of the Christians refusing to sacrifice. But those governors and magistrates, who were either the slaves of superstition, or naturally propense to cruelty, or solicitous to please *Maximian*, now marching with rapid strides to supreme power, took *occasion* from this edict to destroy, either by protracted tortures, or by sentences of death, a great multitude of Christians in most of the provinces.(1) The Christian community being thus debilitated and down-trodden, *Maximian* openly disclosed the designs he had been secretly revolving. He compelled his father-in-law *Diocletian*, and the colleague Emperor *Maximianus Herculius*, to *abdicate* their power, and assumed to himself the rank of Emperor of the East, leaving the West under *Constantius Chlorus.* At the same time he appointed two colleagues in the government, or *two Cesars*, of his own choice, and entirely devoted to himself, namely, *Maximin*, his sister's son, and *Severus*, excluding altogether *Constantine*, the son of *Constantius.* This revolution in the government was advantageous to the Christians of the *western* provinces, and in a measure restored their peace; but the Christians of the *East* were persecuted with increased violence and cruelty, by *Maximian Galerius* and *Maximin.* Hence, the number of Martyrs and Confessors in those regions was great.(2)

(1) The principal authority for this new or fourth edict, issued in the second year of the persecution, is *Eusebius*, (de martyribus Palaest. c. 3. p. 321.) who says: Secundo anno, Urbano tunc provinciam regente, Imperatoris missæ sunt litteræ, quibus generali præcepto (καθολικῷ προστάγματι) jubebatur, ut omnes ubique locorum et gentium publice idolis sacrificia et libationes offerrent. *Eusebius* here mentions only one Emperor; whence it appears, that this edict was [p. 938.] sanctioned by the authority of *Diocletian* only; and this is confirmed by a passage soon to be adduced from *Constantine* the Great. The same decree that was sent to *Urbanus*, the governor of Syria, was unquestionably sent to all the other provincial governors. For *Eusebius* expressly says, it was a καθολικὸν πρόσταγμα—*mandatum generale;* and that it embraced all the provinces of the empire, or required *omnes ubique locorum et gentium* to sacrifice to the Gods. Neither will the numerous examples of martyrdom in the Roman provinces, which are recounted by *Eusebius*, (Hist. Eccles. L. viii.) and by the moderns, *Tillemont* especially, (Memoires, &c. tome v.) admit of any doubt on this subject.—*Eusebius* does not tell us, what punishment the Emperor decreed for those whom no tortures could induce to offer sacrifices. But learned men, who treat of the sufferings inflicted on the Christians prior to the reign of *Constantine* the Great, would have us believe, that Diocletian ordered those who refused to honor the Gods, to be put to *death.* And they probably so judge, because they see that a great multitude of Christians of every class, were everywhere cruelly slain with various tortures, after this fourth edict was issued. And *Eusebius* himself may have led them to believe so, as he, immediately after mentioning the imperial edict, proceeds to state examples of Christians either condemned to be devoured by wild beasts, or to be decapitated, as if he would thereby exhibit the force and cruelty of the imperial mandate. But I have concluded, after attentively considering the whole subject, that the edict *prescribed* no punishment, and much less that of death, as the penalty of refusing to offer sacrifices; and that the governors were only commanded, in general, to *compel* the Christians to worship the Roman deities in every way they could, and by such inflictions and tortures as they might choose. *Constantine* the Great, in his edict preserved by *Eusebius*, (de vita Constant. L. ii. c. 51. p. 467.) after

mentioning these later edicts of Diocletian, and saying that these edicts, as it were *cruentis mucronibus scripta esse*, describes their import thus: Τοῖς δὲ δικασταῖς την ἀγχίνοιαν εἰς εὕρεσιν κολαστηρίων δεινοτέρων ἐκτείνειν παρεκελεύετο Judicibus præcipit, ut ingenii *solertiam* ad acerbiores cruciatus excogitandos intenderent. That this description cannot refer to new modes of capital punishment, or new ways of putting men to death, which the governors were to devise, must be manifest. Neither did Diocletian wish the Christians to be *slain*, but to have them brought back to the religion of their ancestors by coercion and force. The passage must therefore be understood of new modes of torture and suffering; and the Emperor would remind the magistrates, that as experience had shown that the Christians were not moved by the usual methods of torture, they must exert their *ingenuity* to devise new modes of torture, and new forms of suffering, by which the minds of these obstinate persons might be subdued, and they be induced to honor the gods. And that this was the import of the edict, is put beyond all dispute, by the manner of its execution, as described by *Lactantius*, a spectator of it, (Instit. divinar. L. v. c. 11. p. 449.) He [p. 939.] represents most of the judges as being *careful* not to kill any of the Christians; but, as the Emperor had directed the invention of new modes of torture, they, as it were, vied with each other in the ingenuity of their modes of compelling Christians to apostatize: Dici non potest, hujusmodi judices quanta et quam gravia tormentorum genera excogitaverint, ut ad effectum propositi sui pervenerint. Hoc autem non tantum ideo faciunt, ut gloriari possint, nullum se innocentium peremisse, - - sed et invidiæ caussâ, ne aut ipsi vincantur, (namely, by other judges. That judge, therefore, who could not overcome his Christians by his modes of torture, was considered as outdone by others.) aut illi (Christiani) virtutis suæ gloriam consequantur. Itaque in excogitandis pœnarum generibus nihil aliud, quam *victoriam*, cogitant. Sciunt enim certamen esse illud et pugnam. - - Contendunt igitur, ut vincant, et exquisitos dolores corporibus immittunt, et nihil aliud devitant, quam ut *ne torti moriantur*. - - Illi pertinaci stultitià jubent curam tortis diligenter adhiberi, ut ad alios cruciatus membra renoventur, et reparetur novus sanguis ad pœnam. Could there be any stronger proof, than this testimony of the very eloquent man narrating what fell under his own observation, that *Diocletian* did not wish the Christians put to death, but only *worried out* with tortures, until they should apostatize! Whence it follows, that he by no means decreed the capital punishment of such as would not sacrifice. But there are other arguments to the same point. In the Eccles. History of *Eusebius*, (L. ix. c. 9. p. 360.) there is an edict of *Maximin* in favor of the Christians, which is of great weight in this matter. For, first, *Maximin* states the substance of the edict of Diocletian and Maximian Galerius against the Christians, precisely in accordance with our views: Domini ac parentes nostri, Diocletianus et Maximianus, recte atque ordine constituerunt, ut quicunque a Deorum suorum religione descivissent, *publica animadversione ac supplicio ad eorundem cultum revocarentur*. Therefore, they ordered no man to be put to death. And next, he tells us, how the judges in the East obeyed the decree: Ego vero cum in Orientis provincias venissem, comperi quamplurimos homines, qui reipublicæ usui esse possent, ob eam quam diximus caussam a judicibus in certa loca *relegari.* Therefore, in the East, the judges merely sent into *exile* those Christians whom they could not bring to apostasy by tortures. Who does not see from this, that the Emperors did not decree the capital punishment of the unyielding Christians? For if the persisting Christians were willing to die, the judges who should only order them into exile, would act contrary to the mandate of their sovereigns, and would incur their displeasure. But a fine passage in *Eusebius*, (Hist. Eccles. L. viii. c. 12. p. 306, 307.) entirely settles the point. Having stated many examples of Christians most cruelly slain, in [p. 940.] Egypt, Pontus, Syria, and other countries, he adds, that the judges, desparing of effecting anything by inhumanity and cruelty; ad *clementiam* et humanitatem se convertisse. Neque enim fas esse aiebant, ut urbes civium sanguine contaminarentur, - - sed potius decere, ut humanitas et beneficentia Imperitoriæ majestatis in universos diffunderetur, nec posthac nostri capitali supplicio plecterentur: Quippe hujusmodi pœna per Imperitorum indulgentiam (διὰ τὴν τῶν κρατούντων φιλανθρωπίαν) nos liberatos esse. Yet it was a sorrowful *clemency*, which the judges chose to substitute for severity. For, omitting capital punishment, they ordered that the Christians whom they could in no way induce to worship the Gods, should have their *eyes* dug out, or one of their legs *disabled;* and the innocent and holy men, thus mutilated, were condemned to the *mines.* Yet, even this inhuman humanity, proves that the Emperors forbid, tacitly at least, the slaughter of the Christians; and the judges themselves acknowledged it.—This new and horrid edict of Diocletian, therefore, in general terms, directed the magistrates to command all citizens whatever, within their several jurisdictions, to offer sacrifices to the Gods; and such as should resist and refuse to offer sacrifices in the manner of their ancestors, they were *to torture* with every species of suffering and pain, until they would do as the Emperors required. Neither the measure nor the duration of these tortures was prescribed, nor the method of proceeding with those who resisted these tortures with a determined and invincible resolution. And hence each of the judges, according to his personal character and disposition, put a more severe or a more mild interpretation upon the Emperor's edict: some, as we have seen from the decree of *Maximin* in *Eusebius*, only *exiled* those they could not subdue; others, as we also learn from Eusebius, deprived those they could not overcome, of a leg or an eye; others, influenced by furious passion, condemned them either to the wild beasts, or to decapitation, or to other horrid modes of execution: and the most cruel persisted in torturing the Christians variously, until they died from exhaustion. Many, also, for different reasons, proceeded contrary to the will of the Emperor, and at once put to death the Christians whom they had seized. I will cite a noticeable passage from *Lactantius*, (Instit. divinar. L. v. c. 11. p. 448.) which admirably illustrates this subject, and clearly supports our views of the import of Diocletian's edict. Quæ per totum orbem singuli (judices) gesserint, enarrare impossibile est. Quis enim voluminum numerus capiet tam infinita, tam varia genera crudelitatis? Accepta enim potestate (which was not well defined,) *pro suis moribus quisque sævit.* Alii præ nimia timiditate plus ausi sunt, quam jubebantur; (thus did the judges, who condemned the captives to die, which was not commanded:) alii suo proprio adversus justos odio; quidam naturali mentis feritate; nonnulli, ut placerent, et hoc officio viam sibi ad altiora munirent: aliqui ad occidendum præcipites [p. 941.] extiterunt; sicut unus in Phrygia, qui universum populum cum ipso pariter conventiculo concremavit. - - Illud vero pessimum genus est, cui clementiæ species falsa blanditur: ille gravior, ille sævior est carnifex, qui neminem statuit occidere.

But while it is certain, that the governors and judges most unjustly put a great many Christians to death in various ways, contrary to the Emperors mandate, it must also be admitted, that among those put to death, there were not a few, who, by their own fault, drew upon themselves capital punishment. I say nothing of those who attended religious meetings, which, from the commencement of the persecution, was severely forbidden: for these had some excuse for their conduct. But there were others, who *voluntarily* presented themselves before the judges, professed that they were Christians, and most indiscreetly *demanded death*. Says *Sulpitius Severus*, (Historia sacra, L. ii. c. 32. p. 247. edit. Clerici.) Certatim gloriosa in certamina ruebatur, multoque avidius tum *martyria* gloriosis mortibus *quaerebantur*, quam nunc episcopatus pravis ambitionibus adpetuntur. *Sulpitius* speaks rhetorically. For it is equally wrong and contrary to Christian morality, *unnecessarily to seek martyrdom*, and *to aspire after a bishoprick from motives of ambition*. That there were persons influenced by such inconsiderate zeal as actually to seek death, appears from many examples in *Eusebius* and others. I will mention one. After the fourth edict of the Emperor was brought into Palestine, *six young men* of Gaza, hearing that some Christians were to fight with wild beasts, all went to Urban the governor, with their hands tied, confessed that they were Christians, and boasted, that they were not afraid of the wild beasts. They were all put in prison, and after a few days decapitated. And this rash conduct, *Eusebius* commends, (de martyribus Palæst. c. 3. p. 321.) but I do not; nor did the laws of the Church favor this class of people. Is it at all strange, that those who thus insulted the Emperor, the public laws, and the governors, and audaciously provoked those whom Christianity required them to respect, should be punished for their indiscretion, by proud men, high in power, and ignorant of true religion?

(2) I have before stated, that *Maximian Galerius* was induced to persecute and oppress the Christians, not merely by his superstition, but also by his lust of power. He coveted supremacy in the republic, or wished to secure to himself and friends the entire Roman Empire, to the exclusion of the family of *Constantius Chlorus*. And as he despaired of attaining his object without a civil war and great movements of dubious result, so long as the Christians, who were all devoted to *Constantius* and his son, remained secure and powerful, he concluded that they must first of all be oppressed, and deprived of their resources. That I am correct in these views, is clearly shown, if I do not mistake, by what this very ambitious man contrived and executed, while the persecution was everywhere raging against the Christians. He dissembled [p. 942.] his purpose of subjecting everything to himself and friends, so long as the edicts against the Christians were moderate, and did not extinguish all hope of their return to prosperity. But after he had prevailed, doubtless by various artifices,

on his father-in-law, in the year 304, to issue the very distressing edict already described, and there seemed to be no salvation possible for the Christians, he dropped the mask, and openly avowed what before he had kept concealed in his own breast. In the latter part of the year 304, the condition of the Christians had been made such, by the fourth edict of Diocletian, that they could attempt nothing important, and could not raise a civil war in behalf of *Constantius* and his son. For, all the provinces of the Roman Empire were drenched in Christian blood, except only Gaul, and even there the Christians could hold meetings only within the palace. The temples dedicated to Christ were every where prostrated. Meetings for worship or other purposes, could no longer be held by Christians. Most of them had fled the Roman soil, and taken refuge among the barbarians, who received them kindly. See the edict of *Constantine* the great: (apud *Eusebium* de vita Constantini L. ii. c. 53. p. 468.) Those unable or unwilling to flee the country, hid themselves, and could not appear in public without imminent peril of their lives and estates. Their principal men, including the bishops and ministers of religion, were either slain, or maimed and sent to the mines, or mulcted with exile; so that the professors of Christianity were every where without leaders and guides. Their property both public and private had, for the most part, been seized by the greedy magistrates and judges. From a dread of torture and protracted sufferings, many had procured their own death: and others, including not a few presiding officers and men of note or of rank and standing, had apostatized from Christ. The Christians, who had in great numbers been connected with the court of Diocletian or with the army, were all either put to death as culprits, or sent into exile, or detained in prisons. The needy residue, weak and obscure, and consisting of persons of inferior rank or standing, could not possibly disturb the republic, and take arms in behalf of *Constantius.* Therefore, all causes of fear being removed, *Maximian Galerius* freely disclosed his designs, and made manifest that he wished to rule the Roman Empire alone. In the first place, he constrained, partly by threats, and partly by argument, his father-in-law *Diocletian,* to whom he was under the greatest obligations, and also the other Augustus, *Maximian Herculius,* on the Kalends of May A. D. 305, to divest themselves of the purple and the imperial dignity, the former at Nicomedia, and the latter at Milan, and to retire to private life. By what method he effected this momentous change, no one has told us more distinctly and accurately than *Lactantius;* (de mortibus persequutor. c. 17 &c. p. 954 &c.) This being accomplished, he assumed to himself the title of *Emperor of the East,* and left to *Constantius Chlorus* the rank of *Emperor* [p. 943.] *of the West.* He hated *Constantius* exceedingly, and would therefore have gladly deprived him of both life and official power: but *Constantius* stood strong in the affections both of the citizens and the soldiers, and he was guarded by the powerful protection of the army. And therefore, perceiving that he had not forces adequate, either to destroy a man of such vast power, or to depose him, *Maximian* thought best not only to bear with him, but even to elevate him: and he was the more willing to do so, because he supposed the mildness of Constantius left nothing to fear from him; and moreover, as Constantius was in bad health, he hoped he would soon be removed by death. Says *Lactantius,*

(de mortibus perseq. c. 20. p. 361.): Maximianus, postquam senibus expulsis, quod voluit, et fecit, se jam solus totius orbis dominum esse ferebat. Nam Constantium, quamvis priorem nominari esset necesse, contemnebat, quod et natura mitis esset, et valetudine corporis impeditus. Hunc sperabat brevi obiturum, et si non obisset, vel invitum exuere facile videbatur. Quid enim faceret, si a tribus cogeretur imperium deponere. From Constantius' son *Constantine*, afterwards styled the Great, he felt that more was to be feared, he being a young man, and very highly esteemed by the people and the soldiers. But as he resided at the Court of Nicomedia, *Maximian* thought he had him in his power, and that he could easily procure his death, either by assassination or by other means. He indeed actually attempted this repeatedly, and especially in the following year, 306: and from this may most manifestly be learned the general designs of *Maximian*, and his reason for persecuting the Christians. Says *Lactantius*, (loc. cit. c. 24. p. 968.): Insidiis saepe juvenem appetiverat, quia palam nihil audebat, ne contra se arma civilia, et, quod maxime verebatur, odia militum concitaret; et sub obtentu exercitii et lusus feris illum objecerat. But *Constantine*, perceiving the perfidy and plots of the tyrant, sought safety by flight, and went to his father in Britain. And this wise step of the young man alone, frustrated all the plans of *Maximian*, and procured for the Christian religion which the tyrant sought to exterminate, the victory over superstition, and astonishing progress through the whole world. The only benefit, therefore, which *Diocletian* received from the edicts which he issued at the instigation of his son-in-law against the Christians, was the loss of his empire. For *Maximian* would never have dared to assail him and deprive him of the purple, if he had seen him encompassed with Christian friends and ministers, of whom Maximian stood in the greatest fear, and the armies full of Christian soldiers.—After gaining the supreme power, which he had long coveted, *Maximian* took for himself and *Constantius*, without consulting Constantius, and against the will of Diocletian, *two Cesars*, men entirely devoted to him; the one was *Severus*, an Illyrian, and distinguished for nothing but his vices; the other was his sister's son, *Daia*, to whom he gave the name of *Maximin*. The former, under Constantius, governed Italy, Sicily, and Africa: to the latter, his uncle [p. 914.] committed the government of Syria and Egypt.

This great change in the civil government, brought some relief to the afflicted Church. *Eusebius* (de martyr. Palæst. c. 13. p. 345.) expressly says, that the western provinces, namely, Italy, Sicily, Gaul, Spain, Mauritania and Africa, obtained peace, when the persecution had scarcely continued two years. Nor will this appear strange, if we consider that Gaul, Spain, and Britain were governed by *Constantius Chlorus*, the friend of Christians, and a despiser of the Gods; and that *Severus*, to whom the other western provinces, Italy, Sicily, Mauritania and Africa, were subject, although he was a Cesar, was obliged to respect the majesty and authority of the Emperor of the West. Neither was *Severus* himself cruel; though he was a drunkard, and immoderately addicted to voluptuousness. And yet, what *Eusebius* states respecting the peace of the western provinces, must not lead us to suppose, that they all enjoyed equal tranquility and happiness. The Christians inhabiting the provinces under the immediate government of *Constantius*, namely, *Spain*, *Gaul*, and *Britain*, were undoubtedly, either by his command or with his consent, not only freed from the peril of their lives and estates, but also allowed to hold religious meetings, and to rebuild their prostrate temples. That it was so in *Gaul*, is certain. For, as it has been well ascertained that in Gaul no violence had been done to their persons, but only to their sacred edifices, the peace which *Eusebius* tells us was restored to the Gauls, can be understood only as affording them full liberty from the Emperor, of resuming their suspended meetings, and rebuilding their sacred edifices. In *Spain*, where the edicts of Diocletian had been more effective than in Gaul, and where many Christians had been tortured and slain, the same happy state was not produced except in part; as will soon be shown. Yet there can be no doubt, that here also, after *Constantius* attained the rank of Augustus and Emperor of the West, no Christian was molested on accout of his religion; and the bishops and others who had been imprisoned were set at liberty. The Spaniards, though too eager for swelling the number of their martyrs, yet acknowledge that, in the third and following years of the persecution, no person in their country suffered death for Christ. And this is put beyond controversy, by the list of Spanish martyrs compiled by *John de Ferreras*, (Histoire generale d'Espagne, tom. 1. p. 303, &c.) for the list terminates in the second year of the persecution.—In the provinces governed by *Severus* the Cesar, the state of the Christians was less happy. Penalties, tortures and capital executions had indeed ceased, and private meetings were tolerated, and likewise bishops; but Christian temples, and the liberty of meeting [p. 945.] publicly for worship, were by no means allowed. I suppose, this may be inferred from the example of *Africa:* for undoubtedly, the same state of things existed in the other provinces governed by *Severus*, as in this. *Optatus Milevitanus*, (de schismate Donatistar. L. 1. c. 14. p. 14.) states, that a sort of council of bishops was held, apud Cirtam civitatem, in domo Urbani Carisi, post persecutionem : and, that the meeting of this council was early in the Spring of the year 305, is proved by unquestionable documents, and has long been demonstrated by learned men. And therefore, at the time of this council, near the beginning of the third year of the persecution, the war upon Christians had terminated in the province of Africa. But, that perfect peace was not yet restored there, *Optatus* shows in the same passage. For he says, that the bishops met in a private dwelling, *quia basilicae necdum fuerant restitutae.* And a little after, (c. 16. p. 17.) he expressly states, that it was *Maxentius*, who at last gave perfect tranquility to the African church ; and this could not have occurred before the year 307 : Tempestas persecutionis peracta et definita est. Jubente Deo, indulgentiam mittente Maxentio, Christianis libertas est restituta. The persecution therefore, in a measure ceased, in the province of Africa, after the political changes we have described: The refugees returned to their country; the bishops could meet and deliberate on religious matters, without danger of imprisonment or any punishment; the offering of sacrifices was no longer required; and those who would not worship the Gods, were not prosecuted as culprits. And yet, it was after this, that, *Indulgentiam mittente Maxentio, Christianis libertas est restituta ;* that is, they might not rebuild their temples, and they could not openly meet together in public edifices for the worship of God. In short, *Severus* truckled, lest he should appear to disregard the will of *Constantius*, by whose authority he reigned: and he did not order the Christians to be molested, and yet he did not revoke the previous laws against them, nor suffer them openly to profess their religion.

But in the eastern provinces, where *Maximian Galerius* with *Maximin*, reigned, the calamities of the Christians became more grievous. For *Maximian* enacted far more atrocious laws against the Christians than the former edicts, and commanded that all, who could not be forced by repeated tortures to offer sacrifices, should be burned to death in slow fires. *Lactantius* speaks of these laws,(de mortibus persequutor. c. 21. p. 964.): Dignitatem non habentibus, pœna ignis fuit. Id exitii primo adversus Christianos permiserat, *datis legibus*, ut post tormenta damnati (that is, that such as could not be constrained by tortures to forsake Christ, should be condemned, and) *lentis ignibus exurerentur.* This terrible punishment is eloquently described in this passage, by *Lactantius.* And he closes his account of it by saying, that the bodies when roasted by the slow fires, were again burned, and: Ossa lecta et in pulverem comminuta, in flumina et mare jactata fuisse. The testimony of *Lactantius* is confirmed by [p. 946.] *Gregory* of Nyssa, (Orat. de S. Theodoro martyre, tom. iii. p. 581.) He explicitly says, that a decree was issued by Maximian and Maxentius, that such as would not renounce Christ, should be put to death: Ἐκ δόγματος Θεομάχου, πᾶς Χριστιανὸς ἠλαύνετο τῷ δυσσεβεῖ γράμματι καὶ πρὸς θάνατον ἤγετο. Impio decreto sancitum erat, ut quicunque Christianus esset impio scriptô exagitaretur et ad mortem duceretur. What *Gregory* calls δυσσεβὲς γράμμα, as appears from that which is added, was a slip of paper fastened to the forehead of the condemned Christians, on which was written the cause of their execution, doubtless in ignominious terms. *Gregory* does not state the kind of death inflicted: but the *Theodorus*, whose history he recites, after long continued and extreme tortures, was cast into a fire: which goes to show, that the law of *Maximian* mentioned by *Lactantius*, was enforced also in Pontus. And yet, that the procedure against the Christians was not in accordance with this law, in all the provinces, appears from the examples in *Eusebius* and others, of martyrs who perished by various modes of execution. Perhaps, therefore, in certain provinces, for instance, Asia Minor, Pontus, &c. the persevering Christians, by order of the Emperor, were consumed in a slow fire; but in general, only death was decreed against the unyielding Christians, while the kind of death was left to the choice of the magistrates. This conjecture, however, I find to be unnecessary, on reviewing the statement of *Lactantius.* For he does not say, that execution by burning, was *prescribed*, but only *permitted* by the Emperor. The law therefore, only in general, ordered recusant Christians to be *put to death*, but left the judges free to burn them, or to execute them in some other manner.

Maximin, who held *Syria* and *Egypt*, at first professed great lenity towards the Christians. For, perceiving that many of those who refused to sacrifice to the Gods in the East, had been exiled by the magistrates, he commanded the judges not to punish any of the Christians, nor to send them into exile, but rather to endeavor to gain them over to the worship of the Gods by blandishments and exhortations, without violence or terror. This, he himself states in his edict preserved by *Eusebius*, (Hist. Eccles. L. ix. c. 9. p. 360.) And I suppose we may believe him, although some learned men think he speaks falsely. For *Eusebius*, after reciting the edict containing these declarations, adds, that the Christians would not avail themselves of the advantages offered them in the edict; Quod jam antea post pacem Christianis similiter indultam, versutiam ac perfidiam suam ostendisset. Thus *Eusebius* admits, that *Maximin* for a time showed himself mild and placable towards the Christians, and allowed them to live in peace; yet he adds, that this kind treatment was not permanent. The insidious or perfidious peace here referred to, was undoubtedly that peace which is mentioned in the edict. But, not long afterwards, either from his own super-[p. 947.] stition which was very great, or excited by the authority and influence of his uncle, or lastly, from discovering the little success of the lenity he had shown, *Maximin* assailed the Christians everywhere, with such fury, that he seemed to exceed all their other persecutors in cruelty. *Eusebius*, (de martyr. Palæst. c. 4. p. 323, 324.) tells us, that this new or second assault upon the Christians by this Cesar, commenced in the third year of the Diocletian persecution. He sent forth edicts, through all the provinces under him, commanding the magistrates to compel all the citizens, without exception, to offer sacrifices. And thereupon, the judges, dispatching criers throughout the cities, summoned all heads of families to come to the temples, and obey the imperatorial mandate: and those who refused were stretched upon the rack, and at last, if they would not yield, were put to death by various modes of execution. The most sickening examples are described by *Eusebius*. See his Eccles. Hist. (L. viii. c. 14. p. 311, 312. L. ix. c. 2. 3. 4. p. 349, &c.) and his tract on the Martyrs of Palestine, (c. 4. p. 322.) also *Lactantius*, (de mortibus persequutor. c. 36. p. 987. and c. 38. p. 990.)

§ V. **Civil wars, and state of Christians, from A. D. 306 to A. D. 311.** While *Maximian Galerius*, by the slaughter and destruction of the Christians and other tyrannical arts, was seeking to obtain for himself and son-in-law the supreme power over the whole empire, divine Providence suddenly disturbed all his cogitations and all his concealed plans. For in the year 306 *Constantius Chlorus*, his colleague Emperor, whose death he had long anticipated, *died* in Britain, having by his will appointed, as the heir to his empire, *Constantine, his son;* the very man of whom Maximian stood most in fear: and the soldiers, immediately on the death of the father, proclaimed the son *Augustus and Emperor.* To this adverse occurrence *Maximian* found it necessary to submit; but he craftily sought to modify it somewhat, that it might produce the less harm. He unwillingly conceded to *Constantine* the lowest place among the Sovereigns of the Empire, with the title of *Cesar:* and at the same time he raised *Severus,* previously a Cesar, to the rank of an Augustus or Emperor, thus curtailing the power of *Constantine.* But the obstruction which human sagacity opposed to the rising power of *Constantine,* the current of events soon prostrated. *Maxentius,* the son-in-law of *Maximian Galerius,* and the son of *Maximian Herculius,* indignant that *Severus* should be preferred before him, assumed to himself the rank of Emperor, and took for a colleague his own father, whom *Maximian Galerius* had deprived of empire. And [p. 948.] hence arose, in the Roman world, very great commotions and most destructive civil wars; in which, fortune so favored *Constantine,* that he obtained, contrary to the calculations and the will of his enemy Maximian, the rank of Augustus and Emperor. Amidst these civil commotions, the Christians experienced various fortune, especially in the countries of the *East:* for the servants of Christ in the *western* provinces, if we except those of Africa and Italy, felt none of the troubles of those tempestuous times. For those who contended for political power, according as they supposed the Christians might aid or thwart their wishes and interests, showed themselves either friendly or hostile to them.(1) This dubious and fluctuating state of things, *Maximian Galerius,* the author of so great evils and sufferings to the Christians, himself at length terminated. For while laboring under a long continued and distressing disease, previous to his death, in the year 311, he issued a public edict, restoring the Christians to their ancient tranquillity.(2)

(1) The events, both prosperous and adverse to the church, which occurred from the year 306, when *Constantius Chlorus* died in Britain, to the year 311, when the dying *Maximian Galerius* gave peace to the Christians, cannot be correctly understood and appreciated without a knowledge of the great political changes during that period. For these changes, if I do not wholly misjudge, exhibit the causes both of the good and the ill fortune of the christian community: for so great was the multitude of Christians, who increased even amid the calamities they endured, that it would be readily perceived that the party, to which they should adhere and afford aid and assistance, would have the superiority. And hence, those who were eager to reign, either oppressed and persecuted the Christians, whom they feared, or courted, sincerely or feignedly, their favor. *Maximian Galerius,* who very manifestly wished to engross to himself and friends the whole Roman empire, to the exclusion of the family of *Constantius Chlorus,* endeavored to oppress the Christians, who were devoted to *Constantine* and his son, lest they should thwart his designs. And he

would doubtless have attained his wishes, if *Constantine* had not cluded his repeated attempts on his life, by flying to his father in Britain. *Maximian* had to dissemble his chagrin at this unexpected flight; but being sovereign of the greatest part of the Roman empire, he hoped he should be able, without much difficulty, to conquer the young man when bereft of his father, if, without his consent, he should arrogate to himself sovereign power. He undoubtedly reasoned at that time, as *Lactantius* says he did when he granted the imperial pur-
[p. 949.] ple to *Constantius Chlorus*, (de mortibus persequutor. c. 20. p. 962.): *Quid faciet, si a tribus cogetur imperium deponere?* And yet he did not so rely on this expectation, as to neglect other methods of removing the impending danger. For he tried, with blandishments, to entice *Constantine* out of Britain, and allure him to his court. Says *Lactantius*, (loc. cit. c.24. p. 968.): Qui (Constantius Chlorus) cum graviter (morbo) laboraret, miserat (Maximianus) litteras, ut filium suum Constantinum remitteret sibi videndum, quem jamdudum repetierat. But he could not persuade either the father or the son, to comply with his request. And the death of *Constantius*, which occurred soon after, in the year 306, frustrated all his efforts. For, as we are told by very credible writers, (*Libanius*, *Eusebius*, *Julian*, and others,) *Constantius*, by his last will and testament, transferred to his son, as his patrimony, all the provinces which he had governed while living: and the soldiers, having a knowledge of this will, immediately after the death of *Constantius*, proclaimed *Constantine* both *Emperor* and *Augustus*. Nothing could have occurred more disagreeable to *Maximian*. But, as he could foresee that a tedious and hazardous civil war would arise, if he should altogether set aside the decision of the soldiers, he concluded to yield to necessity, and to correct the evils which time might bring forth, by his prudence. He, therefore, took a sort of middle course, which had some show of equity. He assigned to *Constantine* his father's provinces, *Gaul*, *Spain* and *Britain*, with the rank of the fourth among the Sovereigns, and the title of *Cesar*. And *Constantine*, a sagacious young man, and equally afraid of a civil war, contented himself with the constrained liberality of his enemy. But, that *Constantine* might not be equal to his father in power and resources, *Maximian* assumed to himself for colleague, the man who was entirely under his control, *Severus*, hitherto the administrator in Italy and Africa with the title of Cesar, and made him Emperor and Augustus, in place of the deceased *Constantius*. *Severus* had previously governed *Italy* and *Africa*, not independently, but in subordination to *Constantius*: which had been very advantageous to the Christians living under his jurisdiction. For he did not dare to disquiet those, to whom the Emperor of the West, *Constantius*, gave his protection. He now received, with the honor of Emperor, the *supreme power over Italy and Africa*: and from these provinces, if *Maximian* should so order, war might easily be caried into Spain and Gaul, where *Constantine* ruled. The new arrangement of the Roman government was, therefore, wisely contrived to hold *Constantine* in check, and if necessary, to subdue him by war. But, contrary to all expectation, *Maximian* himself was caught by those very snares, which he had laid for *Constantine*. There was then living as a private citizen, on a farm in the vicinity of Rome, *Maxentius*, the son-in-law of *Maximian Galerius*, and the son of

that *Maximian Herculius*, who had unwillingly abdicated the empire, at the same time with Diocletian. This *Maxentius*, a very proud man, was indignant that *Constantine* and *Severus* should be preferred before him: and [p. 950.] therefore, raising a sedition at Rome and in Italy, he not only assumed to himself the rank of Emperor and Augustus, but likewise persuaded his father, *Maximius Herculius*, again to seize the helm of government. There were, therefore, at the close of the year 306, *four Augusti*, three in Italy and one in the East; and *two Cesars*, the one in Gaul, *Constantine*, the other in the East, *Maximin*. The next year, 307, *Maximian Galerius* sent *Severus*, at the head of a numerous and powerful army, against the new Emperors in Italy. But *Severus* was unsuccessful, and, being captured by *Maximian Herculius*, was induced to destroy his own life. *Maximian Galerius* was enraged, but not discouraged, by this victory. *Herculius* therefore, foreseeing that *Galerius* would soon appear in Italy, at the head of a fresh army, to avenge the death of his friend *Severus*, went hastily into Gaul to *Constantine* the Cesar, and offered him his daughter *Fausta*, and the rank of Emperor and Augustus, if he would enter into alliance with him. *Constantine* consented, married Fausta, and exchanged the title of Cesar for that of Emperor. Again, therefore, there were *four* Emperors presiding over the Roman commonwealth, three in the West, and one in the East: and but one Cesar, namely *Maximin*. While *Herculius* was in Gaul, *Maximian Galerius* arrived in Italy with his army; but he could neither take Rome, nor induce his son-in-law *Maxentius*, to receive the purple and the imperial dignity from his hand. He therefore returned to the East, with ignominy, and not without great peril to his life and fortune. After the departure of *Maximian Galerius*, *Herculius* returned to Rome: and, as his son would not be obedient to him, he attempted to expel him from the throne. But he was unsuccessful, for the soldiers fought in defence of *Maxentius*: and therefore, leaving Italy, *Herculius* fled first to his son-in-law *Constantine* in Gaul, and soon afterwards to his enemy *Maximian Galerius*, at that time in Dalmatia. In this very difficult posture of public affairs, *Maximian Galerius*, who was very corpulent, and of course sluggish, perceiving his need of the aid of some active and energetic man, beloved by the soldiers, and competent to meet *Maxentius* in the field and restore the republic to tranquillity; created his intimate friend *Licinius*, a man not distinguished for birth or virtue, but a good soldier, and in great favor with the soldiers, Emperor and Augustus. But this remedy, which the Emperor devised for existing evils, most unfortunately only produced new evils. For, *Maximin*, his sister's son, who had hitherto governed the East with the title of Cesar, when informed that *Licinius* was promoted to the rank of Emperor, was indignant, and the next year, 308, with the consent of his soldiers, he assumed the same rank: and to prevent the rise of a new war, *Maximian Galerius* deemed it necessary to sanction this rash act of *Maximin*. [p. 951.] Therefore, in the year 308, the Roman empire had *six* Sovereigns: and a *seventh* appeared the same year in Africa, in the person of *Alexander*; but his reign was not long. During all these changes and commotions, *Constantine* in Gaul, cautious and provident, was a quiet spectator, his only aims being, to render the provinces he governed tranquil and secure against the incursions of the adjacent barbarians, and to strengthen his power by the attachment of his people to him. In the meantime, his father-in-law *Herculius*, returned from the East to Gaul, and laying aside the purple and the title of Empeor, pretended to be resolved to spend the remainder of his life in quietude. *Constantine* put confidence in the perfidious man, who all the while was plotting another nefarious project. Though an old man, he was inflamed beyond measure with the lust of dominion; and as he saw every avenue to the supreme power closed against him, he contemplated the dethronement of his son-in-law, that he might reign in his place. He therefore made war upon *Constantine*, was vanquished, and for a time feigned penitence and great moderation; but in the year 310, he returned to his old habits, and attempted to murder *Constantine* in his bed-chamber; and being convicted of this crime, by order of his son-in-law, he hung himself in prison. While these events were passing in Gaul, *Maximian Galerius* in the East, was preparing for war against *Maxentius;* and, to raise funds, he imposed very heavy burdens upon the citizens. But in the midst of his great enterprises, and while every where oppressing the Christians, whom he considered as the principal obstacle to his success, he was attacked by a dreadful disease in the year 310, and the next year, 311, exhausted by intolerable pains and sufferings, he ended his days.

What befell the Christians, amidst these various and memorable revolutions in the Roman government, we will now state, so far as we can learn the facts from the writers of those times; who are not indeed contemptible, yet are not very accurate, nor diligent, nor free from partiality, nor well versed in public affairs and the policy of courts. If historians of this period, like *Livy*, *Tacitus* and *Polibius*, had come down to us, we could much better trace the course of events, and mark the steps by which Christianity rose to dominion over the Roman world. The writers, not Christian, such as *Zosimus* and *Aurelius Victor*, only give us dry summaries of events. The Christian writers are more full, especially *Lactantius*, (in his tract *de mortibus persequutor.*) and *Eusebius.* But they are excessive in their praise of the virtues and probity of *Constantine*, and continually heap reproaches on *Maximian* and his friends as well as enemies; and they ascribe everything to God, who, they tell us, avenged the cruelties of *Maximian*, rewarded the piety and wisdom of *Constantine*, and, in a wonderful manner, exalted the Christian religion over the worship of the Gods. [p. 952.] This is pious, and commendable; and the facts stated are true: and yet it is manifest, that human passions and worldly policy, had no small influence in these transactions.

I begin with the West.—*Constantine*, as soon as he had obtained power and the title of Cesar, gave to the Christians of his provinces, full liberty to profess their religion, and to worship God according to the divine prescription. His father, as we have already seen, had forbidden the Christians to be molested: but he had not confirmed this by a public law; nor had he given them the liberty, beyond the limits of Gaul, of assembling publicly for worship, of holding councils, of rebuilding their prostrate temples, or of creating bishops. But *Constantine* freely bestowed on them all these privileges, and this not in a private way, but by issuing a public edict. That edict is the oldest of all his religious statates. Says *Lactantius*, (de mortibus persequtor. c. 24. p. 969.) Suscepto imperio, Constantinus augustus nihil egit prius, quam Christianos cultui ac Deo suo reddere. Haec fuit prima ejus sanctio sanctae religionis restitutae. Nearly the same things are stated in his divine Institutes, (L. 1. c. 1. p. 6.) where he says to *Constantine:* Salutarem—principatum praeclaro initio auspicatus es, cum eversam sublatamque justitiam reducens, teterrimum aliorum facinus expiasti. The first of these passages manifestly describes the nature of the benefit, conferred by *Constantine* on the Christians at the commencement of his reign. For *Lactantius* says, that he—*Christianos cultui ac Deo suo reddidisse.* They had already been freed from the fear of death and of punishment, by his father; but it was *Constantine*, who *cultui eos et Deo suo reddebat*; that is, who restored their lost power of publicly worshipping God, and of course also of consecrating edifices to this worship. *Constantius Chlorus*, therefore, although friendly to the Christians, had not conceded to his Spanish subjects, and perhaps not to his British, the liberty of holding religious meetings, and of public worship; as we have before attempted to prove.—This remarkable kindness of *Constantine* to the Christians, which was the prominent trait in his character, most certainly, did not proceed from any love for the religion professed by the Christians; for at that time he was quite ignorant of this religion. Neither did it proceed from any magnanimity, justice, equity, or any similar characteristics of his mind; for these virtues were very imperfect in him, before he embraced Christianity. I can discover and appreciate, in *Constantine*, before he became a Christian, *prudence, fortitude*, and *skill* in governing; but I also discover in him many things very unbecoming in a good, wise, magnanimous and just prince, and indicative of a *proud, ambitious, cruel* mind, destitute of true virtue. These declarations it may be proper to confirm, by some examples, lest I should appear to assail, without reason, a prince renowned on so many accounts.—I. In the war between him and the Franks and Alemanni, in the beginning of his reign, as *Eutropius* tells us, (Breviar. Histor. Rom. L. x. c. 3. p. 457.) the captured kings of these nations, *Bestiis objecit*, cum magnificum spectaculum muneris parasset. A little after, passing the Rhine, he invaded the Bructeri, a people of the Francic race, slew a great number, and again condemned the captives to [p. 953.] the wild beasts. See the *Panegyrici veteres*, published at Antwerp by Livineius, (Orat. ix. p. 197, 198.) These kings and people had broken their covenants; but such punishments are not indicative of a just and good, but of a barbarous and cruel prince: temperate severity becomes a wise and humane general, even in the most just wars.—II. *Herculius*, when the civil war with his son arose in Italy, went to *Constantine* in Gaul, and offered him his daughter Fausta, with the title of Emperor and Augustus; and *Constantine* very eagerly received both; an act unworthy of a magnanimous prince, and manifestly indicative of a mind swelling with pride and ambition. *Herculius*, whom he knew to be perfidious and tyrannical, had no power of conferring dominion and rank and titles of honor: and *Constantine* must have been greedy of honor, and exceedingly vain, to suppose that he could be elevated and honored by such a man, and to actually receive honors at his hands. And yet, to this man, his father-in-law, patron, friend, and confederate, he would afterwards afford no aid, either against *Maximian Galerius*, or his son *Maxentius*. *Herculius* fled from Italy, and arriving in Gaul implored the good faith of the son-in-law: but the son-in-law could not be moved.—III. A far worse and a blacker crime, undoubtedly, was, his compelling this very *Herculius*, from whom he had received both the purple and a wife, to be his own executioner. Says *Lactantius*, (de mortibus pers. c. 30. p. 977.): *Datur ei* (there was given to Herculius, by his son-in law Constantine,) *potestas liberae mortis:* in the use of which he hung himself with a rope. How cruel a favor for a son-in-law towards his father-in-law! I admit, that *Herculius* had been guilty of a great crime; for he had sought to take the life of his son-in-law; if we believe what *Lactantius* and some other historians relate. But this will not efface the mark of cruelty and inhumanity on *Constantine*. If *Herculius* deserved that punishment, it was certainly most unsuitable for *Constantine* to pass the sentence on his father-in-law, then venerable for his hoary head.—IV. As to his *religion*, I suppose, that before he became a Christian, *Constantine* was of no religion. His father had worshipped the one God, despising the Gods of the nations: and *Eusebius* expressly tells us, (de vita Constant. L. 1. c. 17. p. 416.) that all his children, he (*Uni omnium Regi Deo consecraverat;* that is,) had taught them to worship the one God, and to hold the Gods of the Romans and the other nations in contempt. *Constantine*, therefore, in obedience to the commands of his father, as he himself admits, in his edict preserved by *Eusebius*, (de vita Constant. L. ii. c. 49. p. 466.) wished to be accounted a worshipper of the one God. And yet, when occasion seemed to require it, and lest he should alienate the minds of the people and soldiers from him, he supplicated the Gods, gave thanks to them, and offered them sacrifices and gifts. For example, the insurrection of the Franks, in the year 308, being quelled sooner than was expected, he repaired immediately to the [p. 954.] temple of Apollo—of that Apollo, whose oracles he had ridiculed and detested, when he was a young man in the court of Diocletian, as he himself relates, (apud *Eusebium* de vita Constant. L. ii. c. 50. p. 467.)—he went, I say, into the temple of Apollo, and by most splendid gifts, and by prayers to that God, he manifested his gratitude for the peace bestowed by him on the empire. See the *Panegyrici veteres*, by Livineius, (Orat. ix. p. 204, 205.)—Such being the character of *Constantine*, before his conversion to Christianity, I fully believe, that the favors he conferred on the Christians, from the very commencement of his reign, did not proceed either from his humanity and justice, or from any love for the Christian religion, but were owing solely to his desire to establish his own authority in the empire. Fearing the power and snares of *Maximian Galerius*, whom he knew to be his enemy, he wished to secure to himself firm protection in the Christians, against all adverse occurrences and the machinations of the tyrant.

His kinsman or wife's brother, *Maxentius*, on assuming the imperatorial dignity, followed the example of *Constantine*, and for the same reason. In the provinces which *Severus* had governed, namely *Italy* and *Africa*, after the death of *Constantius Chlorus*, and when *Severus* became an Emperor, the persecutions against the Christians waxed a little more severe. But *Maxentius*, equally with *Constantine*, as soon as he assumed imperatorial power, prudently, and to secure the good will of the Christians, put an end to those movements, and forbid the Christians to be molested. As to *Africa*, we have a substantial witness in *Optatus Mileritanus*, who says, (de schismate Donatist. L. 1. c. 16. p. 17.): Maxentium indulgentiam misisse, atque libertatem Christianis restituisse. By the word *indulgentiam*, we may understand permission to meet publicly for the worship of God, and to create bishops, and build temples. By the word *libertatem*, we may understand *full liberty*, such as they enjoyed before the persecution of Diocletian. For the liberty of worshipping God privately, without fear, they had previously enjoyed under *Severus.*—As to *Italy* and the other parts of the Roman empire subject to *Maxentius*, *Eusebius*, (Hist. Eccles. L. viii. c. 14. p. 310.) gives such an account, as confirms our statement of the cause of *Maxentius'* kindness to the Christians. It was feigned or political benevolence. For he says that *Maxentius* went so far, Ut religionis Christianæ professionem *simularet*, fictam pietatis speciem præ se tulisse, civibus praecepisse, ut a persecutione Christianorum desisterent. And he adds, that his motive was, Ut in eo morem gereret, blandireturque populo Romano. 'Επ' ἀρεσκείᾳ καὶ κολακείᾳ τοῦ δήμου Ῥωμαίων. A great part, therefore, perhaps the greatest part of the Romish people, was Christian, or at least friendly to Christianity: and to secure their aid and attachment, against *Maximian Galerius*, who was meditating war upon him, he not only annulled all the edicts against the Christians, but even pretended to be ready to quit the religion of his ancestors, and to embrace Christianity. He therefore appeared to exceed *Constantine*, in good will towards [p. 955.] Christians: for *Constantine*, though he showed himself friendly to the Christians, manifested no disposition to embrace their religion, but continued to serve the Gods of the Romans.

The state of the Christians was therefore tolerably prosperous in the West. But in the *eastern provinces*, governed by *Maximian Galerius* and *Maximin*, the storm against them raged with the greater violence. This we learn from several writers, and especially *Eusebius*, (Historia Eccles. and de martyr. Palæstinæ.) Yet the monuments of this period that have reached us, though few, leave no room for doubt, that in those provinces, likewise, the state of the Christians was affected by that of the commonwealth; and that *Maximin* especially, was sometimes more indulgent and sometimes more severe, towards the Christians in his provinces, as circumstances seemed to him to demand. In the sixth year of the persecution, A. D. 308, according to *Eusebius*, (de martyr. Palæst. c. 9. p. 332.) the war upon the Christians in *Syria* and *Palestine*, seemed to cease; and even those condemned to the mines, were restored to freedom: but, after a short time, the persecution raged with more violence than before. For new edicts against the Christians, were issued by *Maximin*, which required that the decaying temples of the Gods should be repaired, and that all the people, children and slaves not excepted, should be forced by penalties to eat the flesh sacrificed to the Gods. *Eusebius* confesses, that he does not know the causes of these suspensions and renewals of the persecution. But it will be manifest, to a person consulting the civil history, that in this year, (308,) *Maximin* assumed the title and rank of Emperor in Syria, contrary to the will of *Maximian:* and Maximian appeared disposed to avenge this rash act by a war. Now, so long as Maximian's wrath continued, *Maximin* spared the Christians in his provinces, in order to conciliate their good will. But when *Maximian* was appeased, the new Emperor *Maximin* issued fresh edicts against the Christians; in order to show, that he would employ the power conceded to him, agreeably to the pleasure of the chief Emperor, whom he knew to be hostile to the Christians, and in order to insinuate himself the more effectually into his good graces. This new fury, after a little time, abated: for *Maximin* concluded, he had fulfilled his obligations by his edicts; and he thought it not best to exasperate the feelings of Christians too much, lest they should turn against him, on the demise of Maximian, whose declining and very bad health indicated that his death was approaching. And therefore, in the latter part of the seventh year of the persecution, (309,) and in the beginning of the eighth, (310,) the Christians, (according to *Eusebius*, de martyr. Palæst. c. 13. p. 343.) enjoyed the highest peace, and surprising liberty; so that even those who had been condemned to the mines, now built temples. But this peace was interrupted, in the course of the year 310, by the governor of the province, who informed the Emperor, that the Christians abused their liberty. And hence new calamities occurred, and [p. 956.] many Christians were put to death; of whom thirty-nine were beheaded on one and the same day, by order of *Maximin*. This tempest, however, was short, and soon clemency was thought to be safer policy than severity. For in this year, *Maximian* was attacked by that terrible disease, which the next year put an end to his life: and, as all could see, that the disease must terminate fatally, and as it was feared that, after his death, great commotions and contests for the supremacy would arise, prudence induced *Maximin* to desist from persecuting the Christians. And *Maximian Galerius* himself, the author of the persecution, writhing under a horrible disease, gradually laid aside his cruelty, as his strength and life wasted away. And hence, on the one side the fear of war, and on the other, the fear of death, restored peace and security everywhere to the Christians. See *Eusebius*, (Historia Eccles. L. viii. c. 16. p. 314.)

(2) The disease of *Maximian Galerius* is described particularly, by *Eusebius*, (Hist. Eccles. L. viii. c. 16. p. 314.) and by *Lactantius*, (de mortibus persequutor. c. 33 &c. p. 981 &c.) Nothing can be conceived more distressing. For, a cancer attacked his immoderately fat body, and by eating gradually, amid horrible sufferings, converted it into a living corpse. When various remedies had been tried in vain, and no hope of recovery remained, a little before his death, in the month of April, A. D. 311, by a public edict, in the name of all the Emperors, he abolished the laws enacted against the Christians. This edict is extant in a Greek version from the Latin, in *Eusebius*, (Hist. Eccles. L. viii. c. 17. p. 415.) and the Latin in *Lactantius*, (de mort. perseq. c. 34. p. 984.) In this edict, he permits, *Ut denuo sint Christiani, et conventicula sua* (their sacred edifices or temples) *component* (erect or build). But upon this condition, *Ut nequid contra disciplinam agant.* By the *disciplinam*, he means the Roman religion; as appears from the preamble to the edict, in which he says, that he, Antehac voluisse cuncta juxta disciplinam publicam Romanorum corrigere. Therefore, in restoring peace to the Christians, the Emperor required of them, that they should form no projects against the public religion of the Romans, and should not pro-

sume to assail the Gods, either by words or actions. Indeed, the condition seems to extend still farther, and to require of Christians, that they should not attempt to convert any one from the religion of his ancestors to Christianity.—*Eusebius* and *Lactantius* tell us, that *Maximian*, before he issued this edict, Deo errorem suum confessum esse, atque exclamasse inter dolores, se pro scelere satisfacturum. And if this was the fact, then he confessed, that the Christians' God was justly punishing him for his cruelty to the Christians, and that he was conscious of this divine retribution. But the very edict of the Emperor, which these writers exhibit, militates against the credibility of their statement. For *Maximian* is so far from there confessing that he had done wickedly and unjustly, that he maintains, on the contrary, that every thing he had done against the Christians, had been done wisely and well. And he tells us, that he had aimed to effect, by his laws, Ut Christiani, qui parentum suorum reli- [p. 957.] querant sectam, *ad bonas mentes redirent*. And therefore, in this last act of his life, he represents the Christians as being *senseless;* and he entertained no doubt, that the religion of the Romans was better and more sound than that of Christians. A little after, he explicitly charges the Christians with *stultitia;* and not a syllable does he utter, from which it can be inferred, that any penitence for his conduct had entered his heart, or that he regarded Christianity as the only true and divine religion. He states *two* reasons for changing his policy towards the Christians. *First*, he had noticed that the Christians, while urged by violence and peril to offer sacrifices, lived destitute of *all* religion, and neither worshipped Christ nor the Gods: Cum plurimi in proposito perseverarent, ac videremus, nec Diis eosdem cultum ac religionem debitam exhibere, nec Christianorum Deum observare. And therefore, considering *any* religion, even a corrupt one, to be better than none, he would rather have the Christians follow their own religion, than have no religion at all. And *secondly*, to this he adds another reason, namely, his *clemency:* Contemplationem mitissimæ *clementiæ* nostræ intuentes et consuetudinem sempiternam, qua solemus cunctis hominibus veniam indulgere, promtissimam in his quoque indulgentiam nostram credidimus porrigendam, ut denuo sint Christiani. *Maximian* therefore would not have it thought, that he followed right and justice, but rather *clemency;* and that he was *indulgent* to persons whom he pronounced *fools*, and destitute of sense, and not that he showed himself *just* to the innocent and the good. I can readily suppose, that the friends who were his counsellers, suggested these reasons to him. Yet the concluding words of the edict, undoubtedly, disclose *the cause* which drew this edict from him, and also manifest his views of the Christian religion: Unde juxta hanc indulgentiam nostram debebunt (Christiani) *Deum suum orare pro salute nostra et reipublicæ ac suâ*, ut undique versum respublica restet incolumis, et securi vivere in sedibus suis possint. From these words, it is manifest,—I. That *Maximian* believed, the Christians had some sort of a God.—II. That this God was not the supreme Creator of all things, whom all men ought to worship, but merely the God of Christians, or the God of a particular race, such as many other of the Gods. For the Romans, the Greeks, and all the nations, in that age, believed that each race of people had its appropriate and peculiar God.—III. That this God of a particular race, possessed great power, so that he could bestow health, and avert dangers from the state.—IV. But that this God did not confer such benefits, except at the request of his own worshippers. There can be no doubt, that some one of the attendants on the diseased Emperor, suggested to him, that the God of the Christians, while resident in this our world, restored life to the dead, and health to the sick; and that [p. 958.] these benefits had not yet ceased; for there were many examples of sick persons miraculously healed by the prayers of Christians. And therefore, possibly the Emperor also, by the aid of this God, might survive the dreadful disease which was consuming him, if he should grant peace to the Christians, and ask their prayers for him. The Emperor, being extremely anxious to live, listened to the suggestion; and therefore, when his case was desperate, when the Gods of the Romans had in vain been importuned with prayers and sacrifices, he at last took refuge in the Christians' God; whom, nevertheless, he would not worship. Hence, it was the *fear of death*, and the influence of *superstition*, and not the goadings of conscience for crimes committed, that produced this edict.—On the publication of the edict, the war upon the Christians every where ceased; the prisoners were released, the exiles were recalled, and meetings were everywhere held without opposition. *Maximin*, indeed, would not publicly proclaim the edict, in the provinces which he governed, (as *Eusebius* states, Hist. Eccles. L. ix. c. 1. p. 347.) yet he gave verbal instructions to the rulers under him, no longer to inflict any evils on the Christians: and this, according to *Eusebius*, was as advantageous to the Christians, as if the edict had been published. *Eusebius* tells us, that it was hatred of Christians that prevented *Maximin* from publishing an edict so salutary to them. But I can hardly persuade myself that this was the fact. For *Maximin* did the thing which the edict required, although he would not publish it. It is more probable, therefore, that *Maximin*, knowing the death of *Maximian* to be very near, laid up the edict of the Emperor—who might even then be dead,—intending to wait and see what would occur after his death.

§ VI. **Constantine's Edicts in favor of the Christians, A. D. 312, 313.** On the death of *Maximian Galerius* in the year 311, the provinces which he had governed were divided between *Maximin* and *Licinius*. The former had the Asiatic provinces, and the latter the European. But *Maxentius*, the Emperor of Italy and Africa, meditated war against *Constantine*, that he might render himself Emperor of the entire West. The ostensible cause, however, of the war, was the death of his father *Maximian Herculius*, whom *Constantine* had compelled to destroy his own life. *Constantine*, therefore, prudently anticipating the counsels of his enemy, marched his army from Gaul into Italy, and after weakening *Maxentius* in several conflicts, entirely routed him in the year 312, in a fierce battle, at the Milvian Bridge, not far from Rome: and *Maxentius* in the flight, by the breaking down of the bridge, fell into the Tiber and perished. The victorious *Constantine* entered the city, and not long after, with *Licinius* his colleague, [p. 959.] issued an edict which gave the Christians the fullest liberty of living according to their own principles, institutions and usages. And the next year A. D. 313, he confirmed and defined this liberty more precisely, in an edict drawn up at Milan. *Maximin*, indeed, who governed the East, was menacing the Christians with new calamities, and also preparing for war with the Emperors of the West. But fortune forsook his enterprises. For *Licinius*, encountering him at Adrianople, obtained a complete victory. And *Maximin* escaping by flight, drank poison, and died a miserable death at Tarsus, in the year 311.(1)

(1) These occurrences in civil history, I shall not here amplify and illustrate: for they are well known; and, being supported by the testimony both of Christians and Not-Christians, they are doubted by no one. The justice of the wars,—first against *Maxentius* and then against *Maximin*, even the enemies of *Constantine* do not question; but they equally recount the flagitious acts, the vices and the crimes of both *Maxentius* and *Maximin*. I shall therefore speak only of things relating to the christian community.—*Constantine* with *Licinius*, immediately after the victory over *Maxentius*, by an edict addressed to the Pretorian Prefect, granted to the Christians and to all other sects, perfect liberty to worship God in their own way, to profess their religion, to hold religious meetings, and to erect temples. See *Eusebius*, (Hist. Eccles. L. ix. c. 9. p. 360. 363.) As *Maxentius* was vanquished in the month of October, A. D. 312, and the edict was issued directly after the victory, I think it certain, that the edict was written near the close of the same year. This *first* edict in favor of the Christians and other sects, is lost: but from the *second* edict, which was drawn up at Milan the next year, 313, (of which we shall speak hereafter,) it appears, that the first edict contained some defect, which might deter persons from embracing christianity. Yet what that defect was, the second edict does not definitely state. The words of the second edict, emendatory of the first, are given to us by *Eusebius*, (Hist. Eccles. L. x. c. 5. p. 388.) *Lactantius* also gives us this edict, in Latin, the language in which it was written, (de mort. Persequut. c. 48. p. 1007.) but he omits the Preface, as not being pertinent to his object. The words in *Eusebius* are these: Sed quoniam in eo rescripto, quo hæc facultas illis concessa fuerat, (in which this liberty of retaining and practising their religion, was conceded to Christians,) multæ ac diversæ sectae nominatim ac diserte additæ videbantur, (πολλαὶ καὶ διάφοροι αἱρέσεις ἐδόκουν προστεθεῖσθαι σαφῶς,) quidam eorum, ob hanc fortassis caussam, paulo post ab hujusmodi [p. 960.] observantia destiterunt, (ἀπὸ τῆς τοιαύτης παραφυλάξεως ἀνεκρούοντο) That is—if I do not mistake, they forsook the christian religion, and went over to the other sects. From this statement of *Eusebius*, it appears,—1. That this edict gave absolute freedom of professing their religion, not only to *Christians*, but

likewise to *all other sects;* e. g. Jews, Samaritans, Manichæans, and all others.—II. That these *other sects* besides Christians, were expressly named and designated in the decree.—III. Hence, some *Christians* took occasion to forsake the christian religion, or to neglect the observances of it. This is very obscure: for who can easily understand how some Christians should forsake their religion, because other sects besides the christians were expressly named in the Imperatorial edict? And hence learned men disagree as to the *meaning* of the passage. Some, as *Tillemont*, *Basnage* and others, frankly confess their ignorance of its import: and they charge the edict with obscurity: but perhaps, they might better charge Eusebius' *Greek translator*, with carelessness in translating. I think the meaning of the Emperors will be sufficiently clear, if we compare what precedes and what follows, with the words which contain this apparent enigma. In the Preface to the edict, the Emperors say, that they, in the first edict, Sanxisse, ut ceteri omnes, tum Christiani, sectæ suæ ac religionis fidem et observantiam retinerent, (τῆς αἱρέσεως ἑαυτῶν τὴν πίστιν φυλάττειν.) Now this liberty, granted to the Christians and to the other sects expressly named, some persons explained thus: *That it was the pleasure of the Emperors, that every person should adhere to the sect or religion, in which he had been born and educated, and should not go over to another religion.* And therefore, some who had recently embraced christianity,—Jews, for instance, returned to the religion of their fathers, that they might not appear to disobey the mandate of the Emperors: and other persons of other sects, who had not long before embraced christianity, did the same. This false interpretation of their first edict, the Emperors corrected by a second edict, (preserved by *Eusebius* and *Lactantius*,) the following year, 313, published at Milan, after the defeat of *Maximin* and the establishment of the government of the empire. For in this edict, they corrected ,the ambiguity of the first: and this they do, in terms which show, that we have rightly apprehended the defect in the first edict. For they thus express themselves: Itaque hoc consilio salubri ac rectissima ratione ineundum esse credimus, ut nulli omnino facultatem abnegandam putaremus, qui vel observationi Christianorum, vel ei religioni mentem suam dederet, *quam ipse sibi aptissimam sentiret.* They had just before written: Credidimus ordinanda, ut daremus et Christians et omnibus *liberam postestatem sequendi religionem, quam quis-* [p. 961.] *que voluisset.* Therefore many had before supposed, that it was not the pleasure of the Emperors, that every one should follow the religion which he preferred; but that, on the contrary, they wished every one to adhere to the religion transmitted to him from his ancestors.—In the same edict, moreover, the Emperors expand and amplify the privileges conferred on the Christians by the first edict. They first removed all the *conditions*, with which the liberty granted to Christians in the former edict was circumscribed: Scire dignationen tuam convenit, placuisse nobis, ut, *amotis omnibus omnino conditionibus*, quæ prius scriptis—super Christianorum nomine videbantur, nunc caveres, ut simpliciter unusquisque eorum - - citra ullam inquietudinem ac molestiam sui id ipsum observare contendat. What these conditions *were*, which the Emperors now removed, it is impossible at this day to determine satisfactorily.—The Emperors add explicitly, that what they conceded to the *Christians*, they conceded also to the *other sects*, Ut in colendo, quod quisque delegerit, habeat liberam facultatem.—Afterwards they revert again to the Christians, and, with great particularity, ordain, that their places of worship should be restored to them, without pay; and also the lands, which, before the persecution, Ad jus corporis eorum, id est, ecclesiarum, non hominum singulorum, pertinuerint: for in the first edict, this matter was not stated and explained with perfect clearness. This last part of the edict is drawn up with great accuracy, and shows that it was dictated by one very friendly to the Christians.

As in the *West* there were *two edicts* issued in favor of the Christians, the fisst not very perspicuous, and the second more clear; so in the *East*, the same thing occurred, though in a different manner. *Maximin*, the Sovereign of the East, notwithstanding he hated the Christians, dared not oppose the edict of *Maximian Galerius* favorable to them; yet, after a little time, he assailed them again by concealed artifices. For, as *Lactantius* says, (de mort. perseq. c. 36. p. 986.): Subornabat legationes civitatum, quæ peterent, ne intra civitates suas Christianis conventicula extruere liceret. Quibus ille adnuebat. This *Eusebius* confirms, and more fully explains; (Hist. Eccles. L. ix. c. 2. p. 349.) for he says, that *Maximin* first induced the Antiochians, by means of one Theotecnus, Curator of that city, a wicked and violent man, to request of him, as a very great favor, that no Christian should be permitted to reside in Antioch. And as *Maximin* granted their request, other cities readily followed the example of the Antiochians, and *Maximin* most cheerfully assented to their wishes; and thus a new and violent persecution arose in the East against the Christians. Moreover, the Emperor aided those impious enemies of the christian name, by edicts engraven on plates of brass; one of which, presented to the Tyrians, *Eusebius* has preserved; (Hit. Eccles. L. ix. c. 7. p. 352.) As to these [p. 962.] legations from cities, there can be no doubt; for *Maximin* himself declares, in his rescript to Sabinus, (apud *Eusebium*, Hist. Eccles. L. ix. c. 9. p. 361.) that the Nicomedians, and other cities, did send such legations to him. But whether it was true, as *Lactantius* and *Eusebius* would have us believe, that Maximin *suborned* those legations of the cities, or, as *Eusebius* says, (loc. cit. c. 2. p. 349.): ipsum ad se legationem misisse adversus Christianos; I confess, I do not know. Undoubtedly, the Christians suspected it was so: but whether their suspicion was well or ill founded is, I think, very uncertain. For they had no other evidence for their suspicion, than the ill-will of *Maximin* towards Christians. It certainly might be, that the Antiochians, either spontaneously, or at the instigation of Theotecnus, went to the Emperor, requesting the banishment of the Christians; and that after he had gratified their wishes, other cities, as *Eusebius* himself states, followed the example of the Antiochians. That the Emperor should grant the petitions of the cities, I do not at all wonder. For the supremacy in the empire which he sought, and the war against *Constantine* and *Licinius* which he meditated, made the good will of the cities and citizens exceedingly necessary to him. The narrative of *Eusebius* throws light on the subject. He acknowledges,—notwithstanding *Lactantius* makes *Maximin* the author of *all* the legations,—that only *one* legation, the Antiochian, was suborned by him; and that the others proceeded from the free choice of the cities, following the example of the Antiochians. He also says, that Theotecnus, the Curator of Antioch, by a crafty trick, induced the Antiochian people to send the legation for the expulsion of the Christians from that city: for he had himself consecrated a statue of Jupiter Philius, and he pretended that this God, by his statue, had directed that all Christians, his enemies, should be expelled from the city, and from the fields around Antioch. Now if the facts were so, we must believe, that if *Maximin* suborned the Antiochian legation, which was an example for the others, then Theotecnus acted the part he did, by the command of Maximin. And perhaps this was the fact. But how did *Eusebius* and *Lactantius* get their knowledge of it?—From Theotecnus?—He certainly never disclosed to the Christians this state secret of his master. Whence, therefore, did they learn, that Theotecnus was only the tool of the Emperor? Who does not see, that this charge against the Emperor, turns out to be a mere *suspicion;* and that the Christians had no authority for it? As already remarked, *Maximin* himself, in the rescript in which he mentions these legations, (apud *Eusebium*, Hist. Eccles. L. ix. c. 9. p. 360, 361.) states, that it was with reluctance and sorrow, he conceded to the Nicomedians and to others the power of expelling the Christians: for their petitions seemed to him contrary to equity: but that he was compelled to answer them kindly; for all the Emperors before him had done the same thing: and it [p. 963.] was a thing pleasing to the immortal Gods. In this language there is reference, undoubtedly, to that oracle of Jupiter Philius at Antioch, and to the responses of other Gods, requiring the expulsion of Christians from the cities. And I can almost believe, that *Maximin* does not misrepresent the truth; and that, not he, but the pagan priests, who undoubtedly dictated those oracles, were the real authors of those legations against the Christians. Whoever attentively considers the state of the empire at that time, and the political designs of *Maximin*, will readily perceive, that it was not for his interest, either to irritate the Christians, or to oppose the friends of the Gods: on the contrary, prudence demanded, that he should temporise, and as far as possible, conciliate the good will of both parties. And therefore, as he admits in the rescript referred to, he forbid on the one hand the forcing of Christians by violence and punishments, to worship the Gods; and on the other hand he gratified the cities, which would not endure Christians among them. It is the common practice of the Christian writers, to load the memory of the enemies of Christianity with many and great suspicions and accusations; some of which, indeed, are not to be treated with contempt; but others, if carefully examined, will appear weak and futile.

But let us pass over these transactions, and consider what results followed, in the East, from the edicts of *Constantine* and *Licinius* in the favor of the Christians.—When the edict of A. D. 312, was first brought to *Maximin*, he would not publish it in the provinces under his jurisdiction. This, I would attribute, not so much to his hatred of the Christians,—the cause assigned by *Eusebius*, as to his pride and arrogance. For he wished to be accounted the chief of the Emperors, and superior in rank to *Constantine* and *Licinius:* and therefore, he thought it degrading to his majesty, to publish a law enacted by persons whom he deemed his inferiors. But he addressed an epistle to the governors in his dominions, which is preserved by *Eusebius*, (Hist. Eccles. L. ix. c. 9. p. 360.) differing indeed, in many particulars, from the edict of the Western Emperors, and yet favorable to the Christians. And this epistle shows very clearly, that *Maximin* did not wish to alienate the minds of Christians from him, but rather to conciliate their good will. For he proclaims his humanity and clemency towards them, and declares, that from the commencement of his reign, he had inculcated on the magistrates under him, not to compel any person to worship the Gods by penal inflictions. He says: Saepe devotioni tuae partim per literas scripsi, partim coram in mandatis dedi, ut adversus Christianos provinciarum rectores nihil acerbe statuant, sed potius clementer et moderate indulgeant, seque illis accommodent. He had indeed given kind answers to the delegations from cities that were unwilling to tolerate Christians within their walls: but this he did, unwillingly, and partly from respect to the laws of former Emperors, and partly in obedience to the oracles of the Gods: but, now, he adds in conclusion, it is his pleasure, that the Christians should be treated humanely and kindly.—The Christians did not put confidence in this edict, knowing *Maximin* to be unstable minded, and at one time to oppose, [p. 964.] and at another to favor them, according to the changing state of his affairs, and the condition of the republic. And as the edict did not explicitly give them liberty to erect temples and hold religious meetings, they dared not assume such liberty, and profess openly their religion.—But after he had been vanquished by *Licinius*, in the year 313, he issued a new and more ample edict in favor of the Christians: which also is preserved by *Eusebius*, (Hist. Eccles. L. ix. c. 10. p. 363.) In this edict, he complains, (whether truly or falsely, is uncertain,) that the judges and magistrates did not correctly understand his former edict; and then, he explicitly gives the Christians liberty to rebuild their sacred edifices; and he commands, that the lands taken from them should be restored. —Shortly after issuing this decree, he died at Tarsus. And thus, in the year 313, the Christians of both the East and West were released from all peril and fear, after enduring infinite evils, especially in the Eastern countries, from the year 303, or during ten years.

§ VII. **Constantine's Conversion to Christianity.** About the same time, and after the victory over *Maxentius* at the Milvian bridge, *Constantine* the Great is said to have embraced the Christian religion: and it is the common and ancient opinion, that the sign of a cross seen by him in the heavens, produced and confirmed this resolution of the Emperor. If that man is a Christian who thinks the Christian's manner of worshipping God is a good and holy one, then I have no doubt that *Constantine* was, at that time, a Christian. But if no man should be called a Christian, unless he believes that Christianity is the only true religion, and that all other religions are false, then I suppose *Con-*

stantine became a Christian at a later period, and some years after the victory over *Maxentius*. For, if any reliance can be placed on public records, it is certain that *Constantine* at first considered all religions to be good, and he supposed Christ to be like the rest of the national Gods; but after some time he acquired purer and better knowledge on religious subjects, and he concluded that God ought to be worshipped in no other than the Christian manner.(1) But what is reported of the sign of a cross, or rather, of a Monogramm of the name of *Christ*, seen in the clouds by him and his army, is more difficult to be explained than many imagine; and the inquiring and truth-seeking mind is so perplexed, that it can hardly determine what to deny, or what to believe.(2)

[p. 965.] (1) That *Constantine* the Great sincerely and truly embraced the Christian religion, is put beyond all question, by his deeds, his legislation, his policy and his institutions: nor is there any event in history, except those only of sacred history, which, in my opinion, rests on stronger evidence both of testimony and of facts. If the man, who makes it his chief object through a great part of life to establish and propagate the Christian religion; who resists and depresses the religions opposed to it; who changes nearly his whole system of jurisprudence for its benefit; who, to his last breath, praises and extols and solemnly professes Christ; who commands his children to be instructed and trained up in that religion; who exhorts and excites all his citizens and people to embrace it; who honors and distinguishes its priests and ministers with various benefits, and does many other things of like nature, whereby the Christian religion is sustained and strengthened,—if, I say, *that* man does not deserve the name of a Christian, to whom can that name belong? But that the truth may be obscured and rendered powerless, by the biasses of the mind, is seen in this case. For there are very learned and perspicacious men, who either deny that *Constantine* the Great was a Christian, or maintain that he hypocritically professed Christianity, in order to secure his supremacy in the commonwealth. Some of these are led to such conclusions by their zeal for new religious opinions, some by hostility to the clergy, whom it pains them to see *Constantine* invest with so many privileges and favors; and some by the evils which, they are grieved to see, crept into the church through *Constantine*. Yet they would be thought to indulge no groundless suspicion, and therefore they assign reasons for their opinion.—*First:* Many direct our attention to the life and conduct of Constantine; in which there are doubtless many things altogether unworthy of a Christian man. He slew Crispus his son, and Fausta his wife, on mere suspicion: He destroyed Licinius his kinsman, together with his innocent son, contrary to his plighted faith: He was immoderately addicted to pride, to vanity, and to voluptuousness: He tolerated superstitions, that are inconsistent with Christianity. But the excellent men who resort to such reasoning, e. g. Christian *Thomasius*

Godfrey *Arnold*, and many others,—to speak plainly, trifle with the subject, and misuse the ambiguous term *Christian* to deceive the incautious. *That* man is *properly* denominated a Christian, who not only believes in Christ, but also regulates his life by the precepts of the religion which Christ taught: but those also are *called* Christians, who entertain no doubts of the truth and divinity of the Christian religion, although they deviate in conduct from its rules. That *Constantine* was not a Christian in the former sense, is demonstrated by the vices and crimes laid to his charge: but that he was a Christian in *this* sense of the word, no fair-minded man, who is free from superstition, maintains. Those who call *Constantine* the first Christian Emperor, mean no more than, that he was the first of the Emperors who regarded Christianity as the only true and divine religion. This, *Constantine* might do, and yet act very diffe- [p. 966.] rently from what a Christian ought to do.

Secondly: Learned men who doubt of the religion of *Constantine*, remark, that it was only at the close of life, and when laboring under a fatal disease, (according to *Eusebius*, de vita Constant. L. iv. c. 61, 62.) that he not only received baptism, but likewise was received among the Catechumens by the imposition of hands: from which they conclude, that through life he was a man of no religion, but at last, in the near prospect of death, that he might not appear to die destitute of *all* religion, he requested to be enrolled among Christians. Very many spurn at this reasoning; but in my view, it deserves serious consideration. For it is well known, that the whole Christian community consisted of the *Catechumens* and the *Faithful*. If then *Constantine*, during his whole life, was neither a *Catechumen*, nor one of the *Faithful*, and only a little before his death was admitted a *Catechumen*, and subsequently by baptism received among the faithful, it would seem to follow, that he lived out of the church until the end of life, and of course that he should not be classed among Christians. As to his deferring his baptism till near the end of his life, the fact is certain, not only from the testimony of *Eusebius*, but also of other writers of the highest character and authority, *Jerome*, *Ambrose*, *Socrates Sozomen*, and others. There are indeed some learned writers of the Romish community, e. g. *Baronius*, *Ciampinus*, *Schelstratus*, and many others, to whom Mathew *Furmann* joined himself a few years since (in his Historia sacra de baptismo Constantini, published at Rome, 1742, 4to.)—who, relying on more recent and doubtful authorities, believe, that *Constantine* was initiated with sacred rites, at Rome, by *Sylvester*, then bishop of Rome, in the year 324. But these writers meet with little credence now, even in their own church; and they are solidly confuted by various writers, among whom are the Romish Cardinal, Henry *Noris*, (in his Historia Donatistar. Opp. tom. iv. p. 650 &c.) *Tillemont*, and others. To these add, one who has neatly and carefully summed up the arguments on both sides, and who pretty clearly shows that he follows those that account the story of *Constantine's* baptism at Rome as a mere fable, namely, Thomas Maria *Mamachius*, (in his Origines et Antiq. Christianæ, tom. ii. p. 232 &c. Rom. 1750, 4to.) That *Constantine* was admitted a *Catechumen* at Helenopolis, a little before his baptism, is learnedly and copiously maintained by Henry *Valesius*, in his notes on *Eusebius*, (de vita Constant. L. iv. c. 61

p. 551.) He observes, that *Eusebius* expressly says: Constantinum tunc primum manuum impositionem cum solemni praecatione in templo Helenopolitano suscepisse. And from this he infers, that *Constantine* was then *first* made a *Catechumen.* For, as appears from many passages in the early writers, the bishops created Catechumens by the imposition of hands. In confirmation of this opinion, *Valesius* adds, that no where in the life of Constantine written by [p. 967.] *Eusebius*, is it said, *that he prayed with the Catechumens*, in the church, *or that he received the Sacrament of Catechumens.* Yet there is much less force in this argument, than in the former. If the postponement of baptism till near death was the only difficulty, it might easily be surmounted. For those acquainted with the customs and opinions of the early ages, well know, that *many*, in that age, purposely deferred baptism till near the close of life, in order to go perfectly pure and immaculate to eternal life: for they supposed, that baptism purified the whole man, and entirely washed away all stains and defilement from the soul. And that *Constantine* had some such idea in his mind, is evident from *Eusebius*, (de vita Constant. L. iv. c. 61. p. 557.) where he says: Firmissime credidisse Imperatorem, quaecunque humanitus peccavisset, arcanorum verborum efficaciâ et salutari lavacro *penitus esse delenda.* And hence we find numerous instances in that age, of great men who deferred baptism a long time, and even till their dying hour. See the examples collected by the brothers *Ballerini*, (Notes to *Noris*, Hist. Donatist. Opp. tom. iv. p. 651.) by *Giannone*, (Historia civili Neapolitano, tom. i. p. 128.) and by others. In addition to this opinion, there was another, which had equal influence to cause baptism to be delayed. Most of the doctors taught, that a protracted, painful and difficult *penance* was necessary, for those who, after baptism, became defiled with new transgressions and sins: and that it was not easy to obtain the forgiveness of God, if when once purged and washed, they returned to their old pollutions. Moreover, *Constantine* himself, in his address to the bishops just before his baptism, (apud *Eusebium* loc. cit. c. 62. p. 557.) says, that he had formerly intended to be baptized in the *Jordan*, in which Christ was baptized by John. And this would accord with the superstition of those times, and can easily be believed.—It remains, therefore, only to inquire whether, in fact, *Constantine* first became a Catechumen a little before his death. *Valesius* and those who follow him, think this to be manifest from what *Eusebius* relates, that the bishops laid hands on the Emperor with prayer, at Nicomedia, just before he was initiated into Christian worship by the sacrament of baptism. And it is true, that the Catechumens were made such by prayer and the imposition of hands. But it is no less certain, and is taught in many passages by the ancients, that persons who had long been *Catechumens*, received at certain times, the episcopal imposition of hands. And especially, and most pertinently to our inquiry, the bishops were accustomed to lay hands on the *Catechumens*, just before baptism, either when they confessed their sins, or when they solemnly execrated the Prince of Hell, or *renounced the Devil.* I shall pass by this latter imposition of hands, and speak only of the former. It was a very ancient custom of the Church, that such as were about to be baptized, should previously confess their sins; and upon this, the bishop laid his hands on them accompanied by prayer, and in set words he imparted to them God's forgiveness of all [p. 968.] their former sins. Thus *Tertullian*, (de baptismo, c. 20.): Ingressuros baptismum orationibus crebris, jejuniis, et geniculationibus et pervigiliis orare oportet, et cum confessione omnium retro delictorum, ut exponant etiam baptismum Johannis. The testimonies of *Augustine*, *Socrates*, *Gregory Nazianzen*, and others, who mention this ancient custom, might easily be adduced. Now this alone overthrows the whole argument of *Valesius* from the imposition of hands, viz.: That the bishops laid hands on *Constantine*, before he received baptism; and therefore, he *then* first became a *Catechumen*. For persons, who had been Catechumens many years, when the time of their baptism drew near, were customarily consecrated by a renewed imposition of hands, after confessing their sins. And that *Eusebius*, when treating of the baptism of *Constantine*, speaks of that imposition of hands which followed a confession of sins, and not of that by which persons were made *Catechumens*, is so manifest from his language, that nothing could be more clear. He says: Genu flexo humi procumbens (Imperator) veniam a Deo supplex poposcit, peccata sua confitens, in Martyrio, (in seeking baptism, therefore, *Constantine* followed the ancient custom of the Church, and publicly confessed his sins: and this act of piety was pertinently followed by the imposition of hands,) quo in loco manuum impositionem cum solemni precatione primum meruit accipere. But this passage, I perceive, will not satisfy the more difficult: for they will say, that *Eusebius* distinctly tells us, that *Constantine* then *first* (πρῶτον) received imposition of hands. And as it may thence be inferred, that *Constantine* had never before received imposition of hands, they will contend, that he had never been admitted to the class of *Catechumens*: because, as before stated, Catechumens were created by the imposition of hands. Not to protract the discussion needlessly, I will grant, that the word πρῶτον in this passage of *Eusebius*, is to be taken in so strict a sense as to place it beyond controversy, that *Constantine* had never before received imposition of hands. But, on the other hand, I will demand of these learned men to *prove*, that this practice of the ancient Christians of creating Catechumens by the imposition of hands, was not only received throughout the Christian Church, but also that it was every where regarded as so sacred and so necessary, that no one could be accounted a Catechumen, unless he had been as it were consecrated by that ceremony. Most of the testimonies to this practice, come to us from the Latin writers; while the Greeks who notice it, are very few, and quite recent authors. Therefore, it might be that the Latin Church consecrated Catechumens in this manner, but not likewise the Greek and Oriental Church. But suppose, that the Greek and Oriental Christians did also use this rite; who does not know, that practices of this kind, which depend [p. 969.] on custom rather than on established law, are not observed invariably, but are frequently neglected or omitted for various reasons?—But I will settle the point at issue in a shorter way. The things stated by *Eusebius*, relative to the life and conduct of *Constantine*, put it beyond all controversy, that he had previously been a *Catechumen*. For he constantly performed all the duties of a Christian man not yet baptized, or of a Catechumen; he attended on the religious worship; he gave himself to fasting and prayer; he celebrated the Lord's

Days, and the days consecrated to the memory of the martyrs: and he watched through the night on the vigils of Easter. I omit some other things. And on the other hand, he allowed himself to be excluded from those things, to which Catechumens were not admitted. For in his speech before his baptism, (apud *Eusebium*, de vita Constant. L. iv. c. 62. p. 557.) he testifies, that he had been partaker in the common prayers; but, of course, not in the sacred supper. And therefore, nothing more can be inferred from the language of *Eusebius*, than that he had not been admitted into the class of Catechumens, *by that solemn rite*, the imposition of hands with prayer. And who can deem it strange, that such a man as *Constantine*, was not treated in the common manner? And as he faithfully performed all the duties of a *Catechumen*, what need was there of subjecting him to all the rules and regulations for plebeians? The very learned *Valesius* admits the zeal of *Constantine* in performing all the duties incumbent on unbaptized Christians: and he says, we may hence infer, that the Emperor was a *Christian*, but not that he was a *Catechumen*. How do excellent men, sometimes, deceive both themselves and others! Could any man in that age be a *Christian*, yet not be a *Catechumen?* All the members of the Church, were either the *Faithful*, or the *Catechumens:* and the Christians knew of no intermediate or third class. That *Constantine* was not one of the *Faithful* until near the close of life, is most certain: if therefore he was not a *Catechumen*, how could he be a *Christian?*

Lastly: The learned men who impugn the personal religion of *Constantine*, endeavor to show, from the history of those times, that it was his lust for reigning that induced him to feign himself a Christian; or, that he sought to open his way to supreme power by a feigned profession of Christianity. But this is preferring conjectures, and those too of little plausibility, before reliable records of facts and testimony. If I may be allowed to speak of myself, I have read and pondered the history of those times, with all the diligence I could, and yet I never could discover that the Christian religion ever did, or could aid and further his desire to reign without an associate, which desire I admit was very ardent. He had reigned prosperously and with glory, before he became a Christian, or while he adhered to no religion; and he might have attained the su-
[p. 970.] preme authority, and have performed great achievements, if he had continued in the religion of his ancestors, or persevered in the worship of the Gods. In the first place, nothing can be inferred from his wars against *Maxentius* and *Maximin*, to prove him a dissembler in this grave matter of religion. If *Constantine* had unjustly commenced aggressive wars against *Maxentius* and *Maximin*, and had chiefly used the assistance of the Christians to oppress his colleagues, there might arise a strong suspicion that he dissembled, as to Christianity, from motives of ambition. But the justice of his wars against both *Maxentius* and *Maximin*, is not denied even by his enemies; and it is placed beyond all dispute, by the whole history of those times. Moreover, the army which he conducted from Gaul into Italy against Maxentius, as we shall soon show from *Zosimus*, was not composed of Christians, but principally of barbarians and worshippers of the Gods. And of a similar character was the army with which *Licinius* encountered *Maximin*. These wars, therefore, cannot be

adduced to prove his ambition; and much less are they evidence of that impious trickery with which he is charged. And if any one shall maintain, that after the conquest of *Maxentius*, *Constantine* showed himself so just and kind to the Christians, for the sake of accomplishing, by their aid and friendship, those proud designs which he meditated, he will bring forward a suspicion, which is unsupported by testimony or by any other proof, and a suspicion easily confuted. The man who harbors such a suspicion, does not consider that *Constantine*, after his victory over *Maxentius*, did not exalt the Christian religion above all others, and decide that it is the only true religion; but he merely gave the Christians the power of publicly professing their religion; and the same liberty he gave to all sects and all religions, with no exceptions. Neither does the man consider, that the worshippers of the Gods were, at that time, far more numerous than the Christians, although there were Christians everywhere. There would be some ground for this ill opinion of *Constantine*, if he had commanded all his subjects to follow the Christian religion, and had endeavored to extirpate the ancient religion, or even if the number of Christians in the Roman empire had preponderated over others. My conclusion, after carefully considering all the facts, is, that if the Emperor had wished to attain to supreme power, by the aid of *any* religion, he could more readily and more easily have accomplished his wishes, by pretending to adhere to the *old superstition*, which was favored by the majority of the citizens, than by a feigned adoption of the new religion, which was odious to a majority both of the soldiers and the citizens. So, likewise, the contests between *Constantine* and *Licinius*, which occurred after the subjugation of *Maxentius* and *Maximin*, did not originate from religion, nor were they carried on, and successfully terminated by the aid of religion. And I confidently affirm, that religion was serviceable to *Constantine*, in no one of his political enterprises. And finally, I for one believe, that the judgments of the cotemporary writers are to be preferred before the divinations, however ingenious, of all the moderns. *Zosimus* and *Julian*, [p. 971.] both shrewd men, and well acquainted with all the counsels and acts of *Constantine*, and both, also his enemies, had no doubts that he, in good faith, passed over from the religion of his ancestors to Christianity: indeed, they assign causes, though futile ones, for this defection. These men, certainly, did not lack the means of discerning the truth in this matter, nor the disposition to publish it: and shall *we* account ourselves more discerning and perspicacious than they, when, after so many centuries, and by means of a few documents, we see, as it were, through clouds, a small part of the history of that period?

Although I suppose that *Constantine* was a Christian, that is, that he believed the Christian religion to be the only true religion, during a great part of his life, yet, as to the time when he thus embraced Christianity, I disagree with the common opinion. On this point, nearly all follow *Eusebius*, (de vita Constant. L. i. c. 27. p. 421.) who tells us, that until the war with *Maxentius*, *Constantine* was a man of dubious, or rather, of no religion. And this I can easily believe, for it accords very well with his conduct. But when he was about to march against *Maxentius*, prompted, undoubtedly, by a sense of impending peril, he pondered in his mind, to which of the Gods he should entrust himself and his

fortunes. *Eusebius* says: Cogitare apud se cœpit, quemnam sibi Deum adsisceret. In this, I suppose, he acted sincerely, and not hypocritically. The result of his deliberations was, that he determined to worship the one God whom his father had worshipped, and to neglect the Romish Deities. The grounds of this resolution, in addition to the example of his father, who worshipped the one God, were the adversities and the sad end of Diocletian, Maximian, and the other Emperors, who had sedulously followed the religions of the Gods. These reasons are not forcible, nor creditable to *Constantine.* For he did not abandon the Roman Gods, and betake himself to the worship of the one God, guided by *reason*, or from *conviction*, founded on the numerous arguments which the light of nature suggests; but he merely followed the recommendation of his father, and his hope of vanquishing his enemies and obtaining a prosperous and splendid reign. For, as *Eusebius* reports from his own mouth, he reasoned in the following manner: My *father* worshipped the one God, and he was uniformly prosperous through life. On the contrary, *those Emperors* who worshipped many Gods, after a series of calamities, came to miserable deaths. Therefore, that I may live happily, and be always prosperous in this world, I will imitate my father, and connect myself with the worship of the one God. The man who, by such reasoning, is induced to embrace any religion whatever, appears to me to show a very moderate degree of religious knowledge, and to be more solicitous about the present life than the future. And besides this, there is another thing, which seems to me to detract more from the reputation of *Constan-*
[p. 972.] *tine*, than his contempt for the Gods can add to it. *Constantine* did not know the character of the one God, whom his father had worshipped, and by whose aid he had lived prosperously and happily. And this his ignorance, *Eusebius* does not conceal. For he says, (de vita Const. L. i. c. 28. p. 410.) that the Emperor: Obsecrasse Deum illum, ut se ipsi *noscendum* præberet. He therefore did *not know*, how far the power and influence of his father's God extended, or with what attributes he was invested. It is manifest, both from other sources and from the citations soon to be made from his edicts, that *Constantine* did not regard this God of his father as being that *supreme* and only *author and creator of all things*, whom the Christians adored as a God of infinite majesty and power, but only as a God of finite or limited powers; yet, as more benignant, efficient, and powerful, than all the Roman and Grecian Gods. For a considerable time, therefore, *Constantine* was (in modern phrase) *a Deist;* and one of the lowest and most ignoble class, worshipping a single God, of whom he had no determinate conceptions. But not long after this, if we believe *Eusebius*, he obtained more light. For, as he was marching with his army against Maxentius, at mid-day, he and his whole army saw in the clouds, that celebrated Monogramm of the name *Christ*, or the sign of the cross, with the inscription: Τούτῳ νίκα. *Hac vince.* See *Eusebius*, (de vita Const. L. i. c. 28. p. 422.) Of this celebrated vision, we shall treat formally hereafter. But this divinely exhibited image did not remove all clouds from his mind, or explain to him that God of his father, whom he was desirous to know. Says *Eusebius*, (de vita Const. L. i. c. 29. p. 422.): Addubitare cœpit, quidnam hoc spectrum sibi vellet. This celestial vision, therefore,—and I would have it particularly noticed, did

not profit him at all. The prodigy needed an interpreter: and this function Christ himself assumed. For on the following night, he appeared to him in a dream, with the sign which had been shown him in the heavens, and directed him to make a military standard, in the form of that sign, and to use it in his battles. (Ibid. c. 29. p. 422.) The Emperor obeyed this command, and forthwith caused a standard to be made, resembling the sign which he had seen both waking and sleeping; and he afterwards had it carried before his army in all his battles. *Constantine*, therefore, *now knew* what God he ought to worship. And yet, what is very strange, although he had long been well acquainted with Christian affairs, and been conversant with Christians so many years, he did *not know* what a God, the being called *Christ* was; nay, he did not understand the import of the vision. Says *Eusebius*, (de vita Const. L. i. c. 32. p. 423.): Κὰι τὶς εἴη Θεὸς ἠρώτα, τὶς τὲ ὁ τῆς ὀφθείσης ὄψεως τοῦ σημείου λόγος. Interrogabat, quisnam ille Deus esset, quidve signi illius visio sibi vellet. And yet, as *Eusebius* had just before said distinctly, Christ himself had conversed with *Constantine* in his sleep, and had taught him the meaning of the vision. Therefore *Constantine* sent for priests of the Christian religion; and when he had learned [p. 973.] from them the character of the God whom he had seen, and the power of that sign, he betook himself to reading the sacred books of the Christians, with the assistance of the priests: and he now firmly decided, that Christ alone was worthy of worship and adoration. (Ibid. c. 32. p. 423 &c.) The series of the narration in *Eusebius*, puts it beyond controversy, that all this occurred in *Gaul*, before Constantine had passed the Alps with his army, to encounter Maxentius. And *Eusebius* expressly says, (loc. cit. c. 32. p. 424.): *Post hæc (after all above stated,)* munitus spe bona, quam in illo (*Christo*) collocaverat, tyrannici furoris (*Maxentii*) incendium restinguere aggressus est. Therefore, according to this author, *Constantine* was already a Christian, when he determined on the war against Maxentius; as a Christian, he marched into Italy; relying on the aid of Christ, he fought with Maxentius; and to Christ he attributed his victory; and lastly, after his triumph, he manifested his gratitude to his Preserver, by enacting laws in favor of the Christians. That a large part of this is true, I do not doubt. For, as *Constantine* issued his liberal edicts in favor of the Christians, immediately after his victory over Maxentius, he, doubtless, was then more favorably disposed towards the Christians than previously; and he must be supposed to have attributed his victory to Christ. And yet these very edicts, which evince his good will to the Christians and his reverence for Christ, at the same time prove, that all the things stated by Eusebius *could not be true*, and they show, that *Constantine* was not, at that time, a Christian, except in the lowest sense. For while he believed Christ to be a God, he did not believe him to be the supreme God who controls all things; nor did he consider the Christian religion to be the only way of attaining salvation, but only a good and useful one, and more safe than the other religions. That I may not be thought to speak unadvisedly, I will cite the Emperor's own language, in his second edict in favor of the Christians, preserved by *Lactantius*, (de mort. perseq. c. 48.) *Eusebius*, (Hist. Eccles. L. x. c. 5.) and others: Hæc ordinanda esse credidimus, ut daremus et Christianis et omnibus liberam potestatem sequendi religionem, quam quisque voluisset: quo, quicquid divinitatis in sede cœlesti, (ὅ, τί ποτέ ἐστι θειότητος καὶ οὐρανίου πράγματος,) nobis atque omnibus, qui sub potestate nostra sunt constituti, placatum ac propitium possit existere. The reason why the Emperor concluded to allow all the citizens, and among them the Christians, liberty to follow what religion they chose, was, that he and all the citizens might have all the Gods resident in the *celestial mansion*, *propitious and friendly* to them. And therefore, at the time *Constantine* issued this edict, he believed,—I. That there are many Gods, in the celestial mansion.—II. Among the Gods dwelling in the celestial mansion, Christ is one.—III. His own safety, and that of the citizens and of the whole republic, required, that all these Gods, and Christ among the rest, should be propitious and friendly to the Romans.—IV. Among these Gods, were the Gods then worshipped by the nations of the earth, and [p. 974.] particularly by the Romans.—V. And therefore all these Gods, as well as Christ, ought to be honored and worshipped, lest they should be offended and become hostile to the republic.—From all which, it clearly follows,—VI. That the form of religion approved by Christians, was a useful and good one:—yet VII. The religions of all the Gods, also, had their value: and therefore,—VIII. All the religions of all the Gods, were to be tolerated and treated with respect, notwithstanding they were perhaps not all of equal excellence and dignity. A little after, in the same edict, a sentence occurs, in which the same views are expressed in terms a little varied: Credidimus, ut nulli omnino facultatem abnegandam putaremus, qui vel observationi Christianorum, vel ei religioni mentem suam dederet, quam ipse sibi aptissimam esse sentiret, ut possit nobis summa divinitas, (τὸ θεῖον,) cujus religioni liberis mentibus obsequimur, in omnibus solitum suum favorem atque benevolentiam præstare. The *summa divinitas*, (τὸ θεῖον,) whose favor the Emperor here deems necessary to him, is not the one supreme God; but the phrase must be explained in accordance with what precedes it: and hence, the *summa divinitas* is, what Constantine had denominated, *Quicquid divinitatis in sede cœlesti est.* What he subjoins, viz. that he and his colleague, Hujus divinitatis religioni *liberis mentibus* obsequi, deserves special attention. What does the declaration mean? As the *summa divinitas* is explained by Constantine to include *all the Gods in the celestial mansion*, or *quicquid divinitatis in sede cœlesti est*, it must be evident, that these words can have no other meaning than the following: We, the Emperors, serve all the Gods *liberis mentibus*, both the ancient Gods, and him whom the Christians worship; that is, we confine ourselves exclusively to no one religion, but we favor them all: but to our citizens, we give the liberty of selecting from among those religions, that which they think to be the best.—How far are these views from those of a true and perfect Christian? And, if the religious character of *Constantine* is to be learned from his public edicts, how greatly do *they* mistake, who suppose that after vanquishing Maxentius, he forsook the Gentile religions, and embraced the Christian as being the only true religion? There is not one of all the laws enacted by *Constantine*, during the first years after the victory over Maxentius, which is not easily explained in accordance with the views we have attributed to him. He conferred precious privileges and favors on the Christians and their priests, he spoke respectfully of the Christian religion, and he denominated the church very holy and Catholic. But all this a man might do, who approved of the Christian religion, esteeming it holy and good, and yet did not consider the other religions as false, and to be abandoned. And there is no one of his laws, for several years, from which it may be clearly inferred, that *Constantine* held Christ to be the Saviour of *mankind*, and *his* Saviour, and that he disapproved altogether the religions of the Gods. With his *edicts*, which [p. 975.] show his mind to be fluctuating among various religions, his *conduct* is coincident; and some of his acts could not have proceeded from a truly Christian man. His laws tolerating soothsayers, provided they practised their arts openly, enacted in the seventh and ninth years after his victory over Maxentius, are well known. (See the Codex Theodosianus, L. ix. Tit. xvi. Leg. 1, 2. and L. xvi. Tit. x. Leg. 1.) Although *Gothofred*, *Tillemont*, and others, labor to extenuate the baseness of these laws, yet they do not prevent its appearing, that *Constantine* had not then wholly abandoned the old Romish religion. and settled down in the profession of Christianity alone. Neither do I see, why *Zosimus* should be charged with falsehood, when he states, (Lib. ii. p. 103. edit. Oxon. 1679. 8vo.) that *Constantine*, long after his dominion was established, listened to soothsayers, and put confidence in them. And I suppose, the same *Zosimus* does not impose on the succeeding ages, when in the same place he says, that the Emperor, even after Licinius was slain, Patriis (the Roman) sacris usum esse, non honoris quidem, sed necessitatis caussâ; i. e. lest the Roman people should take offence. For just so ought an Emperor to do, who had publicly declared, that he, *Liberâ mente*, omnis *divinitatis in cœlesti sede* versantis *religione obsequi*; or, was not exclusively devoted to any one of the religions then known in the Roman empire.—I pass over other acts of *Constantine*, unsuitable for a man, who believes no religion to be true but the Christian.

How long *Constantine* retained these vague and undecided views of religion and religious worship, regarding the christian religion as excellent, and salutary to the Roman state, yet not esteeming the other religions or those of inferior Gods, as vain, pernicious and odious to God;—it is difficult to determine. *Zosimus*, as is well known, reports, (Historia, L. ii. p. 104, &c.) that Constantine did not publicly profess christianity, and show himself hostile to the Romish sacred rites, until after the slaughter of his son Crispus and his wife Fausta; which truly detestable crimes were perpetrated in the year 326. The falsehood of this statement, as well as of the cause assigned by *Zosimus* for the Emperor's change of religion, I shall not stop here to prove; for it has long since been demonstrated by many persons, and may be easily substantiated from the laws which *Constantine*, before that time, enacted for the benefit of the christian religion. And yet, in my opinion, *Zosimus* has not herein erred so grossly as learned men have supposed. For, not to mention that the error is of only a few years, who can wonder that a man who understood that *Constantine* practised the Roman worship for many years, and did not hesitate to sacrifice to the Gods, notwithstanding he venerated Christ and was benignant to his worshipers,—should thence infer, that the Emperor went over to the Christians at a later period than was commonly supposed? After well consider- [p. 976.] ing the subject, I have come to the conclusion, that *subsequently to the death of*

Licimius in the year 323, when *Constantine* found himself sole Emperor, *he became an absolute Christian*, or one who believes no religion but the christian to be acceptable to God. He had previously considered the religion of one God as more excellent than the other religions, and believed that Christ ought especially to be worshipped: yet he supposed there were also inferior Deities; and that to these some worship might be paid, in the manner of the fathers, without fault or sin. And who does not know, that in those times, many others also combined the worship of Christ with that of the ancient Gods, whom they regarded as the ministers of the supreme God in the government of human and earthly affairs? From the year above named, commence those laws and actions of *Constantine*, from which most clearly appear, his abhorrence of the ancient superstitions, and his wish to abolish them and to establish every where the christian religion. Previously, he had enacted no such laws, except the single one for the observance of the Lord's day, in the year 321, which partially disclosed the designs he was then contemplating. It was not till this year, (323,) that all persons who, on account of christianity, had in preceding times been exiled or condemned to the mines and the public works, or been stripped of their property, were restored to their homes, their liberty, their reputable standing, and their estates. See *Eusebius*, (de vita Constant. L. ii. c. 20. p. 453, &c.) And it was at the same time he prohibited the sacrificing to the Gods, which had before been lawful; (Euseb. loc. cit. c. 44. p. 464.) and commanded christian temples to be erected, and the decayed churches to be repaired and enlarged; (Ibid. c. 46. p. 465.) But the strongest and most certain evidence, that his mind was entirely alienated from all worship of the Gods and exclusively devoted to Christ, is the Address he sent to all the citizens, on the falsity and baseness of the ancient superstitions; in which he exhorted all people to renounce the Gods, and to worship none but Christ. This very pious Address, worthy of a christian Emperor, is found in *Eusebius*, (de vita Constat. L. ii. c. 48, &c. p. 466, &c.) These edicts were followed up, in the last years of his life, by actions and institutions expressive of Constantine's purpose of extirpating the ancient religions, and of supporting only christiany. For he commanded the temples of the Gods to be every where demolished, the images to be broken, the treasures and goods of the temples (to be confiscated,) and the sacrifices to be discontinued. See Jac. *Gothofred.* ad Codicem Theodosianum, (tom. vi. P. 1. p. 290.)

As I suppose it to be certain from what has been stated, that *Constantine* attained gradually to a correct knowledge of religious truth, that at first, and for a long time, he was only a semi-Christian, but afterwards banished all superstition from his mind, and sincerely embraced christianity; I therefore conclude, that the statement of *Zosimus*, (Histor. L. ii. p. 104.) is not to be wholly disregarded. He says, that after the death of Licinius, a certain Egyptian came to Rome from Spain, and persuaded the Emperor of the truth of the Christian [p. 977.] religion. *Zosimus*, undoubtedly, did not fabricate this story; for what possible motive could induce him? He must have learned it from those acquainted with the events of those times. But that Egyptian did not first bring Constantine to entertain high and honorable views of the christian religion, for such views he had long entertained; but he purified and perfected the Emperor's ideas of Christ and of the christian religion, which had before been somewhat corrupt and superstitious, and he demonstrated to him, that the worship of the Gods was utterly inadmissible. On apprehending and embracing these views, the Emperor took on him the patronage of the christian religion only. I venture still farther, and maintain, that there is not a total destitution of truth in the statement by *Zosimus* of the *manner* in which Constantine was led to desert the Romish religion and attach himself to the christian, notwithstanding learned men have pronounced it a compound of calumnies and lies. Zosimus tells us, that Constantine demanded of the flamens of the Gods a lustration from his gross crimes in regard to Licinius and his own wife and son; and that they told him there was no lustration possible for so great offences; But that the Egyptian Christian before mentioned, told the Emperor, that the Christian religion had power to blot out *all* sins, and to free those who embraced it from *all* guilt. And therefore he willingly embraced so convenient and useful a religion. I admit, that in this narrative there is not a little of ignorance, of envy, and of malignity: and yet I can believe, that there is some truth at the bottom of the fable; and that *Constantine*, after the death of Licinius, first learned, either from this Egyptian or from some others, that Christ has made expiation for the sins of *all men*, by his death and blood, and that the pardon of *all their sins* may be confidently promised to *all those*, who by faith become partakers of his merits. In the first years after his victory over Maxentius, his views of religion generally, and of the Christian religion in particular, were not altogether sound, and they differed not greatly from those of the Greeks and Romans. For, being ignorant of the nature of the salvation and blessings, which Christ has purchased for mankind, he supposed Christ to be a God, who rewarded the fidelity and assiduity of his worshippers with happiness and prosperity, in the present life, and inflicted evils of all kinds on his contemners and enemies. Constantine himself advances such ideas, not obscurely, in his Rescript to Anulinus, (apud *Eusebium*, Hist. Eccles. L. x. c. 7. p. 394.) where he writes, that he had noticed, that despising and depressing the worship of one God, had brought immense evils upon the republic and the citizens; but the reception and observance of it, had conferred great glory on the Roman name, and the highest happiness on the citizens. At that time, therefore, he measured the excellence and worth of different religions by the temporal benefits they conferred, and he signified his approbation of Christianity, because it promised most advantages to the Romans. Nor does *Eusebius*, as before remarked, deny that such were at first [p. 978.] Constantine's opinions. But the Christian teachers with whom he conversed, gradually removed from his mind this great error, so repugnant to the nature of Christianity; and they demonstrated to him, that Christ had not purchased worldly glory, honors, and pleasures for his followers, but had obtained of God for them, the pardon of all their sins, and the expectation of eternal salvation. And thus, having learned at last the true nature of the Christian religion, by the aid of this Egyptian or some others, he was able to perceive more clearly the folly and deformity of the ancient superstitions; and therefore sincerely gave his name to Christ alone. And hence, if I mistake not, arose that fable of *Zosimus*.

(2) The story of *Constantine's* seeing a cross in the heavens, before his battle with Maxentius, is familiar even to the children of all sects of Christians and yet it has exercised exceedingly, very distinguished men, who had the fullest belief in the divine origin of the Christian religion. And *first*, there is dispute as to the time and place, in which the Emperor saw this wonderful sign. On this point, there are two opinions among the learned. Some say, he saw the vision while he was in *Gaul*, and was contemplating a war against Maxentius. These follow the high authority of *Eusebius*, (de vita Constant. L. ii. c. 28. p. 410.) who certainly so relates the story, as to leave the impression, that *Constantine* determined to wage war with Maxentius, *after* he had seen this cross, and *after* he had formed a military standard in imitation of it. For he says, (c. 30.) that the Emperor having placed the sign of the cross before the soldiers, advanced with his army, (and it was from Gaul, he marched,) to restore liberty to the Romans. And he presently adds, that in all his battles with Maxentius, this sign of the cross was borne in the front. And he closes his narrative of the subject, with these words, (c. 32. p. 424.): *Post hæc*, (after all that had been said of the vision of the cross, and the formation of the Labarum in the likeness of it,) munitus spe bonâ—tyrannici furoris incendium restinguere aggressus est. He therefore determined on the war with Maxentius, *after* he had seen the cross; and that determination, all the learned admit, was formed *in Gaul*. What has been adduced from *Prudentius* and others, in confirmation of this opinion, has much less weight, and may easily be confuted.—But *others*, relying on the testimony of *Lactantius*, (de mort. persequut. c. 44. p. 999.) maintain, that this cross appeared to Constantine, *at the siege of Rome*, A. D. 312. on the 7th of the Kalends of November. This opinion was first advanced by Steph. *Baluze*, in his notes on this passage of Lactantius: and he was followed by Anton. *Pagi*, *Fabricius*, and many others. And it is difficult to say, which of the two, *Eusebius* or *Lactantius*, is most to be credited. The brothers *Ballerini*, (in their Ob-
[p. 979.] servations on *Noris*, Histor. Donatistar. Opp. tom. iv. p. 662.) have assumed the office of arbiters in the controversy; and, in order to reconcile *Lactantius* and *Eusebius*, they would persuade us, that Constantine *twice* saw the cross in his sleep, *first in Gaul*, and *then in Italy*, just before the decisive battle with Maxentius. But these learned men will not meet ready credence, since it may be inferred from the language of *Lactantius*, that Constantine had seen no cross, until the dream which he describes. I will dismiss this question, which is of no great moment, and not easily decided; and will proceed to consider the *vision* itself.

Those learned and sagacious men who have disputed concerning this celebrated cross of *Constantine*, may be divided into *two* classes. For, since no one can deny, that the Emperor wished to be regarded as having actually seen that celestial sign called his cross, and moreover, studiously sought, by various means, such as institutions, medals, declarations, &c. to persuade both citizens and soldiers of the reality of the vision; yet there are some, who think his *honesty* in this matter, may be called in question, and, indeed, ought to be. Hence, *Some* regard the story as a *fable*; and they conjecture various reasons for the Emperor's fabrication of it. But *others*, and they are the majority, have no doubts, that *Constantine* actually *saw* what he states: yet those who constitute this party, entertain different views, as we shall see hereafter.

The first who ranked Constantine's story of the cross among *fables*, were the friends and worshipers of the Gods living in the century in which the vision is said to have occurred, *Gelasius Cyzicenus*, (in his Acta Concilii Nicaeni, L. i. c. 4. in Harduin's Concilia tom. I. p. 351.) says, that they boldly asserted, that this vision was to be placed among the fabrications intended to benefit the Christians: Τοῦτο τὸ διήγημα τοῖς μὲν ἀπίστοις μῦθος εἶναι δοκεῖ καὶ πλάσμα. Hæc tota narratio infidelibus *fabula* et *commentum* esse videtur. Against these enemies of the cross, *Gelasius* disputes earnestly; but not as he ought to do, by adducing testimonies, but solely by citing examples of similar visions; which, if true, would only prove that this vision was possible, not that it was actual. Among the moderns, so far as I know, the first who formally denied the reality of Constantine's vision, was John Hornbeck, (in his comment. on the bull of Urban VIII. de imaginibus, p. 182.) But *he* does not employ historical arguments, nor those derived from the nature of things, but merely theological objections. He was combatted by Henry *Noris*, (Append. ad Histor. Donatist. Opp. tom. IV. p. 662.) After *Hornbeck*, very learned men in great numbers, embraced his views. See Jac. *Oiselius*, (Thesaurus numismat. antiquorum, p. 463.) Jac. *Tollius*, (in *Lactantium* de mort. persequut. p. 267. ed. Bauldrii.) Chris. *Thomasius*, (Observat. Hallens. tom. i. p. 380.) Godfr. *Arnold*, and many others: all of whom pronounce the story *incredible*, and therefore deny the validity of the testimony in support of it. But while they rank the prodigy among *frauds*, they disagree as to the kind of frauds to which it should [p. 980.] be assigned. Some suppose it was a *pious fraud* or a religious wile, devised for recommending and confirming the Christian religion: while others prefer to call it a *military wile* or *stratagem*, by which Constantine sought to inspire his soldiers with confidence of victory and heroic valor in the war before them. Of these two opinions, the *first* has, I think, no probability whatever: for, at the time the cross is said to have appeared to him, *Constantine's* great solicitude, most certainly, was, not to establish and extend the christian religion, but to vanquish Maxentius. Besides, Constantine was not then himself a Christian; and he used this vision, not to aid the Christians, but to animate the soldiers. The *other* opinion has more plausibility; and it receives some countenance from the example of a similar artifice employed by Licinius. For soon afterwards, when Licinius was about to engage in battle with Maximin, he pretended, that an angel appeared to him by night, and taught him a form of prayer, which if the soldiers should repeat, they would certainly gain the victory. See *Lactantius*, (de mort. persequut. c. 46. p. 1003.) This *artifice* of Licinius, (for what liberal minded man will presume to say, it was a true vision?) produced a wonderful effect on the soldiers. Says *Lactantius:* Crevit animus universis, victoriam sibi credentibus de coelo nuntiatam. Who that compares the two prodigies,—the cross of Constantine and the prayer dictated to Licinius by an angel,—does not at once suspect, that Licinius copied the example of his colleague with some variation? But those who maintain the common opinion, oppose to this conjecture, the fact that *Constantine* confirmed his testimony by *an*

oath. For *Eusebius* says, (de vita Constant. L. i. c. 28. p. 410.) that Constantine not only declared most solemnly, that he actually saw the cross, but he also confirmed his assertion by an oath: Ὅρκοις τε πιστωσαμένου τὸν λόγον. Who can hesitate to believe the Emperor, a Christian, and an old man, calling God to witness the truth of his declaration? To meet this argument, the opposite side quote *Zosimus*, who has recorded, (Histor. L. ii. p. 102.) that *Constantine often perjured himself: Constantinum saepe pejerasse.* But this charge of an enemy, in this case, is of little weight. And yet I could wish, *Eusebius* had given us the form of the oath used by the Emperor. For it is well known, the word ὅρκος was also used for a mere asseveration; and those well informed in ancient customs, are aware, that the ancients had no very distinct and clear ideas about swearing, and at times placed naked assertions among oaths. But besides this argument from the oath of the Emperor, I have another, which seems to free him from the suspicion of a military artifice, and to support the opinion of those who think Constantine really *saw* something resembling a cross. *Zosimus*, who is certainly good authority in the case, tells us, (Histor. L. II. p. 86.) that the army, which Constantine led against Maxentius, was col-
[p. 981.] lected among the barbarous nations, the Germans, the Celts &c. who at that time, undoubtedly, were ignorant of christianity, and worshipped the Gods of their ancestors: Collectis copiis ex redactis in potestatem barbaris, et Germanis, et aliis Celticis nationibus, itemque de Britanniâ coactis militibus - - ex Alpibus in Italiam movebat. Now to stimulate *such* soldiers and fire them with confidence of victory, a very different artifice was necessary. If he had told his troops, that *Mars*, or some other among the Gods with which they were acquainted, had appeared to him sword in hand, and had assured him of a triumph, he would undoubtedly have awakened their courage. But what influence, I pray, upon barbarian men, ignorant of Christ, would a speech like the following, possess: Take courage, fellow soldiers! We shall be victorious; for I have seen the sign of a cross in the clouds; and Christ appeared to me in my sleep, saying that under the guidance of this sign, I shall be able to triumph over the enemy! If we would not make Constantine a great simpleton, we must believe that he would adapt the fraud, by which he sought to animate them, to their genius, their customs, their capacities, and their opinions. But this vision, which learned men suppose he invented, was totally opposite to the feelings, the habits, and the sentiments of the troops which he was leading to battle; and it was suited to impose on none but Christians.

Those who acquit Constantine of all fraud, and suppose his *vision* to have been *a reality*, differ as to the *nature of that vision.* The majority suppose that he saw it while *awake;* but others say, it was in his *sleep.* Both adduce in support of their opinions high and very respectable authorities. Those who maintain the *first* opinion, rely especially on *Eusebius*, who says, that he received his account from the mouth of the Emperor. Yet there are other and later writers, (the principal of whom are *Philostorgius* and *Socrates*,) who likewise state, that the vision was addressed to the bodily eyes, and not to the imagination or mind; they say, that Constantine beheld in the clouds at mid-day, a column of light in the form of a cross. These testimonies are carefully collect ed by Jo. Alb. *Fabricius*, (Diss. de cruce Constant. § 6. Biblioth. Graecae vol. vi. p. 13, &c.) But all these writers appear to have derived their information from *Eusebius:* and therefore to him, or rather to *Constantine*, whose statements he records, the whole narrative is to be traced. *Eusebius* says, (de vita Constant. L. i. c. 28, 29. p. 410 &c.) that he heard *Constantine* not only declare, but confirm with an oath: Horis diei meridianis, sole in occasum vergente, se crucis tropaeum in coelo ex luce conflatum, soli superpositum, ipsis oculis vidisse, cum hujusmodi inscriptione: Hac Vince: Illud visum milites etiam animadvertisse, quibus cinctus erat: Nescivisse vero se, quid hoc spectrum sibi vellet: At sequenti nocte, Christum dormienti apparuisse cum signo illo, quod in coelo ostensum fuerat, praecepisseque, ut militari signo ad similitudinem ejus, quod in coelo vidisset, fabricato, eo tanquam salutari praesidio in praeliis uteretur. If this narrative is true, Constantine had *two divine visions;* the *one* in [p. 982.] broad *day light*, and when he was *awake;* the other the *night* following, and when he was *asleep.* The first he did not comprehend at the time: but the latter dispelled his ignorance and doubts. For Christ himself interpreted to him the mysterious vision. As all the other writers lived after *Eusebius*, and, as appears from their language, transcribed almost their whole account from him, the whole story rests solely on the fidelity of *Constantine* and *Eusebius*. For though Constantine says, that his *soldiers* saw what *he* saw, yet *Eusebius* derived his information solely from the *Emperor*, and he names no other witness. And here I cannot but remark, that the learned men who confidently affirm, that the *whole army*, as well as Constantine, saw this wonderful sign, cannot *prove* what they affirm, from the language of *Eusebius*. For he does not say, that Constantine's *army* saw that cross, but merely says: *Milites* omnes, *qui ipsum nescio quo iter facientem sequebantur*, miraculi spectatores fuisse. This language, I think, is better and more correctly explained of the *few* men who were *his body guards*, or the praetorian soldiers, that accompanied him on some excursion, than of his whole army. As for *Eusebius*, there is no reason at all to suspect him of any wish to deceive his readers, or that he stated any thing different from what was told to him. He certainly had *no reason* for misrepresenting or fab icating any thing of the kind. Indeed there are some things, which seem to place his fidelity in this narration beyond dispute. *First;* In his Eccles. History, which afforded the fairest opportunity for introducing so important a matter, there is no mention of it whatever. This shows, that when he wrote his History, that is, prior to the year 324, he was ignorant on the subject; and that it was not *then* generally a subject of conversation. *Again;* In his life of Constantine, (L. ii. c. 28.) he frankly acknowledges, that this prodigy seems almost *incredible;* but that it would be wrong to question the Emperor's veracity: which is as much as saying: "I believe the facts were as I have stated, because my most gracious lord bids me believe them: but if another person had told them to me, I would not believe them." A man wishing to deceive or meditating a pious fraud, would not so speak. We are therefore brought back to *Constantine only.* Shall we give credence to this august witness, or shall we disbelieve him? It seems almost sacrilege, to charge so great a Prince with guile and falsehood when under oath. And yet he was but a man; and motives for his using deception can be named. *Constantine* was a *vain* man, and greedy of praise and glory, as his conduct shows; nor do his friends wholly deny it. I therefore think, that it will not be temerity to suppose, he added somewhat to the truth; and perhaps, he changed a *mental and nocturnal vision* into a *day vision* with the bodily eyes, for the sake of appearing *great* and favored of God, in the estimation of the citizens and particularly the bi-[p. 983.] shops. Nor is this a mere naked *suspicion:* it has *some* support. For, *cotemporary writers* of high reputation,—to say nothing of more recent writers,—knew nothing of that day vision of which *Constantine* speaks, but they represent the whole as passing in a *dream.* Thus *Lactantius,* (if, as I suppose, he was the author of the book *de mortibus persequutorum,*) the preceptor of Crispus, Constantine's son, and no less intimate and in confidence with the Emperor than *Eusebius,* tells us, (c. 44.) that the Emperor was admonished *in his sleep,* to mark the shields of his soldiers with *crosses:* commonitus est *in quiete* Constantinus, ut *coeleste signum* Dei notaret in *scutis,* atque ita proelium committeret. Fecit ut jussus est, et transversâ litterâ X, summo capite circumflexo, Christum in scutis notat, quo signo armatus exercitus capit ferrum. This man, therefore, living at court and in the focus of light, had heard nothing about a luminous *column* seen in broad *day,* and bearing the inscription, HAC VINCE. Neither had *Rufinus* heard any thing of it; for he likewise, (Hist. Eccles. L. ix. c. 9.) speaks only of such a dream. If the vision of *Constantine* had been publicly known, and if the Emperor had stated to others what he stated to *Eusebius,* how, I ask, could these men be ignorant of a thing of such magnitude, and substitute a mere dream in place of a true vision? Whatever conjectures or exceptions we may form, it is manifest, from this disagreement of writers of the same age and authority, that common *fame* reported nothing definitely respecting this vision, and what some supposed was a day vision, others considered to be a dream. What inferences may be drawn from all this, I need not explain at length. Consider also the inscription, HAC VINCE, which, it is said, appeared in the air with the cross. This inscription creates so much difficulty in the affair, that the more it is considered, the more certain it seems, that the whole was a *dream.*

Those who think this vision was actually seen by the Emperor with his waking eyes, are again divided in opinion. The majority, following the example of *Eusebius* and the ancients, place the vision among *real miracles;* and they suppose God intended it as a persuasive to the Emperor to embrace the Christian religion. But some, with the late Jo. All. *Fabricius* at their head, place this cross of Constantine among *natural phenomena.* They suppose that the Emperor saw a *solar halo* encompassing the sun, and not being well acquainted with the science of nature, he mistook it for a divine prodigy. The deceased *Fabricius* published a Dissertation, (in his Biblioth. Graeca, vol. vi. p. 11, &c.) in which he displayed this ingenious theory with great fulness and erudition. If all that *Eusebius* has reported from the mouth of Constantine, is strictly true, no one can doubt at all, but that this cross is to be ascribed to the mighty power of God, or to be set down as a *miracle.* For, whence could come those two words, HAC VINCE, except from the boundless power of God? But if we approach this interpretation, we encounter so many and so great difficulties, that we start back instinctively. *First:* Although no mortal can prescribe limits to the divine wisdom, as to the ways in which God shall deal with the men [p. 984.] whom he would bless and reclaim from superstition; yet it is certain, that he always selects the more *sure*, the more *suitable*, and the more *manifest ways*, in preference to the *dubious*, the *obscure*, and the *difficult*. Now I can clearly perceive, (and all who will reflect, must agree with me,) that if God intended to produce a religious reformation in Constantine by a miracle, he could have done it in a far clearer and more certain manner, than by placing the form of a cross before his eyes, the meaning of which, on his own showing, he did not comprehend. *Secondly:* It must appear strange, nay *incredible*, to all men of sound minds, that God should make the victory over his foes, to depend on the sign of a *cross painted* upon the shields of the soldiers. This surely was calculated to beget superstition in the minds of the ignorant people, and to establish them in the worship and veneration of a *cross*, which has no power whatever to produce, or to preserve and augment true religion. More holy counsel, undoubtedly, and more accordant with both reason and Christianity, (I speak confidently: and I think all good and Christian men will agree with me,) I say, God would have given more holy counsel to Constantine, if he had directed both him and his soldiers, to forsake their superstition and impiety, to worship Christ, and with devout supplications to implore his aid; and on such conditions, had assured him of victory. But from such a direction as the following: *Inscribe the form of a cross on the soldiers' shields, and bid them carry it before them, and you will be victorious*, what could result, except the corrupt opinion, that there is a supernatural *power* in the sign of a *cross*, and therefore, that whoever goes into battle protected by it, will be victorious, whether he is a good man or a bad one, a man of sound views or superstitious. I need not say, that if God had wished to prostrate Maxentius by a miracle, he could very easily have effected his object, not only without a cross, but also without any battle and slaughter. *Moreover*, no one will deny, that the miracles and visions of God are always *useful;* neither can he needlessly and uselessly change the laws of nature. But this mid-day vision, which *Eusebius* reports from the mouth of the Emperor, was altogether *vain* and *useless*. For, as the Emperor expressly says, neither *he* nor his *soldiers understood* what it meant. It was therefore necessary, that a divine expositor, the Son of God, should explain the obscure, and consequently, useless prodigy, and should inform the Emperor, in his sleep, the night following, that by this sign God intended, to lead him to fabricate a military standard after the form of that celestial sign. Undoubtedly God foresaw, that Constantine would not understand the import of the miracle: why then, did he not show him a more intelligible and certain sign? Was it, perhaps, that Christ might have some reason for appearing to the Emperor in his sleep? The *dream* also, in which Christ appeared to Constantine, I can never believe was *divine*. For the Son of God would have addressed the Emperor, in a very different manner. What, I ask, did he say? Did he exhort Constantine to believe and to strive after holiness? Did he bid him eschew and oppose superstition and impiety, rule the State with justice and wisdom, repent of his past trans- [p. 985.]

gressions, and prefer the salvation of the citizens before all things else? Not one of all these. What then did he say? He pointed out the way to obtain a victory; he showed Constantine what sort of a military *standard* he must use in his battles. Was such an address worthy of the Savior of the human race, of him who expiated the sins of men by his death? Was it worthy of the Author of peace to mortals, who would have his followers forgive their enemies? But why enlarge? This was the natural *dream* of a soldier and general on the eve of battle, who fell asleep while ruminating on the best method for obtaining the victory. Let us beware, lest by too eager defence of the miracles told us by the ancients in their age, we should do injustice to the majesty of God, and to that most holy religion which teaches us to subdue ourselves, not our enemies.

The opinion of the very learned man, who ingeniously maintains that the cross of Constantine was a *natural phenomenon*, has also its difficulties, which I have not sagacity enough to remove. First, this remarkable man himself admits, that he had much difficulty with those Latin words, HAC VINCE, which Constantine said, appeared to him in the air along with the cross. For who, I pray you, can attribute such a writing to mere natural causes? To surmount this difficulty, the very accomplished Greek scholar attempts a new interpretation of the language of *Eusebius;* who tells us that Constantine stated, that he saw the the trophy of a cross, γραφὴν τὲ αὐτῷ συνῆφθαι, λέγουσαν· τούτῳ νίκα. These words *Valesius* renders: *Cum hujusmodi inscriptione:* HAC VINCE. But the learned *Fabricius* would have us translate them thus: *Eique adjunctum fuisse picturam, indicantem, in hoc ipsi esse vincendum.* He therefore supposes, that the word γραφὴν in the passage, does not mean an *inscription* or writing, but a *picture* or figure. And he supposes λέγειν to be equivalent with to *signify* or *indicate.* And the *figure* indicative of victory, he supposes, was a *crown,* such as every *solar halo* is. And it is well known, that a *crown* was the sign of victory among the ancients. And hence, the idea of this distinguished man and his followers, is, that the words HAC VINCE, were not *written* on the sky, but were enigmatically or symbolically expressed by the *figure of a crown.* That I may not appear punctilious, I will admit that the words of *Eusebius* or rather of Constantine, will bear this interpretation. But 1st, how obscurely and poetically, would the Emperor have expressed himself in this familiar conversation, if he had used such terms to convey his meaning to *Eusebius?* Suppose any man, wishing to tell his friend, that in a dream *he saw a crown,* should say, he saw a figure, which *signified:* CONQUER BY THIS; what should we think of such a man? Certainly, we should conclude that he talked in enigmas, and did not wish to be understood; for he would violate all the laws of familiar discourse. 2dly, It is certain, that Constantine did not wish to have his words so understood. For, on the *Labarums,* on medals, and on the other monuments, he would have [p. 986.] the very *words* HAC VINCE, (τούτῳ νίκα,) distinctly written: which is evidence, that he wished every body to believe, those *words* appeared before his eyes in the air.—3dly, All the ancient writers so understood both him and Eusebius: for their language puts it beyond controversy, that they all believed *Constantine* to say, that, not a *crown,* the sign of victory, but the very *words*

Hac Vince, appeared to the Emperor. Besides, another difficulty of no less magnitude occurs. Among all the crosses hitherto observed by astronomers in solar halos, there has not been one similar to that which Constantine says he saw: so that an example of such a natural phenomenon is a desideratum. From *Eusebius* and from the medals, it is most manifest, that Constantine did not see the figure of a true *cross*, but the *first Greek letter* in the name *Christ*, ss. X, through the middle of which, the *second letter* of that name, ss. P, was drawn perpendicularly, thus: ☧. Now such a figure as this, has never been seen by any astronomer. I may add, that those who make the day vision a *natural occurrence*, cannot suppose the *nocturnal vision* or dream which followed it, to be *supernatural* or divine. For, as natural phenomena have no significancy, who can believe that God undertook to instruct Constantine as to the sense and meaning of such a phenomena? Those, therefore, who believe the dream of Constantine was sent of God, must necessarily believe that the preceding mid-day vision was also divine or miraculous.

Finally, to give frankly my own opinion on this subject, I think, if there is any measure of truth in this famous vision, (which I will not take upon me to deny,) it all pertains to the *dream*. But Constantine, a long time afterwards, to procure for himself greater influence with the bishops, and to gain the reputation of being in high favor with God, *added from his own invention* all the rest; and *Eusebius* recorded the *whole* just as *he* stated. Such frauds, in that age, were common among Christians; nor were they deemed unlawful. Constantine, while ruminating on the perilous war with Maxentius in which he was about to embark, fell asleep. And while he slept, he seemed to himself to behold Christ, having in his hand that *Monogram of his name*, of which Constantine retained a distinct recollection, and promising him victory under the guidance of that sign. When he awoke, he supposed he had been divinely taught the way to obtain the victory, and that he ought to obey the vision. Yet, if any one prefer the supposition, that *Eusebius* either did not correctly understand the Emperor, and mistook what he said of his *dream* to refer to an *ocular vision*, or, purposely added several things to the Emperor's statement, I shall not object to his retaining such a supposition.

§ VIII. **A Short Persecution by Licinius.** The Roman republic appeared tranquil and happy, after the subjugation of Maxentius and Maximin; but soon after a new war for dominion, [p. 987.] arose between Constantine the Great and his colleague *Licinius*, to whom Constantine had given his sister in marriage. But this war was of short duration. For in the year 314, *Licinius* being defeated in two battles, at Cibalæ in Pannonia, and in Thrace, was compelled to sue for peace with his kinsman. But, nine years after his defeats, this turbulent man, who wished to have no associate in the government, both from his own choice and at the instigation of the Pagan priests, assailed Constantine with larger and more powerful forces, in the year 324. To attach those priests the more to himself, *Licinius* not only inflicted very great wrongs upon the Christians of the provinces under his government, but also cruelly put to death not a few of their bishops.(1) But fortune was again adverse to him. After being defeated in several battles, he had no resource but to cast himself on the clemency of his conqueror; and *he*, in the year 325, for reasons not known, ordered him to be strangled. After this victory over Licinius, *Constantine* reigned sole Emperor all his life; and he strove to the utmost, by his counsels, his laws and regulations, and by rewards, to extend the Christian religion over all the nations he governed, and to depress and gradually destroy the religion of the Gods and the ancient superstitions.

(1) Of this renewed persecution of the Christians in the East, by *Licinius*,—not to mention others who touch upon it cursorily, *Eusebius* treats professedly; (Hist. Eccles. L. x. c. 8 &c. p. 396 &c. and de vita Constant. L. ii. c. 3 &c. p. 444 &c.) Among those who touch upon the subject incidentially, I think we are to place *Aurelius Victor*, a Roman, in whose work *de Cæsaribus*, (c. 41. p. 435.) these words occur: Licinio ne insontium quidem et nobilium philosophorum servili more cruciatus adhibiti modum fecerunt. Licinius had nothing to do with the *Philosophers;* nor can ingenuity devise a reason why he should put them to death. *Victor* must therefore refer to the Christian *bishops;* who imitated the Greek Philosophers in their dress, mode of life, &c. nay, as is well known, often assumed the name of *Philosophers.* For, many of these, as *Eusebius* testifies, (ubi supra,) Licinius cruelly and in a servile way put to death, both personally and by his governors. At first, he showed favor to the Christians; as appears from the edicts in their behalf, issued jointly by him and Constantine, and also from some other things. But when he resolved on a second war against Constantine, he became hostile to them; and this, I apprehend, not so much from hatred of Christianity, or from the love of superstition, as from the lust of power, and the hope of subduing Constantine. For, he doubtless, expected, that the vast multitude of the friends and patrons of the ancient religion, [p. 988.] who were exceedingly mortified to see their interests continually decline, and those of the Christians flourish and enlarge from day to day,—would join his party, take up arms, and rush heartily into an intestine war against Constantine, the patron of Christians, if they should see him to be inclined to oppress the Christians, and to restore the ancient religion to its pristine dignity. To this motive, suggested by policy, we may add the exhortations and promises of the Pagan priests. For they, as *Eusebius* tells us, (de vita Const. L. ii. c. 4. p. 445.) when he consulted them: *Respondebant eum victorem hostium et superiorem in bello fore.* And hence, in his oration to his soldiers, (preserved by *Eusebius*, ibid. c. 5. p. 445, 446) in order to animate them, he craftily insinuates, that he had undertaken the war to avenge and vindicate the ancient religion;

and he promises, after gaining the victory, to wholly exterminate all despisers of the Gods. For hitherto he had spared the common Christians, although he had, before the war began, put to cruel deaths the more grave, venerable, and excellent of the *bishops* in his provinces. See *Eusebius*, (loc. cit. c. 2. p. 441.) But this cruelty, likewise, did not so much proceed from a hatred of the religion taught by these bishops, as from *policy*, and the desire of conquest. For he feared that these bishops, whom he knew to be much attached to Constantine, and to have vast influence with the people, if he spared them, would prove traitors and enemies, would communicate information to Constantine, and would excite sedition and rebellion among the plebeians whom they controlled. *Sozomen* perceived this motive in the crafty man; for he says, (Hist. Eccles. L. i. c. 7. p. 409.): Licinius existimabat, ecclesias Christianorum (and especially the presidents or *bishops* of the churches,) id unum optare et studere, ut illum (*Constantinum*) solum Imperatorem haberent. Therefore *Licinius* first expelled all Christians from his palace; and then, proceeding farther, he ordered all military men on duty in the cities, if they refused to sacrifice to the Gods, to be deprived of their military honors. (*Eusebius*, Hist. Eccles. L. x. c. 8. p. 396.) Other enactments, altogether unjust and cruel, followed. Through his provincial governors, he raised calumnies against the *bishops* most distinguished for probity of life and for influence, and then put them to death in new and most cruel ways. Some of the *temples* he demolished; others he ordered to be closed. These were the precursors of heavier calamities and sufferings, with which he threatened the Christians when he should have conquered Constantine. Therefore many of them, to save their lives from peril, fled, and took refuge in the fields and deserts. But divine Providence, by the victories of Constantine, dissipated all his atrocious projects. And this war of Licinius, became beneficial rather than injurious to the Christians. For, Licinius being slain, and *Constantine*, ruling the empire without a colleague, more zealously than ever, protected the Christian cause, and defended it against the assaults and machinations of the old superstition.

END OF THE SECOND VOLUME.

TABLE OF COINCIDENCES.

The paging of the original Latin is noted in brackets at the outer endings of the lines in this translation. But as the figures do not stand out very prominently, and as the paging of the original is most commonly referred to by writers, the following table of the coincidences of the two pagings is subjoined.

Orig.	Transl.	Orig.	Transl.	Orig.	Transl.	Orig.	Transl.	Orig.	Transl.
p. 1	vol. I. p. 8	p. 57	vol. I. p. 76	p. 113	vol. I. p. 145	p. 169	vol. I. p. 216	p. 225	vol. I. p. 283
2	9	58	77	114	147	170	217	226	284
3	9	59	79	115	148	171	218	227	285
4	11	60	80	116	149	172	219	228	286
5	12	61	81	117	150	173	221	229	287
6	13	62	83	118	151	174	222	230	289
7	15	63	84	119	153	175	223	231	290
8	16	64	85	120	154	176	224	232	291
9	17	65	86	121	155	177	225	233	292
10	19	66	88	122	156	178	226	234	293
11	20	67	89	123	157	179	227	235	294
12	21	68	90	124	159	180	229	236	295
13	22	69	91	125	160	181	230	237	297
14	24	70	92	126	161	182	231	238	298
15	25	71	93	127	162	183	233	239	299
16	26	72	94	128	163	184	234	240	300
17	28	73	96	129	165	185	235	241	302
18	29	74	97	130	166	186	237	242	303
19	30	75	98	131	167	187	238	243	304
20	31	76	100	132	168	188	239	244	305
21	32	77	101	133	170	189	241	245	307
22	34	78	102	134	171	190	242	246	308
23	35	79	103	135	172	191	243	247	309
24	36	80	104	136	173	192	244	248	310
25	37	81	106	137	175	193	245	249	312
26	39	82	107	138	176	194	247	250	313
27	40	83	108	139	177	195	248	251	314
28	41	84	109	140	179	196	249	252	315
29	42	85	110	141	180	197	250	253	316
30	43	86	111	142	181	198	252	254	318
31	44	87	113	143	183	199	253	255	319
32	46	88	114	144	184	200	254	256	320
33	47	89	115	145	186	201	256	257	321
34	48	90	116	146	187	202	257	258	322
35	49	91	117	147	188	203	259	259	324
36	50	92	119	148	190	204	260	260	325
37	51	93	120	149	191	205	261	261	326
38	52	94	121	150	192	206	262	262	327
39	54	95	122	151	194	207	263	263	328
40	55	96	123	152	195	208	264	264	329
41	56	97	124	153	196	209	265	265	330
42	58	98	126	154	197	210	266	266	331
43	59	99	127	155	199	211	267	267	332
44	60	100	128	156	200	212	268	268	333
45	61	101	129	157	201	213	269	269	334
46	62	102	130	158	202	214	270	270	336
47	64	103	131	159	204	215	271	271	337
48	65	104	132	160	205	216	273	272	338
49	66	105	134	161	206	217	274	273	339
50	67	106	136	162	207	218	275	274	340
51	69	107	138	163	208	219	276	275	342
52	70	108	139	164	210	220	277	276	343
53	71	109	140	165	211	221	278	277	344
54	72	110	142	166	212	222	279	278	345
55	74	111	143	167	213	223	281	279	346
56	75	112	144	168	214	224	282	280	347

Orig.	Transl.	Orig.	Transl.	Orig.	Transl.	Orig.	Transl.	Orig.	Transl.
p.281	vol. I. p.318	p.357	vol. I. p.432	p.433	vol. I. p.521	p.509	vol. II. p.56	p.585	vol. II. p.125
282	349	358	434	434	522	510	57	586	126
283	350	359	435	435	523	511	58	587	127
284	352	360	436	436	524	512	58	588	128
285	353	361	437	437	525	513	59	589	129
286	354	362	438	438	526	514	60	590	130
287	355	363	439	439	527	515	61	591	131
288	356	364	440	440	528	516	62	592	132
289	357	365	441	441	529	517	63	593	133
290	358	366	443	442	530	518	64	594	134
291	359	367	444	443	531	519	65	595	134
292	360	368	445	444	532	520	66	596	135
293	362	369	446	445	533	521	67	597	136
294	363	370	447	446	535	522	68	598	137
295	364	371	448	447	536	523	69	599	138
296	365	372	450	448	vol. II. p. 1	524	69	600	139
297	366	373	451	449	2	525	70	601	140
298	367	374	452	450	3	526	71	602	141
299	368	375	453	451	3	527	72	603	142
300	369	376	454	452	4	528	73	604	143
301	370	377	456	453	5	529	74	605	143
302	371	378	457	454	6	530	75	606	144
303	372	379	458	455	7	531	76	607	145
304	373	380	459	456	8	532	77	608	146
305	374	381	461	457	9	533	77	609	147
306	375	382	462	458	10	534	78	610	148
307	376	383	463	459	11	535	79	611	149
308	377	384	464	460	11	536	80	612	149
309	379	385	465	461	12	537	81	613	150
310	380	386	467	462	13	538	82	614	151
311	381	387	468	463	14	539	83	615	152
312	382	388	469	464	15	540	84	616	153
313	383	389	470	465	16	541	85	617	154
314	384	390	472	466	17	542	86	618	155
315	385	391	473	467	18	543	87	619	156
316	386	392	474	468	19	544	88	620	156
317	387	393	475	469	19	545	88	621	157
318	388	394	477	470	20	546	89	622	158
319	389	395	478	471	21	547	90	623	159
320	390	396	479	472	22	548	91	624	160
321	392	397	480	473	23	549	92	625	161
322	393	398	482	474	24	550	93	626	162
323	394	399	483	475	25	551	94	627	163
324	395	400	484	476	26	552	95	628	163
325	396	401	485	477	26	553	96	629	164
326	397	402	487	478	27	554	96	630	165
327	399	403	488	479	28	555	97	631	166
328	400	404	489	480	29	556	98	632	167
329	401	405	490	481	30	557	99	633	168
330	402	406	491	482	31	558	100	634	169
331	403	407	492	483	32	559	101	635	170
332	404	408	494	484	33	560	102	636	171
333	405	409	495	485	34	561	103	637	171
334	407	410	496	486	35	562	104	638	172
335	408	411	497	487	36	563	105	639	173
336	409	412	498	488	37	564	106	640	174
337	410	413	500	489	38	565	107	641	175
338	411	414	501	490	39	566	108	642	176
339	412	415	502	491	40	567	109	643	176
340	413	416	503	492	40	568	110	644	177
341	414	417	504	493	41	569	110	645	178
342	416	418	505	494	42	570	111	646	179
343	417	419	506	495	43	571	112	647	180
344	418	420	507	496	44	572	113	648	181
345	419	421	508	497	45	573	114	649	181
346	420	422	509	498	46	574	115	650	182
347	421	423	510	499	47	575	116	651	183
348	422	424	511	500	48	576	117	652	184
349	423	425	513	501	48	577	118	653	185
350	425	426	514	502	49	578	119	654	186
351	426	427	515	503	50	579	120	655	187
352	427	428	516	504	51	580	121	656	187
353	428	429	517	505	52	581	122	657	188
354	429	430	518	506	63	582	122	658	189
355	430	431	519	507	54	583	123	659	190
356	431	432	520	508	55	584	124	660	191

Orig.	Transl.	Orig.	Transl.	Orig.	Transl.	Orig.	Transl.	Orig.	Transl.
661	vol. II, p. 192	p. 727	vol. II, p. 250	p. 793	vol. II, p. 308	p. 859	vol. II, p. 365	p. 924	vol. II, p. 423
662	193	728	251	794	309	860	366	925	424
663	194	729	252	795	310	861	367	926	425
664	194	730	253	796	311	862	368	927	426
665	195	731	253	797	311	863	369	928	427
666	196	732	254	798	312	864	370	929	428
667	197	733	255	799	313	865	371	930	429
668	198	734	256	800	314	866	372	931	430
669	199	735	257	801	315	867	372	932	430
670	200	736	258	802	316	868	373	933	431
671	200	737	259	803	317	869	374	934	432
672	201	738	260	804	318	870	375	935	433
673	202	739	261	805	318	871	376	936	434
674	203	740	261	806	319	872	377	937	435
675	204	741	262	807	320	873	378	938	436
676	205	742	263	808	321	874	379	939	437
677	206	743	264	809	322	875	379	940	438
678	206	744	265	810	323	876	380	941	439
679	207	745	266	811	324	877	381	942	439
680	208	746	266	812	325	878	382	943	440
681	209	747	267	813	325	879	383	944	441
682	210	748	268	814	326	880	384	945	442
683	211	749	269	815	327	881	385	946	443
684	212	750	270	816	328	882	386	947	444
685	213	751	271	817	329	883	386	948	445
686	213	752	272	818	330	884	387	949	446
687	214	753	273	819	331	885	388	950	447
688	215	754	273	820	331	886	389	951	447
689	216	755	274	821	332	887	390	952	448
690	217	756	275	822	333	888	391	953	449
691	218	757	276	823	334	889	392	954	450
692	219	758	277	824	335	890	393	955	451
693	220	759	278	825	336	891	393	956	452
694	221	760	279	826	337	892	394	957	453
695	221	761	280	827	338	893	395	958	454
696	222	762	280	828	338	894	396	959	455
697	223	763	281	829	339	895	397	960	455
698	224	764	282	830	340	896	398	961	456
699	225	765	283	831	341	897	399	962	457
700	226	766	284	832	342	898	400	963	458
701	227	767	285	833	343	899	400	964	459
702	228	768	286	834	344	900	401	965	460
703	229	769	287	835	345	901	402	966	461
704	229	770	287	836	346	902	403	967	462
705	230	771	288	837	346	903	404	968	463
706	231	772	289	838	347	904	405	969	463
707	232	773	290	839	348	905	406	970	464
708	233	774	291	840	349	906	407	971	465
709	234	775	292	841	350	907	407	972	466
710	235	776	293	842	351	908	408	973	467
711	236	777	294	843	352	909	409	974	468
712	236	778	295	844	353	910	410	975	469
713	237	779	295	845	353	911	412	976	469
714	238	780	296	846	354	912	413	977	470
715	239	781	297	847	355	913	413	978	471
716	240	782	298	848	356	914	414	979	472
717	241	783	299	849	357	915	415	980	473
718	242	784	300	850	358	916	416	981	474
719	243	785	301	851	359	917	417	982	475
720	244	786	302	852	359	918	418	983	476
721	245	787	303	853	360	919	419	984	477
722	246	788	303	854	361	920	420	985	477
723	246	789	304	855	362	921	421	986	478
724	247	790	305	856	363	922	422	987	479
725	248	791	306	857	364	923	422	988	480
726	249	792	307	858	365				

GENERAL INDEX TO THE WORK.

A.

C.

D.

E.

F.

H.

33

I.

J.

K.

L.

M.

N.

O.

P.

Q.

R.

S.

T.

U.

V.

W.

No. of pages, ...	512
No. of pages of Contents, &c.	12
Total pages in Vol. 2, ...	524
No. of pages in Vol. 1.	561
Total No. of pages in Vols. 1 & 2. . . .	1,085

Date Due

Emily's Adventures
in Wonderland

Ryan & Julia

CPSIA information can be obtained at www.ICGtesting.com
Printed in the USA
LVOW10s1717150915

454265LV00020B/1459/P

9 781313 725705